4-18-63 - (54-6305)

# BOOKS BY ALLAN NEVINS

## PUBLISHED BY CHARLES SCRIBNER'S SONS

THE DIARY OF JOHN QUINCY ADAMS (*edited by Allan Nevins*)
ORDEAL OF THE UNION, 1846–1854 (*two volumes*)
THE EMERGENCE OF LINCOLN (*two volumes*)
THE WAR FOR THE UNION: THE IMPROVISED WAR, 1861–1862
THE WAR FOR THE UNION: WAR BECOMES REVOLUTION, 1862–1863
A CENTURY OF CARTOONS (*in collaboration with Frank Weitenkampf*)
THIS IS ENGLAND TODAY (1943)
JOHN D. ROCKEFELLER, THE HEROIC AGE OF AMERICAN ENTERPRISE, 1940 (*two volumes*)
STUDY IN POWER: JOHN D. ROCKEFELLER, INDUSTRIALIST AND PHILANTHROPIST, 1953 (*two volumes*)
FORD: THE TIMES, THE MAN, THE COMPANY
  *A History of Henry Ford, The Ford Motor Company, and The Automotive Industry, 1863–1915* (*with Frank Ernest Hill*)
FORD: EXPANSION AND CHALLENGE: 1915–1933 (*with Frank Ernest Hill*)
FORD: DECLINE AND REBIRTH: 1933–1963 (*with Frank Ernest Hill*)
JOHN D. ROCKEFELLER *One Volume Condensation by William Greenleaf of* STUDY IN POWER

## PUBLISHED ELSEWHERE

ILLINOIS (*Oxford Series on American Universities*)
THE AMERICAN STATES DURING AND AFTER THE REVOLUTION
THE EVENING POST, A CENTURY OF JOURNALISM
AMERICAN SOCIAL HISTORY RECORDED BY BRITISH TRAVELLERS
THE EMERGENCE OF MODERN AMERICA, 1865–1877
GROVER CLEVELAND, A STUDY IN COURAGE
HAMILTON FISH, THE INNER HISTORY OF THE GRANT ADMINISTRATION
ABRAM S. HEWITT, WITH SOME ACCOUNT OF PETER COOPER
THE GATEWAY TO HISTORY
FRÉMONT, PATHMARKER OF THE WEST
THE WORLD OF ELI WHITNEY (*with Jeannette Mirsky*)
AMERICA, THE STORY OF A FREE PEOPLE (*with H. S. Commager*)
THE STATESMANSHIP OF THE CIVIL WAR
THE UNITED STATES IN A CHAOTIC WORLD
THE STATE UNIVERSITIES AND DEMOCRACY

## AS EDITOR

LETTERS OF GROVER CLEVELAND
SELECT WRITINGS OF ABRAM S. HEWITT
THE DIARY OF PHILIP HONE
THE DIARY OF JAMES K. POLK
DIARY OF GEORGE TEMPLETON STRONG (*with M. H. Thomas*) (*four volumes*)
LETTERS AND JOURNALS OF BRAND WHITLOCK (*two volumes*)
FRÉMONT'S NARRATIVES OF EXPLORATION
THE HERITAGE OF AMERICA (*with H. S. Commager*)
THE LEATHERSTOCKING SAGA
A DIARY OF BATTLE: THE PERSONAL JOURNALS OF COLONEL CHARLES S. WAINWRIGHT, 1861–1865

# FORD:
## DECLINE AND
## REBIRTH: 1933-1962

# FORD

## *Decline and Rebirth*

## *1933-1962*

BY ALLAN NEVINS
AND FRANK ERNEST HILL

RESEARCH ASSOCIATES: MIRA WILKINS
GEORGE B. HELIKER AND WILLIAM GREENLEAF

*NEW YORK*

CHARLES SCRIBNER'S SONS

PICTURE SOURCES:

Ford Motor Company: 1–8, 11–17, 19–36
Louis Girolami, 18
United Press International, 10
Wide World, 9

# PREFACE

"THE PROGRESS of the world has been in direct ratio to the convenience of communication," said Henry Ford in 1926 at the acme of his success. "We have remade the country with automobiles." For the three preceding years his factories had turned out more than two million vehicles annually. The network of motor highways throughout the United States was rapidly growing, and with the appearance of more than twenty-five million cars and trucks on the roads of the world, striking changes had taken place in industry and social life. It was Ford's distinction that his firm, and he as an individual, had been the chief catalytic agents in bringing about these alterations.

*Ford: the Times, the Man, the Company* (1954), the first volume of the history of the Ford Motor Company, told how their chief initial contributions had been made by the creation of a cheap but durable car, the Model T; by the inauguration of the complex and revolutionary system of industrial activity called mass production; and by the establishment of the five-dollar-day in 1913–1914. The further revolutionary progress of the Ford Motor Company was recounted in the second volume, *Ford: Expansion and Challenge, 1915–1933*.

Up to this time Ford had been a powerful ferment in industrial and social life. His competitors in the automotive industry had learned from him, and all industry had gathered precision and power from the plethora of improved machine tools, the metallurgical advances, and the new factory routines of the Ford Motor Company. But by 1933 Ford had ceased to be a revolutionary leader and was a mere competitor. One strong rival had wrested primacy in the motorcar world from him, and he was being hard pressed by another. "Business today is an explorer's ship," he wrote in 1931; "it is always meeting new conditions." This was unquestionably true. But, he went on to say, in business there was no system of management, and the ship depended "on the man on the bridge." In this he was partly wrong, for while the individual heading a corporation was important, the time had now passed when a single leader could effectively direct a large and complex industrial undertaking alone. This Ford was now attempting to do.

The present volume tells the story of his failure, of how the Ford Motor Company tottered on the edge of disintegration, and of how it was finally lifted from its position of danger by the wise and vigorous management of Henry Ford II (the founder's grandson) to a new state of efficiency and prosperity.

When the authors were working on the first of these three volumes it seemed that nothing could match the miracles of the young automobile industry, of Ford's fabulous Model T, of the moving assembly line and the five-dollar-day. However, the next volume (*Ford: Expansion and Challenge*) with dozens of exhilarating episodes—the Peace Ship, the birth of the Fordson tractor, the rise of the great Rouge plant, the Brazilian rubber plantation, the culmination of Model T manufacture, its passing and the creation of Model A, and the development of a great Ford empire abroad—seemed to be the very heart of the company's story, after which any further record must be anticlimax.

Yet it is questionable if the present volume is not the most poignant and impressive of the three. It contains the moving personal story of an aging genius who battled valiantly but in vain to recover his position of supremacy in the motorcar industry. This account is tragic in that it involves Henry Ford's refusal to use the full talents of his gifted son Edsel, who might have helped him to win success. Edsel Ford did much to strengthen the company, but he was not permitted to do all that he could have done. Ford rejected him as his chief adviser, Edsel died, and the firm, after losing other able executives, occupied a desperate position when Henry Ford II assumed full control.

The story of the Ford Motor Company in one sense then merges into the larger story of the automotive industry and its contribution to American life. But its remaking as a corporation offers an exciting and instructive record. This process, followed step by step, reveals how a great manufacturing business can be built from the verge of disaster to vigorous industrial and financial health. It brings to the reader a group of creative personalities—Ernest R. Breech, Lewis D. Crusoe, John Dykstra, Robert S. McNamara, and others. The present volume is of further interest in describing the creation and role of the Ford Foundation, into which the Ford fortune was channeled, and the transformation of the Ford Motor Company from a business entirely owned by the Ford family into one the majority of whose voting stock is now held by the public.

This book, like the two preceding ones which with it comprise the history of the Ford Motor Company, has been written under the supervision of Columbia University, the authors working on salary and receiving no royalties, but operating with full independence.

The volume owes much to many individuals who in various ways have assisted in its making. Particular credit should go to the three research associates who with the authors have gathered and sifted the abundant source materials used, and have made valuable suggestions both as to the design of the book and as to the completed chapters. We wish to thank William Greenleaf, now Associate Professor of History at the University of New Hampshire, George Heliker, Associate Professor of Economics at Montana State University, and Mira Wilkins, Project Director of a History of American Business Abroad, Graduate School of Business, Columbia University, for their invaluable services.

The Ford Motor Company has freely permitted access to the voluminous records (correspondence, memoranda, and statistics) in the Ford Archives; and for this volume, as for the two preceding ones, the assistance of Henry E. Edmunds, the Archivist and Director of the Department of Research and Information, has been of the greatest service to the authors. The members of his staff have been constantly helpful both to the authors and the research associates. Ford officials from Henry Ford II throughout the company have discussed their work with the authors. We are indebted to James O. Wright, Charles H. Patterson, Ben Mills, J. E. Lundy, Arjay Miller and other officials, and to J. R. Davis, long prominent in Ford Sales, although now retired. Charles E. Sorensen also lent his aid, and Charles A. Lindbergh, closely associated with Henry Ford and the company before and during World War II, gave freely of his time to help with the chapters dealing with that period.

Needless to say, whatever errors or shortcomings appear in this volume are the responsibility of the authors and not of those who have so generously aided them.

A.N.
F.E.H.

Columbia University,
New York,
March, 1963

# CONTENTS

# ILLUSTRATIONS

xvii

# FORD:
## DECLINE AND
## REBIRTH: 1933-1962

# I

## CRISIS OF 1933

### I.

Noonday of March 4, 1933, brought the American people a new president and a new political philosophy. As early as May 1932, Franklin Delano Roosevelt had called for "bold, persistent experimentation" to meet the crisis that had grown from the economic collapse of 1929. In his inaugural address, while asserting that "This great nation will endure as it has endured, will revive and prosper," and that "the only thing we have to fear is fear itself," he proposed "a disciplined attack upon our common problems." In the ringing voice which the radio carried into millions of homes, he announced that, in extremity, "I shall ask the Congress for the one remaining instrument to meet the crisis—broad Executive power to wage a war against the emergency, as great as the power that would be given me if we were in fact invaded by a foreign foe."

The listening crowd in Washington cheered, and the vast radio audience echoed its approval. Roosevelt had correctly appraised the feelings of his fellow Americans, and in his brief, courageous address had won their immediate support. From that hour he was acclaimed as leader, and the measures he and his "brain trust" devised were praised for their decisive character and promptly considered by a receptive Congress.

Henry Ford gave the American public his own message. "We have come to the end of an era of waste and inefficiency," he reported early in February, "and a new era is coming in." He foresaw a period of expanding production, and cited housing in particular. As for the automobile, "We haven't even started," but "the car of the future is in sight." The New Deal and the Ford Motor Company thus began their association with a common optimism. Both their leaders had an

1

instinct for the mood of the American public and could appeal successfully to it—Ford through pithy statements to the press and messages in company advertisements, and Roosevelt through his speeches and the radio "fireside chats" which began on March 12, 1933. Both were apostles of resourcefulness and courage. They had known each other casually in World War I, when Roosevelt as Assistant Secretary of the Navy dealt with Ford as a builder of Eagle boats.

Beyond these areas came a sharp divergence. Ford was an individualist, convinced that ingenuity and effort would bring economic health to his industry and nation. He would denounce, expose, and oppose, but he would not constrain. He believed that the better program, like a creative businessman competing with stodgy rivals, would always triumph. But to become effective, it must develop in a relatively free economic atmosphere. In contrast, Roosevelt leaned toward "a planned economy," and proposed to legislate the depression out of existence. Super-policemen dedicated to driving confusion into order, his governmental agencies would curb many activities which he regarded as anti-social.

The two attitudes were basically in conflict, and an ultimate clash was inevitable. It may be added that neither Henry Ford nor the American people ever lived under a government like that now unfolding its program in Washington.[1]

2.

The onset of the depression late in 1929 had found the Ford Motor Company in a relatively happy position. Three years earlier the decision to abandon the Model T had been forced upon the firm. How reluctantly Ford had accepted this step, how he had developed a new model, how in the period of transition General Motors' Chevrolet had become the most widely sold car, and how in 1929 the Ford Model A had regained supremacy (selling 1,710,734 units to lead its rival by some 400,000) was a story familiar to the country.[*]

At the end of 1929 Ford, the chief automobile producer, had surveyed a scene in which the growth of the industry had been as socially significant as it was meteoric. In 1909 the manufacture of cars had

---

[*] Allan Nevins and Frank Ernest Hill, *Ford: Expansion and Challenge, 1915–1933*, N.Y., 1957, Chs. 15–18.

ranked twenty-first among American industries in dollar value. Two decades later it ranked first. As W. F. Ogburn was to write in 1933: "To think of the automobile as a more speedy substitute for the horse is to underestimate its influence. It has greatly increased and diversified transportation, cut down railroad traffic, . . . lessened the isolation of the farmer, aided the consolidation of small schools and churches, . . . dispersed factories, and has developed a new type of vacation."

Actually, the automobile had changed the nation's civilization on an even wider front. It had played a major part in the surge of progress in all industry, to which it contributed metallurgical advances, improved machine tools, the moving assembly line, and other factory devices making possible mass production. Similarly, the effect of trucks, buses, and other commercial vehicles upon transportation was by no means restricted to the farmer, though he found the truck, tractor and automobile invaluable. The motor car was already beginning to displace the hotel with the motel, and affected numerous American activities from political campaigning to the location of housing. A great national system of motor highways was already developing. The industry early in 1933 used 40,000 dealers, 100,000 garages, and 350,000 filling stations.[2]

As it had mounted on a rising curve of production, the business had collided with the great depression. To understand Ford's mood in March 1933, and the condition of the industry and his company at that time, one must recognize the extent of the devastation that had ensued. Ford himself had at first been scornful of the pessimists who saw a bleak future. Regarding the depression as "not a natural phenomenon but the ignorance of economic health laws," he had asserted that greater production, lower prices, and higher wages would restore prosperity. He derided "over-production," to which many attributed the disaster, as impossible and ridiculous.

Acting on his beliefs, late in 1929 the industrialist had fixed a minimum seven-dollar-day wage for his plants, and in 1930 had announced a $25,000,000 program of factory expansion. These optimistic acts were not effective, although the company for a time seemed to prosper, maintaining its lead over Chevrolet and, indeed, over the entire General Motors production, despite the appearance of a 6-cylinder Chevrolet to compete with the 4-cyclinder Model A. Ford in 1930 sold

1,256,600 units to take 40.33 per cent of the passenger car market, as against 34.7 per cent for General Motors. It held an even larger percentage of the increasingly important truck sales.

But in 1931 the appearance of Chrysler's low-priced car, the Plymouth, and an improved Chevrolet, forced Ford's passenger sales down to 532,041, and despite some loss of volume, General Motors held a firm first place with 43.26 per cent of the total to Ford's 28.15 per cent. Ford had to abandon the seven-dollar-day, and in 1932 its employees worked for a minimum of four dollars. That year the company reached the nadir of its productive activity with only 262,106 cars sold in the United States, and Chrysler pressed it for second place (17.41 per cent to 23.80 per cent).[3]

Ford's experience was little sadder than that of the industry as a whole or of the nation. The industry had shrunk like a leaky balloon. While in 1929 it had produced 5,294,087 vehicles valued at $3,709,515,-000, in 1933 it manufactured only 1,848,013 worth $1,096,946,263—a reduction in value of more than 70 per cent. In 1929 it had paid $733,082,618 in wages; three years later it paid but $252,106,467. The nation had suffered comparably. Its income had dropped startlingly from $87.4 billions in 1929 to $41.7 billions in 1932. Manufacturing as a whole had been struck almost as disastrously as the automobile group. Its income fell in 1931 to 32 per cent of the level in 1929, while the motor manufacturers showed a drop to 30 per cent. However, the automobile industry recovered somewhat sooner, and was already showing an upturn by the spring of 1933.[4]

The three companies we have mentioned, General Motors, the Chrysler Corporation, and Ford, more and more dominated the industry. There were numerous others, but none played a large role compared with the "Big Three." In 1925 the "independents" had sold 24.71 per cent of the automobiles produced in the United States; in 1933 their share was only 10.47 per cent, and was diminishing.

While this decline had begun before 1929, the depression had quickened it. The dark years had expunged a number of such long-familiar companies as the Stearns, Moon, Kissel, Gardner, Locomobile, Elcar, Jordan, and Marmon. Furthermore, in 1933 two of the leading independents went into receiverships—the Overland in February and the Studebaker in March.* Along with the Hudson, Nash, and Packard,

* Both emerged in 1935, after reorganization. See Note 5.

they had enjoyed the best sales. But while the total production for all independents had been only 309,800 in 1932, in that year Packard outsold the Cadillac 11,600 to 9,005, and the Hudson bested the Oldsmobile, Chrysler, Dodge, and De Soto (38,700 to 22,011, 23,282, 35,335, and 26,070 respectively). The Overland cut its prices so low that it met with disaster, but it sold some 26,000 cars in 1932.

Among the leaders of the independents were men whose names were well known to the car-buying public: Roy Chapin of Hudson, John North Willys of Overland, Albert R. Erskine of Studebaker, Alvin Macauley of Packard, and Charles W. Nash of the Nash Motors Company. The veteran R. E. Olds would soon pass from an advisory to an active role in a vain effort to save the struggling Reo. The independents did not lack talent, and some survive today; but all were suffering from the fact that the American family confined itself to one car, and bought increasingly in the lowest-priced field. All in all, the scene showed the big getting bigger, and the small getting smaller. The number of plants revealing a net income had shrunk from 530 in 1929 to 68 in 1932. In the latter year even the big three reported deficits: General Motors $4,559,000, Chrysler $10,162,307, and Ford a soaring figure of $70,831,-153.[*5] The difference between the independents and the Big Three in this period was that the latter had huge cash reserves which enabled them to sustain a loss, while most of the independents could not.

General Motors was the biggest of all automobile manufacturers. When, a few years later, the Federal Trade Commission made its report on the motor vehicle industry, it noted that this company, "although its total assets were slightly exceeded by a few other corporations," exceeded all in its earnings over a twenty-nine year period. It held a position in 1933 of massive strength. In 1929 its assets had stood at $1,324,889,000, and in 1933 they still amounted to $1,183,674,000. The company carried a cash balance of $150,952,000. It was not devoted wholly to motor cars, for it also manufactured refrigerators, aircraft, diesel engines, air-conditioning equipment, and other non-automotive products. Yet cars were its dominant concern. The corporation operated by relatively self-contained divisions, of which in 1933 there were more than 50. Of them 34 made motor cars or parts, and the investment in this sector of the business was about 85 per cent of the total.

---

* It is interesting to note that the Nash Motors, although its sales volume was small, slid through the lean years with profits, its low year being $470,000 in 1933. Kennedy, *op. cit.* 298.

Its chief car divisions in 1933 were the Chevrolet, Buick, Cadillac, La Salle, Oldsmobile (Olds Motor Division), and Pontiac. Not only was the Chevrolet in 1933 the best-selling car on the market, but the five others covered the entire range of automobiles from low-to-high-priced vehicles. The Yellow Truck and Coach Manufacturing Company produced taxicabs, buses, and other commercial vehicles. The chief parts division, serving all the car units, was the Fisher Body Group. In addition to its domestic plants, General Motors controlled twenty-nine foreign subsidiaries, among them Vauxhall Motors, Ltd. in England, and the Adam Opel, A.G. in Germany. The sales of most of these firms were high in their respective countries.[6]

As president of the corporation, Alfred P. Sloan, Jr., a fifty-eight-year-old executive who had sold metal bearings to Henry Ford in 1901, guided his fifty-unit team with consummate skill. William S. Knudsen, who had left a high post in the Ford Motor Company in 1919, acted as vice president in charge of all car and body operations. It was he who, as head of the Chevrolet division, had so developed that car, improving its quality and lowering its price, as to compel Ford to abandon the Model T. Richard H. Grant was the brilliant General Motors sales manager.[7]

Much smaller than General Motors, but nevertheless a giant, and growing rapidly, the Chrysler Corporation, launched in 1925, had already pushed into an uncontested third position in the industry, and was threatening to displace Ford as second. Its total assets were relatively small, standing at $224,596,830 in 1928 and amounting to $145,-416,287 in 1933. But the company's cash position was strong, and its resources in plants and men were impressive. In 1928 it had acquired the properties of Dodge Brothers, thereby gaining factory facilities for large operations, and to its first car, the Chrysler, it had added the Dodge and its own De Soto, both medium-priced. Then, in 1931, Chrysler introduced the Plymouth as a competitor of the Ford and Chevrolet, and thus had four cars of high reputation. Chrysler also had a thriving export division.

More brilliant than any figure in the automotive world since the appearance of Henry Ford, Walter P. Chrysler, now in his late forties, had in the words of E. D. Kennedy "made an opportunity of what might have been a disaster." His own Chrysler was a fairly high-priced car, the Dodge when he bought it was regarded as a white elephant, and he had to create the Plymouth. Yet in eight years, ably assisted by Fred M. Zeder in engineering, and K. T. Keller in production, he had wrought a miracle. Though the company had suffered a deficit in 1932, it kept growing even in the depression. The Plymouth actually increased its sales as the rest of the industry slipped downward.[8]

Ford in 1933 was thus battling not only the depression, but two strong rivals. In 1931 it was clear that Model A could no longer be a winner. Ford did not meet his competitors with a new 6-cyclinder car like the Chevrolet and Plymouth; instead, he leapt to an 8-cylinder motor for the new Ford—hitherto unheard of for a cheap car. The V-8, as it was called, was to last long and enjoy its periods of triumph, but it came into production so slowly that the Ford Motor Company sustained grave losses. For 1931–1933 the deficits, after taxes, amounted to about $120,000,000.[9]

In the darkening scene Ford never lost faith. As the center of the motor car industry, Detroit was a city of the unemployed, in which hundreds of thousands of workers were idle, and at the great Rouge plant, where a hundred thousand had worked, less than 30,000 were busy.* Mayor Frank Murphy, ably administering the stricken city in which businessmen, laborers, and schoolteachers stood in the breadlines, must have seen some kinship between it and James Thompson's City of Dreadful Night. When Anne O'Hare McCormick of the *New York Times* visited the Detroit-Dearborn area in May 1932, she found it grimly discouraging. The great Ford plant on the Rouge, she pointed out, stood for "mass production, mass employment, and mass idleness when production slows down." The automobile industry had shown courage. "Alas, it is not enough. The Rouge plant and the other plants are turning out all the cars they can sell, perhaps more, are employing all the men they can use; but still the slack drags like a dead weight on the city—on the world." Yet Ford, although almost sixty-nine, an aging David without a sure weapon to fell his giant adversary, stood poised for action. He saw the depression as a deeply instructive experience. "We are here to work out something, and we go on from where we leave off."

* Unemployment for the State of Michigan ran to more than three quarters of a million late in 1932.

Ford took his text from his past achievements. Had they not been of Aladdin brilliancy? Pursuing the dream of a cheap but sound car for the masses, he and his organization had developed the moving assembly line and true mass production. They had inaugurated the then fabulous five-dollar-day, lifted the Model T to a position of unchallenged superiority for a dozen years, had developed the first cheap, reliable tractor, later the Model A, and, now the V-8. More than any other agency, the Ford Motor Company had enabled workers of low income to possess motor cars. For most Americans, Ford was a shining archetype of industrial leadership, and was well aware of the fact.

Ford believed that he and his company, having accomplished so much, would with their tested resourcefulness accomplish more. They had the means for doing so. In 1929 the assets of the Ford Motor Company had been computed at $925,000,000, and its investment in automotive plants and equipment about equalled that of General Motors (which, it will be recalled, manufactured other products). The 1933 figures showed $864,389,000 in company holdings. Ford had cash in hand to the sum of $112,679,279, and $74,722,000 in government securities.

The Ford organization in fact controlled an empire. Many Americans, if asked to say what the word "Ford" meant to them, might have replied "The Rouge," and the company's immense plant on the Rouge River some half dozen miles south of the town of Dearborn, Michigan, was the greatest single center of Ford activities. Occupying a tract of 1100 acres, utilizing its own harbor, to which ships could come from Europe or Africa, it contained the largest foundry in the world, a steel-manufacturing complex, a paper mill, a body-making unit for Ford cars, and other buildings engaged in the manufacture of engines and parts for the company's automobiles. No comparable automotive factory existed anywhere else. It used 92 miles of railroad track and a fantastic system of conveyors to bear products-in-the-making from one building to another. Its machine tools, numbering 53,000, required a special work force to sharpen and repair them.[10]

At the center of Ford activity were also the Lincoln factory in Detroit, and the Highland Park plant just north of the city, which had been the birthplace of the moving assembly line and five-dollar-day, but was now partly rented, partly used for storage. Besides these, the company had about 35 assembly plants scattered over the United States.

Because of the depression, only eight of these were active in 1933, and the others were used as parts depots or as sales offices.*

One phase of Big Three practice should be noted. "The Ford Motor Co.," said the Federal Trade Commission report in 1937, "is more integrated than any other vehicle manufacturers with General Motors second in line." Chrysler, who used suppliers extensively, could not compete in this respect with either of its rivals. (The scale of integration in 1933 differed little from that in 1937.) But the opinion that Ford was the most highly integrated automobile company in either year may be questioned. Ford, to be sure, made some of its own iron, steel, engines, and bodies, but contracted with numerous suppliers for many car parts, while General Motors made all but a few of the elements of its own cars.

In addition to main plants and assembly factories, the Ford Motor Company operated a number of village industries. These small units, using some hydroelectric power, produced parts for Ford cars—valves, tappets, springs. They were experimental in character, and not self-supporting. In 1933 there were five village industries, and four larger plants near cities which used some water power. At this time Ford was planning to process soy beans for oils, plastics, and paints for his cars, but as yet had no factories. The company used a Ford Fleet of more than a dozen freighters, and owned iron and coal mines, forests, and wood-working plants on the Upper Peninsula of Michigan. It operated an enormous rubber plantation in Brazil at a constant loss. Ford was completing at no small expense Greenfield Village, with the Edison Institute and Henry Ford museum, a showcase of older American life. Many of these activities were personal, peripheral to automobile making, and expensive.

The Ford automotive enterprises were not confined to the United States, for they had long since spilled over into other countries, so that the total investment in foreign lands by 1933 exceeded $56,000,000.[11] During the depression Ford had neglected none of these activities. New

---

* The number of assembly plants varied from year to year. This number is given in *Automobile Topics*, Mar. 4, 1933, 203. The plants of General Motors and Chrysler were in general of about the same character as the Ford plants. Except for two Ford assembly units, no new factories had been built by any of these companies, a Chrysler-Plymouth plant having been the most recently erected (1928). However, all had improved their factories. General Motors had plants in many states, the total number notably larger than Ford's. In 1937 Chrysler was credited with 20 plants, all of which he apparently had in 1933, and most of which were built before 1925.

assembly plants had been opened, as at Richmond, California, and Alexandria, Virginia, and the works at Dagenham in England had begun operations in 1931. The only activity that he dropped was the airplane operations he had begun in 1925, which had developed the Ford trimotor and blazed a path for modern American commercial aviation.

The officers who worked under Henry Ford during this period were uniformly capable, and in some instances of the highest ability. As we shall see, they labored under difficulties. In happier circumstances, they might have proved themselves fully a match for the officials of General Motors or Chrysler.

Edsel Ford was nominally President of the Ford Motor Company, but his father held the majority of stock and the power, which he sometimes used in a disruptive manner. Edsel, now in his fortieth year, served with great astuteness in planning, advertising, and sales activities, performing an immense volume of useful work. He contributed also to the styling of Ford and Lincoln cars. Had it not been for his participation in this field, the Ford models would have been at a far greater disadvantage in their competition against General Motors and Chrysler products.

The Ford Motor Company gave special attention to the processes of production, over which two exceedingly forceful men presided, Charles E. Sorensen and P. E. Martin, both veterans from early Ford days. Sorensen, now fifty-two, had immense energy and a capacity to drive himself and others. Martin, a little older, seconded his efforts. Sorensen's chief assistant, Mead L. Bricker, would also occupy an increasingly important place in Ford production. A. M. Wibel, long with the company and familiar with production and financial problems, meanwhile gained distinction in the purchasing field as an executive of sound judgment. These were really the giants of the organization, although John R. Davis in Sales and Laurence Sheldrick in Engineering had also shown great abilities. But, as important as any of them, was the director of Ford personnel, Harry Bennett. Small physically, but eneregtic and self-assured, he had entrenched himself as a power beside the throne, unquestioningly carrying out Henry Ford's orders, and posing a threat to Edsel and Sorensen, the two men with the greatest capacity for operating the company.

W. J. Cameron, a skilful speaker and writer, had charge of Ford's personal publicity, which, except for a certain fulsomeness, he managed well. E. G. Liebold, formerly influential as Henry's executive secretary, was now being pushed into the background by the more tactful Frank Campsall. In general, all the Ford officials of the nineteen-thirties had been with the company in the previous decade, and some in an earlier period. Throughout the industry, indeed, the high executives were an older group than the leaders in the first quarter of the century, and showed a declining energy.

Meanwhile, the industry had attained a certain maturity. It had reached the point where motor cars were assumed to be dependable. Durability and safety were taken for granted: speed, comfort, and pleasing appearance were the qualities for which buyers now looked. For the cheaper cars particularly this represented a change. Once the ability of a car to go somewhere and return, however rough the road, had been the crucial test. Now the leading cheap cars offered power with 6- or 8-cylinder engines, provided comfort with springs, shock absorbers, improved suspension, and better brakes, and used streamlining and happy color combinations to present an attractive appearance. Open cars had practically disappeared, and all protected their occupants from the weather. The lower-priced cars cost from $450 to $700, and the medium-priced from $700 to $1500. General Motors covered the middle-class field with the Pontiac, Oldsmobile, and Buick; Chrysler with the De Soto, Dodge, and Chrysler; and Ford in 1933 had no car in this area. The Packard, Pierce-Arrow, Cadillac, and Lincoln were all priced above $2000. However, as the public had increasingly shifted to the cheap car, it was there that the battle for supremacy would be waged. At the same time, it was more and more important that a company offer four or five models instead of one.[12]

Such was the general situation that Ford and his company faced in 1933. As the year began, he was busy building up the production of his new model, the V-8, and was also concerned with public affairs.

3.

In the fall of 1932 the Hoover administration had come under severe challenge. Roosevelt had arraigned it as timid, and promised to attack the depression with vigor. Although Ford belonged to no political party (he had supported Woodrow Wilson in 1916 and Cox in 1920, but Coolidge in 1924 and Hoover in 1928) he approved a continuance of the existing leadership. Notices in Ford plants had read: "To prevent times from getting worse and to help them get better, President Hoover must be reelected." He was displeased when, in a surge of vehement protest, the voters swept the Democrats into power.[13]

The period between the election and Hoover's departure proved trying. Business and industry sank into deeper prostration; unemployment, for which no complete statistics were available, mounted until experts estimated that more than 13,000,000 men and women were idle. In 1930 and 1931 bank failures had accelerated sharply. The number for 1932 (1456) was less alarming than that for the preceding year (2294), but it represented more than twice the average for pre-depression years.* A new crisis was plainly building up, and the whole financial system seemed to be tottering.[14]

A sad illustration of what was happening was offered by Detroit. By 1933 its two chief banking organizations were both in need of considerable funds and drastic reorganization. These were the Guardian Detroit Union Group, Inc., whose principal unit was the Guardian National Bank of Commerce, and the Detroit Bankers Company, in which the First National Bank of Detroit was prominent. Each group included more than a dozen institutions. The Fords had deposits in both, and were involved with the Guardian management.[15]

Although both chains had been assisted by the Fords, and the Union Guardian Trust Company had obtained loans from the newly created Reconstruction Finance Corporation, in January 1933 it brought matters to a crisis by asking for a much larger grant.** Federal appraisers came to Detroit to investigate, and reported that its assets were insufficient to warrant the $37,000,000 requested. Ernest Kanzler and Clifford Longley suggested to Edsel that the Ford Motor Company supply additional collateral by subordinating to other deposits the $7,500,000 which it had in the Union Guardian Trust, and Edsel agreed to do this.[16]

---

* The losses to depositors, $2,113,000,000 for the period 1929–1933, indicate the gravity of the situation.

** According to Edsel, he and his father, or the company, had $32,500,000 on deposit with the Guardian banks, and of $18,000,000 with the Detroit Bankers. Edsel was a director of the Guardian chain, and of several of its banks. Clifford B. Longley, a lawyer who acted on a consultant basis for the FMC, served as the Guardian Group president. Ernest C. Kanzler, Edsel's brother-in-law, was Chairman of the Board. The Guardian companies had suffered cruelly in the depression. The group directors had shifted funds from one unit to another to meet recurring crises. The FMC made temporary deposits which enabled some of the institutions to issue more satisfactory statements, and Edsel and the company had also extended or endorsed loans to such units and the group as a whole which, from December 1930 to January 1933, amounted to $12,000,000. Nevertheless, the situation continued to be desperate. In May 1932 the Guardian Trust Co. got a loan of $5,000,000 from the RFC, which was soon increased to $15,000,000. Then came the application for a still larger loan!

However, the situation was now complicated by the acts of two strong characters, James Couzens and Henry Ford. Since Couzens had resigned from the Ford Motor Company in 1915 and sold his stock four years later, the two men had been wary of each other. While Ford rose in American industry, Couzens had become a force in the political world, and now as senator from Michigan, headed a sub-committee of the Senate Banking and Currency Committee. This was supposed to confer with the RFC on national banking policy, and RFC heads suggested that Couzens be consulted about the proposed loan. Unfortunately, the senator felt that he and his committee had been inexcusably neglected. Asked about the loan, he denounced it. When President Hoover appealed to him to match the subordination of deposits by Ford with an advance of capital that would provide adequate security, he refused; he held that the Union Guardian Trust Company was "Mr. Ford's baby." [17]*

The officials of the Guardian group now hoped that Ford would supply the money that Couzens had refused to advance. But the industrialist was unresponsive. He resented Couzens's attitude, and felt that the new proposal was an imposition upon him, Edsel, and the Ford Company. They had already advanced $12,000,000. On Sunday, February 12, Henry Ford announced that he would not only deny further capital, but would also refuse to subordinate the Ford deposits in the Union Guardian Trust Company. The situation was catastrophic. If the Union Guardian Trust Company failed, it would drag down the entire Guardian chain. This would certainly cause a run on the First National Bank of Detroit, chief unit of the Detroit Bankers Company. This institution, already vulnerable, quickly applied for RFC aid, but in vain.

Banking and federal officials pleaded with Ford, but could not move him. Although in general an individualist and a firm opponent of Federal "meddling," he felt that Washington, with or without Couzens's approval, should save the Union Guardian Trust.** "I am not likely to

* One commentator, Harry Barnard (see note 13), cites a memorandum by RFC President Charles A. Miller, who met with Senators Vandenberg and Couzens and President Hoover to discuss the Detroit banking situation in mid-February, and a letter from Hoover of September 14, 1941. Hoover recalled suggesting to Couzens that, since Ford was willing to subordinate his Guardian Trust Co. deposits, Couzens should advance additional capital to justify the loan. "The Senator showed great resentment to my pressing him, and I replied that if 5 per cent of my fortune would save a panic in hundreds of banks with hundreds of thousands of depositors and tens of thousands of people's jobs in my home town, they could have it tomorrow. He left in great heat."

** Ford was apparently quite receptive to the Government's aiding banks (which he detested anyway), but was opposed to Federal participation in business.

leave my money in a bank in order to prevent Jim Couzens from spouting on the floor of the Senate," he snapped. Furthermore, he added, if the Government did not act, he would withdraw his money "from any other Detroit bank that was open." The situation revived in him a long-standing hostility to financiers. "We must get rid of the idea of making money out of money," he declared, and added: "Money is not a commodity. A million dollars in gold by itself will not produce one copper penny. Put a hen on it and it will not hatch. Water it and it will not grow." A bank, he held, was a repository, and the funds it accepted should be available for withdrawal and use. Otherwise, the depositor was like a man who had left his automobile in a garage, to find when he called for it that it had been half-wrecked in an accident.

Such remarks did not improve the situation. By emissary, Couzens suggested that Ford and he make a loan jointly, but Ford was now adamant. "You tell Couzens I wouldn't have anything to do with anything he proposed," he admonished his secretary.

Temporarily the situation was saved when, late on the night of the 13th (a holiday because of Lincoln's birthday), Governor William A. Comstock of Michigan declared an eight-day bank holiday, which was later extended.[18]

Either Ford or Couzens could have met the crisis, or the two jointly could have done so. The clash of personalities blocked action. Though the public was confused, it tended to sympathize with Ford. Its feeling became emphatic when, on February 24, 1933, Henry and Edsel Ford, in a joint letter, proposed to the depositors and directors of the two chief banks—the Guardian National Bank of Commerce and the First National—to undertake "the creation of two new banks." The Fords would provide the entire capital required, which they set at $8,250,000, but they reserved the right to "select the men whom we all believe will merit public confidence." They added: "The institutions so established will be of the type of financial structure that will merit public faith in the ability of industrial Detroit to rehabilitate itself."

The dramatic timing and boldness of the proposal were characteristic of Henry Ford. The press reported that the banks accepted it, and the public applauded. But four days later, on February 28, officials of the First National rejected the plan, and the Guardian group came to a similar decision. *Business Week,* on April 5, 1933, attributed the action to self-interested financiers. "The bankers didn't want to be rescued.

They knew that the Fords' first move would be to wipe clean the slate of officers and directors, and start over with a new personnel. They knew that both the First National and the Guardian would go into receivership, with offsets of deposits against loans, and stockholders and directors held liable for losses. So the Ford move was blocked."

Meanwhile, another plan unfolded as General Motors purchased all the common shares of an entirely new bank, the National Bank of Detroit, for $12,500,000, and the RFC bought preferred shares to an equal amount, thus creating an initial capitalization of $25,000,000. This institution opened on March 24, 1933, and took over most of the liquid assets of the First National and the Guardian National Bank of Commerce, neither of which reopened. Later in the year, on August 10, a second concern, the Manufacturers National Bank of Detroit, began operations. In this the Fords held a controlling interest. It too won assistance from the RFC. Capitalized at $3,000,000, it absorbed five institutions in Highland Park and Dearborn, establishing branches to serve these communities.[19]

Both new establishments prospered. Ford had made a dramatic offer which he had been prepared to carry through. Although rejected, it won him further reputation. The public approved his championship of depositors, and recalled other occasions on which he had defied "the interests," as in his attack on the Selden patent (1903–1911), his first five-dollar-day wage (which shocked many business and industrial groups), and his rejection of bank loans in the depression of 1920–1921.

4.

Like most Americans, Ford recognized the necessity of Comstock's holiday during the Detroit banking crisis, and must have approved the national bank holiday proclaimed by Roosevelt on March 6. Nothing in his correspondence indicates his attitude toward early New Deal policies like the proposed Agricultural Adjustment Administration (March 16), or the Civilian Conservation Corps (March 21), the Federal Emergency Relief Bill (March 29), or the Tennessee Valley Authority, for which legislation was requested on April 10. But Ford was deeply concerned with the plight of the American farmer (potentially one of his best customers), had shown a persistent interest in the rehabilitation of youth, and in the nineteen-twenties had proposed to develop Muscle Shoals. As early as April 16, he praised Roosevelt's "sincerity and cour-

age" and "the expenditure of his vast energy in the work of his office."
And on May 8, 1933, he put his full moral force behind the administration. In the first of a series of personal messages in company advertisements he said:

A great thing has occurred among us. We have made a complete turn
around and at last America's face is to the future.

Three years—1929 to 1932—we Americans looked backward. All our old
financial and political machinery was geared to pull us out of the depression
by the same door through which we entered. . . . It failed. We now realize
that the way is forward—through it.

Thanks for that belongs to President Roosevelt. Inauguration day he
turned the Ship of State around.

Ford added that "we all look to what is coming," and concluded,
"The best thing I can do for the country is to create industry by building good motor cars." [20]

However, the test of this honeymoon of Ford and the administration
came with the signing of the National Industrial Recovery Act by
Roosevelt on June 16, 1933. The measure was a colossal experiment in
self-regulation by American industry. It embodied a principle that
Hoover had pushed while Secretary of Commerce under Coolidge, and
upon which Roosevelt had touched approvingly in the 1932 campaign.
The measure had been hastily prepared to supplant the Black-Connery
Bill for a compulsory 30-hour week to "spread the work," laid before
Congress in December 1932. Roosevelt considered the Black-Connery
plan too radical, and Ford had condemned it as a device that would
lower the entire national economy. "You just have everybody poor
under that plan," he scoffed.

The NIRA avoided such a disaster by providing for codes to be formulated by the chief American industries, each devising a plan by
which its various firms could live and thrive. Under most codes, quotas
for production were set and under some basic prices were established.
Maximum hours of work were also prescribed, with minimum rates of
pay. Section 7A of the act recognized the right of labor to organize and
engage in collective bargaining. Both the government and labor were
to approve each code.[21]

At this time, the President commanded the greatest popular support
he was ever to enjoy. "The public mind was receptive to action on a
heroic cast," writes one commentator. "The widespread belief that gov-

ernment must intervene to rout the forces of depression . . . opened the way for new and unconventional experiments in economic policy." Business leaders in general cooperated. All code activities were exempt from anti-trust laws. Agreements on prices, hitherto furtively contrived, could now be open. If the depression could be ended by such practices, the New Deal was prepared to approve them.

Under Hugh S. Johnson, a blunt retired brigadier-general of cavalry who had administered the Selective Service Law in World War I, and had later been active in business, the Recovery Administration was launched as a moral crusade. Johnson, whom Secretary of the Interior Harold L. Ickes privately described as "impetuous, high-handed," soon became known as "Old Ironpants" and "Hardboiled Hugh." He invoked public opinion as his prime weapon, and charged into an activity that ultimately produced 550 codes, 200 supplementary agreements, and 11,000 administrative orders. Approximately 2,300,000 employers and 16,000,000 workers were affected. The first code, governing the cotton textile industry, was signed by the President on July 9, 1933. A business upturn in the spring and early summer gave impetus to the conferences which were under way in hundreds of business and industrial areas.[22]

On the very day when the Recovery Act was signed, Ford indicated to the press that he felt grave reservations. "We know that President Roosevelt wants to do the right and helpful thing," he conceded, but spoke sharply of men "whose particular genius is to try to run other people's business." The government "has not any too rosy a record in running itself this far." It was well and good to try to improve business practices, but "I was always under the impression that to manage a business properly you ought to know something about it."

The statement could have given no comfort to Johnson. He knew all too well that other firms in the automobile industry were unenthusiastic about a code. Their business had improved early in the year. They did not need legalized price-fixing, for they had neither cutthroat competition nor overproduction, while Section 7A of the new act was repugnant to firms that had long united to maintain the open shop. As E. D. Kennedy pointed out in his history of the industry, all "saw in the National Recovery Act a present menace and a potential disaster."

Happily for Johnson, the public was firmly supporting NRA and the companies comprising the National Automobile Chamber of Commerce were disposed to make a code. If they did not, they might receive one from Washington, which popular opinion would perhaps force them to accept. On June 15, the forty-seven members of the Chamber directed their president, Alvin Macauley, to appoint a sub-committee for drafting a "unified trade policy" under the act. On June 22, representatives of five companies, including General Motors, Chrysler, and Ford, met under Donaldson Brown, who was a vice president and the finance chairman of General Motors. The Ford Motor Company was not a member of the NACC (later the Automobile Manufacturers Association), but its Lincoln Motor Company had maintained an affiliation that had existed before Ford acquired it in 1922. The latter now agreed to cooperate in studies preliminary to the drafting of a code, and assigned Herman L. Moekle of the Treasurer's office and Louis Colombo, a lawyer representing Ford, to act for the Lincoln company. This pleased both Johnson and the NACC, and Johnson especially, for Ford's reputation over the country was high and he controlled almost 24 per cent of the industry's production. His example, if favorable, might influence other industries, speed the general process of code-making, and enhance the prestige of the NRA.[23]

Johnson left no stone unturned to win Ford's cooperation. He had known the industrialist in World War I, and had admired his high minimum wage, eight-hour day, and five-day week. "Mr. Ford," he wrote later, "had established the principles of his own NRA, so far as hours and wages are concerned, years before the depression." After a long-distance telephone conversation, he made a secret flight to Detroit, conferred with Ford at the Dearborn Inn, and believed he had won his cooperation. Sorensen, aware of the meeting, had the opposite impression: he recalled later that Johnson "got nowhere." The differing versions of the event are reconcilable. Ford was a master at creating an impression while making no commitment. "I must somehow have misunderstood him," wrote Johnson later. All too soon Ford was to deny any pledge of the support the general thought he had won.

Meanwhile, the code was completed. It was not wholly satisfactory to the administration, for the rights of labor could be deftly denied under a so-called "merit clause." Ford did not sign, but Edsel was favorable, and Johnson was not utterly discouraged, reasoning that Ford had not *refused* to sign. "Mr. Ford," said the general, "says he approves of everything done and being done by this administration." Two days later, on July 29, Johnson must have been shaken in this belief when the manufacturer commented disparagingly on the code.[24]

## 5.

Actually, Ford had already reached a decision not to sign. Moekle and Colombo were favorable, and Arthur Brisbane, the brilliant Hearst columnist, long a Ford admirer and adviser, felt that Ford would sacrifice nothing in signing. Edsel was favorable because, as Moekle said, "Some of us felt that by going along . . . we would probably be able to get Government business." This was no small consideration, for besides the many long-established federal agencies, such new creations as the Federal Emergency Relief Administration and the Civilian Conservation Corps would use motor vehicles extensively in their work. If the Ford Motor Company did not sign, it would not receive the Blue Eagle emblem of the NRA, and would not be eligible to bid for government business.

But Ford feared to commit himself. Despite the "merit clause" in the code, he distrusted Section 7A. Quite as great a deterrent were his suspicions of the NACC. The Chamber had succeeded the Association of Licensed Automobile Manufacturers, which had tried to enforce the Selden patent. Ford had never joined it, never became a party to the useful NACC cross-licensing agreement, and had never permitted a Ford car to be shown in the annual show sponsored by the Chamber. Now, in 1933, he suspected an alliance between the New Deal, the big financiers, and his rivals. He did not proposed to come under their control. During the nineteen-thirties he jotted down in a little notebook certain comments that indicate his thinking. "To kill competition To regulate output," runs one. And again, "The whole thing is the most vicious attempt on the part of i.n.b.s. [international bankers?] to take over our government that was ever planned." Another jotting: "I do not think that this country is ready to be treated like Russia for a while. There is a lot of the pioneer spirit here yet."

The code, under the NACC as administrator, authorized an examination of the books of motor car producers. It did not fix production quotas, but Ford knew that other codes had, and believed that if the New Deal favored such a practice, it might be adopted. Since 1919, all company stock had been held by him and his family, and he did not propose to sanction an invasion of his business privacy.[25]

It did not matter that these considerations had no real validity. To Ford they were dangers, and he was willing to lose some benefits in order to be free of them. "Henry Ford," writes Peter F. Drucker, "was

both the last Populist and the greatest one." Populism, the reform movement of Ford's youth, was comparatively a "leftish" philosophy, but its
roots lay in rural unrest and protest, and while it demanded government protection of the people from monopolistic railroads, banks, and
manufacturers, and from unscrupulous middlemen, it never proposed
restrictions on the individual producer. It wanted free competition.
Ford, in his days of power, unlike other captains of industry, still held
to this doctrine.

As he refused to sign the code, he became the symbol of the individualist; an unpopular symbol with the administration, but not with
its opponents or even some of its adherents. The competitors of Ford,
having signed the code, were now receiving the stickers, placards, and
other materials supplied by NRA, and had a right to display the Blue
Eagle. Chrysler, in a full-page advertisement, boasted that it flew from
"every flagstaff" of his factories. "Proud and glad to do our part," ran
the Chevrolet slogan. Ford was the non-conformist. Johnson publicly
regretted this, and when asked what would happen to objectors "who
won't go along with the new code," he barked injudiciously, "They'll
get a sock in the nose!"

His remark suggested an impending clash. But for some time the administration still hoped that Ford would sign and even made overtures
to win his acceptance. He was invited to send a representative to the
hearings on the code held in Washington in mid-August. Later in the
month, Roosevelt, through Prince Louis Ferdinand of Germany, expressed concern about Ford's position. But the latter yielded no ground.
Instead, he began to formulate a policy which he was soon to follow:
to *observe* the code without accepting it. When the pact was finally
signed by the President on August 27, Ford was in a good position to
meet all its provisions, or better them.

Johnson was dissatisfied. Ford, he asserted, must sign if he wanted
the Blue Eagle, and on August 29 he set September 5 as a deadline for
full compliance. Regardless of whether or not Ford "observed" the
code, or even improved upon it, the government would purchase none
of his products. Johnson also appealed to the public. "I think the American people will crack down on him when the Blue Eagle is on other
cars," he said bluntly. "No corporation is rich enough and no group
strong enough to block this nation." [26]

He and the administration now seemed to be waiting for the impact of public disapproval to work upon the heretic. The press applied the pressure they hoped for. "In a fight between the eagle and the flivver," asked the Cleveland *Plain Dealer,* "who wins? Our bet is on the eagle . . . because the bird of the air rather than the bird of the roads has the moral backing of the public." In Pittsfield, Massachusetts, the *Eagle* conceded that the NRA was a "socialistic experiment," but concluded: "Right or wrong, that is the path we have elected to lead us out of the depression woods, and the laggards must be compelled to join up." The *New Republic* intimated that the government's plan was the forward-looking solution, and Ford's attitude an individualistic protest. Would the New Deal be able to harness the wild horses of pioneer America? The New York *Daily News* held Ford's acceptance to be essential. "If Mr. Ford can tell it (the New Deal) to go to hell and get away with it, it won't be long before some of the other big boys will do the same thing." [27]

In October, Charles Edison, son of Ford's friend and idol Thomas A. Edison, attempted to mediate. Evidently he wrote the industrialist about the code, and the latter replied at length. In a four-page, single-spaced letter probably composed by Cameron, Ford pointed to his enlightened labor record. "I have never bargained with my men, I have always bargained for them." He refused to welcome government interference in his business. "The nation has never seen a stranger spectacle," he remarked, "than press and people shouting victory because powerful major industries promised . . . to pay as much as $14 or $15 a week." He added later, "The code minimum wage is hardly a good dole." He had kept quiet because he did not want to diminish any measure of success which NIRA might be able to achieve. Signing? "There is nothing in the law requiring a man to sign; the only requirement is to obey."

Charles Edison showed the letter to Roosevelt, who said that Ford had missed the point. "If Henry will quit being a damn fool . . . and call me on the telephone I would be glad to talk to him." Young Edison reported this in a telephone discussion with Cameron. Ford had only to nod and the White House doors would open. But he was unresponsive, and in a letter of October 9 Edison threw up his hands. "As a Clearing House, I'm something of a flop." He felt that Ford was making a mistake.[28]

The government still had one potent weapon which the President himself invoked in a ruling of October 26, that unless the Comptroller-General dissented, the government under the NIRA could not buy products manufactured by firms that had not complied with industry codes. This was aimed at Ford by striking at his dealers. Many had signed the code, but of course their cars had been produced by a recalcitrant parent firm. "A billion dollar concern," exploded Johnson, "which does not subscribe for a Blue Eagle cannot hide behind a $10,000 company that does subscribe." He also talked of legal steps if Ford did not meet a request by the NACC for information on wages, employment, and working conditions.

Johnson's outburst was touched off by a bid on light trucks for the CCC submitted by the Northwest Motor Company, a Ford agency in Bethesda, Maryland. The War Department had already ordered the rejection of all bids involving Ford products for its new motorization and aviation program. However, the bid of the Northwest agency on a lot of 500 trucks for the CCC was, according to its owner, at least $169,000 less than that of the next lowest bidder, the Dodge Brothers. When this offer was refused, he protested that no manufacturer was associated with him, and threatened to sue.

The Ford Motor Company at once took the offensive. In statements issued on October 27, it accused Johnson of assuming the airs of a dictator, and pointed out that the Ford Motor Company had fully complied with the law. "Signing the code is not the law," it insisted. "Flying the Blue Eagle is not the law." Johnson, it asserted, "proposes to charge the American taxpayer a higher price in order to give Government business to a concern that pays lower wages than the Ford Motor Company does. . . . Johnson is not boycotting us. He is boycotting 5,300 American manufacturers [Ford agents who had signed the code] who cooperate with Johnson." [29]

Midway in the controversy, the Veterans Bureau announced that it had accepted a bid on one Ford car, and would buy it. "The bureaucratic machine has slipped a cog!" commented one newspaper. The bid fell under a judgment by Comptroller-General John R. McCarl that government contracts must go to the lowest bidder despite the President's ruling, and there was no question of McCarl's authority. As the *New York Times* remarked, "The Comptroller-General is solely an agent of Congress and his rulings . . . . cannot be set aside by the President." As a result, early in December, the CCC awarded the

Northwest Motor Company a contract for 818 trucks. However, Ford's success was short-lived, for early the following April, McCarl accepted a new executive order of March 14, 1934, which definitely forbade the consideration of bids involving Ford products.[30]

Ford never wavered in his refusal to sign the code. To some extent he was doubtless encouraged by the growing support he won from the public. He and Edsel had received some reproachful letters. "While the people at large provide the Ford Motor Company with protection and opportunity to do business," wrote one correspondent, "you can no longer operate a large enterprise with its many social as well as economic responsibilities like a plutocrat of former years." But most exhortations were of the opposite character. "Johnson's position weak," telegraphed one supporter. "Sincerely hope you stick to it and win." Wrote another: "Henry Ford should be commended for the great exhibition of real Americanism that he is now displaying . . . in his bloodless duel with the NRA." "I hope you lick hell out of the NRA," declared still another well-wisher. "Permit me to congratulate you upon your stand with the present damned rotten administration."

Fervent praise for Ford as a folk hero was mingled with these exhortations. "May the power, or deity, or God, that has guided you throughout your life, from your humble start . . . to the leadership you now command, guide and keep you always!" prayed an admirer.[31]

Journalists added their encouragement. "Henry Ford is literally a young man at seventy," said the influential Arthur Brisbane in a broadcast on the industrialist's birthday (July 30, 1933), "young physically, of course young mentally. When I last saw him, a short time since in Dearborn, he went up the long flight of steps two at a time . . . and when a younger man said, 'That is dangerous for your heart,' Mr. Ford replied, 'Make your heart get used to it.' " In the *New York Times,* Gladys H. Kelsey reported that Ford "now has become the bright and shining knight of the motor capital, which watches with approval of some hopefulness his latest tilt with generally accepted standards in his defiance of the NRA." Will Rogers had his jest: "When you start jerking the Fords out from under the travelling public, you are monkeying with the very foundations of American life." [32]

The Ford sales campaign was meanwhile going well. It was aided indirectly by the opening of Greenfield Village, with the Edison

Institute and historical museum, on June 12, 1933, and by the celebration four days later of the thirtieth anniversary of the founding of the company. While the corporation had no exhibit at the World's Fair in Chicago, one was being considered, and the Johansson precision gauges, manufactured by Ford, were on display in the Science and Industry section. Visitors to Chicago were made welcome at the large assembly plant there.

The advertising campaign opened in May with a series of letters from Henry Ford to the public. Emphasizing the quality of the car, he stressed past Ford accomplishments, and prophesied the dispersal of heavy industry "in village and country." But, he continued in July, "the past does not especially concern me; it has all been preparation for the future." In August: "We did not invent the 8-cylinder car. What we did was to make it possible for the average family to own one. As always, we have done the pioneering work. . . . Motor manufacturing practices will follow the trail we have blazed."

As the year closed, sales showed an increased volume, but no betterment of the company's position with respect to its rivals. Doubtless Ford was satisfied. He knew that had he been able to sell freely to the government, the record would have been brighter. He had played heretic at a price. But he was willing to pay it, for he had maintained his independence, and he must have suspected that his defiance was not without advertising value. Every day brought him reminders of the unique position he had achieved. It was reflected in news stories. Long-standing Ford customers praised his cars. Men, women, and children told him their troubles, sent him poems of praise, and begged for aid in an immense variety of projects. The assumption that Henry Ford could meet any practical problem and even achieve the impossible was widespread and persistent. One letter which found its way through the Detroit Board of Commerce to Edsel's office illustrates the widespread credulity in the Ford legend:

There is a story in our town that that large star in the west is a light put up by Mr. Ford every nite in honor of Mr. Edison. I have watched it several nights until it disappears; is there any truth in the story we here would like to know, if it isn't much trouble will you answer this
and oblige
Mrs. S. A. Leiby
Rd. 2 Box 41-B, New Castle, Pa.[33]

Before the New Deal could fully harness "the wild horses of pioneer America," this type of faith in a rugged individual would have to be modified.

## 6.

In the succeeding months, Ford gave little attention to the NRA. For the Northwest Company, its head, R. P. Sabine, continued to submit bids which the government rejected, and the Ford Motor Company brought suit to compel the Interior and Agriculture Departments to consider such offers. In June 1934, a court decision supported the government. When the issue was revived that summer in anticipation of a purchase of 3570 trucks for the Works Progress Administration, Johnson made it clear that "observing" the code was insufficient and Ford did not bid.

He was far more interested during 1934 in pushing his new V-8, Lincoln, and truck models. These had been features of a "Ford Exhibition of Progress" which opened in New York on December 9, 1933. In presenting them, the industrialist gave the administration a friendly pat, admonishing his dealers over a forty-one city telephone hookup: "We have all got to pitch in and do all the business we can to help the President pull the country out of the hole." The following month, he approved the purpose of the NRA "in trying to make industry do what we were doing twenty years ago," but remarked that it "hadn't tackled the fundamentals yet." [34]

In the fall of 1934, President Roosevelt made his third attempt in a little more than a year to arrange a personal meeting with Ford. (After his first invitation through Charles Edison, he had written in November 1933, directly to Ford, who courteously refused on the ground that, because of the NRA, a visit would be misconstrued.) The President had doubtless seen Ford's comment that "the President was doing the best he could in an extraordinarily difficult situation." He knew that Ford had approved the general purpose of the NRA, though not its operation. The two men had exchanged birthday greetings.*

Roosevelt could scarcely have hoped to persuade Ford to sign the

---

* Ford also kept in touch with former President Hoover, who had presided over the Greenfield Village Edison semi-centenary celebration in 1929, more than four years before the village was opened to the public. Ford telegraphed him on Oct. 21, 1934: "At this hour five years ago you kindled the fire in the Lincoln Courthouse in Greenfield Village. The fire is still burning." Hoover replied appreciatively. (Acc. 587, Box 7)

code, for the NRA was crumbling and Johnson resigned in September. Evidently the President planned to promote a general friendliness that might be useful for the future. Henry Ford was, after all, a national institution, and when the next war crisis came his importance to Roosevelt and the nation would be reëmphasized. The President wrote, on November 8, that he was giving some thought to the placing of industries in small towns. "I know of your great interest in this. . . . It would be fine if you could come down to Warm Springs while I am there [which was to be soon] in order that we may have a good talk about this and other matters. I hope Mrs. Ford can come down with you."

Ford declined the invitation, pleading Clara Ford's ill health, but wrote that Edsel and his wife would be happy to come. The President sent his cordial acquiescence. As a result, on November 24, the Edsel Fords arrived for friendly talks. They watched while Roosevelt took a dip in the glass-enclosed swimming pool of the Warm Springs Foundation, contributed by Edsel and his wife some six years earlier. They enjoyed a picnic at Flat Shoals. But the talks did not go far, for when questioned about the NRA by reporters, Edsel spoke in his father's words: "We have not signed an NRA compliance certificate," he said, "and have no intention of doing so. However, we are complying 100 per cent and more with the code requirements." [35]

On November 1, 1934, Henry Ford announced his program for the coming year. He would spend amply on advertising and plant expansion, produce "a million cars or better," and await the result confidently. "So far as the Ford Motor Company is concerned, the depression is over." He believed that it would be better for the country as a whole "if American industrialists would just forget these alphabet schemes and take hold of their industries and run them with good, sound, American business sense."

During 1935, a new glass factory, a hot strip rolling mill, and a new cold sheet finishing mill rose at the Rouge, while the entire power plant there was thoroughly modernized. On January 23 a work force of almost 70,000 men was employed at the plant, the largest since 1929. The sweep upward since January 1933 had been dramatic. Despite his refusal to sign the code, Ford had prospered, making an improvement which outstripped that of his two rivals.

As in 1923-1924, he was even proposed as a candidate for the presidency. "I have high regard for Mr. Hoover," wrote one admirer in late October 1935, "but Mr. Ford will take the votes." A Vermont printing company sold stickers: "The People's Choice: Henry Ford for President, 1936." While no man of sense took this fantastic activity seriously, it may have fortified Ford's belief that he would find support were a renewed attack made upon his independence.[36] His approbatory mail may also have encouraged him in believing that he might pursue unscathed another line of action that was far more vulnerable than his course on the NRA: a labor policy that was out of harmony, not merely with New Deal ideas, but with the basic trends of the time.

# II

# THE TROUBLED MARCH OF LABOR

To WEATHER the brief storm over its relations with NRA was easy enough for the Ford Motor Company; but meanwhile a far graver tempest was gathering, and about to burst on its head with staggering fury.

Although a just solution of its labor problems was fundamental in the long run to the public position of the company, the relations of management with the workers during the nineteen-thirties were destined to be tragically unhappy. From the beginning of the decade, labor in the automotive industry showed a growing determination to achieve better organization, fuller civil rights, and fairer hours and wages. Despite the depression, it was less and less willing to submit to the harsh treatment which it got in many factories, and not least that of Ford.

## 2.

The first years of the Great Depression found a young Detroiter, who had just left Dayton University with a diploma and a reputation as football tackle, working in the Chrysler factory to support his wife and baby. His name was Richard T. Frankensteen, and he was soon to become noted in the labor movement. Paid only 49 cents an hour or $3.92 a day, he had to borrow money to pay for the delivery of his child. He had often read the statement which Walter Chrysler kept posted on the bulletin boards: "Our door is always open. Come in and present your problems. We will discuss any matter with you." But when he submitted a statement upon living costs to the Works Council, with a request for better pay, the vice president in charge of labor relations rebuffed him.

"We don't control the price of butter, Mr. Frankensteen," he said.

"We have nothing to do with the question whether your wife is as frugal as another man's wife. We don't control the level of rents. All we can say to you is that we pay a competitive going rate—and if we paid more, we'd be out of business."

To Frankensteen this retort was illuminating. "It made plain to me that the only answer was to organize," he said later. "*We* workers had to take care of the competitors." Industry-wide unions alone would put a stop to competitive wage cutting.[1] Everywhere in the country workers thrust into poverty, like Frankensteen, took heart from Roosevelt's belief in the need for strong unions, and from the protections promised in Section 7A; everywhere they cast about for leadership.

When they looked back, they saw the necessity for resolute effort. The position of the unions before the stock market crash of 1929 had been weak, and the next thirty months of deflation and unemployment had worsened it. The whole trend of the twelve years of Harding, Coolidge, and Hoover, in fact, had been disastrous to labor. Workers had bitter memories of great strikes lost—the steel strike, the railway shopmen's strike, coal strikes; of adverse court decisions; and of an open-shop campaign heavily financed by capital under the label of "The American Plan." They remembered how ruthlessly various sick industries like Southern textile manufacturing had exploited their hands by low wages, the production "stretchout," long hours, and the use of children.

In the automotive field labor felt a special bitterness, for nowhere, not in the plants of the smaller companies, not in those of Chrysler, not in the many factories of General Motors, had unionism gained a firm hold. For years Ford had represented an exception, and unionism had approved him, but in the early 1930s his high wage policy had collapsed, and his doctrinaire opposition to labor organization, activated by the opportunistic Harry Bennett and his squads of spies and *provocateurs,* was rapidly promoting a condition where unionism was needed for the protection of the rank and file of workers.

Meanwhile, the American Federation of Labor under William Green had certainly not offered unskilled or semi-skilled toilers any shining beacon of hope. Based on craft unions, it had largely ignored the men and women of the mass-production industries. Between 1920 and 1933 its membership had sunk from slightly more than 4,000,000 to only 2,125,000. Representing the best paid workers in the most prosperous industries, it was essentially conservative. In strike after strike, it had failed to give hard-pressed workingmen any useful aid: the strikes of miners, textile hands, packing-house employees, and Andrew Furuseth's seamen's union. It had allied itself with employers in shielding them from agitators and promoting the efficiency of labor.[2]

In no area, moreover, had the AFL attempted less down to 1933 than in the automotive industry. William Green and other leaders had dreamed at times of organizing it, but they never translated their dreams into bold action. Instead, they let selfish divisions cripple all effort. For example, when the carriage-makers' union strove in the 1920s to enroll auto workers, it met the rivalry of the blacksmiths' union, painters' union, upholsterers' union, and a dozen other crafts, all claiming and receiving Federation support. This factionalism, with the stony hostility of employers, kept union membership insignificant. In 1929 the carriage-workers' union had only about 1500 adherents in an industry employing half a million people, and other craft unions were as feeble. The AFL leaders never even began to interest a majority of automotive employes in their hazy plan for federal unions, and General Motors and Ford were so fiercely hostile that Green dropped the scheme.

As the depression plunged thousands into despair, radical elements had inevitably pushed forward to offer an aggressive program. Communists had been active in the Passaic strike of textile workers in 1925–1926, and in 1926 had temporarily taken over the International Ladies' Garment Workers Union in New York City. When the long-suffering "lint heads" of North Carolina cotton mills struck against a 55-hour week and other abuses, Communists had seized their opportunity. They had played an important part in the labor struggles in Gastonia and Marion, marked by violence which caused a number of deaths. In the automobile industry they had gained a precarious foothold in 1929 by seizing the old Automotive, Aircraft, and Vehicle Workers' Union, which they rechristened the Auto Workers' Union, and they had formed a few cells elsewhere within the industry.[3]

It would be easy to overstate the strength of the Communists in American industry in general and automobile factories in particular, for they were never numerically powerful. But they showed a capacity for trouble-making out of all proportion to their numbers. They made the most of the Trade Union Department of the Communist Party, from which William Z. Foster mobilized all their forces to press two related campaigns: the organization of wage earners and the whipping up of discontent among the unemployed. Communist interest in workless men was for obvious reasons even greater than in workers. Under Marxian theory, jobless people were natural products of the crisis in capitalism that led to revolution; they could be incited to angry outbreaks that would intensify the class struggle and hasten the overthrow of the old order. While Communist leaders thought unions valuable as agencies for teaching discipline and unity to the workers, this role was merely transitory. The final goal was not collective bargaining with employers, but a politico-social assault that would overthrow the entire capitalist structure. Red organizers, therefore, put fiercer effort into establishing a network of Unemployed Councils than into augmenting the ranks of the Auto Workers' Union.[4]

Like the steel, cotton textile, lumber, and machine-tools industries, automotive manufacturing seemed by 1932 a fertile field for Communist seed. Employment had dropped catastrophically. In September 1932, the automobile factories were using 60.8 per cent fewer hands than a year earlier. Probably half the men were making less than $1,000 a year. Arbitrary discharges, espionage, exhausting speed-ups, and the petty tyrannies of foremen poisoned the atmosphere of most plants. Amid the general discontent, an important part of the Communist effort in 1931–1932 lay in the staging of "hunger marches." In St. Louis, New York, Akron, Albany, Los Angeles, and other cities these demonstrations disturbed sober citizens and angered the police. Nowhere was material for a "hunger march" more abundant than in Detroit.

Largest of these factories was the immense Ford complex on the Rouge; and Communist leaders would find special zest in levelling a blow at it and its famous head. Renowned from China to Chile, it had become a symbol of both the shining achievements of capitalism, and the regimentation of workers. Henry Ford seemed to multitudes, ever since the five-dollar-day of 1914, a liberator, but to multitudes of others the assembly-line made him a tyrant. Any demonstration against him would resound around the globe. Benjamin Gitlow, head since 1929 of the American Communist Party, tells us that for a long time party officers had received urgent cables from the Comintern—hundreds in the aggregate—urging unionization of the industry and special efforts to attack Ford.[5]

Any important success in Detroit would elude the Communists until clashes with the police, bloodshed, and martyrdom flowered out of their demonstrations. They needed another Haymarket Riot! Mayor Frank Murphy of Detroit, later Governor of Michigan and Justice of the Supreme Court, grasped the fact, and for reasons of shrewd policy as well as respect for civil rights ordered city officials to permit parades, and avoid interference with orderly meetings—to the great irritation of the frustrated Communists. Riots were so conspicuously absent that hardly even a case of nosebleed was recorded. The minions of "plutocratic tyranny" were not playing the game. If they were not goaded into rash action, all the talk of class war would collapse ignominiously.[6]

To avert this calamity, the Communists arranged another "hunger march" through Detroit and Dearborn to the gates of the Rouge on Monday, March 7, 1932, and to improve the chances of trouble took care not to ask either city for a permit.[7] Several thousand men arrived at the rendezvous in Detroit, some on foot, some by jammed streetcars —refusing to pay their fares and shouting "Charge it to Ford!" They fell into a mile-long line, banners waving and placards wobbling above them. Progress through Detroit was orderly, for Murphy provided a police escort to the Dearborn boundary. As the marchers swung up Miller Road in Dearborn toward the Ford employment office, however, trouble began. The police deployed across their path, and ordered them to disperse. The genesis of this display of Dogberryism is not clear, for previous demonstrations had been held in front of the Rouge plant with no untoward results. Some observers thought that Dearborn officials had been irritated by the failure to apply for a permit; others that the police were angered by the evasion of car-fares; still others that a bit of recent brick-hurling and window-smashing had convinced the authorities that it was time to take a stand. Gitlow asserts that the marchers intended to occupy the plant, using machinery to barricade its doors.[8] If word of this had gotten out, the police might have decided that it was best to act promptly.

At any rate, they followed the order for dispersal with a discharge of tear gas. The March wind flung it back into their faces; and as Harry Bennett, in charge of the plant security, writes, "A free-for-all developed quickly, and in a short time the Dearborn police had the devil beat out of them." The marchers pushed on up Miller Road. As they swung forward the Dearborn fire department rallied with hoses to aid the police, and a frantic telephone call brought contingents of Detroit patrolmen to the scene.

The upshot was a sharp, bloody battle at the Rouge gates, accounts of which are confused and contradictory. The one certain fact is that four demonstrators were killed by gunfire, twenty more wounded, five of them seriously, and a substantial number of police and firemen injured by bricks, stones, and clubs. Only the police used firearms, and the question whether they were justified in this is undeterminable.[9]

Bennett has furnished the most vivid story of the affray. He and ex-Governor Green were reviewing some motion pictures in the plant—Henry and Edsel being away at lunch—when he heard that the fire department was dousing a mob on Miller Road. It was a bitterly cold day. He tells us that he had a vision of wrathful headlines over photographs of ice-coated victims. "That's going to be some more nice publicity for the Ford Company!" he exclaimed, and hurried out to stop the violence. Finding the fire chief, he expostulated. The chief, after growling, "Why, they're a bunch of Communists," nevertheless turned off the water. Pleased with this success, Bennett decided to reach the marchers, address them, and persuade them to go home. He drove up to the line and got out of the car. When a woman brick-thrower told him, "We want Bennett, and he's in that building," he retorted: "No, you're wrong; I'm Bennett." Instantly a shower of slag descended upon him. As he fell, he instinctively seized one of the leaders, 19-year-old Joe York, district organizer of the Young Communist League, and pulled him down too. At that moment the Dearborn police at the plant gate and the Detroit police on the overpass opened fire, instantly killing York.

Continuing to display more energy than discretion, Bennett clambered to his feet only to be knocked unconscious by one of the mob. This was fortunate, as he later concluded, because if he had not fallen, one side or the other would have killed him.[10]

Though Charles Sorensen was not present, he was able to assure Sir Percival Perry that Bennett was the only member of the staff outside the plant at the time, and that he was trying to quell the riot. "It was absolutely necessary for the police to rescue him." Bennett had to be taken to the Henry Ford Hospital. A story later circulated by labor partisans pictured him as driving into the parade firing a tear gas gun, and responding to a shower of stones with his revolver. He had meant well, but after the original blunder of the police and firemen in using tear gas and hoses to halt an orderly march, his impetuous self-exposure had made matters worse.[11]

Of course the Communists exploited all the propaganda values of the tragedy. Taking care to postpone the funerals to Saturday, they used the intervening four days to whip up emotion. Ten thousand people paraded down Woodward Avenue to East Ferry Avenue in downtown Detroit, their band playing the Russian funeral march of 1905 and the *Internationale*. Ten thousand more gathered at Woodmere cemetery, almost in the shadow of the Rouge plant, and as the bodies were lowered thousands raised their clenched fists in the Communist salute. Speakers exhorted the crowd to march on Detroit City Hall the following Monday to protest to Mayor Murphy and the city council against police "murders." [12]

This attempt to blacken Murphy was outrageous, for he had befriended the workers and scrupulously protected the rights of radical groups. He told the *New Republic* that organizers of parades did not even need permits if they served due notice of their intentions. "In Detroit mass meetings and parades are held as a matter of right— police merely supervise and regulate." He welcomed grievance committees at City Hall. But the Communists, hoping to destroy so able a democratic leader, raised the cry: "Smash the Murphy-Ford Police Terror." [13]

A Wayne County grand jury, after investigation, brought in a moderate and sensible report. It laid the responsibility for organizing the march squarely on men connected with the Communist Party. It also concluded that the conduct of the demonstrators was reckless and illegal, and that the Dearborn police had acted with good intentions if poor judgment. Although the rioters did considerable damage to Ford property, the grand jury found that no Ford officer had resorted to the use of force. The most incisive newspaper comment, by the *New York Times* of March 13, 1932, applied to the industry as a whole —indeed, to all American industry. The misery which generated such explosions, the editors pointed out, arose from the fact that masses of wage-earners had been suddenly plunged into unemployment and penury. "Not half the men who were employed in 1929 are working today, yet most of them and their families are still in Detroit, hoping against hope and leading a hand-to-mouth existence."

Until the jobless multitude was given jobs, unrest would persist. Some hope for a temporary remedy was placed in a prompt showing of the new models of Ford and other automobile companies, which might help stimulate a revival of buying. Throughout the spring and summer of 1932, however, the situation remained grim—grim enough to encourage Communist leaders to maintain a systematic siege of Detroit. This was directed partly by William Z. Foster as representative of the Comintern, and partly by Earl Browder, general secretary of the national party organization. In Detroit several men were perniciously active: William Weinstone, a political organizer of great shrewdness, Maurice Sugar, an aggressive labor attorney, William K. Gebert, a leader of the Polish radicals, and Joe Kowalski, long editor of the Polish journal *Voice of the People* (*Glos Ludowy*). But the real authority lay overseas. "Everything the Communists did in Detroit," declares Gitlow, "was done according to plan in much the same way as a military high command carries on its operations. The plans were first formulated in Moscow. . . . Never, in important operations, were the Detroit Communists left on their own. Special emissaries were sent out by the Comintern . . . . to guide them." [14]

Fortunate it was that the Presidential campaign this fall of 1932 gave masses of suffering voters an outlet for their anger, and still more fortunate that it brought into power a president with a broad constructive program. But the happiest fact of all was that the workers, even in stricken Detroit, remained fundamentally anti-revolutionary. Though the old American economy had temporarily failed them, they still believed in it.

### 3.

The underlying conservatism of most wage-earners was soon emphatically illustrated. Just after Roosevelt's victory a strike occurred in the Briggs Manufacturing Company, which made bodies for Ford and had leased a section of the Highland Park works. The Ford heads knew they were safe from any work-stoppage in their own plants, for the employes were completely unorganized, and the city was full of men hungry for a wage envelope. But labor conditions in some supplier factories were so much worse than in the large automobile establishments themselves that a spasmodic explosion took place. Late in January 1933, the Briggs workers, without visible organization, without funds, and almost without hope, spontaneously dropped their tools. They felt that they could endure no more. Average hourly earnings had fallen as low as ten cents, for they labored under a piece-work system which included no pay for "dead time" when materials were unavailable, even though they had to remain at their work stations. Men stumbled home after a frustrating day with eighty or ninety cents.

As the Briggs strike forced about 40,000 Ford men out of work, the uprising spread. Some 3000 body workers in the Hudson Company quit, demanding a 20 per cent rise in wages. At the important Motor Products plant 1200 men walked out. The Murray factory and others were compelled to close. Although at most only 9000 Briggs workers struck, perhaps 60,000 men were made idle altogether.[15]

The Briggs strike was doomed to early failure, for in the trough of the depression even desperate men lacked the means to fight long. It showed effective strength for only a week. The first days of February found Briggs gradually increasing its production with strikebreakers, and by the 15th its output was normal. But although the workers were defeated and about half of them lost their jobs, they accomplished two results which deeply impressed the Detroit community.

Their revolt showed, in the first place, that wage-cutting had reached an intolerable stage. The press and public were insisting that pay *must* turn upward. *Business Week* commented that labor, like other commodities, had its rock-bottom price. "This first 'depression strike' is the beginning of a balancing process which establishes the limit of pay and hours and treatment which men will stand."[16] The Briggs Company, while rejecting the major demands, was compelled to grant a minimum wage of 25 cents an hour, with pay for "dead time." In other plants where sympathetic strikes occurred or were threatened, management had to make concessions. At least two companies cancelled proposed wage cuts to avoid strikes, and heads of the Hudson Company agreed to negotiate with a workers' committee.

The second result of the body workers' strike was a demonstration that these impoverished men had no Red leanings whatever. To all Communist approaches they turned a hostile shoulder. Some mean-spirited efforts by the employers to fix a Communist label on the walkout aroused the anger of the Briggs strike committee. It was the Briggs Company, they declared, which had fostered radicalism by permitting inhuman conditions in its plants. "We dare anyone to accuse us to our faces of being other than true American workingmen, with any other motive than that of seeking living wages and reasonable working conditions." [17] The strikers saw that self-help through collective bargaining was their only future hope. As they received no encouragement from the American Federation of Labor, some of them were ready to hew their own path.

A month after the Briggs strike broke down, those workers who had fought to the last incorporated what they hoped would become a general mass-production union, the Automotive Industrial Association, its doors open to all workers regardless of race, color, creed, or skill. It announced its intention of helping "stem the tide of Radical Communism now spreading through the country," and of promoting co-operative relations with employers which might avert strikes. The AIA continued during 1933 to solicit unskilled membership. Other unions arose. Just after Roosevelt was inaugurated, the Mechanics' Educational Society sprang into life, and soon enrolled 25,000 members among skilled tool and die makers. A little later that year, a body called the Associated Automotive Workers became active.[18]

These new groups were small and weak, their future uncertain. So were the carriage-makers' union and craft unions incorporated in the American Federation of Labor. In short, so far as the automotive industry went, labor organization was still embryonic. But light lay ahead. Roosevelt's NRA attempted to meet not only the aspirations of the social reformers who thought that wealth should be redistributed to improve purchasing capacity, and the requirements of businessmen who hoped to regain prosperity under codes of fair practices, but the demands of labor for a floor under wages and a ceiling over hours, and for a guaranteed right to organize for collective bargaining. When, on May 8, 1933, Roosevelt spoke to the nation over the radio, he declared that his program included plans for giving wage-earners a fair return, and the power to bargain collectively through agents of their own choice. And when next month he signed the Recovery Act, with its epochal guarantee of organizational rights in Section 7A, labor's hopes ran even higher than general public enthusiasm for the measure.[19]

4.

The critical question for labor was whether industry would carry out in good faith this colossal experiment in self-regulation, based upon codes to be negotiated with the workers as well as government. Or would it use its superior power to "chisel" on labor, hours, and other matters? We have noted the general excitement throughout industry, as Hugh S. Johnson took office, over the formation of codes;[20] and labor shared this excitement, for its future was at stake. Automobile workers among the rest began nervously laying plans for action, and the Automotive Industrial Association, the Mechanics' Educational Society, and a newly formed body, the Federation of Automotive Workers, all scrutinized the possibilities of the situation.

Ten days after Roosevelt signed the law, the American Federation of Labor held a meeting of several of its craft unions in Washington, and during the initial week of the NRA placed William Collins, its first full-time organizer in this field, in Detroit. This appointment commanded no enthusiasm in the automobile shops. Collins was too much wedded to craft-union ideas, too contemptuous of illiterate foreign-born workers, and too deficient in energy, to make a good organizer in a mass-production industry. Although he had the assistance of several full-time aides in Michigan, and of part-time organizers in Cleveland and other cities, he made little progress. Such workers as came forward were enrolled in local unions, usually one to each plant, with direct AFL charters. Six locals were thus formed in Detroit by the end of July 1933, but they had to operate in clandestine fashion, Collins not daring to give the men union cards for fear of company retaliation.[21]

Because the industry had always been aggressively open-shop—and Detroit an open-shop city in general—the central issues of the automobile code concerned labor. This Hugh Johnson quite realized as he strove to bring the manufacturers, including Henry Ford, into line. According to Harry Bennett, Ford formed a prejudice against the NRA when Pierre Du Pont, whom he disliked, urged him to sign the code; and it is clear that his distrust of the NACC was also a consideration. The fundamental fact, however, was that he, like all the major automobile manufacturers, had an intense aversion to the provision for recognition of the unions; that it was Section 7A that most disturbed him. "Apparently his objection to the code," stated a New York *Sun* dispatch, "is that it requires him to recognize the right of his employes to organize as they please for the purpose of collective bargaining." [22]

Labor watched helplessly as, after much debate, the NACC filed the proposed automobile code at the end of July 1933. The industry discussed and modified it in open hearings the next month, and on August 27 the President approved it. Labor watched helplessly again as all the manufacturers subscribed to it except Ford. Apparently he had placed himself in a special category of non-cooperation; but actually, no vital distinction existed between his position and that of the general group of automobile-makers. Neither the group nor he had any intention of accepting Section 7A. While Ford, with more blunt honesty than tact, repudiated it openly, the other manufacturers set about nullifying it by evasion. The automotive industry was simply not ready to give up its whip-hand, the open shop.[23]

Ford was encouraged in his outright repudiation, and the other manufacturers in their evasion, by the impotence of the workers. Lack of time to organize, the lukewarm temper and poor strategy of the AFL, and a realization that the huge floating population in the Detroit area was ready to "scab" in any dispute, made these mass-production workers a mere drifting herd. When President William Green rose in the hearings on the NACC code to offer a few mild amendments, the employers treated him as a toothless mastiff. And when representatives of the Automotive Industrial Association and the Federation of Automotive Workers presented demands that would have given the code a semblance of partnership and equity, they were just as contemptuously ignored, for everybody knew they could only wag a forefinger. As an AIA participant later said: "The code was simply drawn up in complete disregard of labor. It was signed with equal disregard." [24]

The employers at first tried to throw Section 7A out of the window. That is, they proposed to amend it by a stipulation that they should "continue the open-shop policy heretofore followed and under which unusually satisfactory and harmonious relations with employes have been maintained." At this Hugh Johnson exploded in anger. He declared: "There can't be any language that uses 'open shop' or 'closed shop' or any of that." Donald Richberg, general counsel of the NRA, supported him with a reasonable objection. Organized labor, he said, had always given the words 'open shop' just one interpretation—it meant a shop closed to union men. The employers' stipulation would therefore be construed by labor as a refusal of compliance with the law: "It is improper to incorporate in the code any phrase subject to such construction." [25] The companies thereupon fell back to their second line of defence, a demand, in effect, for a guarantee of full liberty in hiring and firing. This was embodied in a "merit clause;" they would select, hold, and promote employes, the clause ran, "on the basis of individual merit" without regard to their affiliation or non-affiliation with any labor or other organization.[26]

This right to hire and fire without respect to seniority, as labor leaders pointed out, flung the door wide open to the destruction of unions. "Merit" in an employe would coincide miraculously with non-membership in any union; troublesome union leaders would conspicuously lack "merit." But the government had to accept the code on the theory that a poor agreement was better than none. It knew that the manufacturers, who anticipated no great advantages from the legalization of cooperative trade practises, were prepared to say: "If we have to abandon the open shop, then we will do without any code." [27] At heart, many of them would have liked to follow Ford's example and reject the Blue Eagle, or, as he called it, "Roosevelt's Buzzard." They simply lacked his callousness and his sense of invulnerability to public opinion.

Roosevelt, therefore, approved the code with the inclusion of the "merit clause," its original language but slightly changed. William Green persuaded himself that a little face-saving phraseology, declaring that the clause should not be used to weaken collective bargaining "by interpretation," was an adequate safeguard. Practically nobody else in labor, management, or government shared his view.[28] Officers of motor companies wore the satisfied smile of the Nigerian tiger. When management in other industries demanded similar "merit clauses," Hugh Johnson shamefacedly called the concession to the automobile manufacturers "a slip," and Richberg announced that it established no precedent. In discussing the negotiations for the soft coal code, Johnson declared emphatically that such language "would be allowed in no other industrial agreements." [29]

In short, the automobile oligarchs were given preferential treatment (though the steel industry also made it plain that its principal companies would not recognize the unions). One automobile journal jubilantly announced that the code was "the first victory of industry over organized labor" under the Recovery Act.[30] As it took effect September

5, labor found the code largely nugatory. It provided for a 35-hour week, except in seasonal rushes, when work might be stretched to 48 hours, and for wages ranging from 41 to 43 cents an hour. This pay level was manifestly below the average of the industry, and still further below the average of Ford, General Motors, or Chrysler. Henry Ford crisply stated of the code: "If we tried to live up to it, we would have to live down to it." To emphasize this fact, on the day it took effect, he announced wage increases varying from 40 cents to $1 a day. Company records, indeed, showed that ever since July he had been bringing details of his hours and wages arrangements into conformity with the code standards, or above them. The conclusion of one careful student that the wage-hour requirements in the automobile industry were unlikely either to augment purchasing power or to spread work seems indisputable.[31]

So far as these requirements went, the Ford Company could easily have accepted the code, and had they stood alone Henry Ford would probably have signed it. And so far as the collective bargaining stipulation of Section 7A went, no great moral distinction can be drawn between Ford and the other employers. While he impudently flouted it, they quietly and slyly buried it.

The principal tool in this adroit burial, the "merit clause," worked well. In the fall of 1933 the companies that signed the code began discharging men in a way which proved their inveterate hostility to labor organization. When they rehired help after layoffs, they favored non-union men over union members of greater seniority. Though labor leaders protested against this and against sundry violations of the rule as to hours, such abuses increased during 1934. Another burial-tool was the formation of company unions to deflect the workers' movement into easily controlled channels. Employers in many industries began creating labor organizations that were typically confined to the wage-earners of a single plant, and were easily controlled; and in this the automotive companies of the NACC were not behindhand. They argued that such "kept" unions had the advantage of low dues, friendly relations with employers, and freedom from interference by outside labor leaders. Clearly they also had the disadvantage of total inability to fight. These facts led some men later to term the auto code "as rotten an egg as was ever hatched by the Blue Eagle." [32]

5.

While the Ford Company went its independent way, its peculiar in-
tolerance for unions found some striking illustrations. In September
1933, most of the 2500 unorganized workers in its assembly plant at
Chester, Pennsylvania, spontaneously walked out and formed an AFL
local. On orders from Dearborn, the manager thereupon posted notice
that the works were closed indefinitely, and refused to discuss the dispute with the employes' committee or the mediator of the National
Labor Board of the NRA. Although the indignant chairman of this
board, Senator Robert F. Wagner, recommended drastic action, the
government did nothing. The complaints of the hard-pressed strikers
aroused much public indignation in Pennsylvania. Yet, by hiring strikebreakers and inducing some men to return, the plant was able to reopen
in mid-October.[33]

When it opened, the managers recalled only 800 of the more than
2000 who had quit work. After ten days of waiting, a union committee
gained a hearing, but its pleas on behalf of the unemployed hands fell
on deaf ears. The manager, on November 10, finally handed the committee a statement that he would take back former workers only on
the basis of merit, "without discrimination," and would not treat with
any union deputation. Union officers, appealing to the NLB for help
in making collective bargaining a reality, and to the AFL for support,
got no assistance from either. Finally, learning that their secretary was
probably a Ford spy, the union disbanded. Henry Ford had swiftly
crushed the first invasion of his domain.[34]

Pickets from the Chester works meanwhile, at the end of September,
induced employes at the assembly plant in Edgewater, New Jersey, to
launch what was primarily a sympathetic strike, although the Edgewater people had special grievances as to pay and hours. Within a few
days, about 1600 out of 2000 men and women quit. Here the AFL already had a local, and although its heads at first strove to prevent the
walkout, later they did their best to make it a success. This time the
Ford Company used more subtle methods. The managers, after a
month's wait, met with union representatives, so that the NLB ruled
that its requirements as to collective bargaining had been met; but the
strikers declared that they were treated so evasively that no true bargaining took place at all. Intra-company correspondence shows that,

while the managers publicly denied any discrimination against union men, privately they were reporting to Dearborn on the implementation of a discriminatory policy.

Edsel Ford was consulted, but he had no influence whatever on the unyielding attitude of the executives. The best admonition he could offer went no further than: "Be careful—Section 7(a) of code." In the end, the Edgewater strike simply guttered out. It lost its chief *raison d'être* when the Chester strike failed, while the plant heads found that 1200 workers were enough to meet their current needs. Again, many men were left jobless, and the union was crippled.[35]

Company after company, throughout the automotive industry, offered a callous defiance of Section 7A that grew into a national scandal. Union leaders were ejected from factories, and union organizations ignored. Early in 1934 the discontent in the Buick, Hudson, and Fisher Body plants had become so acute as to threaten strikes. While unrest in the Ford works was serious, Ford's restoration of the $5-a-day minimum wage for 47,000 workers did much to cut the ground from under union leaders.[36] Companies in the NACC reduced the working week while maintaining the daily pay level. But these concessions did not satisfy automotive workers who felt outraged by the discharge of union men, the disregard of seniority, and the total veto which auto factories put upon collective bargaining. On March 13, 1934, sixty union officers descended upon Washington with warnings of an insurrection unless the wholesale violations were ended; they would call strikes, widespread, immediate, and determined, if the government did not act.[37]

This was a crisis. The chances of national recovery, which then seemed roseate, might be shattered by such a blow. At first, the NACC was unyielding. Discussing the issues with Hugh Johnson and William Collins, its heads declared flatly: "The industry does not intend to recognize the AFL as such."[38] They would enter into no contract with the Federation. The automobile workers, equally determined, held angry meetings in various cities to support their representatives in Washington. On March 20 the alarmed President called both the labor and industry leaders to the White House, seeing them separately. Talks dragged through several days. Of the two groups, the labor men were still decidedly the weaker, for organization had been slow, and the continuing depression left the labor market glutted. They were also the more reasonable. Collins, reflecting the characteristic conservatism of the AFL, telegraphed the locals in the factories to postpone their walk-out, while the manufacturers continued to sputter arguments in favor of the open shop, and to declare that they would never permit employes to form "unions of their own choosing" for collective bargaining.

In these circumstances the "peace plan" which the White House got both sides to accept, and which Roosevelt announced on March 25, 1934, was nearly as one-sided as the code. Under his scheme, the employers agreed to bargain with freely elected representatives of worker groups; but what groups? One sentence read: "The government makes it clear that it favors no particular union or form of employee organization of representation." This gave company unions a position never contemplated by the authors of Section 7A. Worse still, the plan provided for proportional representation of different groups on the bargaining committee. That is, "kept" company unions, AFL unions, independent unions like the Automotive Industrial Association, and other groups should elect members on a pro rata basis.

This provision gave management an ideal opportunity to divide the workers and set one group against another. It stimulated the creation of more company unions. The new peace arrangement also established a board under the NRA to deal with alleged infractions of the rule (now reaffirmed) which forbade discrimination in the hiring, retention, or discharge of workers. Obviously the value of this board would depend on the zeal and courage of the members. Leo Wolman, Professor of Economics in Columbia, was appointed chairman, Richard Byrd, secretary of a General Motors local, the labor representative, and the able New York attorney Nicholas H. Kelley, the employer member. It leaned so strongly toward conservatism that Alfred P. Sloan of General Motors commented: "All's well that ends well." [39]

Roosevelt hailed the peace plan in the automobile industry as an encouraging development in a dark time, declaring that it had charted a new path in social engineering, and furnished the best basis yet found in any large industry for a just and comprehensive system of industrial relations. This was calling Apples of Sodom a deliciously nutritive food. To be sure, at first the AFL officials offered the approving purrs expected of them. President Green cooed that at long last the automobile managers had conceded the right to organize, and had promised true collective bargaining; William Collins telegraphed Federation men in Flint to give up all thought of striking—"It's the biggest victory they

ever won." But perceptive labor men did not find the plan at all satisfactory, and agreed to it only for two reasons: the sole alternative was
a strike which they were not strong enough to carry to victory, and they
still felt a certain faith in Roosevelt. "He asked us to trust him," said
Byrd, "and we will." The Washington correspondents of the *New York
Times* and the St. Louis *Post-Dispatch* had no illusions. They correctly
reported that the drive of labor for a fair balance of bargaining power
with the rulers of the automobile industry had reached its Second
Manassas.[40]

The defeat proved crushing, partly because the President's plan gave
company unions full status, and, where they were numerically strong,
a high representation; while it did nothing to strengthen the unions
truly representative of labor. General Motors had lost no time in organizing its own employes' association and a "works council" in every
plant where it could muster a following. Chrysler had done the same,
blithely announcing in the fall of 1933 that 86 per cent of its workers
had voted in favor of a "joint shop council" plan. Other automotive
corporations cajoled or pushed their wage-earners aboard the same
bandwagon. The company unions, as one employe bitterly remarked,
could obtain such marginal benefits as larger milk bottles for lunch
and cleaner factory windows, but on really important issues their com-
plaisance made collective bargaining a farce.[41]

Another reason for the heaviness of the defeat was that the Wolman
Automobile Labor Board proved feeble and sometimes utterly helpless
in trying to protect labor. It soon became a target for the bitterest denunciation. The main reasons why it lacked vigor, of course, were that
organized labor had little strength, and that the President had put no
government power behind it. Doubtless its able chairman did his best
in a murky situation. Wolman had been a member of the NLB and
an adviser of Sidney Hillman, and united fine civic spirit with wide
practical experience. One labor leader who knew him at the time credits him with high intentions. "He seemed to me the type of man sincere enough in trying to do a job, but he just didn't know where he was
going."[42] A major question of policy at once arose, however, on which
his decision struck dynamic labor leaders as completely wrong. Should
the board deal first with employe representation, which would make
possible true collective bargaining on hours, wages, and working conditions, or should it first take up the cessation of discrimination in

hiring and firing? Supported by Kelley, Wolman gave priority to cases of discrimination.[43]

The workers' dissatisfaction precipitated a spring freshet of strikes in 1934. Early in April, employes of Motor Products Corporation walked out, closing Hudson Motors as well. This was at the height of the production season, a favorable time to strike. Before the month ended, the Mechanics' Educational Society (tool and die makers) called out Chevrolet employes in St. Louis and Fisher Body workers there and in Cleveland. The Chevrolet strike at once spread to the General Motors assembly plant in Tarrytown, N.Y., and the Fisher Body strike to the Buick factory in Flint, Mich. Many automobile workers were incensed over the delays of the Wolman Board in checking and certifying the endless lists of union members—50,000 by April 12, it was said—sent to it for collective bargaining purposes. Although in May the AFL heads reached agreements with General Motors and Fisher Body which represented some real achievement of equal bargaining rights, the underlying discontent persisted. In the fall of 1934 one labor leader, J. W. Pickering, expressed his chagrin in burning terms:

It has been conclusively proven in the last six months that industry did not live up to their part of the agreement and never intended to do so. They flagrantly violated every clause and part of their agreement by the simple expedient of interpreting the agreement to fit their needs. They would not recognize any outside union nor bargain collectively; concentrated all their efforts in building up of company unions through coercive methods; and then said complacently to the Union committees . . . to take the matter up with the Auto Board, knowing full well the Board's limited powers and reluctance to promulgate any rules or decisions that would interfere with the industry's policies.

And a still more prominent labor leader, Homer Martin, was shortly to write Father Coughlin:

I heard the President of the United States, Franklin D. Roosevelt, whom I greatly admire, declare that the worker's right to organize would be enforced. Yet I have witnessed the failure of the Board appointed by him. In these past nine months hundreds of workers have lost their homes, suffered the horrors of charity, seen their families go without proper clothing, even die because they did not have adequate nourishment, when their only crime was to join and work for their own organization.[44]

### 6.

To all believers in the right of workers to bargain through unions of their own choosing, the situation in the automobile industry at the beginning of 1935 was depressing. The limp organizational efforts of the AFL had broken down. Membership in its automobile locals had fallen to about 20,000. The Wolman board in April completed plant elections to provide a basis for the proportional representation that had been part of the President's peace plan, but the Federation boycotted the polls, in which it ran a disgraceful fourth. At the end the board announced that nearly nine-tenths of the 163,000 workers voting had chosen representatives unaffiliated with any organization. The low total of participants, out of about 400,000 workers in all, was itself discouraging.[45]

Of the two Gibraltars of management, General Motors had yielded a little to the unions, Ford nothing. Both had obstructed the efforts of the NLB and ALB. Both were seats of long-continued and well-entrenched abuses; of uneven wages, of the speed-up, of industrial espionage, and of "driving" tactics by harsh foremen. In both, the private policeman, the stool-pigeon, and the scab flourished. Espionage in General Motors had attained proportions as intolerable as the spy system managed by Harry Bennett in the Ford works. The La Follette committee, investigating impairments of the civil rights of workers, found that in the thirty-one months from January 1, 1934 to July 31, 1936, General Motors spent $994,855 on private detective services. Spies reported on even the reading habits of workers, and attended picnics of Fisher Body employes.[46]

With Henry Ford, Bennett, and Sorensen maintaining their severe regime, the atmosphere of the Ford factory on the Rouge was particularly noxious, and the hostility to unions especially virulent. One intelligent Irish worker named John Fitzpatrick declared that the frigid Sorensen-Bennett ban on communication went far beyond a no-talking rule. "There was no association with any other man. Any association with other workers in the department, or line, or at the bench where you were working, was frowned upon. There was a feeling in the mind of everyone that he was an individual with no connection during working hours with any other man." First at Highland Park, and later at the Rouge, he was depressed by the power of the omnipresent service men under Bennett: [47]

> Once you got by the gate the tension began, because in there, no matter how good a man you were . . . a service man would come up to you, tap you on the shoulder, and tell you to pack your tool box and go off to Miller Road—this meant the Employment Office. There, in the service man, was the supreme authority so far as your job was concerned—right there at the gate when you walked in.

At the end of his first day, Fitzpatrick was so numbed by the mood of fear which enveloped the Ford factory that he mumbled to himself: "Well, two weeks will be enough here." Though he remained to attend trade school and learn the skills of a die sinker, his hatred of the tyrannical service men and foremen became more intense every week. He saw that only a strong union could stand up to these malevolent satraps. "The foremen never had to give a reason. There was no one to appeal to, because you were an individual. No man had any sense of security, even in his own trade. . . . During the layoffs in the depression there was a terrific amount of favoritism. Actually, as far as seniority was concerned, I doubt if very many knew how to spell the word, let alone give any meaning to it."

This worsening of labor relations in the Ford factories, this change from the decent attitudes of young Henry Ford and Dean Marquis early in the century to the despotism of the elderly Ford, Sorensen, and Bennett in the thirties, made even a company union impossible. None was proposed. Any effort to form an independent union was crushed as quickly as the spies discovered it.

In the winter of 1933–1934, for example, the Mechanics' Educational Society began to recruit tool and die workers in the Rouge, soon enrolling about 200. They met furtively outside the factory, each member knowing only a few others. Of course, informers quickly told the company heads. When these officers began quietly transferring men into John Fitzpatrick's section in Department 711-J of the Rouge, neither he nor the few MES men known to him suspected the truth: every one was a fellow member, although most of them did not recognize one another. The transfers went on for six weeks. Then suddenly all of the 250 men in the section were discharged simultaneously! It was only when the MESA leader called a meeting that these employes comprehended what had happened.

In time, one by one, they were called back to work, possibly because Ford was unable to find satisfactory substitutes, possibly because the MES threatened to appeal to the Automobile Labor Board. The union, however, was broken.[48] This was the way in which Sorensen and Bennett translated into fact Henry Ford's complacent statement upon unions: [49]

"I have never sought to prevent our men from joining any association—religious, racial, political, or social. No one who believes in American freedom would do that. When our men ask about unions, I give them the same advice as when they ask about any of the other schemes that are always being aimed at men's wages. I say to them: 'First, figure out for yourself what you are going to get out of it. If you go into a union, they have got you, but what have you got?'

"We think our men ought to consider whether it is necessary for them to pay some outsider every month for the privilege of working at Ford's. Or, whether the union can do more for them than we are doing."

The most important automotive strike in the spring of 1935, in the Chevrolet plant in Toledo, proved humiliating both to the Wolman board and the AFL, but it did demonstrate a rising solidarity among the workers. Led by a Federation local, employes dropped their tools April 22, asking for a signed contract, seniority rights, a five-day week, pay rising from seventy cents an hour, and abolition of the speed-up. They refused to have anything to do with the Wolman board. President Green, while declaring the strike unauthorized, said that he would support it. For a time it seemed brilliantly successful, and must have given Ford officers some apprehension. Since the Toledo factory supplied transmissions to Chevrolet and Buick, its paralysis closed down General Motors plants in Atlanta, Kansas City, Fort Smith, Arkansas, Janesville, Wisconsin and Tarrytown, and the Toledo union hoped to extend its organization to all the closed establishments. But this the AFL would not countenance. Through the organizer it sent to the city, the Federation persuaded the Toledo men to make a separate peace.

One significant gain, however, the strikers did achieve. Besides a tiny rise in minimum wages, they forced the management to recognize a shop committee of nine, to be freely elected by the workers. Unionism was moving slowly, but it was moving.

For labor, this spring of 1935 might in fact be called the proverbial dark hour before the dawn; if not a radiant, at least a hopeful dawn. A rapid sequence of events, which perceptive Ford officers should have found big with portent, gave workers in the mass production industries an entirely new standing and power.

The first event was the destruction of the NRA by the Supreme Court's decision in the Schechter Case on May 27, 1935. Its termination brought no sorrow in the automobile unions, which had protested against Roosevelt's two extensions of the life of the code. The second resounding event was the passage by Congress of the National Labor Relations Act or Wagner-Connery Act in July, preserving all the guarantees of Section 7A and putting teeth into the old provisions. That is, Congress now ensured all employes the right to self-organization, collective bargaining, and other activities for mutual aid or protection, with stern penalties for all violations. The law severely punished such measures as General Motors and Chrysler had used to cripple free organization by company unions or veiled discrimination, and outlawed the open shop attitudes and practices of which Ford and his company were the most brazen champions. A National Labor Relations Board of three members was given almost dictatorial powers of enforcement.

To make the Wagner Act effective in the mass production field, labor required powerful all-inclusive unions, and as the third great event of 1935, the Committee for Industrial Organization stepped upon the stage. The long-pent resentment of all types of workers in many fields over AFL lukewarmness in meeting the challenge for organization under Section 7A boiled up in decisive action. That resentment was nowhere keener than among automotive employes. The plant locals which the AFL had chartered were so badly neglected by the national organization that for months they had been on the brink of revolt. Earlier this year they had compelled the executive council of the Federation to authorize the president and secretary to organize a national or international automotive union; and a month after the Wagner Act became law, their pressures forced William Green to grant a charter creating the United Automobile Workers of America.

This new UAW, with the law now firmly supporting it, carried some promise. But the terms of its charter were too narrow to suit most labor men, for it embraced only the workers engaged in manufacturing and assembling automobile parts, and excluded many others in the plants. A host of resentful automotive employes also objected to William Green's appointment of an old-line organizer, the before-mentioned Francis J. Dillon, as head of the UAW. They were ready to join a broader movement.

At the Federation convention in Atlantic City in October 1935, the revolt which gave birth to the CIO swiftly got under way. The breezes blew in cool from the ocean, but the issue of craft-union vs. industrial-union organization burned with intense heat. John L. Lewis of the United Mine Workers characterized the record of the Federation as twenty-five years of unbroken failure. He punched one obdurate craft-union apostle in the jaw. The last convention, he vociferated, had seduced him with fair words: "now I am ready to rend my seducers limb from limb." With him, as he stalked from the hall, went three powerful bodies, the 500,000 members of his United Mine Workers, the 200,000 of David Dubinsky's International Ladies' Garment Workers Union, and the 150,000 of Sidney Hillman's Amalgamated Clothing Workers.

Immediately afterwards, eight heads of international unions met in Washington and announced the formation of the Committee for Industrial Organization. From his Washington headquarters Lewis on November 2 indited a crisp note to William Green. "Dear Sir and Brother," it ran, "Effective this date, I resign as vice-president of the American Federation of Labor." [50]

Ford and General Motors officers well knew what enthusiastic faith their workers placed in the Wagner Act and the CIO. The feeling among auto workers was unmistakable. By April 1936, some 30,000 of them had elected delegates who met in a national convention of the UAW in South Bend, Indiana. William Green appeared in a futile effort to hold their fealty to the Federation, but Lewis had already delivered a stirring address in Cleveland to a great gathering of employes, and the CIO received an enthusiastic endorsement. The delegates summarily ejected Dillon from office, and chose in his stead Homer Martin, a former Baptist minister of college training who had found his true vocation when he began organizing Chevrolet wage-earners. Quick, intelligent, and courageous, if also impulsive and reckless, he understood how to appeal to the ordinary mass-production laborer. His chief defect was indecisiveness in times of crises, and, on occasion, poor judgment.

As the United Automobile Workers joined the CIO, a new wave of organizational activity was sweeping all the mass-production industries. John L. Lewis, of pugnacious jaw, beetling brows, and kindling rhetoric, directed the strategy, with capable lieutenants in every area. In the steel industry Philip Murray, a man of Scottish shrewdness and persistence, succeeded early in 1937 in getting not only Big Steel—the major corporations—but many lesser companies to recognize his union. In Southern factories Sidney Hillman obtained a broad foothold for the United Textile Workers. Maritime workers, rubber workers, transport workers, and other groups, filling up their ranks under the CIO aegis, claimed the collective bargaining rights guaranteed by the government.

But a fight impended. Though it was clear that the UAW would soon organize much of the automobile force, it was also clear that whereas the United States Steel Corporation had surrendered to unionism without a fight, the automotive companies were in a mood to resist stubbornly. Henry Ford, Walter Chrysler, and Alfred P. Sloan were not yet ready to match the enlightened attitudes taken by Myron Taylor and Thomas W. Lamont in the steel industry; Ford least of all. The automobile business had grown up more recently than steel, and lacked maturity. It gave a larger place to personal autocracy than steel had done since the time of Carnegie and Frick. As battle loomed ahead, labor began to prepare for it. During the summer and fall of 1936 some of the locals of the Mechanics' Educational Society affiliated with the UAW, and so did the Associated Automobile Workers of the Hudson and other factories. Most important of all, the Automotive Industrial Workers' Association, which was strongest in the Chrysler plants and was led by Richard T. Frankensteen, voted to merge with the UAW.

Labor was at last strong enough to wage its struggle for union recognition and other benefits with the power to deliver heavy blows, and with what its rank-and-file deemed a probability of success. Indeed, it delivered heavy blows even in 1936.

## 7.

The first demonstration of its vigor was its swift success in an autumn strike in the Bendix plant in South Bend. Here the UAW enrolled more than 2500 of the 2600 employes, and prepared to take a poll of the force, under protection of the National Labor Relations Board established by the Wagner Act. It was confident that this would make it the authorized agent in collective bargaining. When the Bendix management applied for a court injunction, more than 1500 men in November occupied the plant, and refused to move. After a week the company capitulated, giving the UAW full recognition.

Meanwhile, the Chrysler workers in the Dodge plant in Detroit were winning a still more signal triumph. The UAW there, charging discriminatory hiring and firing, took votes which pronounced almost unanimously in favor of a strike. Frankensteen obtained the help of skilled CIO agents in preparing for a walkout. Then, in the nick of time, Chrysler surrendered! It reinstated three discharged men, provided work for others who had been laid off, and promised strict observance of the seniority rule. A two weeks' sitdown strike at the Midland Steel Products factory in Detroit won a similar victory, covering wage increases, seniority, and union recognition. Finally, in December 1936, the Kelsey-Hayes Wheel Works were brought to terms in a five-day occupancy of the plant by strikers.[51]

Henry Ford doubtless observed that the automobile workers were showing not only a new energy, and a new confidence in government support, but a new unity. They stood together; when the Midland Products men quit work, the Chrysler and Dodge Unions announced that they would handle no substitute materials from other plants. The workers also had a new weapon in the sitdown strike. If its legality and ethics might be debatable, its effectiveness was unquestionable. The rapid march of labor in the smaller units of the automotive industry encouraged—nay, exhilarated—the CIO leaders. The reduction of Chrysler in particular delighted them. The two main fortresses of conservative management, however, General Motors and Ford, still remained unstormed, for GM had yielded only a few outworks, and the Ford Company nothing whatever.

The busy production season starting just after Christmas was obviously the strategic moment for attacking these powerful bastions of the open shop. General Motors was chosen as the first objective. Its profits in 1936 came to nearly $228,000,000; its average wage for workers the previous year had been $1150. On December 28, 1936, the first gun boomed in Cleveland. All the 700 workers in the Fisher Body plant there, making tops for General Motors cars, downed their tools, and more than 1000 stayed in the factory. Two days later the strike spread to the Flint branch of Fisher Body.

Henry Ford knew that his turn would come next. But before we deal with this stirring drama, we must examine the whole business and engineering position of the Ford Motor Company in meeting many trials; a checkered story of mingled progress and regression at home, and of tremendous difficulties abroad engendered by the worsening international situation.

# III

# CHALLENGE OF THE FUTURE

IN MIDSUMMER of 1936, Alfred P. Sloan, Jr., President of General Motors, reported to his stockholders that for the quarter ending June 30 the net earnings had been $88,108,372—a sum equal, after the payment of preferred dividends, to $2.00 a share on the common stock. "This," remarked the *New York Times* financial reporter, "is the largest amount earned by the corporation for this quarter since 1929." In contrast, the Ford Motor Company for the entire year 1936 showed a profit of $17,930,000.

A profit is a profit, and even small gains were then prized. For the preceding ten years Ford had operated at an overall loss of approximately $26,000,000. The company in 1936 made less than a fifteenth as much as its chief rival, and what was worse, had been toppled from second to third place as a manufacturer of passenger cars, holding only 22.44 per cent of the market as against 30.2 per cent the year before. Chrysler had pushed ahead of Ford with 25.03 per cent, while General Motors led with 43.12. These figures rang an alarm that every Ford executive could hear.[1]

What they could do in response was not clear. The possibility of dramatic recovery existed, for the V-8 in 1937 might to some extent repeat the Model A's performance in 1929. But various factors worked against such an accomplishment. Among the strongest were the attitudes and actions of Henry Ford himself.

### 2.

A successful car begins with engineering. Ford himself recognized this. "I believe that true management begins with the product and its making," he said in 1931, "and that into them must go the largest measure of leadership, for the pressure to better both the product and its

55

method of manufacturing must be continuous." Ford in 1936 commanded sound means of production, but his engineering facilities were mediocre compared with those of General Motors. Such facilities comprised buildings, technical equipment, and men, and the procedures in which all were used.

We may begin with the men; and something should first be said of Ford's personal habits and the manner in which he followed company activities. As already noted, he now ignored his former executive secretary, E. G. Liebold, whose decline in favor dated rather mysteriously from the Detroit bank crisis, and dispatched office work with the aid of Frank Campsall; while in matters of policy he already leaned on the audacious and energetic Harry Bennett. Edsel was influential in business and sales, and Sorensen in production.

One important means by which Ford obtained information and directed the work of the company was his luncheon table in the Engineering Laboratories Building at Dearborn. At this circular board gathered daily the principal men concerned with the engineering, manufacture, and sale of Ford cars. By a tacitly established order of seating, at Ford's right was his son Edsel, and on his left, Sorensen. Then in order to the left from Sorensen were seated W. J. Cameron, P. E. Martin, Hudson McCarroll, Laurence Sheldrick, A. M. Wibel, John Crawford (Edsel's executive assistant), B. J. Craig (Secretary-Treasurer of the company), and William C. Cowling (Sales—later replaced by J. R. Davis). Thus Ford could talk directly to the heads of Manufacturing, Personal Publicity, Engineering, Purchasing, Finance and Sales.

Ford, who had made an effort to convert his officials to his own choice and amount of edibles, ate "rabbit food." Most of the others frequently sampled it. Sorensen in contrast might order beefsteak and pie a la mode.

The group assembled at 12:55 p.m. precisely, and at 12:59 Ford would come in, walk around the table, and shake hands with every man, including occasional visitors. Then all would sit down. Conversation was controlled. No subject was brought up unless Ford himself, or Edsel, introduced it. However, a wide range of topics, mostly serious, was in general covered, most of them dealing with company matters, and Ford got thus an immense amount of information, especially on engineering and production. Here, too, he might make decisions about new work or operations already in progress. To be a regular attendant at this luncheon table marked a man as a chief official of the company. However, Harry Bennett rarely appeared.

To return to engineering, Ford himself nominally directed it. But while he always had plans for the future, and was usually pushing a dozen projects, these were haphazardly selected, and much of the work was as confused as a pre-holiday railroad station. Under Ford, Laurence Sheldrick served informally as engineering head. He had directed the work on Model A, and now supervised what might be called product engineering. That is, he took little part in purely experimental activities, but guided coming company models from blueprint to finished cars. Under him other men were assigned to various areas. Dale Roeder dealt with commercial vehicles; Joseph Galamb with body design; Eugene Farkas, Cornelius Van Ranst, and others with engines; Howard Simpson with tractors. It should be borne in mind that Ford disliked titles and organization, and that all these arrangements were informal.

As if practice were not already sufficiently loose, Ford rarely permitted an experimental task under one man to start without surreptitiously launching someone else on a similar project, to promote competition.

The confusion which attended this whimsical procedure was compounded by the allotment of quarters for work. After completing his impressive engineering building in 1924, Ford had assigned space in it capriciously. There being no central offices, the men took their quarters apparently by accident, while a radio station, the Johansson blocks, the *Ford News,* and publicity and executive offices were jumbled with laboratories and experimental sections. The effect was bewildering. The name of Ford engineering was written large and bright, but to find the living activity was difficult. "Although all designs for Ford and Lincoln cars originate in the Ford Engineering Laboratory," wrote Hartley Barclay in 1936 in his *Ford Production Methods,* "there is no single large building devoted exclusively to research. Much of it *may* originate in one of the fourteen laboratories scattered throughout the Rouge plant, and it rightfully belongs as near as possible to the production of work under construction."

Dale Roeder recalls an episode that reveals the engineers themselves groping for order. Once in Sheldrick's office he raised the question of a plan for engineering activities. With a cloak-and-dagger air, his chief pulled a chart from his desk which showed his own effort at clarification. "Don't let anybody ever see this," he warned, "because we're not allowed to have an organization chart." [2]

The lack of organization was accentuated by certain gaps in basic equipment. Dynamometer facilities were inadequate, there was no wind tunnel,* no provision for testing car and engine performance under varying temperatures, and no test track for new vehicles. General Motors had all these facilities. "I determined that no money should be spared in equipment and personnel," said Alfred P. Sloan in reviewing its policy toward research activities.[3]

A further deficiency in Ford engineering lay in the relative dearth of college-trained men. The company method as fostered by Henry Ford was to take a promising high school graduate and complete his training in the shop. The candidate usually took correspondence school courses in addition. Many such men remained mechanics. In this respect they resembled Ford himself. "I did not consider Mr. Ford an engineer," remarked Roeder. "He was an excellent mechanic and he had a tremendous amount of ideas." Like him, many of his assistants in the engineering field lacked the intensive technical training that the universities were now giving.

To be sure, the company did employ a number of college graduates. Roeder had a thorough academic training and had taught engineering at Ohio State. McCarroll, J. L. McCloud, Frank Riecks, Emil Zoerlein, and Howard Simpson were all university men. On the other hand, Sheldrick himself, and such other engineers as William Pioch, P. E. Haglund, Frank Johnson, and E. A. Walters acquired their advanced training on the job, and showed high ability.

The mixed group was notably effective. If some members seemed to fit into the old-fashioned shop where design and production were fused, this bound them closer to the product and made for a better cooperation with foundry and production crews. Sorensen, himself a graduate of the school of hard knocks (which he gave even better than he took) watched design closely as well as production.** He was well-equipped to cooperate with the Ford engineers, and properly utilized, they might well have challenged the best that General Motors or Chrysler could do.

---

* The Ford aviation group (1926–1933) had employed one for aircraft design, and particularly that of the trimotor plane. However, this seems never to have been used by the automobile engineers.

** Howard Simpson in his reminiscences says: "Sorensen came around to the Engineering Laboratory just as often as Mr. Ford, sometimes with him, and sometimes separately."

However, they worked under handicaps. These stemmed mostly from Henry Ford, and comprised his fetishes, his taboos, and his methods of supervision.

Among fetishes, he believed the transverse spring to be best (as in theory it was), that use of the torque-tube drive was imperative, and that only mechanical brakes were safe. Among taboos, he opposed anything that General Motors or Chrysler had developed first. Instead of studying, adapting, and bettering what they had done, he resolutely ignored it. He even frowned on the mention of a rival firm. Daniel J. Hutchins, an able official in Sales, recalled his snapping once: "Now you're working for General Motors. When you start talking about them, that's what they want—to get your mind off Ford and over on General Motors." Specifically, Ford was hostile to hydraulic brakes, longitudinal springs, the Hotchkiss drive, and the 6-cylinder engine.

Finally, he followed design and development closely, and often made objections or suggested changes before an engineer had more than started. This confused, exasperated, and often discouraged his designers.[4]

Ford's mounting age was undoubtedly a factor in hardening his prejudices and accentuating his tendency to petty interference. According to Sorensen, the V-8 engine was "his last mechanical triumph." Neither Ford nor many of his contemporaries were aware of any diminution in his powers, but the truth was that he was now living in a world that had absorbed all the improvements his own generation had made, and in an industry led by younger men of greater vigor than his. They appraised any new advance, and at once set out to better it. In Roeder's opinion their crews were more modern and aggressive than the Dearborn organization. He felt that Ford worked against himself. "The engineers were not given the freedom of design or the freedom of expressiveness in design."

With Model A, the Ford group had momentarily captured the market. Unfortunately, believes Roeder, they rested on that achievement. "We retained the Model A type of design in brakes, in chassis, and so forth." But Chevrolet and Plymouth promptly "moved in with suspension ride, hydraulic brakes, and styling, and capitalized on advancement. . . . In other words, Mr. Ford had become a retiring, conservative force in engineering." In the nineteen-twenties Ford had been years ahead of his competitors. "Now he was following them, by 1934 or

1935, I'd say." [5] This situation was not helped by the depression, during which the engineering force was slimmed, so that Ford could watch every member and exert his growing tendency to meddle.

As a compensation for its shortcomings in engineering, the Ford organization in the nineteen-thirties was active in testing new manufacturing methods, evolving new products, and providing improved plant facilities.

It has already been noted that plant additions and improvements were made in 1935. These included the rebuilding and enlarging of a blast furnace (which added from 500 to 800 tons of steel a day to Ford output), the expansion of steel-making facilities at a cost of $10,000,000, the rebuilding and modernization of the Rouge glass plant, an increase in coke capacity, and a modernization of the Rouge power plant. Altogether, $37,000,000 was being spent on such projects. Ford was meanwhile building a tire plant erected under the supervision of E. F. Wait, who came from the Firestone Tire and Rubber Company to operate it, and began production on December 21, 1937. It was a highly modern factory which eventually made 5000 tires a day and brought the price for the industry down by about $2.50 a tire! In 1937 the company launched a second expansion program which gave it a new pressed steel plant, an increase in Rouge power units, and a new tool and die shop.[6]

Throughout the mid-thirties Ford engineers and technicians were experimenting with new enamels and plastics, patenting a rear-engine car, perfecting a new method of rust-proofing metal parts, and developing the manufacture of cast steel. This was utilized where forged steel had previously been employed, as in crankshafts and cylinders, and marked a notable step forward, for cast steel showed superior strength and endurance, and made possible impressive reductions in time and cost.[7] But such accomplishments, while more astonishing for being wrought without adequate research facilities, merely emphasized the need for them.

When we look beyond the laboratories to the market place, we can note the impression which Ford engineering made on the sellers of Ford cars and on the customers who bought or rejected them.

### 3.

The point of contact between the Ford Motor Company and the public was, of course, the dealer. He displayed Ford wares, did no small amount of advertising at his own expense, sold the cars, and heard the complaints of dissatisfied owners. For all makers of automobiles, the loyalty and efficiency of dealers were of paramount importance.

The Ford Motor Company by 1931 had a dubious reputation in its relations with dealers, for it had always ridden them hard. Although they had suffered severely during the period between Model T and Model A, when they had no cars to sell, after the prosperous year 1929, Ford, who thought that a good car sold itself, cut their commission from 20 to 17½ per cent, and compounded the injury by sharply increasing the number of Ford agencies. He soon found that he was losing dealers to General Motors and Chrysler, and in June 1931 chose a new sales manager in William C. Cowling. The commission to dealers was raised, and was now a flat 22 per cent, which was better than Chrysler (21 per cent) but lower than General Motors (24). Cowling was still the head of sales for Ford in 1936.

He had taken over the post reluctantly, for his previous work had been entirely in traffic and administration. However, he was a good public speaker, and cherished a determination to revitalize sales activity by harmonizing the company-dealer relationship and at the same time demanding a vigorous effort from the dealers. Fortunately, Cowling could count on the support of John R. Davis, who had been a more logical candidate for sales head. Davis's experience reached back to 1919—almost to the fabulous days of Norval Hawkins. Cowling and Davis travelled about talking to assemblies of dealers to win back their confidence. The two itinerant sales executives found a very restive group of Ford agents. "These men," recalls Cowling, "were looking at other companies and going to other companies." He and Davis painted a bright picture for the future, with the new V-8 car and improved general conditions. One salesman recalls that Cowling was "quite an orator," who while speaking would pace back and forth before a long speaker's table. Gradually a better feeling was established between the company and its representatives on the firing line.

The Big Three maintained sales organizations which were fairly similar in size and methods. Chevrolet and Chrysler each used about 10,000 salesmen, while Ford had 9500. All by contract possessed complete power over their dealers, and all used it. The Federal Trade Commission, studying them during the period 1932–1938, found that all compelled their dealers to open new showrooms and garages, to take more cars than they could usually sell, to buy selling aids they did not want, and to intensify used-car activity to deal with the ever-mounting volume of second-hand automobiles.

Of the three, General Motors had the most liberal attitude, using a little less pressure than the others, paying more attention to the complaints of dealers, and giving them fuller service. Its Chevrolet represented in part the findings of a Customer Research Staff which had studied public taste and given its findings to the Engineering Department. If Walter Chrysler employed less extensive research facilities, he conceded nothing in pioneering spirit, and already had a brilliant record in the introduction of automotive improvements. Both Chevrolet and Plymouth put the accent on appearance and comfort. Ford met them reluctantly on this ground. He preferred to stress power, price, and economy of operation.[8]

The Big Three all offered financial arrangements through which dealers could sell cars on credit, or borrow money themselves. The General Motors Acceptance Corporation had been established in 1919. Ford had formed the Universal Credit Company, directed by Ernest C. Kanzler, in 1928, and Chrysler had used an independent organization, the Commercial Credit Company, since 1926. All the manufacturers tried to make the use of these agencies by dealers mandatory.

Henry Ford had reluctantly approved selling cars on credit, although Edsel had early recognized it as essential, and all Ford dealers had employed it for years. During the banking crisis of 1933, although the UCC was in sound condition, Ford had insisted on getting out of that company.* He sold his interest to the Commercial Investment Trust Corporation, but in a statement at the time explained his action rather plausibly: "We are essentially manufacturers, and the finance company is essentially a banking business. We wanted to separate the two." He praised the Universal and indicated that its relationship to the Ford Motor Company would continue as before. This was reaffirmed by Cowling on May 17, when he wrote the branches: "Universal Credit Company will continue exclusively to serve Ford dealers and their customers."[9]

---

* Actually, the UCC Annual Report for 1932 shows that the corporation had made money that year. When Ford told Kanzler that he wanted "to get out of it," the latter explained the sound condition of the subsidiary, and that the FMC would in no case be responsible for UCC's debts to the banks. When Ford proposed to "close it up," Kanzler suggested: "Why not sell it?" (Ford, with a majority interest, could have ended UCC's life.) Ford agreed—for cash! In the middle of a depression, this was difficult to find, but Kanzler negotiated a sale to CIT. "It was a terrible mistake on Henry Ford's part to have sold the finance company," he said later. Actually, it was a triumph of Ford's prejudice over his business interest. (See Note 9.)

We may now return to the sales struggle of the nineteen-thirties. When the Ford V-8 appeared in 1932 it did not spring from the factory shining and faultless. While the engine represented a notable feat, it showed the usual "bugs" of a new product. Some of the immense castings necessary were faulty and had to be replaced.* The engine mountings permitted too much vibration. There was trouble with piston rings and high oil consumption. The ignition was faulty and the water pump functioned badly. Ford had insisted on placing it in the cylinder head. "In other words," said Sheldrick later, "you were trying to pull hot water out of the engine at the top rather than push cold water in at the bottom." The arrangement was disastrous in a hot climate where the water became steam and the pump failed. Agonized protests rocketed up from the Southwest. Finally, Ford himself recognized that the pump should be placed "on the entrance side of the system" where the water came into the block.[10]

In addition, though Edsel by a hard battle for pleasing design and smooth riding had won his father's grudging cooperation, the Ford cars were not quite as attractive in appearance, or as pleasant for passengers, as their rivals.

By 1933, many of these defects had been remedied, but the public had not forgotten them. In addition, Ford dealers faced certain difficulties traceable to Ford's past actions and utterances. Although he had settled the Sapiro case in 1927 by an apology for his anti-Semitic activities, many Americans of Jewish origin still refused to buy a Ford car. Hollywood organizations hesitated to use one in a motion picture or for carrying equipment or personnel. Similarly, Ford's past outbursts against tobacco, particularly the cigarette (as in his pamphlet *The Little White Slaver*) made his salesmen unwelcome in many tobacco manufactories and agencies. They also at times found it difficult to sell trucks to breweries because of Ford's denunciations of liquor. Rabid New Dealers shunned Ford cars, and the time would come, in the late 1930s, when his resistance to the unionization of his plants would affect sales. All these factors counted keenly when times were poor and the struggle for supremacy intense. In 1933 Ford raised his total sales to 313,225, but although the Ford car outsold the Plymouth, it did not gain on the Chevrolet, and its percentage in the low-priced field dropped from 37.3 to 30.1. For the first time, Ford was now third, Chrysler second.

* The V-8 engine block was one casting—at the time a notable feat.

The prohibition on sales to the government was a serious element in the showing, but so was the lack of diversification in company products. Ford offered two cars only, and its Lincoln sales were low, only 2112 in 1933. Chrysler produced four models (Plymouth, De Soto, Dodge, Chrysler), and General Motors six (Chevrolet, Pontiac, Oldsmobile, Buick, LaSalle, Cadillac). When the Model T had sold almost as many units as all other makes combined, the single car was no disadvantage. But that day had passed forever, and Edsel, Wibel, and Sorensen were beginning to think of new types that might be manufactured, particularly in the middle-priced field.

Nevertheless, the V-8 in 1933 laid a foundation for a better year to come. On August 26, in the National Elgin Stock Car Race, the first seven cars were Fords. This gave the dealers something to talk about, as did economy tests. Against a Chevrolet in a New Hampshire competition, a V-8 won by averaging 28.18 miles to a gallon of gasoline.* At the same time, the company offered a cheap factory reconditioning plan of engines and other parts.[11]

With 1934, a happier era began. The V-8 that year, Ford proudly asserted, was "the best we've ever put out." With an improved engine, the car had greater power, more speed, and quicker acceleration than its predecessor, featured a new ventilation system and better brakes, and showed improvements in style and comfort that reflected Edsel's influence. "Can a champion come back?" asked *Advertising and Selling,* and noted that "Ford is definitely out to regain the leadership which Chrysler's Plymouth and General Motors' Chevrolet have taken from him." (The Plymouth, of course, had never outsold the Ford.) A varied advertising program by Ford was to fortify the merits of his automotive products.

The company began the year by reducing all truck models from $5 to $40 a unit. At the same time, it announced a V-8 production schedule of 55,000 units for January, the highest for that month since 1930; and it was promoting an improved Lincoln in 21 body types.** Dearborn late in 1933 had witnessed "The Ford Exhibition of Progress," a display of "the evolution of the motor car," with Ford car and truck models,

---

* The competing Chevrolet got 24.0 miles per gallon. Its dealer in Exeter, N.H., put an advertisement in the local paper: "To V-8 owners: A Stock Ford did it. Why doesn't yours? Bourne Chevrolet Co., Exeter, N.H."

** These included various models, all with V-12 engines on 136 and 145 inch chassis. Ford advertising listed 11 types of Ford cars, the basic models being coupe, roadster, sedan, phaeton, cabriolet and victoria. De Luxe models raised the number.

and this was now transferred to New York as a prelude to an extensive trip about the country. While newspaper advertising called attention to the display, a million direct-by-mail circulars were sent to truck owners. Radio broadcasts twice a week, featuring Fred Waring's Pennsylvanians, rounded out the program of publicity.[12]

As the year advanced, the company found new events to advertise. On February 24, 1934, V-8's took the ten first places in the Gilmore Cup Race for stock cars ($3500 in prizes). About the same time it announced plans for an impressive exhibit at the Chicago Century of Progress World Fair. When on March 13 all Ford plants restored the five-dollar-day, Henry Ford was especially happy to announce the step. "No one loses anything by raising wages as soon as he is able," he declared. "It has always paid us. There is no economy in cheap labor or cheap material. The hardest thing I ever did was to reduce wages."

He soon afterward denied that he would follow the example of his competitors, who had just raised their prices. "When prices go up, business goes down," he said crisply. "Higher wages are not an additional cost under proper management." Sorensen and his assistants, who had to produce at a profit despite higher wages and rising costs, could not have brushed the matter aside so casually. However, the final result was good for Ford sales. After his rivals had raised their prices and Ford had held his, the V-8 at $525 for the roadster and $610 for the victoria represented on the average, as *Motor* put it, "a favorable price differential of $60 at a time when a dollar was a lot of money to a lot of people." As the magazine went on to point out, "Most of the emphasis is on price . . . rather than on quality desirability."

Meanwhile, with the Ford exhibit travelling all over the country, the tempo of newspaper advertising was deftly stepped up. Then in June the Chicago World's Fair was opened. Here the Ford Motor Company utilized an 11-acre tract with an 1100 foot frontage on Lake Michigan. A five-acre park, the Ford Gardens, had been laid out adjoining the company's buildings. Of these the central unit was the Rotunda, a spectacular structure which was later to be rebuilt at Dearborn for permanent displays and offices.

The Ford showing was ambitious, and stressed five principal displays: former industrial methods, illustrated by exhibits from Greenfield Village; the Ford Drama of Transportation, set in the Rotunda and presenting 67 vehicles from an Egyptian chariot to the V-8; an industrial demonstration comprising 40 manufacturing operations; a soybean exhibit; and the Road of the World, a visual display of highways from ancient to modern times, culminating in free rides in Ford cars on an elevated road. In the park an orchestra shell with surrounding seats brought the Detroit Symphony Orchestra to guests, who could hear it for twelve weeks during afternoon and evening hours.[13]

By the end of the summer the company's diligent efforts had paid off. Ford had leapt from third to first position in the distribution of automobiles. "Leading the industry in sales for the first time since 1931," remarked one trade journal, "Ford is now 25,000 units ahead of Chevrolet." A temporary record of industrial peace had doubtless aided the Ford campaign. The company's rivals had clashed with organized labor and were struggling through a thicket of strikes, which stemmed from the employers' alleged obligations under the NRA code. Ford had never signed the code, had no obligations under it, had restored the five-dollar-day, and despite considerable unrest among his workers, had encountered no strikes. As autumn began, the company sponsored the World Series broadcasts (Detroit Tigers vs. St. Louis Cardinals), and established the Ford Evening Hour, a program of good music seasoned with brief talks by W. J. Cameron on Ford ideas and achievements.

In the end, Ford was not to hold its hard-won first place. Toward the close of 1934 Chevrolet came up with a rush to nose into the lead by 4500 cars. But the Dearborn company had done well. It had sold 532,589 cars and 128,250 trucks, 660,839 units in all, and had captured 28.20 per cent of the total market. It exceeded the Chrysler totals by more than 100,000 units, thus going into second place. General Motors led with 852,375 passenger cars and 157,507 trucks.

The Ford engineers and manufacturing executives had been working hard on the V-8, and the 1935 models won the praise of expert observers. "The Ford is longer, larger, more commodious and far more beautiful than ever before," wrote James Dalton in *Motor* at the beginning of the year. The company still quoted prices below those of its rivals. Dalton pointed out that since it was entirely owned by the Ford family, its dynamic head "has no stockholders to whom he must make an accounting and is under no obligation to pay dividends." Perhaps, he suggested, the family did not live for money alone. "Pride rather than profit undoubtedly is the primary actuating motive of the Fords—Henry and Edsel. . . . It may be that they want more than anything else to show the world they can again sell half the automobiles made in the United States."

The V-8 not only showed better lines, but offered a new clutch, improvements in the engine, and better spring suspension and distribution of passenger weight. It started more quickly and drove faster than its rivals. The new car, chanted Ford advertisements, "is the only car in the low-price field with a V-8 cylinder engine." Advertising remained generous, and early in the year Ford profited by an extended strike that interfered with Chevrolet production. Dealers exploited their opportunity, never relinquished the advantage they obtained, and outsold Chevrolet by 826,519 to 656,698, Plymouth finishing third with 382,925 cars.[14]

Again the victory had been based primarily on price. And this fall Ford took a step forward in strategy by introducing the Lincoln Zephyr, which Cowling termed "a sensational, completely new motor car." It had a 122 inch wheel base and a 110 h.p. motor against the regular Lincoln's 145 inch base and 150 h.p. motor. Selling at $1275, it invaded the medium-priced field, essentially giving the Ford dealers a third car.

Had the Dearborn strategists taken this moment to introduce a Six, and change from mechanical to hydraulic brakes, from transverse to longitudinal springs, and from torque tube to Hotchkiss drive, working meanwhile for a smoother ride, the race for supremacy might have swung drastically in favor of the Ford Motor Company. For 1936 both Chevrolet and Plymouth were making every effort to excel in appearance and comfort. Plymouth boasted of a "shockless" steering mechanism, a superior spring suspension, rubber-cushioned bodies, increased horse power, and better insulation. Chevrolet introduced its first hydraulic brakes, a solid steel top, "shockproof" steering, a new high compression motor, and rust-proof fenders. Ford, however, did not rise to its opportunity. It clung stubbornly to mechanical brakes, now definitely a liability, and to transverse springs, and while improving its body lines, raised its prices! [15]

Doubtless this last step was a highly important element in the ensuing setback to Ford. Doubtless, too, the industry and public had gone through a period of experimentation which had left them convinced of the superiority of hydraulic brakes. The emphasis of Chevrolet and Plymouth on comfort and style was also bearing fruit. Ford records show that the public was increasingly insistent upon smooth riding. Complaints from customers at this time include groaning or seizing brakes, body backlash, overheating of the engine, and other indications of the uneven performance of the V-8.

One salesman of the period, Walker Williams, recalls another cause of declining sales, the determination of numerous Ford dealers to make sure of a profit from trade-ins. "I'm going to sell fewer cars and make more money!" was their slogan.

The used car was a strategic and often an explosive factor in the sales area. Most customers had one, and a highly important consideration with them was the allowance the dealer would give for it if they purchased a current model. Of course, logically he should pay only a sum that would enable him to sell the used car at a profit. In some instances, to sell a new car, he might take a small loss on the old one. But to make this a regular practice spelled danger. The trade-in could quickly become a devouring monster, destroying a dealer's business while it grew in volume (if there was a slight loss on each transaction, the greater the sales total the greater the eventual disaster!). On the other hand if an agent would not bid on used cars, a rival might take his business. Ford dealers in 1936 tended to make only profitable trades. "It looks like [they] are only taking the cream," wrote Russell Gnau, Sorensen's assistant, to the production chief, "and are not willing to trade like Chevrolet and Chrysler dealers." This was a prejudiced opinion, for Sorensen's office tended to think that all Ford dealers were lazy; still, it may have had a certain amount of truth at the particular time.[16]

The central sales office did not give up as the situation showed signs of deteriorating. It worked diligently to arouse the dealers and get them to help themselves. Early in the year, it prescribed an "R & G [renewed and guaranteed] used car procedure" for the benefit of dealers. It also had a vigorous plan for new car selling, "See 'em, Tell 'em, Sell 'em," starting a contest on March 26, for the best exemplification. In April it put out a new carburetor which would allegedly increase gas mileage by from 10 to 15 per cent. In May, discounts to Ford and Lincoln dealers were raised to 24 and 25 per cent, respectively, and that month the entire branch system was reorganized. Improvements were also made in the interior appearance of both the Standard and De Luxe V-8 models.

Nevertheless, the year was not a success. The sales of the Lincoln Zephyr were encouraging, for while two years before only 2170 Lincolns were sold, in 1936 the total was 18,994, of which 17,715 were Zephyrs. However, the sale of Ford cars reached only 748,000, while Chevrolet leaped ahead to 930,000. Ford led Plymouth (499,580), by a wide margin, but again fell to third place for total output in the industry as Chrysler's full line (851,974) outsold the Ford (764,126), and held 25.03 as against 22.7 per cent of the market.[17]

4.

Undoubtedly by mid-1936 the Ford dealer was convinced that he worked at a disadvantage, and knew why. Cowling recalled that Henry Ford instructed him to sell the mechanical brake as the only safe one, "and I religiously tried to do it." However, he found the dealers unreceptive. They not only clamored for hydraulics, but declared that the Ford car was less attractive than its competitors. Fortunately, the situation was soon to be altered for the better in several ways.

The most fundamental was the removal of the production aspect of engineering from the Laboratories Building in Dearborn to the Rouge plant, some five miles distant. Sorensen and Edsel had come to a tacit cooperation, recognizing that if the company were to survive, it would have to do so despite and not because of Henry Ford. According to Sheldrick, "they felt that they would have to get things that pertained to the operation of the business out from where he could tamper with them too much." Sheldrick vaguely mentions "signs of senility," but that term is too strong. Ford's behavior was rather obsessive: the testimony of Farkas, Roeder, Simpson, Thomas, and numerous other Ford engineers is that his tendency to interfere had become almost psychopathic. Roeder says that the occasion for the transfer was the redesign of the 1937 Ford in 1936, while Sheldrick was in Europe. At any rate, early in 1937 such engineering as immediately affected production was established in new headquarters at Gate 4 at the Rouge. Purely experimental engineering remained at Dearborn.

The change provided a certain freedom. Ford was still dictatorial upon vital matters, but as Sheldrick puts it: "He couldn't pop in so often. . . . We were able to get things done, get them built up to finished form before he could upset them." One reason for this lay in Ford's keen concern with experimental engineering which was still kept in the Laboratories Building. Stopping there, he was likely to become interested and forget the five-mile trip to the Rouge.

Another avenue to improvement was opened by the Ford truck and allied commercial vehicles (buses, delivery wagons, and the like). The Ford truck had originally been the creation of Ford customers, who built special bodies for the Ford chassis, and finally all but forced the company to design various types of vehicles for hauling. Henry Ford had never given the truck the same interest he bestowed on the Ford car. Roeder, working with commercial vehicles, found that he could win a relatively easy assent to changes in them that the industrialist would never have permitted in a passenger vehicle. Frequently Edsel approved them, assuming that his father would ignore the commercial branch of the company's business. He did. By 1935 Roeder had installed longitudinal springs at the rear end of the truck; the *Ford News* of December 1934 offered a paean of praise for transverse springs on one page, and a salute to longitudinal springs on another! Roeder also got the position of the water pump altered for trucks. Before long, all changes adopted for the truck and proved useful with it found their way to the car.

The Ford truck, incidentally, had done somewhat better in competition than the car, leading Chevrolet in 1930, 1931, 1932, and 1935. However, it was now on a downward curve, and after 1937, when it once more outsold its rival, never again attained that distinction. In the 1930s its sales were uneven, but good in prosperous years, running above 180,000 in both 1935 and 1937.[18]

Finally, the engineering department acquired some highly prized testing facilities. With the move to the Rouge, Sheldrick set up a satisfactory dynamometer room for testing engines. Soon afterward, with Wibel's assistance, he procured a Four-Square axle-testing machine. "This was something we had needed terribly all through the years. We had no way of loading an axle and testing it." Another innovation was the wind tunnel. The evidence upon its introduction is cloudy: Esper, later in charge of wind-tunnel work, says that Sorensen had seen one employed for car design in Europe, and persuaded Ford to construct it for full-sized vehicles in the Engineering Laboratories Building. This was completed in May 1936, and by 1938 was equipped with devices which could produce either extreme heat or extreme cold. "We could bring the temperatures of the tunnel down to 20 degrees below," remarked Sheldrick. ". . . We did an immense amount of valuable work."

Last came the test track. The lack of such a facility had been a scandal among both company engineers and production executives. Late in 1936 Roeder was driving Edsel and Henry Ford on Monroe Avenue in Dearborn. Henry asked him where they had been doing their testing, and Roeder replied that it had been done on the public roads, an increasingly dangerous practice. They turned into Oakwood Avenue, and were aproaching a gate to the Ford airport, opposite the Dearborn Inn. "Turn in here," said Ford. They did so, and drove around the immense landing tract. "We will have a test track in here," said the industrialist, and almost immediately one was begun. It was not at first satisfactory, but was rebuilt in the late nineteen-forties.[19]

The question arises, Why did Ford permit the transfer of all active engineering to the Rouge, and the gradual sabotage of some of his chief ideas? Sheldrick believed that Sorensen effected the shift to Gate 4 with the plea that it was essential to smooth production. This is more than plausible. A new model every year was now the norm, and to get it out required both hard work and close cooperation between the engineering and production staffs. Sheldrick notes also that Ford was concerned with other activities, and that with increasing years he was at times forgetful of or even indifferent to matters affecting the main factory. Abundant evidence supports these suggestions, and Ford's other activities deserve attention.

One of them was Greenfield Village, where exhibits and historic buildings spoke for Ford to the public. Its opening in 1933 had been preceded by a decade of collecting and planning on Ford's part, while for the rest of the nineteen-thirties he was busy acquiring further exhibits, and overseeing its management. Of the four schools he established there, the Scotch Settlement was opened in 1929, the McGuffey in 1934, the Ann Arbor House in 1937, and the Miller School in 1943.[20]

A second project in which Ford was interested was the cultivation and processing of soy beans. He felt that the crop had a great dietary importance, could aid the farmer, and had a definite place in his own business. While he had begun experiments in 1929, they were carried on for some time in an informal fashion at Dearborn. But in 1935 a complete processing plant was established at the Rouge and in 1938 two others began operations at Saline and Milan, Michigan, for the extraction of oil from the bean, and the making of plastic units for Ford cars. These came to include lever knobs, horn buttons, switch handles, and distributor housings. In 1939 the Ford Motor Company grew about 100,000 bushels of soy beans, and bought an additional 500,000 bushels.[21]

A third and far more extensive activity that commanded Ford's energies was his village industries. They embodied a dream that he had cherished before World War I, that first took form in 1919 in a small plant operated by water power at Northville, Michigan, on the River Rouge. For the village industry, as Ford defined it, a rural location and available water power were both essential. Usually an old grist mill stood on the site that he selected, and was remodelled for manufacturing purposes. Northville made valves for Ford automobiles. Before 1933 Ford had established five such units, and four larger ones not called village industries, but all on rivers, all operated in part by hydroelectric power, and all manufacturing parts for the Ford car: Iron Mountain on Menominee River in Northern Michigan, Green Island on the Hudson, Hamilton on the Miami in Ohio, and the Twin City plant on the Mississippi.

True village industries were supposed to provide work for people in rural areas, who would use short periods to operate their farms. Ford himself had been reared on a farm when few machines existed; he had always felt a deep desire to aid farm people. The Model T, developed to negotiate the execrable roads of the American countryside, proved of tremendous benefit to rural areas, and the Fordson tractor had served in plowing and cultivating. When he launched his village industries, Ford boasted that he would "take the factory to the country," and check the migration of farm boys to the towns. Of course the Rouge at first represented an exercise in decentralization: originally an offshoot from what was then the main plant at Highland Park, it had been dropped seven miles from nowhere and had a port of its own. But it became a rather fearsome example of concentration, and Ford thought of his village industries as expressing an opposite trend—the scattering of operations in small units.

During the 1930s Ford unquestionably intensified his interest in small plants. After 1935 no year passed in which he did not found at least one new unit. In six years he constructed 13 (including his two soy bean plants), and in 1938 could contemplate a list of 212 possible sites which E. G. Liebold had prepared. W. J. Cameron in his Ford Sunday Evening Hour and in magazine articles discussed the "decentralization" which such activity represented. Even *Fortune* picked up the term. "Mr. Ford now feels that he has learned all centralization can teach," it remarked late in 1933. "The next step is decentralization."

But while Ford and Cameron talked of the breakup of industry, the total impact of all the little plants making valves, ignition coils, wire springs, gauges, generators, starters, and so on was feeble, and the term "decentralization" was not properly used for them. Compared with the real decentralization which would occur under Henry Ford II, that represented by the village industries was a trivial activity, employing fewer than 4000 workers in the smaller plants, and only about 10,000 altogether, including Hamilton, Ypsilanti, Green Island, and Twin Cities. Furthermore, it completely lacked the financial control which gave the decentralization of the later period its chief significance. Nobody had any financial authority over the village industries, which Ford operated for personal satisfaction. We can only guess at their gains and losses.

However, they were important in that they contributed to the decentralization of Ford's own activity. They, Greenfield Village, the soy bean experiment, and a fourth project to be dealt with later, the tractor, all engaged his attention and even his passionate interest, and gave him less time for the V-8 and the Ford truck.

The rural plants beside streams, employing from a dozen to several hundred men, might even be said to have his affection. He loved to examine sites for new units, and to supervise their preparation when once selected. He loved to help in converting old mills into operating plants, for they lured him as surely as any circus ever lured a small boy. "Henry Ford could not resist the temptation of buying the old grist mills," recalled an aide. He loved no less to visit the plants in operation and to discuss the advantages of these little factories in comparison with metropolitan establishments. He praised the character of the workers—"the men are keen and contented and like their work" —pointed out that no families were on relief in such communities, and extolled the promise of the establishments for the nation as well as the industry: "With one foot on the land and one foot in industry, America is safe!" [22]

Partly because of Ford's age, partly because of the small scale of the operations, partly because no plan was ever made to build them into an important functional role in the Ford economy, the village industries of the nineteen-thirties are merely a decorative part of the Ford story. But while their master was concerned with them, and with his new tractor project, his engineers, guided by Edsel and Sorensen, were staunchly trying to meet the challenge of their competitors.

## 5.

The Ford campaign for 1937 was launched in November 1936 with a mammoth reception at Detroit and Dearborn to Ford dealers of the United States and Canada. Additional visitors came from Europe and Asia to attend the unveiling of the new cars and trucks. So severely did the incoming throng tax hotel facilities, for it was estimated at 7000, that many dealers were compelled to use their Pullman cars as rooms.

On the morning of November 6 some 300 buses and a host of taxis and private cars brought the visitors to the Detroit Coliseum where the new models were to be revealed. Sales Manager Cowling introduced Henry Ford, who spoke his usual single sentence of greeting, and Edsel, who at greater length proclaimed that it was the Ford practice to make "the best possible car for the price, and always make a better car at a lower price."

Finally the auditorium was darkened and a pencil of light picked out a V-8 emblem on the center of the elevated stage, an imposing structure with a ramp by which cars could ascend the platform or be driven down from it. From the V-8 emblem a golden-haired sprite unwound herself (a twelve-year-old from a Greenfield Village school), and summoned a group of elves and gnomes who approached with various car parts. These they threw into a cauldron in the central portion of the platform, from which steam began to emerge as engines, radiators, fenders, and other elements were tossed in. Finally the fumes cleared, the elves disappeared, and the first 1937 model, the V-8 club coupe, rose, traversed the stage, and finally made its exit down the ramp and off the Coliseum floor. Other types appeared, including the new Lincoln Zephyr and a variety of truck models.

That afternoon at Greenfield Village the dealers presented a Cape Cod windmill to Henry Ford, and in the evening attended an elaborate dinner in the Coliseum, at which bottles of wine stood on every table. Recalling Henry Ford's long opposition to alcohol and the authoritative tone of the Sales Department in the past, one dealer exclaimed, "Oh, boy, this is a liberalized company!" Unquestionably their visit, which included a tour of the Rouge the following day, stirred them for new effort.[23]

The 1937 Ford embodied numerous improvements. First of all, it offered customers a choice between 60 and 85 horsepower engines, both V-8's, and the smaller undoubtedly an answer to the demand for a Six. Body and engine were rubber-mounted. A new brake, a better steering gear and wheel, and numerous minor improvements, made a car that any dealer could talk about.

The varied efforts the company had undertaken in 1936 to revitalize the selling organization were now counting. "The public reaction to the Ford V-8 line is great," announced Cowling a week after the assembly at the Coliseum. "Now it is squarely up to you as dealers to see that the public gets what it wants by making it easy for the buyer to buy." Proper handling of used cars was stressed. Meanwhile, the discount for dealers on Ford passenger cars was raised from 24 to 25 per cent, and on trucks from 22 to 23 per cent. Cowling telegraphed in February: "We want leadership Lincoln and Lincoln Zephyr as well as Ford." He pointed out that the Lincoln Zephyr market was far greater than commonly supposed.

The Ford drive was successful for more than half a year, though it then slowed down as the nation slid toward the sharp recession of late 1937–1938. The total results by comparison with 1936 were gratifying. The Ford car, with 765,933 units sold, stood barely 2000 below Chevrolet, and if trucks were included, Ford led 955,309 to 951,714. Lincoln-Zephyr sales had mounted to 25,186, an excellent showing for a medium-priced car, which promised well for the future.

But the company was still making little money. Indeed, the profit of $6,760,967 after taxes in 1937 was little more than a third of the almost $18,000,000 it had made in 1936. In addition, the brakes of the V-8, too hastily approved, were noisy and showed a tendency to seize. The outlook was not happy.[24]

It was at this time that Cowling retired as sales manager. He himself offers no explanation for his departure. Henry Ford, however, had become impatient with him, and he may have served as a scapegoat for the year's indifferent record. The dealers no longer responded to his oratory, while throughout his administration they had tended to rely on Davis, who knew the business of selling thoroughly. For them it was a happy event when Edsel on December 22, 1937 informed the branch managers: "I take great pleasure in announcing the appointment of Mr. John R. Davis as General Sales Manager of the Ford Motor Company." [25]

A highly important segment of the Ford business all this while was conducted overseas; and from the uncertainties of the domestic outlook we must turn to the chaotic foreign scene.

# IV

## OVERSEAS DOMAIN

THE Ford interests had become by 1930 an empire of world-wide dimensions, and like other far-flung empires, in the ensuing decade it met heavy strains and vicissitudes. If the central capital of this empire was in Dearborn, its chief proconsular capital lay at Dagenham on the Thames, and if supreme authority was exercised by Henry Ford, Edsel, Sorensen, and their aides, their governor-general for Europe and the Near East was Sir Percival Perry in London.

Every political upheaval of these stormy years mirrored itself in new problems for Ford's overseas possessions. At moments these were so vexatious that the Dearborn executives must have wished they could jettison the whole complex foreign operation. They knew well, however, that the business was of primary importance to them. Ever since Europe had bought the first awkward Ford contraptions at the dawn of the century, the profits on sales abroad had contributed to prosperity and stability at home. The world-wide demand for the Model T had done much to swell dividends paid and capital reinvested. As the Great Depression gripped the United States, the European, Latin-American and Oriental markets took on a more imperative value.

Fortunately for Dearborn, just before the depression set in the European business had been placed on a new and improved basis. Three cornerstones of that foundation had been laid in 1928: Henry Ford's recall of Sir Percival Perry to the helm, hailed by Sorensen as "the best news you could have brought me," the commencement of the Dagenham factory, and the adoption of the "1928 Plan." The fourth cornerstone was supplied when a special small English car was put into quantity production in 1932. Bright hopes for the future were attached to these basic arrangements. Some of them were to be shattered by the deepening economic depression and the international turmoil created by Hitler, Mussolini, and Franco; none was to be realized in just the form contemplated; but the objectives were sound, and the effort to achieve them commands admiration.

The "1928 Plan" for reorganizing the European businesses, of which Sir Percival Perry was the principal author, was intended to give the various Ford companies clear direction and an efficient degree of unification. It was also intended to do something to "Europeanize" them, at least in their outward aspect.

Familiar with the automotive business in various countries, Perry saw that harmony should be imposed on a generally uncoordinated group of activities. After World War I the Dearborn authorities had chopped their enterprises in Europe, North Africa, and the Near East into a dozen divisions, all independent. The French, German, Spanish, Italian, Dutch, Belgian, and other concerns operated with little regard for each other, and the oversight exercised by Dearborn through traveling auditors and district supervisors, occasional roving agents, and an intermittent flow of letters and cables, lacked consistency and force. It was thought that this form of operation exposed the foreign units to nationalistic attack. It was asserted that they seemed too much American; and that they were obviously managed from the United States. All of them kept the name Ford—though General Motors adroitly bought up foreign companies and names, notably Vauxhall in England and Opel in Germany. Most of these defects Perry hoped to remedy.

2.

Under the "1928 Plan" the Ford Motor Company, Ltd., of England, acquired the assets of the existing Ford companies in Britain, Germany, France, Italy, Spain, Ireland, Belgium, Holland, Denmark, Finland, and Sweden. A huge aggregation!—and though it was presently reduced in one direction by the removal of the French and German companies from Perry's immediate supervision, it was extended in others by the inclusion of Portugal, Egypt, Roumania, Turkey, and Greece. As an integral part of the plan, substantial quantities of the shares of its existing Ford companies in Britain, Germany, France, Spain, Belgium, Holland, Denmark, Sweden, and Finland were sold to the public, the British company retaining a controlling stock interest, directly or indirectly, in the continental companies. The plan made the great plant at Dagenham, which was in operation by 1931, the center of manufacture, sales, and service activities throughout Europe and its periphery. Dearborn was to design the cars, Dagenham was to manufacture both knocked-down components and complete models, and continental companies were to assemble knocked-down parts and distribute the product. The assumption was that British manufacture would be cheaper than American, for concentration of European work in Dagenham would permit the adoption of mass-production methods, while labor would cost less, and no transatlantic freights need be paid.

With the astute and genial Perry in charge, some of the initial expectations were realized. All inquiries, messages, and orders flowed through what was called "The Office of Sir Percival Perry," an administrative agency whose jurisdiction ran from Cork to the Polish border and the reaches beyond the Bosphorus. Sitting as chairman of the boards of directors of all the associated continental companies except the Swedish, Perry mastered their plans and influenced all decisions.

He, of course, took orders from Henry Ford, from Edsel, whom he much admired and who paid special attention to European affairs, and from Sorensen, a warm friend who seldom hesitated to play the role of benevolent despot to all European managers. Sorensen once caught up an English official who attempted some unwise initiative by a terse telegram: "Are you aware that we are controlling design over here?" Perry also took advice and guidance from high engineering and sales experts in Dearborn. Nevertheless, he had a fairly free hand in choosing European subordinates and shaping policies. He saw to it that the boards of the associated companies included men whose prestige would help diffuse an impression that the concern must be fairly autonomous.

These were boards, in fact, that he alone of the Ford executives could have selected. The English group, for example, included Lord Illingworth, a great textile manufacturer, Sir John T. Davies, director of the Suez Canal Company, and Roland D. Kitson, director of the Bank of England. The Spanish company enlisted the Conde de Guell, onetime cabinet minister; the Dutch company R. J. H. Patijn, former general treasurer of the finance ministry; the Belgian company Camille A. Gutt, later managing director of the International Monetary Fund, and the German company Dr. Heinrich F. Albert, one-time Minister of National Economy. The French company was managed by Maurice

Dollfus, a prominent Paris banker. Edsel was a director of all the European companies, Sorensen of most of them, and Henry Ford of one, the British organization. The essential coordination of activities came from Edsel, Sorensen, and Perry.[1] Nevertheless, the interposition of the office of Lord Perry between the various continental companies and the parent firm in the United States, and the issuance to the public of substantial minority shares for the British and continental companies made substantial problems as well as some benefits.

3.

A man of less sagacity than Sir Percival, less energy and imagination, might have fumbled some of his complicated responsibilities. He might have mismanaged the great Dagenham enterprise, might needlessly have offended the proud Frenchmen, Spaniards, or Italians with whom he worked, might have neglected Denmark in favor of Turkey, or might have irritated critical Americans. This last error would have been fatal. Edsel visited Europe in the troubled summer of 1936, "a great encouragement" according to the leading German director. Sorensen was repeatedly in Europe, and a visitor to Dagenham wrote back to Dearborn: "They sure look up to him as being the last word over here."[2] Perry had to satisfy Herman Moekle in Auditing, A. M. Wibel in Purchasing, Tom Naubert in Service, and Russell I. Roberge in charge of Overseas Sales. These tough-minded men made personal inspections in Europe, sent members of their departments over to help solve specific problems, and sometimes called their Dagenham counterparts to Dearborn for consultation.

But Perry always kept the confidence and liking of the two Fords and Sorensen. He made a fast friend of Ernest Kanzler, Edsel's brother-in-law. It is also clear that his grasp of the complex undertakings from the Thames to the Nile was consistently adequate and his vigilance unfaltering.

As industrial generalissimo, he had to supervise car and truck manufacturing at Dagenham, the tractor factory at Cork, the older assembly plants at Copenhagen, Barcelona, and Asnières on the Seine, and the new assembly plants constructed in 1930–1933 at Amsterdam, Antwerp, and Cologne. He had to give advice upon sales outlets stretching into Poland, Turkish Armenia, and Algeria. He had to meet the competition of General Motors and every important European manufacturer. It made a heavy load, but he and his chief aide, A. R. Smith, shouldered it vigorously. They expected the European market to grow, which in uneven fashion it did. When profits appeared in various countries Perry had to devise some solution for the difficult problem of double taxation. Though fully cooperative with Dearborn, Perry never hesitated to assert dissenting opinions. Had he been given a decade of normal economic and political conditions, he would doubtless have brought the "1928 Plan" to general success. But in the Europe of the nineteen-thirties, it was the abnormal which rapidly became normal. Old principles of equity, courtesy, and international cooperation were discarded with a ruthlessness that made business a jungle.

Yet despite depression, fascism, and war, Perry wrote a remarkable record. One immediate difficulty concerned the basic car design. When Dagenham began production in 1931 Dearborn staked everything on the Model A, a vehicle unsuited to the island market. In older days the Model T had done well on narrow English roads; the Model A was too large, too heavy, too costly. Rising horsepower taxes and increased costs of motor fuel had created a demand for economical cars, which the Morris and Austin competitors were meeting with brilliant success.

Perry began asking for what was called a "baby Ford"—a car of small-bore engine, 7.5-foot wheelbase, light weight, and 8-horsepower. With the logic of facts supporting him, he carried his point; united American and British effort created a prototype which embodied some characteristic Ford engineering; and the Dearborn heads approved it early in 1932. That spring and summer Dagenham was retooled, and in autumn the new vehicle found a warmly receptive market.[3]

This was the *avant-courrier* of the long line of light English Fords that were to become familiar on roads from Perthshire to Natal, from California to New Zealand—the Anglias, Prefects, Consuls, and others. At £120 for the two-door 8-horsepower model, it sold briskly both in Britain and on the continent. This car, with the three sizes of truck and van models offered by Dagenham, quickly brightened the European picture.

It was high time, for losses from handling the Model A had brought the English company to the verge of receivership and compelled it to borrow approximately $1,500,000 from the Belgian company. Now a period of prosperity ensued which lasted, more and more shakily amid gloomy world events, until the opening in 1939 of World War II. In 1933, a bitter year in the United States, the English company made a profit which approached £1,400,000 or $7,000,000, doubly welcome amid the deficits of the time. To be sure, a third of this was attributable to profits on exchange following President Roosevelt's devaluation of the dollar, but even so, the result was gratifying. Perry was able to wipe out all debts and bank a comfortable surplus.

In the next three years, down to 1937, Perry was able to demonstrate the potentialities of the Dagenham factory and its small cars. At the fast-growing, shinily modern, well-planned plant, he built the first 1440-pound-pressure power station in England, and soon afterward completed the coke ovens and blast furnaces. Meanwhile, he introduced in 1934 a 10 horsepower De Luxe Ford which British buyers received enthusiastically, and the following year created a sensation by pricing his 8-horsepower automobile at £100, or less than $500 at the current rate of exchange. Neither Austin nor Morris could sell a fully-equipped car at this low level.

Other evidences of returning confidence appeared. In 1933 Perry moved the manufacture of Fordson tractors from Cork to Dagenham, and in the two years 1935–1936 doubled his tractor sales with 18,000 units. In the same years, unit sales of automobiles made at Dagenham also almost doubled, giving Ford in 1937 one-sixth of the British market. The hard-pressed British economy profited that year from the employment of 12,650 workers at Dagenham, almost twice the 1934 roster. Ford Ltd. paid dividends of 5 per cent in 1934 and 1935, and 6 per cent in 1936; * and they would have been greater had not Perry continued to invest much of his earnings in new construction and improved equipment, a policy which harmonized with Henry Ford's in Dearborn. He plowed some profits also into an extended program of social-welfare benefits. The company in 1935 adopted a pensions scheme, and two years later began giving its workers holidays with pay. These and certain minor innovations raised the total cost of fringe benefits to more than £225,000 in 1937; a rather large figure, as Edsel Ford suggested, when compared with net profits that year of £375,000, but in Perry's eyes none too large.[4]

Considering the times, the progress of Dagenham and the English company down through 1937 could in fact be termed thoroughly satis-

* On a capital of £9,000,000.

factory. The factory that year made some 65,500 passenger cars, or as noted, nearly twice the 1934 total of 35,800. In the production of commercial vehicles it was not gaining, for its 8-cylinder truck sold slowly in a country which preferred four cylinders; nevertheless, it produced 18,153 trucks and vans. In the previous autumn it had brought out a new V-8 car of 22 horsepower which, intermediate in size between the 10-horsepower Ford de-luxe and the 30-horsepower V-8, had not proved popular as against the small English car.

It was possible during 1937 to spend more than £1,200,000 on expansion of the Dagenham plant, which had now become impressive. One building alone covered 28 acres. The powerhouse produced enough heat, light and power for a city of 160,000 people. The coke ovens carbonized 800 tons of coal a day, while the blast furnace daily devoured 2000 tons of coal, limestone, and iron ore to provide metal for the vehicles. The 1800-foot jetty on the Thames, the largest and best-equipped on the river, could rapidly load export cars into 12,000-ton ocean-going ships.

It was still the proud boast of the English company that its 8-horsepower Anglia was the cheapest car in the world. At £100 it undersold the Fiat at £116, the Austin 7-horsepower at £118, the Morris 8-horsepower at £120, and the Opel Cadet at £125. The demand for the Anglia enabled the directors to keep their dividend at 5 per cent for 1937. But the next year prospects darkened. This recession year found American industry dropping again to low levels, so that before it ended Dearborn had chalked up a severe loss. Though Great Britain weathered the new storm a little better, the profits of the English company were reduced to less than £170,000. It was now plain that adverse economic and political factors were costing the Ford Motor Company, Ltd., the place that Perry had hoped it would take on the continent, and every indication pointed to still gloomier times. Difficulties rose in a thorny hedge on all sides.[5]

4.

It was the misfortune of Perry and Ford that the newly reorganized foreign operation was caught in all the strains generated by world-wide depression, rising international antagonisms, the brutalities of dictators, and the legislative greed and panic that built so many quotas and tariff walls. No country was guiltless of selfish follies; certainly not the

United States, trying to collect war debts while at the same time raising high customs barriers. Companies doing an international business were cockboats tossing in the wake of a terrible storm—for the depression, the dictators, the economic nationalism, and the savage conflicts were an aftermath of the World War. While the "1928 Plan" had merits which peace and prosperity would have brought into relief, its imperfections, some the fruit of inadequate preliminary study, some of excessive optimism, were starkly exposed by the stresses of the era.

The blind world in which Coolidge and Baldwin dozed was supplanted by the savage world of Stalin, Hitler, and Franco. Even if the old order had continued, Perry would have met grave difficulties; the times compounded them.

His first harsh embarrassment stemmed from the fact that the continental companies did not find it convenient and profitable to buy from Dagenham rather than Dearborn. For one reason, the small English car did not suit many continental buyers so well as the American type of vehicle. Their distances, established tastes, and tax arrangements still made the heavier automobile preferable in many of their markets. And in the second place, Dagenham failed to demonstrate the anticipated economies in manufacture over Dearborn. Since its output remained low by American standards, its unit costs were high. English workmen, while precise and dependable, also did a smaller day's work than the Yankees. These facts more than offset the transatlantic freight costs.

Meanwhile, the imponderable element of prestige counted. In finish, size, speed, and reputation, the American car was much more impressive than the British. Anxious to please their customers and earn profits for their home stockholders, the continental companies clamored to buy in the cheaper market. Dearborn yielded and, in the spring of 1934, decreed that European affiliates might patronize both Dearborn and Dagenham at will.

Perry's second major embarrassment was that the continental companies became increasingly reluctant to channel their communications with Dearborn through his London office. Knowing that ultimate decisions upon design, finance, markets, and other vital matters must come from Michigan, they wished to be heard and answered directly. National pride intensified their feeling; a Frenchman found it easier to defer to the *fons et origo* of Ford power than to an English lieutenant. Many continental managers felt strongly on the subject. Yet as unitary control in Europe by a man of ability in close touch with all companies had manifest advantages, the problem except for France and Germany remained unsolved in the priod preceding World War II.

A third difficulty had no special reference to the 1928 Plan. No matter what comprehensive scheme of European organization had been adopted, it would have required some shrewd artifice or advice of counsel to avoid double or triple taxation of profits. Each nation, struggling in a blind melée, was intent on keeping the last centime or groschen for itself. Nearly all of them raised taxes on foreign companies, blocked or limited dividend transfers, impeded the exchange of capital, goods, and persons, and in general harassed "alien" businesses. From the start, Perry sought to minimize these effects by the creation of a strategically placed holding company, and was in part successful.[6]

But taxes on dividends were only part of the picture. All over Europe levies on horsepower, on steel and other materials, on appurtenances, and on gasoline (which in Italy helped force vehicles to the use of coal and wood as fuel), limited business, while quota-laws complicated the situation.

A modification of the 1928 plan was unavoidable. France and Germany led the way. In both countries the demands of government and public for the fullest utilization of domestic materials, suppliers, labor, and management, and the lengthening array of official restrictions, made it imperative for Ford subsidiaries to reduce their dependence on Dagenham. They had to manufacture for themselves, or perish. The result was that in 1934 Ford Ltd. sold to Dearborn most of the stock in the French and German companies, and these companies began independent manufacturing. Their withdrawal from English supervision tore a great gap in the unified system of production and sales that had been the basis of the 1928 Plan. Dagenham's loss of important market areas meant an enhancement of its unit costs, and a surrender of its firm coordinating grip upon finances, purchases, and sales in western Europe. But the step had become unavoidable; Europe had never been more disunited, its peoples more feverishly nationalistic, its ideas more fixed upon a favorite word of the time, autarchy.

Dagenham nevertheless kept much of its domain, strengthened by the new assembly plants at Antwerp and Amsterdam; and as we have indicated, it widened its activities in the East. In the early 1930s the sales and service center established in Istanbul in 1928 came under English control. Perry's European representative, F. S. Thornhill Cooper, then suggested that new and separate organizations be established for Greece, Roumania, and Egypt, areas previously given inefficient service from Istanbul. During the first seven months of 1932 Bucharest saw Ford Romana SAR begin operations; Alexandria saw the Ford Motor Company (Egypt) commence handling sales and service; and a sales company was incorporated in Athens. They all reported directly to Perry. In the same year Ford Lusitana, a wholly-owned subsidiary of the Spanish Ford company, took charge of the selling and servicing of cars in Portugal. Early returns from all these operations, except the Turkish, were encouraging. On its 1937 business Ford Romana, with Bulgaria and Yugoslavia in its sphere, paid a 20 per cent dividend, and Ford of Egypt at its fifth annual meeting in the spring of 1938 confirmed an interim dividend of 100 per cent, and paid a final dividend of the same amount.

Year by year Perry, surveying his wide territory, was able to compensate for losses in one area by profits in another, and usually to emerge a gainer. In 1934, for example, the Italian, Turkish, and German companies (with the last-named writing off some debts) operated at a loss. But the Danish and Swedish companies paid dividends of 7 per cent and 8 per cent respectively; the Dutch company declared a 12 per cent dividend; and the flourishing Belgian and Spanish companies (the latter, alas, soon to be engulfed in civil war) rewarded their stockholders with 25 per cent dividends. The total earned profits paid into the holding company exceeded £160,000.

Such a record of expansion and profits in one of the years of the European depression testified to Perry's abilities, and to the virtue of resiliency in the 1928 Plan, which yielded ground here to gain ground there. In 1937, as the depression slowly lightened, the Irish, Italian, Turkish, and Portuguese companies turned barren pages while the Spanish company could not even hold its annual meeting or publish its accounts. For the year, the subsidiary companies and the Near Eastern Branch had to report a small loss of £4,935, but Perry was able to write: "The Holding Company continues in a strong position. Its cash resources have been largely applied in making loans to the Company for asset expenditures of Dagenham."

This year Perry had to record of the Greek and Roumanian profits: "Cannot be transferred owing to currency restrictions." Holland was historically one of the world's staunchest defenders of freedom. Yet he had to write of Dutch activities: "Obstacles which handicap the free development of automobilism are continually increasing. . . . Further increase in petrol tax, the forthcoming introduction of a concessioning system for passenger cars and trucks, and the law regulating the number of working hours for paid drivers . . . [have] hampered the development and financial results of the company." Business could still be done, but within a vicious circle of ever-narrowing restrictions which nations imposed in self-defense or in retaliation. The United States by its Smoot-Hawley tariff had led the march. Because American tariffs shut out European manufactures, European peoples could not buy American products, and American farmers ceased to purchase either American or European wares. And over the world hung a darkening threat of war.[7]

A really graphic impression of the growing chaos can be obtained only from an examination of the history of the individual companies. It is a record stormy in France, portentous in Germany, and bleak indeed in most of southern Europe, but brightened in most places by courageous effort.

5.

Direct management of Ford interests in France, as noted, was the concern of the big, handsome Paris financier Maurice Dollfus, who had valuable friendships in industry, banking, and government. Unlike Perry, he did not possess thorough familiarity with automotive procurement, engineering, and marketing, and had to turn to Dearborn for advice and decisions in these areas. He never commanded the full confidence of Sorensen and the Fords as Perry did, and was watched more closely. But he possessed abounding energy and resourcefulness, was unhesitantly loyal to the Ford organization, and showed as much conservatism on issues of labor and free enterprise as Henry himself. His experience in French affairs enabled him to thread his way through the snarl of economic and political regulations with remarkable sureness. Though his problems must sometimes have driven him distracted, he never despaired.

Since by 1934 French laws and tariffs forced the company to undertake its own manufacturing, Dollfus and his directorate (still headed by Perry) faced the alternatives of erecting a great new factory of their own, or acquiring by purchase or partnership a plant of some existing company. They chose a partnership. After separating from Dagenham, Ford SAF made an agreement with the elderly but enterprising manufacturer E. E. C. Mathis, whose small car enjoyed a fair sale, to form a new company called Matford SA. It would lease the Mathis factory at Strasbourg, lease the Ford assembly at Asnières, and combine the skills and patents of the two firms, using new funds which each engaged to invest. Incorporated September 27, 1934, Matford had a capital of 20 million francs, soon rising to 60 million. Dollfus became managing director, and the Ford group, controlling 60 per cent of the shares, chose a majority of the directors.

This Ford preponderance gave Mathis some concern. A man of fine sensibilities, he was proud that he had been one of the world pioneers in the automotive industry. Since 1901 he had built up a great reputation, but in 1934 his financial position was weak. However, he wrote to Edsel in the summer of that year, just before the merger was complete: "I cannot remain blind to the fact that I am running a risk—which, I repeat, I am doing with my eyes open." He added that he would not accept the hazard if he did not feel that he was in just hands. "According to the terms of the agreement, you could even go so far as to stop producing Mathis cars and thus break our engagements after five and a half years; in this event, the good will of my firm would be completely destroyed, and even my name might be given oblivion." Little did he guess how close he was coming to prophecy.

The whole arrangement was of necessity one-sided, for Ford SAF brought the new company much greater values than did Mathis SA. To be sure, Mathis claimed fourth place in the French industry. But this did not mean much. His Strasbourg plant and machinery were in Sorensen's judgment antiquated and of little enduring value. In the last analysis, he gave the merger only one essential asset, a French identity for an American-ruled company. The Ford group later asserted that he never contributed a cent of capital to the new enterprise, but received dividends far higher than he could have obtained had he continued business alone; Ford SAF meanwhile adding 35,000,000 francs to capital, and giving the operations invaluable technological expertness. Had it not been for the alliance with Ford, he would probably have gone bankrupt.

But Mathis did bring his name and his reputation throughout France, and thus imparted a Gallic color to the Ford enterprises that was important to their survival in the heated nationalism of the time. Nine months after the merger agreement, the directors could tell stockholders in the annual report for 1935: "We think we may state that the aim of our general policy during the past few years, which has been to make a French national work, is fulfilled."

Unfortunately, while Mathis's name was valuable in currying favor with the patriotic public and the government, it was a feeble prop in selling cars. As the Asnières-Strasbourg plants began humming in the fall of 1934, they at first produced the Ford and Mathis cars separately. Buyers flocked to acquire the French version of the Ford V-8; they turned a cold eye upon the 4-cylinder Mathis. A year later Dollfus prevailed upon the directors to drop the Mathis trade-name, and concentrate the company energies upon a single 8-cylinder car of French design to be called the Matford. Naturally, this cut Mathis to the heart. He was further discomfited when, over his opposition, Dollfus began pushing the Ford V-8 cars so strongly that their French distribution increased by one-third in 1936.[8]

In his grief Mathis wrote the elder Ford, whom he held in regard as a fellow-pioneer: "Nobody can better understand than you, my dear Mr. Henry Ford, how painful it is for a businessman to witness the utter smashing up—without any reason or advantage for his partner— of a firm which bears his name and to the success of which he has devoted the efforts of his entire life."[9] But Dollfus remained adamant, and informed Sorensen in mid-1936 that he was taking no notice of what Mathis said or did. It became evident that the best solution would be the purchase by Ford SAF of the whole Mathis interest, and negotiations upon terms got under way.

While vexed by these internal disputes Matford successfully met its chief external trials. It achieved a workable relation with the French authorities. The Ministry wished Matford to make an all-French product. Dollfus, giving earnest assurances that he was moving toward that end, won a grant of time and other concessions. Over the voluble opposition of Citroen, Renault, and Peugeot, the government allowed

Matford first to import quantities of machine tools on special license, exceeding its quota, and then in 1936 permitted another importation of 600 tons of body parts above quota. As Dollfus explained to Sorensen, the authorities were indulgent because Matford was offering employment when labor was in distress, and because they accepted his promise to halve importations from the United States, and shift to a purely French basis as soon as possible. By the end of 1935 Matford was in fact producing practically a French car. Most of the raw materials were French, the V-8 motors, transmissions, and rear axles were Strasbourg-made, and much of the body work was done by French suppliers.

Equally important were Matford's successes in the labor field. In the spring of 1936 the leftist alliance called Front Populaire, with Leon Blum its chief architect, won a decisive majority in elections to the Chamber, and in June Blum became the first Socialist premier of France. His program, which included a 40-hour week and the nationalization of the principal war industries, met stubborn conservative opposition. To overrule it, the workers began massive sit-down strikes.

"For the first time in the history of this country," Dollfus wrote Sorensen on June 3, "plants and properties have been occupied—up to now peacefully—and the consequences may be, and in my opinion will be, far-reaching." The employes, while careful to damage nothing, were determined to stop production until their demands were met. Yet no strike occurred at the Strasbourg factory, and the Asnières employes walked out for only five hours on June 2, apparently to show their support of workers elsewhere rather than to express grievances of their own. Dollfus believed the reason why they all reported for work on the 3rd was that most of labor's demands had already been met by Henry Ford of his own free will. As the strikes spread and lengthened, Matford operations were inevitably affected by the shutdown of suppliers' plants, Asnières closing for a week and Strasbourg being interrupted three hours. But the competitors, Renault, Peugeot, and Citroen, were closed for longer periods.

One result of the strikes was thus an increase in Matford prestige throughout France. While labor disorders had racked most important industries, Matford had been almost untouched, never halted deliveries a moment, and at once went back on a full employment schedule. For the country as a whole industry and labor reached agreements, under

the aegis of the Blum government, which lifted wages an average of
12 per cent, gave workers paid annual vacations of a fortnight, enforced a 40-hour week, brought in compulsory arbitration without prejudice to the right to strike, and broadened the social services. Because
Matford's standards were already high, for it had always operated on
a 40-hour week, the new levels cost it less than most firms. Hourly
wages went up 10 per cent at Asnières and 17 per cent at Strasbourg,
and monthly wages 6 per cent. Throughout France, as inflation gained
pace, and capital fled the country, repeated wage increases became
necessary. Before 1936 Matford had again increased the Asnières and
Strasbourg payrolls by 12 per cent, and between July 1936, and the
following February, certain employees received as many as four separate increases. But since even greater advances were forced on
competitors, Matford gained rather than lost ground.

International tensions were meanwhile increasing. Mussolini invaded
Ethiopia in October 1935, and nine months later the Spanish civil
war began. Hitler's reoccupation of the Rhineland early in 1936
brought Europe to the verge of war. One Dearborn production expert
who happened to be in Strasbourg saw French troop trains, machine
guns, and heavy artillery moved into the city, heard air-raid sirens
tested, and agreed with Hitler that the first blows of the next war
would be struck so swiftly that the League members would not even
have time to assemble. Though Sorensen cabled, "No sense to our
boys leaving Strasbourg," most observers concluded that the city was
unsafe for a great industrial unit. This feeling reinforced the growing
desire in Ford SAF to cut loose in some fashion from Mathis—perhaps
by buying him out, perhaps by refusing to renew the lease on the
Strasbourg plant—and to erect a new factory. Attempts at purchase
took protean forms during 1936–1937, but negotiations proved abortive
because Mathis demanded terms that Edsel Ford and Sorensen refused
to meet. Bargaining over a new lease also broke down on a whole array
of controversial points—rental payments and lease terms, a Ford option
to buy the plant, the purchase of shares, and the disposition of machinery.[10]

By midsummer of 1937 the Ford-Mathis rupture was complete, and
Dollfus served notice on Mathis that Matford would not renew the
Strasbourg lease when it expired in 1940. Some hard feeling was nat-
ural on both sides. But actually both had gained something: Mathis

had made more money than he could have earned alone, and Ford SAF had effected an entrée into the circle of the French automobile industry. Making the best of his painful situation, Mathis in July, 1938, agreed to sell his Matford shares for thirty million francs in cash, and six million in Ford SAF shares, leaving his claim for heavy indemnity to arbitration. Out of this claim, even though the arbitrators ruled that he had no case, he finally got an additional five and a half million francs, or roughly $122,000. In view of what quickly happened to Strasbourg, he did fairly well.[11]

Under darkening international skies, with war moving inexorably closer, Ford SAF now drove ahead with plans for its own basic factory. Dollfus had found a sixty-acre site on the Seine near Poissy, fifteen miles from Paris, which seemed to him ideal, and which could be had for only $170,000. The sound cash situation of Ford SAF enabled it to pay part of the cost of construction and equipment. Certain sums could be transferred to it from Matford for this purpose, and the resourceful Dollfus, with his banking connections, could borrow other sums. When Sorensen pointed out the perils of debt, Dollfus had figures to show that the company's position was excellent and its future possibilities "immense." Obviously, he remained hopeful that peace would last.

"Our volume of business has practically doubled," he wrote Sorensen in March, 1938; "at the same time Renault is down, Peugeot stagnant, Citroen is the only one with ourselves flourishing." He wished to place a new small car on the market, and believed that expansion in this direction would create a rich new volume of trade.

Dollfus's enthusiasm brought everyone to his aid. Edsel Ford and Sorensen approved his proposals, the latter suggesting that plans for the German Taunus might also serve for the new French car. Perry and the other directors of Ford SAF fell into line, and on May 2, 1938, unanimously voted to build at Poissy a plant for manufacturing not only the two V-8 models already current, but an additional 4-cylinder car. The estimated cost of $4,000,000 would be met mainly by using Ford SAF accumulations and by borrowing from within the Ford empire; for example, 30 million francs from the Belgian Ford Company. In the spring of 1938 serious strikes, and that summer fresh Nazi threats, played havoc with business. When the Czechoslovak crisis in September threw all Europe into turmoil, many Frenchmen joined the colors, and mobilization halted normal activities. But in the relief after Munich large elements believed with Daladier and Chamberlain that peace had been assured for their time, and it was again safe to make long-range plans. Dollfus wrote Henry Ford on October 3: "The return of Mr. [Edouard] Daladier to France from Munich and his pilgrimage the next day to the Arc de Triomphe where the unknown soldier is buried, was indicative of the sense of dignity and cohesion existing now here."

During the fall work was initiated on the Poissy plant so vigorously that by the end of 1938 contracts had been let, grading and pile-sinking were progressing, and some construction was under way. The atmosphere in France had sharply changed. When the left-wing groups refused to endorse the Munich pact the Popular Front disintegrated; Daladier's government defeated the attempt at a general strike in November; and a pronounced shift to the right took place. Partly because of defense needs, the government showed a greater friendliness toward industry. Dollfus took new heart. Whereas he had feared that the disturbances of the year would cost Matford and Ford SAF heavy losses, the companies taken together showed a small gain. He could hope, moreover, for a profitable share in the growing defense effort. A smaller Dagenham on the Seine might be useful to France in many ways.

It was in relation to the defense program that the French company wrote the last gallant page of its pre-war history. Just after Munich the Minister of National Defense told Dollfus that Matford should at once make plans for emergency work in the event of war. Great Britain was seeing to the construction of "shadow plants" for defense. Taking this cue, the Ford directors in December 1938 discussed a defense-production plant which would run at a minimum level in time of peace, "but would be ready to take over all our installations in case of hostilities, and would thus assure the continuance of our companies while making a wholesome contribution" to national safety. They agreed to place it outside the exposed Paris area. But what should it begin making? Dollfus had already suggested the answer: airplane engines. "There is a terrible shortage of these motors in France," he had written early in 1938, "Hispano-Suiza and Gnome being the only two firms producing them, and in very small quantities indeed." Now, at the beginning of 1939, Guy La Chambre, the Air Minister, besought him to ask the Ford interests to come to his aid.

"I know of Henry Ford's passion for peace," La Chambre stated.

"We are nevertheless convinced that both he and Mr. Edsel Ford . . .
will readily understand that such contribution as you may make can
only be a most important factor in the cause of peace." [12]

March found Dollfus in Florida on Edsel Ford's boat, discussing the
matter with Edsel and Sorensen. They agreed that he should go ahead
and negotiate with the French government. He then hurried to Dearborn to develop his plans with P. E. Martin, B. J. Craig, and Moekle,
who sent six Dearborn technicians to France to look into production
problems. In May Dollfus, back in Paris, was reporting to Edsel that the
new undertaking had made encouraging progress. The government
had decided that the plant was to manufacture Rolls Royce engines,
and Rolls Royce executives were very cooperative. The French authorities showed a rising anxiety for early deliveries. By mid-May they
wanted 1200 engines, and were ready to spend 89 million francs to provide the machinery. Sorensen and Edsel Ford expressed concern lest
the French government keep itself in a position where it might cancel
the contract after the Ford interests had spent colossal sums on it, but
Dollfus reassured them.

Thus, as war approached, Ford SAF rapidly matured its plans for
defense production. On June 23, 1939, it incorporated under French
law a company called Fordair to manufacture the airplane engines, this
being a wholly-owned subsidiary; in fact, its alter ego. A month later
it purchased a well-constructed factory in Bordeaux, which with equipment cost 6,500,000 francs, and which Fordair could use at once. The
shareholders of Ford SAF agreed to raise the capitalization from
130,000,000 francs to 300,000,000, and to borrow 44,000,000 by issuing
debentures. Large government contracts for trucks came in. The deepening crisis found the Ford interests in France rising to their opportunities and duties. At the beginning of September they controlled four
plants—the leased Strasbourg factory, the Asnières assembly, the partly
completed works at Poissy, and the newly-acquired Bordeaux factory.
The deed on this last-named property was executed August 28th. Six
days later, France and Britain were at war with Germany, and the
emergency plant would be put to an immediate test.

Dollfus protected the Ford investments in France with skilled hands.
The picture was darker in Germany, where the government used nationalism as a politico-economic weapon to bludgeon industry into sub-
mission to the Nazi party and the Nazi Reich. Between 1933 and 1939

the Ford Company had the cruel choice of subscribing completely to the decrees of a totalitarian Reich, or closing its operations with the loss of a huge investment. Even if it accepted the first alternative, the management would be imprisoned within ever-narrower limits defined by the state, and the influence of the Fords, Sorensen, and Perry would decrease to the vanishing point. In the end, either choice might lead to the same result: practical confiscation.

It was no specific antagonism to Ford or his company that decreed this harsh policy. On the contrary, Hitler expressed admiration for Ford's methods and envy of the results they had wrought in the United States. "I am a great admirer of his," he told one German about to visit Dearborn; "I shall do my best to put his theories into practice in Germany." He recalled that he had once hated people driving in huge, luxurious cars. "But I have come to the conclusion that the motor car, instead of being a class-dividing element, can be the instrument for uniting the different classes, just as it has done in America, thanks to Mr. Ford's genius." [13]

But the Hitler regime was determined to create a totally self-sufficient economy, geared to a production quickly convertible to war uses. The Reichsverband der Automobilindustrie issued in rapid succession three directives: first, that practically all automobile parts must be made in Germany; next, that the cars must be made entirely of German materials; and finally, that all cars must have standard parts, interchangeable from one German automobile to another. General Motors during 1934 met all these requirements in manufacturing its Opel, but Ford lagged behind. We must remember that Ford began with what was primarily an assembly plant at Cologne, putting parts imported from England and the United States into an American-type car. Under stringent German pressure it did a little manufacturing in 1931, and then in 1933–1934 a great deal more, severing its Dagenham connections and expanding its operations to large-scale manufacturing; Dearborn at the same time acquiring the majority stock ownership previously held in London. Cologne was then in a position to buy increasing quantities of materials and parts within Germany. But it moved more slowly than German nationalists liked, and failed to win full Reich approval.

Some of its difficulties grew out of the weak state of the company at the time of Perry's take-over under the 1928 Plan. Its manager, Edmund C. Heine, a naturalized American citizen, was an arrogant pro-

Nazi who offended American and English superiors without winning strong German friends. He floundered into such a sea of difficulties that Dearborn sent its auditor, A. L. Byrns, in 1935 to inspect the Cologne activities. It was a scarifying report of general deterioration that Edsel, Moekle, and Sorensen read. Heine's management, reported Byrns, had dismissed capable executives without replacing them, had overemphasized distinctions of class and blood as a criterion of merit, had let the salary schedule fall behind the times, and had practiced gross favoritism. Members of the bloated office staff could seldom be discharged no matter how inefficient. The company had paid large amounts for legal fees and representation.

Other difficulties stemmed from the general Ford policy of trying to force American models upon the European market; the policy from which Perry had revolted in undertaking the small British car. As Dr. Albert put it, Ford suffered because it did not appear "on the scene in the German cloak from the outset." Instead, it sold not only the Köln (basically the English small car) and the Rheinland (the American Model B), but, keeping the American labels, the Model A and the Ford V-8.

A comparison of General Motors and Ford was eloquent. Although they began selling automobiles in Germany at the same time, by 1935 practically half the German buyers took the Opel cars with their domestic name and materials, while Ford had only 4.5 per cent of the market. The far-sighted Alfred P. Sloan of General Motors had seen as early as 1923 that special national tastes, laws, and standards of living would have to be met, and had worked toward cars entirely foreign-made and foreign-designed. However, in most countries Ford had nevertheless competed with General Motors on better than even terms.[14]

Sorensen summarily displaced Heine in 1935, appointing as the new "temporary manager" Erich Diestel, a businessman of brains and experience. He held a law degree, had been private secretary to Dr. Albert, the strongest director of Ford-Germany, when Albert was head of the North German Lloyd, and was a director of the Hamburg Electricity Works. As mayor of Altona he had political standing. The fact that he had never been concerned with manufacturing, selling, or servicing automobiles worried some subordinates. It was said that he had never even owned a car and could not drive one. "I have never seen anybody know less about the automobile or automobile business," declared one of his engineers. He was also a total stranger to Ford ways, men, and policies. But these deficiencies did not prove a heavy disadvantage, for in the first place he had abundant resourcefulness, which quickly earned him the title of full manager, and in the second, Dr. Albert, a man of dominating personality, continued to play a coordinate role in company affairs. He gave Diestel advice, carried on an extensive correspondence with Edsel and Sorensen, and helped make all basic decisions.

The most vital prerequisite in rehabilitating Ford interests was to obtain the government's recognition of the Cologne cars as German products. Some evidence exists that Dr. Albert, who had been forced out of the North German Lloyd by Nazi hostility, had since made his peace with Hitler. At any rate, he flung himself wholeheartedly into the effort to meet the government's demands. It was too bad, he wrote Sorensen, that the Cologne company had waited to be prodded into Germanizing its product; and too bad that Heine had described the cars as German when they still contained much foreign material—"this misrepresentation will always be cast in our teeth." With the cooperation of the Fords, Sorensen, and Perry, Dr. Albert and Diestel sought to dissipate both the popular and the official prejudice against their cars, the Eifel (an adaptation of Model Y) and the German-made V-8.

They made progress. By an early date in 1936 no Ford car exceeded the official limit of 5 per cent for foreign parts, and in most cars the foreign material, chiefly the steering-shaft and gears, was under one-half of one per cent. The company meanwhile tried, as the government wished, to enlarge its exports. It received a supposedly secret export subsidy from the Reich, sufficient to reduce its billing prices to Barcelona. Perry also agreed to help the hard-pressed German company by opening Denmark, Rumania, and Bulgaria, previously Dagenham enclaves, to German cars and parts, with a resultant increase in Cologne's exports.

But one Reich demand the Cologne management could not satisfy: that for a standardization of parts on the basis of Reich norms. Albert and Diestel agreed to it in principle, but not in practice. The step, they argued, would involve expensive retooling, would destroy the interchangeability of parts with other Ford cars, and would so weaken Cologne as to undermine Ford's potential contribution to the German economy. They pleaded for some concessions, some elasticity. But Nazi decrees were absolute, and the government made Ford's non-conformity the official reason for still withholding approval of the cars.

This refusal could have serious results, and it heightened Dr. Albert's interest in a scheme he had already been considering: a merger with the Stoewer Works in Stettin, which owned large facilities, including a body factory adaptable to Ford needs. The Stoewer heads had proposed a union, and Albert saw in it not only physical but political advantages. Because high Reich officials had placed several orders with Stoewer, Ford reenforcements of plant, technological skill, and capital would be appreciated in the right quarters. Moreover, Albert, who was now tiring of Diestel, believed that the Stoewer manager would make an excellent new administrator for the combined enterprise. All this Dr. Albert argued to Edsel Ford and Sorensen in person during a special visit to Dearborn in March 1936, and they gave his plans general assent.[15]

For a time, indeed, it seemed that the merger would go through. Sorensen visited the Stoewer works, liked them, and approved of a Ford loan of half-a-million marks for their expansion. But then came some disagreeable revelations. For it was suddenly learned that the Stoewer officials had misrepresented the assets and profits of the company, had understated its debts, and had spent nearly all the half-million marks within two months. Perry and the Americans at once rejected the plan, and Dr. Albert terminated all relations with Stoewer.

This fiasco left the Cologne company still exposed to government hostility, though some of the official acquaintanceships which Dr. Albert had made during his negotiations were useful. Fearing a resurgence of animus against Ford products, he advocated a series of protective moves. He would go the whole road in standardization, would seek orders for Nazi-type "defense," would stimulate the export business, and would in general comply with the demands of the government. He would also, it soon appeared, get rid of Diestel. That executive had applied for party membership, concealing the fact that he had Jewish ancestry—a fact which Nazi investigation promptly revealed. It would be wise, Albert declared, "to meet prevailing opinion without delay," and discharge Diestel. Apparently he himself shared this sickening type of "opinion."

Fortunately, Sorensen and to a lesser extent Perry questioned Dr.

Albert's stand on this matter. The downright Dane, who sometimes had thoroughly correct intuitions, enjoyed one now. Dr. Albert, he wrote Perry, "is altogether too impressed with the necessity of cooperation with Government authorities." He was determined to stand behind Diestel, whom he thought the ablest man in the German company. "Dr. Diestel has a very good grasp on our business. He senses our ideas and carries them out better than anybody we have had up to date." And calling Albert to Dearborn, Sorensen forced him to give way, to admit that he might have been wrong, and to promise to give the manager a free hand and to refrain from excessive interference.

With Diestel's authority confirmed, the German company could take judicious steps to meet its pressing problems. The Reich officials were always comparing Ford unfavorably with Opel. The Opel management, well selected by General Motors, had standardized its entire output, had built a new truck factory in accordance with Nazi wishes on a strategic site near the heart of Germany, and in other ways had cooperated handsomely with the government. Under the sunshine of Reich approval, it not only sold nearly half the automobiles manufactured in the country, but received several profitable government contracts. Since it could not transfer its large profits outside the country, it invested them in modernization and expansion of plant, to the further delight of the Nazis. Why couldn't Ford of Germany do as well? Neither the man in the street nor the Reich leaders could understand why it did not imitate Opel, and gained an impression that it did not *want* to.[16]

Diestel nevertheless made some advances. Sorensen allowed him to standardize the V-8 engines, and all the new models, although he forbade standardization for the two main existing models (C and Y) until further investigations could be made. Sorensen and Perry also lent a hand in stimulating the volume of German exports. Both Dearborn and Dagenham bought materials from the Cologne factory—Dagenham, for example, sent one order in 1936 for $250,000 worth of magnetos and other parts. Proposals that the German company be allowed to sell in continental markets where Ford-England was particularly active caused some friction. Sorensen urged Perry to "sacrifice" some of his sales and assist Cologne; and though the Englishman demurred, Edsel, Sorensen, and Roberge finally persuaded him to agree.

It is probably true that, as Roberge believed, the choice lay between increasing sales from Cologne and closing the German operations. Diestel and his associates were laboring under still other difficulties, one special worry being the quota restrictions on raw materials. In the autumn of 1936 the plant seemed likely to close for want of rubber, and later on copper, iron, and steel gave the management equal anxiety. Only by putting frantic effort into barter arrangements did Dearborn fill the needs. Political antagonism meanwhile closed Czechoslovakia to German goods. Other nations, like Poland, fixed strict import quotas on German shipments. Under these pressures the German company, professing warm appreciation of English "courtesy," moved more and more into fields once held by Dagenham or Dearborn alone, and in this way saved itself. During 1936 Ford exports from Germany rose nearly fourfold (by 283.25 per cent), and in the following year they increased again. Prices had to be kept down to Dagenham levels, but some of the exports seem to have enjoyed government subsidies.

Though Ford's German operations precariously survived, and still more precariously grew, Dearborn never could feel really happy about them. They existed by grace of a government as dictatorial, capricious, and brutal as any of the annals of mankind. But finally the Reich acknowledged the German character of the Cologne car. In January 1937 the Ministry of Economics published through its Propaganda Office a statement of recognition.

This may have been because the Nazis now had strong reason to wish the use of Ford facilities. As 1938 opened, they were negotiating with Dr. Albert, and he was corresponding with Ford leaders in America, upon the possible manufacture of a truck able to carry three-ton loads on paths of all kinds, however rough, muddy, and broken the country; in short, a truck for war purposes. It was to be assembled at some safer place than Cologne, in the interior of Germany. Naturally, Henry Ford objected, and Edsel also opposed it, but Sorensen seems to have been only less eager than Albert to gain the business.

The upshot was that the special war truck was vetoed. However, in April 1938, the directors of Ford of Germany agreed to erect an assembly plant in the Berlin area, where both ordinary trucks and V-8 passenger cars would be built. The following June the government promised to give the company an order for about 3,150 of its ordinary type of truck to be completed by March 1939. The government was also ready to place orders for large lots of passenger car chassis to be assembled in Berlin. Relations with Dr. Albert with the Reich authorities were now, as he put it, "satisfactory." With the war at hand, the German subsidiary of Ford, like the German subsidiary of General Motors, had been drawn into close relations with the Nazi overlords. On November 24, 1938, Diestel heard Field Marshal Goering, head of the Four Year Plan, explain to a conference at the Air Ministry just what he expected of the automobile industry, and Colonel von Schell asserted that the army would at once require 30,000 trucks.[17]

At this point the management changed. A Dane and a German, their names Erhard Vitger and Robert Schmidt, with Diestel's resignation on December 15, 1938 succeeded him as joint managers of the company.

### 7.

The Ford organization meanwhile met substantial calamities in Spain and Italy—calamities which it was powerless to avert or combat.

During the early nineteen-thirties the Spanish company, Ford Motor Iberica, made what Edsel Ford termed a splendid record of sales and earnings. By 1936 it had nearly one-third of the Spanish market, its deliveries exceeded those of any other European company except the British, and its earnings were better than those of the Belgian, Dutch, or Danish concerns. It had only an assembly plant at Barcelona. Its growth, however, and the pressure of the Spanish government for home manufacture with home labor and materials, led Perry to lay plans for expanding this assembly into a fully-equipped factory. At the beginning of summer in 1936 all the prospects were bright.

Then fell the thunderbolt; on July 18 began the bloody and bitter civil war. Spain was soon rent into hostile districts across which implacable armies, assisted on the insurgent side by Hitler and Mussolini, and on the government side by Stalin, fought with terrifying cruelty. For nearly a week Perry heard nothing from Barcelona, deep in the loyalist zone. Then in August news trickled in, first through George Jenkins, the American manager, who fled to London, and later in letters from Juan Ubach, the assistant manager who remained in charge. Anti-fascist committees controlled the plant, and had confiscated some vehicles and spare parts; production had been interrupted; but the employes were still being paid, and they promised that the plant would be restored to its owners when the war ended. During August the workers furnished the Catalonian government, which was on the loyalist side, twenty armored cars, each topped with a machine-gun turret. That same month Ubach and the Ford workers met the request of the loyalist government for 1,133 new cars and trucks, to be used against the insurgents.

Perry saw that he faced a question of cardinal importance. Should he try to keep aloof from the conflict, a strict neutral, forbidding the Spanish company to meet demands from either belligerent, and ordering the outside companies to sell no cars, trucks, or parts to any Spanish army? Ubach wished to keep on supplying the loyalist government, and soon asked Perry to send him the needed parts. Jenkins, on the other hand, after hurrying to Lisbon to help manage the Spanish subsidiary in Portugal, besought Perry to prevent Barcelona from giving any avoidable aid to the loyalist "reds," whom he accused of dark crimes; and he circulated a letter asking all Ford dealers in rebel Spain to communicate with him—he was obviously ready to supply them from Portugal.

After some natural hesitation, Perry concluded that Ford could no more avoid involvement with both sides than the numerous other suppliers of all types of goods, who continued shipping them into Spain. He wrote Ubach to take no part whatever in politics, but to submit to coercion by the authorities controlling Barcelona, and not try to resist. He sent the same instructions to Jenkins: "Our Company takes no interest in politics, but, obviously, has to bow to Authority." Throughout 1937 and 1938 Ford products went to both belligerents. Production in Barcelona for the loyalists was tardy in recovering its pre-war pace, but by May 1937 Ubach delivered 150 units, and under duress continued to supply the Catalonian authorities. Jenkins meanwhile shipped Ford products from Portugal into rebel-controlled areas. At first he was allowed to sell fully-built cars only to dealers outside peninsular Spain, including the Canary Islands, Morocco, and Gibraltar, parts alone going into the peninsula. But Jenkins, eager to help the rebels, reminded Perry that Opel cars would take much of the Spanish market if Ford abandoned it, and Ford Lusitana was soon authorized to send cars, trucks, and tractors to accredited dealers in insurgent-held areas against payment in dollars and pounds. Perry even asked Diestel in Germany to assist the Portuguese company. Almost 6000 automotive units, with a large number of spare parts, reached Franco's forces through Ford Lusitana.

Rebel bombing of Barcelona did minor damage to the Ford assembly plant. Early in 1939 Franco's troops captured the city, and threw Ubach into jail, from which British efforts soon obtained his release.

The end of the civil war in March 1939 terminated a nightmare in the history of Ford Iberica. Perry reported to Edsel Ford that balancing the 7.6 million pesetas in profits brought forward from 1935 against the wartime losses of 1936–1939 resulted in a total deficit, at the end of 1939, of nearly 11.7 million pesetas. The only satisfactory asset of the company had been its Portuguese subsidiary. The war also left a legacy of government ill-will. Franco disliked the company because it did not give him his war supplies on credit, as General Motors, Chrysler, and other American firms had done. Ford Iberica made strenuous efforts to placate him, its directors in May 1939 agreeing to proceed with plans for the manufacturing plant, and its officers assuring the government that they had never *voluntarily* had any dealings with the "reds." Perry also offered to send Spain much-needed parts, and to supply the government with trucks. But the ill-feeling long remained.

While digesting their losses, the Ford executives had also to give up their hopes of immediate expansion. Ubach reported that foreign capital in Spanish enterprises would probably be kept below 35 per cent, and a visit of Roberge and Moekle to Madrid confirmed the information. Plans for factory reconstruction were set aside for reëxamination. And events elsewhere on the European continent soon pushed interest in Spain and Ford Iberica into the background.[18]

The Italian story was almost equally depressing. Perry's hopes for the activities of Ford Ltd. in Italy had initially been buoyant, and Dearborn had shared them. By the early 1930s the Ford interests had invested nearly a million dollars in land, assembly operations, and sales offices in Genoa, Trieste, Naples, Livorno, and Bologna. But Mussolini's government was determined to protect the Fiat company from foreign competition, and especially Ford's dangerous rivalry. By 1936 the government had imposed an advalorem duty of 300 per cent on Ford products, lifting the cost of a Ford car in Italy to five times that of a similar model in the United States! After losing nearly $700,000 within a single twelvemonth, Sorensen and Perry agreed in 1934 to a "gradual evacuation" of Italy, and the following year Sorensen was prepared to terminate activities altogether. Perry was not quite so pessimistic. He reported that although he had reduced the Italian organization to skeleton proportions, he believed that an improvement must soon take place. "Conditions are so bad that there will have to be a change in the economic Government, as all authorities seem to agree that Mussolini's attempts to make Italy economically self-supporting have been a disastrous failure." Unhappily, the worst was still to come.

When Mussolini loosed his attack upon Ethiopia in October 1935, the situation became impossible. Throughout the first nine months of the year Italian forces on the Red Sea littoral had been making heavy purchases of Ford trucks and other units from the Egyptian Ford Company, which served that area. At least 2200 ton-and-a-half trucks, according to the *New York Times,* went to Mussolini's troops, and total truck sales by the Egyptian company shot up to 4767 in 1935 as compared with 802 the previous year. The dictator had massed a quarter of a million men in East Africa. His blow, supported by bombs and poison gas, outraged decent people, and Henry Ford, true to his pacifist principles, at once applied his own private sanctions. He stopped shipments of war material to Italy, taking this step a month before the League declared its futile partial embargo. Moreover, Ford maintained his stand even after the League backed down.

This brave action had some effect. General Rodolfo Graziani declared at the end of 1935 that he would have been well on the road to Addis Ababa had Ford not prevented him: "We paid for 800 Fords in advance, but the sale was cancelled when Henry Ford began his private sanctions." Governmental and popular hostility rose like a wave. When Rome imposed still higher duties on Ford products brought into Italian ports, it expressed both its developing policy of economic nationalism and the current resentment against Henry Ford's position. Perry, seeing the restrictions grow, hastened to reduce the Italian operations to an absolute minimum. He cut expenses so radically that losses for the years 1934–1939 totalled only $31,000; but even so, he could only lament, "Our experience in Italy has been most disastrous." [19]

Other southern countries contributed to the melodrama of the troubled time. In the Near East and Balkans the Ford management experienced enough intrigue and adventure to stock a dozen E. Phillips Oppenheim novels. The Istanbul operation suffered not only unprofitable days, but official allegations of dishonesty, for the government in 1935 accused its heads of evading some customs duties and cheating on others. Litigation ensued which finally vindicated the company, but drained all its cash reserves. In Greece the Ford manager had to flee the country when the government investigated his affairs in 1938, the company forfeiting the bail it had posted. The Bucharest branch likewise came under a financial investigation, but without untoward result. Only in Roumania and Egypt, the former with an assembly plant, and the latter with merely a sales and service organization, were substantial profits achieved in the later nineteen-thirties.

The small northern countries, all reasonably stable parts of the Dagenham domain, continued to do as well as the depression and political turmoil permitted. Till the end of the nineteen-thirties Belgium remained a reliable market for the English company, and so did Holland and Denmark. The Swedish market expanded, while Finland and the Baltic states granted favorable import quotas to Ford Ltd. Perry, to be sure, had a few sharp collisions with his lieutenants in these countries. The Belgian director Camille Gutt, one of the financial wizards of Europe, repeatedly matched his wits and determination with Sir Percival. In particular, when the Belgian company was asked to allow the French concern to find a large debt merely by handing over preferred shares, without outside guarantee, Gutt in 1938–1939 successfully resisted. By threats of resignation, he and the other Belgian directors forced a revision of terms on the French debt. Perry also had a long wrangle with the manager of the Dutch company, G. J. J. Both, a stubborn individualist who did not wish to accept orders from Dagenham. After the resignation of Both in 1937, a new Dutch head showed more docility.[20]

## 8.

Though the English company remained the firmest element in the European situation, and kept its dividends at first 5 and then 6 per cent until the war began, it had to conduct a heavy struggle in its home territory. One discouraging fact was that Lincoln cars, which as a purely American product Perry never really liked, sold badly in Britain. They were distributed by a wholly-owned subsidiary, Lincoln Cars, Ltd., incorporated in June 1936, and marketed for the first two seasons at a distinct loss.

At the same time, Ford Ltd. failed to find a profitable demand for its trucks. This, Perry insisted, was because Dearborn compelled the company to use an 8-cylinder engine when British buyers almost universally preferred a 4-cylinder type, consuming less gasoline and oil. Not until Henry Ford and Sorensen gave way in 1937 and began hammering out a design for a 4-cylinder motor did the outlook improve. The fact that more and more continental companies, as we have seen, purchased materials and parts locally, told heavily against the English company. Exports by Ford Ltd. fell so low in 1938 that Perry spoke grimly at the stockholders' meeting the following spring of the "tragic degeneration of international trade."

The small cars did as well as could be expected in view of the recession of 1937–1938, which was as serious in Britain as in America, and the increased competition by other makers. In every type of car Ford Ltd. tried to offer lower prices than its English rivals. It also showed continuous enterprise; in September 1937 it introduced a new 8-horse-power model with a reconstructed body and improved engine, and in October 1938 bought out still another model, the 10-horsepower Prefect.

But after the mid-thirties the number of home competitors thickened. Alongside those old rivals, the Austin and Morris, appeared small cars made by Vauxhall (General Motors), Hillman, and the Standard Motor Company, splitting the market among six leading English firms instead of three. At the same time, Opel cars flooded into English sales-rooms. The Reich, eager to create a favorable balance of trade, subsidized the export of German automobiles by special payments, and by giving a false value to the International Mark. In vain did British manufacturers denounce such dumping, for low-tariff Britain was reluctant to add to its restrictions. The best shield was the widespread prejudice developing against German goods.

Resolutely confronting its adversities, and relying on the solid merit of its cars, trucks, and tractors, the British company did well even as Hitler plunged Europe into war. When 1939 ended, it had made a trading profit for that year—eight months peace, four months conflict—of £2,753,500; and after deducting heavy sums for taxes, depreciation, and other charges, its net profit stood at £606,000. These figures included no receipts from its subsidiaries. It had earned more than 10 per cent on its shares, and paid dividends of 6 per cent. This was a happy improvement over 1938, the year of recession, Munich, and enhanced fears of war. While new horsepower taxes had hit the V-8, Lincoln, and Mercury sales hard, the company had profited from large mid-year orders by the government for a reserve supply of Fordson tractors. The Minister of Agriculture explained to the country that the

Ford company was the only one in Britain with sufficient capacity to meet national requirements within a reasonable time. Ford Ltd. carried forward into 1940 the sum of £1,044,000. Perry, looking back over the stormy decade, could feel he had done well.[21]

Others thought so too. The New Year's Honours List of 1938 had transformed Sir Percival Perry into Baron Perry of Stock Harvard. Showers of congratulations, American, British, and continental, fell upon him. Yet his greatest services to his country lay ahead.

The outbreak of the war had witnessed, in all the lands engaged, the mobilization of the Ford companies to support the national effort, and of necessity, they fought on both sides. In Germany the company had profited from an increasing solidarity with the government. With more than 4200 employes at Cologne, and a sale of nearly 37,000 units, it paid its first dividend in 1938. During 1939 the new Berlin factory went into operation under such close Nazi control that the American executives could learn little about it. One Dearborn engineer, V. Y. Tallberg, was refused admission as a foreigner. Roberge had a great deal of trouble entering the place, and when he did get in, could not find what the German government was making there. Beyond question, in 1939 a major part of Ford production in the Reich, despite Henry Ford's stern objections, was shifted into channels at least indirectly useful to the German war effort.

West of the Rhine, in Dollfus's principality, the two complete plants at Asnières and Strasbourg, and the incomplete facilities at Poissy and Bordeaux, were equally useful to the French war effort—as long as that effort endured.

It was Dagenham that was to play the largest role in the war, for it had the greatest facilities, ablest direction, and fullest assistance from America. Important executive changes improved its administration. In January 1939, Lord Perry had resigned from the work of European coordination to give all his time to his British chairmanship. The manager, A. R. Smith, and Secretary, H. S. Cooper, were added to the directorate, on which Sir Malcolm Campbell had recently taken the seat made vacant by the death of Sir John T. Davies. To fill the places opened by the promotions of Smith and Cooper, Patrick Hennessy, a man of remarkable energy and acumen, was made the new manager, and J. M. A. Smith the new secretary.

Shortly afterward, to meet the war threat, Perry transferred the holding company from Luxembourg to a less vulnerable position. With the consent of the English Treasury, he liquidated the Société d'Investisse-ments Ford, transferring practically all its assets and liabilities to the Ford Investment Company of Guernsey. In close rapport with the government, its officers vigilantly braced for an ordeal, Ford Ltd. took the shock of war with Germany.

What, in the large view, was the pre-war contribution of the overseas enterprises to the vigor, breadth, and prestige of the Ford Motor Company? Henry Ford, Edsel, and Sorensen would have said that it was very considerable. These enterprises were in a vulnerable position. All suffered from the rampant economic nationalism of the day—tariffs, import quotas, and exchange restrictions; all helped their nations prepare for conflict; and some in time faced obliteration. Nevertheless, the Ford undertakings in Europe and the Middle East, like the always-prosperous Ford Motor Company of Canada with its subsidiaries in Australasia and other parts of the British Commonwealth, helped give the parent corporation current stability and future hope.

They did much for the magic of the Ford name all around the globe, so that natives in Malaysia, fellahin on the Nile, and peasants in the Tyrol knew it nearly as well as Chicagoans did. They pumped moderate but real profits into the Dearborn treasury at times when American profits were disappointing. At the end of 1937, for example, the directors of the English company paid £326,250 to shareholders—and Dearborn owned a majority of shares; while that same year Dagenham carried forward a balance of £912,994. They laid the foundation for sound future companies, particularly in Britain and Germany, to emerge from the storm of war. They made some useful contributions to automotive design, broadened the range of Ford vehicles, and helped keep alive an interest in half-neglected products like the tractor. Labor relations were for a time decidedly more advanced in Britain than the United States, while the Canadian company made special boast of its "human engineering." The total Ford Motor Company capital in foreign branches became a reserve of some magnitude; at the end of the war, indeed, the investment in the British and Canadian companies was computed at $24,903,000.[22]

The total contribution to strength, stability, and flexibility was large. How much it was needed will become clear as we turn back to examine the situation in Dearborn.

# V

## A COMPANY IN THE DOLDRUMS

For six and a half years Cowling had been head of sales activity, with more emphasis on inspiration than administration, which for the most part fell to Davis. As Davis now took charge, a change of atmosphere was apparent, as when in a desperate final quarter the football coach sends in a player who holds the enthusiasm of the team. Edsel believed in Davis, and spoke the literal truth when he announced his appointment "with great pleasure." The branch managers and dealers shared this feeling. One official said later, "Cowling was only a mouthpiece, while Jack Davis had the complete respect of our dealer organization." [1]

He needed that and his own utmost efforts, for he had taken up a faltering activity at the low point of a depression. Yet he pushed forward confidently with the sale of 1938 cars. Asserting that more people bought the 1937 V-8 than any other 1937 make,* he announced that its successors "are *better* cars, for Ford improvement goes on constantly." He particularly urged an effort to establish the "thrifty-sixty," stating early in January that this vehicle with the smaller V-8 engine cost "less to run than any other Ford ever built," would do from 22 to 27 miles a gallon, and would reach a top speed of 75 miles an hour.

Davis had various plans for improving the dealer organization and raising Ford sales. But he knew that a multitude of used cars clogged every dealer's quarters. Selling would be difficult enough without this handicap, and with it might be impossible. Feeling that the used cars must be moved, and that an industry-wide effort would be required to dispose of them, he asked Edsel if there were any objection to his approaching the Automobile Manufacturers Association (to which Ford, it will be recalled, had never belonged.) "They won't listen to you,"

---

* Including trucks, this was true; in passenger cars, Ford sales lagged 2107 units behind Chevrolet.

109

Edsel protested. "Maybe not; but may I talk with them?" Edsel agreed, and Davis approached Alvin Macauley, the AMA president, won his approval, and then convinced the AMA board that a Used Car Week early in March would serve all automotive manufacturers.

The result was salutary. By agreement, the poorest cars were burned, the conflagrations of these "clunks" arousing the interest of many communities. The Ford organization had taught its dealers so much about used cars that it led all companies with a sale of more than 57,000 vehicles, reducing its used car stock by 22,804 units.[2]

Davis was now free for the first time in his experience to plan a program of improvement. He began at once to rewrite the existing contracts with dealers, incorporating additional incentives and protections. He also set about improving both the business and sales techniques of Ford representatives. He distributed a monthly bulletin on accounting, a "Manual of Business Management," and other printed aids, while in his letters to branch managers he preached expert salesmanship, which to him meant careful preparation and a clear objective. He warned against an overemphasis on used cars, pointing out that some Ford dealers were buying and selling them to the injury of their new stocks. "We are not granting the use of Ford sign to used car dealers," he stated. He also outlined the best methods of disposing of trade-ins, including their reconditioning with the use of company specialists as advisers.

It was an auspicious beginning, which would later be fortified by the introduction of a new car. Meanwhile, however, certain forces were building up within the company to interfere with sales activities, with engineering, and with manufacturing.

2.

The position of Harry Bennett in the Ford Motor Company has already been noted. As related in *Ford: Expansion and Challenge,* he had steadily strengthened his standing, and emerged into moderate prominence about 1927. At the time of the episode at Gate 4 in 1932, he already wielded considerable authority, and this incident increased it. "He had mercurachrome put on his cuts and went to see Ford and the latter was impressed," said Bricker afterwards. At any rate, Bennett now assumed a position of rapidly increasing importance in the company.

He already controlled Ford personnel, and showed clearly that he understood the strategic power that this control gave him. With the formation of the UAW, the creation of NRA, and the passage of the Wagner Act, labor problems in the Ford Motor Company suddenly became of as great or greater moment than those posed by engineering or sales. Henry Ford was deeply concerned. He had worked for the election of Landon in 1936, and Republican defeat only intensified his determination to oppose the New Deal. He felt that he needed a right-hand man whose views tallied with his own, and who could carry out Ford policy with unflinching firmness. He regarded Edsel as unqualified, both because his views were conciliatory, and because of what his father felt to be an inherent lack of "toughness." Bennett quickly stepped in, saying what Ford wanted to hear, and crisply acting upon it. Black, who as head of advertising was close to the son, states that Edsel resented being thus shut out, and Sorensen in his autobiography is in emphatic agreement. He himself, up to now the most influential executive in the organization, both personally with Ford and functionally because of his work, was too busy with manufacturing and overseas activities to take on the additional burden of labor. But he had not been asked. Bennett was the chosen man.

The small, quick-moving, athletic Bennett, who on occasion knocked down men almost twice his weight, apparently did not know the meaning of fear. "If I had to enumerate his outstanding qualities," said the not too friendly Sorensen, "I believe I'd put fearless personal courage first." All evidence supports this statement, but courage was not Bennett's only asset, or even his most important one.[3]

By the nineteen-thirties the personnel chief had gathered about him a force of men to police the Rouge plant and serve him in general who have been well described as "broken bruisers, ex-baseball players, one-time football stars, and recently freed jailbirds." Henry Ford still believed that he could rehabilitate criminals by giving them jobs. Bennett, in hiring such men, was thus carrying out Ford's philosophy. At the same time he cultivated police, FBI officers, and state parole officials, and pushed an acquaintance with a variety of influential figures in the Detroit underworld. This again pleased Ford, who felt that Bennett might thus protect his son and grandsons, and on occasion the interests of the company.

Bennett had an office in the basement near the entrance to the Rouge plant, and later in the Administration Building opposite the Rotunda.

Here he kept one or more revolvers, and a target which on at least one occasion he used in a friendly match with Ford. Irate Bill Klann, an able Ford executive who left the company late in the nineteen-twenties, once in a sudden quarrel stopped Bennett's attempt to draw a weapon by knocking him against the door.[4]*

Bennett was by no means satisfied to confine himself to personnel and labor problems, though for some time they were nominally his only provinces. According to numerous Ford executives he always had larger ambitions, and in time aimed at the control of the entire company. The question of Bennett's attitude toward Edsel and Sorensen might admit of some difference of opinion. Bennett later professed friendliness toward both, but Sorensen paints a different picture; and the testimony of many others and the subsequent course of events all indicate that he worked vigorously to pull Sorensen down and to neutralize Edsel as a factor in company control. By the late 1930s he had begun his drive for supremacy. He had rather impressive resources for extending and solidifying his power.

For example, by 1937 he had the authority to employ and discharge all but a few men on the Ford payroll, and could approve transfers and expense accounts. Sheldrick was bitterly aware of Bennett's prerogatives. "He had to approve all travel vouchers. . . . One could not hire, fire, raise, or transfer a man [without Bennett knowing of it and confirming it]. I could not send a man on a trip, I could not make a long distance call, I could not send a telegram if he didn't want me to do so."

Such powers could never have been exercised had Bennett not consolidated his position as Henry Ford's counsellor and action-agent. As his position became accepted, it gave him almost unlimited opportunities. If Bennett wanted an official discharged, a piece of construction begun or halted, or a general policy altered, he seemed to speak for Ford, and sometimes said so. "Often we suspected that he wasn't speaking for Mr. Ford," said Bricker, "but we couldn't check on it." If anyone had checked with Ford, the latter would probably have supported Bennett regardless of the facts, and the questioner would have been on the way out of employment.[5]

One of Bennett's methods of extending his influence was to put other

* Klann, outraged because Bennett called a certain worker his brother-in-law, denied the statement; whereupon Bennett accused Klann of calling him a liar and reached for the pistol.

officials in his debt and then exert pressure upon them to appoint persons loyal to him, or let contracts to bidders he might suggest. Davis in Sales found himself facing requests that he appoint certain men as branch managers or dealers. His successor, Doss, was even asked to discharge a good man in order to make room for a Bennett candidate. After Bennett in 1930 got Harry Mack into the Sales organization, Mack appointed a number of dealers, and was used by Bennett as an agent for distributing favors. If the head of Ford Security wanted a car given to someone, Mack would deliver it. No record of sale would ever appear, but by various means the exact value of the car was established for accounting purposes. Both Davis and Edsel were well aware of these irregularities, and as time passed they waited for an occasion for discharging Mack.*

Another method used by Bennett was to watch the acts of persons he wished to discredit and casually drop apparently haphazard information about them into Ford's ear. This procedure could turn Ford against a person, or move him to adopt a policy Bennett suggested. Sometimes Bennett even persuaded his contemplated victim to do something that he knew Ford would not like. In *We Never Called Him Henry,* he disclaims responsibility for 90 per cent of the acts which made him unpopular with fellow employes, asserting that he was merely obeying orders. However, he does not tell how many of these orders were the result of Bennett's own influence on Ford.[6]

Davis repelled the efforts of Bennett to extend his foothold in the Sales Department, and Wibel gave him small comfort in Purchasing. Yet both men on occasion had to meet Bennett's wishes in the form of Ford mandates. Meanwhile, Bennett did very well for certain favorites in the Ford plant, where he could dispense contracts for supplying fruit, ice cream, and food. Some concessions were held by characters from the Detroit underworld: Chester LaMare, for example, supplied great quantities of fruit.[7]

Bennett's supporters among Ford officials included Ray R. Rausch, Richard Kroll, and William Comment in production, Russell Gnau in Sorensen's office, and the Ford secretary and treasurer, B. J. Craig, who would trot over to Bennett's office at a phone call to see what was wanted. Through Captain O. A. Johnson and his deputy Norman J. Ahrens, the cocky young personnel director exercised control over the

* Edsel recognized that Bennett was the real offender, but to discharge him was impossible.

Ford Fleet. Equally friendly to him were the metallurgist and engineer, Hudson McCarroll; Ford's man of all work, Ray Dahlinger; and his personal secretary, Frank Campsall (who took walks with Bennett). Bennett had planted other men in various places, such as Frank Holland (useful in labor disputes), Leonard Saks (personnel), Stan Fay, Jim Brady, John W. Thompson, and Clifford Prevost. Thompson was to direct Ford publicity in the nineteen-forties, and Prevost was to serve as Ford representative in Washington. Bennett worked closely with I. A. Capizzi, whose law firm represented Ford in many matters.

Cooperation with Bennett did not mean approval of his activities. No Ford official could afford to offend him. When in the late nineteen-thirties no less a person than Sorensen made at least one attempt to speak to Ford against Bennett, he was coldly checked. Bennett was exactly what Ford wanted. "Henry Clay," he told Davis's successor H. C. Doss, "what I like about Harry is that if I want something done he will do it; I don't have to tell him twice." As a result of Bennett's position in the company, fortified by his personal influence over Henry Ford, he could command almost anybody's cooperation, willing or otherwise. This was particularly true as he assumed a leading role in labor matters.[8]

Bennett's increasing influence was plain to anyone who watched the guests in his luncheon room. Among the regular attendants at his oblong table on the top floor of the Administration Building were Harry Mack, Ray Rausch, Stan Ray, and Russell Gnau. The sports world was likely to be represented by men like Harry Newman or Mickey Cochrane. Guests from the underworld regularly appeared—Palma or Tocco or some of their friends—and a police official or state probation officer might turn up. Here, too, a number of Ford executives sometimes ate. Bricker, Davis (before he became Sales Manager) Wiesmyer, or Logan Miller would all come on occasion, for they realized that it was politic to do so. Davis recalled that if he went to one of the other tables in a larger adjoining room, Bennett would find occasion to say: "What's the matter, Davis? Don't you like us?" It saved trouble to go voluntarily. At Bennett's table the talk would be of sports, crime, or police work, and never of the automobile industry, although most of those present were of course active in it.

The damaging impact of Bennett on the Ford organization, at once insidious and pervasive, was most clearly observable in its effect upon

Edsel's status. Long president of the Ford Motor Company without exercising the full powers supposed to go with the office. Edsel by the early 1930s had achieved a position of strength. He had a pretty free hand in styling the Ford cars, directed advertising and sales (as he had long done), and ran the business organization of the company. While Henry Ford still dominated engineering, even in this field Edsel exerted a helpful influence, and would continue to do so until his death. But as he gave promise of larger stature, Bennett began to manipulate men and conditions to thwart him.

Bennett declares that in any opposition he offered Edsel, he was prompted not by his own wishes but by Henry Ford, and for this assertion there is some support. Sorensen and others recognized that Bennett was often only acting as Henry's agent. Ford believed for many years that Edsel lacked iron—that to become the executive he should be, his character must pass through a hardening process. Henry used Liebold, Sorensen, and finally Bennett to help him shape his son to something nearer his own image; to become a hard, decisive, quick-thinking industrial leader.

He never succeeded. Edsel had his own character, and remained true to it. He had deliberately made up his mind that filial loyalty required him never to oppose his father once Henry had made a decision. "If that's the way father wants it, that's the way it's going to be," he would say. Recognizing that "my father built this business," he found the corollary clear: "It's *his* business—" to operate as he saw fit. This deference wherever his father's wishes were concerned did not mean that Edsel was weak. Fred Black speaks effectively upon this point. "When I say that Edsel's . . . character was as definite as his father's, but only in a different way, I'm expressing a summation of opinion, not merely my own. Those of us who were at all sympathetic toward Edsel, felt that he was a *fine* executive, and well capable of heading the Ford Motor Company and of being its president." * For the immediate situation, deference to father meant tolerance of power in Bennett.

As the 1930s advanced and Ford with increasing age became more stubborn in his ways, the "hardening" of Edsel continued. It was doubtless guided to no small extent by Bennett, who began to see himself as

* Edsel had one admirable trait his father lacked. If an unpleasant job were to be done, Henry Ford farmed it out to someone else. Edsel invariably accepted responsibility for it. "I'll do my own dirty work," he would say.

Ford's successor. He wanted to "fence Edsel in" so that he heard less of what was going on in the company. He was working meanwhile to establish more "Bennett men" throughout the company, and increasingly to dictate who should be employed and who should receive agencies, concessions, and commissions. There were numerous ways of doing this if Henry Ford would approve. For example, when the University of Michigan let its football coach Harry Kipke go, Bennett empowered him to purchase certain car accessories for the company—with the result that Bennett himself was startled to see how much Kipke prospered.

Bennett in time began to find or place men loyal to him in various phases of production. This naturally annoyed Sorensen, who unfortunately for himself assumed that Bennett was so ignorant in that area that he could never pose any threat there. Actually, Bennett had no need to match Sorensen's knowledge: all he required was power to act, for he could get agents with the abilities and skills he lacked. The same was true for other company activities. Thus Bennett's power was increasing at dozens of different points, if often in what seemed petty ways.

A situation was being created which dangerously affected a number of such high executives as Edsel, Sorensen, Martin, Wibel, and Craig and which brought dozens of second-rank executives face to face with Bennett's power, and taught them not to oppose it. Almost invariably they were at first startled and upset, and what they saw shook their confidence in the company. "I often wondered how an organization could tolerate an individual like that around," said Anthony Harff, Bricker's secretary. "He always seemed to be tearing down instead of building up." This was also the feeling of more important officials like Wagner, Black, Logan Miller, Bricker, and Davis.

The situation was sharpened by rumors that Bennett used Ford materials and labor to build one of his houses, and abused the company for the benefit of his favorites. Of the former allegation no proof exists; but the charges of manipulation and favoritism were true. As Moekle says, "The real harm was that these stories . . . had a very, very bad effect upon the morale of the organization." They were particularly injurious in that many employes who saw that Edsel was being increasingly thwarted had long regarded him as their hope for the future. "The loyalty you had was because of Edsel," said Harold Hicks, who left the company in 1933. "You really worked there, hoping and praying for the time when Edsel would be in charge." Toward the end of the nineteen-thirties that day began to look incredibly distant, and almost a mirage.[9]

### 3.

The year 1938 found all the chief motor companies under indictment for favoring specific finance companies. Reports arose that Ford and Chrysler would sign consent decrees, and in November the Department of Justice announced tentative agreements with both. Under these agreements the firms promised not to advertise particular finance corporations as handling the sales on an installment basis. General Motors meanwhile firmly refused to accept such a decree if it meant a divorce of its affiliate, the General Motors Acceptance Corporation, and this refusal put Ford and Chrysler at a temporary disadvantage. However, their dealers continued to use CIT (in the case of Ford) and CCC (in the case of Chrysler), among the other finance companies available to them.

Spring brought to a climax an effort that had been hopefully pushed for several years. The company had been developing a small car, below the V-8 size and power. The objective was to reach a level of customers not tapped by even the $540 Ford. This would introduce a third Ford car and perhaps increase sales sufficiently to regain for Ford its former preeminence.

Farkas engineered the model. He used the smaller V-8 engine, and the 92-A, as the car was called, emerged narrower and shorter than the regular Ford, and 600 pounds lighter. The first completed model, as Farkas recalls, was "a sweet-running job." But difficulties arose. The small motor cost but $3.00 less to manufacture than the larger. The remainder of the car was also cheaper only as it used less material, for practically all the essential elements were common to both the 92-A and the V-8. Wibel calculated the possible saving in each car at a mere $36. Since the 92-A would have to compete with year-old larger used cars, this was not enough. As Gnau telegraphed Sorensen, who was disturbed by news of the suspension of work on the small car, "HF and EB cannot see their way clear that this car could be built so that there would be enough difference between the price of the 112" [the standard V-8] and what they could sell the small one for." So by mid-

April the project was abandoned, signifying that the company would not expand the range of its models downward.

This may have been a matter of regret to Davis, but he was working diligently to strengthen the dealer organization, and had enough to occupy him. In June he issued a sheet, "July Sales Program," which outlined a detailed plan for dealer activity. He also kept close count of the demonstrations reported by dealers, and urged more of them, with one daily demonstration by each dealer as a minimum. "Where branches are maintaining this average splendid results are being achieved." Meanwhile, he sought a more constructive relationship between the branches and the dealers on the one hand and the General Sales Department in Dearborn on the other. The work was experimental, but the *FTC Report* of 1939 on the industry, emphasizing injustices to dealers, soon made his efforts timely. By August he had held three regional meetings at which dealers were urged to express their views frankly on everything from cars to contracts. From this flowed the Dealers' Councils later organized by the company. Here General Motors, under Sloan's encouragement, had led the way.[10]

As the fall showing of 1939 models approached, Davis thus had a stronger organization, with increasing confidence among the dealers. He could bring them good news from the engineering and styling departments. Besides improvements in the engines and marked advances in style and comfort, the entire line of cars was equipped with hydraulic brakes, a change that popular opinion and the representations of Edsel, Wibel, and Sorensen had forced upon the reluctant Henry Ford. It expunged one of the chief selling arguments of rival dealers, and gave Ford representatives new confidence.

But the important event of the year was the appearance of the Mercury, a car in the medium-price field designed to compete with the Pontiac and Dodge. Sheldrick gives Edsel credit for the idea, although of course Ford executives and salesmen had for some time recognized that a greater variety of cars was desirable. A new frame and a new motor adapted from the V-8, but larger and more powerful, were developed for the model. The time seemed appropriate, for the Lincoln Zephyr had just shown that the Ford organization could sell successfully above the low-price level. In June, July, and August, the Zephyr led all cars in its class in sales—the Buick, Packard, and La Salle.

On September 29 the Mercury, still unnamed, was announced to

Ford branches and dealers, and Davis outlined a selling plan, designating four types of agents. One was to handle all Ford products (the Lincoln, Lincoln Zephyr, Ford, and the new car), and presumably comprised the strongest Ford dealers. A second group was to sell quality cars only (Lincoln, Lincoln Zephyr, and the new car). A third group would offer only the Ford and the new car; and the fourth group would handle Ford business only, but with permission to market the new car if opportunity arose. The first three groups would receive a discount of 25 per cent, and the fourth 20 per cent.

On October 6 the Mercury was formally announced to the branches by name as a new car in the lower medium-price range, to be added to the Ford-Lincoln line shortly before the New York Automobile Show. "It will have a wheel base of 116 inches (as against 112 for the De Luxe V-8), a V-8 engine more powerful than any hitherto marketed by the Ford Company, hydraulic brakes and numerous advanced mechanical features." It would show flowing lines, a wide and roomy interior, and "luxurious" upholstery. Announcement to the public and dealers was made by Edsel on the same date.

The car was widely advertised and discussed in newspapers and trade magazines, shown on October 17 to managers and assistant managers in the Rotunda, and made available to dealers for showings on November 4. *Motor* in its November issue described it as resembling the Ford in general design, but with special characteristics. The public liked it, and although some dealers privately called it "an overgrown Ford," all felt that it was something they could sell. Davis, late in October, sent dealers a printed pamphlet, which stressed coming improvements in their position, eliminating "destructive influences such as the crowding of agents," and went on to discuss "the most attractive, the most compete and the most saleable line of merchandise we have ever offered." He emphasized the fact that with the Mercury, Ford was entering an entirely new field. The provinces occupied by the Lincoln Zephyr and the Ford must not be invaded by the new car. (The Mercury in five types sold from $920 to $1180, the Ford from $540 to $920, the Lincoln Zephyr for $1360 and up.) "This car has been brought out to *expand*, not to divide, the business which belongs to Ford and Lincoln Zephyr." Davis then told how to display and sell the Mercury. Salesmen should be hired to devote "their entire efforts to this field," and a service organization developed to handle needs and complaints of Mercury

owners. The energy with which the Mercury was introduced and marketed should be borne in mind for comparison with the promotion of
another Ford model years later, the Edsel.[11]

The final showing for the year 1938 was not good, but in the recession no company had prospered. Total Ford sales reached 387,514, including 6835 Mercurys, these having been available for only a month.
Chevrolet bettered the Ford car sale (363,688) by more than a hundred
thousand (464,337). But Davis was working to improve his sales force,
and at the year-end sent branch managers a request for suggestions that
might be passed on to the Engineering Department. This invitation to
offer constructive criticism marked a new trend in the attitude of the
General Sales Office.[12]

4.

The beginning of 1939 found the grip of the depression relaxing. Reports for March revealed the best sales month since July 1937, for all
told, 75,400 units had been sold. Soon a meeting in New York laid plans
for a summer sales drive, for which the company offered generous
prizes. Speaking to the managers and their assistants Davis asked: "Is
this the kind of help a factory should furnish dealers? If not—what?"
He quoted Consumer's Research reports from 1934 onward to show
that Chevrolet had its numerous weaknesses. "We magnify our own
difficulties and discount the other fellow's," he concluded.[13]

By May the Ford exhibit at the New York World's Fair was attract-
ing tens of thousands of daily visitors. On the highest ground of the
exposition area, close to the symbolic Trylon, the company's allotted
area comprised almost seven acres. The Fair was staged in an atmosphere of somewhat unnatural gaiety, for while the talk was constantly
of peace, Munich had occurred only seven months earlier, and Hitler
had promptly occupied the Sudetenland. Henry Ford remained an
extreme representative of many Englishmen and Americans who refused to believe in the imminence of war. At the time probably Edsel
and Sorensen somewhat uneasily agreed with him; after hostilities began in Europe they would begin to recognize the danger of American
involvement while Henry still resolutely rejected such a possibility. In
1938, however, no one associated with the Ford exhibit showed aware-
ness of international tension.

Above the entrance to the company's exhibit hovered a twenty-five-foot statue of Mercury in stainless steel. Inside, the exhibits were devoted to establishing the institutional character of the Ford Motor Company. They found a climax in "The Road of Tomorrow," an elevated highway encircling the entire main building, over which visitors could ride in Fords, Mercurys, or Lincoln Zephyrs. The entrance building showed the first Ford car of 1896 and other exhibits. A mural 70 feet long and 30 feet high, by Henry Billings, gave a comprehensive impression of Ford activities, the more vivid in that certain machine parts—such as the V-8 engine—were incorporated in the design.

Beyond the entrance building lay the Industrial Building, in which numerous manufacturing processes involved in the making of a car were demonstrated. Actual parts of a foundry, a rolling mill, an industrial farm, testing procedures, and the Henry Ford Trade School were in operation. From the Industrial Building the visitor moved into an enormous patio, around which Ford cars were displayed, while a central fountain by the sculptor Isamu Noguchi expressed in abstract forms the power of the automobile. At one end stood an enclosed bandstand where the composer Ferde Grofé conducted concerts afternoon and evenings.

In all this the influence of Edsel can be perceived, for he was much interested in the Ford exhibit. Late in April he rented a residence on Manhasset Bay, near the homes of Walter Chrysler and Alfred P. Sloan, Jr. He saw the public give an ample response to the Ford display; in August, four months after the opening, Davis reported that 4,953,610 persons had been guests, 1,138,000 riding "the Road of Tomorrow." [14]

The summer sales program had meanwhile scored such a success that at the beginning of August every branch had exceeded its quota. Ford executives approached the showing of 1940 models in Dearborn in September with confidence. They showed no organic engineering changes, but had been sufficiently altered to eliminate the "bugs" discovered in the 1939 car, and featured new styling, a finger-tip gearshift on the steering post, sealed-beam headlamps, better brake drums, greater seat and leg room, and improved spring suspension. The ensuing September meeting at Dearborn was successful in generating enthusiasm among the branch managers and their assistants about "Ford for Forty." Full information on the new models was presented and the new test track at the Ford Airport was demonstrated. Built under the inexpert direction of Dahlinger, it was a rudimentary affair, with stretches of dry asphalt, wet asphalt, and standing water which eventually the Engineering Department would have to rebuild. The gathering brought in more inquiries from dealers than ever before, with 40,000 orders, and Davis felt justified in setting a 1940 goal of 900,000 vehicles.[15]

But the meeting had been marked by an episode which was to shake the entire sales department. As Davis was speaking on the final night, at the Dearborn Country Club, Harry Mack and several companions entered the room. Mack had a right to be there as head of the Dearborn branch. They made a great deal of noise, and Davis asked in vain for quiet. However, he finished speaking, and since the program had been completed, left for home. According to G. J. Crimmins, Mack and his friends had supplemented the wine served at dinner with liquor of their own, and were in a contentious mood. In the locker room downstairs, Mack encountered Dick Powell, an able executive and powerful man, and pushed him aside. Powell protested, and the two exchanged blows. Powell knocked Mack down and according to report beat him rather badly. Later he in turn was attacked by Mack's friends. Mack at least went to the hospital.

During the next few days the incident was widely discussed. Edsel and Davis felt they could scarcely avoid disciplinary action, and this seemed an opportunity to get rid of Mack. They decided to do so, and Davis called him in and discharged him. But the two had not reckoned sufficiently on Harry Bennett. The personnel head sprang to Mack's defense like a parent defending an incorrigible child. By telephone he accused Davis of responsibility for the fighting at the Country Club because as Sales Manager he should have been there to prevent it. He also charged that Davis had provoked the trouble, and informed him that Henry Ford wished to see him in Bennett's office at once.

Davis found Ford there, who asked what had happened. As Davis started to tell him he was constantly interrupted by Bennett, asserting that the facts were not as Davis gave them. Finally, according to Davis, Bennett made a completely false assertion, and Davis snapped, "Harry, you're a liar!" Bennett cried: "Nobody calls me a liar!" and raised his arm as if to strike. Ford quickly ducked under it and disappeared, leaving Davis with the impression that he had wanted to bring about a conflict and was pleased.

Bennett still held his arm poised. "Why don't you hit me?" demanded Davis, who, although aware that Bennett was a boxer, was in very good physical shape and confident of holding his own. But Bennett did not hit him.

It is possible that he recognized the justice of Davis's position; later he was to write that he liked him, and had suggested a friendly settlement. Davis felt that Bennett's subsequent conduct showed no animosity. At any rate, later in the day Edsel called Davis to his office in considerable agitation. "Father is in a terrible state of mind," he said. Edsel felt that the discharge of Mack must stand, but something would have to be done to placate Henry Ford (and of course Bennett). He outlined a "temporary solution," which he acknowledged to be unjust, but which was acceptable to his father. Davis would be transferred to the Pacific Coast with salary unchanged, to manage the Long Beach branch and supervise all West Coast sales. Doss, who meanwhile had succeeded Mack as head of the Dearborn branch, would be made sales manager. Something would have to be done for Mack. Later Davis would be reinstated.

Davis agreed; "I had faith in the Ford Motor Company and in Edsel Ford," he said later. He called the change his transfer to Siberia. He advised Edsel to appoint Mack head of the Service and Parts Department. "He can't do much harm there." Edsel consented, announcing Mack's transfer on October 16, and just before Christmas Doss's appointment as sales manager.[16]

Davis's demotion at the very time when sales prospects had brightened checked the momentum of the Ford organization. At the same time Sorensen's position was definitely worsening, although he did not admit it. He was now deferring to Bennett and some of his agents rather than risk a conflict.*

As for the sales organization, Doss, an honest and able manager, continued the new policies, but the branch heads and dealers never forgot Davis, whom they trusted above any sales head since Norval Hawkins. Fortunately, they had not seen the last of him. But it is time to turn to another of Henry Ford's outside interests, which was further to complicate the affairs of a company that at times seemed a rudderless vessel on a stormy sea.[17]

---

* This is the testimony of Haglund, Wagner, and others in their reminiscences. Sorensen deferred to Rausch, who was in charge of the open hearth, avoided getting involved in labor negotiations, and advised Edsel not to.

5.

"What the country needs right now," said Henry Ford in the fall of 1937, "is a good tractor that will sell for around two hundred and fifty dollars."

This remark must have startled Ford's associates. True, the tractor had once been almost as much a passion with him as the cheap car. After experimenting since 1906, he had brought out the Fordson in 1917 to help Britain till her unused land, and had sold it both in Europe and the United States. But in 1928 he had shifted production from Dearborn to his plant at Cork, and again in 1933 to Dagenham. A few Fordsons were imported into the United States, but the Ford Motor Company seemed to have forgotten the machine. In June 1935 Sorensen had said to a reporter, "Tractors? The average farmer seems to think he can get along without one, but he won't do without an automobile." Now the seventy-four-year-old Ford was returning to a great project of his youth.[18]

By December 1937 he was furiously at work "on a new low-priced tractor of unusual design." Actually, with Howard Simpson as his engineer, he had experimented with such a unit for years. The Fordson, carelessly operated, could tip over backwards. Ford was looking for something safer and different, and apparently soon believed that Simpson had produced it. At Dearborn on January 7 he displayed to newspapermen a machine partly designed by Simpson. It was a three-wheeled type with a V-8 engine, and Ford demonstrated it to newsmen, "as pleased as a small boy with a fire engine." He asserted: "I don't care if we can't make a cent of profit. The main thing is to get something started."

However, he soon set aside this tractor, and became interested in a four-wheeled type designed by another engineer, Karl Schultz, which also proved unsatisfactory. Simpson was all but frantic. His boss was alternately rejecting sound advice and asking for what seemed impossible—and sometimes getting it! For example, he wanted four-speed transmission with overdrive so designed as to occupy the same space as the standard transmission. To protest, he replied: "Nothing is hard to do unless you think it is," and Simpson astonished himself by accomplishing the feat! But he felt he was getting nowhere, for he was constantly being pulled off promising projects to try a wholly new approach. He said later: "Spending all the time on it myself I had no doubt that I could go ahead and design a job if he had left me alone long enough." But this was not to be. Of course, his poison was meat to Sheldrick and Roeder. While Ford pushed the tractor they had more freedom with their cars at the Rouge.[19]

And then Henry George Ferguson appeared on the scene. Born in northern Ireland in 1884, Ferguson had been named for the American single tax advocate then speaking to large audiences throughout England and Ireland. The child developed into a flamboyant, unpredictable adult with a passion for mechanics and grandiose ideas about himself and his work. At twenty-seven, in 1911, he formed a company in Belfast, Harry Ferguson (Motors), Ltd., to merchandise and service automobiles, implements, and later tractors. An admirer of Henry Ford, he had sought an interview with Sorensen when the latter came to London in 1917 to advise on Fordson activities. Ferguson already had ideas about tractors and the Dane gave him some encouragement, emphasizing especially the advantage of having the working tool (plow or cultivator) directly attached to the tractor instead of being drawn behind it on wheels of its own.

With the assistance of William J. Sands, Ferguson worked out two devices. One was a "linkage" system by which a plow was directly attached to a standard Fordson tractor. Ferguson showed this invention to Ford in 1920–1921, and later formed the Ferguson-Sherman Manufacturing Corporation which made and sold several versions of these plows for use with Fordson tractors. The second device was a combination of the linkage with a hydraulic cylinder in the tractor by which the driver could raise or lower the implement by means of hydraulic control. This permitted the farmer to cultivate as deeply as he desired, or to raise the tool entirely above the ground for transport, an advantage that the Fordson had never enjoyed. Tools coupled to the tractor went back with it to the barn instead of being perhaps left to rust in the fields.

By 1936 Ferguson had persuaded an English manufacturer, David Brown, to build a tractor using this hydraulic control, but it did not sell well, and the inventor began to seek backing in America. He knew that Ford was interested in a tractor, and in October 1938 demonstrated a Ferguson-Brown model for him at Dearborn. He could not have timed the showing better. Ford had rejected two models of his own, and was ready to be convinced by an outsider. In the good Michigan soil of Ford's Dearborn farm, Ferguson showed with complete success the advantages of the linkage system and the hydraulic lift. The latter in particular fascinated Ford. Ferguson reënforced the exhibit with a lecture proclaiming that his tractor would "revolutionize agriculture and bring about a new economic life for the world."

According to Ferguson, a compact was soon made—a "gentlemen's agreement." Ferguson was to put "everything I have in the world into your hands for its [the tractor's] manufacture. I will place my services wholly and absolutely at your disposal for future design, for manufacture, for education, for distribution, for a new world economy." In return Ford was to put his "resources, energy, fame and reputation behind the manufacture of the equipment, and . . . manufacture a good machine at low cost, in volume, based on my [Ferguson's] ability to create the sales throughout the world." Either party on notice could terminate the agreement. This version is Ferguson's recollection of what occurred, and is the only account that exists, since by the time the story was told, Ford was no longer alive. There had been no witnesses. Ferguson asserted that Ford fully concurred, declaring: "That is a good idea. I will go along with you on those terms." [20]

The exact nature of the agreement was not understood by the engineers and other Ford officials, but they were not worried about it. Their chief had negotiated similar compacts in the past, to his advantage. Such was his understanding with Henry and Wilfred Leland antedating his acquisition of the Lincoln Motor Company. In the arrangement with Ferguson all might have gone well had Ford lived and retained his full mental powers; as matters stood, the agreement was not (putting it mildly) to work out happily.

Sorensen was out of town when Ferguson's demonstration took place, but on his return was met at the Dearborn railroad station by Henry Ford, who fairly effervesced about the new tractor. Sorensen was not greatly impressed. He thought the machine too small, not rugged enough for the varied soils of the United States, too expensive to manufacture, and antiquated in design. However, he agreed with Ford that Ford engineers could make a usable product of it.

After a vain attempt by Schultz to incorporate the hydraulic lift and the linkage ideas into his "KF" tractor, the Ford Motor Company assembled a formidable engineering team to produce a satisfactory model. Sheldrick directed the project, on which Roeder, Simpson, McCarroll, and numerous others worked. Ferguson joined them with four assistants.

Later Ferguson asserted that he and his engineers "were the designers, planners, and inventors in every detail" of the new tractor. Sorensen called this a complete fabrication. There is no question that Ferguson and his men participated in the designing process, for copies of some of their suggestions remain; but not only Sorensen, but all the Ford engineers, declare that final decisions lay with Ford, and that he accepted little from Ferguson. The latter, as Roeder puts it, "came in with an idea and it was completely re-engineered by the Ford engineers, for production jobs. . . . As far as the tractor-engineered design itself is concerned, that was a Ford deal. Ferguson brought up the idea of the plow, the linkage, and the hydraulic system." Thoms put it more briefly: "We took the Ford tractor and fitted the Ferguson lift on it."

At the time, apparently, there was little friction between the two groups. Tooling was the next step, and on this Ford was estimated to have spent $12,000,000, Ferguson nothing. The process was entirely in Ford's hands. The Ford Motor Company also helped the inventor to finance his distribution company, the Ferguson-Sherman Manufacturing Corporation, which included the Shermans who earlier had distributed the Ferguson linkage plow for the Fordson. This soon became Harry Ferguson, Inc.; the Shermans dropped out. The new company would have charge of sales, and would procure implements for the tractor. Ford collected nothing from it until sales were made. Similarly, the Ford organization assisted Ferguson to find dealers, many being Ford agents.[21]

The 9-N (as the unit was known at the plant) was called "the Ford tractor-Ferguson System." The title satisfied both parties (and by inference apportions credit much as suggested above). By June 1939 it was ready, and a quasi-public demonstration was given on the 29th. Ferguson spoke to a limited number of newspaper men and prominent Detroiters, extolling the machine.

Unfortunately, the rate of production for the first year was not so high as anticipated: only 35,742 units were made as against an expected 63,750. Production increased in 1941 to 42,910, but the lower output necessarily raised the cost, and eventually the price. Ferguson protested vehemently. Actually, Ford was making every machine at a loss. In view of the war, Edsel wanted to stop production, but Henry Ford insisted on continuing despite the mounting deficits. He was making little money on motor cars, but before he could count a profit on them, he must pay his losses on the tractor.[22]

6.

Doss issued his first telegram to branch managers on December 27, 1939. In a few days he would have the figures on sales for the year, showing that the company, although presenting a far better record than in 1938, was still in third place, with 481,496 Fords, 65,884 Mercurys, and 19,940 Lincolns, making a grand total of 567,320 cars. It was a good performance, and particularly so for the Mercury, a completely new automobile, yet Chrysler had outsold the company, and Chevrolet, with 598,341 units disposed of, had outdistanced the Ford. The organization was still fighting—chiefly to keep the Ford ahead of the Plymouth, and to establish the Mercury.

In commercial vehicles General Motors was also leading. Ford had surpassed Chevrolet in the sale of trucks in 1935 and 1937, but trailed badly in 1938, and in 1939 sold only 128,889 to Chevrolet's 169,457.[23]

There was always the possibility of a brighter future. In 1940 one hope lay in a Ford Six, long asked for, which was authorized about the time the Mercury appeared. The story runs that some visiting dealers pleaded with Edsel to produce the engine, and that he agreed. At this point his father appeared, and the son explained to him the promise he had made. "Go ahead," said the older Ford. "You're the boss." Aside from working on a 5-cylinder motor and starting a six to rival the regular model that Sheldrick was designing, he did nothing about the new motor, and it was duly offered in 1941 as an alternative to the V-8. By that time the production of civilian cars had been sharply curtailed, and would be halted entirely in a few months.

Doss's active leadership in sales was to last little more than a year, although the effects were visible for two. He did well. Making his reputation in the 1920s as head of the Kansas City plant, he had resigned rather than be a party to the reduction of discounts ordered in 1930. Later he had returned to the company, and had performed brilliantly at the Chicago branch. Henry Ford liked him (Bennett says that Doss was his choice), and for a time he had a fairly free hand.

He was forced to make concessions to Bennett, who eventually re-installed Harry Mack as head of the Dearborn branch. He saw Edsel increasingly circumscribed in his office as president. However, the beginnings of war work, in which Bennett at first took no part, gave Edsel a greater sense of freedom and importance.

In 1940 Ford sales rose to 644,162 and in 1941 to 702,656, with the Ford car selling 542,755 and 602,012 respectively. The Mercury climbed first to 80,418 and then 81,874, a respectable accomplishment which gave it 2.19 per cent of the total passenger car sales for the country. The Lincoln maintained its position, which was an inferior one. The total Ford sales did not win the company second place in either year, although the Ford car still maintained a comfortable supremacy over the Plymouth. What might have happened had the war not come is a matter of guessing. Doss thought the Ford curve was rising sharply, but to hope that was the duty of any sales manager.

One fact seems certain: the Lincoln Zephyr had not met the hopes of company officials, or fulfilled its early promise. In 1937 it contributed to a high mark of Lincoln sales (25,243), but then declined, and seems to have killed the sale of the regular Lincoln, which dwindled to hundreds. By tacit consent the Zephyr did not survive the war period, and the Lincoln later won back some of the ground it had lost.

Actually, the war had begun in Europe before Davis left, and soon all the automobile companies would be engaged in defense work. Thus by 1940–1941 the industry may be said to have reached another important milestone in its growth. What had happened to it during the troubled nineteen-thirties, and what at this point was the place of the Ford Motor Company among the makers of motor cars?

A glance at the increasing number of automobiles parked in American cities or traversing the highways was sufficient evidence of a massive growth in the use of gasoline-driven vehicles and the facilities for servicing them. The statistics of numbers of cars were no less impressive. Not until 1941 were the manufacturers of automobiles to sell almost as many new units as in 1929 (4,596,000 to 4,624,879 twelve years earlier), but the volume for the middle and late 1930s exceeded that of the 1920s prior to 1929, and more used cars were in circulation than ever before. The total number of automobiles and trucks in use had increased (34,472,000 for 1941 to 26,502,508 for 1929).

More important was the expansion of the American road system.

During the 1930s, working on highways was a chief activity for both the WPA and the CCC; unemployment became an implement for improving transportation. In this period about $100,000,000 more Federal money a year was spent on road-building than during the nineteen-twenties, a rise of about 50 per cent. In 1937 a top expenditure of $520,798,487 was made. Up to 1930 a total of 92,828 miles of road had been completed under federal auspices, of which 90,000 were of a high type surface. During the nineteen-thirties 167,742 miles were built, of which 160,000 were of "high type" (presumably concrete or asphalt). During the same period the mileage of state highways rose from 315,000 to 560,000.

The increase in roads was more than quantitative, for it gave the automobile new power as well as new places to go. Cars went faster, and in addition valiant efforts were made to make them go safer. Signs for the guidance of a motorist were now a norm—not only those telling him distances and destinations, but also those which warned him of bad curves and of intersections. White lines marked the center of roads and the states insisted on specific hand signals to indicate turns or stops (unfortunately these were not as yet uniform throughout the country). In addition, the motorist making an extended trip could procure maps and information on traffic laws, points of interest, and places to stay overnight. While the motel had yet to achieve a smart and expensive status, there were numerous cabins and private homes where the automobilist could stay.

Meanwhile the improvement of the car had been steady. Power had increased with better engines, and an automobile that had made 30 miles an hour in 1925 could now cruise at 50, and attain maximum speeds much higher. Most of the improvements of the decade have been noted: hydraulic brakes, the Hotchkiss drive, better transmissions, springs, and other agencies for smooth riding. The 4-cylinder motor, still popular abroad, was rare in the United States, where sixes, eights, and twelves were featured. The sealed-beam headlights arrived for practically all 1940 models, and were appreciatively hailed.* Of the cars in general that year one writer, noting that mechanical changes were few, remarked that the manufacturers "make good power plants better, easy riding still easier, and handling qualities . . . still more

---

* They provided better visibility, and utilized, as today, the short-distance beam when approaching other cars, and a longer, 50 per cent brighter one for clear roads.

enjoyable and safe." The cars were lower slung than ever, more deftly streamlined, and featured controlled ventilation within the automobile. Running boards had largely disappeared. The automatic convertible had ousted the open car. Except for this and the sedan, cars showed a smooth arc at the rear. While colors were usually solid, there was a movement under way to brighten the motor world with a variety of shades, often matched by the color of the upholstery. The 1940 Mercury provided a choice of eight colors: black, Como blue, Mandarin maroon, Sahara tan, cloud mist, Folstone gray, Lyon blue, and Yosemite green. The Lincoln Zephyr came in nine colors, and while the V-8 offered only black, cloud-mist gray, and Lyon blue, it would soon give more choices.

The car of 1940 had thus attained maturity, and the whole industry was stronger, more resourceful, and more responsive to public demand. Prices remained low. The 1940 Ford started at $600, and the medium-priced cars (Pontiac, De Soto, Packard, Nash) could be bought for $783 up. Alfred Reeves, speaking for the industry, boasted that in October 1940 the price of cars since 1908 had fallen from $1.25 to 25 cents a pound, and the average car price from $2130 to $778.

In this new motor world the Ford cars still maintained an important position, despite the strife inside the company, and its low standing with the government, labor, and other groups of customers who resented Ford's utterances and policies. "Ford," was still a powerful word, commanding the loyalty of millions. Edsel's well-directed efforts had improved the mechanical character of company cars, and their appearance. In the difficult circumstances in which he, Sorensen, Davis, and Doss labored, they had done well. If the Chevrolet and Plymouth slightly excelled the V-8 in refinements, it showed power and the new Six economy.

The company had fought not only its competitors but also its own leader. Henry Ford's vitality during most of this period had been extraordinary, but it had not been channeled into the production of better cars. Had he not been absorbed in interests outside the automotive field, or at its edges, he might have guided his firm more ably. Again, he might merely have insisted the more strongly on his tabus and fetishes; and his preoccupation with Greenfield Village, the soy bean, the village industries, and the tractor may have permitted others to accomplish something creative.

The Ford organization in 1940 was still dynamic. It must not be confused with that of 1945. Roeder, who later joined in the reorganization of the company, looked back from the 1950s on the earlier engineering group with something of nostalgic pride. "They had an enthusiasm about their work," he recalled. "I think there was more enthusiasm among the engineers and the people working with them than I have ever seen since we have . . . set up an organizational structure in which each person has certain responsibilities for certain things. I think most of this enthusiasm was due to the fact that we were a relatively small group as compared with today. There was a spirit of wanting to get the job done. There wasn't a lot of paper work involved. . . . You got direct decisions and as soon as you got a decision you were able to go ahead." [24]

The pride in the distinction of being a Ford man was also part of the spirit, whether in engineering, manufacturing, or sales. Henry Ford had always been the symbol of his company's creative character, and in emergencies a dynamo to revive and extend it. He was a symbol still, for though no longer an active leader, he jealously guarded his position as founder and imperator. All his outside obsessions were draining money from the company, and the unacknowledged but bitter strife between Bennett, Sorensen, and Edsel was eating at the vitals of the organization like the fox under the Spartan boy's cloak. The Ford Motor Company had no real single head, no clear purpose, no capacity to focus its strength on a drive ahead. Sheer momentum and the real abilities of its best officials kept it doing far better than might have been expected, but it was really waiting for a mind and hand that could once more give it direction, assurance, and power.

In following the story of Ford engineering, production, and sales, we have had to neglect the unfolding of the labor struggle. It was in dealing with the massive forces of unionism that the Henry Ford–Harry Bennett regime showed its worst side, and it was in this troubled area that the final acceptance of a new order was most sudden and startling.

# VI

# A NEW DEAL FOR LABOR

THE world in these fast-changing times was never allowed to forget that Henry Ford's labor views did not change. He resolutely clung to his condemnation of unions, holding that he could best look after the welfare of his "fellow workers." He specially detested the closed shop; he proclaimed himself entitled to hire and fire as he saw fit; and he made it clear he intended to provide good wages and working conditions within the line that he thought his revenues permitted, but not beyond. All in all, he insisted on giving orders, not negotiating agreements. Like many another industrialist, he was unable to comprehend that sometimes the fountains of the great deep were broken up, and it became necessary to steer his ark to a new Ararat.

It was in a grim tri-cornered struggle that he clung to the past after 1936. One combatant was the United Automobile Workers, a vital element of the CIO; another was the Roosevelt Administration, determined after its tremendous victory of 1936 to enforce the Wagner Act; and the third was the Ford Motor Company. Since the government had invincible power, the outcome was certain. But as Ford fought to defer his fate, the issue for a time appeared doubtful.

The opening offensive of John L. Lewis's CIO in midwinter of 1936–1937 gave Ford notice, as we have seen, of what lay ahead. Its battle against General Motors seemed David against Goliath—and had the same end. First closing the Fisher Body works in Cleveland and Flint, the strike spread rapidly to the Buick, Cadillac, and Fleetwood plants in Michigan, and soon paralyzed nearly all the company's operations in Indiana, Ohio, Missouri, and Georgia. By mid-January 1937 some 115,000 workers were out. General Motors fought with every weapon at its command. It appealed to conservative sentiment, procured injunctions from the courts, and like the textile employers in the South, occasionally resorted to violence, as when it enlisted some hardfisted adherents called the "Flint Alliance." But its resistance proved futile against the new leadership of the strikers.

Temporarily the command of the United Automobile Workers was highly effective. Its head, Homer Martin, young, bold, confident, was at his best in a dramatic contest like this. A natural exhorter, his oratorical powers cultivated by years in the Baptist ministry, he knew how to appeal to mass-production workers. This cleancut, athletic leader was ready to work to exhaustion; his fearlessness, sincerity, and tenacity offset his weaknesses—impulsiveness in speech and action, excessive good-nature, and naiveté. The UAW'S secretary, George Addes, a tougher negotiator and a more vigilant administrator, made good some of his deficiencies. Richard Frankensteen, physically power- ful and ambitious, had executive energy, and other organizers, includ- ing Walter Reuther, once an employe in the Ford plant, and his brother Victor, felt an enthusiastic belief in impending success.[1]

Their tactics included a defiant use of that efficient new device, the sit-down strike. The workers simply dropped their tools, and sat at their places in passive resistance. Thus they shut out scab substitutes, enjoyed shelter and warmth, and gained a greater sense of solidarity. The method had already been tried in local strikes in the Hormel Packing plant in Minnesota and the Goodyear factory in Akron, and had won the day in the Bendix Corporation strike in South Bend. Now it was employed on a national scale.

Though President Green of the AFL declared the sitdowns out- rageous, speakers in Congress denounced them as trespass and robbery, and the lower Federal courts ultimately pronounced them illegal, notably in the Apex Hosiery Case, employers found it difficult to cope with them. When efforts were made in Michigan to get Governor Murphy to use the militia to oust the sitting employes, he wisely offered instead to mediate the dispute. In Flint the Fisher officials turned off the heat, and removed ladders by which the strikers were being supplied with food. A battle of workers against company guards and city police ensued, in which clubs, tear gas bombs, and riot guns were used—and the strikers held their own. Under a truce arranged by Governor Murphy, the sitdowners agreed to evacuate the plants, but General Motors promised not to resume production in them.[2]

By February 1, 1937, about 140,000 of the 150,000 workers in General

Motors were idle, and the company was losing its season's profits. On that day strikers in Flint, where the truce had broken down, seized the key plant which assembled motors for all Chevrolet cars—"Chevrolet IV." This was a decisive blow. John L. Lewis thereupon arrived in Detroit to help UAW leaders conduct a series of conferences with General Motors officials, and on the 11th the great corporation substantially capitulated. It recognized the UAW as bargaining agent for its own membership, and opened the door for negotiation upon wages, which were soon raised. It also granted seniority rights, and promised a study of the speedup to eliminate its abuses. News of this settlement elated labor circles and electrified the country.

Then in March, Ford executives anxiously watching the scene saw the CIO win further resounding victories. Early that month some 60,000 of the 70,000 Chrysler employes struck and sat down in their factories. Governor Murphy, struggling for a settlement, finally induced John L. Lewis and Walter Chrysler to confer amicably. Chrysler always liked to talk of his start in overalls, and though he was an aggressive man who headed one chapter of his autobiography "Full Authority Is What I Want," he really liked to keep close to his workingmen. On April 8, he also surrendered. His company would recognize the UAW as the principal though not exclusive bargaining agent for his workers, and would give them approximately the same wages, hours, and working conditions that the General Motors force were obtaining.[3]

Meanwhile, the American public was astonished by news that another industrial behemoth, the United States Steel Corporation, had yielded to the mere threat of a strike. In March, as the Steel Workers Organizing Committee (SWOC) prepared its blow, the executives raised the white flag, consenting to unionization and a 10 per cent increase in wages. The labor heads for their part promised not to use unfair tactics in enrolling additional employes in the CIO ranks. For this peace treaty Myron Taylor as chairman of the Steel Corporation board and John L. Lewis and Philip Murray as labor chieftains divided most of the credit, but some of it belonged to Thomas W. Lamont of the House of Morgan, which was in a position to exert pressure. Taylor and Lamont knew that disagreeable revelations of company espionage and gangsterism would accompany a strike, and appreciated that a new day in labor relations was dawning. The agreement included an 8-hour day and 40-hour week. As Jones & Laughlin and some 40 other steel companies followed, SWOC was soon able to lay claim to the enlistment of 400,000 steel workers.[4]

### 2.

But after these early successes mass-production labor reached the entrenched lines of hardjawed Bourbons, obstinate upholders of the old regime. The five companies of Little Steel stood like a stone wall, Eugene Grace of Bethlehem and Tom Girdler of Republic refusing any concession. Republic Steel in May and June 1937 spent $44,000 to arm its plants with guns and grenades. The country read with horror of the Memorial Day battle at the South Chicago works of Republic, when the police fired on peaceably marching strikers, killing ten, wounding thirty or more, and brutally clubbing others. It read of a riot in Massilon, Ohio, where one Republic worker was killed, 13 were injured, and 160 were arrested. The strike against Little Steel spread throughout seven states, involved 83,000 employes, and caused so much disorder that most Americans sympathized with President Roosevelt when he wished a plague on the houses of Tom Girdler and John L. Lewis alike. Nothing since the textile strikes of 1934 had caused so much turmoil. Finally the Little Steel executives by terroristic methods defeated the union effort. Later on, the National Labor Relations Board condemned these methods as illegal, and compelled the corporations to rehire discharged employes and accept collective bargaining, but temporarily reaction had triumphed.

Meanwhile, a wave of strikes was engulfing the land—more than 4700 of them during 1937.[5] In June alone, labor disputes cost nearly five million man-days.

Henry Ford instantly took his stand with Grace, Girdler, and other opponents of the new dispensation. His hostility to the administration and the UAW knew no bounds. Frances Perkins, Secretary of Labor, told a cabinet meeting late in April that a tacit agreement had been made by which no strike would be called in the Ford works, on the understanding that Henry would in due course submit to the Wagner Act and deal collectively with his employes, but she did not know the full facts in a complicated situation. When the Supreme Court that month upheld the Wagner Act, Ford exploded to an interviewer from the Detroit *News* that it was "just one of those things that help fasten control upon the necks of labor," and that he would resist it to his last dollar. But he, too, was oversimplifying his position.[6]

Henry Ford in this crisis had a fateful choice to make. He might accept Edsel's advice and try to negotiate a favorable agreement with the UAW. Sorensen tells us that this spring the two had long heated wrangles, in which the son showed increasing readiness to oppose his father, who at almost seventy-five betrayed his age. They quarreled so violently that Sorensen avoided their meetings, or left as quickly as he could escape. Alternatively, Ford might cling to his anti-union prejudice, and use a harsher man to implement his policy. He of course took this second road even at the cost of estrangement from Edsel, for he had the illusion that most employes and most public sentiment would support him against the UAW program. "Our workers won't stand for it, I won't stand for it, and the public won't stand for it," he declared. He took heart from the fact that the public was really growing fearful that the balance of power between labor and management was being too heavily upset, a Gallup poll in April 1937 disclosing that more than two-thirds of the people queried hoped the Supreme Court would declare sitdown strikes illegal. And he took further encouragement from the fulminations of the conservative press against the flood of labor disputes, which it later pronounced responsible for the recession of 1937–1938.[7]

Henry's decision was firmly announced, but it had subtle undertones. Immediately after the Supreme Court validation of the Wagner Act, he called in Edsel and Sorensen to issue his ukase. He knew how strongly Edsel had hoped to treat with the UAW leaders, and that in its current radio campaign to enlist automobile workers the UAW was praising Edsel's comparatively enlightened stand. He knew also that the UAW was falsely asserting that Sorensen was a union man at heart, who still carried his patternmakers' card. Benjamin F. Fairless had been startled to hear that Myron Taylor had acceded to John L. Lewis's demands, and Henry Ford did not mean to be thus taken by surprise. He told Edsel and Sorensen that the law must be defeated by evasion and delay. They were not to meet with any union officials, not to discuss labor questions with anybody, and not to give any press interviews. If hard beset, they could take a trip away from Detroit.

"I've picked someone to talk with the unions," he said, in effect. "I want a strong, aggressive man who can take care of himself in an argument, and I've got him. He has my full confidence and I want to be sure that you will both support him. He is waiting in Charlie's office now." They drove to Sorensen's office—and Edsel recoiled in dismay when they found Harry Bennett there. As they discussed the Wagner Act, Bennett bubbled with enthusiasm over the possibilities for exercising his special gifts. He assured the other three that he could handle Homer Martin dexterously, worm his way into the inner councils of the UAW, sow confusion, stave off a decisive break, and prevent any working arrangement.[8]

His real assignment, it was plain, was to delude, demoralize, and delay, combining Fabian and Machiavellian tactics. It was perhaps his first cunning efforts to beguile the trustful Homer Martin that gave Miss Perkins her mistaken hope of Ford's ultimate acquiescence. Edsel listened to Bennett sick at heart.[9]

It is clear that Edsel was more rebellious than ever before in his dutiful life: hostile to a contest against the law, hostile to the methods contemplated, and hostile to the grant of broad new powers to Harry Bennett. The antagonism between Edsel and Bennett fell just short of open war. Feeling that his father's dulled perceptions and defective judgment were being abused, that a great property affected with a public interest was being mishandled, and his rightful place being brazenly usurped, Edsel was humiliated and desperate. His wife and mother, seeing that the situation was killing one of the finest men in Detroit, suffered with him. It was at this time that Clara Ford, hearing how Bennett had gotten Henry to share his revolver practice, burst out angrily, "Who is this man who has so much control over my husband and is ruining my son's health?"—then collapsing in tears.[10]

The feud between father and son poisoned the atmosphere of the plant in 1937. Bennett fomented it by carrying tales to Henry of Edsel's recalcitrance, while he made systematic efforts to weaken the son by knifing all who supported him. When Sorensen found that he too was being spied upon, he went to Bennett with a hot protest. He added that if Bennett would only consult Edsel fully upon his activities in labor affairs, they might have peace in the family and the Rouge plant. As it was, Edsel had to make it plain to labor leaders that he felt no respect for Bennett's decisions and tactics. But Bennett was obdurate. "I am following orders," he declared. When Sorensen asked if he had been instructed not to discuss labor with Edsel, he said no, he was his own boss. But in this, as in everything else, he clearly followed Henry's perverse wishes, merely giving them his own malicious emphasis. The long tragedy of Edsel's life was deepening.[11]

When Henry Ford, Bennett, and Sorensen determined to obstruct the Wagner Act, they gave every branch of the Ford empire a clear understanding of their intentions. Every shop, every assembly plant, every office, knew the policy; the executives were expected to obey without question. Later the National Labor Relations Board (NLRB) emphasized this fact: [12]

Since the respondent's operations and its main policy emanate from its main office, the kind of inaction on the part of employers which the act clearly contemplates could have been achieved with little effort throughout the respondent's system. But the policy makers did not choose this course. Instead, they determinedly sought to defy the law by formulating and sanctioning a highly integrated and amazingly far-reaching program of interference, restraint, and coercion . . . in an orbit within which the Congress had declared that employees were entitled to enjoy unhampered freedom.

### 3.

The first sharp demonstration that Ford intended to be as obstructive as Girdler occurred in the memorable "battle of the overpass" at the Rouge on May 26, 1937. Up to that date resistance to the UAW drive for members had followed a familiar pattern: the discharge of a few men at a time for union agitation, the distribution of cards warning workers that if they joined unions they would "put their necks in an iron collar," the growl of foremen that membership would prove perilous. Spokesmen for the UAW evinced caution, for while they boasted in early spring that they had a sufficient base in the Rouge plant to ensure a permanent organization, and predicted that workers would soon flock into the union, they were not yet ready for a full drive. They were weaker in the main Ford factory than they had been in General Motors or Chrysler.[13]

In mid-May, however, Walter Reuther, Richard Frankensteen, Ed Hall, and other leaders began definite action to organize the Rouge. On the 24th they opened union headquarters in Detroit, where, according to Frankensteen, the police showed none of the ugly hostility encountered in Dearborn. They also obtained a permit from Dearborn City Hall to distribute handbills at the Rouge gates on the 26th.

At once, Bennett undertook defensive preparations. Reporters and photographers of Detroit newspapers, arriving at the plant early that day, talked with Bennett and Everett Moore, nominal head of the Service Department, who remarked ominously that "some loyal employes" might resent the handbill distribution, and that if these loyalists grappled with the union distributors, "it won't be the fault of the Ford Company." At the Rouge gates newspapermen noted groups of brawny men placed to command every entrance.

Union headquarters were warned that the situation held grave possibilities. Ed Hall, who had planned to accompany Reuther and Frankensteen, received a telephone call from John Gillespie, one of Bennett's associates who happened to be an old friend. "Ed, I like you," Gillespie said, "and I don't want you to go out there today. Something is going to happen. . . . It's going to be extremely unpleasant." Hall reminded Gillespie that he had a license to carry two revolvers. "If any of your stooges out there lay a hand on me," he said, "I'll blow them so full of holes they won't make a good sieve." Nevertheless, the union organizers met at noon and reconsidered their plans. Among the workers present were women, and to reduce the likelihood of violence, they agreed to do the actual distribution of handbills.

Early in the afternoon most of the organizers left for the Rouge plant by street car. Reuther, Frankensteen, Richard Merriweather, Ralph Dunham, and a representative of a civil rights organization, the Rev. Mr. Raymond P. Sanford, drove in a car to the main entrance at Gate 4, Hall being detained by a committee of women who called at his office. They arrived more than an hour before the change of shifts, which would give them their best opportunity to distribute their circulars; and Reuther and Frankensteen went to the street overpass at the gate, where they posed for the photographers. Lounging here were a number of powerfully-built men, including Angelo Caruso, boss of the Down River gang in Detroit, Warshon Sarkisien and Ted Greis, professional wrestlers, Oscar Jones, a boxer, and several members of Ford Service. Another lounger, Wilfred Comment, carried handcuffs in the rear pocket of his trousers.[14]

As the photographers finished, several of this group strode up peremptorily: "This is Ford property. Get the hell off of here." The union men moved toward one of the exits to obey. But they suddenly saw it blocked by other approaching guards, and as they paused were

1. Henry Ford in the Ford Engineering Laboratory, holding a V-8 water pump

2. The 1935 V-8 Phaeton De Luxe

3. Upper left. Henry and Edsel Ford at a building site

4. Lower left. The original Rotunda at the World's Fair, Chicago, 1934

5. Above. Edsel and Henry Ford with the 1935 V-8 engine

6. Right. Charles E. Sorensen

7. The Styling Building and Styling Rotunda at Dearborn, Michigan

8. The River Rouge Plant, Dearborn, Michigan

9. Ford Security-men (LEFT) and UAW men at the Rouge just before the Battle of the Overpass. Walter Reuther and Richard T. Frankensteen are second and third from the right.

10. Signing the Ford-UAW contract. Left to right: Philip Murray, President of the CIO; Harry Bennett; and R. J. Thomas, President of the UAW

11. The M-4 tank. C. E. Sorensen appears in the doorway at the extreme left.

12. Willow Run assembly line

13. The Ford glider

14. Willow Run building and airfield

15. Lord Perry, C. E. Sorensen, and Heinrich Albert in the mid-1930s

swiftly slugged from behind. At once they became victims of a systematic beating.

Reuther was knocked down, kicked in the face and body, picked up and thrown down again, kicked some more, and finally thrust down the flight of iron steps leading from the overpass. Frankensteen's coat was pulled over his shoulders to pinion his arms; then, as photographs showed and onlookers testified, he was kicked mercilessly in the head, groin, and kidneys, and when prostrate was gored in the abdomen by the heels of his assailants. Merriweather's back was broken, and Dunham was gravely injured. As a girl who was kicked in the stomach vomited at the foot of the steps, a mounted policeman rode over, and in what seemed to the Rev. Mr. Sanford a pleading voice, told one of the Ford men: "You mustn't hurt those women; you mustn't hurt those women." Union people scattered hastily. The episode was over in a minute; but like other violent scenes of the time—the killing of a worker by national guardsmen in the Toledo Electric Auto-Lite strike, the Memorial Day clash at Republic Steel, the driving of sit-down men from the Hershey Chocolate factory—it was preserved by vivid photographs, which newspapers and magazines spread before the whole country. In due course witnesses described the affair to the NLRB. The Battle of the Overpass gained a lasting fame in the history of the labor struggle.[15]

The NLRB shortly filed a complaint against the company for discharge of union workers, use of violence, and other actions hostile to collective bargaining, and the company responded in characteristic fashion. Spokesmen, including W. J. Cameron in the Ford Sunday Evening Hour, denied the charges. Ford attorneys, assisted by Frederick Hill Wood of New York, who had argued the Schechter case before the Supreme Court, challenged the Board decisions on such points as the admission of hearsay testimony and whenever feasible appealed to the courts. After listening to witnesses present on May 26, the Federal examiner made a scathing report; and before 1937 ended the Board found the Company guilty of violating the Wagner Act, ordering it to stop interfering with union organization, and made it reinstate a number of discharged employes with back pay. Company heads denounced the decision, Henry Ford declaring: "Anybody who knows the Ford Motor Company knows the things the Board charged never happened and could not happen here." They further announced that they would not comply and would appeal the decision, whereupon the NLRB itself went to the courts.[16]

But the UAW had temporarily been turned back. Confident that his Rouge plant was safe for the time being, Henry Ford could mount guard over his peripheral properties. The course of events in Kansas City and Dallas meanwhile proved that he and Bennett were ready to break the union wherever they had power.

In Dallas the social and economic atmosphere was unfavorable to unionism, partly because conservative white people feared that the organization of mass-production workers would give the Negro better status. When the sitdown strikes alarmed Ford, the Dearborn office sent one Warren Worley to work with loyal Dallas employes in espionage and union surveillance. The service department organized an "inside squad" of thirty men ready for concentration at strategic points to meet trouble. Foremen distributed a booklet, "Ford Gives Viewpoint on Labor," setting forth Henry's belief that "predatory money interests in New York" controlled the unions. On June 23 two UAW organizers who appeared at the factory gate encountered Worley's squad, and were severely beaten with orders to get out of town and never come back. Two days later, another beefy group of factory men, its champion tug-of-war team, were relieved from ordinary duties to constitute an "outside squad," armed with blackjacks, pistols, whips, and lengths of rubber hose called "persuaders." Officers of the plant called two mass meetings, at which they warned workers that anybody who took John L. Lewis's side would find that he had slapped a grizzly bear, and that "if it takes bloodshed, we'll shed blood right down to the last drop." [17]

The "outside squad" thereafter ran rampant without police hindrance, seizing every opportunity to use its weapons on union organizers, members, or even sympathizers. Some men were mauled on the streets, and others frightened out of Dallas by threats of assault. A member of the squad later testified to some 25 or 30 beatings all told. An attorney representing the organizers, W. J. Houston, who on July 10 was set upon by Worley and others, has left a horrifying account of how he was hit from all sides, how when he fell to the pavement he was kicked mercilessly in the head, groin, and limbs, and how his assailants jumped up and down on his stomach. Emerging from the hospital a wreck, he decided to move from the city. Another labor

man, organizing employes for an AFL union, was also attacked by the
Ford squad and given a savage beating. After ordering him to leave
town, they threw him into a field where a passing motorist found him
and took him to the doctor.

At no time did the police interfere with the "working over" that
the service force gave union men—a term that meant the use of whips,
fists, or blackjacks. Indeed, the police often informed Worley of the
arrival of labor organizers from other cities. On the few occasions
when a victim dared swear out a complaint against the police, they
showed blithe confidence that the courts would dismiss the charges.
One of the most flagrant instances of the subversion of law and order
was an arrangement which Worley's forces made with the park police
to disperse a meeting held by the Textile Workers' Organizing Committee to view a new film called "Millions of Us." In the brawl which
followed, the projecting equipment was demolished, the film and
sound records were destroyed or stolen, and the projectionist was
tarred, feathered, and dumped behind the offices of a newspaper where
photographers were waiting to take his picture. Only when the governor sent some Texas Rangers to Dallas did the anti-union violence
partially subside.[18]

Kansas City offered much the same pattern of Ford intransigence,
municipal inertia, and union helplessness. One partial excuse could
be made in both centers for the city authorities: struggling against
depression and unemployment, bearing heavy relief burdens, and
apprehensive of radicalism, they found it all too easy to side with the
big industrial unit that gave people work, paid large taxes, and
protected the existing order.

During the General Motors strike UAW organizers became active
among Ford's Kansas City assembly hands. The head of the plant,
H. C. Doss, kept well informed and expressed concern to Dearborn
because the "union boys are getting bolder." He wished to discharge
a number of men to "scare the others." A superintendent told the
secretary of the local union to keep his mouth shut because "there are
plenty of tough boys here that will crack your skull for you," and
when the secretary was transferred to another job, the foreman was
told to "work his tail off" and not let him talk to anybody. The Kansas
City Star, printing Henry Ford's advice to workers to avoid unions,
predicted that anybody who joined them would eventually be de-

capitated. Dearborn, however, instructed Doss to move circumspectly, and suggested that he be careful in discharging men to make sure that they were "released for some infraction of the rules." [19]

Indeed, for a time this spring, as the strikers won in General Motors and Chrysler, and as Big Steel surrendered, the outlook for unionization of the Kansas City plant seemed fairly bright. When early in April the UAW, resenting some extensive layoffs, called a sitdown strike, Ford and Bennett felt real concern, and sent John Gillespie to confer with a UAW vice-president in Kansas City. The two agreed orally upon an arrangement which represented a union victory, restoring all the men to their jobs, providing for consultation with the union before further discharges, and granting a general wage increase. By the end of May 1937 the UAW claimed that 2000 of the 2500 workers in the plant had taken out union cards. Plant and union officers held frequent conferences on their problems, including the elimination of processes which had resulted in numerous cases of lead poisoning. A system of genuine collective bargaining seemed to have been established. All this, however, was illusory, for company hostility never really flagged.

In July company employes received two circulars reminding them of Henry Ford's dislike of unions, and the following month a company organization, the Blue Card Union, directly supported by the Ford treasury, began to solicit membership. When the plant temporarily closed in September for a change of models, its officers began spreading ominous rumors. Ford, they said, planned to build a new assembly plant in St. Louis which would cost Kansas City a thousand jobs. As many frightened employes began withdrawing from the UAW, the Ford superintendent notified its heads that Dearborn had instructed him to cease dealing with the union. Obviously, Henry Ford and Bennett were determined to stamp out the organization. When the UAW responded by accelerating its drive for new members, with considerable success, the superintendent in October urged Dearborn to close the factory for three months to "clear up the present situation"— that is, to eliminate the union. Bennett and P. E. Martin agreed to this and shut down the plant. And when the union defiantly proclaimed a lockout strike, the company discharged all maintenance and production workers, and announced the transfer of operations to Omaha.[20]

This was a body-blow to Kansas City. The city manager, H. F. McElroy, hastily telegraphed Bennett in protest, flew to Detroit to confer with the Ford executives, and surrendered as abjectly as General Hull had given up Detroit to the British in the War of 1812. While Ford and Bennett consented to reopen the Kansas City factory, he agreed to provide full open-shop conditions for them. Hurrying back to Kansas City, he announced that he had found Mr. Ford anxious not to invade anybody's rights, but merely to protect his employes, and he would see to it that "men who wish to work are permitted to do so without interference." No doubt Bennett, who maintained that the Ford Company had closed its assembly because the Kansas City police were excluding all non-union workers, had talked to him in no uncertain terms. What the city manager's announcement meant was that a previously neutral municipal government would now use its police power to protect strikebreakers and disperse pickets. McElroy had succumbed to the Ford threat—though it should be realized that he probably felt he was under almost irresistible pressures. He had to think of 2500 jobs, 2500 weekly pay-checks, 2500 families exempt from relief, 2500 wage-earners buying in stores and keeping them in business. He had to think also of the city's future, for loss of the plant to Omaha would have been a disaster.[21]

No sooner had McElroy returned and the assembly reopened than the city atmosphere changed. When the union renewed its strike December 10, the police forbade all picketing. They arrested union men trying to form a line, scattered a crowd of demonstrators at the plant by using tear bombs, and notified union leaders that if they caused more trouble, the force would not stop to make arrests—it was "going to beat their heads in." Armed crews of loyal Ford employes helped keep the plant open. Just before Christmas the Jackson County sheriff took from such a 28-man crew 12 short guns, 14 revolvers, and 60 other weapons, but the prosecuting attorney released them without bail.

In vain did Homer Martin telegraph the city authorities in outraged protest. "A striker caught with a slingshot was sentenced to the municipal farm," he exploded, "but, with company backing, thugs can carry an arsenal fit for the army and you release them until you decide whether you will issue charges. Of course, you won't issue charges." He added: "On the lighted cross of the magnificent City Hall hangs the broken body of Justice."[22]

Temporarily, Ford had won an almost complete victory in Kansas

City. In the depression atmosphere desperate men were easily hired, and the system of armed patrols conveyed them safely through the factory gates. Much public sentiment, uneasy over the sitdown strikes, opposed to the New Deal, and receptive to the general ideas of the Liberty League headed by Hoover and Al Smith, supported Ford. The company union made steady advances. As Christmas approached, UAW workers who knew of Henry Ford's reiterated statements, who read about the terrorism in Dallas, and who realized that only Blue Card men stood much chance of permanent employment, changed their allegiance. The police force stood by to protect them, and the grateful company collected donations to buy Christmas presents for policemen. By New Year's, the UAW had been rendered powerless in the Kansas City plant.

This amounted to defiance of Federal law, and the NLRB was quick to catch up the gage that Ford had thrown down. On January 31, 1938, the board issued a complaint charging that the company dominated the Blue Card Union, that it had locked out 967 workers and refused to reinstate them, that it had subjected 114 other workers to penalties for union activities, and that in general it had practised interference, restraint, and coercion in violation of the Wagner Act. The board at once (February 14) opened hearings in the case. Its procedure was necessarily slow, however, and meanwhile the union remained impotent. As at the Rouge and in Dallas, the UAW had been checked.[23]

For a time, in fact, it seemed that the opposition to the new national labor policy headed by Henry Ford, Eugene Grace, and Tom Girdler might gain a substantial victory. Many people regarded Ford's championship of the open shop as a heroic defense of American individualism. The recession which deepened in the winter of 1937–1938 was imputed by many businssmen and even some sober economists to the labor turmoil. Congress in December defeated the Black-Connery minimum wage bill in the first check given to a major Administration measure in the House. The infiltration of a few unions by gangsters, Communists, and men intent upon gaining power at the expense of both industry and labor had aroused wide public resentment. An early historian of the NLRB declares that it met "the almost unanimous opposition of the nation's press, the hostility of influential columnists, the organized action of certain lawyers' groups, the public and private

activities of a few Senators and Representatives." The governor of
Oregon declared that his state's development had been hamstrung by
the Wagner Act, its evils "magnified a thousandfold by faulty and
insincere administration on the part of the NLRB." [24]

The board did commit some grave errors of judgment, prolonging
its deliberations and offending influential groups. It originally claimed
that it had full discretionary authority to carry out the policies of the
law without judicial restraint so long as it kept to the remedies contemplated by Congress. The Supreme Court soon ruled that judicial
definition of the board's powers was in some instances necessary, and
in the celebrated Board case against Fansteel Metallurgical, it refused
to uphold an order requiring Fansteel to reemploy men who, according to the court, had forfeited their claim to jobs by "high-handed
tactics." The courts also had to deal with a frontal conflict between
the Wagner Act and the Norris-LaGuardia Act, which forbade use of
the injunction against labor. That is, the NLRB could certify a certain
union as the legal bargaining agent with an employer; but a competitive union which had lost the board-conducted election could then
picket the plant in an effort to compel the employer to deal with *it,*
and nobody could enjoin the second union from such activity. The
NLRB encountered procedural difficulties, moreover, in pressing its
cases. [25]

Another issue which temporarily weakened board authority was that
of free speech. In a case of 1939, based on the Battle of the Overpass
and other misconduct at the Rouge, the board presented as evidence
some of Henry Ford's statements, including the "Fordisms" he printed
on little cards. That spring the Civil Liberties Union criticized the
board's order against such anti-union propaganda as a denial of Ford's
right of free speech, and the New York Federation of Women's Clubs
attacked the board on the same ground. This was at a time when
businessmen were vocal for amendment of the Wagner Act, even
Roosevelt's former lieutenant, Donald Richberg, making that demand.
Company attorneys quickly seized upon the principle of free speech
as justifying resistance to part of the board's orders, and the Federal
Circuit Court early in 1941 upheld their contentions. [26]

Meanwhile, labor's struggle against Ford was crippled by factional
dissensions within the UAW. Under the sunshine of the successes
against General Motors and Chrysler a crop of ambitious new labor

leaders sprang up, eager to take advantage of the new opportunities. They saw that Homer Martin lacked administrative grasp, and was too benevolent to be suspicious of plausible enemies; and this distrust increased when he was naively drawn into some dubious private negotiations with Henry Ford and Bennett. He doubtless entered on these parleys because he agreed with certain other labor leaders in the winter of 1937–1938 that union weakness, the hunger for jobs aroused by the recession, and the strength of Ford's security forces under Bennett, made any successful strike in the Rouge impossible. He was quite right in this conclusion. The very layout of the plant was such that a sitdown effort to seize control was not feasible and the working force was notoriously honeycombed with informers who would give prompt warning of an impending strike. The first weeks of 1938 found employment in the Detroit area tragically scarce, tens of thousands reverting to relief, and union coffers almost empty. In that black January 200,000 of the 250,000 UAW members in Detroit were out of work; of the 87,000 men normally employed at the Rouge, only 11,000 were on full time. Postponement of a labor drive against Ford was imperative, but it accentuated the union mistrust of Martin, and gave his antagonists an opportunity.

These rivals, who included Richard Frankensteen, Wyndham Mortimer, and Walter and Victor Reuther, asserted that Martin was too emotional, too rash, and too deficient in power of ruthless action to be an effective commander in the crisis. He had been excellent for the first histrionic drives, but was unfitted for the long, hard campaign in prospect. A tougher, stronger man should head the UAW. Frankensteen, whose rugged physique had quickly recovered from the overpass scrimmage, thought he was the man. Mortimer, leader of a disruptive Stalinist element which ironically called itself the Unity Group, and included the Reuther brothers, was ready to play much the role that the notorious Harry Bridges had taken in the West Coast CIO. Walter Reuther, young and keenminded, hoped to use his presidency of the Detroit West Side Local to seize the UAW reins. All three, but especially Frankensteen, were unabashed opportunists. Frankensteen, after first taking a position in support of Martin, soon turned to cooperation with Reuther and his associates.[27]

The power grapple, marked by feuding in the locals and bitter exchanges in the press, kept the UAW in turmoil throughout 1938–1939.

Each group accused the others of treason to labor objectives. Martin and his aides during 1938 convoked two mass rallies of Ford workers which, according to Reuther, were intended not to strengthen the union, but to tighten Martin's authority. The drive against Ford, Reuther charged at the UAW convention of 1939, became a political football. "It was a political football because many people in high places in our union at that time realized that anybody who organized the Ford Motor Company" could dominate the CIO, and one of Frankensteen's lieutenants "absolutely went out to create a political machine instead of a Ford organization." No wonder, Reuther added, that workers would not contribute to a fund to organize Ford employes, for they saw their money was being misused. To this Frankensteen retorted that he had fought for what he thought right, and that it was his foes who were shortsightedly selfish. "They forgot Ford was the man they were fighting, and started to fight me."

This internal struggle, largely paralyzing the strength of the UAW throughout the late 1930's, forced Martin upon the defensive and encouraged him in his conciliatory talks with Henry Ford. The spectacle of dissension became pitiable. When the faction-torn executive board of the union made decisions which it immediately reversed, public opinion was disgusted. The readiness of Mortimer and others to play the Stalinist game so antagonized conservative labor officials that a group of them in the summer of 1938 asked John L. Lewis to intervene. In August the executive board expelled Mortimer, Frankensteen, and Ed Hall from the UAW, and early the following year matters went from bad to worse. Martin, facing certain defeat, led his followers out of the CIO to form a new union affiliated with the AFL, which he asked the NLRB to accredit as the bargaining agent for automobile employes. The directors of the UAW-CIO promptly stripped him of his presidency and thrust him into outer darkness, also expelling George Addes, and elected the reliable R. J. Thomas as UAW president.[28]

A struggle between the rival unions ensued. As a result, opposition to Ford, and true collective bargaining in other automotive companies, remained in a state of semi-collapse during 1939. When Harry Bennett went on vacation this year, the *Nation* (February 11) congratulated him. The growing uproar in the UAW, it remarked, must provide pleasant background music for his trip. "For the third successive season the Ford Company has managed to escape an organizing drive, and no small part of the credit goes to Mr. Bennett's skilful manipulation of factional differences within the union." It might better have said that the discredit went to selfish and shortsighted union leaders.

Yet the NLRB was meanwhile pressing cases against the Ford Motor Company which strongly affected public sentiment, for they offered disturbing evidence upon conditions within the Ford domain.

4.

The sluggings on the overpass in July 1937 had been given front-page reports by the newspapers all over the country. So the following November were the beatings of a score of UAW agents for distributing CIO leaflets. Arrests of more union agents in the ensuing months—268 in December, and 352 in January 1938—were again headlined all over the land. In its decision against Ford just before Christmas in 1937 the NLRB declared that Bennett's service department maintained a surveillance over employes even outside the plant, and was ready to crush by force any sign of union activity. "The River Rouge plant has taken on many aspects of a community in which martial law has been declared, and in which a huge military organization . . . . has been superimposed upon the regular civil authorities." The country in these years saw a great deal of strong-arm vigilantism, with company police and community police working in harmony, in all sections; in Southern textile-mill areas, Pennsylvania and Illinois coal fields, and California fruit and vegetable districts. It was exposed in newspaper articles, magazine reports, and most memorably of all in John Steinbeck's *Grapes of Wrath;* and the Ford Motor Company got its full share of harsh publicity.

Events in Dearborn, Kansas City, and Dallas gave currency to a new term, the Ford Terror. This meant not only the use of violence, but the creation of an atmosphere of dread and intimidation. In 1938 a book by a responsible labor leader equally opposed to Communist and Fascist tendencies, Benjamin Stolberg, succinctly described it: [29]

There are about eight hundred underworld characters in the Ford Service organization. They are the Storm Troops. They make no pretense of working, but are merely "keeping order" in the plant community through terror. Around this nucleus of eight hundred yeggs there are, however, between 8000 and 9000 authentic workers in the organization, a great many of them spies and stool-pigeons and great many others who have been browbeaten into joining this industrial mafia. There are almost 90,000 workers in River Rouge, and because of this highly organized terror and spy system the fear in the plant is something indescribable. During the lunch hour men shout at the top of their voices about the baseball scores lest they be suspected of talking unionism. Workers seen talking together are taken off the assembly line and fired. Every man suspected of union sympathies is immediately discharged, usually under the framed-up charge of "starting a fight," in which he often gets terribly beaten up.

Harry Bennett's power extends beyond Dearborn to Detroit. In certain localities in Michigan judges and other State officials cannot run for office without a petition with a specified number of signatures. Bennett simply puts such petitions on the conveyor belt, and in one afternoon the prospective candidate has all the signatures he needs.

This statement was essentially accurate. Throughout the 1930s the depression accentuated a deterioration of working conditions which had begun in the previous decade. This was true of all mass-production industries and especially all automobile manufacturing, but it was particularly true of the Ford plants after their refusal to emulate General Motors in accepting collective bargaining, and particularly galling to Ford workers who knew something of the happier early days and the oldtime image of Henry Ford as a friend of the workers.

Job insecurity made union organization more difficult, and espionage more effective. The long lines of unemployed at the gates reminded every arriving worker that he could be replaced in a moment. For the country as a whole, National Industrial Conference Board estimates showed that while unemployment was worst in the spring of 1933, with nearly 16,000,000 out of work, it remained high in March 1936 (with about 10,775,000), and went higher still in March 1937 (almost 11,400,000). The Detroit labor market was especially depressed in 1938, for overproduction of cars the previous year had given dealers an excess stock which numbed the whole automotive industry.[30]

Of all labor grievances at the Rouge, none was sharper than the speed-up. Martin, Sorensen, and other bosses had always driven their men, but never so much as now. A flip of the switch would put the assembly line into higher gear, compelling workers to strain themselves to the utmost. Comfort, physical health, and nervous stability all had to be forgotten. J. M. Waggoner, manager of the Lincoln plant, tells us that men fearful of losing their jobs really exerted every nerve.

"No doubt about that! We could get more work out of a man. You could go up to a man and say, 'Listen, instead of ten bodies today, I want twelve bodies today.' And you got them!"

The foundry became known as the madhouse. Open hearth workers who had once expected to dismantle 130 used cars a day for scrap lifted their quotas to 190, while the superintendents urged them to go on to 225. Finishers of crankshafts early in the 1930s had turned out five to seven every sixty minutes for 75 cents; in 1935 they were turning out eleven and being asked for twelve, while the hourly wage had dropped to 50 cents. Only workers near the water-fountains had time to get a drink. A hammer-man reported in 1935 that the speed-up had become so exhausting that the labor turnover in the previous year had been ten men for each machine.[31]

Always over the men hovered the fear of slowing down and losing their jobs, of becoming gray-haired and superannuated, of illness, breakdown, and the soup-line. No worker trusted his neighbor, who might belong to Bennett's spy system. None expected much mercy from his foreman or superintendent, for they were also under pressure. The bosses told them that times were hard, the company was straitened by competition, costs must be cut, and production must rise; their records were sharply scrutinized. The speed-up broke countless men not only physically, but nervously and morally, for it was founded upon a disregard of human dignity which left them in a frustrated rage against the machines that drove them, the company, and the whole industrial system.

Logan Miller, who was assistant-superintendent of the Rouge plant 1935–1941, records that he developed a nervous stomach which affected all parts of his body—"what they called Forditis." Many workers not only in the Ford plant but other automobile factories termed this ailment the "shakes." The wife of a General Motors participant in the Flint sitdown strike told an interviewer: "You should see him [her husband] come home at night, him and the rest of the men in the buses. So tired like they was dead, and irritable. My John's not like that. He's a good, kind man. But his children don't dare go near him, he's so nervous and his temper's so bad. And then at night in bed, he shakes, his whole body, he shakes." Another wife chimed in: "Yes, they're not men any more. My husband he's only thirty, but to look at him you'd think he was fifty and all played out. And unless we have the union things will get worse." [32]

All the automotive companies, including Ford, were accused of wrecking the health of employes by the speed-up and the stretch-out (that is, the assignment of a greater number of machines to each man to tend), and then dismissing these prematurely aged hands as unfit. Dr. I. W. Ruskin, after a study of the health of auto workers, told the UAW convention in South Bend in 1936 that "the intolerable speed-up" had resulted in a prevalence of neurosis. He added bitterly: "These men with aching bodies and shivering nerves, with their mental faculties warped and deteriorated, are cast out of industry without a qualm. To the employer this human scrap has no salvage value; he does not give it the same interested consideration that he gives to metal scrap or other salable commodities." The companies denied such assertions. A Ford study showed that among approximately 86,000 workers in its plants in the Detroit area in 1935, excluding Lincoln, nearly 37,500 were 40 or older, 25,900 were 45 or older, and about 12,000 were 50 or older.[33] The true grievance of labor lay elsewhere.

It was accurately stated by John Reid, secretary of the Michigan Federation of Labor, when he explained that industry wanted younger and younger men. "Persons 40 or older may keep their jobs if they are employed, but new men of similar age will not be hired." This assertion is well supported by statistics from Ford and other companies. The large automobile factories did not discriminate against older men when discharging workers, but did discriminate against them in rehiring help. Figures from the Rouge plant for six months beginning April 1937 show that of 3451 persons hired, 63 per cent were 30 or under, and only 207 were 50 or older. One consequence of this displacement of older men was that they often played a specially energetic part in organizing unions, and another was that they insisted on making "seniority rights" a fundamental union demand.

Few of the Ford practices angered experienced workers so much as the cavalier disregard of long years of service.[34] One foreman tells us: "Seniority or anything like that never entered our minds; we just kept who we thought were the best men." H. S. Ablewhite of the employment office records that men were called back to work without system. "They just took the list and called them as they came, with no seniority at all." Men with two, five, or ten years in the factory behind them might stand in line and see others who had never been inside the doors get the new jobs. Few employees, however, would have accepted Ablewhite's assertion that employment depended on nothing more than accidental inclusion in a list. Workers past forty were convinced that arbitrary discharges or layoffs, followed by rehiring, constituted a method by which the company deliberately rid itself of older men, and still others would have said that it was a method of keeping wages down. Many believed that under the Bennett regime jobs were handed out to men with the right connections, including friends of influential politicians of the area.

That hiring and firing was sometimes used to lower the wage level is attested by statements of responsible Ford men. Charles Patterson asserts that he and others in the Spring and Upset Building were taken to an employment office and put through its routine, including a physical examination, discharged and rehired, just so that their pay might be cut, Patterson's dropping from $14 a day to $10. Theodore R. Mallon declares that one of the tasks of Ray Rausch in the days of Bennett's ascendancy was to reduce compensation. Laying off a well-paid man, he would say, "Come on back and we'll give you $6 a day." Mallon adds: "They would fire the men with high-paying jobs and hire them back at a lower salary if they were willing. A lot of them expected they'd have to take a cut, but they didn't expect to be shoved around like a dog."

Many discharges, of course, were founded on suspicion of union allegiance or sympathy. A tap on the shoulder by one of the service men, a walk to the employment office for pay, and the rebel, real or supposed, was out. He might be luckier, at that, than some of the suspected organizers who were transferred to the Rouge assembly line for "toughening up." J. M. Waggoner tells of five or six trimmers sent out for disciplining. "I don't know what happened to them over there, but when they came back you wouldn't even know they were the same men. They had black eyes and pushed in noses for arguments. . . . They really dressed them down, these fellows we thought were organizers." [35]

Henry Ford when younger had long prided himself on the considerate treatment he gave his workers, and on a pay scale which had made Ford men the aristocrats of industry, owning homes, automobiles, bank accounts, and insurance policies. Now all this was gone.

It could be said, of course, that the depression wrecked the prosperity of many wage-earners in all the great industries, and that the general drop of income was something Ford men simply shared as a common catastrophe. The severity of that drop can be demonstrated by a few statistics. Before the depression skilled Ford workers earned from $2500 to $3000 a year, and unskilled or semi-skilled men from $1200 to $2000. But by the beginning of 1935 the wages of the skilled had been cut by at least $800, and of the unskilled by at least $200. The year 1937 began as a comparatively good one in the automobile industry, with demand rapidly recovering. That year the average hourly pay in the Ford factories was 87.95 cents, and the average pay for a 40-hour week $35.18. Of course a majority of employes never worked the fifty weeks that would have given them $1759, or even thirty-five.

By that year most workers for Ford, as for General Motors and Chrysler, had lost their homes, exhausted their bank accounts, and cashed in their insurance. The Ford Company cannot be blamed for the depression, or for seasonal layoffs. Its pay scales had improved since 1935. Nevertheless, from 1937 to 1941 Ford wages were one or two cents an hour below the average in the industry, and even further behind the leaders in the automotive field. So far had it lost the spirit and standards of the five-dollar-day! [36]

The Ford scene, to be sure, still had some cheerful aspects. The great Rouge plant was clean, freshly painted, and efficient; it was well lighted and well ventilated. Its machinery, usually of the latest design, was shielded to prevent accidents, and its safety record, despite an outbreak of lead-poisoning in 1935 among solder workers, was excellent. Its first-aid stations and hospitals were models of their kind, and seriously injured workers could be hurried to the Henry Ford Hospital. No factory in the land had better drinking water, more spotless toilets, or shinier floors. In employment policy, the company maintained a proud record of giving work and self-respect to persons blind, crippled, epileptic, or otherwise physically handicapped. It furnished new opportunity to paroled or discharged convicts. It continued to offer the Negro worker a chance that he found nowhere else. When the third annual conference on the economic life of the Detroit Negro in 1935 reported that the city's 120,000 Negroes were not allowed fair employment,

Donald J. Marshall of the Ford Motor Company replied that 8000 of its 80,000 employees were Negroes. The company still trained ambitious boys in the admirable Ford Trade School, whose diplomas had a national prestige.[37]

Ford's friendliness to veterans meanwhile earned him judicious praise. In the autumn of 1933 the company arranged with the American Legion of Wayne County to hire 5000 veterans on the simple presentation of a letter from the post commander certifying to membership. Press reports told of thousands of men standing in lines, eager to pay their dues in order to obtain a job. One reason for the decision of the UAW not to move directly from its victory over General Motors and Chrysler against the Rouge was the lack of any inner core of union organization at the Ford factory. While of course union weakness stemmed in part from the stern hostility of Henry Ford and the vigilance of Bennett's service men, it was also related to the fact that many thousands of employes had substantial reason to think of Ford with gratitude. Many would have accepted Theodore A. Mallon's statement: "Things were really okay except the men couldn't call their souls their own"[38]—a cruel exception, but one which left hope for better times.

## 5.

The good fortune of Henry Ford and Bennett in the factional quarrels of the opposing labor forces was short-lived. After Homer Martin's deposition as head of the UAW and the elevation of R. J. Thomas to his place, that union gained in cohesion and strength. Leading his rival AFL union, Martin fought a losing battle; during 1939 his strength ebbed away and in April 1940 he was forced from the field. By fall that year—the fall in which Roosevelt's New Deal policies won another decisive victory—the UAW confronted Ford and other industrialists with solid ranks and rising confidence.

During the period when he still held considerable power, Martin had made an agreement with Henry Ford, which accomplished little except to perplex all onlookers. The fact that while yet president of the strife-torn UAW, in the fall of 1938, he began negotiations with Ford and Bennett, seemed to some enemies proof that he was either a dupe of the crafty heads of the company, or a fellow-conspirator in their plans to destroy the UAW. Neither hypothesis seems tenable. His long career shows that he was honest and highminded, and though he was much too confiding, he tried hard to assure himself of Ford's good faith. He hoped, and thought Henry also hoped, that a settlement would prevent further violence like that of the Rouge overpass. He believed that Ford's old interest in the lot of the workers might be re-awakening. He knew that Edsel continued to exert pressure on his father, and that the recent organization of a company union, the Ford Brotherhood, Inc., was interpreted by some observers as a move by Edsel, Sorensen, and W. J. Cameron to undercut Harry Bennett.[39]

Homer Martin also knew that many people believed the CIO unions destructive, and that the continuance of sitdown strikes—for the country in the spring of 1938 witnessed them in other important plants—stimulated a wide public demand for curbs on labor. William Allen White blamed the Roosevelt Administration for the sitdowns, Herbert Hoover expatiated on the days lost, and the United States Chamber of Commerce demanded curative legislation. Sorensen constantly urged union heads to make good their promises of increased production. "I wanted to be friends with industry," Martin later said. He tried to make his union helpful: "We stood for honesty; for a workman doing a decent day's work. The result was we built up production; we built up sales—we felt that was our job." [40]

The motives of Henry Ford in the negotiations are more enigmatic. Bennett, we may easily believe, played a Machiavellian part, but Ford was a man of many moods, and it is never safe to underrate his psychological complexities. He felt gusts of real sentiment for his workers—very fitful gusts, to be sure. William Mielke, who had held a responsible position in the Rouge, tells us that one day in these years he met Henry, who asked what he thought of conditions there. "I answered that I was glad he asked the question," Mielke records. "I had in my pocket a list of the things that I considered worthy of improvement, and proceeded to reach in my pocket for the list. He departed abruptly with both hands up in the air. . . ." Some occurrences this year could have appealed to his better nature. In April his fiftieth wedding anniversary brought him many tributes, including a number from workers. In July Detroit gave two weeks to the celebration of his seventy-fifth birthday, with many references to his oldtime idealism and humanitarianism. He was awarded the Watt Medal by the Institute of Mechanical Engineers. But how much all this touched him is conjectural.[41]

What is certain is that Martin reached a tentative agreement with

Bennett and Ford, purely oral, late in December 1938 that early the following month Local 600 at the Rouge publicly announced it, and that its impact upon the UAW was mixed, some members of the executive committee approving and more disapproving it. Its complete terms are hazy. But it seems clear that Ford agreed to recognize the UAW as bargaining agent for its own members, to allow the wearing of union buttons, to reinstate workers who had been discharged for union activities, and to establish a machinery for adjudicating grievances. Martin in return agreed to withdraw all UAW suits before the NLRB, and to dissociate the union from personal damage actions filed by union members. This would save Ford from heavy legal expenses, and from the blow to his prestige which the Supreme Court's approval of NLRB rulings, now universally anticipated, would deliver.[42]

It is also certain that the agreement never stood any chance of becoming effective. The distrust of most union men for Ford and Bennett was too deepseated to permit acceptance. They pointed out that until the compact was reduced to writing, the union depended entirely on Ford's good faith, that it did not establish full recognition of the UAW, and furthermore that it left minor questions unsettled. Martin asked that a special convention meet in Detroit by March 1 to pass on the agreement, but a hostile majority of the board fixed it for March 20 in Cleveland under conditions which made defeat certain. When Martin thereupon led his followers into the AFL, Ford and Bennett showed no willingness to make a similar agreement with his new union, and indeed, by various acts did a good deal to detach his remaining adherents. In the spring of 1940 he resigned, and practically disappeared from labor history. He had made a reprehensible mistake in accepting personal favors from Bennett and writing him an effusive note of thanks.

His successors in Ford AFL union very shortly surrendered their charter (September 1940) and announced their allegiance to the UAW-CIO. From that moment Ford faced a firmer labor front than for years past. The union immediately put fresh energy into its plans for a drive against the company. It was able to subject the firm to a merciless fire of unfavorable press releases, a barrage of legal suits, and continuous pressure from the federal government. Michael Widman was taken from the United Mine Workers to direct the campaign, and equipped with $100,000 pledged by the UAW and CIO jointly. Whenever the company discharged workers for what the union asserted was union activity, Thomas or Widman wrote eloquent letters of protest to Henry or Edsel Ford, and distributed copies to the press. They took many of the cases to the NLRB, confident that the courts would sustain the board in ordering discharged employes reinstated with back pay, and the company's only means of avoiding this result was to anticipate the order by voluntarily re-hiring the men. At the same time, the UAW did its utmost to discredit the company with the federal authorities.

Union spokesmen, whenever Ford bid on a defense contract, called public attention to the supposed Nazi sympathies of some Ford officials, and their repeated violations of the Wagner Act. Sidney Hillman, representing labor in the Office of Production Management, argued that if a choice existed between a company that obeyed the law and one that did not, the former should get the contract. Early in 1941 Ford's bid on a ten-million-dollar truck contract was rejected because of his labor record. This increasing aggressiveness of the union did much to bring hesitant workers into its ranks.[43]

The new boldness reached its culmination in the winter of 1940–1941, when hundreds of proselytizers and organizers were thrown into the Ford domain. They included richly colorful personalities who later became legendary. One was Norman Smith, a gentle, shabby, tireless man who wore an old suit and old shoes into shreds, but who could talk to tough mill workers until they cried; another was William B. Taylor, a Marlborough of labor strategy, who tirelessly bent his keen mind to planning campaigns and organizing forces; and still another was Harry Ross, who mapped the city and plants by streets and departments, and concentrated volunteers at every vulnerable point. At first timid employes pulled down their shades and would not answer the doorbell, while others paid their dollar dues under assumed names, but courage grew. Success in organizing workers outside the plants encouraged sympathizers within them to join the union openly.

"They just popped up all at once," later recalled Al Smith, superintendent of the motor building. "They started blooming all over the place; regular men, who had been working there for years. The first thing you knew, the son-of-a-gun was around there signing up guys and one thing and another, and of course he wasn't even suspected because he was an old employee." Converted men began to wear their union buttons, and if Bennett's force tore them off, pinned them right on again. Admittedly some employes were still cowed, while others—notably Negroes—who were specially grateful to Ford, gave a cold shoulder to the organizers, but the initiative had passed from the company to the UAW. Moreover, the economic revival that attended the beginning of the European war and an immense American defense effort so reduced the competition for jobs that wage-earners, feeling a new security, became more defiant of the plant police. Bennett could no longer crack the whip.[44]

Success brought helpers from many quarters. Ministers and priests gave the UAW outspoken support, and provided opportunities for organizers to enroll members. Clubs, lodges, and fraternal bodies took a friendly attitude. Foreign-language groups of various types gave union agents facilities for approaching men of their own national origin. The *Michigan Labor Leader,* an organ of Catholic trade unionists which emerged in September 1939, published editorials cheering on the UAW. When the union in the fall of 1940 made its first demand for a NLRB election to designate an agent for collective bargaining, the company attorney rebuffed it, pointing to the obvious fact that the membership was a minority group. But by January 1941 the UAW felt strong enough in the Lincoln plant to file an election petition with the NLRB, and six weeks later did the same for the Rouge and Highland Park plants.[45]

At this point the Supreme Court delivered a decisive blow by handing down in mid-February 1941 a judgment completely upholding the UAW and NLRB in their suit and orders against the Dearborn plants. Percy Llewellyn, president of the Rouge Local, was restored to employment, and soon raised the UAW membership in the Motor Building to 95 per cent of the force. When he was discharged again, the men threatened a sitdown strike unless he was brought back, and the company yielded. Superintendent Al Smith told him: "You walk around the building and see that everybody is satisfied. . . . Go any place you want to. Talk to anybody you want to as long as you promise me there won't be any trouble." Llewellyn later described the result. "I was signing guys up at the rate of hundreds a day after that. I'd go around and talk to them; come back and work ten minutes on the job and start off again. I set up my committeemen, my stewards, and all the union machinery. At the NLRB election I think we were closer to 100 per cent than any building in the Rouge."

Henry Ford stood on the verge of defeat. On March 8, in Georgia, he reiterated his old shibboleths: he would "never submit to any union," his real assailants were "the outside forces," and ever since the Selden patent fight the same Wall Street group had been "out to get us." But in Detroit, the company heads were forced into more and more concessions, and even so, every day a clash became more probable, for confident union members thirsted for open battle. Harry Ross recalls that they would burst into Michael Widman's office shouting, "They have fired more of our people; they have fired our organizers. Let's strike them, let's close them down!" [46]

### 6.

On April 1, 1941, came a spontaneous explosion. John Fitzpatrick, furthering union activity, was talking with workers on the afternoon shift when he learned that 1200 or 1500 men had gathered at the superintendent's office in the rolling mill. Hurrying thither, he was told that the union chairman in the mill and seven others had been discharged, and that workers had at once shut down at least three buildings. "Maybe this is it!" Fitzpatrick thought. He directed the men to protect the furnaces and other plant property, but to encourage employees in other buildings to drop their tools. Meanwhile, UAW headquarters in Detroit had been deluged with telephone calls: "A-Building stopped work;" "Rubber plant closed by the company;" "Axle plant men walked out." The whole Rouge, except for a few units like the foundry, where the union had never gained strength and the Negroes formed a group favorable to Ford, was paralyzed.

When Reuther, Widman, and others reached the Rouge and saw 50,000 men gathered in a mass refusal to work, they knew that the movement could not and should not be halted. At 12:35 A.M. word was sent to leaders in the plant: "You are officially on strike." The rank and file were told to march through the Rouge on Road 4 to Miller Road, and then to local headquarters on Michigan Avenue, cheering and singing "Solidarity." They did just that. "It was a thrilling moment," Fitzpatrick has recalled, "a wonderful experience, to walk out along with all those men determined on one thing, through Gate Four, with service men standing there looking at us and not daring to say a word. No supervisor, no officer of the Ford Motor Company, neither Harry Bennett nor any service man, dared say us nay."

Union leaders, though happy that the strike had arisen spontaneously among the men with their enthusiastic support, had been shrewd enough to prepare a strategic plan. They never considered a sitdown. Knowing that they could not picket the gates, some of which were approached by overpasses and protected by machine-guns on the roofs, they had decided that the only course was to block the five highways leading into the wide Rouge plant. A few cars placed across the roads as one shift went out and another came in would create a barrier, and thousands of halted automobiles would pile up before it. This plan was executed. Within a few hours car-barricades effectively obstructed all the roadways. Non-strikers remaining inside the Rouge, notably about 2500 Negroes, found the road-blocks and picket lines an obstacle to egress. They could do nothing but stay there, brandishing home-made weapons, sleeping on improvised mattresses, and accomplishing considerable plant damage, until the tension eased.[47]

Henry Ford, meeting Sorensen on April 2 at Willow Run, sourly remarked that the strike could not have been averted and might do more good than harm. On his orders, Sorensen kept clear of the Rouge, and soon flew to Miami. Edsel came back from Florida only to receive strict orders from his father to leave the labor situation to Bennett. Nevertheless, Edsel succeeded in exerting a decisive influence in the situation. All the older executives were in a truculent mood: Sorensen had the bizarre idea that the union had produced the strike by terrorism, Henry Ford wanted to arm the non-strikers and use tear gas if necessary, and Bennett was eager to put Ford's service gangs behind Henry's commands. Edsel was alarmed by the possibility of pitched battle. He pleaded with his father, he kept Bennett on the telephone, he argued, he protested, and as Bennett puts it, he "insisted" on a moderate course.[48]

In the atmosphere of intense excitement surrounding the Rouge, bloody encounters on April 2 and 3 seemed momentarily imminent. On the first morning non-striking employees inside the plant tried twice, at seven and again at nine, to smash the picket lines by mass assaults through the plant gates. As Dearborn police watched helplessly, workers wrestled and pummeled each other in a wild melee, but each time the union forces beat back their assailants. Sporadic fights between strikers and service men kept breaking out. Old scores were paid off, Angelo Caruso, prominent in the overpass beating of Reuther and Frankensteen, being stabbed. Steadily the union strength grew.

UAW headquarters ran out of buttons as unexpecetd numbers of workers surged in and paid their dues. Radio station WJBK, under union auspices, reported every half-hour on the progress of the strike and carried messages to maintain morale.

Inside the besieged plant the service men, with Bennett and Ray Rausch in charge, played on the fears of the Negroes and others, telling them that if they tried to leave they would be beaten by the UAW pickets as scabs, but if they stayed they would have security, food, and pay. Within a short time, however, discipline crumbled so badly that the inmates became less a garrison than a mob. As food supplies ran low, the stronger men seized and hoarded all they could; gamblers started crap games; and reckless Negroes raced new cars wildly through the plant. In the drafting room blueprints were tossed into great piles to make pallets. The inmates, in fact, made such a shambles of the works that maintenance crews later took several days to repair damage and clear up the debris. Genuine danger existed that a race riot might grow out of the conflicts between strikers and non-strikers. To avert this disaster, the UAW assured everybody that it had many Negro members, and that any race feeling was artificially inspired by company bosses and jealous AFL men. Walter White of the NAACP meanwhile used a union sound truck to speak to the Negroes within the plant, fruitlessly urging them to leave under safe conduct.[49]

Bennett employed the first days of the walkout in trying to reach a public sentiment which he well knew to be hostile, and to obtain help from public officials who gave him a frigid gaze. He issued statements calling the union workers Communists and "lawbreakers," determined to wreck the defense program. His telegram to the President asking for assistance in ending terroristic mass picketing, violence, and other interferences with the Ford defense effort met no response. When the company's counsel, I. A. Capizzi, hurried to Washington to talk with Secretary of War Henry L. Stimson, saying that the strikers had done $100,000 worth of damage at the Rouge, and pleading for government intervention, he also accomplished nothing. While the President and Secretary Perkins kept informed upon the stoppage, Roosevelt said that he did not consider it a serious interference with defense work. For a time Bennett looked hopefully to Governor Murray Delos Van Wagoner, but after ordering all the available State Police to Dearborn to help maintain order, the governor resolutely declined to molest the strikers. By the night of April 3, Ford executives knew that the city, state, and national government would keep their hands off.[50]

Realization of this fact meant that the drama, with all its complexities—its racial overtones, its news-stories luridly slanted against Ford or the UAW according to the bias of the journal, its openings for a small but venomous Communist element,[51] its test of Federal labor policy—would be short. At the heart of the drama stood a half dozen men: the fast-decaying Henry Ford, the sinister Bennett, the determined Philip Murray, Walter Reuther, and John L. Lewis, and the public-spirited Edsel Ford, now more deeply aroused than ever before. When on the third day the union laid down its terms, Bennett ignored the offer. But Edsel courageously insisted on negotiation, and Bennett chronicles the result: "Though Mr. Ford and Edsel were far apart on this, Mr. Ford gave in to Edsel's wishes. I don't think the CIO would have won out if it hadn't been for Edsel's attitude."

For the union won. On April 11 Henry Ford telephoned Sorensen, who jotted in his diary: "Strike settled." On what terms? The Ford Motor Company agreed to an election under the NLRB to enable Ford employees to specify the union to represent them in drawing up a contract; and the company promised then to discuss the contract. The scene was set for a denouement which would astonish the nation.[52]

## 7.

A mass meeting of the UAW ratified the settlement, and on April 13, 1941, wheels began turning again at the Rouge. Six weeks later, on May 21, after feverish canvassing in which Bennett and his aides worked for the AFL against the CIO, the election was held. Its outcome was decisive. In the Rouge the UAW received 51,868 votes, or practically 70 per cent—it being significant of the intensity of feeling among the workers that of nearly 78,000 ballots cast there, only 34 were blank. The AFL vote in the Rouge was 27.4 per cent, a tribute to Homer Martin and evidence of the lingering attachment of certain groups to Ford. But only a pitiful trifle of 1958 votes, or 2.7 per cent, were cast against both unions.[53]

This tiny vote for Henry Ford's no-union principle, writes Sorensen, was crushing news to the aged founder. It was "perhaps the greatest disappointment he had in all his business experience; . . . he was never the same after that." But many of the glimpses we have of Ford in this spring of 1941 are of a man who had already suffered a slight stroke (1938) was soon to have a second and more serious one, and was feeling the effects of increasing age (he was to be seventy-eight in July). We see him asking whether a long-dead associate had really died; saying petulantly to Governor Van Wagoner after he refused to intervene, "Well, you've got a plant—what are you going to do with it?"; telephoning Sorensen after his surrender to union terms that the CIO had lost everything; and still assuring people that "the Jews" were persecuting him. Now he knew that his uncompromising policy had suffered total defeat. His associates were bad losers. Capizzi declared that the company "must now deal with a Communist-influenced and led organization," greedy for millions "with which to finance its drive to control all American industry," and Bennett chimed in: "It is a great victory for the Communist Party, Governor Van Wagoner, and the NLRB." Of course they all read the writing on the wall.*

Negotiations for a contract began June 1, 1941, in Detroit, were shortly transferred to Pittsburgh so that Philip Murray might participate, and ended in Washington on June 20. Harry Mack of the sales department, Capizzi and his assistant Frank Nolan, and several others represented the company, Bennett occasionally participating; R. J. Thomas, George Addes, and Murray were the chief UAW representatives. By June 18 a formal contract was ready. Bennett took it to Henry Ford, "who when he got the sense of the document," as Sorensen significantly puts it, walked out in utter rejection. Next day, he took Sorensen on a tour of the buildings, saying nothing, until in late afternoon he called Edsel to a conference in Sorensen's office. There he talked bitterly of the contract, winding himself up until at the end he burst out that he was not going to sign.

"I don't want any more of this business," he said. "Shut the plant down if necessary. Let the union take over if it wishes!" Sorensen calmly pointed out that the government, which had large contracts with the company, would seize and operate the Ford works. If that happened, Ford responded, it would be in the motorcar business, and he would be out. "Close the plant!"

* In Kansas City, too, the workers won. On May 21, 1941, the NLRB ordered the reinstatement of most of the employees who had been discharged there, with payment of back wages. It seems safe to estimate that in Kansas City the company paid as much as $1,500,000 for back pay, lawyers' fees, and the cost of the NLRB proceedings. To this had to be added a large loss of sales because of a consumer boycott, and the further loss of prestige and good will. The bill for temporarily breaking the Kansas City union came high.

Thus spoke Ford on June 19. But on the 20th company representatives in Washington signed the contract. On the 21st this was front-page news all over the land, and an amazed nation read with it Edsel's statement that the UAW victory in the Rouge election had rendered full compliance imperative: "As the company views the situation no half measures will be effective. We cannot work out one scheme of things for some of our workmen and another scheme for the remainder. So we have decided to go the whole way." The NLRB's publication of the terms on June 24 showed that Ford had indeed gone the whole way.[54]

Under the contract the Ford Motor Company granted a union shop for all workers throughout the country, with the exception of a few such classifications as foremen, and agreed that all new employes must join the UAW if not already members. Ford also agreed to deduct initiation fees, monthly dues, and special assessments from pay envelopes—"the checkoff." Service men were thereafter to wear distinguishing uniforms, caps, or badges to eliminate secret spying. As for wages, the company promised to adjust them to the highest level of any competitor selected by the UAW—which chose General Motors for production workers, and other corporations for employes in glass, rubber, cement, and additional specialties. More than 4000 discharged workers were to be awarded back wages. In return, the UAW consented to drop or settle out of court all cases pending against the company for violations of the Wagner Act, or for personal assault. A procedure for adjudicating grievances was created, so carefully devised that the UAW thought it safe to allot only one steward to every 550 workers, as against one to every 200 in other unionized plants.

Why had Henry Ford thus suddenly reversed his whole past policy? Why had he given the UAW the most generous contract it had ever achieved?—Chrysler, for example, had not granted it sole bargaining rights. The answer is that the reversal was not as sudden as it seemed, and that a broad complex of considerations entered into it.

Ever since the shock of the NLRB election and its proof of the workers' discontent, Henry had been in a mood to listen to the insistent arguments of Clara and Edsel, and to weigh certain unescapable truths. That his mind was far from closed had been shown at one point by his agreement with Homer Martin, and at another by his surrender to Edsel's insistence on a peaceful termination of the April strike. Though more petulant and erratic than before his stroke, he was in all probability more easily influenced.

Sensitive to public opinion, he realized that if he let labor troubles paralyze his great plant just as it flung itself into the defense effort, the people would condemn him. Moreover, he knew that the deeper the NLRB dug into the multitudinous complaints against the company, the more unpleasant evidence, disagreeable headlines, and customer distrust he would have to face. With some 2600 employes asserting that they had been dropped for union activities, the bill for retroactive pay became longer every day that he remained defiant. He might explode in a wild declaration that he would close the Rouge, but actually he could never endure watching his proud creation stand idle. And then he had been irked to see how General Motors and Chrysler had leaped ahead of him; perhaps he now decided that by a bold stroke he could do more than they had done, gain more enthusiastic support among workers, and put them in an embarrassing position.

And while he deliberated, his wife and son unquestionably brought steady pressure to bear. On the night of June 18, when he came home to tell Clara that he had ordered Sorensen to shut down the Rouge, she was in a mood to endure no more. She knew how Edsel was suffering; she had a sharp vision of rioting, casualties, and denunciatory press reports. According to Sorensen's report of what Henry told him, she turned on her husband in frantic desperation. If he refused to sign a peace agreement, she said she would not stay to see the ensuing violence; she would leave him. "And," said Henry, "I felt her vision and judgment were better than mine." Very possibly this is part of the explanation of the *volte-face*. So speaking, Clara would have added the final decisive element to a complex of forces and ideas that at long last compelled Henry Ford to face the realities of a new era.[55]

It was high time, for the defense program of the government, to which we now turn, had placed the company in a position in which unified, harmonious effort was essential.

# VII

## SHADOW OF WAR

On August 28, 1939, while Franklin D. Roosevelt was sending urgent messages to Warsaw, Rome, and Berlin with a hope of resolving the Polish-German crisis, Henry Ford made a confident assertion. "They don't dare have a war and they know it," he said. Three days later German tanks, rolling across the Polish border, began a conflict that was to widen as it raged, and last for six years.

For Europe and America, despite the Ethiopian and Spanish Wars and the turmoil in the Orient, the focus of interest in foreign affairs had increasingly become Hitler's Germany, and the invasion of Poland marked a dramatic culmination of the Nazi surge for *Lebensraum*. Ford was well acquainted with the regime; for his own plants in Germany had been affected by its anti-Semitism and the subordination of all industry to a strong nationalistic policy. The re-introduction of compulsory military service, the occupation of the Rhineland, and the annexation of Austria had clearly shown its aggressive character. But apologists for Hitler continued to insist that the excesses of his rule would subside as he won a rightful place for his state in Europe.

Ford was the readier to accept such theories because he had always admired the enterprise, orderliness, and industrial skill of the Germans. Liebold, who still served him in various ways, was German in descent and sympathies. Poultney Bigelow, an eccentric American of Fascist tendencies who corresponded and visited with Ford, stood on familiar terms with the former Kaiser. Prince Louis Ferdinand, Ford's friend, supported Hitler while deploring his extreme acts. Such were Ford's connections and attitudes that on his seventy-fifth birthday, July 30, 1938, before a cheering crowd in Dearborn, he accepted the Grand Cross of the German Eagle from Fritz Hailer, German vice-consul.[1]

To the instant chorus of condemnation led by eminent American

Jews, Ford offered a temperate defense. The medal, he protested, came from the German people, who "as a whole are not in sympathy with their rulers in their anti-Jewish policies." (According to Liebold, Ford made this distinction when the decoration was proposed. "You tell them I'll accept anything the German people offer me," he had said.) His acceptance of the cross, he assured reporters, did not "involve any sympathy on my part with Nazism." He added: "Those who have known me for many years realize that anything that breeds hate is repulsive to me."

He had indeed opposed both dictatorship and conquest. "Through wars and dictatorship," he had stated early in 1936, "whole nations have ceased to be free." His opposition to war had been manifest for more than twenty years, and represented a deep conviction that Americans should avoid any conflict except one in defense of America itself. So firm was this feeling that the Munich accord of September 30, 1938, pleased him. Not long afterward he told reporters at Dearborn with a quizzical smile, "I'll bet anyone even money that there will never be another war." The seizure of Czechoslovakia the ensuing March found him still asserting that the best service Americans could render the world was to keep out of foreign conflicts.[2]

Ford had not restricted his anti-war activities to occasional statements. As early as 1932 he and Clara had taken an interest in the "moral rearmament" drive of the Oxford Group established by an American clergyman, Dr. Frank N. D. Buchman, in 1921, to promote an intensive, personal practice of Christianity. This body, as the threat of a European war grew, had made peace and understanding among nations a prime objective, and Buchman had succeeded in enlisting the support of eminent persons in many countries. By 1936 he was directly in touch with the Fords, and on July 15, 1939, obtained a signed statement for public use. "There is enough good will in the people to overcome all war, all class dissension, and all economic stagnation, when that good will shall be hitched to the affairs of men and nations," Ford declared.

Buchman hailed the declaration as a "Magna Charta," and on Ford's seventy-sixth birthday sent a rhymed greeting in his own hand.[3]

Soon to become associated with Ford in opposing American participation in European affairs was the renowned aviator Charles A. Lindbergh. He had met the manufacturer on August 11, 1927, not long after his dramatic solo flight across the Atlantic, and had taken both Henry and Edsel Ford aloft in the *Spirit of St. Louis*—Henry's first taste of flying. Lindbergh later recalled that Ford at the time was a living legend to him, for he had driven a Ford car at the age of eleven, and had followed the industrialist's career with interest. He was surprised when Ford accepted his invitation to make a flight, for the *Spirit of St. Louis* had been designed for a single occupant, and Ford "had to sit, bent over, on the arm of my pilot seat." But "he seemed to enjoy the flight very much." Some months later, as one of a group establishing an air line from New York to Los Angeles, the aviator selected the Ford trimotor as the best available commercial plane, and the new company ordered ten of them (1929). Lindbergh saw Ford on several occasions in these years, and discussed the possibility of building a larger aircraft with perhaps four motors to replace the trimotor. He and his gifted wife, Anne Morrow Lindbergh, repeatedly stayed at Fair Lane with the Fords.* While they later lived and traveled abroad for several years, Ford retained his interest in them, and in the summer of 1937 helped sponsor an observance of the tenth anniversary of the solo Atlantic flight.

At this time (1938) Lindbergh was about to begin a tour of European countries to observe their programs in aviation. In August he visited Russia, spent part of the following month in Czechoslovakia, and in October arrived in Berlin to attend a meeting of the Lilienthal Society for Aeronautical Research. He completed a tour of the plants and air fields of the Reich, and on October 19 accepted the Service Cross of the Order of the German Eagle, with Star, the second highest decoration in the field given by the German government. Field Marshal Goering, chief of the Reich air force, made the award.

The presentation was a complete surprise to Lindbergh, and he probably recognized that its acceptance might not be popular in the United States. One news report stated that his wife on seeing the deco-

---

* Lindbergh recognized the dynamic quality Ford showed in meeting industrial problems. He particularly remembered a statement by the industrialist, as it was reported to him, made in the late nineteen-twenties just after the death of a young pilot whom Ford had known. Ford had announced at a conference on the type of airplanes the company should build: "We're going to make monoplanes because they're simpler. We're going to build them of metal because metal's the thing of the future. And we're going to have more than one engine because we're not going to have any more forced landings." Lindbergh said, "Here Ford had laid down three fundamentals that have formed the base of successful air transport development." At the time, none of these was fully accepted. Lindbergh recognized that Ford's decisions were intuitive, not scientific, and "often erratic," but on occasion, as in this case, startlingly right.

ration exclaimed, "The Albatross!" with reference to Coleridge's ancient mariner. Sure enough, Lindbergh like Ford was denounced for accepting an honor from Hitler's Reich. Premier Molotov of Russia at once condemned him; J. A. Ubank, an American authority on aeronautical law, commented disapprovingly; and later Secretary of the Interior Harold L. Ickes and the playwright Robert E. Sherwood reproached both Ford and Lindbergh. In accordance with his consistent policy, the flyer did not reply to these attacks.[4]

Early in 1939 he returned to the United States. He held a commission in the Army Air Corps Reserve, and at the request of General H. H. Arnold made a survey of American aircraft facilities and progress, for the most part without pay, that spring. Later he testified before the House Appropriations Committee on European military aviation, and the relative position of the United States. His conclusion was that America, while not inferior in aeronautical workmanship, lagged "in quality as applied in the performance of military aircraft," and that "the production of military aircraft in Europe today is far ahead of our own production." However, he felt that the geographical position of the country protected it from attack. We should not compete with Europe in output, but should at once develop our "applied and fundamental research." Chiefly as a result of Lindbergh's report, on which Air Force recommendations were based, the Committee on June 12, 1939, asked for an appropriation of $292,695,547 to help the country regain "its aeronautical research leadership." Lindbergh termed the program "very conservative." [5]

While he was thus on record as favoring more preparedness than Ford, he recommended a purely defensive activity. He had never discussed publicly the involvement of the United States in a European conflict, but privately he regarded this as a sinister possibility, and after the invasion of Poland accepted an invitation from the Mutual Broadcasting System to state his attitude.

"I speak tonight," he told his listeners on September 15, 1939, "to those people in the United States who feel that the destiny of this country does not call for our involvement in European wars. . . . We must keep foreign propaganda from pushing our country blindly into another war." America had joined in World War I, but had not cooperated fully in establishing a permanent peace. That mistake should not be repeated. "We must either keep out of European wars entirely or stay in European affairs permanently" (a possibility then completely unthinkable to most Americans). If we entered it, the war would demand a full national effort—men as well as munitions. Western civilization would be endangered, and the United States should hold aloof to preserve as much of it as possible.[6]*

He had voiced a view of which Henry Ford could fully approve. Ford was one of those who wanted no "involvement in European wars," and five days later he in turn spoke against current proposals for modifying the neutrality act of 1935 to permit France and Britain to purchase war materials in the United States for cash. "It is foolproof," Ford said on September 20 of the existing law. "If we change it one iota we will take the first step toward getting us into war." He spoke to reporters along similar lines at the American Legion convention in Chicago on the 25th. "If we start shipping that stuff over there we'll be in the war right away," he warned. He pooh-poohed the conflict, which he declared would end if the United States did not enter it. "If I were put on the stand I'd say there isn't any war today." [7]

However, Congress amended the law to permit the purchase of war materials, and Roosevelt signed the new act on November 4. The President was committed firmly in private and increasingly in public to assisting the allies as opponents of dictatorship and protagonists of freedom. Severe restrictions still guided American ships and American citizens in the war zones. Large defense funds voted early in 1939 were supplemented, and in August Roosevelt appointed a War Resources Board to survey national industrial and military resources and propose a plan for their use.

### 2.

By this time the German *Blitzkreig* had subdued the greater part of Poland. The Russians, with Hitler's grudging consent, had poured into the eastern third of the country. Simultaneously they made demands upon Finland for an exchange of territory, and when on November 30, 1939, these were rejected, invaded the small republic. Despite astonishing resistance, by the following March they had subjugated it. Mean-

* On Dec. 6, 1959, Lindbergh defined his 1940 position to the authors. "I was not opposed to the United States taking part in European affairs on what I considered a rational basis. I was definitely opposed to dabbling in them. . . . Incidentally, I have never been basically an isolationist. This became a political term, loosely applied to anyone opposed to American entry in the war. There were 'Isolationists' and 'Interventionists,' and in this political sense I was an Isolationist."

while they had also occupied the Baltic states of Lithuania, Latvia, and Estonia, setting up governments which were quietly extinguished in the summer 1940 when the three states were absorbed into the Soviet Union. The half year had offered a chilling demonstration of the brutalities which weaker nations might suffer from strong totalitarian powers. Henry and Clara Ford contributed through a glamorous Finnish friend, Dagmar Rinie, to the aid of Finnish soldiers and orphans.[8]

In the winter of 1939-1940 the conflict abroad, popularly known as "the phoney war," seemed to merit Ford's scornful appraisal, for none of the great powers except Russia was active. Hitler proposed that his opponents recognize a *fait accompli* in Poland and make peace; Britain and France refused. Both sides were building up power to strike, and Hitler refrained only because of forbidding weather. The United States had increased its army and navy, and participated in an all-American conference at Panama City, while Roosevelt was studying the recommendations of the War Resources Board. Public opinion polls in November showed 62 per cent of all Americans favoring aid to the Allies short of war. Yet although the expansion of American industry for defense production had begun, deliveries of aircraft had been slow.

With April 1940 the entire situation changed. Like a thunderbolt the Nazi forces struck undefended Denmark, began an invasion of Norway, and on May 10 crashed into the Netherlands. In a few days the invaders had occupied these countries and driven on into Belgium and France. While the German campaign was in its early stages, on May 16, Roosevelt sent a special message to Congress calling for the intensification of defense activities. He proposed to lift the production of aircraft to 50,000 planes a year: "Our defenses must be invulnerable, our security absolute." He asked for a billion dollars, and a special fund of $200,000,000 which he himself might employ.[9]

Congress promptly appropriated one and one half billion dollars for defense and established the Office for Emergency Management to coordinate governmental agencies for preparedness. Seven heads for various undertakings were appointed by Roosevelt. The most important to Ford and in the opinion of the nation was William S. Knudsen, president of General Motors, who on May 28, 1940, became Commissioner for Industrial Production.

Ford could no longer belittle the war. His devotion to peace had nothing of the conscientious objector's philosophy. When in 1917

American participation in World War I seemed certain, he had abruptly ended his pacifist activities and offered his factories to the government for military production. But the situation in May, 1940, was not parallel, and he still opposed American entry in the European conflict. In this he agreed with Lindbergh, who in March, through an article in the *Atlantic Monthly,* and a nation-wide broadcast on May 19, reiterated his belief that America should remain aloof from the struggle. The flyer approved the building up of the nation's military strength —air, land, and naval. Since February he had conferred with Ford on occasion, and had discussed the role that the Ford factories could play in a sound preparedness. Ford was now to speak upon this point.[10]

On the very day of Knudsen's appointment he indicated that the Ford Motor Company might help to strengthen the nation. He told reporters that "with the counsel of men like Lindbergh and Ricken-backer [chief American "ace" in World War I] . . . and without meddling by Government agencies" it could "swing into a production of a thousand airplanes of standard design a day." He emphasized that he was talking about defense activity only and that the United States must not be drawn into the war. "A lot of pressure is being brought to push us into it . . . but I am confident we can keep out." The statement on the Ford potential for aircraft production understandably startled the nation. But it should be pointed out that while he had mentioned Lindbergh and Rickenbacker as advisers, his appraisal of Ford capacity was wholly his own. Said Lindbergh later: "Certainly I had nothing whatever to do with the preposterous idea of the Ford Company making a thousand planes a day."

Nevertheless, the announcement produced swift and spectacular action. One result of it was a trip to Washington by Edsel Ford on May 29, 1940, at the request of Secretary of the Treasury Henry Morgenthau, Jr. Edsel saw other government officials, and soon Frank Campsall, Ford's personal secretary, was in communication with the War Department. On June 7 he received the following telegram:

In response to your request the War Department will be very pleased to send a pursuit plane of a design this country would need in an emergency to the Ford Airport at 11 A.M. next Monday together with an engineer . . . The War Department and the National Defense Commission deeply appreciate your offer to further the national defense program.

Louis Johnson, Assistant Secretary of War.

When the plane arrived on the 10th, Henry and Edsel Ford gave it immediate attention. Henry stated that it did not appear more complicated than he had expected. Edsel, saying that the company would make preliminary studies to see what could be done, left that day for Washington to confer with Knudsen. The two had been on friendly terms in recent years, cooperating in various civic projects. In Washington on the 11th Edsel told newspapermen that his company was prepared to start production as soon as it received contracts, and reminded them that it had manufactured aircraft "until a few years ago" (actually, from 1925 to 1933).[11]

Now a second project, apparently advanced by Knudsen, quickly terminated the first. In mid-June Edsel Ford stated that his company's interest was in aircraft engines rather than in airplanes, and it was revealed that Ford would manufacture 6000 Rolls-Royce motors, a number soon lifted to 9000. Sorensen was summoned from Florida to examine an engine and consult on the question of its manufacture. "When I saw it," he recalled later, "I knew that its fine workmanship and high performance would appeal to our organization." He telephoned Henry Ford. The British were to get 6000 engines, and he was somewhat surprised when Henry, being told of this, agreed to accept a contract. "I believe the enthusiasm Edsel and I showed for the project influenced his decision." Lindbergh may also have had an influence, for he had told Ford that the Rolls-Royce was the best available service engine to compete with German models.* The Ford Motor Company Ltd. of England was also studying the motor with a view to producing it. Plans were at once made for tooling and production in America.

Then suddenly Ford reversed himself. Hardly had an announcement of the contract been made when Lord Beaverbrook in London stated that the Ford company had undertaken to produce 6000 engines for Britain. Sorensen insists that "we had not accepted an order from England," and implies that the American government only was to deal with Ford, and later release the allotted number of units to the British. However, the Defense Advisory Commission on June 25, 1940, declared that separate contracts were to have been made, and that this detail had been explained to Edsel.

---

* In recounting what he had told Ford, Lindbergh (letter to authors, Nov. 13, 1959) emphasized the difference between *service* models as opposed to *prototypes*. American prototypes (experimental models not yet in production) were he felt quite equal to European engines.

Ford himself had clearly not so understood it. To manufacture for a foreign belligerent was repugnant to him, and his age, health, and emotional state put him on edge. He was almost seventy-seven, and the stroke he had suffered two years earlier had had its effect. Pride in the capacity of his organization, a desire to contribute to American defense, and Sorensen's and Edsel's enthusiasm had all prepared him to accept the Rolls-Royce assignment. But his fear that America would enter the war, and his dislike of Roosevelt as an apostle of involvement, were almost psychopathic. Any mention of participation, says Sorensen, "upset him almost to incoherence." On June 19 he denied that the Ford Motor Company would manufacture for Britain and on the 24th summoned Knudsen and Sorensen to Dearborn, joining them in Edsel's office.

"I won't make any of those Rolls-Royce engines for England," he announced.

"But, Mr. Ford," remonstrated Knudsen, "we have your word that you would make them. I told the President of your decision, and he was very happy about it."

The mention of Roosevelt was unfortunate, though Ford had already made up his mind. "We won't build the engines at all," he snapped. "Withdraw the whole order. Take it to someone else."

Knudsen, says Sorensen, left the office "purple with rage." His was an embarrassing position. Meanwhile, Ford had whipped himself into a state of anger and suspicion. He concluded that Roosevelt was controlled by a sinister league of American corporations interested in European industry, who were resolved to push their country into the European conflict.[12]

The abandonment of the contract was announced on June 25, after it had cost considerable work by Ford engineers and executives. The company suffered in reputation: the tone of the press was regretful, and a deluge of angry letters poured into Dearborn. These, still preserved, fill three inches of one of the folders devoted to Edsel's affairs. "Just a pal of Hitler's! . . . You are another of the back-stabbing Americans!" was typical of the bitterest comment. Many correspondents reported "shock and surprise," and announced their determination never to purchase another Ford car. These letters, probably unseen by Henry Ford, may well have disturbed Edsel.[13]

Ford emphasized that he was not refusing to aid the defense program. "We are not doing business with the British Government or any other foreign government," he said on June 27. "If we make 6000 Rolls-Royce engines it will be on an order from the United States Government." Such an order, he noted, had not been received. He pointed out that he had offered to produce for "defense purposes only," and would hold to that policy.

Meanwhile he ordered work continued on an aircraft motor which had been started early in June as a power plant for the pursuit planes he had expected to manufacture. On June 28 he "talked about airplanes" with Lindbergh, who was visiting the Fords and inspecting company factories. The Rolls-Royce contract was soon taken over by the Packard Motor Car Company, which executed it capably.*

From Dearborn the Lindberghs went on to the Wayside Inn at Sudbury, Massachusetts, from which on July 10 Charles wrote Ford appreciatively of his recent visit. A meeting with you, he said, "always leaves me with a feeling of renewed strength and encouragement. . . . You, more than anyone else I know, have shown that man need not necessarily be dominated by the machines he has created." He was encouraged by the anti-interventionist attitude of the American Legion, and mentioned that he had written Sorensen about aircraft manufacturing problems, offering any help he could give. He then offered Ford a 1927 Franklin car, presented to him by its manufacturers, if the industrialist wanted it for the Greenfield Village museum. Ford accepted the car and sent Lindbergh in exchange a new Mercury.[14]

By early August Ford had developed his aircraft engine to a point where success seemed assured. The company had refused a tentative proposal, made in July by Donald Douglas of the Douglas Aircraft Company, to manufacture 2500 bomber planes, because, as Sorensen put it, "We must enter this field on our own, with our own engineering." On August 12, 1940, Knudsen offered Ford a second opportunity in defense production, involving an American product and a contract with the American government. Would the company build the new

---

* A word needs to be said about Ford experience with the Rolls-Royce aircraft engine. In the spring of 1939 a group of Ford engineers, headed by Walter Wagner, had gone to England to assist the Ford's French company to manufacture the motors. They gathered valuable information, and were prepared to help with American production. Wagner tells of Henry Ford coming into a room at the Rouge where plans were being made, and telling Sorensen to call the entire project off. Later, says Wagner, Packard tried to engage him. Sorensen refused to release him, but permitted him to give some information to Packard. After France was overrun, the Ford Motor Co. Ltd. in England undertook to build Rolls-Royces.

Pratt & Whitney 18-cylinder air-cooled aircraft engine? "Don't make it!" was Henry Ford's first response. Sorensen and Edsel remonstrated with him. Blueprints for all parts of the motor were not yet available, and Sorensen pointed out that Ford could perhaps improve minor points of design, and could certainly set new standards in manufacture. Ford yielded, and a tentative agreement for 4000 engines was announced on August 16, 1940.

On the 20th Edsel, Sorensen, Bricker, Wibel, McCarroll and others visited the Pratt & Whitney plant at East Hartford, Connecticut, to study the adaptability of the engine to mass production, and two days later notified the War Department that they were ready to proceed. In the next few weeks they received letters of intent which together covered the project in full, along with the allocation of $14,000,000 by the government for a special plant to produce the engines.

The Ford Motor Company was now an important unit in the defense program, for meanwhile it had undertaken experimental work on other military devices. However, it was participating under vigorous labor protest. As early as May 27, 1940, the UAW-CIO had pledged cooperation in the defense program, but at the same time called attention to what it called Ford's "Nazi sympathies." From that time forward, as we have noted, every defense contract brought an attack from labor on Ford's refusal to obey the law. But Knudsen ruled that Ford's compliance with the law was a matter for court decision, and that the defense program must not be impeded during the legal settlement of the issue. Meanwhile, Ford factories continued to operate, the UAW protests seeming to have been of no effect on the work force.

The new aircraft engine factory, for which ground was broken September 22, was placed on one of the few remaining open areas of the immense Rouge plot. The project grew impressively in the process of being born, so that the final building covered an area 360 by 1408 feet, with a wing for test cells 270 by 952 feet. The total floor space of 1,286,344 sq. ft. (two stories) dwarfed that originally planned, and the buildings alone (unequipped) cost $39,000,000. As the entire structure had to be erected in winter weather, a roof-high, temporary wall was constructed, largely of tar paper, as a protective shell, and within this "box" coal braziers burned night and day to keep the temperature above freezing. The entire building was air-conditioned to promote cleanliness and control temperatures and humidity for the delicate machine operations required. Plants at Highland Park, Memphis, St. Paul, and Kansas City were equipped for parts production.

By April 1941 the installation of machinery was under way in the completed shell of the building, and late that month a limited production of parts began. An aircraft school accommodating 1100 trainees was operating by June. By August 23, 1941, the first complete engine was assembled, and 323 were built by the end of the year.[15]

Up to this time the project had provided the Ford organization with triumphs, frustrations, and confusion. Its engineers had quickly suggested better materials for various parts of the engines, and improved routines of production. They had proposed superior methods for machining both the crankshaft and the propeller shaft. They strengthened the rocker arms and connecting rods by prescribing more durable metals. By introducing a tungsten tip for the distributor finger, they increased its life by one-half. With 10,000 precision gauges they greatly simplified the processes of inspection. These changes had been accepted promptly, for Pratt & Whitney had a high opinion of Ford production techniques.

But some Ford proposals ran counter to all past aircraft experience, and were met with a lifted eyebrow. One was the Dearborn decision to cast centrifugally rather than forge the cylinder barrels of the engine.

Sorensen and his associates had long since experimented with cast and forged products, and felt complete confidence that a cast barrel would be superior. In addition, it would be cheaper, permitting notable savings in both time and materials. But Pratt & Whitney rejected the cast barrel because it had never been used in aeronautical engine construction. Even the Air Forces viewed it dubiously, and Assistant Secretary of War Robert A. Lovett wrote Sorensen that they "cannot give up the tested known for the experimental unknown." The cast barrel must have a 150-hour trial before it could be accepted. When the test was given, the barrel passed it triumphantly, and Ford was authorized to use it. But to Sorensen's surprise, when on November 5, 1941, he asked Pratt & Whitney if they wanted to adopt it, they declined, stating that they must await a test at the front! Sorensen exploded: "I will go on record anywhere in the world that the cast barrel is better!" But apparently Ford had to be satisfied with using the part in its own engines.[16]

This was a frustration. So was the difficulty of getting nearly 1200 specially built machines required by the factory for effective production. Although Ford had a high priority, these came slowly, as they had to clear through the War Department, which had an enormous accumulation of orders for such materials.

Meanwhile the factory was in considerable confusion because of the lack of proficient foremen and workers. Despite the training school, which comprised 16 classroome and 11 laboratories, and had begun teaching employes in June 1941, the scarcity of really competent personnel was painful. The labor force was an unleavened lump of wholly inexperienced workers who eventually numbered 26,000, including 3000 women, and only by degrees could it be made an efficient group. Many foremen had been promoted too suddenly, and were unfitted to guide the ignorant rank and file. L. S. Hobbs, the Pratt & Whitney engineering manager, noted in October 1941 a lack of able officials and seasoned workers, and concluded that the difficulties of the factory stemmed from this fact. Time, he observed, must and would correct it.[17]

In the summer of 1940 Ford engineers, at the War Department's request, had been active in developing a final design for the jeep.* Dale Roeder, in charge of Ford truck design, says that activity on the jeep— the tough, all-terrain vehicle for which Willys-Overland and American Bantam companies had produced earlier models—was going forward in July. In October the Army supplied specifications, and Ford, Willys, and Bantam all built cars and received orders for 1500 vehicles each. The overall design selected was Ford's, the power plant that of Willys. On this final revised design the Ford bid for 15,000 units was high, and for a time the company did nothing further in this field.

Ford also worked on the model of a reconnaissance car, or midget truck, a half-ton vehicle with a low silhouette that could make 60 miles an hour, carrying an anti-aircraft gun and three men with light field pieces. A contract for 1500 cars was signed in December, and on February 28, 1941, Edsel Ford drove the first unit off the assembly line. By this time the Army had also become interested in a "swamp buggy," a jeep that could traverse soggy terrain, and work was soon under way at the Rouge on this conveyance. In this work the UAW leaders had demanded that Ford recognize the law and deal with the union, but were

---

* Not then so called. Sheldrick asserts that "that name was created right in the Ford Motor Company months later."

ignored. The Army proceeded with the contracts, President Roosevelt refused to interfere, and no evidence exists that union activity notably slowed down the company's production.[18]

Meanwhile Henry Ford had maintained his opposition to American entry into the war. In August 1940 Lindbergh had become a member of the America First Committee, dedicated to keeping the nation out of the conflict. When Ford and his wife joined, Lindbergh wrote on September 22, 1940, thanking him. "Your stand against entry into the war has already had great influence, and if we are able to keep out of it, I believe it will be largely due to the courage and support you have given us." He sent Ford Anne Morrow Lindbergh's book, *The Wave of the Future*. In this slender volume, while disclaiming sympathy with totalitarian excesses, Mrs. Lindbergh suggested that Germany, Italy, and Russia had taken account of needs and hungers which the democracies had ignored. They had "discovered how to use new social and economic forces. . . . They have felt the wave of the future and they have leapt upon it. The evils we deplore in these systems are not in themselves the future; they are the scum on the wave of the future." America, she pleaded, must avoid the war and build "a strength of growth, reform, and change."

Ford continued his active opposition to American involvement. On November 21, 1940, he asserted that the Europeans had been duped by "greedy financial groups," but that "we should not meddle in the affairs of any people." In January, however, he supported a strong defense program, and in February actually urged aid to the Allies and the Axis alike! He hoped they would become exhausted, and that the United States could then "help them both make a just peace." In other words, his policy was to strengthen America, but to see that its sword was never lifted to join an attack, but only to parry one.[19]

Early in August 1940, before a crowd of 40,000 gathered at Soldier Field in Chicago by the Citizens' Committee to Keep America out of the War, Lindbergh urged that the United States offer "a plan for peace" which would incorporate "terms of mutual advantage." He advocated cooperation with Germany if necessary. In February 1941 appearing as a witness against Lend-Lease legislation before the Senate Foreign Relations Committee, he protested that his sympathies lay with Britain, but argued that an Allied victory would mean a long-protracted conflict. "This is why I say I prefer a negotiated peace to a complete victory by either side." American help, he believed, could not lift British air strength to a level with Hitler's. After the war, in 1948, in a brief book, *Of Flight and Life,* Lindbergh summarized his position in 1939–1941. "I advocated that democratic nations stand by and arm," he wrote, "while Nazi Germany and Russia fought out their totalitarian ideas." [20]

The case which Ford advanced, and which Lindbergh argued more fully, was never weighed coolly by most Americans. Events charged their minds so that they saw salvation in an active opposition to the German dictatorship. They felt that non-participation worked for Hitler, and was pusillanimous. As a result, many called both Ford and Lindbergh Fascists. In New York the pro-Ally daily *PM* published articles asserting that Fritz Kuhn, leader of the German-American Bund, had once been a Ford employee, and that Harry Bennett and W. J. Cameron were still engaged with him in anti-Semitic and pro-Fascist activities.

Ford executives indignantly denied all the charges except the employment of Kuhn, who had worked briefly at the Ford Hospital in 1927, and the complete falsity of the other accusations was demonstrable. Actually, it was difficult to attack the popular image of Henry Ford, and he suffered little. Lindbergh fared worse. His honorary membership in the Lafayette Escadrille was cancelled, he was adversely criticized by government officials and the press, and felt compelled to resign his reserve commission. Only much later was it widely recognized that his position was both consistent and honest, that he had steadily urged a strong defense program, and like Ford when war came was ready to serve his country. But Lindbergh will appear later in the story of Ford war activities. [21]

### 3.

Shortly before Christmas 1940, Dr. George J. Mead, Director of Procurement for the Aeronautical Section of the Advisory Council for National Defense, with Major James Doolittle of the Air Force, called upon Ford and Sorensen in Dearborn. Would the Ford Motor Company undertake to build 1200 Liberators? Talks followed. Henry Ford would not discuss the manufacture of these bomber aircraft with any of the aviation companies (note the earlier rejection of Douglas's overtures), but he respected Dr. Mead and spoke freely with him. When

Mead proposed that Edsel and Sorensen go out to California and look over the Douglas and Consolidated aircraft plants, Ford agreed. "Those planes [i.e., any built by the Ford plants] will never be used for fighting," he told Sorensen. "Before you can build them, the war will be over."

It was arranged that early in January 1941 Sorensen, Edsel, and his sons Henry and Benson should fly out to San Diego, the site of the Consolidated plant, Mead picking up Sorensen in Florida with an Army plane. At San Diego the party would be joined by William F. Pioch and Harry Hanson, specialists in engineering and factory construction, and other Ford men. Already the undertaking, although tentative, was assuming titanic proportions.[22]

Edsel was eager for his sons to follow Ford activities, particularly those related to defense activity. Henry II, who was now twenty-three, had attended Yale for four years, at first specializing in Engineering, then in Sociology, and serving as manager of the crew in his final year. However, he lacked sufficient credits to graduate, and left college to begin work in the Ford Motor Company. Benson, now twenty-one, had gone to Princeton. He had enjoyed the full use of only one eye, fell behind in his studies, and in his sophomore year (1939–1940) undertook a program of extra work to keep up with his class. This effort seemed headed for failure when in September 1940 Benson with Edsel's approval left college and began work with his brother in the company. The youngest son, William Clay Ford, only seventeen, was attending the Hotchkiss School at Lakeville, Connecticut. Josephine Ford, Edsel's daughter, was a student at Chatham Hall, Chatham, Virginia.[23]

Edsel enjoyed a close relationship with his children. To an acquaintance who wrote him in 1939 praising the young men, he replied: "They are turning out satisfactorily from my point of view, and I hope they will continue to do so." He was aware of their limitations. When a Yale correspondent reported in late 1939 that Henry II was doing well in his studies, the father answered wryly: "It is almost time for him to do so, having but a few more months left at New Haven." His correspondence with Princeton shows that he understood Benson. Observing that Benson had never learned to concentrate on studying, he added: "He is very shy about asking advice, and would rather go blindly along alone than to approach the proper parties for counsel." Edsel showed the fullest respect for Benson's independence, discussing his problems with him, but leaving final decisions to Benson himself. In the summer all the children were usually with their parents at Seal Harbor, Maine, and during winter holidays often joined them at Hobe Sound, Florida.[24]

Henry II had been married in June 1940 to Anne McDonnell, whose parents lived in New York City, with a summer home in Southampton, Long Island. They were wealthy, and Anne had thirteen brothers and sisters. Before the marriage, Henry accepted the Roman Catholic faith of his wife. Edsel and Eleanor Ford made the young couple a wedding gift of a Grosse Pointe residence, and transferred to Henry 25,000 shares of Ford Motor Company stock, "in recognition," wrote Edsel, "of the fact that you are finishing your college career this month, and after being married will join the Ford Motor Company as your future business, and also because of the fact that you are at the present time a Director of the Company."

Benson early in 1941 became engaged to Edith McNaughton, daughter of the Lynn McNaughtons of Grosse Pointe. Her father had been a vice-president of the Cadillac Motor Company. They were married July 9, 1941.

By the end of 1940 both young men had spent some months in the engineering department of the company. Sheldrick recalls that they worked first in the dynamometer room, and "didn't pull any punches about getting their hands dirty . . . and their clothes all messed up." They served under Leonard Williams, a Negro technician. Harry Bennett strongly objected to this, but when Sheldrick reported the fact to Edsel, the latter said: "That's good for the boys. Keep them right there; that's all right." Then they joined the crew experimenting with the jeep. Sheldrick took Edsel to watch the tests of the first completed model, and arranged for Henry and Benson to drive it out of a patch of tall grass and underbrush right up to their father.

"He got the biggest bang out of that. . . . That was the one time that I saw Edsel when he was thoroughly enjoying himself. He was awfully proud of his boys." [25]

To return to the California expedition, the Fords and the Government officials arrived in San Diego on the morning of January 8 and inspected the Consolidated plant. That same day Edsel and Major Reuben H. Fleet, President and General Manager of Consolidated, announced that their firms would cooperate in aircraft production, Ford making bombers "either in whole or in part."

However, this was little more than a declaration of hope. Sorensen had studied the plant with realistic eyes. "I liked neither what I saw nor what I heard," he recalled years later. Consolidated's goal was a bomber a day, or 350 a year. "It was painfully evident that it did not have either the plant or the production methods to meet this quota," and even if it did, this meant three years to produce a thousand bombers, though the Air Force wanted them in as yet unannounced thousands. The plane was "custom made," with little attempt at mass-production. The final assembly took place out-of-doors on a structural steel fixture. "The heat and temperature changes so distorted this fixture," Sorensen recalled, "that it was impossible to turn out two planes alike without further adjustment." The prospect of successful production of parts by Ford was dim, for if made to uniform measurements they "would not fit properly under out-of-doors assembly conditions."

Sorensen was grimly discouraged, and said so. "How would you do it?" he was asked. He promised to have a plan by the following morning.

Compared with the Ford car, Sorensen perceived, the bomber was like a skyscraper to a garage. Yet he believed that mass production could be achieved, and set himself the goal of a bomber an hour. He had already gathered all the information he could about the structure of the plane, its major units and sub-units, and the time required for various operations. That night on paper he broke the bomber into essential units and roughly schemed the production of each. By early morning he had sketched the floor plan of a plant which would provide for these operations, and feed the sections and parts into an assembly line. It was a new thing under the sun—as startling for the aircraft industry of 1941 as Eli Whitney's scheme for the manufacture of rifles with interchangeable parts had been in the machine shops of the early 1800s. But Sorensen had complete faith in its feasibility.

At breakfast he showed the sketch to Edsel, outlined the undertaking, and won full approval. They then went to Fleet's office "to shoot the works on a $200,000,000 proposition," backed only by a penciled sketch. Henry and Benson Ford went with them.

Sorensen began by announcing that the Ford Motor Company was prepared to build B-24's. Fleet countered by suggesting that Ford manufacture parts for Consolidated to assemble. He proposed a contract for a thousand wing sections. "We'll make the complete plane or nothing," Sorensen asserted.

He laid his proposal before Mead, with the sketch. If the Air Force would spend $200,000,000 on plant and equipment, Ford would build a factory capable of turning out one Liberator bomber an hour. Mead was immensely encouraged. This would mean 540 planes a month instead of 520 a year. Fleet, apparently dazed by the audacious scheme, agreed to give Ford a license to produce, and to furnish blueprints. Mead and his associates "did not question our ability to go through with an undertaking of such magnitude." It soon developed that blueprints for the entire bomber did not exist, and Sorensen promised to send out engineers and draftsmen to provide a full set. Returning to Dearborn, he laid his plan before Henry Ford, who, fascinated by its scope, agreed to proceed, but stipulated: "Make a complete plane only." [26]

### 4.

To establish the Ford Motor Company as a primary aircraft manufacturer was not easy. The government was eager to enlist its engineering skills and manufacturing capacity, but was dubious as to its building entire planes. On Thursday, January 31, a group of Army officers led by General Oliver P. Echols, Chief Procurement Officer for the Air Corps, arrived at Dearborn to confer on procedure. The Ford representatives were asked to draw up a letter outlining their proposals. They suggested as the first step an "educational order" to Ford for certain parts, and as the second a Ford program for making all parts of the plane, which would be supplied to Consolidated and Douglas for assembly in new plants to be erected in Oklahoma and Texas. The third step would be for Ford to make completed planes.

The Army approved the first two steps and on Monday, February 4, in the Detroit *Times,* Echols made an announcement to this effect. Of the third step he said: "We are naturally hopeful, but we have not agreed to go along with it." However, the newspapers gave no small attention to the idea that complete planes would be made by Ford.

Sorensen kept pressing for Army approval of this final step. He wrote Dr. Mead on February 10 urging that a decision be made.

Consolidated meanwhile urged the government to make it the "prime contractor," with authority to sub-contract, to distribute design information, and to make final recommendations as to all proposed changes. Finally in late February the Army authorized the building of a bomber assembly factory, and although the announced purpose was to make assemblies of wings, fuselages, noses, stabilizers and so forth which were to be used for completed bombers at Fort Worth (Consolidated) and Tulsa (Douglas) plants, the ultimate production of complete bombers by Ford was assumed by Sorensen, and the factory planned accordingly. A schedule was soon agreed upon whereby the new establishment would turn out 100 bombers a month, 50 each, in knocked down parts for Consolidated and Douglas.

It may be added that once again labor was unable to make a large defense contract an occasion for imposing its legitimate demands upon Ford. The government refused to stipulate recognition of the union, and Hillman condoned its failure to do so. "If anything interferes with the national defense program," he stated, "we ought to lay that aside. But whenever there is a choice, we ought to deal with people who are obeying the laws." [27]

Sorensen envisaged a mile-long plant, and while the company owned land in the vicinity of Dearborn on which to build one, he, Henry Ford, and the Army all considered the Ypsilanti area preferable. Some four miles to the southeast of that town and twenty-one miles from the Rouge, Ford owned a considerable body of farmland. Here a little stream called Willow Run meandered through clumps of woodland and cultivated fields to the Huron River, which emptied into Lake Erie. In the summer of 1939 Ford had established a summer camp there for underprivileged boys.

Willow Run thus offered a nucleus of land for the factory and the landing field which must adjoin it. Additional acreage could be purchased at reasonable prices. The immense airdrome which the B-24's would require could be placed there more easily than near Dearborn. "Out there in those wide open spaces we had plenty of elbow room," said Harry Hanson, who represented the company in planning the entire development. With Ypsilanti, Ann Arbor, and other towns nearby, there seemed also to be a local labor supply, whereas the Detroit-Dearborn area was studded with defense plants and workers for them were already scarce. (Actually, Willow Run was to draw heavily on the Detroit region for its work force.) Even in January 1940 Ford agents had been busy getting options on additional tracts, but Sorensen noted on February 6 that actual purchases would be held up until "this matter [of a full agreement with the government] has been all settled." [28]

As soon as a letter of intent covering the projected plant was received late in February 1941 the additional tracts of land were acquired, and plans were made for the factory and airport.

"A year ago," remarked a writer for *Time* in March 1942, "Willow Run was a lazy little creek west of Detroit, surrounded by woodlands, a few farm houses, a few country schools." On March 28, 1941, flocks of workers and machines invaded this bucolic region, and began uprooting trees and filling and leveling. The tracts of timber were extensive, with many large oaks, maples, and elms. Roy Schumann, then a Ford employe, recalled how the fallen timber was piled in logs on the site. Henry Ford appeared, appraised the situation, and said: "Well, let's build a sawmill and saw up the timber right here." So a mill arose, and the trees were minted into lumber on the spot. Little of this was used for the permanent factory, but much went into temporary structures and housing. The clearing and leveling continued for three weeks; then on April 18 the ground was broken for the buildings.

Considerable alterations were made in the plans for them, for the first schedule of 100 bombers a month, fixed on May 20, 1941, was raised in September to 205 units per month (65 each for Consolidated and Douglas and 75 flyaways), and later was lifted above 400 a month. In consequence, the cost of the factory rose from $11,000,000 to $47,620,000. Meanwhile Hanson, aided chiefly by Pioch and Stanley Hill, worked out the final scheme for the placement of manufacturing operations and their relation to the assembly line. Albert Kahn, the architect, then produced blueprints for the great ground floor, and sketches of the factory elevation.

Hanson had taken a large part in the creation of the Rouge plant, and had helped guide the construction of the British Ford factory at Dagenham, England. But Willow Run challenged him with the largest single structure he had ever helped to devise—"the most enormous room in the history of man." Sorensen's mile-long building never materialized (although a mile-long assembly line eventually did), but the huge L-shaped home of the B-24 had a length of 3200 feet and a maximum width (at the base of the "L") of 1279 feet. The total factory area utilized 3,503,016 square feet, and with the hangars 4,734,617. Slightly over 80 acres were devoted to factory, and 109 acres to hangars. The landing field occupied 850 acres, with seven concrete runways, one of 6250 feet.[29]

It would be fascinating to trace in detail how more than three square miles of rural Michigan was metamorphosed by conferences, mathematical calculations, steel, concrete, and machinery into a modern center of production scheduled to produce thousands of enormous planes for the uses of war. The sequence of operations was complicated. Ford technicians—seventy at a time—were gathering vital information at Consolidated's San Diego plant. Sorensen, Hanson, Bricker, and their assistants were inventing a flow of manufacturing never before attempted. Their agents were meanwhile hunting down the structural steel, glass, aluminum, and bricks for the shell of the factory, and finding or designing and building the machine tools essential to its operation. Like a thousand rivulets, but with a force as calculated as it was varied, these activities were running toward final accomplishment. And they ran with incredible speed, for the ultimate goal, the quantity production of bombers, must be quickly attained.

Problems arose. Sorensen had what he himself termed "the wild idea" of building the fuselage upright, which for a portion of the plant would have required a ceiling put by Hanson at one hundred and fifty feet. He was "talked out of that," and the fuselage was made in parts.

Again, the exact site of the factory had to be shifted and the building somewhat altered so that it lay entirely in a single county and did not straddle the boundary of two. "We aren't going into that other county," Hanson told Kahn, "and have a sensation over taxes." The draining of the airfield proved an intricate task, and required 70 miles of pipe, starting with four-inch and ending with an eighteen-foot outlet. Transportation and housing headaches are part of a later story. But for a time the plant was an island in a sea of Michigan mud.[30]

All during the spring and early summer of 1941 Ford technicians had been busy at the Consolidated plant in San Diego, correcting the blueprints for the innumerable parts of the plans, and studying the methods employed in the bomber factory. The Ford experts and the aircraft workers achieved cooperation, but the two had widely different ideas as to manufacturing procedures. A limited acceptance of Ford practices took place. "Consolidated are adapting Ford methods and ideas in their shops and offices," wrote Roscoe Smith from San Diego to Sorensen in April 1941, "and there is considerable comment in circulation to the effect that Ford has got them off their 'fanny.' " This statement was unduly optimistic. Consolidated did go so far as to abandon the outside assembly plan, and finally established an indoor, sequent assembly in August. But an inherent conflict remained between the aircraft engineers and technicians and the automotive men.

Before Ford could manufacture for Consolidated and Douglas, an agreement on the construction of the plane had to be reached. Experts for the three companies conferred, and accepted a breakdown into 69 units. Ford divided many of these still further. While Consolidated planned two sections for the fuselage, Ford eventually recognized 33. The wings, originally divided into a center wing section and two outer panels, were in Ford procedure further subdivided. In general, Douglas procedure tended to be closer to Ford's than that of Consolidated. (Of course the aircraft was of Consolidated design). The Dearborn technicians soon made suggestions designed to simplify and improve the bomber, and of twenty proposed up to August 29, 1941, fifteen were accepted. The Air Forces * had more confidence in Ford ideas than did Consolidated, and were a factor in the acceptance of changes.

The Ford goal—the moving assembly—required orderly pressures of manufacture and easy access of workers to their tasks. Sorensen was outraged by the Consolidated method of dealing with the fuselage as he found it in San Diego. Later he contrasted this with the Ford method:

With that section in two parts, wide open, we could install all the electric wiring and hydraulic piping, also install and check up on the tail section. These sections could be set up on a conveyor, then brought to a point where the two halves could be joined, by riveting.

Consolidated people's method was the exact reverse. They made a unit, then dragged all wiring and hydraulic fittings through the door. Very few

---

* After June 20, 1941, by Army Regulation 95-5, the Army unit dealing with aviation was designated "The Army Air Forces."

men could work in that space; and I described the pulling of wiring through the door as "like a bird building his own nest while sitting on it."

Consolidated abandoned this practice after the breakdown was made, but the contrast between simplification and unnecessary complexity in assembly is clear. The August assembly line of Consolidated represented an advance based more on Douglas than Ford practice, and Ford followed it to a large extent in establishing its own line later.

Another case in point involved construction. When the Ford engineers got the blueprints for the pivot used to retract the landing gear of the B-24, they were amazed and shocked. One Ford representative described it later as "a collection of about half a dozen pieces of steel, a couple of large sized tubing members, and some flat pieces all of which had to be welded together." Almost one hundred welds had each to be X-rayed. The tubing was already difficult to obtain, and would soon become more so. Ford re-designed the unit in three pieces, centrifugally cast. "We used it all during the war and I think there was one instance of failure attributed to it."

Further instances of Ford ingenuity in manufacturing and assembly were to appear. But the chief point of dispute between the two companies stemmed from the character of their employes and the previous industrial experience of the organizations.

Except for a few of the rank and file that had survived from trimotor days, Ford could count on no skilled aircraft workers. William B. Mayo, who had directed Ford aviation from 1925 to 1933, was dead, and Harold Hicks, the aeronautical engineer, had left the company. Furthermore, Ford engineers prescribed for all products exact specifications as to materials and dimensions, and used a maximum of tools and fixtures in manufacture. Since the work was precise and mechanically guided, relatively unskilled labor could be and was used for production. Such labor was the only kind available in quantity in 1941. Ford, therefore, demanded accurate blueprints for all components (there were 700,000 rivets and 1,550,000 other parts), and proposed to use the maximum of machine tools, fixtures, and hard-metal dies.

In contrast, Consolidated could command a highly skilled work force, had hitherto brought the materials to the plane, used rubber or soft-metal dies, and depended on the ingenuity and knowledge of the workers to alter parts and make changes when these were essential. If Consolidated officials recognized advantages in Ford planning routines, they were adamant in rejecting Ford methods of manufacture. Elaborate fixtures and hard-metal dies were highly expensive, and might have to be scrapped if extensive changes in design occurred. Since such changes were almost certain, and Consolidated could quickly adapt to them, its staff regarded the elaborate Ford plans for production as little short of lunacy.

Another element in the situation which the Air Forces recognized, but which Consolidated did not admit and of which Ford was not aware, was the fact that the Liberator was not an outstanding bomber. The older Flying Fortress (B-17) was of superior design, but the Liberator was slightly faster and carried a bigger load, and nothing else was available, for the much superior B-29 was still to be developed. The Liberator was a makeshift. Pilots called it a "clunker," and knew that in time it must be replaced. Consequently an elaborate tooling job for such a plane seemed to informed men, even if they were sympathetic to Ford, a dubious procedure. Actually the Liberator was to serve for more than three years, so that in the event the Ford assembly line was justified.[31]

When Roscoe Smith returned from San Diego in late July with more than two hundred men who had worked with him in San Diego, he found at Ypsilanti the steel skeleton of a factory, its brick walls soon to rise. The last concrete floors were being poured. On May 1 a spur from the New York Central railroad had been laid to the site, and materials could be delivered.

Smith had been appointed to operate the factory, with the able Logan Miller as chief assistant. He knew that initial orders for machine tools had been placed only a month earlier, and the first arrived on August 12. Sewers had been laid at the airport. He saw that as yet nothing could be done at Ypsilanti, and collected a small work force to start the piecemeal manufacture of parts at the Rouge airport. On September 7, he began to transfer workers to Willow Run, where he installed the tool room and some punch presses. Meanwhile he was preparing to open a school at Dearborn for training workers. By November a limited production of parts had begun.

Thus the vast undertaking was under way, but as 1941 drew to a close no part of the plant was completed, the landing field was unfinished, transportation to the new factory was lacking, most of the necessary machine tools were undelivered, the work force—some thought 100,000 employes would be needed—was almost non-existent, and there were no facilities near Ypsilanti to house them.[32]

### 5.

Already by mid-1941 the Ford Motor Company was committed to the manufacture of aircraft engines, had assisted in the development of the jeep and produced a number of those vehicles, was designing a swamp buggy, was putting out reconnaissance cars, and was deeply involved in its adventure with the B-24 bomber. Yet before the end of the year the organization was to undertake two more assignments in defense work.

One was to assist with the design and manufacture of tanks. By the summer of 1941 the Army was preparing to end production of its M-3 (medium) tank. Useful to the British in early North African campaigns, this unit had shown basic defects in fire mechanism and power, and particularly in its engines. Some of these, air-cooled, had whirled up clouds of dust that blinded the drivers of vehicles behind them. Diesels and a combination of five motors had also been used with unsatisfactory results. The Army had designed a new tank, the M-4, which carried its 75 mm. gun in a freely revolving turret, while the crevice between the tank and its turret, vulnerable in the M-3, was protected by a collar. However, no satisfactory power plant for the new machine had as yet been evolved. As early as July Army officials had come to Dearborn to consult with Ford about production.

It will be recalled that in June 1940 Henry Ford had begun to develop a liquid-cooled motor for his hypothetical 1000-a-day pursuit plane, and that after the plane was abandoned he had continued to develop the engine, confident that one day it would be used by some type of American airplanes. He had invested about $2,000,000 in the project, and by July 1941 had a motor practically ready for use. The basic design was evolved by an engineer named Cornelius Van Ranst. Sheldrick called him "a dreamer of the first rank, and a clever, clever designer," but thought that he lacked the toughness to stick with a design to the finish. Others had a better opinion of Van Ranst. And in this instance he had produced a brilliant design with a cylinder block and crankcase in one aluminum unit. The result was lightness combined with strength. A novel valve system helped to make the engine outstanding.

The discussion of tanks, with its overtone of worry about power, now in mid-July of 1941 turned attention anew to Van Ranst's engine. Edsel Ford and Sorensen discussed the possibility of using it for the M-4, called in the engineers, and decided, says Sheldrick, "that by taking eight cylinders of the twelve-cylinder aircraft engine . . . we could make an excellent tank engine." Van Ranst was told to plan an 8-cylinder adaptation. A week later, on July 22, Sheldrick had business in Washington, and took along some drawings of the proposed model. At dinner he showed them to Major Emerson Cummings of Army Ordnance.

Cummings was immediately interested, and Sheldrick went back to report. No contract was drawn. "We were feeling quite patriotic about that time and we just started working on it on our own." Sorensen summoned the engineers, set a date, and snapped: "All right. Get busy and don't drag the seats of your pants. Tanks are being built and the Government has no engine for them." [33]

While this work went forward, the company was asked how quickly it could begin tank production. Edsel, Sorensen, Wibel, and Sheldrick went to Washington, and on September 17 inspected a model of the M-4. The design was not final, and automotive firms were asked to make suggestions. Sheldrick objected forcibly to the final drive housing in the front of the tank. He convinced Army officials that his position was sound, was told to redesign that unit, and had a new nose prepared by Ford engineers which was accepted October 20.

Meanwhile, on September 19, the government had asked for a sample of the new Ford engine, and on October 10 the company agreed to manufacture the M-4. It proposed on October 23 that negotiations cover armor castings, armor plates, and a tank assembly plant costing $45,190,000. The Rouge steel technicians had developed a method for manufacturing armor with water-cooled dies. These prevented warpage (which had attended manufacture by water cooled sprays), and cut the time involved from two hours to less than eight minutes. On December 9 the government guaranteed adequate advances to build facilities for the production of 400 tanks a month. The M-4 thus became a Ford design in part as to body, and wholly as to engine; for the GAA-V-8, as Van Ranst's model was called, soon became the standard power unit for all medium tanks. [34]

In the fall of 1941 the company was questioned on its ability to provide quantity production for the M-7 Anti-Aircraft Gun Director. With Germany still dominant in the air, this instrument then seemed of immense importance. It was a mechanism developed by the Army and the Sperry Gyroscope Corporation. "In its use," recalled H. J. Robinson years later, "if a plane flies into sight, even though it is only a dot in the sky, and the operators of the M-7 can get the plane in their telescope, it is doomed. The M-7 figures not only the range, plane speed, altitude and direction, but also how much the gun 'lead' must be . . . sets the fuse in the shell and lights a red light on the gun to let the gunner know that it is on target and he can fire." Seven or eight of every ten shells would register hits. Naturally the device was bewilderingly intricate: it required 1820 parts and 11,130 pieces. A total of 276 aluminum or die castings, 721 gears, 380 nickel alloy shafts, 549 ball-bearing sets, and 39 instrument dials were involved in its construction.

Army Ordnance was doubtful if the M-7 could be mass-produced, but believed that if any firm could perform the task, it was the Ford company. Conferences at Dearborn and the Sperry plant on Long Island led to an agreement under which Sperry promised to provide complete information and waive license fees. Ford technicians studied Sperry's methods of manufacture, and set up a complete M-7 at Dearborn for observation and demonstration. A contract for 400 directors was received by the company October 8, 1941, and four six-story buildings at Highland Park were set aside as a plant.[35]

## 6.

As 1941 advanced, the shadow of war deepened over America. In January Roosevelt told Congress that the United States must be the "arsenal for democracy." The Lend-Lease bill, providing seven billions for defense and Allied aid, had been passed and signed. Defense orders had been increased. Willow Run now faced a quota of 205 bombers a month, and contracts for parts and planes already reached a total of $480,000,000. While America was not in the war, Ford had already undertaken work with aircraft engines, bombers, amphibians, reconnaissance cars, and M-7 directors.

The defense program even touched the Ford family. On March 4, 1941, the Detroit draft board made an appointment for Henry II, and it was said he would not ask for deferment. Benson was registered with the Macomb County Board, and was expecting a questionnaire. On April 5 Henry II was put in Class I, the birth of his first daughter on the 3rd not affecting his status, and later in the month he was an ensign at the Great Lakes Naval Training School. Benson, called in May, was rejected because of his defective left eye. "I would have been glad to go," he said, and later, after much difficulty, he was able to do so.

The activity of his plants in the defense program did not alter Henry Ford's attitude toward American participation in the war. On December 3 he called for a federated world, comparing it to the union of American states. "Europe," he said, "is finding that she cannot live unfederated today." At the same time he reiterated his love for peace. "I still hate war as I always have," he declared. Asked how he reconciled this attitude with the increasing defense production of Ford factories, he answered: "It's the law of the land, isn't it?" [36] Four days later came the event which swept the United States from a policy of assistance to the Allies into the role of active belligerent.

# VIII

## ARSENAL OF DEMOCRACY

By December 7, 1941, the military resources of the United States were immensely greater than they had been two years earlier. From a force of 188,535 the Army had grown to 1,450,998 men, and for the first time in American history a peacetime draft was operative. The Navy, also enlarging, would reach a personnel of 640,000 as 1942 advanced. Though the blow at Pearl Harbor resulted in heavy losses, new construction of ships and aircraft promised a dynamic future. Most important of all, the industrial power of the land had been organized for defense. From the Atlantic to the Pacific plants were manufacturing guns, tanks, and aircraft, each a nucleus of strength which could expand, or aid in the fathering of new factories.

In his radio address of December 9, President Roosevelt emphasized the vital role of production, which must serve both the United States and its Allies. He called for a 7-day week in every industry, the enlargement of existing plants, and the building of new ones. "The United States can accept no result save victory, final and complete." [1]

While numerous industries were engaged in defense production, the automotive group already held a preëminent place. General Motors, Ford, Chrysler, Packard, Willys and others were producing aircraft engines, shells, tanks, and military vehicles. More important, they were the high priests of production, whose knowledge of factory layout, machine tools, and the moving assembly line insured the quantity output that held the promise of victory.

"In the five weeks before Pearl Harbor," a monthly bulletin published by the industry stated in March 1942, "the War Department alone contracted for $3,500,000,000 worth of military supplies from automobile plants." In July the same periodical pointed out that 981 automotive plants in 31 states were active in the war program.

197

Just after Pearl Harbor the Ford Motor Company received exhortations from Washington to increase the production for which it had contracted. Edsel Ford telegraphed in reply to an appeal from Jesse H. Jones, Federal Loan Administrator: "We fully realize gravity of situation and importance of earliest completion and operation of our aircraft motor and bomber plants." On the 13th the *New York Times* reported that the company had adopted a 24-hour, 7-day week. "A full shift was working tonight at the Pratt & Whitney aircraft factory . . . and construction crews were operating under floodlights at the bomber plant." Stated Edsel: "We have taken this action in response to the Government's declaration of an all-out effort in the war." [2]

Government officials also began to schedule higher quotas for items then on order. The Army Air Forces wanted to get 100 aircraft motors in December, 250 in January, and 450 in March, and to step up production by an extra 100 each succeeding month. (Sorensen demurred because of the Army's failure to deliver crucial machine tools.) The Ordnance Department wished to raise the output of M-7 antiaircraft directors to 50 by July 1942 and a total of 1021 by January 1, 1943. Quotas for tank engines and the new M-4 tanks were both sharply raised. [3]

At the same time Government agents began to negotiate for entirely new equipment. On December 19, 1941, the National Defense Research Committee brought to Dearborn drawings for an amphibian jeep which they hoped Ford would perfect and produce. The company agreed, and in sixty days completed a three-man model which operated on land or water, passing crucial tests on the Huron River near Ypsilanti. Federal officials were delighted. Vannevar Bush, Director of the Committee, termed the feat "an excellent piece of engineering . . . carried out in a prompt and effective manner." In June 1942 Ford signed a contract for 5000 vehicles.

Similarly, the company was soon to undertake the production of a supercharger for aircraft engines, a smelter to make magnesium, an aluminum foundry to produce castings for aircraft motors and the Ford tank engine, a new steel mill for tank body castings, the manufacture of the universal carrier for the British, and the production of gliders for the Air Force.

Meanwhile, the quota of cars for civilian use had been steadily curtailed, and early in January the War Production Board cleared the way for the total conversion of the automobile industry to war by halting all light truck and passenger car production at the end of that month. On February 10 the Ford Motor Company turned out its last private car. "The same assembly line that made Ford automobiles is now to be used for jeeps and staff cars for Army officers," reported the press.

Other companies were now manufacturing for war. Like the millions of men and women then leaving school, office, and factory to don uniforms, the officials and employees of the industry were changing their occupations and attitudes. They would fashion new products, some in fantastically strange plants. Their purposes, skills, and work forces would alter, and for almost four years a new civilian car would be as extinct for them and the American public as the passenger pigeon or the unicorn.[4]

### 2.

While all Ford activities had centered on the manufacture of automobiles, trucks, and tractors, the company could command an unusual range of materials, plants, and skills. Its coal and iron mines, tracts of standing timber, sawmills, the Ford Fleet, the steel and glass complex at the Rouge—these together offered a great diversity of resources. The three main plants at the Rouge, in Detroit (Lincoln), and Highland Park were supplemented by 34 Ford branches and 29 village industries scattered across the country. Sixteen of the branches were assembly units, 18 service parts distributors. Altogether the company controlled 23,341,000 square feet of floor space, and tapped numerous reservoirs of labor. The 123,477 employes of January 1942 could be greatly increased and in November 1943 actually numbered 203,398, although only 15 of the branches were to be Ford-operated. (The government would buy or lease most of the remainder for war work.) Three old plants not included in the 34 branches would be rented to aircraft manufacturers. The Ford tool and die shop, one of the largest and best in existence, represented an investment of $14,000,000, was admirably organized and manned, and commanded a large assortment of precision tools.[5]

The total resources, while less varied than those of General Motors (which had manufactured refrigerators, diesel engines, radios, railroad equipment, and cables as well as trucks and cars) were thus impressive; and equally impressive were the resources in personnel. Most of the Ford employes were self-made high school graduates who had completed their schooling on the job. They were used to attacking new problems and facing severe handicaps. It was second nature to them to appraise a situation, set a goal, and plan its attainment, taking into account materials, processes, tools, and men. This was true of engineers like Sheldrick, Farkas, and Roeder, and of executives like Sorensen, Bricker, and Robinson. All had applied Ford's principle that almost any project could be analyzed and carried through, and that accepted ways were always to be challenged.

Such qualities were valuable in the manufacture of war materials, where every product was new (usually not only to Ford men but to the designers), and a challenge to originality in production methods. "We didn't know too much about it . . . and we had an entirely new approach," said Frank C. Riecks. "Lots of times we would cut corners when somebody else wouldn't even try." Actually they knew a lot. Metallurgy, casting and forging, the role of jigs, fixtures, and machine tools—which they could skilfully adapt, or if necessary invent—were all in their experience. They understood the importance of exact blueprints for precision work. They had learned the infinite possibilities of plant layout, even to the point of remaking the entire interior of a factory. And since their planning always terminated in timed procedures keyed to tools and fixtures, they were usually clamoring from the start for the machinery without which mass production was impossible.[6]

Such was the fact with the Pratt & Whitney aircraft engine, the first large assignment the Ford Motor Company undertook, and one of its most important.

3.

"We have buildings, jigs, and fixtures all timed to meet our machinery requirements," telegraphed Sorensen on December 15, 1940 to Lt. Col. A. B. Johnson in Washington, even while the new engine building was rising within its heated tarpaper shell. "Any machines you hold up on us now means engines are held up. If machinery could come in faster . . . it would mean that tools and fixtures would be adapted earlier which all means earlier engines. Come here and let us show you the plan." Thus in the beginning stages of the project

Sorensen was trying to speed up the delivery of equipment. He knew that elaborate tooling was the essence of the high production he hoped to achieve.

As noted earlier, machine tools were at a premium even in 1940, and early in December 1941 an Office of Production Management representative reported that the plant had only 27.8 per cent of the machinery it required. Sorensen was telegraphing Knudsen: "Machinery requirements on both bomber and Pratt & Whitney engines are the controlling factor for increasing early deliveries. . . . Give us all the help you can." Meanwhile Brig. Gen. George C. Kenny of the Air Forces Material Division was demanding greater production, tool or no tools! Sorensen must have felt that he had been told to lift himself by his bootstraps.[7] In January 1942 the partially equipped factory turned out 287 engines. But the lack of tools was not the only impediment to production. The work force continued to present a difficult problem.

This had three aspects. Although the settlement of the preceding June had established UAW-CIO as the approved bargaining agent in all company shops, provided for the orderly settlement of grievances, and even granted a union check-off, slowdowns and stoppages continued to retard production. Many of the rank and file felt that every complaint required such action; and local union leaders, while not authorizing the practice, tended to support it once it was under way. No less a person than Philip Murray, President of the CIO, lectured 600 Detroit union officials for failing to help enforce "one of the finest labor contracts in the country," urging: "We don't want any slowdowns or stoppages in production. These have got to be stopped." He was applauded, but the strikes continued.

A second difficulty had developed as the local draft boards had taken Ford workers in large numbers for the armed forces. Sorensen protested against this as early as December 1940. Pointing out to Major I. D. Brant, State Advisor on Occupational Deferments, that the company was already teaching 2500 young men (before the formal opening of the aircraft engine school), he stated: "I believe you will understand that when the airplane engine plant is ready for operation, we cannot go out into the street and pick up a lot of mechanics." Brant promised cooperation, and perhaps saved some workers, but from January 1 to October 31, 1942, a total of 9219 Ford employes entered the military services! This made a mockery of the Ford effort to prepare workers in school and shop for their role in production.

The third difficulty with the work force, that of finding sufficient leaders (mostly foremen) and trained operators, was related to the second, but as output goals were constantly raised and the trained employes available were spread thinner, it took on its own special importance.

Nevertheless, constant progress in monthly production was achieved, and by September 12, 1942, the original contract of October 31, 1940, for 4236 engines had been completed. Subsequent contracts were being filled, and by December the plant was delivering 805 engines a month. This compared with the Nash schedule of 700 R-2800's, and Pratt & Whitney's own quota of only 600! Yet despite Ford's protests that it had many other war contracts to meet, the Air Forces pressed the company for a larger output, and set a goal of 3400 a month to be attained by the spring of 1941.[8]

To meet such a schedule, the Rouge aircraft engine plant alone was quite inadequate. The current production would have to be more than tripled. Sorensen at once diverted the production of parts to company plants at Highland Park, Kansas City, St. Paul, Memphis, Hamilton, Ohio, and Green Island, N.Y., and to five village industry plants in Michigan. Ford officials dismantled and shipped more than 2000 machines to these places to speed manufacture. The new contract based on the revised schedule made Ford the largest producer of high-powered aircraft engines in the country.[9]

E. J. Wedge had supervised the early stages of the aircraft engine project, working competently under all handicaps. Now, however, as the undertaking expanded to mammoth proportions, confusion developed, and finally H. J. Robinson, former manager of the Lincoln plant, came in to assist and eventually replace him. The great enterprise needed his magic touch. He set schedules, developed training for foremen, and replaced a large number who had been elevated hastily and did not know "how to make out a time sheet correctly." Before long he had coordinated the complex task and made possible a dramatic rise in production. He too faced great difficulties. The masses of poorly trained workers, all forced under company contract to be union men, proved particularly difficult, and their ignorant unrest culminated on March 14, 1944, in a wildcat strike which threatened to paralyze the entire Rouge operations. They attempted to set up a road block barring entrance to any part of the plant. The company took stern measures to check this disorder, and the UAW officials cooperated. The management penalized 31 employes, and the union, after making its own investigation, wholly approved of the action. The effect upon the workers was good, and there was little more difficulty with them at the aircraft engine plant.[10]

By 1944 Ford led all American engine manufacturers in horsepower shipments, 56,658,000 monthly to Curtiss-Wright's 54,288,000. Moreover, it steadily reduced its man hours per unit. In November 1942 the man hours required to make one engine were 2,330.59; two years later only 1,027.17 hours were required, and by June 1945 only 905.27. Significantly, Curtiss-Wright was using 40,100 employes to produce less than Ford did with 26,100. After V-Day in May 1945 output at the Ford plant fell off, and ceased that August. The grand total produced in the four active years was 57,851 engines. This came to 7.2 per cent of all American aircraft engines made during the war (802,161).[11]

4.

The M-7 anti-aircraft director was in a preparatory stage at the time of Pearl Harbor. Reconversion of buildings at Highland Park was in process. The gathering of a highly skilled work force at a time when skilled mechanics were as rare as machine tools, the establishment of a school, and the planning of an assembly process—these activities marked the project during its first months. Nevertheless, a completed model was delivered on June 16, 1942, and approved. Manufacture was temporarily blocked by delays in the delivery of vital tools, and by confusion resulting from poorly coordinated effort, for 45 to 50 groups had been working on the project, and had become quasi-independent units. However, H. J. Robinson came in, quickly won the authority his predecessor had lacked, and by July 1943 had established order and efficiency, so that 105 directors a month had been produced. A goal of 10 a day was set. General Gordon Wells of Ordnance wrote to express pleasure "at the increasing rate of production and the high standard of quality of the directors, spare parts, and assemblies." [12]

But the entire contract was soon cancelled. The Allies now dominated the air, and defense from enemy planes was less urgent. More important, an electronic type of director had been developed which by radar could locate hostile aircraft in cloudy, foggy, or rainy weather, or at night. Altogether, 802 M-7's and 400 M-5's (a simpler unit of

English design) had been produced. Termination of the project freed Robinson for the aircraft engine program.[13]

American entry into the war had also found the tank program short of the production stage, though preparations were well along. Facilities for manufacture had been developed at Highland Park (314,144 sq. ft.) and the Rouge (189,200 sq. ft.)—an aluminum foundry at the Lincoln plant and an armor plate building at the Rouge (finished July 12, 1942) being vital to the project. Production followed rapidly. On April 25 the first GAA engine was completed, a tank model was ready May 13, tests were successful, and on June 4 the first tank rolled off the assembly line, two months in advance of schedule.

The Ford Motor Company made only 1683 M-4 tanks and 1035 M-10 tank destroyers, a second vehicle which it agreed to produce in the final contract of May 5, 1942. A number of reasons combined to cause a cancellation of its contracts. The government seems to have felt that Fisher Body and Chrysler could adequately manage the supply of medium tanks, and the Ford commitments with respect to both aircraft engines and bombers produced a shortage of workers which seemed to warrant reduction of the overall program in some important respect. Fisher by early 1945 had produced 16,000 tanks and tank destroyers and Chrysler 20,000, indicating their ample capacity. Ford, however, continued to supply two vital elements, armor plate and engines, for the M-4's. All told, it manufactured 26,954 engines for the regular tank-makers,[14] on a model that was a distinctive contribution to the war program, justifying the foresight and persistence of Henry Ford. Because he had developed it at his own expense for a year and a half, Army Ordnance had a superior engine available at a time of critical need early in 1942.

Other vehicles manufactured by Ford for the Army, Navy, and for Great Britain included the universal carrier (13,893), G&T military trucks or reconnaissance cars (77,915), Navy cargo trucks (2219), bomb service trucks (7053), and ordnance cargo trucks (6000). At the company's plant in Chester, Pennsylvania, tanks produced by various manufacturers were processed for shipment overseas. A total of 155,000 units were handled there, and 55,980 at the Richmond, California, plant.

In addition, the company became a major manufacturer of jeeps. Though it had failed to win a sizable order for these vehicles late in 1940, when another opportunity came the bid was closely figured, and its acceptance made Ford a large-scale producer. In addition to facilities at the Rouge, the company utilized others at Dallas and Louisville, each of these plants delivering 95,000 jeeps in a total production of 277,896.[15]

Despite its creative contributions in the form of the amphibian, the tank body, the tank engine, the jeep, and the reconnaissance car, the Ford organization delivered relatively few vehicles to the armed forces. Of 2,665,196 units manufactured for the services, Ford contributed only 387,737. Sheldrick felt that the Army brought the company its headaches, and shunted the big orders for routine production to General Motors and Chrysler. "The feeling was quite prevalent among us that we were getting all the dirty work and dirty jobs." Officials in rival companies had the same feeling about themselves; the armed forces were making the best decisions they could and pleased nobody. Ford, however, did not get the vehicle orders.[16]

### 5.

In addition to its aircraft engine and bomber projects, Ford was to undertake one more assignment in aerial warfare which came rather late and gathered momentum just as the director project was cancelled. This was the manufacture of gliders.

In the first period of American defense activity, 1939–1940, Army officials had regarded the glider, on which the Germans had worked diligently as a carrying unit for parachute troops, as an untested and even frivolous craft. From 1933 on the Army had forbidden its pilots to fly these motorless airplanes!

The Germans had used gliders to some extent in their 1940 European campaign, but first employed them intensively during their invasion of Crete in May 1941. They had adopted the glider train (a series of gliders towed by a motored airplane) from the Russians. Their assault on British positions in Crete was marked by the use of 15,000 troops, carried in gliders which were cut loose from planes near the point of attack to make their own landings. Despite gross errors which sacrificed a considerable percentage of the troops, the operation was successful and demonstrated beyond doubt the effectiveness of the glider in battle.

As a result, the Army Air Corps and Marine Corps acted quickly.

Twelve officers undertook a three-week course in glider flight training at civilian schools, and programs were then developed for both services. At the time of Pearl Harbor the United States still had no troop-carrying gliders, but the Waco Aircraft Company of Troy, Ohio, was designing models for training, and others for carrying men and equipment.[17] Once in the war, the Army studied the glider as potentially important in its overseas activities. On all important fronts American troops would eventually have to invade enemy territory, and every means for achieving concentrated striking power would have to be utilized.

On March 8, 1942, Lieut. Col. P. H. Kenny of the Army Air Forces discussed at Dearborn the possibility of having the Ford Motor Company manufacture a cargo type of glider, carrying either men or armament, in quantity. Ford engineers were sent to Wright Field and the Waco plant to study the possibilities of mass production. The company possessed an excellent site for glider production at Iron Mountain, in the Northern Michigan peninsula, where it had both a sawmill and a large wood-working plant. These had been shut down soon after Pearl Harbor, but a considerable work force, with able officials, was still available. The plant was close to sources of plywood, used in the wings.

Ford engineers received the "go-ahead" signal from the Army on March 27, 1942, and on April 4 procured blueprints for a 15-man glider. A letter of intent for 1000 of these CG-4A units was received April 21, with $19,000,000 as the estimated cost, a sum which did not include the reconversion of the Iron Mountain plant. "The Government was very reluctant to give us any money for conversion," said Walter G. Nelson, in charge of the project, later. "At one time we were about $250,000 in the red as far as the Government was concerned." But eventually this outlay was fully reimbursed.

Acting for Nelson, engineer Thomas Stephenson went to Troy to get a complete set of prints. At the Waco plant he talked with Francis Arcier, the chief engineer, a veteran English aircraft designer who years earlier had helped develop Handley-Paige planes. The glider company had been reluctant to license Ford, and Arcier greeted his visitor sardonically. "I suppose the next thing Mr. Ford will do is to make a man of soybean meal!" But Stephenson won the WACO designer's respect, and he became immensely helpful.

Because of limited space in the Waco drafting rooms, drawings for the glider had been made to half scale. At Dearborn, re-drawn to full scale, they showed innumerable errors—"literally thousands of them," Nelson recalled. If Ford had not insisted on the full-scale blueprints a very faulty product would have resulted. Arcier was appreciative, helped to make corrections, and revised his opinion of Ford proficiency. "He became a very, very firm friend of ours," said Nelson. "He gave the Ford Motor Company full credit for the success of the glider program." [18] Ford engineers at Dearborn planned a production layout and designed numerous jigs and fixtures, one of which cut an original eight hours of work for the gluing and drying process to ten minutes.

The first glider model was built at Dearborn while conversion of the Iron Mountain plant was in process, and on September 16, 1942, was towed into the air at the Ford airport for its test flight. All of the machine except compass, radio, and landing gear (supplied by the government) had been built and assembled at Dearborn. The fuselage was of tubular steel construction, covered by fabric, the wings of plywood, the floor of wood. Fifty feet from nose to tail, the craft had a wingspread of 84 feet, and with full load weighed 6800 pounds. It could carry 15 fully equipped soldiers, or a reconnaissance car, or a 75 mm. howitzer. In the presence of Henry and Edsel Ford and of company and Army officials, the model, with two Army officers at the controls and two Ford engineers as passengers, was cut loose at 8500 feet. It maneuvered for 45 minutes, banking, diving, and climbing. It was promptly accepted.[19]

Ford methods of tooling and assembly were viewed with misgivings by Army experts. "They were extremely critical of the theory of construction," recalled Nelson. "We had several delegations up here [Iron Mountain] trying to find something wrong with our construction." But their doubts concerning the magic fixture that had reduced one eight-hour job to ten minutes were soon quieted: "In all their tests the glue-joints were about 100 per cent perfect; they couldn't find a thing wrong with it. All they could criticize was the theory, and finally they changed their minds even about the theory."

Assembly line production began in December 1942, and by late January Ford had produced 12 gliders. The volume rose to 60 in March, 85 in April, 110 in May, and 130 in June. Additional contracts carried manufacture to August 1945. Tests proved parts of Ford-made craft interchangeable, and finally the Army shipped Ford gliders to other contractors, stipulating that all parts of their products must

be interchangeable with those of Ford models. In June 1943, at government request the company began a 30-man glider which was accepted
on January 6, 1944. Only 100 of these were manufactured.

The glider assumed high tactical importance in American plans and
operations during 1943. "Glider pilots and airborne troops will be in
the forefront of attack," declared General Arnold. "The importance of
these swiftly moving troops cannot be overestimated." His words were
borne out by the use of gliders in North Africa in late 1942. An American airborne division shared in the invasion of Sicily early in 1943,
and at Port Moresby in New Guinea 3600 troops were delivered by air
in twenty-four hours when a Japanese threat demanded reënforce-
ments. Gliders were again used in the invasion of Italy, and played a
vital part in the invasion of Europe on June 6, 1944. Later they appeared in the ground-air invasion of Holland. According to company
officials, Ford gliders were popular at the fronts. Nelson liked to quote
a master sergeant's letter: "Our people, when they see crates marked
'Ford' say, 'Thank God for the Ford glider.'"

Nelson estimated that the time for building a glider was halved by
Ford tooling and assembly, while the cost, set first at $25,000 a unit,
was reduced to about $10,000. The rapid increase in the Ford produc-
tion pace was reflected in the rising proportion of Ford gliders to the
whole. In 1942 the company built less than one per cent of all CG-4A's,
in 1944 36.6 per cent, and in 1945, 50 per cent. Including 30-man
models, the total Ford production amounted to 4,291.

According to Maj. Gen. James M. Gavin, the CG-4A shared with
the British glider, the Horsa, the honors of the most successful motorless craft used in World War II. He found each "amazingly rugged
in view of the landing speed it had" (60 m.p.h. on rough terrain). One
unfortunate feature was a device on which Ford engineers had prided
themselves, a nose that opened for the unloading of reconnaissance
cars or howitzers, for according to Gavin "four out of five gliders
ended up against fences, stone walls, or trees, thus making it almost
impossible to remove the combat cargo." Later designs which provided
tail openings did not reach production until after the war.[20]

6.

Despite the variety of its activities, Ford at war was identified in
the minds of most Americans with the huge Liberator factory planned

at Ypsilanti. The vision of great bombers rolling off the assembly line like motor cars to overwhelm the enemy became an indelible national image. And this promise of American strength seemed to be confirmed as the mammoth factory began operations at Willow Run.

Beyond question the American aircraft industry of 1940 was unprepared to shift from experimental to quantity production. As the historians of the Air Forces point out, it "had continued to operate on a handwork basis. . . . Its resources in 1940 were too limited to have permitted an expansion on the scale required. The additional resources and managerial and engineering talent, and, to a large extent, of machinery and facilities, came chiefly from the giant automobile industry."

But there was a startling difference between possessing great industrial resources and applying them to a wholly new objective. *Mill and Factory* early pointed this out in quashing the glib talk that the automobile industry could produce by merely pressing a button. "Mass production without thorough preparation is and forever will be impossible." The warning was little heeded, but Ford officials, struggling to make their miracle at Willow Run, would later recognize its validity.[21]

Sorensen and Henry Ford led a drive that blended the fervor of a mediaeval crusade with the complete modernity of an industrial experiment never before attempted. Sorensen *knew* he could mass-produce the B-24. As for his chief, a California aircraft executive remarked, "I believe Ford would drop a hundred million dollars to get his bombers out." Yet neither thought the task easy. The long sojourn of hundreds of Ford engineers and production men at San Diego, the thorough breakdown of the plane, the precise blueprinting of parts, and the intensive tooling prescribed by company engineers and executives prove that the task as a whole was regarded with respect approaching awe.

Roscoe Smith, surveying it in December 1941, must have realized that Sorensen's magic factory was a remote if not visionary structure. Access to the uncompleted building at Ypsilanti could be won only over poor roads. The bomber school was still a plan, and would begin at Dearborn on December 29, 1941, with 100 students. A school building at Willow Run? Ground for it would not be broken until the coming January 24. When on January 4, 1942, the nose fuselage was put under construction at the Ford Airport, the main plant at Ypsilanti was not even completely roofed over.

"It was all new," recalled A. M. Wibel, in contact with the project from the start as a high company executive. In addition to the lack of a trained work force, an important factor was the extensive use of aluminum throughout the plane—a metal that Ford personnel had worked with very little. Another was the necessity to break in numerous officials (for those at San Diego had been a mere handful) to direct the almost innumerable aspects of this alien undertaking.

The case of Walter Wagner is illustrative. A tooling expert and able executive, he had studied the Rolls-Royce engine in Europe with American manufacture in view, and had tooled the Ford tank engine. About the end of 1941 he was offered a post in Houston, as plant manager at three times his Ford salary. Sorensen heard of it, called Wagner over to the aircraft engine building, and seized the lapel of his coat.

"Listen," he said, "you belong to us. I've got something for you. I'm going to take you over to the bomber plant and you're going to be a superintendent."

"But, Mr. Sorensen," protested Wagner, "I don't know a thing about airplanes."

"Who the hell does over there?" demanded Sorensen. He turned the bewildered Wagner over to Bricker, long his right-hand man. Bricker had charge of all war work and was advising Smith about Willow Run. "Make him Logan Miller's assistant," the Dane said.

Bricker and Wagner, who were old friends, went out to Willow Run and entered the factory building. It was like an enormous cave with workers and machines scattered about and gaps in the roof. Bricker led the way to a large open space strewn with numerous machine parts.

"I think the first thing we ought to do is to get this thing together and working," he remarked.

"What is it?" asked the dazed Wagner.

"You mean to say you don't know what this thing is?" Bricker demanded with pretended astonishment. "Where have you been?"

"I've been at Lincoln. I told Sorensen I didn't know anything about airplanes."

Bricker grinned. He said: "This is a machine that does all the operations on the center wing. It does twenty-eight operations. And we have got to get it going because it feeds all our lines. We can't make airplanes without it."

The episode flashes a clear light on the confusion at the great plant. If the operation was formidable, so was the chaos of this period when the very roof was incomplete, when tools were being received, fixtures set up, and men learning to know their future gigantic worksite.

Nevertheless, the preparations for production went forward urgently. Construction of the main building, of the flying field, and the first hangar was soon pushed to a conclusion. The airplane school, the administration, the personnel and other buildings were begun. By the middle of January the center wing fixture which Wagner had seen as a mass of scattered parts had been assembled for operation. Although numerous tools were still lacking, parts of the first bomber had been started. The rudder, the center wing leading edge, the outer wing panel and elevator were all in process during February, and on March 31 a limited shipment of parts was dispatched to the Douglas plant at Tulsa.

Even before the great main structure had been completed Smith, Pioch (in charge of tooling), and the plant engineers had made their plans for production. The big factory at Willow Run was L-shaped. The base of the L, 1280 feet in width, housed the die and punch presses, the tool room, machine shop, and several manufacturing activities. Starting thence, the assembly progressed along the much narrower arm of the building for almost 3000 feet and through 15 stations. As the planes advanced, sub-assemblies on either side fed in essential parts. The total of all assemblies, 5460 feet, technically realized Sorensen's "mile-long plant." At Station 8 the 55-foot center wing section was mated with the fuselage. For this operation the fixture Wagner had seen scattered about in pieces was employed. A number of "towers" were used to anchor it, each sunk eighteen feet in concrete to insure complete stability. The fuselage and center wing section were positioned so that each fitted into place at the exact angle required and to the thousandth of an inch. Only one check was required to insure accuracy. The fuselage and center wing were thus united, the rivet holes automatically punched, and other operations conducted to finish the section. Then the landing gear was lowered, and from that point every plane went forward on its own wheels.

Since at this stage the bomber had only the 55-foot width of the center wing section, two lines of "ships" moved along while engines, empennage, and gun turrets were set in place. Then the double line gave way to a single line where outer wing panels, ailerons, flaps, and propellers were added. A floor drive carried the plane forward, and conveyors overhead added various units until the finished B-24 emerged at the eastern end.[22]

Such was the plan. It had great theoretical and many practical advantages over that of Consolidated Aircraft, which established an indoor assembly that became operative in December. Consolidated used a long, narrow building which constricted both manufacturing and assembly operations, and its planes were still to a considerable extent "custom-made." In installing the center wing section it could not employ a floor-based fixture, because the plant's proximity to the sea produced changes of level. It provided cumbersome cradles to hold the units, measuring scales, and sighting by transit, a procedure which required a group of highly skilled workers and much delicate adjustment. The Ford fixture represented a revolutionary change. "With this machine," said Logan Miller, "we reduced a 36-man, 1500-hour job to three men working 26 minutes." Many of the other 1600 machine tools and 7000 jigs which Ford used effected tremendous savings. One point of superiority in Willow Run practice was that all Ford dies combined blanking operations with the making of holes for rivets, and as many as 781 punches were built into one die. Consolidated workmen bored most of these holes by hand.

Ford had superlative equipment for making hard dies, and its officials were completely familiar with jigs and machine tools, many of which were designed by Ford engineers. These engineers were scornful of rubber and soft-metal dies, noting that the soft-metal units quickly became inaccurate, and had to be repaired with loss of time and production. Nevertheless, the Consolidated group regarded the Ford designers as madmen. How long, they asked, would this elaborate tooling take, and what would be its cost? How many bombers could have been built by more conventional methods in the meantime? Again, what would happen when changes in design junked these expensive tools, as would frequently happen? These questions were pertinent, particularly the last, and Ford in the end had to deal with them.[23]

Unfortunately for Roscoe Smith, when he took charge of bomber production he walked into a disruptive struggle for power in the company. His allegiance was to Sorensen. But while Sorensen was in complete charge of constructing the factory, and through Smith, of production, another man handled all personnel and labor relations, and plant security. This was Harry Bennett, who was not inclined to yield any fraction of his powers, but anxious rather to increase them. When he and Rausch ordered the installation of certain equipment, Smith succeeded in having it removed. Thereupon Bennett became an implacable opponent of Smith, at the same time finding numerous points of disagreement with Sorensen. One morning early in May 1942 the three were discussing their differences in Smith's office, with Bricker present. Bennett became angry and squared off as if to attack Sorensen, who started to leave. Smith, fearing violence, stepped between the two as Sorensen went out, and Bennett struck him in the eye, knocking him against the door frame and to the floor. According to Smith, this was the only blow struck; other accounts say he rose, and was knocked down again. Sorensen, ejaculating "Harry, I'm surprised at you," hurried out. Smith never returned to Willow Run.*

Bricker now took over the administration of the plant. (He telephoned Smith that he must leave, and had him returned to his former work with small plants.) No one questioned his ability, but the change was salutary, as both Bricker and Logan Miller got on well enough with Bennett. Furthermore, as Wagner stated later, the widely-experienced Bricker was "more of a commander," who had a way of getting results. "He would delegate responsibility and believe me, it was respected. . . . We always recognized Bricker as a big man." [24]

One of his first problems was the shipment of knocked-down parts first to Douglas, and later to Consolidated. Each of the assembly plants for the aircraft companies was far larger than Consolidated's San Diego factory, measuring about 4000 by 400 feet. It was a question how the precious materials could most safely be transported. After transit by rail was considered and rejected, large trailers were employed for the 950 miles to the Douglas establishment, each 63 feet

* One account of the Bennett-Smith fracas states that Henry Ford was then at Mackinaw, and that both Bennett and Sorensen tried at once to reach him. Bennett alleged that he succeeded, and gave his account. After listening to it Ford is said to have remarked, "Well, Harry, I still think you hit the wrong fellow."

long. Eventually 86 trailers were employed, four being required to transport a complete plane. The journey required four days.[25]

Bricker took over the management of Willow Run on May 19, 1942, although he does not seem to have been designated as official head until some ten months later. By May 25, 1942, nearly 15,500 employes were working there, 1874 of them women. The current schedule adopted in February called for an eventual production of 405 planes a month—100 knockdowns to Consolidated at Fort Worth, 155 to Douglas, and the remainder to be finished at Willow Run. This was of course a future goal, for production could not gather momentum until 1943. The immediate objective had been one complete knockdown and one flyaway to Douglas in May, and not even this was achieved. The first plane in parts did not leave for Tulsa until July 12, and the first flyaway was not delivered to the Army Air Forces until September 10.[26]

The difficulties which impeded production at the plant were not limited to the completion of the buildings and air field, the slow delivery of tools, jigs, and fixtures, the lack of trained men for aircraft work, and the final tooling of the plant. Other problems loomed large: relations with workers, their housing, and their transportation from the Detroit area to the factory. The latter was in a sense an aspect of the labor problem also.

It has already been shown in connection with the aircraft engine plant that Ford had a contract with the UAW, and that all employes at Willow Run were automatically members of the union. However, Bennett and his security force were in charge of personnel, and according to numerous union officials and workers who later testified upon conditions in the bomber factory, were attempting to prevent union control.* The Reuther plan, proposed in December 1940, and revived as a proposed basis for action after Pearl Harbor, had undoubtedly caused some friction. It contemplated the pooling of idle automotive resources for use in aircraft construction under joint control by government, industry, and labor. Knudsen had been cool to it, but various writers and political figures (Dorothy Thompson, Raymond Clapper, Paul V. McNutt, Leon Henderson and others) had favored its consideration. Both the automobile and the aircraft

* One union observer later stated that "my impression was that the Company was always hopeful that the UAW would never really sink its foot in out there."

companies emphatically rejected it, asserting that they could not share the direction of their activities with labor: as C. E. Wilson put it, the "coordinated exchange of facilities and men would be 'socialization.'" Reuther, a professed Socialist, wanted this. However, it was clear by mid-1942 that he had lost his fight, and only a residue of bitterness on the part of labor officials remained.

At the time Bricker took control, the union was operating under a regional director, and employes belonged to Local 600 or Local 849. Eventually, on May 30, 1943, Local 50, called "The Bomber Local," took over all Willow Run employes. A year earlier, the management-union relationship was muddied by the ignorance of thousands of new workers, and by Bennett's devious attitude. He was hiring numerous southerners who, he hoped, would disregard union obligations. The union was trying to bring some order into the chaos. It formed an Educational Department early in 1942, which offered courses in collective bargaining, union history, and so forth, and in June set up a Recreation Department which promoted clubs and classes in the arts. The company was meanwhile operating its airplane school. Sporadic wildcat strikes broke out against various abuses and lack of facilities. The work must have been attended with considerable confusion because of these factors, with the rift between Bennett and Sorensen augmenting it![27] At the same time, the drafting or enlistment of workers was already posing a disruptive threat which would grow in size as time passed.

As for transportation, which became an urgent matter as more and more employes came from the Detroit area, both Michigan Avenue (U.S. Highway 112) and the Ecorse Road offered access to the plant once connecting links were completed. The first was opened on July 26, 1942. However, the vital necessity was an express highway to Detroit. Hanson had gone to Washington while the factory was being built to lay the case before Assistant Secretary of War Robert P. Patterson, and the construction of the road was commenced September 11, 1942, with Patterson speaking at the dedication ceremonies. The artery was completed in the spring of 1943. However, workers who spent from 40 to 50 minutes getting to their jobs often preferred more accessible factories which were also clamoring for employes.[28]

This raised the question of housing for the workers in the Ypsilanti area. Estimates of a work force of 110,000 at peak production were made, and even Sorensen calculated that 90,000 would be required, with 30,000 employed by sub-contractors in other areas. In May 1942 practically no housing had been provided, although some workers had rented rooms in the vicinity, and others were using trailers. "Living space within the radius of ten miles of Willow Run simply does not exist," reported the *New York Times,* and the Detroit Housing Commission and the Federal Housing Authority moved to launch a $35,000,000 project which would provide homes for 75,000! The Ford Motor Company and local government agencies opposed this, and eventually private builders were permitted to supply houses, dormitories, and trailers. By 1943 fairly extensive facilities were available, but throughout 1942 housing remained a momentous problem.[29]

By September 1942 the plant was practically complete. The main building was tooled and ready for volume operation. On the other hand, the work force was still less than 20,000, and composed largely of workers with little or no industrial experience. The Airplane Apprentice School, its building near the great factory completed in June, was teaching thousands of "students." By November 7 it had 3701 enrollments and 19,842 graduates, but while it prepared men and women for a variety of tasks, those it fed into the plant still needed the seasoning of actual work. Meanwhile, only four knockdowns had been sent from Willow Run to Tulsa by October 1, and only eighteen flyaways had emerged from final assembly. By the end of the year production was mounting, with 107 bombers sent south or offered at the factory to the Air Forces; but many of these needed modifications, and the net credit for the year was only 56.[30]

Willow Run was now a busy and exciting scene which seemed to be fulfilling the fabulous promise of its inception. Out of the rural landscape had risen its buildings and airport: the immense main factory of steel, brick and glass, the administrative units, the huge No. 1 hangar (another was to come) with hospital and dormitory, a power house, and the authoritative sweep of the flying field with its more than mile-long concrete runways. Actually it was not the biggest plant built for World War II. In Chicago Chrysler was even then designing a larger one, with 19 buildings and a main factory so huge that "Willow Run could be set down (inside it) . . . with enough room left to lay out twenty baseball diamonds." But this giant complex never caught the public imagination, for Willow Run already had gripped it, and held preëminent place in the pride and hope of the land.

Henry Ford and Sorensen were almost daily visitors at Ypsilanti. "Mr. Ford would be on our tail all the time as to why the stuff didn't come off the assembly line," recalled Wibel. Edsel was frequently there, with other Ford officials who came to observe and plan, and on April 3, 1942, Charles A. Lindbergh had arrived to take up duties which included flight testing and experimentation.*

Already politicians, journalists, high Army officers, and even royalty were coming to gaze in wonder or assess progress: Donald Nelson of the War Production Board; Sir Oliver Littleton, British Minister of Production; W. Averell Harriman of Lend-Lease; King Peter II of Yugoslavia; Captain Randolph Churchill, son of Winston; and Lt. Gen. H. H. Arnold of the Army Air Forces. Franklin D. and Eleanor Roosevelt made a dramatic surprise inspection of the factory on September 18.

Parking lots were filled with workers' cars, women in coveralls mingled with Army inspectors, helmeted flyers hung about the hangars; engineers made their way to their quarters on the mezzanine floor, and union stewards and security police argued about factory conditions. Already half-finished planes moved from station to station, gathering engines, guns, and wings like gigantic champions donning their armor for the battle.[31]

7.

Accomplishment was growing, but not at a rate to warrant exultation. Already there were murmurs of doubt. In mid-November 1942, the *New York Times,* reporting Charles E. Wilson's induction to the War Production Board to supervise aircraft manufacture, remarked: "One of Mr. Wilson's chief headaches was expected to be the Ford

---

* Lindbergh's chief duty was to observe the operation of the factory and make suggestions for improvement. However, he did experimental flying, both with B-24's and the P-47. Emile Zoerlein tried to lift the plane's ceiling of 32,000 feet, and Lindbergh did much of the test flying. By substituting a plastic distributor head for the hard rubber head, which had disintegrated at high altitudes, Zoerlein raised the ceiling to 40,000 feet. Lindbergh also taught Bennett how to fly, and remembered that while the antagonism between Bennett and Sorensen was obvious, in Henry Ford's presence both were like members of a happy family. While Lindbergh was at Willow Run, Ford suggested building a big four-engined transport, and wanted the flyer to take charge of the project. Lindbergh suggested a small plane to parallel the Model T. Ford was not interested. It later developed that he wanted the big plane for flights by himself and Lindbergh, and gave up the idea when Lindbergh showed no interest. The flyer was made aware of Ford's willingness to attempt the impossible when Sorensen called him by telephone and spoke of Henry Kaiser's plans for a huge flying boat. "Why couldn't we build one?" he demanded. "Why couldn't we build a flying boat with a thousand-foot wing span?" Lindbergh suggested starting with one of 500 feet. "You fellows are always blocking me, always blocking me," Sorensen growled, and hung up.

bomber plant at Willow Run which has not been turning out bombers or even—in the desired quantities—the parts which it was supposed to supply for aircraft companies." It suggested a cause for the failure in excessive concern with the assembly line methods. British aircraft experts were cited: "it is impossible wholly to have mass production of combat planes because of the rapid improvement of design." The Senate investigating committee under Harry S. Truman made its second visit, and independently Senator M. C. Wallgren of Washington remarked on February 15: "Apparently there has been practically no production to amount to anything." A sardonic punster caught the mood of anxiety by re-naming the plant "Will It Run?"

Actually, output was mounting. In January 1943, 31 bombers were completed; in February, 75; in March, 104; and April would turn out 148. To be sure, this was far short of the 405 planes a month the Army had set as a goal in 1942, and the new proposal of February 26, 1943, for 535. Still, it was progressive accomplishment, and we know now that President Roosevelt, who had investigated the Willow Run situation, was satisfied as to the production that might be expected.[32]

The chief cause of slowness was lack of manpower. The work force was growing; it stood above 30,000 in January, and would mount to 42,331 in June, including 10,000 women (this was to be the high figure). But the force was less than it seemed. As early as December 1942 the *Times* reported: "The Ford Motor Company's bomber plant at Willow Run is hiring all the suitable men who apply, but is losing more than it hires." Seven months later Sorensen reported to Wilson that for July 1943 he had hired 3078 workers, but that 3614 had quit. They were leaving because of poor housing, or the long rides to and from Detroit, or the demand of the armed forces for recruits.

Enlistments and drafting had indeed been disruptive. By April 1944 some 8000 Willow Run employes had been lost to the services. The drafting of skilled workers was particularly harmful. Sorensen wrote Donald Nelson in March 1943: "We have had as many as seven . . . specialists drawn out of the most important departments in the assembly in one day, and without a moment's notice to us." In addition, on any given day absentees represented about 15 per cent of the workers. For example, in June 1943, in a work force of 42,331, an average of 6334 were absent. Though it was now clear that the plant would need less than 70,000 for volume operation, manpower during the first nine months of 1943 represented a desperate problem.[33]

An important decision was made early in March. "If enough workers could not be brought to the job," remarked a commentator, "the job would be taken to the workers." Happily, at certain Ford plants in the Detroit area and elsewhere, labor was available. The first step was taken on March 12, when tools and fixtures for the outboard fuel accessory doors were transferred from Willow Run to the branch plant at Hamilton, Ohio. Finished parts from this new work site were received at the main factory a month later. Satisfied with this experiment, Bricker made another: on April 17 he moved fixtures for the engine dress-up from Ypsilanti to the Lincoln plant in Detroit, which was about to suspend tank manufacture. On May 12 he put the stabilization assembly job into the former Rouge tire plant (tire-making equipment had been shipped to Russia). This operation alone freed 1100 Willow Run workers for other jobs. Further decentralization saw the production of nose side-panels and fuselage tail cones shifted to Highland Park, and nose rings and air ducts to Lincoln. Outside contractors were also invited to bid, and as a result fixtures for the pilots' glazed enclosure were sent on April 14 to the Pittsburgh Plate Glass Company of Capital City, Missouri. Numerous other firms were awarded subcontracts.[34]

For a time these measures were not clearly reflected in total production, although by June 1943 this reached 190 planes a month, and by August, 231. The Army, Consolidated, and Douglas all wanted higher output. Sorensen's restiveness under their importunities was increased by a letter from Hugh Fulton, counsel for the Senate's Special Committee Investigating the National Defense Program (Truman Committee), which he received on July 9 with an advance copy of the Committee's forthcoming report. This spoke sharply of Willow Run. After praising Consolidated, Douglas, Boeing, and Vega, it noted the slowness of Ford. "The production line was set up similar to an automobile assembly line," ran one passage, "despite the warnings of experienced airmen. This was probably a mistake." It asserted that "the Ford Motor Company did not take full advantage of the opportunities to send workmen as distinct from engineers to the Consolidated plant at San Diego." It also stated that until recent months Ford "had not produced at Willow Run a plane which was capable of use at the front," and that the Army had permitted "freezing" the design to get out such bombers as had been completed. It concluded with a grudging admission that the company was now producing "in substantial numbers."

Sorensen, asked to comment, made a singularly docile reply. He stressed only the successive raises in the production schedule. Actually, many criticisms of Ford were false or distorted. All types of experts had been sent to San Diego. Aircraft men, who had shuddered at the idea of a moving assembly line, were violently prejudiced. No evidence whatever exists that Ford bombers could not have been used for combat. All bombers were subject to modification for front-line use, and eventually the Air Forces set up 28 centers for this special work. Thus far "freezing" had affected only small blocks of planes, and in the end it applied to all aircraft producers.[35]

Despite a rising output, August seems to have marked a psychological "low" for Bricker and Sorensen. Undoubtedly the disruptive struggle for power in the company was felt at Willow Run. Restlessness among the workers,* and a sense of confusion and lack of morale on their part, grew out of the vastness of the entire task, and their sense of the slightness of their own contribution. Soon workers were taken on trips through the entire factory, got a sense of the complete job, and enjoyed a feeling of elation. As yet, however, many were bewildered.

On August 11 a formidable group assembled at Willow Run to confer on schedules. It included Knudsen, now a lieutenant general, Brig. Gen. Charles E. Branshaw of the AAF Materiel Center at Wright Field, several colonels and majors assigned to procurement, and Sorensen, Bennett, Bricker, and Logan Miller.

Knudsen asked if the plant could produce 405 flyaways and 100 knockdowns a month by December. Bricker replied that for such an output 62,000 workers would be needed, but suggested that 285 flyaways and 100 knockdowns were possible. This met the W-5 schedule, while Knudsen's query looked to the later 8-L. Sorensen pointed out that Ford had numerous war contracts, and that scheduled production should represent "potential reality rather than a challenge to the contractor." The government had kept raising the schedule, but had been

---

* It will be recalled that this was a period of high employment at Willow Run, and also of high absenteeism and departures. A foreman's wildcat strike on June 20, 1943, while lasting only a day, emphasized the dissatisfaction of the workers. They sensed the lack of accomplishment which had earlier been a fact, and this erupted on Oct. 9 in accusations by two union leaders that the record at the plant was "the outstanding failure of the war." By that time production was zooming, and the company's counteraccusation that the charges were "verbal sabotage" had point. Ford officials were trying to make living conditions at Willow Run better, setting up a store and a recreation center for residents. Probably some of Bricker's pessimism stemmed from the fact that with Rausch, Bennett's henchman, in charge of production at the Rouge, he seemed often to meet delays when requests wre made for men or materials.

consistently slow to provide the facilities needed for greater production. He might have added that changes had always been difficult because it was practically impossible to get complete blueprints for them from Consolidated. In view of the difficulties of assembling and maintaining a work force, finally the decision was taken to base the schedule on existing resources. At the same time the Army agreed to help the company find additional subcontractors.

Actually, the growing experience of Ford workers and the extension of subcontracting were beginning to count. Outside plants working on bomber parts were now employing upwards of 22,000 workers, and together with Willow Run, engaged at peak 68,933 persons. As the main factory adjusted to the swelling stream of materials from the outside, feeding them smoothly into moving assembly, production shot upward. It reached 254 a month in September, 308 in October, and 365 at the end of 1943.[36]

Willow Run now entered upon its period of glory. The work force, smaller but immensely more efficient, responded to improved direction. The mile and more of machines performed the former work of hours in minutes. Bricker finally won the adoption of a sensible block system by which at first 50, then 100, and finally 400 bombers were produced before any changes in design could be made. This, in his words, was "one of the most essential controlling factors in smooth and fast production." Labor difficulties subsided with better plant conditions, and better roads, buses, and housing. Both the Air Forces and Ford had inspectors, who, as Richard Kroll later recalled, "got on like cats and dogs." But he standardized procedure so that no alteration was possible except by decision of competent authorities, and general harmony reigned.

The plant was exciting, dynamic, and immensely human. The great march of the assembly line with its formidable machines was impressive even to those who, like Lindbergh, saw it almost daily. It dazed or awed the visitors who continued to pour through: judges, officers of the Free French, OPM officials, Edsel Ford, Irving Berlin the song-writer, Eddie Rickenbacker. "Try a little harder," Rickenbacker told the employees. "Do a little more."

They were a fantastic but impressive crew, these workers. Captained by such seasoned Ford officials as Bricker, Logan Miller, Wagner, Kroll, B. M. Laney, and Charles H. Patterson, they included Negroes, at least two American Indians, men past seventy, and thousands of women. Florence Pang, a Chinese riveter, needed only 8 points to gain her M.A. at the University of Michigan. F. T. Hinkley, in charge of a crew at 77, discovered and remedied defects in the nose-wheel door. Bernice Krome, who found the riveting of bomb door track assemblies difficult, as she had to adjust the squeeze rivet with her fingers, and sometimes injured them, dreamed that she used a mirror to locate the bottom points of contact for the compressor. She tried it next day, it worked, and mirrors and a pilot light were quickly installed on riveting machines.

One day a high-ranking British general, spangled with medals, was being taken through the plant. When he came to the fuselage section in a sub-assembly he mounted a pair of steps, and found himself looking down on a trim blonde in tight-fitting blue slacks who was completing electric installations on the floor of the unit. She glanced up and saw him. "Hello, honey," she said. The general stared at her stiffly. Inspecting him further, she inquired, "Where didya get them ribbons?"

There were continuous conferences ("He may be a liar, but he's a damn good engineer!"), disputes, settlements, and endless activity in the engineering section where changes were being mapped. Outside, planes were making trial flights, the great parking lots were filling and emptying, buses bound for Detroit or coming in were disgorging or ingesting passengers. In Hangar No. 1 the plant hospital was busy with the injured, the railroads brought in trainloads of materials, and the great trailers took off with loads for Tulsa or Fort Worth.[37]

As his oldtime boasts began to come true, Sorensen recovered his confidence. When on September 25, 1943, General Branshaw had asked him about "all possible means for improving your past record," the Dane telegraphed a truculent reply. He noted that Knudsen and Wilson had just visited Willow Run and commended its performance. "Your telegram today is proof that you are not capable of judging what this plant can do. The only knowledge you possess is what some clerk passes on to you. If the matter of understanding was of real import you would be here instead of sending telegrams."

Sorensen now seized the initiative and sent General Arnold a schedule which promised 400 planes in December and 500 the following May. Startled, Arnold in effect asked the Dane to calm himself. "We feel that your proposed schedule is very optimistic and out of line with our experience to date."

But Willow Run now completely confounded all doubters. Production soared. The plant consistently exceeded schedule, and a series of congratulatory telegrams reflected the elation of government officials with its performance. On March 3, 1944, C. E. Wilson of the Aircraft Production Board telegraphed: "The APB notes with pride that our confidence in your company's ability to maintain a fine sustained production record has again been proven. . . . our sincerest congratulations."

From that time forward Willow Run was the leading producer of heavy bombers, and eventually had to cut down its production. Sorensen states that its potential was then 650 planes a month, or almost 8000 a year. In its final months, the plant was retooling for the manufacture of the B-24N, a single-tailed bomber which incorporated numerous changes in design. In the spring of 1945 it received the Army-Navy "E" for superior performance.[38]

Ford never established full harmony with Consolidated, which as long as possible, sought to hold its position as prime contractor, with the right to "distribute design information . . . and advise the Air Corps in regard to the effect on deliveries." It tried to forbid the manufacture of flyaways by Ford, and to keep Ford manufacturing parts for Consolidated and Douglas. In April 1943 it insisted strongly on its right to initiate all changes. This attitude was steadily resisted by Ford, which of course won the right to make complete planes. Consolidated also showed a disinclination to furnish detailed drawings and blueprints for changes, since it still depended on mechanics in the shop to complete these. Ford, needing exact guides for its less skilled workers, continuously protested this practice. Even had it commanded trained aircraft experts, there was of course no assurance that they would complete a new detail in the same way as the Consolidated group. Certain parts of the plane would then not be interchangeable.

In a three-page memorandum to the commanding AAF general at Wright Field, Sorensen on April 29, 1943, pointed out that drawings for changes were often not available and almost never complete. The effort to get them was very wasteful. Yet when Ford was finally forced to make its own specifications, there was a howl from Consolidated, and often from AAF headquarters. "Since the Willow Run Plant is to become the major producer of B-24E airplanes," he argued, "with a capacity of . . . more than twice Consolidated-Vultee, and is already tooled for this high production, it seems that more engineering authority should be delegated to this plant." He proposed that changes be made with the approval of the local AAF engineering officer, Consolidated's own resident engineer at Willow Run, and Ford engineers, but only in cases where Consolidated drawings were not available. The difficulty continued, but Ford apparently won the right to make its own final drawings in emergencies.[39]

By 1944, Ford was making 48.5 per cent of all the B-24's produced, and in 1945, 70 per cent. The total, including knockdowns, was 8685. Its employes produced 80 pounds per month per person of aircraft material as against 60 for the industry. The quality of its product was high. As early as December 1942 Carl A. Brant, AAF representative previously assigned to both Consolidated and Douglas plants, testified that "in many departments the quality of workmanship now exceeds that of Consolidated in San Diego." With further experience, the level of proficiency rose.[40]

What should be said of the total Willow Run performance? Unquestionably in late 1942 both Sorensen and Henry Ford recognized that the plant had fulfilled neither their nor the public's expectations. It was said then that the daring plan for moving assembly production was a mistake. But what was the alternative? There was only one—that Ford, while improving plant layout and introducing some tools and fixtures, should in general have followed aircraft practice indicated by Consolidated. Would this course have increased production in 1942 when more bombers were badly needed? And if so, how much?

The question cannot be answered simply. Those who were ready to give an affirmative reply in 1943 apparently forgot that Ford had no work force experienced in aircraft construction such as Douglas, Consolidated, and North American all commanded. The size of the project was fixed by the Army; nothing would have been saved in buildings, airports, housing, or roads. Tools would have been somewhat more easily procured, but Ford knew the type of tools it used and made many of them, and if it had used others, the workers would have needed far more intensive training. Even North American, profiting by Ford help, took ten and a half months to produce its first bomber, and it had seasoned aircraft workers. (Ford produced a knockdown in fifteen months from the time ground was broken at Willow Run.) Ford's internal politics and labor troubles were perhaps as much a cause of delay as its production plan. A limited production might have been achieved in the fall of 1942, with perhaps 100 planes instead of 56. Lindbergh believed that by using more conventional methods Ford could have lifted its early production, and Roscoe Smith felt that use of more rubber dies would have been cheaper and conducive to a quicker start.*

However, the moving assembly line was something that Ford engineers and production men understood. It could be manned with quickly trained workers. It was more accurate. What may have been lost in 1942 was rapidly made up in the ensuing months. The final performance speaks for itself; there was nothing to compare with it. The real villains at Willow Run were the size of the establishment (dictated by Army), the delay in the delivery of tools and fixtures, the isolation of the site with its twin problems of housing and transportation, the shortage of workers (partly the fault of local draft boards), friction with labor, and the struggle for power in the Ford company. Given the tools and dependable even if ignorant workers, Willow Run could have achieved volume months sooner.

Perhaps a fair summary of the entire undertaking is that of the authors of *The Army Air Forces in World War II*:

The Ford venture at Willow Run was unique in its application of automotive mass production methods of aircraft assembly on a scale far beyond anything yet attempted. For a variety of reasons, many of them beyond its control, the company encountered great difficulties in adapting the B-24 to mass production, and perhaps the strongest criticism of its efforts is the length of time it required to reach mass production. At one time, in September 1943, the Materiel Command . . . seriously suggested that the government take over the management of the plant. Although this was found to be inadvisable, the War Department applied strong pressure which apparently had salutary results.

Ford made a notable contribution to aircraft production, delivering a total

---

* Production figures show that Consolidated at both San Diego and Fort Worth produced 1140 planes in 1942. Since its production was already more than 300 a year, and its facilities were greatly expanded, and since Ford could not have achieved any production before July, the 514 planes it might have produced had its workmen been trained, must be reduced very greatly because they were not trained. The figure of 100 seems about as much as could have been expected.

of 6,791 B-24's between September 1942 and June 1945 . . . (and) 1,893
'Knockdown' units . . . Ford reached a peak production of 428 B-24's in
August 1944, produced 92,568,000 pounds of airframes in 1944, the largest
total produced by any single plant in the country. . . . Although some aircraft manufacturers questioned whether the same results could not have been
accomplished in less time and at smaller cost, it seems clear that the Ford
experiment was ultimately successful.[41]

## 8.

Ford war production, while varied and great in volume, did not
equal that of a number of other corporations. The War Production
Board in 1945 noted that among the hundred principal organizations
contributing to the armed forces as measured in expansion of facilities,
E. I. Du Pont de Nemours & Co. led all others with an expenditure of
$915,985,000 (of which $845,570,000 was publicly financed), while General Motors was a close second with $911,704,000 in war plants ($809,-
926,000 publicly financed). Ford ranked eighth, with $371,657,000 ex-
pended ($355,473,000 advanced by the government), and Chrysler
stood ninth with an outlay of $313,293,000 ($304,238,000 of which were
federal funds). These figures fix the volume of Ford accomplishment
in the national activity.

The totals were impressive: 8685 Liberator bombers, 57,851 aircraft
engines, 277,896 jeeps, 93,217 military trucks, 26,954 tank engines, 4,291
gliders, 2718 tanks and tank destroyers, 13,000 amphibians, 12,500 armored cars, 13,893 Universal Carriers, 2400 jet bomb engines, 87,000
aircraft generators, 53,000 superchargers, 1202 anti-aircraft directors,
magnesium and aluminum castings, and gun mounts. Though Ford
made no ammunition, no guns, and relatively few motor vehicles, it
led in the manufacture of high-power aircraft engines and large bombers. It was also the leading manufacturer of gliders, and supplied engines of its own design for the medium tanks made by Chrysler and
General Motors. It contributed the final body design of the jeep, assisted in re-designing the medium tank, and designed an amphibian
and a reconnaissance car.

General Motors and Chrysler also manufactured a great variety of
war material. They too contributed greatly to design and methods of
manufacture. Chrysler produced tanks, antitank guns, anti-aircraft
guns, aircraft assemblies, aircraft engines, trucks, ammunition, and

other materials. General Motors turned out carbines, machine guns, 90 and 105 mm. cannon, aircraft engines, tanks (both medium and light), tank destroyers, shells, trucks, landing craft parts, P-75's, marine engines, bomb sights, propellers, superchargers, armored cars, and so forth. Other automobile firms like Packard, Willys, Nash, and Studebaker made important contributions. The part played by the automotive industry in the war was vital.[42]

Considering the internal condition of the Ford Motor Company at the time that the United States entered the war, its accomplishments were particularly notable. The boldness and originality of Henry Ford, and specifically of officials like Sorensen, Bricker, H. J. Robinson, Edsel Ford, A. M. Wibel, Sheldrick, Roscoe Smith, Van Ranst, and Logan Miller gave an organization that was already eaten with dissension a sudden new efflorescence. A number of these men left in 1943 and 1944, and the company from which they were thrust was then to stagger in confusion. Their participation in the war was not unlike the last full charge of a renowned regiment that never again would assert itself in so triumphant a manner.

# IX

## POWER IS THE PRIZE

"FOR months," remarked a news magazine early in 1944, "the world-straddling empire of Henry Ford has quivered and groaned like a leviathan with acute indigestion." A more accurate metaphor might have been drawn from Gibbon's pages on Byzantine history. The empire had shaken for years because its aging sultan, refusing to bestow his sceptre on his son, had let his chief vizier and the head of his janissaries or palace police contend for it. *Time* referred to the struggle for power within the Ford Motor Company between the tough big manager, Charles Sorensen, and the tough little service chief, Harry Bennett, who to be sure occupied different spheres.[1] Their rivalry became more pronounced with every passing year, for time itself was a factor. Henry Ford was nearing eighty when the United States entered the Second World War. A few weeks after Pearl Harbor, Edsel had an operation for stomach ulcers, and while still very active in the company his health was dubious. With the question of the succession unsettled, and with Henry's strength precarious, a vacuum was developing in the center of authority, and no man knew how it would be filled.

Inevitably, an atmosphere of uncertainty, intrigue and apprehension enveloped the company. Everyone knew that Sorensen's service ran back to the third year of the corporation and the bright early days when James Couzens was financial chief and Walter Flanders production manager. He was later to declare that in Ford history the years 1925–1944 were "the Sorensen period," and during most of that period he was indeed a dominant and domineering figure.[2] Bennett, as we have seen, had recently emerged to challenge his position. Both had risen rapidly because, as both assert, they caught Ford's ideas instantly and obeyed him implicitly. Sorensen professed respect and liking for Edsel, but if Bennett ever respected anybody but Henry he failed to make it clear. Both knew that, although Edsel was widely admired as one of the finest leaders in American industry, his father had an unshakable conviction that he lacked the steel needed to drive the company forward against competition, labor, and government restrictions. Sorensen later wrote that, as Henry failed, he himself wanted the power of a regent, but only to conserve the vast Ford property for Edsel's heirs. However that may be, Bennett wanted power to keep it, wield it, and enjoy it.

Most contributors to the legend of Henry Ford have found it convenient to assign Sorensen most of the blame for the rough management of labor before the 1941 surrender to the CIO, and Bennett the blame for the company's dissensions and gangster atmosphere. Sorensen's hostility to unions was explicit in words and acts, and one reason why he never negotiated labor problems was simply that he had no taste for negotiation. To him union leadership was "a high-pressure group, surrounded by smart lawyers," and its claims that an all-union shop would bring greater efficiency were an impudent imposture. He was an aggressive driver, whose tyrannies in handling workmen won him general dislike as "Cast-Iron Charlie." It could be said, however, that he was as bluntly direct as a pile-driver. Bennett, with equal harshness and a readiness to use violence which earned him the hatred of thousands, had less grasp—for nobody ever doubted Sorensen's abilities —but more subtlety. He was a figure that Machiavelli would have appreciated. Brassy, companionable, self-assertive, he remained at bottom coldly cynical and reticent, with depths in his personality which he kept veiled. Nobody was ever quite certain that he might not suddenly drop his friendly mien, uncoil, and strike. He carried about him an aura of secrecy, darkness, and mystery; performing functions that were often vague and unpredictable, and using methods equally undefined and arbitrary, he stalked the Rouge horizon like a malign satrap.

Inevitably, as the company in the 1930s drifted toward third place behind General Motors and Chrysler, and lost the reputation for benevolence which Henry Ford had given it in the era of the five-dollar-day, people cast about for a simple explanation. They decided that the malevolent influence of a few men, and especially Bennett, was responsible. We have seen that the struggle for a place of power near Henry's throne involved most of the high executives, and as one by one various men fell before Bennett, they also attributed the company's troubles to "the little fella" in the tightly guarded basement office.[3]

This simplification of a complex set of forces satisfied the desire of people to find a villain in the plot, giving them a handy "devil theory" of Ford decline. But it ignored the fact that from 1919 up to the present time the company had known only one master, Henry Ford. Moreover, it overlooked the unusual set of circumstances which from the late 1930s permitted Bennett to reach for power.

Foremost among them was the failure to create a modern corporate system of administration which could guide the company expertly through style changes, the labor problems of the Depression, the growth of government controls, and the Second World War. No man had done more than Henry Ford to concentrate industrial power and accelerate production. Yet no leader in manufacturing had clung more stubbornly to an antiquated administrative system totally unequal to the demands of the new era. The family business under one-man domination, typical of the era before 1860, had become old-fashioned with the rise of great modern corporations. The most successful industrialists were men who, like Rockefeller and Carnegie, took partners of brains and force comparable with their own, and adopted every improved managerial device.

The contrast between the Ford Motor Company and General Motors was eloquent. In General Motors, Alfred P. Sloan, Jr., though the principal single figure from the 1920s, for fourteen years president and beginning 1937 chairman of the board, was never an autocrat. Ownership rested with a large body of stockholders; the best executives procurable were put in charge of the various divisions and given ample authority; scores of technological and business experts were hired; and from 1937 on production managers, taking their cue from Sloan and Knudsen, treated labor with some respect. But Henry Ford insisted on the personal authority of a czar.

Years earlier he had distrusted independent-minded executives like Norval Hawkins and Ernest Kanzler, and got rid of them abruptly.* He had come before 1920 to feel unhappy with men who thought primarily of the company's social values and its responsibilities to the community and workers: men like Samuel S. Marquis of the sociological department, Clarence W. Avery, a key figure in devising mass-production techniques, and, later, Edsel Ford himself. He had always disliked

---

* The able Kanzler he disliked not only for his independent and progressive ideas, but for his influence as brother-in-law and close friend of Edsel; I. A. Capizzi, legal counsel, asserts that he "detested" Kanzler.

university men and experts of every category. Organization, form-keeping, and the steady pooling of brains and experience were all repugnant to him. Every decision had to be made by Henry Ford himself, or subject to his approval or veto: the idea that a managerial group might assume large responsibilities and fix company policy through regular organization channels was alien to his temperament.

Ford was constitutionally so unable to relinquish or delegate authority that even when he gave the presidency to Edsel for the long period 1919–1943 he in no way really surrendered the sceptre. As long as he remained vigorous, showing flashes of intuitive genius, he could keep his archaic administrative mechanism creakily effective. But as he reached seventy-five his first stroke portended a clear physical and mental decline, it was followed three years later by a second and more serious one, and later still, in 1943, as Bennett tells us, he "began going downhill" rather sharply. Hope of continuing vigor vanished. Instead, another kind of hope arose in the mind of Sorensen, and above all, in that of Bennett.[4]

Coupled with Henry Ford's refusal to relinquish authority even as his health deteriorated was a noticeable hardening of his temper. Once he had been the eager idealist of the Peace Ship and Sociological Department, anxious to apply his power and prestige to the enlargement of economic opportunity and the improvement of living conditions in a new mass-production society. By the later 1930s, however, he regarded a similar idealism in the conscientious, artistic-minded Edsel as weakness. His sympathy with Liberty League opponents of the reforms of the New Deal, his adamant resistance to the unions 1937–1941, and his refusal to listen to executives anxious to tell him of abuses in his plants, indicate how largely he had abandoned his former values. He became increasingly cynical and intolerant. The Peace Ship failure, the ridicule he met in the Chicago *Tribune* trial, the impugning of his motives in his well-meant Muscle Shoals venture—these early experiences had helped to undermine his faith in others' judgments and throw him back on his own instinctive decisions. Absolute power, gained with complete ownership of the Ford stock in 1919, had promoted his dogmatic isolation, and increasing age set a final seal upon it.

In *My Life and Work* he had written that "a great business is really too big to be human," and now he was illustrating the fact. And in time he began to entertain suspicions of some insidious conspiracy against him. He became convinced that malign forces—Wall Street, international Jewry, Communists, Labor plotters, wild-eyed Washington bureaucrats—were trying to "take over our plant." At first he offered such theories only as tentative "views," quick statements that flashed into his mind in the exhilarating exchanges of a newspaper interview, and only occasionally did he give them sustained support, as in the anti-Semitic campaign of the Dearborn *Independent*. But though down to 1932 he retained nearly all his old abilities, his tendency to suspicion grew. Bennett makes the statement, for what it may be worth, that in 1942 he even saw a "plot" in tentative government housing plans at Willow Run, and "blew his top." [5]

Disappointed that Edsel did not pattern himself after the three iron leaders, Bennett, Sorensen, and Henry himself, and mistrustful of the "Grosse Point crowd" near his son, he would not drop control lest Edsel transform the company. Bennett, though he describes instances of cooperative action, was more and more overtly Edsel's opponent. He frankly expressed his contempt for "the white-collar officials up in mahogany row," meaning if not Edsel, at least B. J. Craig, Edsel's assistant John Crawford, and a few others. Once Henry had accepted gifted subordinates, and turned to them for advice; by 1940 he accepted only Sorensen, P. E. Martin, and Bennett, and took advice and support from Bennett alone.

## 2.

Ford himself, then, and the archaic shape he had given his industrial enterprise, were primarily responsible for the decline of the company. They had created the vacuum in high executive talent. By 1939 any discerning observer would have pronounced the company in danger of becoming unsuccessful, and would have noted a decline in its reputation. This would have been the fact whether Harry Bennett had been in the company or not. The cold, ruthless head of the aging sultan's security force was a protean figure, but above all an opportunist. His rise to palace power, culminating in a thrust for supreme authority at the end of the war, was not the product of a Hitlerian plot laid down in *Mein Kampf* outline early in his career and then remorselessly executed. Rather, he found a situation ripe for his abilities, and exploited it with dexterity and determination. Like the musician he was, he played by ear, turning every opportunity to his own advantage until he came as close to mastery of the company as Aaron Burr came to mastery of the American presidency.[6]

The situation having been created for one of the most remarkable coups in industrial history, the establishment of control over a billion-dollar corporation, the steps by which Bennett used his chances possess an interest which requires their examination in detail.

In 1939 Bennett, only 47, was at the height of his powers. As we have already noted, he had risen in the school of hard knocks, pushing forward entirely by hard effort allied with innate ability, and Ford undoubtedly admired his self-made quality. For all his restless, devil-may-care qualities, Bennett knew the value of discipline, and was as ready to take buffets from his one superior as to administer punishment to others. That he had only one superior Henry made clear. When Ford had first sent him to the Rouge, he had said: "There may be a lot of people over there who want to fire you, but don't pay any attention to them. I'm the only one who can fire you." [7]

This simple understanding lasted for nearly thirty years as a purely personal link. Contrary to many statements that he never went on the company payroll, he was placed there on August 23, 1915, and remained there. While he asserts that for twenty-eight of his thirty years with Ford he got "peanuts for a salary," it was said that the paymaster always kept a large sum in cash—first $10,000, then $25,000—available to him for special expenses, and he tells us that "Mr. Ford maintained my homes for me." An informed guess puts his wage in 1940 at $1500–$1600 a month with occasional bonuses. At a nod from the chief, he was licensed to interfere anywhere; Ford, he states, "had me jumping around from one task to another." Talking to an executive, Ford once remarked that managing a great plant was like stirring a pot of molten metal with an iron rod to force the dross to the top, and the executive concluded that he used Bennett as his long rod.[8]

Bennett's appearance and bearing contributed to the respect engendered by his vague, unlimited powers. Short, muscular, moving with springy energy, taking in everything with his hard blue eyes, he had a combative aspect. His features were sharply chiselled, the cheeks and nose scarred from his fighting days, his jaw, chin, and thick neck pugnacious looking. He combed his thinning dark-brown hair to disguise the evidence of growing baldness. His erectness made the most of his five feet seven inches, and his brisk nervous walk added to the effect of wiry strength given by his 160 pounds; as a matter of fact, he kept in the best physical trim. Ever alert, he could use his mind and his fists with equal rapidity. Even in repose his expression wore a certain defiance, and his voice ranged from a hard friendly bark to a high angry snarl.

His dress comported with his character. He liked natty suits, colored silk shirts, snap-brim felt hats, large Western belt-buckles, and bow ties (this last, it was said, because he had once been nearly strangled in a fight when his antagonist seized his four-in-hand). He looked the prosperous man he was. By 1940 he owned a good deal of property, including his lavishly decorated home, "The Castle," near Ann Arbor, several retreats elsewhere in Michigan, and a ranch in California. He made some of his parties at the Castle, in Detroit night-spots, and on his yacht a subject of talk by his conviviality and boisterous practical jokes. However, he carefully protected the privacy of his home life, his wife, and his three daughters, and he sometimes relaxed in sedate domesticity, painting, drawing, and playing a variety of music instruments. He was a good hunter and fisherman.

The center of Bennett's factory activities was a small, plain office in one corner of the administration building. Visitors to the "little fella" waited in an anteroom under the sharp scrutiny of several muscular service-men. They could watch a large Gamewell board with winking lights which, connected to every patrol station in the Rouge, showed at a glance the position of Bennett's security forces. Direct telephone wires reached other strategic persons and places in the plant, and short-wave radio kept Bennett in touch with high Ford executives even in their own cars. The latch to his inner office was controlled by his secretary and by a button under his desk. Once inside, a visitor might be disturbed by what he saw:

At one end there are some files and a long table covered with a model of the Rouge plant. On one of the files is a small contraption about six inches square, the well-known target at which Mr. Bennett occasionally shoots lead pellets from an air gun shaped like a Luger revolver. The target was copied from one designed by Mr. Ford for his own use and has been so constructed that if Mr. Bennett hits the target, as he almost always does, the pellets are deflected toward a slot in the back and do not go ricocheting around the office.[9]

Proud of his marksmanship, Bennett would sit tilted back with one leg on the desk and the other folded under him, methodically shooting the points off a row of pencils aligned on the desk edge. It was reported that just to prove his skill he shot a pencil in half from a friend's fingers; when irritated by a boxing-commissioner who ignored the rule against smoking, he shot the cigar out of the offender's mouth with his .38; and to express his dislike of straw hats he once shot two holes in one held by a caller. He temporarily worried other visitors by keeping in his office two young tigers which the showman Clyde Beatty gave him. "For several years I raised lions and tigers at home," he tells us, "and often took one into the plant with me."

But the room was primarily a work center, and one explanation of Bennett's success was his industry—his ceaseless attention to detail, his meticulous control over all his subordinates. Everybody sought his little office: governors, mayors, prominent industrialists, journalists, police chiefs, detectives for the F.B.I., salesmen, gangsters, movie stars—and usually at least once a day, Henry Ford himself. Bennett kept in rapport with well-informed men in government, business, labor, and the underworld. He knew more about affairs touching Ford interests than Henry's former secretaries, like Liebold, had ever dreamed of knowing. Telegrams from Ford centers throughout the country, letters from workers, reports from agents who were watching Ford workers or officers, confidential memoranda from newspapermen and local politicians, all reached his hands.

From this center decrees meanwhile went out enforcing a stern discipline upon his agents. Each service-man must keep his beat: perhaps the laundry one day, Gate Four the next, guiding visitors through the Rouge on a third, and inspecting fire precautions on the fourth. Everyone reported at intervals daily through the communications system to Bennett's office. Undercover men spied on service-men who in turn watched the workers and to an increasing extent the executives as well. Bennett alone knew the full intricacies of the network. He kept no records, made no written reports, and was responsible only to Ford, whose capricious interest was in results rather than the methods used to achieve them.

### 3.

Whatever the methods, whatever the resulting decisions, Bennett could not have continued his activities without Henry Ford's constant approval. Upon Ford's silent assent or explicit decree rested the fabric of plant police, espionage agents and secret communications, the structure of iron rules, arbitrary enforcement, and steady threat. The relationship between Bennett and Ford was of the kind certain to spring up in any coercive organization under despotic rule: the autocrat needs his Venetian Inquisition, his Gestapo, or his Cheka; and its head, no matter what name he may happen to bear, becomes so powerful that he is tempted to employ his apparatus recklessly. By industry, loyalty, and all-embracing knowledge, Bennett established a fairly complete ascendancy over his master, his relationship being, as he puts it, "progressive." "I became his most intimate companion, closer to him even than his son," he declares.

Ford, though never inclined to explain his trust, did indicate its completeness. Various people remember him referring to Harry as his "loyal right arm." As Henry became older, more rigid, and more suspicious, he leaned on Bennett as the one lieutenant who best knew the facts, and who acted on them in Henry's own spirit. One competent observer, Charles Voorhees, was convinced that Ford thought his aide and echo completely right: "He believed, I think, to the end that Harry Bennett was perfect." Utility, congeniality, intuitive perception of Henry's mental processes, all played a part.[10]

We should never forget the utility, for Bennett did get things done. His legitimate responsibilities were broad and onerous: to protect the plants against fire, fraud, waste, and "irregular intruders," to manage the laundries, to assist all visitors, to maintain a clearing-center for information, to reduce friction and superfluous effort, and in an emergency to keep the works running. Where a blunderer would have let the Rouge suffer from interruption and breakdown, Bennett's efficient measures helped keep it moving smoothly. He had a broad range of legitimate duties, moreover, associated with Ford and his family. He looked to Henry's protection, his transportation, and his freedom from annoyance. His vigilance against the possible kidnapping of Edsel's children, a cloudy subject, may or may not have been an important function; Ford thought it was. During the 1930s Bennett travelled widely to establish business relationships, conclude negotiations, or perform other duties that Ford wished handled discreetly. He went to Canada to bring an important executive back from a drinking bout and to investigate reports that Ford boats were being used by rum-runners. He acted upon letters threatening bodily harm to members of the Ford family—Henry Ford got an average of five a week in the early 1920s; he made quiet inquiry into troublesome marital problems or political involvements of company personnel; he found out why a particular branch suddenly lost energy.[11]

Because Henry as one employe put it, "didn't want anybody meddling with his personal affairs or his person," he specially relied upon Bennett's shrewd, unobtrusive efforts to shield his circle. In the confused years of the Prohibition era, when bootlegging, gang warfare, and robbery flourished, many criminals looked upon the Fords as ripe victims. In March 1924 Detroit police arrested extortionists who had threatened to blind Henry's grandchildren unless Edsel paid a heavy sum, and a few months later burglars stole valuable jewelry from Edsel's well-guarded residence on East Jefferson Avenue. To both Henry and Edsel the threat of kidnapping was so real that Ford is reported to have told Bennett: "Never mind the plants. If anything happens to them we can build new ones. But we've got to make absolutely sure that nothing happens to the children." As Bennett realized that merely guarding the children was not enough, and that he must gain prior information upon any effort to seize them, he left for a long vacation. "Before he got back," a Detroit newspaperman later wrote, "he had visited practically every major city in the United States, and some of the smaller ones where gangs were established." He saw and talked with men who were well informed on underworld activities, letting them take an accurate measure of his strength and ruthless determination.[12]

Whether they liked him or not, and most of them apparently did, they respected him. Current reports declared that he cemented their trust by various services to men in trouble, anonymously hiring legal counsel for some, and giving jobs to others as they left jail; while he used his influence to have contracts, concessions, and even Ford agencies awarded to a few useful agents. They repaid him by conveying timely warning of any scheme for robbery or kidnapping which came within their ken, which enabled him to take appropriate action. In his own book he relates that a reporter for the Detroit *News* gave him a tip "from a West Side mob" that gangsters were about to attempt a robbery of the pay-office at the Rouge. When the expected car-full of bandits drove down Miller Road, which bisects the Rouge, he halted it. "There's a whole arsenal in there waiting for you," he said. "If you go in, there are going to be a lot of people killed, and some of them will be you." They hastily drove away.

On another occasion a hoodlum whom he had thwarted shot him;

but while in the hospital, it was said he received a photograph of the culprit, suddenly and mysteriously slain, with the message, "He won't bother you any more, Harry." [13]

Bennett never concealed from his associates, and least of all Henry, the fact that he had influential relations with the underworld. Shortly after a supposed attempt on Henry's life by men who forced his car off the road, Bennett told the press that his connections were such that within twenty-four hours after the hatching of a plot he would know of it. Some paroled convicts on the company payroll retained channels of communication with gangsters. Joseph A. Laman, a notorious male-factor who had turned state's evidence in the prosecution of a kidnap-ping ring, and who on release from prison found a job at the Rouge, sent Bennett effusive thanks for his "kindness and generosity." [14] Ches-ter LaMare, the short, swarthy Sicilian with pretensions to leadership in the Detroit underworld, gained the fruit-supply concession in the Rouge plant under circumstances which so outraged Fred H. Diehl, head of the purchasing department, that he resigned. Admitting that "Chet didn't know a banana from an orange," Bennett defended the arrangement as an experiment in rehabilitation, and later declared that it protected the company from the violence of racketeers then ruling the Detroit fruit business. LaMare, however, died in 1931 in a typical Mafia execution.

Part of Detroit in these years, like part of Chicago, was a jungle. The huge Rouge plant, which sometimes employed a hundred thousand men, could not escape hiring many jungle-denizens. All automotive factories, in fact, found that hoodlums infiltrated labor unions, Com-munist cells, and other groups. As a result, an atmosphere of uneasi-ness invested industrial sections of the city. If Bennett told the truth in declaring, "Mr. Ford made me his agent in dealing with the under-world," he was assuredly accurate in adding: "He gave me a job that a number of times almost cost me my life." [15] That his work strength-ened Ford's predilection for him there is no doubt, and it equally heightened the impression he gave of mysteriously formidable power. Some relationships led him into avenues which he later left well-cloaked. When the Kefauver Crime Commission questioned him in 1951 upon his acquaintance with two notorious figures, Anthony J. D'Anna and Joe Adonis, it found him utterly uncommunicative. Yet nearly everyone knew that D'Anna owned part of the E & L Transport

Company, which had a franchise for the transport of Ford vehicles; while Adonis was credited with control of the Automotive Conveyance Company, which received a car-hauling contract at the Ford plant in Edgewater, N.J.

Certainly "the little fella" took full advantage of the seeming requirement for hard-jawed, big-shouldered men. He increasingly staffed the service department and stiffened the ranks of petty bosses with recruits from all the rougher groups within reach. He himself writes: "We had many former pugilists." Among those who stood the best chance of landing positions under him were footloose policemen, detectives, and police inspectors, with no questions asked as to reasons for leaving their former employment. Bennett always maintained: "We don't tolerate rough stuff or thugs in the Ford organization." He always defended, and this with reason, Ford's humane practice of giving paroled convicts another chance in his factory. "They're a lot of tough bastards," he said, "but every goddam one of them's a gentleman." [16]

His "gentlemen," who knew just why they had been hired and to whom they were responsible, deepened the grim, corrosive character of life in the great plant. So much plant-security work was right and necessary that it was difficult to make tenable complaints until the line between legitimate and illegitimate activities became almost indiscernible. Rules for handling "irregular intruders" were interpreted to warrant the rough ejection of union organizers. Reduction of friction within the factory came to mean an industrial discipline, verging on terrorism, so rigorous that it drained workers of initiative and vitality. Prevention of theft and fraud received a double-standard application which punished some men with brutal harshness while it left favorites their easy perquisites. Steps taken against "wasted effort" led to the hateful "speed up" and "stretch out." Much of this shackling, hectoring, and policing of employes involved threat of violence or its actual use, and after the passage of the Wagner Act some of it—as Ford well knew—was in direct violation of federal law.

Quite aware of the general fashion in which Bennett managed internal discipline, Ford found it best to pretend that he was ignorant. We have seen that when A. M. Wibel asked him, "I wonder if you know all the facts?" he cut this veteran associate short with the rebuke: "I don't want to know the facts." On another occasion he said that he was not going to spend hours listening to "petty gripes." [17]

4.

Not only did Bennett become Ford's combined police officer and drill-master; he moved into the function of hatchet-man for various rough tasks. If Ford wanted an executive fired, a supplier forced into line, or a union group broken, he had only to hint at his wish. By the 1930s this function was perfectly understood throughout the Ford organization, where Bennett's presence, felt everywhere, was hated and dreaded at all levels.

"The feeling of the average person toward Bennett was fear," Frank C. Riecks has commented. "This included supervision . . . They felt if they should hit Bennett head on, they might be out of a job." With Bennett's adroit ousting of important men whom he saw as rivals or dangerous enemies we shall deal later. But it is to be noted here that he served Henry in the abrupt dismissal of many a lesser executive. At first he would openly ascribe the act to his chief, saying: "Joe, Mr. Ford doesn't want you here any more. He has asked me to fire you." As this course provoked troublesome appeals to Ford, he changed his tactics, discharged the man, and took the responsibility himself. Occasionally he declined a specially troublesome assignment; when Ford directed him to "bounce" Edsel's brother-in-law Ernest Kanzler, for example, he refused. But more often he took pleasure in the task.

He enjoyed it, for one reason, because he had his own personal antipathies. He had disliked Marquis and all he represented. He had no use for the cultivated W. J. Cameron, whose Sunday evening hour on the radio offended him, and made what he calls "endless attempts" to get him discharged, so that finally hostility grew until Cameron refused to speak to him. He loathed Liebold, and Edsel's assistant John Crawford. In his discharges, nobody was sure whether he gave orders in his own right or as Ford's deputy. Everyone wondered, "Just how powerful is Harry Bennett alone?" One Ford executive had the answer: "Mr. Bennett is just so powerful that nobody around here wants to risk finding out." [18]

In many respects, as the years passed, Bennett became something near a substitute son to Henry Ford, and a spoiled son at that; for Henry's relations with Edsel did not improve. When Edsel's brother-in-law and co-planner Ernest Kanzler was abruptly ejected, close observers had been startled by the sudden glimpse of a deep gulf opening

between father and son. That gulf remained.[19] Despite all Edsel's for-
bearing loyalty, relations between them could never again be quite the
same. Edsel's wife remonstrated with the old man, Clara was deeply
troubled, and Edsel's own grief was often clear. Far from seeing that
the son's superb tolerance, combined with his determination to continue
struggling for a more progressive administration, really proved his
strength, the father in a growing conviction of Edsel's weakness turned
to Bennett as the tough, realistic, hard-hitting type he had wished Edsel
to be. And as Bennett became a daily companion, earning Henry's approval at every turn, he achieved the status of lieutenant, son, and crony
combined. Henry telephoned him early every morning, often carried
him to work, and telephoned him again nearly every evening at nine-
thirty. He took any criticism of Bennett's policies, alleged dishonesty,
and violent acts, as criticism of his own management; and as it was
hard to tell where one authority ended and the other began, he was at
least partly right.

The crony relationship was important, for Ford enjoyed his com-
panionship with the cocky, hardheaded service chief. They would meet
sometimes at one of the Ford farms of Greenfield Village to take long
drives together. At other times they would sit in Bennett's basement
office talking, sometimes several hours. They discussed factory problems from the same point of view. "Ford delighted in the game of cops
and robbers," writes one commentator, "and the service department
was that." Or they would take up politics or the light jottings of a Detroit *Free Press* columnist called "Iffy the Dopester" whom both liked,
or one of Ford's many hobbies. Although Ford often urged both Sorensen and Bennett to take vacations, whenever they went away he felt a
gap in his life. Bennett on one of his California trips received a letter
from Henry's secretary reporting: "The boss wishes me to ask how
you are, etc. I think he misses his daily talks." A writer for *Reader's
Digest* elicited a direct indication of esteem when, riding in the rear
seat of a car driven by Bennett, he asked: "Mr. Ford, of all the men you
have met in your whole business and industrial experience, which one
has seemed to you the most remarkable?" Ford silently pointed straight
at Bennett.[20]

All in all, the Ford-Bennett relationship was a curious mixture of im-
pulses practical and emotional, reasoned and instinctive, selfish and un-
selfish. The two men respected each other's skills and efficiencies, liked

each other's crassness, and saw in each other the strengths needed to cope with a brutal world. A pathetic element may be found in Henry's attitudes. Lonely, disillusioned, uniting the most brilliant gifts with the most hopeless limitations, he was groping for some stay, some support. Bennett's attitude, on the other hand, offers little to win our respect. He was loyal to Ford, even to risking his life for his chief, so long as loyalty paid—and no longer, as he proved by signing a vulgar volume of depreciation after Ford's death. He respected Ford's genius, admired his achievements, and liked some of his human traits. But here again he was selfish; he wanted so desperately to share Ford's power, he was so ambitious to seize the levers of authority, that his final determination was to make himself the ruling head.

### 5.

The decline came late but with shocking rapidity. As noted earlier, on Ford's seventieth birthday in 1933 his physical and mental health was sound. Down to his seventy-fifth birthday in 1938 associates marvelled at his spry stair-climbing, quick nervous agility about the plant, and alert responses. Even after his first stroke that year, he seemed much his old self, and his attorney I. A. Capizzi noticed no deterioration.* Then early in the new decade came a change, which after a second stroke in 1941 became pronounced. Herman Moekle noticed early in the war that he was slower in gait, that he did not spend as much time on the job as before, that on a trip he began to chill and needed wraps, and above all, that lapses occurred in his mental grasp. E. F. Wait also marked a serious decline early in the war. Though Ford had known him and Logan Miller for some time, and had always shaken hands with them and offered a pleasant word, suddenly he forgot their names and had to ask after their identity. "There were noticeable periods," Wait records, "when his mind didn't seem to be quite clear." Sorensen fixes the period of marked deterioration as beginning just before Pearl Harbor. "From now on the previously set opinions about Wall Street and international bankers, the Roosevelt New Deal, scheming motor car compatriots, foreign wars, and his son Edsel's quiet determination to live his own life, hardened into an obsession which occasionally flared into hallucination." [21]

---

* Sorensen writes: "After his stroke he became a querulous, suspicious old man. He scented conspiracies to grab his business. Often his memory failed him." But this was undoubtedly after the second stroke in 1941. *Forty Years,* 313.

It is not strange that the calculating man closest to Ford, and best able to gauge his mental atrophy, should weigh more intently than ever the chances of dispossessing him of his erratic sceptre. The years of the Mad Hatter were beginning; anything could happen.

Administrative confusion became worse after Henry's second stroke, and the areas of administrative vacuum more numerous. Ford had always been reluctant to define spheres of authority, and had often delighted in issuing contradictory orders; now his capriciousness made the managerial process a turmoil of uncertainties, fears, and cross-purposes. Sometimes even Ray Dahlinger, manager of Ford's farms, would issue orders to executives, "Mr. Ford told me to tell you." This was a far cry from the early days of the company with its printed admonition: "Verbal orders don't go."

Often it was impossible to verify a second-hand directive, for Ford was hard to find, seldom entering his two offices, and poking about wherever the fancy took him. Once run down, he would often break off any question with an impatient, "That's all been decided—don't bother me about it." For self-protection his executives banded together in little clusters of power, which watched each other jealously and engaged in covert warfare. Charles Martindale relates that a little later, in 1945, a young man was set to drafting an organization chart for the company. He found the task impossible. "He'd bring it to me with tears in his eyes," states Martindale, "and gave up because there was no way of knowing who reported to whom." [22]

This chaos was to the advantage of Bennett, for timid men turned to him for protection. Furthermore, as guardian and shaper of Ford's isolation, he could determine the form of what small resources of leadership the old man still had to give the executives. Bennett was still outside the "round table" group which lunched with Henry in the executive dining room in the Dearborn Engineering Building; but as he saw Ford constantly, he could impose his will on the chief better than this luncheon cabinet. He was ready by 1939 to engage even the once all-powerful Sorensen. Fred L. Black informs us that during this year he heard Sorensen begin to tell Ford something that Bennett was doing, of which Sorensen strongly disapproved. "Mr. Ford, with an ice-cold tone in his voice and steely look, said, 'What is the matter, is he stepping on your toes?'"

And Bennett was equally ready to drop into Henry's mind insinua-

tions derogatory to Edsel's ideas and attitudes. Another veteran executive recalls that once, riding with Edsel, after a humiliating dispute
over policy, the tortured son dropped his usually perfect self-control.
"The hurtful thing about all this," Edsel burst out, obviously fighting
his tears, "is that father takes Harry's word for all this and he won't
believe mine. Who is this guy anyway? Where did he come from? He
is nothing but a gob. You know, we built that Navy School down there
to keep him out of the service because he was in the reserve corps."
Sorensen states that relations between Edsel and Henry were now
strained "almost to the breaking point." [23]

One self-respecting executive after another had left the company in
disgust, had been forced out, until only the thinnest middle echelon
existed between ownership at the top and technicians below. Several
of these technicians were highly capable; William Pioch in designing
machine tools, Harry Hanson in construction work, Roeder in engineering commercial vehicles, and Mead L. Bricker in production.
Others were so clearly objects of Bennett's hostility, like Sheldrick and
Wibel, that their lives were unhappy and their futures dark. Compared
with General Motors, the company was deficient in men of talent and
tested character.

When promising men rose at the Rouge they were all too likely to
make a rough exit. We have already seen that William C. Cowling, for
almost seven years sales manager for Ford, left the company late in
1937; Bennett tells a callous story of exactly how this event occurred.
Ford executives were permitted to get their cars reconditioned in the
factory at moderate cost, and Cowling brought his in. Bennett then (he
states by Ford's instructions, but it is impossible to say who was prime
mover in such matters) kept precise track of the time spent on the
car, and added charges for the time that he and Henry spent overseeing
the job. "When the car was finished, we sent Cowling an enormous
bill." The sales manager promptly notified Bennett, "You can keep the
car," sold an unfinished house he was building, and after a further
prod, left, taking with him his long years' experience.* We have already recorded the transfer of his successor, John R. Davis, to California because he discharged Bennett's favorite Harry Mack.

Beginning in the autumn of 1940, production first for defense and

* There were other and more important reasons for Cowling's exit, as indicated in Chs. 3
and 5.

then for war absorbed much of Edsel's and Sorensen's energy. While Henry was at first lukewarm or obstructive, they believed wholeheartedly in aiding the vast international effort; Sorensen regarded it as the greatest challenge of his life, and Edsel's enthusiasm heightened the already great respect that onlookers felt for the young man. As Willow Run got under way, it required all Sorensen's tremendous drive to meet the government schedules, and Edsel supported him as his failing health permitted. Ray S. Rausch was high in production management at the Rouge, and though Sorensen speaks well of him in his memoirs, the universal impression was that he stood with Bennett, helped Bennett plant his men throughout the factory, and was ready to act against Sorensen in promoting Bennett's ambitions. Among Bennett's most regular luncheon guests in his private dining room were Rausch and Russell Gnau, Sorensen's personal secretary. Gnau also had moved so far into the Bennett camp that practically everybody in the upper ranks believed that he was working to undermine Sorensen—everybody with the exception of the overworked Sorensen.

As Henry Ford's attitude toward Edsel became increasingly harsh, Sorensen had the courage to expostulate with him. "Again and again," he writes, "I tried to impress upon him, without success, that his attempt to drive Edsel into line by using Harry Bennett to annoy him and check his every move was breaking down Edsel's respect for him." He added that it was ruining Edsel's precarious health. What was even worse, Henry was showing a jealous antagonism toward Edsel's sons. When late in 1940, Henry II, recently out of Yale and just married, began to work at the plant along with his brother Benson, men might have supposed that the grandfather would be overjoyed by this promise that the Ford line would continue in control of the great property, and would greet the boys affectionately. Instead, Sorensen tells us, he first said that he did not wish them around, and when they stayed on, treated them with brusque indifference. This attitude did not displease the man who exulted that he was closer than a son to Henry.

Perhaps Sorensen overstates the tension between Henry and Edsel, but some weight must be given an incident he recounts. He relates that in 1941, just after Sorensen, Edsel, and the two boys visited the Consolidated bomber plant in San Diego to study its methods, Edsel came in from a talk with his father. He was overwhelmed with anxiety, for Henry had bidden him to get the boys out of the Rouge—to California, to any other place, the farther away the better. They might stay on the payroll, but they should get out at once! At this, Sorensen writes, he telephoned for a meeting with Henry. When he went, he took Edsel along. As they entered the office, the old man, caught by surprise to see Edsel there, betrayed himself by what Sorensen calls a look of hatred; probably dismay would be a more appropriate word. The outraged manager told Henry not only that he was completely opposed to the exile of the boys, but that if it were carried through, he would leave the company. This ended the matter; but Edsel could not forget it, and the memory still oppressed him when a little later Henry II entered the Navy, and Benson joined the Air Force.[24]

<h2 style="text-align:center">6.</h2>

With the war raging more hotly, the Ford contribution to the Allied cause growing more important, and Sorensen so overburdened that he twice fainted in the plant, events reached a partial climax in the spring of 1943. Edsel's condition had become serious when his stomach ulcers gave way to cancer, and he fell ill with undulant fever contracted from non-pasteurized milk of the Henry Ford farm, where the herd had received no regular tuberculin tests. His father refused to believe that he was in danger. If he would only change his diet and mode of life to that which Henry Ford had found best, if he would stop worrying, listening to men of the wrong type, and opposing Henry and Bennett, he would soon get well. Disgust, discouragement, and anger possessed the best Ford executives as they heard Henry express these views.

One of the best men was ejected from the organization in April— A. M. Wibel. His rigidly honest administration of purchasing, sympathy with liberal ideas, and intimacy with Edsel and Sorensen, all made him repugnant to Bennett. This fine-spirited man, who had worked his way up from a machinist's bench since 1912, had apparently always pleased Henry, and certainly no rational basis existed for his dismissal. He had been elected a vice-president and director along with Sorensen in 1941, thus becoming a figure of national repute. Some men in the company, however, did not want a first-rate administration of purchasing, and poisoned Henry's mind. When an irresponsible agent made trouble in his department, Wibel brought hot accusations against Bennett—and his discharge followed. His loss, which was telegraphed over the country, was a shock to both Edsel and Sorensen, for it meant that one of the company pillars was gone.[25]

Another event of this troubled April is detailed by Sorensen. On the 15th, the day before the manager was to leave for a short Florida vacation, Henry Ford telephoned him. He wanted Sorensen to take Edsel, then almost too ill to move about, in hand, and change his whole attitude toward Bennett, toward Henry, and toward life. "Some job!" ejaculated Sorensen. Of the seven-point program which Henry laid down, five points might have been dictated by "the little fella" himself. Roughly jotted by Sorensen, they ran as follows: [26]

a. Discord over handling labor relations (to end).
b. Wibel and his attitude toward Bennett, says Wibel is through.
c. Bennett in full accord with Henry Ford. Henry Ford will support Bennett against every obstacle. Seeing labor leaders.
d. Bennett's job, no one else.
e. Change relations with Bennett.

When Sorensen saw Edsel next morning he hardly needed to say: "It is evident where Mr. Ford is getting these ideas." Edsel sadly explained to him the full reason for the recent decree that Wibel should get out. Bennett had demanded that Wibel give a lucrative order to some supplier whom he favored, Wibel had angrily refused and appealed to Edsel as president, and Edsel had ordered Harry to stop his interference with purchasing and stick to personnel and labor relations. Henry Ford's telephone call was an additional answer to the son's show of spirit! Agitated almost to the breaking point, Edsel discussed the propriety of resigning and leaving the company. Had he done this, Sorensen would have resigned also, and with Henry II and Benson in the armed services, Bennett would have been left in complete control.

Fortunately, Edsel's forbearance and Sorensen's willingness to talk bluntly to the father averted the calamity. As the old man showed a momentary contrition, the manager and the son—almost equally harassed, stricken, and anxious—went their ways, one to a brief vacation in Miami, the other to the hospital. For nearly a year the son had felt that his illness would have a fatal termination.

On May 26, at 1:10 in the morning, Edsel died at his home in St. Clair Shores of a complication of ailments: stomach cancer, undulant fever, and a broken heart. His father only a week earlier had refused to believe the truth. His death—he was only 49—sent a wave of sorrow through Dearborn and Detroit, for all who knew Edsel loved him. Henry took it with composure, but Sorensen, who went to the funeral, broke down. He always believed that if Henry had treated his son with wise consideration and affection, he could have had a long life. Among those at the funeral was Edsel's brother-in-law, Ernest Kanzler, who had witnessed the tragedy, and was now resolved to do what he could to prevent the future deterioration of the Ford company.

Bennett, according to his own story, was asked by Henry if he would come to the funeral, and replied that he would not be so hypocritical; "I knew," he adds, "that Edsel had despised me." But he had the decency to state that Edsel's departure had left many orphans about the plant. Few coffins have been surrounded by so much bitterness of heart.

What would happen now that the crown prince, so long the center of all hopes for a better regime in the Ford empire, had died before the mentally failing monarch? The presidency had to be filled at once. On May 27, the day before the funeral, Henry telephoned Sorensen that he would take over the position—at nearly eighty, after two strokes! The manager could hardly believe what he heard, and according to his own story at once told Frank Campsall, Ford's secretary and one of Bennett's supporters, that he would give Henry no help in reorganizing the company; he knew that if he did so he would simply implicate himself in putting a sinister group, using a broken figurehead, in control. This declaration frightened Bennett, who drove post-haste to Willow Run to see Sorensen and smoke him out. Was he maneuvering to succeed Edsel as president? Was he, the real binding force in the plant for so many years, trying to bring pressure upon Henry Ford by threatening a disruptive course? Though Sorensen said no, Bennett and his aides still feared him.[27]

And at this critical moment Henry Ford sanctioned still another extraordinary act, the execution of a codicil to his will which was kept secret from the family. The document was drawn by I. A. Capizzi. The company's counsel at the time of the Chicago *Tribune* suit, Alfred Lucking, had been succeeded by various men. One was Clifford Longley, a sagacious lawyer who had shared the anxiety of Edsel and his assistant John Crawford to arrange a farsighted plan of management for the Ford properties when Henry and Edsel died, and who had taken a large part in drafting wills for both in 1936 which, as we shall see later, kept control of the company within the Ford family by creating a foundation. Longley remained Edsel's attorney, but other counsel entered the picture. One was Louis Colombo, a leading Detroit attorney who attracted Henry Ford's attention by his brilliant conduct of a case, and who was retained by the company. In 1940 he was succeeded by Capizzi, another able lawyer with years of public-spirited service on the staff of the county prosecuting attorney and state attorney-general. Working with Bennett in dealing with labor problems prior to the settlement with the CIO, he became well acquainted with him. It appears that someone, divining in Henry Ford's mind an intense dislike for the foundation plan, had advised him against it, with the result that either Henry or Bennett, or both, considered drawing up a counter-scheme. When Edsel died this had not yet been done.

But it was done now. Capizzi was summoned to a meeting in an office at Willow Run. To the best of his recollection some years later, both Bennett and Sorensen were present. He recalls this because the crucial problem of the presidency was still unsettled, and he noted the strong feeling between Sorensen, who apparently thought he should succeed, and Bennett, obviously opposing Sorensen because this would reduce his power. "At any rate," runs an approved summary of Capizzi's recollections, "it was reported to him by Bennett that . . . Mr. Henry Ford was concerned that Henry Ford II would come too much under the influence of Kanzler in the operation of the company and that therefore Mr. Henry Ford was interested in setting up a means whereby the operation of the company would vest in others until Henry II and the other grandchildren were old enough to manage the company themselves." Capizzi advised the group that such purpose could be accomplished by a provision in Henry Ford's will setting up a board of trustees to operate the company after his death.

Significantly, Capizzi adds that the only information he got concerning Henry Ford's wishes came from Bennett; he never talked with Ford himself on the subject. It is also his recollection "that Mr. Bennett finally persuaded Mr. Ford to step in and become president of the company in order to assure his [Bennett's] position of power." However this may be, it was Bennett who asked Capizzi to proceed with the codicil. Of course he did this—the family knowing nothing of the matter. Of the nature of the codicil, whatever the circumstances, there is no question whatever. It nullified the foundation plan by creating a trust, under which the Ford Motor Company was to be controlled by a board named by Henry Ford for ten years after his death. None of the grandchildren appears in the list of trustees later set down by Bennett.* Although Capizzi believes that the codicil named no secretary of the Board, Bennett explicitly declares that he was to hold that position of special power.[28]

One heartening fact was that the women of the Ford family were now playing a determined role in the drama. Edsel's wife had not watched her husband's years of suffering, and heard his anguished denunciations of Bennett, without resolving that her sons' rights should be respected until they could take full management. Clara, as close observers noted, had been expostulating with Henry, denouncing Bennett as persecutor of her son and evil genius of the plant, and taking Mrs. Edsel Ford's side in insisting that the grandsons be trained for control. Both were women of character, whose self-assertion now counted. Another encouraging element in the situation was the government's active interest. As the war reached its crisis, Washington had no intention of letting the tremendous production energies of the Rouge and Willow Run be crippled. President Roosevelt and the war production chiefs wished to see Henry Ford set aside by able, earnest, trustworthy men. But could such men gain control in time?

On June 1, 1943, the stockholders held a meeting, with Henry Ford and his grandsons Henry II and Benson present. This meeting re-elected the three Fords and Sorensen as directors, and chose Mrs. Edsel Ford, Mead L. Bricker, Harry Bennett, Ray S. Rausch, and B. J. Craig as new members of the board. Later that day the board elected the elder Henry Ford president, Sorensen vice-president, Craig vice-president and treasurer, and Herman Moekle assistant treasurer and secretary. This, in view of Henry Ford's age, was a makeshift arrangement which Sorensen, who states that he wished to see Henry II chosen president, regarded as absurd. It might prove worse than absurd, for as Bennett reached for enhanced power, he would feel

---

* Bennett, Capizzi, Sorensen, Liebold, Dr. Ruddiman, Lindbergh, Frank Campsall, and Roy Bryant; Carl Hood soon being named in Liebold's place. *We Never Called Him Henry,* 174. This list is to be regarded dubiously; John S. Bugas, who later saw the codicil, states that Lindbergh was not named in it.

able to count on the support of the elder Ford, Rausch, and Craig.[29]

"Like all palace shifts," commented a writer in *Time,* "this one had backstairs significance. Greatly increased was the already great influence of Bennett. Lessened was the influence of Sorensen, long nourished by the late Edsel Ford. . . . Sorensen has held the only production seat on the board. Now he must share that chair with Rausch, close friend of Bennett." [30] As a matter of fact, he had to share it with both Rausch and Bricker. Nobody knew what the immediate future would hold.

# X

## END OF A LEGEND

WHEN Secretary Knox approved Henry II's release from the Navy to the Rouge plant in the hot August days of 1943, Detroit observers were betting that Henry would encounter the same frustrations that Edsel had met, that the atmosphere of plot, counterplot, and general apprehension would paralyze his good intentions, and that he would probably not have the fortitude to stick to his post and win control. The situation would have confused anybody. Company power rested with three men. One was Henry Ford, whose physician, Dr. McClure, according to Sorensen, had declared that he was so sick that he should not be allowed to come around the plant or transact any business; the second was Sorensen, whose intimate cooperative relationship with the elder Ford was being wrecked, but who for various reasons clung to his managership of production; and the third was Harry Bennett.

Legal authority, to be sure, rested with the board of directors, but Bennett tells us that its meetings were meaningless when Henry Ford did not attend, and farcical when he did. "Mr. Ford would come in, walk around, shake hands with everyone, and then say, 'Come on, Harry, let's get the hell out of here. We'll probably change everything they do, anyway.'" Young Henry, momentarily impotent, had to feel his way cautiously. When later he was asked about the extent to which his father and grandfather had talked to him about plant affairs, he replied significantly that he had talked with his father. He went on: "It may have been in 1941 or a little earlier I told him that things were in a mess, and that it would have to be cleaned up." Edsel, then profoundly discouraged, merely replied that it couldn't be done.[1]

Although Henry II said that his brother Benson knew more about the Rouge than he did, he by no means returned to the company in ignorance of its condition. He had seen enough of the factory before his enlistment to know its routines. Then, while attending the Naval Training School at Great Lakes, he had taken time to follow the principal Ford developments in detail. He had requested Sorensen's secretary, Russell Gnau, to supply not only steady operational reports, but news of everything he heard and observed.

"By the way, ask Bagley to send me the production cards for the 25th and 26th of April, which I am missing and need for my records," Henry II wrote Gnau on April 30, 1941. "I am keeping our production sheets to see how things go, so don't forget." On May 5, just as he finished his grueling course,—"this man's navy is plenty tough"—he had asked again for a steady flow of information. He had deduced from the turbine contracts and the doubling of government orders on the R-2800 motors that automobile manufacture would almost disappear in 1942. "I really miss not getting out there and into all these things, and especially so as I was just beginning to understand how things worked out, and was just getting into a little bit of everything and possibly a little too much of some things." [2]

Obviously, the young man had not only comprehended that he might soon play a principal role in the company, and had not only felt disturbed by the losses of 1941, but showed a keen interest in the automotive industry and an ambition to meet its challenges. He "really missed" the Rouge, he had a grim conviction that much was wrong there, and he had learned too much for comfort about some men's activities. As a director, a listener to his parents' talk, and a roving employe without a desk of his own, he had formed a clear idea of some of the main roots of the trouble.

Henry II had used a short leave to visit the Rouge plant on June 4, 1943, and Russell Gnau had promptly set down a report on the call for Harry Bennett, who was busy with some Navy officers. Again the young man had shown how closely he was following the business. When Gnau remarked that he must have stirred up the management when he complained that the company was making no money, he replied that the average of the profits over the past ten years had been far below Chrysler's. The two had talked about current operations, turnover, and the long lag between shipments and receipt of payments. Gnau then showed Henry II detailed material on the bomber construction at Willow Run and the assemblies at the Rouge, the Lincoln plant, and outside, inquiring whether he had received the facts before.

"No," responded Henry II, "Dad never gave me much information on what was going on." He had known enough about the company position, however, to express uneasiness. "We are OK now," he had remarked, "but what is going to happen after we finish our government contracts?" He stuck stubbornly to his doubts after Gnau tried to reassure him by saying that they would have the greatest post-war job in the world in making tractors. "Automobile manufacture is the really important matter," he had said in effect, "and I do not think we are doing enough development work to get ready for it. You say Gregorie has plans for a new car on the drafting board. Well, you should get on with it."

And Henry II had made one statement of great significance for the future of the company. As Gnau records it: "Henry mentioned the fact that he thought it would be a good idea to bring in a lot of young men. Said we should bring young college graduates into the company for training. We told him we didn't think a college education was necessary except for a professional man, and if a boy had a good high school education that was equipment enough for us to develop him. He said most other companies brought in college boys." [3]

Moving into Edsel's office on his return, Henry II took over part of his father's staff, began to master various duties, and learned to put up with Sorensen's grim patronage and Bennett's hostility, expressed in an odd combination of cajolery and harassment. He "worked for Sorensen," he said later, and disliked him and his methods. He kept away from Bennett as much as he could, and like Edsel detested him.[4] Tramping around the Rouge and Willow Run, cheerful, democratic, and observant, the young man got acquainted with workers, foremen, and superintendents. One reason why Secretary Knox released him from the Navy was that high government officials hoped that he might put an end to the growing chaos in management, for the discharge of experienced and trusted officials had shocked war-production men in Washington. Another reason lay in the intercession of Ernest Kanzler and other anxious Detroit observers. Young Henry's logical first move was to become familiar with personnel. Sorensen, helping in this, was also useful in accompanying him to the capital, and seeing that he met bankers, industrialists, and such high officers as General "Hap" Arnold. They impressed him; and, writes Sorensen, "wherever this 25-year-old young man went he, too, made an impression—a good one."[5]

To be sure, Henry II, who despite his evident ability was as mild in manner and as modest as his father, did not at first seem to be a person of tremendous force. His education, however—the Detroit University School, Hotchkiss School, and nearly four years at Yale, had given him breadth of view. Affable and unassuming, he made friends readily. His athletic five feet eleven and large head made him a striking figure in any gathering; his clear direct thinking, combined with his patent honesty and a certain charm inherited from his mother, enabled him to deal persuasively with audiences. He had a marked capacity for hard work. "The unanimity in praise of his modesty, earnestness, and simple human likeability," declared a writer in *Fortune* in the spring of 1944, "is almost alarming." [6] He was a complete realist—nothing and nobody fooled him—and he had one of Henry Ford's primary traits, tenacity of purpose. Outside observers who had expected little of him, and Bennett's inside group with its hopes that he would prove weak, found him growing rapidly in poise and assurance.

No realist could have missed seeing the mismanagement and confusion at the Rouge against which Henry II had protested to his grandfather. The dislocations of war were unavoidable, but apart from this, much was basically wrong. In the absence of a system for fixing accurate ratios among demand, materials, and working force, personnel was bloated in some departments and starved in others, with a particularly deplorable shortage of expert engineers. The financial statements had latterly been kept from all but a few men, partly because they would have damaged public prestige, and partly because incompetent or dishonest officers knew they might prompt an investigation. One of Bennett's lieutenants said darkly of the balance-sheets: "You never know what someone will do with one of these things." No proper cost controls existed. "Can you believe it?" Henry II later asked one magazine writer. "In one department they figured their costs by *weighing* the pile of invoices on a scale." [7] Production had planned output on a certain projected volume, sales planned its marketing on another, and purchasing bought its materials on a third projection. The company might run at a third of its normal volume, and still employ two-thirds of its normal work force.

Henry II was equally a realist concerning the high officers of the company. He soon took well the measure of them all, and trusted few. Fully aware of the character and designs of Bennett, for his father had talked to him about the man, he knew by personal experience how the service chief could manipulate evidence. He recalled later: "When an important policy matter came up, Bennett would get into his car and disappear for a few hours. Then he'd come back and say, 'I've been to see Mr. Ford and he wants us to do it this way.' I checked with my grandfather and found out that Bennett hadn't seen my grandfather on those occasions." [8] The reminiscences of Sorensen and Bennett for 1943–1944 are often so directly contradictory that neither can be given full credence, but Sorensen's carry much the greater weight, and one of his passages has revealing force. Convinced that Bennett expected to browbeat and thwart Henry II as he had frustrated Edsel, he watched the situation carefully:

One morning I was with him when he got a telephone call from Bennett. He was getting an earful and could hardly get a word in. Not wishing to listen, I stepped into the outer office and went back when Henry II put down the receiver. Not a word was said about the phone call. He was under fire—I could see that—but young Henry was composed and resumed his talk with me as though nothing had happened. The boy can take it, I said to myself happily; everything will work out all right.

## 2.

Time continued to play an important part in the drama. For one reason, the condition of Henry Ford, nominally president, steadily worsened, and his erratic ways could do untold harm. Henry II, making every effort to maintain cordial relations, took care to say nothing that could be carried to his grandfather to create misunderstanding. He even leaned backward to be agreeable. As late as the summer of 1944, speaking before Ford dealers in Massachusetts, he paused to comment on Henry Ford. "He is in excellent health. He puts in a full working day, including Saturday. He goes to Willow Run practically every day, and has put a lot of his effort into that plant, and I believe the outstanding results accomplished at Willow Run reflect his personal supervision. . . . He is going along toward our common objective, Leadership. All our programs have his complete endorsement." Several aspects of this statement are significant: the young man's tactful care to praise Henry, his willingness to help maintain the innocent fiction, good for dealers' morale, of Ford's competency, and his emphasis on leadership in "our" programs. [9]

Time had already eroded the uneasy Bennett-Sorensen partnership, and converted it into a tacit antagonism. The two men shared an ironfisted temper, and while Edsel lived and Henry Ford remained vigorous they had regarded each other with a certain respect and even some tolerance; but the moment that control of the Ford empire became doubtful, their jealousy ripened toward enmity. Sorensen, a powerful constructive force, and a man of strict standards in company matters, was irritated by evidences of graft in plant operations. He was deeply offended by the ousting of his veteran comrade Wibel. He saw with a sense of outrage the renewed purge immediately after the death of Edsel; a purge in which Bennett's adroit manipulation of Henry Ford's senile resentments played a main part, and which led toward Bennett's establishment of undisputed sway. Bennett got rid of the public relations counsel whom Edsel had personally brought to the company a year earlier, and who had given some attention to news articles favorable to Sorensen; his place being taken by John W. Thompson, a subordinate who had kept Bennett's good will. During Edsel's final illness Bennett began maneuvering against John Crawford, Edsel's right hand in office affairs, a man of integrity and vision who had never concealed his contempt for the service chief; and Crawford quickly left under pressure—Bennett calls it Henry Ford's pressure. Fred Black, who had capably staged the company exhibits at international expositions, and who shared Crawford's contempt for Bennett, was abruptly ejected.

In the discharge of one of the most valuable men in the company, the skilled engineer Laurence Sheldrick, Sorensen was himself maneuvered into playing a part. Like other episodes of the time, it has mysterious aspects. Few happenings in plant affairs were now strictly rational. Sheldrick's own story is the most trustworthy account. He relates that Henry II, soon after his arrival, asked about his father's ideas on post-war automobile design. Sheldrick then told him of Edsel's keen interest in plans, and showed him various designs embodying Edsel's ideas. He gathered later that some talebearer carried word of this to Bennett and Henry Ford. At about the same time Henry II proposed to Sorensen that he go with Sheldrick to Aberdeen, Md., to talk with Federal ordnance officers with whom the company was doing business. This Sorensen approved, saying, "Fine, but I think I'd better clear with your grandfather first, though." Arrangements were then duly made by which Sheldrick and Henry II were to meet in Washington on September 14, and to go on to Aberdeen. Little did Sheldrick surmise that plans had been made for his swift decapitation.

In the light of the sequel, Sheldrick could only conclude that Henry Ford and Bennett had peremptorily ordered Sorensen to pick a quarrel with him and force his departure. For on the 13th Sorensen called Sheldrick into his office. He roughly charged the engineer with showing a mass of material on post-war design to Henry II. To this Sheldrick replied that young Henry knew of its existence and had asked for it. Sorensen then accused Sheldrick of making young Henry a "warmonger" by sending him to Aberdeen: "You know how his grandfather feels about that." Sheldrick responded that he was merely trying to serve the company, and that General Motors had shown more zeal in cooperating with the government. "There you go talking about General Motors again," snapped Sorensen in his nastiest tone. "If you think they're so goddam good, why don't you go work for them?" To which Sheldrick made the only self-respecting answer possible: "All right, if that's the way you feel about it, I guess I'm through"—and walked out of the plant.[10]

Nobody knew better than Sorensen that the removal of Wibel, Sheldrick, and the designer Gregorie, who soon followed them, were body-blows to the Ford Company. Ernest G. Liebold went too, a little later. He had long ceased to count in company affairs, and his association with the German-American Bund had brought him under the surveillance of the F.B.I., but the circumstances of his dismissal were unnecessarily humiliating. He showed keen resentment, refusing to consent to the customary press notice of a "resignation," and making his own statement that he had been discharged without cause. Bennett, as he says in his memoirs, had long hated him. Thinking of Wibel, Crawford, Sheldrick, and Gregorie, Sorensen later wrote: "The picture was clear; the team was breaking up. The captain was a sick man, unable to call the plays. The line coaches were gone. Anyone who made a brilliant play was called out." *[11]

---

* Sorensen, *Forty Years*, 328 ff., is emphatic upon the sharp deterioration in Henry Ford's physical and mental condition beginning in 1943; Bennett, *We Never Called Him Henry*, 162 says that in that year "Mr. Ford's health began going down hill." E. F. Wait and others in the company bear this out in their dictated reminiscences. Talk about the decline became so prevalent that Drew Pearson repeated it in a broadcast, only to meet such sharp denial from Henry Ford that he withdrew his statement; *N.Y. Times*, August 25, 26, 30, 1943. After this year Henry Ford had his bright days, and increasingly his bad days. When Lord Perry visited Dearborn, he was distressed, as he told the authors, by a retrogression that he called physical, mental, and moral.

He knew during this autumn of 1943 that his own days were numbered. Like a great oak half-undermined by subterranean waters, he
shook, careened to one side, and stood at the point of toppling.
"Throughout this period," writes E. F. Wait, "you could see him
losing power." Slight after slight had been put upon him by Henry
Ford and Bennett. When President Roosevelt's train had visited
Willow Run on September 18, 1942, Bennett had taken complete
charge of the arrangements: the formation of the parade, path of
automobiles, pace, and stops. FDR's train had pulled up alongside
the plant. After the automobiles completed their circuit of the Rouge,
FDR and Henry Ford entered the President's private car together,
leaving Sorensen outside. He did not gain entry until he went to his
office to get a miniature plane of aluminum that had been used as
a model at Willow Run, fetched it to show the President, and after
some parley with the secret service men, was admitted.

Again, when General Knudsen announced a visit to the plant,
Sorensen directed Logan Miller to prepare a courteous reception for
him. Next day Miller, calling at Bennett's office, found Henry Ford,
Lindbergh, and Bennett conferring together. When he mentioned that
Knudsen was coming that afternoon and that Sorensen wished to
welcome him, Ford burst out: "Logan, don't pay any attention to
Sorensen! Don't pay any attention to him; tell him to go to hell!"
Bennett added a good deal more in the same vein, and both loudly
declared that they would not stay to meet Knudsen.[12]

"It must have been a terrific ordeal for him," states Wait, "but never
by word or deed did he show in any way that he was hurt." The Dane
remained impassive as Bennett, using his malign influence over Henry
Ford, steadily disabled him. The service chief effectively pinioned
Sorensen's arms just before Henry II's return, for on June 18, 1943,
he had himself appointed assistant to Sorensen for administrative
problems, and his associate Ray R. Rausch made assistant to Sorensen
for production.[13] The two, with Henry Ford, thus hemmed Sorensen
in. Long the general production chief, he had latterly aspired to general administrative direction—but now his power was reduced and he
was largely confined to Willow Run. Overworked, often under terrible strain with his bomber program, and half ill as he drove it to
success, he saw that he must soon go.

In November 1943, he told an uncomprehending Henry Ford that
he wished to be relieved on January 1 to go to Florida. According to

his own story, he advised his chief to make Henry II president without delay, and warned him that Washington was grumbling over the plant's loss of key men and the resulting confusion. Perhaps he made some impression upon Ford's mind, for on December 15, Henry II was elected vice president. But when on, or just after, New Year's Day Sorensen said goodbye, Henry Ford's only comment was, "I guess there's something in life besides work." Still seeming not to understand what was happening, the elder Ford left for Ways, Georgia. Sorensen had not resigned, and we can only guess whether he really wished to step out. But from his winter home in Miami, he declares, he kept asking Henry Ford, through Campsall, for "release"; and on March 2, 1944, he got his answer.

It came through Campsall: Henry Ford wished him to resign because he had been ambitious for the company presidency! Sorensen, doubtless furious, of course instantly offered his resignation. Its announcement on March 4 was a shock to the whole industry, and to war-production heads in the government.[14] Lord Perry in England was grieved, and one of the heads of the Morris Works there wrote Sorensen: "Many of us thought you and the Ford Motor Company were synonymous, and it must indeed have been a wrench to part company with what has been a monumental life's work." Sorensen tells us that Charles E. Wilson, one of the heads of the War Production Board, telephoned that the President wished him to take charge of the Ford Motor Company for the government. Determined Federal action could have arranged this. Sorensen adds that he not only refused to be a party to any such plan, but protested against government removal of Henry Ford, "much as that removal was desirable," and expressed faith that Henry II would see the remaining war work of the plants carried through. Through friends in Washington, he asserts he made his view prevail.

To what extent the dramatic exit of Sorensen at the height of the war crisis was a product of the machinations of Bennett, to what extent it represented another erratic impulse of Henry Ford, and to what extent other factors counted, nobody can tell. After Edsel's death no one in the company was in a position to stand up for Sorensen. He himself, after inquiry, concluded that Clara Ford made the decision. This view gains some support from Ernest Kanzler's statement that Clara's hostility to both Sorensen and Bennett, since Edsel's death, had become implacable. It is certain that she now began to act decisively in her husband's name, and it was high time she did. In this course Mrs. Edsel Ford would strongly have supported her.[15]

Sorensen's departure had the quality of a denouement in a tragedy. For decades he had been Ford's principal lieutenant. He stands with James Couzens, C. Harold Wills, Norval A. Hawkins, Walter Flanders, and Edsel Ford as one of the little group of true builders who, using the erratic genius of Henry Ford, lifted the corporation to international fame and power.

Of all the men who served Henry Ford after he acquired complete control of the company, Sorensen was the most powerful, and stands alone as the most dynamically ruthless. By his account he had played a role in the greatest single achievement of the Ford Motor Company, the consummation of the mass-production process which transformed modern industry. He and Edsel had been Perry's staunchest supporters when that energetic architect of the European fabric was regarded with dour suspicion by petty men at the Rouge. He had been a leader in the war-activity of the company. Nobody ever questioned his grasp, drive, or vision. These qualities, edged with harshness, had been knit into every element of Ford activity, but most of all into factory production, a field in which he stood with Knudsen, Flanders, and Zeder of the Chrysler company as master. As he now walked the same plank he had helped prepare for many another worthy man, he could guess what chagrin, frustration, and sense of injustice had possessed them too.[16]

### 3.

Sorensen's and Sheldrick's expulsion, clearing the ring, left the surviving antagonists in this murky, undeclared war face to face: Bennett and Henry II. Lesser officers grouped themselves about these two. To be sure, something in Bennett's motivation, conduct, and aims remains unknown, and men may err in attributing to him the completely Machiavellian, not to say Mephistophelian, role given him by journalists addicted to black-and-white portraiture. We can say, however, that his continued activities in this critical hour, like his past actions, did not belie this portraiture.

The dislodgment of Sorensen was generally accepted as proof that Bennett's star was rising to the zenith. "With Sorensen out," commented *Time,* "there is no one in the empire now, outside of Henry and Henry II, Ford vice-president, to challenge the absolute power of the one-time sailor, boxer, and Ford bodyguard, Harry Bennett." He was "the winner." The event inspired *Fortune* to publish an article on "The Ford Heritage" which, while not fully informed, showed how most people interpreted it, and sounded an ominous note. Detroit was full of rumors, it stated, that Henry Ford was waiting to see how much ability his grandchildren showed, and if they flashed in the pan, "he intends to leave his voting shares in a trust, and one of the trustees will be Harry Bennett." The writer had somehow smelled out the codicil! A column in *Iron Age* expressed the view that Bennett would become actual operating head of the Ford works and all outlying activities at home and abroad.[17]

Unquestionably Bennett held strong cards in his hand. He and his own junta, his palace guard: Ray Rausch, Harry Mack, Russell Gnau, and Stanley Fay. He had his well-placed plant police, seeded with bruisers and thugs. Above all, he had the codicil, for what it was worth, and his domination over Henry Ford's uncertain mind. When in his reminiscences he tells us that a public remark by Henry II acquiescing in government wartime controls over the industry "enraged" the grandfather, we may wonder if Bennett did not promote the rage. Henry Ford's obsession with the idea that his beleaguering enemies were held back by Bennett's wall of defense was somehow sedulously nourished. One of Ford's remarks chills the blood. "The Jew and Communists," he said, "have been working on poor Harry until he's almost out of his mind." He needed a vacation. "Then he'll come back all ready to keep on fighting the ones who are trying to take over our plant." This harmonized with his statement to Fred L. Black: "The Ford Motor Company would be carried away, there wouldn't be anything left, if it wasn't for Harry." [18]

Using these cards, Bennett after Sorensen's ouster expected to enlarge his authority rapidly. Henry II, he believed, might prove weak enough to drift under his tutelage. He told the press that the two of them could soon fill the gaps left by Wibel, Sheldrick, and Sorensen. "There are a lot of geniuses around here, and I hope Henry Ford II will learn to back them as his grandfather did." [19]

Ominously, on the heels of Sorensen's resignation came that of another officer whose departure the best men at the Rouge regretted. H. C. Doss, the capable sales manager, left in frustration and anger. Considering the fact that during the war the output of ordinary automobiles practically ended, he had maintained his long record of effective work. Early in 1944, however, Bennett and Rausch decided that a general sales manager was not needed, and he should give way to five or six regional managers, each supreme in his field. Doss was offered the South, with Atlanta as center. When he remonstrated that a half dozen regional managers would be certain to quarrel, Bennett told him that he should act as coordinator. The vagueness of his proposed authority offended him. Still more did his discovery that two men allied with Bennett's group were travelling in the Southwest looking for lucrative dealerships into which they might put their friends. "That was just about all I could take," he records; "more than enough." Henry Ford II did his best to dissuade him from going, but he left with only a last word of advice:

"The regional scheme will wreck the organization," he told the young vice president. "You will need a first-rate sales manager. Get Jack Davis back here just as soon as you can and put him on the job." [20]

Ominous, too, was the celerity with which, as soon as Sorensen left for the Florida vacation which became resignation, Raymond R. Rausch moved into the production chief's vacant office. This tall, bulky, balding executive of fifty, looking his shrewd, stolid Dutch ancestry, took over Sorensen's work at the Rouge, with attention not only to Ford vehicles but the tank division and Lincoln division. Mead Bricker was left in control at Willow Run. Both were company veterans, Bricker having made his permanent connection with Ford during the First World War, and Rausch having come in 1921; both owed much to Sorensen, who spoke well of them. Rausch, however, had luffed in the direction of Bennett while Bricker held a straight course. Both were directors. "Mr. Rausch evidently did things for Mr. Henry Ford," recalls J. L. McCloud, "generally with Harry Bennett or Ray Dahlinger as intermediary." He had tucked himself under the elbow of Power, and close company observers wondered that Sorensen, before his ouster, had been so naively unconscious of Rausch's unfriendly activities. Bricker's support of Sorensen's policies had never been questioned. [21]

### 4

While Bennett clutched a strong poker hand, Henry II held all the aces—if he had the insight and nerve to play them. "I didn't know how secure I was," he said later, [22] but he commanded half a

dozen elements of potential strength. For one, from the moment he
was elected a vice-president in December 1943 a great many employes
in the lower echelons of the company's management regarded him as
the imminent head. Did not his name give him a prescriptive right to
the presidency? For another, war production leaders in Washington
had learned from Sorensen and Kanzler * to look to him, and to the
extent that he proved capable, they would give him firm support in
directing the plant's war work. In Bennett they had no faith whatever.
As a third element of strength, Henry's grandmother Clara, his mother
Eleanor, and his brothers Benson and William Clay stood united
behind his leadership. Clara, who as Sorensen surmised had now
seized the reins from the nerveless grasp of old Henry Ford had not
only an inflexible hostility toward Bennett, but a fiery pertinacity
when aroused in defense of family interests; Eleanor, a brilliant
woman, had seen her husband so cruelly maltreated that she was
resolved to fight to the last for her sons. The two women were one
—and they controlled large blocks of voting stock.[23]

Most important of all, Henry II had his own abilities and fighting
temper. Doss, in resigning, had said: "I don't like to leave you and
I wouldn't leave you if something could be done with this Bennett
situation." Henry II had replied: "I don't blame you a damn bit, but
there is nothing much I can do about it now. Some day I will!" That
day began to dawn when he was elected vice-president. Backed by his
mother and grandmother, early in 1944 he began to do something
about the situation. His power was enlarged when on April 10 the
board appointed him executive vice-president, the post next in rank
to the presidency. That same month he became a director of the Ford
Motor Company of Canada, and in July vice-president.[24]

His triple task was to establish correct policies, eliminate the vicious
elements in the administrative system, and find capable, honest aides;
three interconnected objectives. Time pressed; June would bring
D-Day in Normandy and the capture of Saipan in the Pacific, and it
was clear the company would soon face the multiform tasks of peace.
As Henry II knew in general outline what policies he must pursue,
the first step was to bring to his side aides of ability and insight. By
good fortune two men of ripe plant experience were at hand, Mead
Bricker and Logan Miller; a third helper was given him by some

* Kanzler was in the WPB until June 1943, a fact of importance.

curious circumstance, John S. Bugas; and a fourth he added by his own exertions, John R. Davis. Men of capacity and integrity, they espoused with enthusiasm Henry's purpose to institute a regime liberal in temper, scientific in method, and efficient in teamwork.

The appointment of Bugas to the plant had elements of mystery. This energetic graduate of the University of Wyoming had practised law in Cheyenne, joined the Federal Bureau of Investigation, served J. Edgar Hoover in Alaska and the South, and finally, at thirty, taken over the FBI in Detroit in 1938. His investigations uncovered thefts and other malpractices in the war work of Willow Run and the Rouge. Possibly his efficiency impressed Harry Bennett with the idea that he might be useful. More probably Harry thought that it would be well to have Bugas right at hand so that Bennett's office could watch and (as he puts it) "cope with" him. At any rate, soon after Henry II came to the Rouge, Bennett hired Bugas to help deal with industrial relations—that is, labor. Once Bennett had him on the payroll he tried to neutralize him. "I was as isolated as a tuberculosis germ," Bugas later said. But to Bennett's discomfiture, the newcomer quickly became one of the best aides of Henry II—alert, progressive, right-minded.[25]

Bricker, a useful, honest, and forceful executive much disliked by Bennett and Rausch, could deal with production almost as ably as Bugas could handle labor. It was plain, however, that they needed reinforcement. Henry II wanted more lieutenants, and going over old plant records and talking with veteran workers, concluded that Doss was right in saying that John R. Davis was needed to manage the sales department. Visiting the Coast, Henry asked him if he would come back to Dearborn. Davis politely refused; not only did he like California, but he feared that his oldtime enemy Bennett might still be strong enough to ruin him. But Henry II insisted. Seeing the root of Davis's reluctance, he promised that they would fight to victory together, or take defeat together. "Put it on this basis," he said in effect. "If I stay, you stay. If you go, I go. The company and I need you. We shall share the same fate." Davis came.[26] Then, the struggle still undecided, came the crisis.

Shortly after Bugas joined the company, Henry II suddenly learned that some document connected with his grandfather's will existed which, if valid, would have the effect of placing control of the property in the hands of trustees for ten years after Henry Ford's death. He was staggered. The document (he did not know it was a codicil) had been kept secret from Edsel's family. Bennett, he gathered, would dominate the trustees, a group largely his friends. In depression and anger, he came to Bugas to talk matters over. This, he declared, was the last straw. He was ready to quit the company, sell his stock, and write Ford dealers all over the country advising them to cancel their connection.

"I tried to calm him down," a magazine writer quotes Bugas as saying. "Finally he agreed not to do anything drastic until I talked to Bennett and found out what it was all about." This is an accurate synopsized version of what passed between them.

Going to Bennett, Bugas told him that Henry II had learned of the secret alteration of the will. This statement in turn staggered Bennett. He showed great agitation and even perturbation. With some remark about not wanting young Henry to feel "bothered," he said: "You come in here tomorrow and we'll straighten the whole thing out."

The next day, relates Bugas, a strange scene was enacted in Bennett's office. Bennett showed Bugas the original typewritten codicil, and a carbon copy of it; for as Capizzi states, Bennett had asked the attorney for a second copy. Then Bennett placed the original on the floor, and set a match to it. The two men watched it burn. When the flame expired, Bennett swept the ashes into an envelope, which he dramatically handed to Bugas, saying, "Take this back to Henry." [27]

In due course Capizzi heard from Bennett of the destruction of the codicil, and asked an explanation. "It wasn't any good anyway," said Bennett. "Why?" asked Capizzi. "Because," rejoined Bennett, "Mr. Ford had carried the instrument around in his pocket for a long time and had made a lot of scribblings on it, including verses from the Bible." He added that Ford, writing in Capizzi's name as trustee, had misspelled it. The attorney came to the conclusion that Ford had never signed the document. If this was true, Bennett's theatrical gesture cost him nothing.

The secret existence of so explosive a document, thus revealed, galvanized Henry II, his family, and his company lieutenants into more urgent action. During the summer and fall of 1944 he, Bricker, Bugas, and Davis spent long hours discussing plans for the future, and strengthening their position. Henry and Davis made their before-mentioned July trip to rally the dealers of New England behind the post-war effort, for the production of passenger cars was recommencing. Young Henry's obvious grasp of company affairs and energetic program for new models impressed everyone. A Maine dealer who followed the tour with attentive eye wrote Davis: "From the smallest to the largest establishment you have always heard the phrase, 'I want to see the boss.'" Another commented: "Mr. Ford's talk. . . . gave us proof that the business is still in good hands. He shows a remarkable grasp of the business in such a short time." Still another called him "a grand young man with plenty on the ball." During the autumn Henry II and Davis travelled together to the Atlanta branch, where Henry announced that the company, as part of a $150-million program of expansion, would erect a great parts depot to supply the Southeast. Davis had shown acumen in rebuilding the field organization of dealers, calling back to service many experienced men.[28]

That winter Henry II and his aides continued their labors. They held their most confidential conferences in a corner of the high-ceilinged Detroit Club, safe from eavesdroppers.[29] Early in 1945 Henry called R. I. Roberge into his office. All indications pointed to an early end of the war, for the Russians had captured Warsaw, and on March 7 American troops crossed the Rhine at Remagen; and Henry felt that Roberge should give all his time to plans for resumption of export trade and foreign production, while G. J. Crimmins should devote himself to the renegotiation and termination of war contracts. The first outlines of an orderly administration were appearing in company affairs. No longer could it be said, as E. F. Wait tells us men had said just after Sorensen left, that the situation was terrifying; that "the place was running wild." On the contrary, a firm hand was becoming evident. James Dalton, editor of *Motor,* had just written: "Next to the founder of the company Henry Ford II is the dominant figure in the Ford organization." He did not know that the founder had dropped out.

One zone of friction as late as May 1945 remained—the Rouge. As the termination of the bomber contract approached, Mead Bricker, in charge at Willow Run, ordered his aide Logan Miller to return to the Rouge. "There," states Miller, "I more or less wandered under special assignment." Rausch still assumed that he was in control of the Rouge, and arrogantly acted on that assumption. From all appearances, Bricker had little authority there and Miller still less. But Rausch unquestionably knew, when on June 2 Henry II announced design changes in the cars for 1946, just where supreme power lay. A significant incident brought matters to a head. Bricker one day gave Logan Miller an urgent week-end task in the tool room, supervised by one of Rausch's subordinates, Joe Durling. Durling of course took word of the job to Rausch, and after his own and Bennett's pattern of conduct, Rausch told him, "Forget it!" Thereupon Miller reported the cancellation of the assignment to Bricker, and added a resentful question: "If you have no authority around here, what are you kidding me about?"

The sequel, as he relates it, was dramatic. "I saw Mr. Bricker go into Mr. Rausch's office, where a few men were sitting. The double-door closed. Finally those doors flew open and out came the group of men as though somebody had exploded a bombshell. That to me indicated that somebody else was taking charge at the Rouge plant in place of Rausch. I never asked where Bricker received his authority." He did not need to ask; Henry II stood behind Bricker. Soon after the last B-24 rolled off the Willow Run line on June 27, Bricker was fully established as production chief of the great Rouge plant displacing Rausch, who however still remained in the company.[30]

By force of character, brains, and toilsome attention to detail, Henry II had fairly established his mastery over the company business. Meanwhile, Clara Ford had labored to convince old Henry that the time had come to transfer the presidency to his grandson. He was peevishly reluctant. Finally Mrs. Edsel Ford, according to her brother-in-law, took decisive action in support of Clara. "If this is not done," she proclaimed, "I shall sell my stock!"—and the old man gave way. He summoned young Henry to Fair Lane for an interview. There he announced that he was ready to step aside, and let his grandson assume the presidency.

"I told him I'd take it only if I had a completely free hand to make any changes I wanted to make," Henry II said later. "We argued about that—but he didn't withdraw his offer." The young man went at once to the Administration Building, where he bade Frank Campsall to prepare his grandfather's letter of resignation and to call a meeting of the board of directors the following day to act on it.[31]

That day, September 21, 1945, the board held one of the most important sessions in its history. Henry Ford, now a mere adumbration, was present; so were Henry II, Bennett, Bricker, Craig, and Mrs. Edsel Ford. Campsall had the elder Ford's resignation ready, and delivered it.

As the paper was unfolded, Bennett, who knew what had been decided, watched with bitter chagrin. He rose abruptly as Craig finished the first sentence, hurled an angry word of congratulation at Henry II, and started to bolt to the door; but others prevailed on him to stay until the decisive vote was taken. "Before the directors' meeting had completely broken up," writes an informed journalist, "Young Henry strode down the mahogany panelled corridor to Bennett's office. He was inside alone with Bennett for several minutes; when he came out Bennett was no longer the boss of Ford, though he was allowed a face-saving directorship for another month." According to Bennett, the meeting took place in young Henry's office. Whatever the scene, Bennett made a last venomous speech to the new president: "You're taking over a billion dollar organization here that you haven't contributed a thing to!" He could have offered no better revelation of his character and aims.[32]

### 5.

The central figure of this gathering, in the historical view, was not the triumphant and vigorous new head, and not the plotter so decisively worsted, but the broken old man who was led from the directors' room, all his glories ended. Already people were referring to Henry Ford in the past tense. A participant in a Detroit program in his honor had written his speech as if Ford were dead, and had frantically changed his tenses at the last moment.[33] What decisively ended in the board room was old Henry's presidency; what had already begun to end was the Ford legend that had been born with the efflorescence of the Model T nearly four decades earlier, and the proclamation of the five-dollar-day seven months before Europe broke into flames in 1914. An era terminated as he stepped out of the room.

No informed man could doubt that Henry Ford's resignation closed perhaps the most impressive and certainly the most spectacular career in American industrial history. Nor could anyone doubt that his worldwide fame had been built on solid and enduring foundations. He had established the Ford Motor Company in 1903 as a daring venture in which few men dared embark their capital. After years of grueling struggle, making one successful car after another, the best labelled A, N, and S, his mechanical genius had produced the Model T, which precisely filled a ravenous national want. The insatiable demand for his automobile enabled him to erect at Highland Park one of the most shining, well-planned, and efficient factories on the globe. It enabled him and his associates to evolve there the magic instrument of industrial fecundity termed mass production; a magic still little understood, for many people equate it with quantity production, which is only one of its half-dozen leading components, but a process which has altered the world, and particularly America. From the early profits of the Model T and mass production bloomed the five-dollar-day, which the London *Economist* has called the greatest single step in the history of wages.

The five-dollar-day embodied a simple but inspired formula for the renovation of the economic and social life of industrialized nations. Mass production meant an opulence of manufactured goods; steady price reduction on these goods meant enlarged consumption, profits, and wage-paying capacity; and higher wages meant increased buying power to maintain the cycle. Once its efficacy was demonstrated, the formula seemed as obvious as Columbus's method of making the egg stand on end. Until it was tested it appeared so unworkable that most manufacturers thought it grotesque, and Ford had to battle his partner Malcomson before he could give it a trial. Ultimately it became the drive-wheel of the affluent society. People might say that the Model T was a happy mechanical accident, that mass production was the creation of many ideas and talents working in unison, and that the five-dollar-day was a sudden impulsive decision; but genius went into each of these achievements, and the genius was Henry Ford's. It was the genius that his close and by no means uncritical associate Dean Marquis called a "supernormal perceptive faculty."

The Henry Ford who became not only world famous, but a world force, before 1915, was on the whole an attractive figure. Complex, wayward, mercurial, with a streak of meanness engendered by his hard early life, and prejudices that arose from ignorance, he could in spite of his glaring faults be called an idealist. He proved his interest in the workers not only by high wages but by making Highland Park and later the Rouge almost model plants in brightness, cleanliness, good air, and safety; still more by the thoughtful if sometimes overstrict welfare work of his Sociological Department. He proved his hatred of monopoly by his overthrow of the Selden patent, and continued to demonstrate it by making his patents and processes free to all. He proved his hatred of war, "a habit, and a filthy habit," by his Peace Ship, which he hoped might help end the insane butchery in Europe. His interest in schools and educational institutes, which he endowed in England, the South, and Michigan; his zeal in developing his industrial museum and Greenfield Village in Dearborn; his efforts to promote better agriculture and wholesome habits in recreation; his devotion to George Washington Carver and Martha Berry; his labors to demonstrate the social value of "village industries"—these showed facets of a true idealism. The Ford who loved old machines, old folksongs, old schoolbooks, and old dances, who built winter shelters for rabbits and grew corn for crows, who detested snobbery and class lines, and who was contemptuous of money, was thoroughly likeable. It is not strange that Americans devoured books on him, and that Russian moujiks and Turkish mechanics wove wistful dreams about his name.

The years hardened him; his worse side wrestled more frequently with the better, until, after paralytic strokes lamed his mind, it seemed to master him. But responsibility for the change rested partly with his environment, with scheming and malicious men, and with changing times. Because rural Michigan of the eighteen-seventies had denied him a proper education, his ignorance laid him open to the lamentable suspicions of his anti-Semitic campaigns. The same ignorance, and the influence of reactionary men, made him a victim later of ideas fiercely hostile to government regulation, to New Deal reforms, and to organized labor. Meanwhile, the milk of his idealism had been curdled by cynical or spiteful attacks. Many American newspapers, he once burst out, were outrageously unfair. "They misquoted me, distorted what I said, made up lies." Part of the press had gibed at his Peace Ship beyond all warrant; business reactionaries had cast base aspersions on his motives in lifting wages to $5 a day; politicians and editors had made blackguardly attacks on Edsel as an alleged draft-dodger. The ridicule which accompanied the trial of his libel suit against the Chicago *Tribune* would have seemed degrading to even a less sensitive man. Then, too, the 1920's were unquestionably crasser and more conservative than the preceding era, and the change in atmosphere affected him.

After the stroke of 1938 the old idealism showed itself only in rare flashes, the old kindliness and philanthropy in few words and fewer deeds. His hostility to labor, his surrender of plant control to hard-fisted men, his comradeship with Bennett, the countenance he gave to violence and injustice, and above all, his tragic persecution of his own son, placed him in a melancholy light. The growing senility of his last years was so carefully concealed that people failed to make due allowance for it. But as he now moved off the stage, tolerant observers knew that his career would have to be viewed as a whole, and that in judging his darkened later years the creative decades could not be forgotten. In perspective, those decades counted far the most, and would be remembered when much that followed was forgotten.

# XI

## OUTER EMPIRE: WAR AND PEACE

THE world convulsion which ended car manufacturing at the Rouge and threw all the energies of the company into war work, of course tore asunder the Ford international network. But abroad as at home, the war years cleared the ground for a hopeful new beginning.

We have seen that Europe in 1939 was dotted with Ford factories, assembly plants, and sales agencies, those in France and Germany autonomous but most of the others controlled from Dagenham. We have seen that despite crazy nationalist restrictions, which ruined the Ford effort in Italy and crippled it in some other lands, the European business as a whole had achieved a precarious prosperity. It had probably enlisted in the various boards of directors a larger number of important European figures—former cabinet ministers, high bureaucrats, renowned financiers and industrialists—than any other business in the world. Its three principal executives were as capable as any of those working in Dearborn. In Germany, Dr. Heinrich Albert was shrewd, aggressive, sleeplessly active, and skilful in trimming his sails to use every favoring political breeze. The impression his letters leave is of a strong business leader, though interested in furthering his own ambitions. In France, Maurice Dollfus, the polished Parisian banker with valuable connections in finance and government, was a big, emotional, likeable man. Ablest and most experienced of all, Lord Perry exercised from his offices in Dagenham and Regent Street a sway marked by consistent grasp and vision.

When fighting began, this Ford domain was necessarily divided against itself. Its various heads had to be patriotic Britons, Frenchmen, Germans, Danes, and so on; its plants had to be used for national purposes. Dearborn's control was first weakened, then in large part lost. Henry Ford tried until Pearl Harbor to keep the American man-

273

agement neutral and pacifist; as he had crippled Graziani's attack on Abyssinia by refusing to deliver trucks to the Italian army, so he would gladly have crippled the war effort in any other land. He of course failed. Yet while national requirements took iron precedence, and while Dr. Albert and Lord Perry became sworn enemies, the Ford domain retained a certain unity. Its managers felt a dual allegiance; most of them never forgot their loyalty to Dearborn, and expected to see the old fabric restored as soon as the tempest subsided.

Before long, executives and workers in the Nazi-occupied lands underwent a poignant personal ordeal, for they had to serve a cause which at heart they hated. Our story, however, begins before this.

## 2.

"I hope that the year upon which we have just entered will bring us peace," Maurice Dollfus had written Edsel from Paris on January 11, 1940, "but I am quite certain that I am voicing the opinion of the entire French nation when I say that there will be no peace without victory; no compromise seems to us possible; but a quick war seems quite a possibility." [1]

This was in the midst of the "phony" war or *Sitzkrieg,* when many Europeans shared his wistful opinion that the conflict would soon end. Hitler, observed Neville Chamberlain, had missed the bus. When Dollfus wrote, the Ford enterprises in France and Britain were being converted to war purposes, and nearly ready to begin manufacturing at capacity.* Ford, Ltd., of Britain, was finishing a "shadow factory" on the Manchester Ship Canal, where it would soon write a record of lustrous efficiency in producing Rolls-Royce airplane engines. The Dagenham factory was pouring out tractors, and beginning to fill orders for trucks and infantry-carriers. Across the Channel, Dollfus had evacuated the machinery and most fixed installations from Strasbourg to Bordeaux, and Matford was manufacturing engines and transmissions for trucks and aviation-engine parts. Meanwhile, Dollfus also pushed work on the new plant at Poissy near Paris.

By early spring of 1940 the Ford works at Bordeaux and Poissy hummed day and night to help the republic to victory. Dollfus, though

---

* The Ford Motor Company of Canada of course also flung itself into the Dominion's war effort.

suffering from diabetes and repeated heart attacks, labored incessantly. The manpower shortage compelled him to hire large numbers of women, whom he found hard to recruit. He also found it difficult to obtain permission to pay them decently on government account, for women's pay in France had traditionally been poor; but by a stubborn battle, the Ford management got their wages raised to a level only one-fifth below the average for men, instead of the usual two-fifths. While the Fordair section at Bordeaux made parts for the Hispano-Suiza airplane motor (for the contract on the Rolls-Royce engine had been dropped in favor of the Hispano-Suiza) the Matford section made truck engines and transmissions, and parts for a 20-mm. anti-aircraft gun. Half-built Poissy took over the assembly of trucks from Asnières. By the beginning of March the Ford works, in spite of horrible difficulties in procuring raw materials, were supplying the French military with 35 trucks a day, and by the end of the month were approaching 50.

How different the picture a few months later! All French factories were now serving the Nazi overlords. Control of the automotive industry in France and other conquered lands was vested in a General Von Schell, under whose authority the German Ford manager, Robert Schmidt, now German Commissioner, for such work, stalked through the Poissy plant giving Dollfus his orders. Though Schmidt had often called himself anti-Nazi, he now boasted of the quantities of machinery he was shipping to the Nazi chieftains from the subjugated nations. He seems at first to have wished to control plant management in detail, but the German government intervened, and after some efforts to push Dollfus about, Schmidt had to let him resume his position as managing director of Matford with little interference. Nevertheless, the proud Dollfus who in January had declared he would never compromise was forced in July to become an acquiescent Dollfus, doubtless boiling inwardly, but obedient.

"I was the first Frenchman to go to Berlin," he reported to Edsel on August 31, 1940.[2] His interview there with General Von Schell was entirely satisfactory to both. He was told that he need fear no confiscation of the plants, could keep them running full-tilt, and would get adequate payment for everything he made. The passive attitude of Henry and Edsel Ford, conforming to official American neutrality, he added, had helped mightily in this consummation. Von Schell, while emphasizing the need for trucks, let him make 100 4-cylinder passenger cars. Beyond question, he predicted, the factories' output would be limited only by shortages of raw material and transportation.

Under German orders, the machinery that had been laboriously shipped from Strasbourg to Bordeaux was crated and shipped back to Poissy—all but some installations which Schmidt earmarked for Cologne. It was the Atlantic ports that were now exposed to attack. Dollfus still expected an early peace in Europe, but it was to be achieved by complete Nazi victory, and he was pleased when high Germans consulted him on their plans for remaking all European industry.

The Nazi reduction of Denmark and Norway, the sweep through Holland and Belgium, the defeat of the French armies and capture of Paris, had been accomplished with stunning rapidity. Begun April 9, 1940, the conquest had been completed by June 15. In the overwhelming Nazi onslaught the various Ford works suffered little damage, though the factory in Antwerp received three German bombs. Except for minor dislocations and the shutting off of overseas supplies, Ford properties in the five nations could be operated as before—and speeded up by the Nazis.

For both military and political reasons, the Danes were at first given more lenient treatment than other peoples. The manager of the Danish Ford company, H.C. Møller, received permission, as he wrote Dearborn, to abstain from turning out "real war supplies such as arms, ammunition, armored vehicles, parts for airplanes, and so on." He would continue to assemble Ford automobiles as long as his supply of parts held out, but when they were gone, would have to supply what Germany wanted, or dismiss his workers. All other factories from Copenhagen to Poissy had to follow Nazi orders forthwith.[3]

### 3.

While it was of course Nazi policy to squeeze as much in supplies, food, military material, and labor out of the prostrate countries as possible, the new rulers of Western Europe were wise enough not to copy Hans Frank's brutal decree in the East: "The Poles shall be the slaves of the German Reich." They wished the main industrial plants to continue production under their general dictatorship, but without loss of plant autonomy.

Under the army command, Robert Schmidt exercised an elastic control over the Ford businesses in Germany, Holland, and Belgium. Doubtless his experience in the Cologne factory had taught him that the best way to get results was to give executives complete freedom. His powers as Commissioner were absolute, comprehending all those formerly vested in the manager, directors, and stockholders. However, he and Dr. Albert assured Edsel Ford in a cable of late June that Schmidt would use this power "to safeguard your interests in plants in occupied territory." [4] In Amsterdam Schmidt kept the Ford manager, C. G. F. Stenger; in Antwerp he continued the Belgian manager, James Van Luppen; and in France, he soon had to give Dollfus, who hated him, but cooperated with other Germans, a free rein.

After the French Government signed the armistice with Hitler at Compiègne on June 22, 1940, the Vichy defeatists, Petain, Weygand, and Laval, began their long collaboration with the German leaders. The anxious Dollfus had to cooperate with both Berlin and Vichy. He was glad to get assurance from the Vichy leaders that they would give him as much protection as if his company were "a purely French concern," and at the same time, intimations from Berlin that his works, as an American and Ford property, would receive special consideration from the Reich authorities. For his first two months of operations under the swastika, he reported profits of more than 1,500,000 francs. The Germans needed all the five-ton trucks he could deliver, and by August he was selling them large numbers, with quantities of spare parts.

An ambitious design had been developed by Schmidt and Dr. Albert to reorganize all the Ford companies of Western Europe into a cooperative group dominated by Cologne. In the New Europe which would emerge from Nazi victory, Cologne would take the place which Dagenham had once occupied, and Schmidt would assume the role played by Lord Perry. Indeed, Schmidt had exultant moments in which he saw German power reaching beyond a humbled Britain into the United States. He told Ford's representative, the Swedish-born V. I. Tallberg, at their last interview in the fall of 1940, that after the war "they would all be taking orders from us, *including Dearborn.*" (So at least Tallberg states). [5] Schmidt and Dr. Albert even suggested to Edsel Ford that the stock of the Ford companies in Europe ought to be redistributed at once, giving the German concern control.

For the time being in 1940–1941, the Germans acted primarily to

coordinate the productive resources of the various plants. They intended that Cologne, Antwerp, Amsterdam, Poissy, and Asnières
should divide by planned ratios the manufacture of trucks, engines and
other products demanded by the Reich. To facilitate the work they
should freely exchange materials and machines. Although thus far the
Amsterdam and Antwerp plants had carried on only assembly operations, under the new arrangement they would undertake manufacture,
or at least the machining of parts, the necessary equipment being transferred from the French factories. Since the trucks made in Amsterdam
and Antwerp would be identical with those produced in Cologne, and
the Poissy-Asnières trucks would differ from them only in frame, front
axle, and a few other features, all the factories could exchange parts.
Of course Schmidt and Albert expected their great establishment on
the Rhine to dominate the complex.

"They are both full of ambition for the Cologne company, and
maybe for themselves as well," Dollfus warned Edsel, "and by the way,
do not mind that it should be known." [6]

Edsel, seeing that the plan would place all the Ford properties of
Western Europe permanently under the control of two headstrong
Germans, turned a chilly face toward it. He did not wish to say a flat
no, for Dr. Albert had reminded him that under international law an
occupying power had the right to seize factories in enemy territory and
force them to make war material. But he did write that while the idea
of doing machine work in Amsterdam and Antwerp seemed sound, he
did not approve of the transfer of French equipment—its ownership
already complicated—to the low countries, and despite Schmidt's enthusiasm, he did not see his "dream" as Schmidt saw it.

Dollfus was naturally still more hostile to the scheme of German
hegemony over the automotive industry of Europe, and opposed it as
firmly as he could. As an oldtime rebel against Dagenham's control,
as a man proud of the business he had built up in the face of Citröen
and Renault competition, and as a Frenchman, he could not bear the
idea of letting the French company become a minor cog in a Teutonic
machine. He was outraged by the way in which Schmidt had, as he
put it, "emptied Asnières of the best part of its valuable stock to the
profit of Antwerp and Amsterdam." [7] He kept his communications
with other Nazi officials open, and it seems certain that he insisted to

them that he could maintain efficient production only on an independent basis.

He had his way, for at least temporarily the German command took his side against Schmidt. They valued Dollfus's zeal. On January 25, 1941, the German and French authorities both recognized the independence of the French company, and limited Schmidt's powers to those of a liaison officer. Since the efficient Poissy plant had been completed and production centered therein, and since the five-ton truck had won full military acceptance, the Ford business had become larger than that of any competitor in the country. "We are doing well," Dollfus wrote Sorensen at the end of May 1941; "we are even progressing to the point where there is no doubt that we have now taken a position which is undoubtedly very much above the one that we had in France before the war." He reported to Edsel that "our business is now exclusively run by ourselves," [8] and that the plants in Belgium, Holland, and Scandinavia depended on the French company for parts.

Any artificial consolidation—even any drastic rationalization—of the European automotive industry by the Nazis would have been a mistake, for the German and French plants needed separate managers giving them full-time attention. In Cologne, Schmidt and Albert themselves joined a supplier in turning out turbines to government specifications, a fact which they concealed from Dearborn. The branch assembly plant which Ford-Werke had opened in Berlin was producing in 1940 a heavy infantry-carrying vehicle called the SPKW, again without the consent of Dearborn. As a pacifist, Henry Ford would certainly have protested indignantly against such activities. The Ford Cologne plant manufactured trucks for the Germans.

Meanwhile, the Poissy-Asnières plants by March 1941 were making 400 trucks monthly and sending enough parts to Amsterdam and Antwerp to enable them to make another 400 units. This volume of business exceeded any peacetime figures for the Ford interests in France. In August, Ford SAF sold the Asnières assembly plant at a handsome profit, and began enlarging the Poissy facilities, adding a foundry to them. That autumn the fusion of Ford SAF and Matford was ratified by the stockholders, and on the heels of a Vichy order for 400 trucks for Africa, a new subsidiary was created, called Ford Afrique.

In short, war business was benefiting both the French and German Ford companies in the precarious, artificial, and hectic way in which war always stimulates large sectors of industry. At the end of 1941 Doll-fus reported net profits of 58 million francs, an impressive figure even when we discount it for inflation. The Cologne plant turned out 16,500 units in 1940, chiefly trucks, while the new Berlin branch that year pro-duced 1072 troop-carriers. Early in 1941 the German company almost trebled its capital, and at the end of the year paid a 5 per cent dividend on the enhanced total. Amtserdam and Antwerp were both making profits, and declared dividends for 1940 of 8 and 5 per cent respectively. It is unnecessary to say that this war-born prosperity of the continental concerns put no money into the Dearborn treasury. In reorganizing the Cologne company the Germans bent a jealous eye on the American control with 56 per cent of the stock, and when dividends were de-clared anywhere under their sway the Government obstructed transfers of money across the Atlantic.

Communications between Dearborn and the German-held plants became more and more tenuous. The American company could of course not ship automotive materials through the British blockade, nor did the British allow the Cologne company to discharge its debts to Dearborn by sending over wheels, bearings, glass, and other merchan-dise. Perry's group, incensed by Dollfus's collaboration with the Ger-mans, made no effort at clandestine communication with him. For a time early in the war Dearborn had shipped parts for civilian cars and trucks to France and the low countries, sent the Swedish and Finnish companies parts by way of Petsamo on the Arctic, and supplied Portu-gal. The Americans even departed far enough from neutrality to send vital machine tools to Dagenham. But while Germany was fighting and losing the Battle of Britain, Dearborn was not in a position to in-fluence business on the European continent.

By the late spring of 1941 Hitler had brought the whole Continent from Russia to the Pyrenees under German control, and all the Ford properties there were held in a tight Nazi grip. Hungary, Slovakia and Roumania had aligned themselves with the Reich in the autumn of 1940. On March 1 Hitler's troops entered Sofia, and Bulgaria joined the Axis. In April he sent his armies smashing into Yugoslavia and Greece. The Ford factory in Budapest was set to assembling trucks for the Ger-man forces. The Roumanian company under its Austrian manager,

E. R. Wachner, whom Perry had vainly tried to displace, bowed to Nazi purposes. Before May Day the Germans broke the back of Greek resistance, hoisted the swastika flag upon the Acropolis, and took over the Ford operations in Athens. Thus when the Nazis, on June 22, thrust into Russia, all the Ford facilities on the continent except the Danish plant were directly serving Hitler.[9] Still Henry Ford clung to his neutrality. Passage of the Lend-Lease Act on March 11 had meant nothing to him, and when he repudiated a statement by Lord Beaverbrook that he had agreed to build 6000 Rolls-Royce airplane engines in the United States, he aroused indignation not only in Britain and the Dominions, but among multitudes of Americans.[10]

The moment Pearl Harbor brought the United States into the war, all the Ford plants under Nazi control became enemy property. Except for occasional roundabout word from Dollfus, the Dearborn office lost touch with them. News in March 1942 that American planes had bombed the Poissy factory pleased Ford men as much as anybody else. The American Ford Company had for some time been producing materials for American defense, and now it became inextricably linked with Ford of Dagenham in the common cause. For during the two years before Pearl Harbor, Dagenham had been writing a gallant record.

4.

When the war began the British Government had been reluctant to place orders with the Dagenham factory because of its seeming vulnerability. Its 66-acre bulk sprawling along the north bank of the Thames, its 16 acres of glass roof gleaming in the sun, its plumes of smoke rising from the chimneys by day, its blast furnaces glowing like rubies against the velvet night—how could Nazi bombers miss them, especially as the broad winding river offered a perfect guide under moonlight? Nevertheless the company aspired to produce, and painfully perfected a blackout. It employed Royal Air Force experts in camouflage to paint the roofs so that to aerial eyes the factory looked like part of the drab Essex marshland, with roads winding through it. Still the ministries hesitated, and except to fill a pre-war order for 3000 tractors to be used in a Plough-for-Victory campaign, the great plant at first made little contribution to the war. Its new Anglia, a war-economy car selling at £126 to £136, was popular, but steel and other materials were strictly limited, while the blackout, gasoline rationing, and travel restrictions cut deeply into the market.

But the day of frenzied activity soon arrived. As the German armies swept to the Channel and Winston Churchill came into power, Dagenham—like every other resource—had to be used to capacity. Placed under full war pressure in June 1940, it was soon producing up to 130 war vehicles a day: half-ton vans, two to five-ton trucks, and two-and-a-half-ton infantry carriers. The introduction of a four-wheel drive made them all efficient in heavy mud or sand, so that drivers in North Africa testified: "But for Ford we could never have gotten along." Even slag from the Dagenham blast furnaces was used to surface air-base runways and make roads. The new Manchester factory, producing its first Rolls-Royce Merlin engines in June, was soon turning them out in a stream which delighted Beaverbrook, Minister for Aircraft Production.[11]

When heavy Nazi bombing began, the air raid precautions at the Ford plants proved unexpectedly effective. Shelters were built, sirens installed, and drills held. In September 1941 raids cost the Dagenham factory 377.48 hours, and a new system was introduced, the "alarm within the alert." New shelters and blast walls were built alongside the production lines. After the sirens sounded, men kept working till bombs actually fell near. Thus in October Dagenham was alerted for 350.24 hours, but the men dropped their tools only 145.41 hours, and figures for hours worked were still more favorable in November and December. The most dangerous spots were the power house, where a moderate-sized bomb might explode the boilers and destroy everything, the blast furnace, the coke ovens, and the foundry room. But the men, wearing steel helmets, toiled grimly through long stints—for early in the winter of 1941 Dagenham abandoned the 8-hour day for two 12-hour shifts. Throughout Britain the 72-hour week had become common, and many workmen stood to their jobs even longer.

The worst night, that of the great raid on London April 17, 1941, was successfully weathered. The Dagenham plant was hit by numerous incendiaries, and three high-explosive bombs. One incendiary bomb pierced the power house roof to fall among the machinery. A worker pulled it from the turbine with his bare hands, and others were using sand to extinguish it when it exploded; four men were wounded, but the turbine remained unhurt. On another rough night a parachute mine fell through the roof of the radiator department, with a number of fatalities, but improvised machinery was installed in a few hours, and radiator-production was only half-stopped for two days. At the rising Manchester factory between December 23, 1940, and May 7, 1941, thirty bombs fell, with the result that a policy of dispersal was adopted, the assembly departments being housed separately from the others. Considering the fact that the German Air Intelligence had an aerial map made on October 25, 1940, showing the precise position of Dagenham, Ford operations suffered astonishingly little from raids, a fact that could be credited in large measure to the courage of the workers.

Partly because larger facilities were needed, and partly because dispersal lessened the danger from air attack, Ford Ltd. opened a number of new plants. The company had long done some work in building engines, chassis, and frames for Bren gun-carriers. To expand this it acquired an old factory in Leamington, dating from 1777, where fireplaces, cookers, and stoves had been made. Modernizing it and adding a foundry comparable to that of Dagenham, Ford workers were soon producing tracks for the gun-carriers. A tramway shed at Wigan and an airplane shed at Cramlington were taken over and refitted for assembling cars and trucks from parts which the Canadian and American plants hastily diverted to England on the fall of France.

During the war Ford Ltd. supplied the British forces with large numbers of heavy trucks, light trucks, vans, troop carriers, and Bren-gun carriers.* The mechanization of agriculture in Britain, with its saving in manpower and expansion of food supply, would have been impossible without the tremendous output of Ford tractors. On D-Day 140,000 tractors were at work in Great Britain, and 85 per cent of them bore the Ford stamp. Of the 34,000 Rolls-Royce Merlin engines which Ford manufactured, each requiring 10,000 separate parts, not one was rejected by the Royal Air Force. Hilary St. George Saunders writes of the Bren-gun carriers that by the end of the war, "every light carrier running on tracks, wherever it might be, in Africa and Italy, in France and Germany, in India and Burma, wherever in fact the far-flung British armies stayed on their triumphant feet, had either been built by the Ford Motor Company or was driven by a Ford engine produced at

* From September 3, 1939, to VJ Day, Dagenham produced 144,495 wheeled vehicles delivered to the government; 41,700 vehicles for essential civilian transport; 23,598 vehicles for export needs; 13,942 Bren-gun carriers and other track vehicles for the forces; 136,811 Fordson tractors; 93,810 new engines; 157,010 reconditioned engines; and many thousand tons of spare parts. See the history of Dagenham's war effort by Hilary St. George Saunders.

Dagenham." Altogether, the company played no unimportant part in the march to victory.

Henry Ford became so unpopular after his sharp repudiation of Beaverbrook's statement that he was going to manufacture Rolls-Royce engines for Britain that Dagenham had to take steps to improve public sentiment. The *Daily Mail* cabled him that the general feeling was one of consternation and distress. Prompted by Perry, he cabled back that the American plants were already doing preliminary work for home defense, and would bend all their energies to it when required. Meanwhile, "Ford Motor Canada and England are using their facilities to the utmost for producing military equipment for defense British empire and will continue to serve their countries as they should." Ford Ltd. simultaneously advertised in the London press: "The vast resources, human and mechanical, of the great Dagenham factory are engaged in urgent national work to the utmost." When Perry suggested that Henry and Edsel Ford might help in the Battle of Britain by furnishing a fleet of fully equipped emergency food vans for bombed areas, they readily agreed, and paid for 350 such vehicles—the fleet finally numbering 450. But it was the huge effort at Dagenham and Manchester which did most to change the public attitude to cordial appreciation.[12]

To keep the factories running the number of women workers was constantly increased, while the government readily excused essential men from the armed forces. Women came to Manchester from Crewe and Liverpool, London and Coventry. A fuller solution of the labor problem was meanwhile found in an old principle of Henry Ford's. The plants gave on-the-job training to people from every background: to clerks, typists, retail salespeople, domestics, boys, foreign refugees. When the Manchester works reached full production, two-fifths of the 17,000 employes were women, and seven-eights had been unskilled when hired.

As was to be expected, wartime profits were substantial, but were greatly reduced by severe taxation. The year 1940, for example, chalked up gratifying results. The "trading profit" came to £2,785,500. A reserve for excess profits tax of £920,000 was set aside, and had already been deducted when the net profit was stated as £1,125,000. From this net figure an income tax had to be subtracted, which reduced the profit to £390,000. The company then declared a 6 per cent dividend, the same as the previous year and the year following. When this was distributed it also was subject to income tax—in fact, a tax of 50 per cent. Altogether, the government profited a good deal more than the stockholders, and this was the story throughout the conflict. Month by month, too, money had to be invested in expansion. It was a much-enlarged Dagenham out of which the Duke of Devonshire on November 10, 1943, drove the 100,000th tractor built there since the war opened.

New facilities, new methods, and a new spirit lifted Ford Ltd. during the war to first place in the British motor industry. Sir Patrick Hennessy (knighted for his work on aircraft production) complained when the Battle of Britain ended that life was less exciting than during the heavy bombings, but he found compensations. As lend-lease arrangements, at first cumbersome and full of delays, became systematized, the Ford works profited. Relations with the government were completely harmonious. Fresh enterprises fed a sense of adventure: the first jeep assembled in England, for example, was put together by Ford Ltd., in the Wigan shed in June 1942. A. R. Smith, under whom the Manchester works lifted production of the Merlins to 10,000 a year, used to express amusement because the Ford Company, which had boasted of making the best low-priced, mass-produced car in the world, used the same methods to manufacture the elaborate engine of the Rolls-Royce concern, reputedly the finest high-priced, hand-made piece of machinery on the globe.

### 5.

While Ford of England wrote a story of rising confidence and achievement, the record on the continent embraced dissension, sporadic damage, and finally a close approach to ruin. After America entered the war, Schmidt came into complete control, ignoring Dearborn. He decided what manufacturing and trading each plant should do, what changes in capital structure should be made, and what dividends were to be paid. He set production levels in Cologne, Amsterdam, Antwerp, Bucharest, and Budapest, though not in Paris. A man of force, ambition, and shrewd intelligence, at times he seemed arbitrary and ruthless, at other times considerate. Ruthlessness was almost inseparable from all German activities at the time.

The French company in particular came into serious and protracted conflict with its German masters. On May 26, 1942, Dr. Albert of the Cologne plant was appointed administrator of the French properties, with Major Henz Tannen, his assistant, the effective director. Tannen, recognizing that Dollfus was experienced and cooperative, at first gave him a free hand. Under their joint supervision, French Ford production was dispersed among a variety of factories—Poissy-Achères, Poissy-Robespierre, Neuilly, Ivry, Corneuve, Bourges—to lessen the perils from bombing. Unfortunately, the transportation costs and higher overhead, with new purchases of machinery, cost the French company serious temporary losses. Dollfus, who was allowed to appoint managers for the new plants, wrote Edsel that "the history of our company during this war seems like a novel." He soon found villains for the novel in his German bosses.

As bickering increased, the outraged directors of Ford SAF entered in their minutes for February 1943 a protest against the threat of dictatorial "foreign interference in the management of our company." They added that while collaboration among the associated Ford companies, such as Schmidt wished, was desirable, the Cologne managers had impeded it by failing to give assistance to French plants injured by bombing. Moreover, the German authorities had halted reconstruction work at Poissy in the last days of 1942 on the ground that the French heads were not following their instructions. During 1943 the Franco-German disputes became more acrimonious, reaching a critical point after Lieut-Colonel Herbert Beckers took Tannen's place that fall.[13]

The essence of the Nazi complaints was that the French were working too inefficiently to meet their schedules. The production of Ford SAF had steadily declined: 4693 units in 1940, only 3799 in 1941, only 2993 in 1942, and a disastrous 1591 in 1943. Dr. Carl H. Wiskott of the Hauptausschlauss Kraftfahrzeuge, a Prussian in temper if not blood, landed on Beckers with the force of a piledriver. The wretched Dollfus and his associates, he scolded, had failed to plan their purchasing, to coordinate other parts of their program, and to keep the German headquarters for foreign industry informed of their activities. Wiskott knew enough American slang to demand more "pep;" "Ford SAF is entirely lacking in it." He also wanted system: the failure sprang from "bad scheduling and lack of cooperation, even inside their own plant." He quoted Shakespeare to warn Beckers that " 'There is something rotten in the state of Denmark.' " This was in October 1943. On December 1,

Wiskott became so furious over erroneous figures for Dollfus's labor needs that he stopped all transfers of workmen. To Beckers he burst out:

"It should now be plain to you how carelessly the people have been working at Ford SAF." [14]

Doubtless some of the French staff deliberately dragged their feet, and labor shortages also caused delay. One important source of trouble, however, was the effective Anglo-American bombing. On March 8, 1942, an American air attack on Poissy closed the plant for the rest of the month. It had just gotten into production again when, on April 2, a double attack smashed much of the new construction, and badly damaged the machinery. The result was the dispersal already noted. It had hardly begun when on April 29 Poissy was again bombed, this time more severely than before. The western end of the machine shop, 6000 square meters out of 25,000, was entirely destroyed, part of the roofing on the other 19,000 was blown away, and about a sixth of the assembly building was demolished. As news of the raid reached the outside world through Vichy, American newspapers carried descriptions and pictures, and A. M. Wibel jubilantly informed Sir Patrick Hennessy that "Poissy certainly got a good hammering." Shortage of materials made rebuilding a slow and tedious process.

The Bordeaux factory suffered some damage in 1942, and repairs had to be discontinued early the next year for want of cast iron and steel. Then on May 17, 1943, Allied planes within fifteen minutes dropped seventeen bombs on the plant. This was fortunately at noon, when workers were getting lunch at a neighboring building, so that nobody was killed. The destruction, however, was heavy. Offices were wrecked, large portions of the buildings devastated, and stored materials ruined. After the architect had estimated the damage at thirteen million francs, or about $260,000, the directors agreed (June 2) that reconstruction under existing conditions was impossible.

Ford's Cologne plant meanwhile miraculously escaped serious damage until the very end of the war. The Dearborn executives, reading of the great raids on Germany in 1942, and especially of the British attack on May 30 when more than a thousand planes plastered Cologne with two thousand tons of high explosives, guessed that their factory must "look like a sieve," but they were mistaken. In 1943 the Allied air force intensified its attack on western Germany and the Ruhr, dropping more than ten thousand tons of bombs there in one thirty-day period beginning in May. Cologne was the target again and again, and on June 24 received two thousand tons of bombs, which started fires that could be seen a hundred miles away. Still the Ford works went scot free. Not until August 19, 1944, when American, British, Canadian and other Allied troops were pressing across France, did the factory receive a direct hit, and even then the damage was mainly broken glass. In October it was hit again, but without serious results. Under Nazi orders, steps were taken to disperse Ford-Werke machinery among neighboring shops on the right bank of the Rhine.[15]

The German company, under Robert Schmidt's continuing direction, did much better than the French. The Berlin assembly plant, after making 765 SPKW vehicles in 1941, was closed, and its machinery returned to Cologne. Production there was concentrated on two types of three-ton trucks, the V-8 Rhein with a 90 horsepower engine, and the 4-cylinder Ruhr with an 87 horsepower motor, and on a half-tracked vehicle, the Maultier. With a working force of from 3500 to 7000 men, including French, Italian, and Russian prisoners, output was slowly raised. In 1941 Cologne produced 14,330 units, in 1942 it made 14,762, and in 1943 the total was 17,202. About 10,000 of the Maultier half-tracks were turned out. This was a weak showing compared with the British output, but good in view of the fact that the Germans started with a poorer factory, had nothing like the Allied reservoir of materials, and lacked a Perry.[16]

The Amsterdam and Antwerp plants, ruled by Schmidt with an iron hand, meanwhile made parts and assembled trucks, while a forge and foundry near Liège assisted them. The Budapest company grew under German control, and with large war orders was a profitable enterprise until late in 1944, when Soviet troops approached the city.

Dr. Albert was arrested in September 1944 by the German authorities, who accused him of implication in the July uprising against Hitler. Spending months in jail, denying everything, he was lucky to be released shortly before the Allied victory. In the final movements of the war the Ford properties naturally experienced sharp vicissitudes, and suffered a good deal of injury. The allied armies, advancing across France, liberated Poissy on August 28, 1944—the date when Ford SAF once and for all emerged from German domination. The Poissy-Achères factory was shelled with considerable damage, though nothing irreparable. When SS units in Carrières attempted a counter-attack with the object of destroying all industrial facilities in the area, Ford workmen helped to repel them. Other Ford plants in the Paris area— at Neuilly, Corneuve, and Ivry—were little hurt. The Bourges factory barely escaped disaster, for all installations and buildings in a wide area around the arsenal in which it was placed were dynamited by the retreating Germans, but the factory itself escaped.

Simultaneously, the Russians were moving into Bulgaria, Yugoslavia, and finally Hungary. As they began encircling Budapest in the first days of 1945, the Ford-Werke officials realized that the city would soon fall into Soviet hands. Feeling it important to get their valuable machinery out of Hungary, they hastily organized a new subsidiary in Austria called Ford Motor Handels *and Werkstatten,* and barely in time moved the installations and stores of spare parts to Salzburg. Here the Allies captured them. The Allies also saved the Danish Ford plant, which almost to the last had stubbornly resisted doing war work for the Nazis. Near the end it was forced to begin the manufacture of tugboats, but saboteurs blew up the first trial craft that was finished. German military police at once occupied the premises (November 23, 1944), to the great annoyance of the Danish management; but only five months later, in May, the Danes fervently welcomed their British rescuers.

The final American advance on Cologne did the properties there more harm than they had sustained throughout the years of bombing. The American Third Army entered the Ruhr Valley on February 22, 1945, seized Trier on March 2, and on March 5 pushed into Cologne. As the troops stormed up the approaches to the Rhine, they shelled the main Ford plant, and this artillery exchange with the Germans almost destroyed it. The principal factory was smashed, the administration building was set on fire, and machinery, fixtures, electrical communications, and materials were ruined. On the 6th the American forces took possession of a paralyzed industrial center. During January and February 1945, it had succeeded in making only 170 units, or a pitiful average of four each working day. It remained paralyzed when on May 7, 1945, Germany's surrender brought the war to a close.

Nevertheless, no herculean effort would be needed to put Ford-Werke of Cologne back into operating condition. The essential fact for the company on the morrow of European peace was that most Ford

properties could be placed in early production, and that one, the Dagenham complex, had attained unprecedented size and vigor. The ensuing
years were to prove, however, that factory walls, machines, and materials were not enough; that men and methods were needed to restore
the automotive industry to prosperity.

6.

The difficulties of reconstruction—and the three years from mid-1945
to mid-1948 could well be called a transitional reconstruction period—
were amply illustrated by the German and French companies. Tottering with weakness, vexed by the political and economic troubles of the
two countries, needing young new executives, they faced a hundred
problems. In recent years Edsel Ford and Sorensen had tried to give
them constant oversight and advice; now Edsel was dead, and Sorensen retired.

The once-busy establishment at Cologne made a valiant effort at immediate resumption of work. Officials hurried over from Dagenham to
supervise the reopening of the factory, first under American military
control, and then under the authorities of the British zone of West
Germany. Fixtures were rebuilt, and machinery that had been evacuated to other towns was slowly brought back. By the end of 1945 the
plant had a considerable force at work making cars and trucks, and
reconditioning old motors, chiefly for the British Army. Erhard Vitger,
a Dane, who had been joint manager with Schmidt, was appointed
manager and custodian of Ford-Werke in September 1945. The resourceful Dr. Albert, whose reputation had benefited from his Nazi
arrest, and who could plead the value of his experience, became temporary head of the Berlin office of the company; but he was now 72
years old, and in such infirm health that he would play little further
role in the German Ford company.

The obstacles to be overcome were terrifying. All of Robert
Schmidt's talents were lost in June 1945 when he was arrested for his
Nazi activities; and when he was released three months later the American military government still forbade him to have any connection with
Ford-Werke. In time he did come back to the company, inspiring Tallberg to make an acid comment on the ease with which people forgot
war offenses, but his activities were limited. Altogether, the Allies arrested about forty Ford-Werke officials, and until 1947 kept a "denazi-

fication committee" busy about the plant, examining and sometimes removing men accused of Hitlerite activities. Much physical rebuilding meanwhile had to be done under almost insurmountable shortages of raw material, of healthy workingmen, and of skilled foremen.

The reëstablishment of markets and trade facilities in a world impoverished by six years of war, and increasingly rent by the hostility between the Soviet Union and the West, also offered difficulties which were enhanced by the hatred with which countless people regarded German representatives and goods. And, of course, the military occupation and the division of the Reich into four distinct zones presented impediments not only to the flow of materials and products, but the exchange of men and ideas. Little by little, Germany struggled to her feet and made an amazing economic recovery. As she did, lusty Teutonic rivals to the Ford-Werke in making and selling cars appeared.

The French company began with some important assets which the Germans lacked. The Poissy factory, badly damaged but soon restored, was not only favorably situated, with rail and river facilities close to Paris, but ideally planned. Dollfus, the manager, now sixty, was at the the height of his powers—"a brilliant opportunist," as Ford executives soon reported, and a man of imagination. He used his influential financial and political connection to obtain for the Ford works a position as one of the six automotive plants licensed under the "Monnet plan" of French reconstruction and he almost overnight achieved a dominant place in the making and marketing of trucks. His wartime "collaboration," one of the innumerable acts of French necessity, was soon forgotten. As he grew older he was retained as Chairman of the Board.

Poissy was soon producing 3.5-ton and 5-ton trucks in quantity, and before long added an improved version of the pre-war passenger car. Its total production rose from 6000 units in 1945 to about 10,000 the next year, and 13,000 in 1947. But these figures, it will be seen, were far from staggering; in fact, Americans could regard them as miniscule. And the French company labored even more than its associates in neighboring lands under all the disabilities of European exhaustion. Machines, materials, men, workmen, managers, were grievously hard to get. The Bordeaux plant was found to be too badly wrecked for restoration. All in all, while Ford prospects brightened in Germany, they remained gloomy enough throughout the nineteen-forties in France.

Ford management in the Low Countries faced serious political troubles. As soon as the war ended, the Dutch Government brought charges of collaboration with the Nazis against the manager of the Netherlands company and three other executives; and the directors suspended these four leaders from duty until in the spring of 1946 the public prosecutor dropped the cases. The Belgian government likewise arrested the Antwerp Ford Manager. He remained under investigation until in November 1947, when Brussells halted the inquiry and left him free to resume his old position the next year. The Danish company, which had no political involvements to regret, got under way in automobile production early in 1946, and that year and the next marketed about 7000 vehicles.[17]

Sorriest of all was the situation in southern and eastern Europe. The Spanish company and Spanish market had still not recovered from the effects of the civil war, and even the Portuguese subsidiary did not offer the Ford representatives in Barcelona much comfort. Italy was picking herself up slowly from the dust. The Bologna sales office found buyers in the first full year of peace for only 278 automobiles and tractors, and in the second only 336—a measure of the poverty and confusion of the land. Poland and the Baltic states were trapped behind the iron curtain. The Budapest plant, badly damaged in the final combats, with machinery gone, was in Russian hands, and Ford would no longer do business in Hungary. Nor would the Ford companies in Athens and Bucharest resume activities, for they were now liquidated. In Istanbul the branch had shut down during the war. The Egyptian company alone was on the verge of an extensive expansion.

Ford properties throughout Europe, in brief, shared all the troubles of the stricken and divided continent, political and economic, and the most important of those on the continent did not begin full recovery until in 1948 the United States implemented the new Marshall Plan of economic cooperation with a four-billion-dollar appropriation.

Dagenham, of course, was able to extend the record of solid growth and expansion which it had written during the conflict. From the outbreak of war to V-J Day, all the Ford plants together in England had produced goods valued at more than three-quarters of a billion dollars. Though nearly 200 bombs had struck the Dagenham works, and 41 employes had been killed and scores injured, the wheels had never stopped turning. Conversion to peacetime schedules was achieved with exemplary smoothness. In 1946 the company's exports exceeded the pre-war record of 1937, and the following year Sir Patrick Hennessy announced that although manufacturing totals were not published in Britain, "it is clear that we were the largest producers in the motor industry." Lord Perry had closed the wartime factories at Manchester, Wigan, and Cramlington, but he retained the foundry at Leamington for steel, cast-iron, and malleable iron, brought up his old Kelsey-Hayes supplier plant at Dagenham, which had long given him wheels, hubs, brake drums, and the like, and acquired another parts-factory at Walthamstow.

To supervise the areas principally served by Dagenham-controlled companies was now a large task, for as the conflict ended Ford Ltd. resumed its supervision over all the European companies except those of France and Germany. Perry looked forward to imminent retirement, but a group of able executives, tested in peace and war, stood ready to take his place. The chiefs represented ten-year steps in age. Lord Perry had been born in 1878, Sir Rowland Smith and Sir Stanford Cooper in 1888 and 1889 respectively, and Sir Patrick Hennessy in 1898. For their services to the country during the war, Hennessy had been knighted in 1941, Smith in 1944, and Cooper in 1945. This trio was amply equipped to give sound and progressive leadership to Ford Ltd. in the post-war period. Lord Airedale, formerly Sir Roland D. Kitson, was made deputy-chairman of the company in 1947 as an understudy to Perry, whose foot was on the doorsill.[18]

Perry's exit in 1948 closed an era in the foreign business, but the creation by Henry Ford II of the International Division of the Ford Motor Company had already opened a new one. The year of the Berlin airlift, of Harry Truman's election, and of the launching of the Economic Cooperation Administration in Europe under Paul Hoffman, was also a year of new explorations and fresh plans in Ford's overseas affairs.[19] To that hopeful story we shall turn after we have reviewed far more hopeful and fundamental developments at home.

# XII

## REACHING FOR ANSWERS

WHEN Henry Ford II took up the reins of power after the dramatic events of September 1945, he drove a chariot which to discerning observers resembled the fabled one-hoss shay at the moment before its collapse. He had rid the company of Bennett but the organization was tottering. Some thought it in even worse state than that. "You've got to remember," insisted J. R. Davis later, "that when young Henry came in here the Company was not only dying, it was already dead, and *rigor mortis* was setting in."

Many facts supported this extreme statement. Deaths, resignations, and discharges had torn the managerial fabric of the firm full of gaps and tatters. Authority, never clearly defined at Ford, had been further obscured in the Sorensen-Bennett, Rausch-Bricker struggles for power, and in numerous areas could not be identified; minor officials and workers would obey "any superior person." Fear and uncertainty hovered paralyzingly over most operations. The young president later estimated worker efficiency at one-third below normal.[1]

In addition, the company faced a depressing array of problems. Reconversion to effective peacetime production demanded great expenditures for machine tools, factory remodeling, and new plants. Scarcities of essential materials, government controls of purchasing and selling prices, and the honest but disruptive disagreement of executives on policies represented hurdles which would prove difficult to clear. The company would require brilliantly successful new cars, yet its engineering talent had never been so depleted. Financial management, because of Henry Ford's hostility to systematic accounting, was confused and almost chaotic. The tractor, production of which had continued during the war, had never shown a profit for Ford, and did not promise one now. The Ford-Ferguson relationship was very unpromising. Various activities started by Henry Ford outside automotive production continued to register losses. Finally, with the exception of the war years, company operations since 1930 showed an overall deficit, and greater losses seemed certain before a gain could be achieved.[2]

The great potentially constructive factor in the situation was young Ford himself. He commanded wide interest, which in the main was friendly, yet tinged with doubt as to his competence. He had lacked the credits to graduate from Yale. Now twenty-eight, he had as yet gained only a limited experience in the automotive world. Modestly he had described himself as "a young man reaching for answers," a phrase which seemed to denote both the seriousness of the situation and his unreadiness to deal with it. His smooth, almost boyish face suggested a victim rather than a victor. "Whether a company the size of Ford," commented *Steel* just after his accession, "can weather the major upheavals in top personnel of recent years without a considerable period of consolidation and readjustment remains to be demonstrated."

Ford, while modest, seemed to brush such doubts aside. On the day of his accession he announced that his main objective was "to put the Ford Motor Company back into first place in production and sales." Actually, he had important resources at his command.

The first was a cash balance on June 30, 1945, of $685,034,892. This would permit constructive spending, although even that immense sum could melt away if the company did not soon turn deficits into profits. He had strong plants in the Rouge, the Lincoln plant in Detroit, Highland Park, and the Ford assembly factories. Already plans for expansion and modernization were under way. In his uncle Ernest C. Kanzler he had found a mature and able adviser. Finally, Henry Ford II had complete courage, for while recognizing the black outlook, he was not daunted. "I knew it could be turned around," he said later. "It never occurred to me that I couldn't do the job." His grandfather had run a one-man show. "But I wasn't my grandfather, and . . . I was anxious to build a team around here so that we could get the thinking of eight or ten top fellows."

Another resource lay in his stubbornness. This and his courage matched similar traits in his grandfather, just as his readiness to work with others matched the cooperative trait in his father. He also had an impulse to find new ways of solving old problems, and a capacity for quick, sound decisions. All these qualities were to be important to the new Ford Motor Company, for dozens of projects and years of time would be required to bring it back to enduring health.[3]

Ford's first step was to gather around him a temporary "team." In contrast to his grandfather's dislike for titles, on September 27 he sent a directive to all chief Ford officials announcing the men who would head Ford activities: Manufacturing, M. L. Bricker; Sales and Advertising, J. R. Davis; Purchasing, C. H. Carroll; Engineering, R. H. McCarroll; Foreign Operations, R. I. Roberge; Accounting, Auditing, and Finance, B. J. Craig and H. L. Moekle; and Industrial Relations, J. S. Bugas. In this group Ford had only three men of the highest ability, Bricker, Davis, and Bugas, while he had wanted "eight or ten." But he was forced to work with what he had, and the team represented a step toward order.

On October 3, 1945, he called these men, with the exception of Roberge, to a meeting of a General Planning Committee, soon to be termed the Policy Committee, which began the discussion of company problems. Five days later he announced the appointment of Earl Newsom as Public Relations Counsel, a step he had weighed for some time. "I wanted someone I could consult on such matters," he said later. Newsom had an extended experience in the public relations field, and since 1935 had operated his own agency in New York. For several years he was to occupy a creative role in shaping Ford policy. Ford had tried to employ him earlier, but Newsom had pleaded too full a schedule— possibly because he was wary of serving an executive who lacked complete power. At any rate, once Henry II had become president, Newsom agreed to work with him.[4]

At the same time that he took his first measures in organization, the young president was completing the purge of Bennett men. This was essential to company efficiency, for the masses of officials and workers could not believe in a new order until the entire group that had surrounded Bennett had left the organization. Bugas offered to undertake the discharges, but the new captain dissented. "No, that's not the way. I have to do it myself, or I'll be known as the guy who couldn't face up to his responsibilities." He sent Rausch out to California, an exile which led to his resignation on October 12, 1945. Meanwhile Gnau, Harry Mack, and others had ceased to be Ford employes. But while Ford adopted a positive policy, it was not to be vigorously enforced for almost a year.[5]

The new company made progress. Too many matters associated with reconversion—costs, manufacturing problems, strikes, purchasing, re-negotiation of war contracts, general finances—crowded in on Ford to permit the thorough study he knew must precede essential changes. But he had grasped the fact that the basic way out of the confusion lay in disentangling activities that had been lumped together. This process would become known as decentralization, and in a limited, almost groping way it was followed that fall. For example, J. R. Davis at the first meeting of the Policy Committee urged that "in all cases complete separation must be had between the sales organization and the manu-facturing organization." He had particularly in mind the fact that branch managers were directing assembly plants as well as the sales force in their areas. On October 18 Ford himself suggested a separate Lincoln Division, which would have its own purchasing, cost, and sales departments—in fact, would control every phase of its activities except engineering. T. W. Skinner was appointed its head. It is significant that the word decentralization appears in these early Policy Committee minutes.

The president was not forgetful of his problems in the large. He be-gan to discuss them with Ernest Kanzler, and, says his uncle, to gather information for the future from numerous sources. But most of his energies were necessarily deflected to the problem of producing and selling the first postwar Ford car. This vehicle and its manufacture and sale were to become a test of the company's capacity.[6]

### 2.

The car pre-dated the elevation of Henry II to the company presi-dency. It came into being soon after the German surrender early in May, while victory over Japan was still to be won. At that time, on May 25, 1945, the War Production Board gave the automobile industry permission to make 200,000 vehicles before the end of the year. The only difficulty was that the manufacturers would have to find the ma-terials for these cars! The Ford Motor Company was allotted a quota of 39,910 units. By June 2 it had completed "a hand-made model," the first to be shown by any manufacturer.

This was actually an improved 1942 car with a 100 horsepower in-stead of a 90 horsepower engine, better springs and brakes, and various "cosmetic" improvements. Nevertheless, it seemed a significant achievement at a time when the number of available civilian vehicles was dwindling, and the eyes of the motorists were turned toward the future. "It is just like Henry Ford to be the first under the wire," commented the Kansas City *Times*.[7]

Plans for production were pushed energetically, and despite scarcities of materials, strikes, and the priority of war work, the company manufactured a considerable number of cars. They could not be sold, as the Office of Price Administration had first to determine what should be charged for them. However, the Japanese surrender on August 14 wholly altered the situation, for at once most controls on raw material prices were removed, and the industry was permitted to manufacture in unlimited quantities. Its leaders now hoped to turn out 500,000 cars before the end of the year instead of 200,000, and the Ford Company expected to more than double its previously scheduled output. "If production is not interrupted again," remarked Henry Ford II on August 15, "we will be able to produce between 75,000 and 85,000 passenger cars, as well as 50,000 trucks by Christmas."

By peacetime standards this goal was pathetically small. In cars it represented a yearly rate of about 250,000, and the company had often exceeded that total in a month. But the situation was highly abnormal. Steel and other crucial metals were in short supply, the remaining price ceilings on raw materials were often disruptive, and labor was demanding higher wages. Any factory reconverting to peacetime production faced the constant possibility of delays and stoppages.

Only a few days after Henry Ford II's optimistic statement his company felt the effect of these difficulties. A strike at the Kelsey-Hayes Wheel Company in Detroit, one of its vital suppliers, dealt it a severe blow. The Rouge plant limped along, but it could not produce cars without wheels, and on September 6 laid off 25,000 men, and on the 15th 50,000 more. Young Ford was disgusted. "In two and a half months," he declared, "we have produced less automobiles than we could in three hours of normal production"; a result attributable to "these continued outbreaks by irresponsible labor groups."[8] Though the Kelsey-Hayes strike was settled on October 8, three days later a thousand millwrights walked out of Detroit factories and slowed reconversion, while a strike in the Aluminum Company of America began. On November 20, Kelsey-Hayes ceased deliveries on the plea that they were manufacturing at a loss. "We are making every possible effort to build cars and provide jobs," stated the harrassed Bricker from a welter of difficulties.

It was amid such confusion that on "V-8 Day," October 26, the company formally unveiled the 1946 car, now further improved from its June prototype. At once a flash of light illumined the gloomy situation. More than 300,000 persons placed orders for the car on October 26th and 27th, "although," as a company release noted, "they had no knowledge whatever of what the cars would cost." Ford personnel bent to the task of producing the 80,000 cars previously set as a goal. However, they struggled against a continued rash of strikes and stoppages (none in their own plants) which by November 27, 1945, included fifteen Ford suppliers, covering products from ball bearings and plate glass to crankshafts and transmissions.[9]

Meanwhile, the OPA had set prices for 1946 cars, which were to be on the average no higher than those charged in 1942. This restriction was a point of pride with the government agency, which was striving desperately to prevent inflation, and which contended that automobile manufacturers had profited sufficiently during the war to afford a temporary loss, sure to disappear once volume production was achieved. The government also proposed to assist manufacturers by lowering the discount to dealers by 4 per cent. Its argument for this measure was that whereas before the war the dealer had lost money on trade-ins, now the terrific demand for all types of cars would enable him to make a profit and he could well accept a lower commission. "The OPA," ran a statement from the Ford Policy Committee minutes October 29, just after Henry Ford II returned from a trip to Washington, "seems to be of the opinion that any price rise permitted the manufacturers should be absorbed by the dealers in their discount allowance."

Both manufacturers and dealers protested emphatically against this proposal, and the Ford Motor Company firmly opposed it. "We want you to know," said J. R. Davis in a message to Ford agents, "that we have done everything possible to prevent any reduction in the dealers' margin, as we feel that the automobile dealer needs the same discount margin as he had previously." Davis believed all dealers would need money for new sales facilities and higher labor costs.[10] Nevertheless, the government maintained its position, and later actually increased the reduction.

As a result of all these difficulties, the Ford Motor Company by the end of 1945 had been able to produce only 34,439 cars. On January 29, 1946, Henry Ford II telegraphed John W. Snyder, Director of War Mobilization and Reconversion, explaining why the output had been so pitifully low. "Time and time again," he stated, "we have been forced to shut down operations because suppliers could not get us parts and materials for cars and trucks. Some of them have stopped making our parts because they lost money at ceiling prices. Some are slowed in their production by strikes or losing their employees because they cannot raise wages. Some cannot now get steel." Ford then threw a bomb into the situation. Pointing out that his company was losing $300 a car, chiefly because it could not achieve quantity production, but partly because the prices it must charge were unrealistic, he proposed the prompt removal of all price controls. This would stimulate production, and goods in quantity would soon end the threat of inflation.

Snyder in reply expressed sympathy with Ford and agreed that "the ultimate answer to our inflationary pressures is production," but staunchly defended the temporary continuance of price controls, writing that their removal would unloose chaos. The prices Ford must charge, he added, were based upon a 1941 volume of production: "If they prove inadequate, you will be entitled to an adjustment in your ceiling prices." [11]

Ford knew the OPA too well to hope for such relief, and on February 8, in a speech to the Commonwealth Club in San Francisco, told the public of his difficulties. The company goal had been 80,000 vehicles by Christmas; the achievement had been little more than 30,000. "We take a good deal of satisfaction from the fact that more than half of all the cars and trucks that have been built in this country since V-J Day have been Ford products." But why was the total so small? He brought out the fact that while his company had not experienced any strikes since the war, it had suffered from a loss in labor productivity. The most popular Ford car had required but 87 man-hours to build in 1941, but the total had risen to 102 in 1942 and 128 in 1945—this being a large factor in a rise in manufacturing costs from $512 to $962. And the total cost of a car that OPA had priced at $728 was now $1041.26.

But, Ford stated, the Ford Motor Company did not propose to cease operation, nor would it take its case to the people over the heads of government agencies. No, it would continue to produce, and attain as great a volume as possible; it would continue to report its difficulties to the OPA, would try to increase the efficiency of its labor, and even if no change came would do its best to live under existing conditions. But, he concluded, "we may lose very substantially in 1946." [12]

This challenge, which no other automobile manufacturer had made so frankly, brought a sharp retort on February 15 from Chester Bowles, then head of the OPA. In a news release Bowles placed Ford's comments among those "launched every year at this time by the few selfish groups which have worked continuously to undermine the American people's bulwark against economic disaster" (i.e., the OPA.). He pointed out that on August 31 last most ceilings on automotive parts had been removed. The implication was that Ford's troubles stemmed from inefficiency. On February 19 Bowles continued the attack in testimony before the House Banking and Currency Committee. Conceding that Ford was losing $300 a car on all the vehicles he produced, he asserted that this was attributable to his not producing in volume, a failure that was no fault of the OPA. He noted that as long ago as the previous summer Ford had asked for a 55 per cent increase in prices. [13]

Ford was in Los Angeles at the time Bowles testified, but Newsom, Martindale, and Crimmins discussed the situation with each other by telephone. Newsom, talking from New York, was emphatic in advising that Bowles should be promptly and fully rebutted. He got in touch with Ford, who as a result, on the very evening of Bowles's appearance, sent a long telegram to Brent Spence, Chairman of the Banking and Currency Committee.

His firm, Ford asserted again, was doing everything possible "to stop the present trend toward inflation;" that is, it was seeking quantity production. It had had no strikes since V-J Day. Shortages of steel had been one factor curtailing volume. As for the removal of price ceilings on most automotive parts, this was too often ineffective, because manufacturers who sold suppliers materials still operated under ceilings, and so, as to certain parts, did the suppliers themselves. One part could affect the making of the entire automobile. "When you fix prices," Ford pointed out, "you control every production operation. Fixing the price on a casting made in an Alabama foundry may mean forcing a wheel manufacturer in Ohio out of business and stopping an assembly line in Detroit." Some suppliers had simply quit, leaving the Ford Motor Company to seek new sources. As for the requested 55 per cent increase, Ford pointed out in a separate telegram to Bowles that the application had been made while the nation was at war, and the number of cars to be manufactured was limited to a total of 39,910; during peacetime no application had been filed. But in the postwar period production had been at just about the wartime level, and costs "almost exactly what we estimated." These facts, said Ford, "illustrate the point I have been trying to make in my public statements—that high costs and high prices of automobiles are caused by low volume production." High volume had thus far been impossible to establish, and, Ford implied, would not be attained while price controls remained. "When you say that only 10 to 25 per cent of our parts are under OPA price control you miss the point. Shortages on only a few parts can stop the whole assembly line." [14]

The battle continued. Under a new order by President Truman and a new OPA head, the Ford Motor Company on March 11 finally received permission to raise the prices of its cars, and a second raise was permitted May 22. As labor and other costs rose and a coal strike and parts shortages suspended company work for 32 days, these increases failed to make the company's operations profitable. But Ford had emerged from the controversy with Bowles as the moral victor, with extensive Congressional and popular support. He had shown the alertness and ability to speak out strongly for his cause. In fact, after taking power as a young man of little experience and doubtful talents, he had now advanced to leadership in one important sphere not only for his own company, but for the automotive industry.

3.

When Richard T. Leonard of the United Automobile Workers approached the Ford Motor Company in the late fall of 1945 proposing negotiations for higher wages, he must have been startled by the reply he received. Signed by Mel B. Lindquist of the Industrial Relations Department, it pointed out that in 1941 the company had agreed to accept a union shop, with checkoff provisions for its plants. It had since acted as a diligent agent for the UAW, collecting in four years $7,779,-924.65. It had hoped thus to eliminate "a great deal of friction, dispute, and downright industrial strife," but had been disappointed. Instead, it had been the victim of 773 unauthorized work stoppages. "We therefore propose," concluded Lindquist, "that you come to our forthcoming negotiations prepared to give us some better plan for giving the company the same degree of security as we have given the union itself."

This was an audacious demand. The union was then devoting scant thought to its obligations, and a great deal of attention to its own needs. The widespread demand for higher wages was justified, for the cost of living had been mounting steadily. UAW leaders had recently laid the question of better pay before their members, who by a vote of 11 to 1 had authorized their agents to begin negotiations for a 30 per cent increase, and to strike any plants that refused to bargain. Leonard was shocked by Ford's counter-demands, and accused the company of taking "a mediaeval attitude." [16]

Nevertheless, when a strike was called on November 21 it was General Motors that became the victim. Its attitude on a wage increase had been unyielding, and it was the biggest of the "Big Three." Moreover, Ford had not refused to negotiate; representatives of the union and the company had held informal meetings early in November, and began formal consultations a day before the GM strike began. The feeling of the union had perhaps grown a shade more friendly toward Ford than toward General Motors and Chrysler. The Ford management had given it an excellent contract in 1941; Bennett was now gone, and the spirit of decency which Henry Ford II had fostered throughout the company, and various liberal utterances he had made, promised a better day.

Leonard and his associates soon discovered that in its insistence on employer rights the company was wholly serious. Both Henry Ford II and John Bugas, directing Industrial Relations, believed that better protection for their company was imperative, and they translated this belief into thirty-one specific demands upon the union at the outset of the negotiations. Furthermore, they emphasized UAW responsibility. "The union could make labor history, particularly at this time, when the public is crying for responsible labor leadership," ran a company statement published on the morning of November 24. Finally, on the 28th the Ford negotiators proposed a simple financial solution: the union should pay $5.00 a day for every member who took part in an unauthorized work stoppage!

The Ford position had been presented so plausibly, and so wholly on the basis of union responsibility, that the UAW felt unable to ignore or reject it. After all, it did claim full authority over its members. The company's argument was that "the union can control its membership in the matter of unauthorized stoppages, slow-downs, and controlled production, but has failed in this responsibility during the life of the present agreement." Leonard did not concede this. He felt that "final responsibility would be a serious menace to the life of the union and we cannot put the weapon in anyone's hands." But he affirmed that the union no less than the company wanted to avoid unauthorized strikes. On December 9 he promised publicly to submit a union proposal to cover the situation, and did so the following day. The plan comprised the discharge of leaders of unauthorized stoppages, and the "docking" of participants (instead of the union) $3.00 a day for the first offense and $5.00 a day for the second. Bugas for the company said that he was "encouraged," but would have to study the offer. "Our position is very clear," he stated. "For four years we have given union security through union shop and checkoff. Continuation of this union security depends upon the union, in turn, tangibly guaranteeing company security." [17]

Meanwhile, Ford agreed to discuss wages. In a letter to the union on December 12 Bugas pointed out that the time was inappropriate because the company was uncertain of its future costs and volume of production, and was losing money on everything it manufactured. However, a week later Ford conceded that "the problem of meeting family budgets" was vital for its employes, and decided "to risk another $33,000,000" in granting a raise of 15 cents an hour. However, this was conditional. It was to take effect only when total Ford production (including Lincolns, Mercurys, and trucks) reached 80,000 units a month, it was contingent on a satisfactory agreement on company security, and it was to stand for two years regardless of the prices that OPA might permit the Ford Motor Company to charge for its cars.

The union rejected the offer, alleging that it was insufficient to meet the rising cost of living, that it would block further wage increases for too long a period, and that it was little better than an offer recently received from GM. As negotiations went forward, federal officers were encouraged by the absence of bitterness; nevertheless, a great gap remained between the two sides. The company was still talking of security and worker efficiency; the union was attempting to disassociate these matters from the wage issue, and to paint the financial future of the company as assuredly bright. The UAW predictions must have been received with wry smiles by Ford officials who knew that average losses of $300 a car were disastrous, and gave no sign of abating. Over Christmas negotiations were adjourned until January 8, 1946.[18]

The day after they were resumed, Henry Ford II indirectly took a vital part in them. At the annual meeting of the Society of Automotive Engineers in Detroit on the 9th, he spoke on "The Challenge of Human Engineering." Prepared with Newsom's assistance, this address sounded a call for a united attack by labor and capital on their common problems. Early in his remarks, Ford made his position on labor unions crystal clear.

I assume . . . that all of us agree that Labor Unions are here to stay. Certainly we of the Ford Motor Company have no desire to "break the unions." . . . We want to strengthen their leadership by urging and helping them to assume the responsibilities they must assume if the public interest is to be served. . . . Union leaders today who have the authority to affect industrial production on a vast scale enjoy a social power of enormous proportions. If they are going to be real leaders they must accept the social obligations that go with leadership.

Ford called for "industrial statesmanship—from both labor and management," which should replace an existing tradition of industrial antagonism. He denounced the idea that conflicts were inevitable, or that strikes helped to "clear the atmosphere." The rights of both management and labor should remain undiminished, but their inevitable differences of opinion should be settled peaceably. "There is no reason why a union contract could not be written and agreed upon with the same efficiency and good temper that marks the negotiation of a commercial contract between two companies." He laid down a six-point program for common effort to attain a common goal—"to make at lower and lower cost more and better products to sell for lower and lower prices;" and he called for a successful attack on industrial problems "by giving the same hard-headed attention to human factors that we have given so successfully in the past to mechanical factors." [19]

The timing of the speech was perfect. It won instant praise, even from one union official. "It is the best speech I've heard in ten years," stated George F. Addes, secretary-treasurer of the UAW.* This was

* Comment also came from industrialists. The Detroit *Free Press* of Jan. 11, 1946, reported Henry J. Kaiser as saying: "I think it was a stirring address, beautifully phrased . . . I think he had a great deal of courage to tell the world he understood we had to adapt ourselves to a modern way of living—that we couldn't go backward, we had to go forward."

undoubtedly gratifying to Ford, although any such approval was not apparent at the bargaining table. However, his recognition of the place of the union in the automotive world must have been received with satisfaction by UAW officials in general, while his demand for a spirit of cooperation had appealed to public opinion, and strengthened the company's demand for security.

After continued negotiation, an agreement on wages was reached on January 26, providing an average 18 cent per hour raise, or a 15.1 per cent advance over 1945 wages. Chrysler the same day signed a contract providing an 18½ cent increase. (Ford wages had been slightly higher.) The final Ford agreement, with provisions for company security, was consummated February 26, and Bugas expressed his satisfaction over the results:

> The union has undertaken to control its membership to prevent illegal work stoppages. . . . The contract provides that any employee found guilty of instigating, fomenting or actively supporting or giving leadership to illegal work stoppages is to be subject to discharge.

Action could be taken by the company without use of the grievance machinery otherwise essential in disciplining employes, though this could be invoked if the accused person denied the charges made against him, and the union supported his denial. But this was unlikely. The UAW by now had its fill of unauthorized stoppages.[20]

Ford and Bugas had reason for satisfaction. True, they had increased their labor bill by $41,000,000 a year, but Chrysler had accepted a comparable increase, and General Motors had already offered to do so. (The union rejected an offer of 18½ cents, demanding the 19½ cents recommended by President Truman's special board. The GM strike was settled March 13 with an 18½ cent raise and other benefits that union officials believed worth more than the extra cent.) In return, they had won gains in some respects less tangible, but having immense value. The entire atmosphere of the labor front had been changed. Ford's position was clear on full union recognition, and this fact, along with the better attitude of foremen and superintendents toward those under them, had paved the way for greater work efficiency. The union had agreed that better pay demanded better effort, and had approved and acted on the company security issue. It was firmly disposed to hold its members tighter and lead them better.

There had been an agreement in the spirit that Ford had advocated on January 9.

Finally, just as Ford had won national recognition as an industrial spokesman against price controls, so he had also won a similar eminence in the labor field. Evidence of his growing stature in the public mind came with his selection by the Junior Chamber of Commerce early in January as "Young man of the year." Just as no other voice from the industry, young or old, had been lifted so effectively against price controls, so none had been so clear and effective on workers and management.[21]

### 4.

But while he was rapidly acquiring stature as an industrial leader, Ford had made little headway in his most challenging task—the revitalization of his company.

As already noted, he had taken clarifying action by placing definite responsibilities on men and administering the Lincoln Division as a separate unit. But many high posts in the company were filled by executives without the highest ability; this was the fact in Purchasing, Engineering, and above all, in Finance, where wretched confusion remained as a legacy from Henry I and his opposition to paper work and to financiers. Young Ford had become bitterly aware of the company's financial shortcomings in seeking precise information for his battle with the OPA, for he couldn't find what various items cost. "We had to know our costs," he remarked years later, "in order to put the Company on a profit-making basis. Anyone could see that." [22]

Nonetheless, Ford took his first step in remodeling the company as a result of pressure from the outside. Early in November 1945 he received a telegram from a group of officers in the Army Air Forces. The message informed him that "we have a matter of management importance to discuss with you," and gave as a reference Robert A. Lovett, Assistant Secretary of War for Air. In the opinion of one member of the group which sent it, the communication "bordered on impudence."

At this time hundreds of thousands of men were being discharged from the armed forces, and Henry Ford II was receiving requests for employment from a number of them. Many were taken into the Ford Motor Company, but few were to play notable roles in its history. The group in question did, since eventually it brought to Dearborn ten persons, six of whom were to become vice-presidents in the organization, and two presidents.

Definite leader among the ten was Charles Bates ("Tex") Thornton, who in 1945 was head of the Office of Statistical Control in the Air Forces, and was said to be the youngest officer in that body ever to become a full colonel. At thirty-two, he had now held that rank for several years. His had been a revolutionary influence in the Army's air branch. When he joined it the right arm of the organization was unlikely to know what its left foot was doing, and he had built up an office which made every useful fact about planes and their use available practically on demand. Furthermore, he articulated plans for the future and charted disbursements. Often he briefed General Arnold and other Air officials prior to their appearance before Congressional committees.[23]

In the course of his work Thornton had arranged for the Harvard Business School to participate in training selected officers for the Air Forces. He had then brought the men so schooled into his organization. As peace approached he and two others studied the records of perhaps fifty officers, and selected seven they considered the "most promising." That made ten, and the full group discussed their postwar futures. They had worked brilliantly together during the conflict; why not continue their association in peace? They were sure that the techniques they had developed in the Air Forces would be valuable in business. After discussing various plans and putting out a few feelers, they found themselves considering an invitation from Robert R. Young to join the Alleghany Company.*

To some of the group this prospect was not attractive. But about that time the youngest, George Moore, heard from his father in Detroit, who was acquainted with B. J. Craig of the Ford Motor Company, that there might be an opportunity for them there. This appealed to the men who had been cool to the Alleghany offer. Ford had a name, a national function, and a reputation for accomplishment. All finally agreed to make a pitch for it. Should Moore's father speak to Craig? No, they decided in a surge of confidence, they would go right to the top: "Phooey! We'll just wire Henry Ford directly!"

---

* They had felt considerable uncertainty as to what they should do. They considered setting up a firm of their own—something in business research comparable with the A. C. Nielson Co.—or purchasing an interest in one that already existed.

So they sent the telegram, with some doubts whether they would even get a reply. Their brash approach had been a long shot try which they could afford to make because of the Alleghany offer. But the following morning Thornton found himself speaking by telephone with the Ford district sales manager for Washington, D.C. "Mr. Ford is very much interested," he was told. Could not he and his group go to Detroit to discuss the matter? Thornton and George Moore made a hurried visit, and then, late in November, eight of the ten arrived in Dearborn to meet Henry Ford in the Rotunda dining room.

The full group, besides Thornton and Moore, consisted of Wilbur R. ("Gene") Andreson, Charles E. Bosworth, J. E. Lundy, Robert S. McNamara, Arjay R. Miller, Ben Davis Mills, Francis C. Reith, and James O. Wright. Moore was the junior at twenty-six, Wright the oldest at thirty-four. They represented a considerable variety in geographical origin and practical experience. Wright, a Virginian, had been trained in law. Thornton, a Texan, and Reith, an Iowan, had done well in business. Mills, from Oklahoma, had worked in responsible positions for the federal government. Three had been teachers. McNamara, a Californian, had joined the faculty of the Harvard Business School; Arjay Miller, from Nebraska, had lectured on business at U.C.L.A.; Lundy, Iowa-born, had served in the Economics Department at Princeton.[24]

When the group arrived in Dearborn neither Mills nor Andreson could be present, but the others were all in uniform, and while military figures had been a common sight about Ford plants, these relatively young men, one a colonel, four lieutenant colonels, two majors, and one a lieutenant, must have caused a wave of interest as they walked into the Rotunda. There they were welcomed by A. G. Coulton, manager of the Office Service Department (a branch of Bugas's Industrial Relations division), who told them that Ford would appear shortly. He came in with Bugas, met the group, and talked briefly with them. They were impressed by his quiet confidence. Although vague as to what he expected them to do, he seemed positive that they would work with him, and "before we knew it," one of them recalled, "we were coming." Another remembered that after hearing Ford, he told himself, "This is for me."

Ford offered to assist them in finding residences. It will be remembered that as far back as 1942 the young president had favored getting college graduates to join the company. In one sense he himself was a new man in an old company, which he meant to remodel, and one of the visitors felt that Ford recognized his loneliness, and welcomed some men of his own age who were also strange to the company and might help him recast it. Nevertheless, Ford with characteristic thoroughness had inquired of Ernest Kanzler as to the character of his guests. As a former official of the War Production Board, Kanzler was well acquainted in Washington, knew Lovett, and was familiar with Thornton's work. He arranged for Henry to talk with Lovett about the young men, and the two had a "long discussion." [25]

The visitors saw no more of Ford on this occasion. That evening, after a dinner with Bugas, they returned to the Detroit Athletic Club, where Bugas proceeded to question them. "We were pretty well grilled," recalled one. After all, Bugas had to protect Ford; he saw "ten of these squirrels come marching through the door. What were they up to?" The questions were answered frankly, for nobody had anything to hide, and apparently Bugas was satisfied. Later he was to be of great help to the newcomers.

After he left, the group began to feel a sense of uncertainty. "Are we safe with Ford?" they asked each other, and appealed to the legally trained Wright. Should they demand written contracts? He advised against it. "If we can't trust Henry Ford we are in a pretty hopeless position," was his conclusion. Deciding that he was right, they resolved to stick with the verbal agreement they had made. This involved the question of salaries, and by agreement with Ford, Thornton on his return to Washington telegraphed what was to be paid each member, and Ford accepted the "package." The men were to report for work on February 1, 1946, and arrived a day early.[26]

Since none of the group knew the automobile business in general or the Ford Motor Company in particular, their first duty was to get acquainted with both, and Coulton arranged with Thornton for an orientation program. At first planned to comprise a month's study, beginning with Accounting, Auditing, and Disbursement, it actually went on for more than four months. Thornton insisted that it be thorough, for he knew what an immense task of reorganization must soon be undertaken. The ten were soon going from department to department with full authority to ask questions of the officials in charge.

Quickly it became apparent that their quest was arousing some deep suspicions. The rumor had got about that they were "hatchet men," gathering information to be used for the discharge of selected employes. Superintendents giving them facts about their work perspired from tension, and as they read from papers their hands shook. When Thornton's group earnestly assured these men that their sole purpose was to gather information about the company for their own enlightenment, their professions seemed to carry little conviction; however, they had no difficulty with men like Mead Bricker or Logan Miller.

Their perpetual questioning and their relative youth soon won them a sardonic nickname. They became "the Quiz Kids." The title annoyed some of the group. "I detested it," said one of them. "We weren't kids, and we weren't quizzing anybody. We were asking a lot of questions because it was the only way we could get the information we needed." Most of the ten were more amused than annoyed, but the designation and a variant, "the Whiz Kids," stuck. The group took notes on what they saw, and met by night to digest through discussion what they had learned by day. The experience was highly intensive, and extremely profitable.[27]

To all of them the Ford Motor Company was a shocking revelation of inefficiency. It was "completely different from what we ever imagined." Financial controls "in any terms in which we were thinking" simply did not exist. Early in their study they asked an official in the Controller's office what the financial results would probably be six months later, and received the reply: "What do you want them to be?" The Quiz Kids were amused, amazed, and scandalized. What kind of financing was this? Soon Arjay Miller had an opportunity to study the records involved, and when he had finished the others crowded around him and asked the same question. He smiled and replied: "What do you want them to be?" It seems that the financial records were so kept that they could be juggled to produce whatever result was desired![28] Again, the organization of practically every part of the company was hopelessly confused. In the Air Forces the distinction between staff and line—the men who planned and the men who carried out the plans—was of course fundamental, as it was in good business theory. In the Ford Motor Company, however, it was ignored. In almost every instance the men who planned had also duties in connection with execution. This was true in manufacturing, engineering, and even selling.

The newcomers learned immensely from their four months of study. It has been said that when it was completed they knew more about the company than any of its established employes, and they probably did have a broader view of activities as a whole, and their interrelationships, than many Ford officials. Naturally they did not begin to know as much about operational details as men like Bricker, Logan Miller, Tallberg, Wiesmyer, or Robinson, who had long been familiar with numerous company activities, and had gained an intensive practical experience. But the young men became very well informed, and grew eager to participate in what they saw as an urgent process of reorganization. Up to April they had had no word as to what their first activities might be; but late that month rumors began to circulate which indicated that drastic changes were under way which would affect the whole company.[29]

### 5.

Henry II had every reason to feel that his acquisition of the Thornton group had brought the firm a useful reservoir of talent. He seems never to have considered—although Thornton may have—that it could serve as a chief force in remaking the company. He knew that however high the abilities of the newcomers might be, they were mere infants in the automotive world, and would remain so for some time to come. Ford saw that his primary need was a general director of operations, to work under him—a man who knew automobiles and the men who made them far better than did he. When he hired the Thornton group he doubtless hoped, as will soon appear, to have such an executive at work on their arrival. This director would help him place them in the organization, just as he would help procure the brilliant men Ford needed in engineering, purchasing, finance, and other areas.

He discussed this problem with Ernest Kanzler, who along with Edsel Ford had begun as early as 1919 to plan an efficient organizational structure for the Ford Motor Company. As recounted in the second volume of this history, the original Henry Ford frowned on this activity, and Kanzler's departure in 1926 was not unrelated to his efforts to systematize a firm that its head wanted to keep loosely organized, although the chief cause of his departure was his attempt to procure the abandonment of the obsolescent Model T and the substitution of a new and better car. After leaving the company, Kanzler maintained an intimate friendship with Edsel, and as director of the Universal Credit Corporation was in close touch with the Ford business. Altogether, he was a well-informed and seasoned adviser. Henry conferred with him about both the general situation and important particulars related to it. "We talked a lot," said Kanzler later. There was never any question of the older man returning to the company, for Kanzler had his own pressing interests. However, the president did discuss with him the important right-hand lieutenant whom he needed. Eventually he had a number of names to consider.[30]

As early as January 1946 Kanzler had suggested for this post Ernest R. Breech, President of the Bendix Aviation Corporation. He himself had become a director of Bendix several years earlier, and had progressed from a casual to a cordial acquaintanceship with its president.

Breech's career had fitted him for Ford's consideration. Born in Lebanon, Missouri, the son of a blacksmith, he had worked his way through two years at Drury College, Springfield, Mo., left school to go into business, and then studied advanced accounting and business law at the Walton School of Commerce in Chicago. He won his certificate as public accountant, joined the Yellow Cab Manufacturing Company, and when it merged with General Motors in 1925 became an employe of that organization. Rising to be general assistant treasurer, he soon became president of its aeronautical division, North American Aviation, and then in 1939 a vice-president of General Motors. During the war he took over the presidency of Bendix, which was partly owned by GM, and tripled its production in a year. It manufactured a considerable amount of automotive equipment. Breech thus had a varied experience. Though particularly strong in finance, he had the general reputation of being a "management trouble shooter." It was even intimated that he was in the line of succession to head General Motors. He was forty-nine years of age, had been in the GM "family" for twenty-one years, was now practically his own boss, and was happy in his work.[31]

Ford and Breech knew each other, for Breech had heard Ford speak, and in April 1945 had solicited business from him. Ford was by now a regular Bendix customer, and a rather important one. The two met casually at automotive meetings, and Ford liked what he had seen of Breech. He had come to a decision that he wanted a General Motors man, and it was probably at his request that Kanzler sounded Breech out in December 1945 or January 1946, finding him unreceptive. Breech suggested Knudsen as a possible man for the Ford job, but when asked if he himself would be interested, replied: "Not under any circumstances." Henry II talked with Knudsen but did not make him an offer. Nor does he seem to have been attracted to any other men in the automotive field.

He apparently remained convinced that Breech was his man, and did not consider that one rebuff ended the question of getting him. Breech later recalled that in February or March 1946, when in Los Angeles, he encountered John Bugas, whom he knew. Bugas asked him, "Has Henry got in touch with you?" "No," replied Breech. "He wants to see you," said Bugas. Not long after he had returned to Detroit, Breech got a telephone call from Ford, who asked if he could see him. Breech offered to go to Dearborn, but Ford said no, he would come to Breech's office in the Fisher Building. They made an appointment for Monday, April 7. Palmer Nichols was in the office when the call came, overheard part of the conversation, and volunteered: "He's going to offer you a job." Breech exclaimed, "My God, I hope he doesn't!" and bet Nichols a dollar that Ford wouldn't.

Breech had what he considered the best of reasons for not wanting to become associated with the Ford Motor Company. It was part of his business at General Motors to watch competitors, and he had perceived during the late nineteen-thirties that the Ford organization was deteriorating badly. He had watched its efforts, he said later, with "contempt and pity," and repeated the phrase by way of emphasis. Furthermore, he had heard numerous stories about the captious treatment of Ford officials, had seen many able men leave, and although "the Ford name was magic," was definitely prejudiced against the organization. One of his business associates whom Breech respected and who had done much business with Ford, "condemned the organization, their methods, both of manufacture and of doing business generally," and indicated that they lacked good management, that their machinery and processes were obsolescent, and that their costs were unduly high. Above all, Breech was satisfied where he was. But since Ford was a good customer, he thought he should in courtesy listen to whatever he had to say.[32]

Henry Ford II was waiting when Breech arrived at his office at 9:15, and came quickly to the point: he intended to remodel the Ford Motor Company along the lines of General Motors, which he credited with "the outstanding automobile management," and wanted Breech to take charge of the operation. Breech asked in what capacity. "We'll make you executive vice-president," replied Ford. Breech asked nothing about terms. "I knew I wasn't coming," he recalled. "I liked my job at Bendix. I named my own board of directors. I was having a good time." The only thought in his mind was, "How am I going to get through this, and keep a good customer?" But Ford stayed on despite Breech's tactful refusal. He was firm in wishing to proceed along the lines marked out by GM, and he wanted the man. Actually, he had a stock option plan in his pocket, which he would have used had Breech shown the slightest receptivity. But he did not give up even when his mission seemed hopeless; instead, he asked if Breech would not come out to the Ford offices, look the situation over, and give him some advice. This Breech readily promised to do.

He made the trip a week later, on April 12. Ford took him to the test track where he saw prototypes of the new Ford cars, and drove one around the course. Then he went to inspect the company's balance sheet, which he remembered later as "about as good as a small tool shop would have." The controller, when asked about "standard volume," didn't know what he was talking about. Breech saw that the company was losing about $10,000,000 a month, and that practically every phase of it needed attention. He tried to think of someone he could recommend but could only think of GM men. Moreover, he began to feel a personal obligation. "I was the cleanup man for GM, but this one was *really* a mess." Ordinarily, it might have been hopeless, but the postwar period with its unusual demand for cars would make it possible for the company to make money even while it was getting its house in order.

He told his wife, "Well, here is a young man that is only one year older than our oldest son. He needs help. This is a great challenge. . . . I hate to take on this job, but if I do not do it I will always regret that I did not accept the challenge." [33]

The opportunity which the Ford Motor Company represented made an immense appeal to the technician in him, as a difficult operation does to a surgeon who knows that perhaps only he can perform it successfully. Ford now told him he could write his own contract, and produced his stock option plan. William Gossett (a New York attorney who was general counsel for Bendix), Kanzler, Clifford Longley (Ford's lawyer), Breech, and Henry II all worked on a possible agreement. The difficulty was that no valuation had as yet been placed on Edsel's stock, and the Ford lawyers felt that the estate could not sell, though they thought the Ford Foundation could. Breech actually came to the point of buying 30,000 shares at $40 a share, but finally decided against it because he felt that the company wouldn't earn enough. "Just think of what I missed!" he exclaimed later. The agreement was finally made without any reference to a stock option plan, although Henry II stated that he felt a "moral obligation" with respect to it. Breech got a higher salary than he had drawn at Bendix, and the promise of job security.[34]

In this situation Kanzler played an important part. Both principals were at times hesitant. Breech, facing the prospect of breaking his association with General Motors, and working for one man, wondered what would happen if he and Ford did not agree. To a large extent this doubt was met by having the contract "set Breech up for life," with other safeguards. Then when the document was ready to sign, Henry had second thoughts. Kanzler recalled how one evening he parted with Ford and set out in his car. Ford remembered an important point he had to discuss, and pursued Kanzler down Woodward Avenue, delayed by traffic lights. Finally he caught up and unburdened himself: "My lawyer says I'm abdicating when I make Ernie vice-president." But Kanzler reassured him that he was not, and after a fresh talk, Breech assured him there would "certainly be no misunderstanding in that connection." At the end he told Ford, "Well, I will be with you; my answer now is Yes."

Minutes of a special meeting of the board of directors for May 16, 1946, state that Breech had agreed to join the company on July 1. Ford had now found the answers he was seeking, and could feel that he had resources for rebuilding. Much was to happen even before Breech arrived; the long period of disintegration and confusion was coming to an end.[35]

# XIII

## TO REBUILD A COMPANY

No MORE than Henry Ford II did Breech propose to remake the Ford Motor Company by himself, or with only the talent he would find there. Before giving a final answer to Ford, he had asked two men, "Will you go to the Ford Motor Company with me?" Both agreed. Not by accident they were expert in the two areas where the Ford organization was weakest—finance and engineering.

Lewis D. Crusoe, born in Minnesota, had received his B.S. degree from the University of Detroit, which he had attended by night. When graduated, he had already served four years with the Fisher Body Company, a division of General Motors, where he later rose to the position of divisional controller, acting also after 1930 as assistant treasurer of General Motors. He had gained an immense knowledge of labor, overhead, cost accounting, tooling, sales, and management in general. A slight, thin man with a pleasant manner but sharp tongue, he was precision in the flesh and demanded accuracy of those who worked with him. Though he had retired at fifty to raise pure-bred cattle on a farm near Cheboygan, Michigan, the next year (November 1945) he had come back to work as Breech's assistant at Bendix. When Breech asked him about going to Ford he was startled: "We [at General Motors] looked on Ford as Mr. Khrushchev looks at West Germany," he recalled years later. But his position at Bendix was temporary, and he replied: "Ernie, I can try it; I can't get hurt." [1]

The second man to whom Breech appealed, Harold T. Youngren, was one he had known as engineer of the Oldsmobile Division, and later as the able chief engineer for the Borg-Warner Corporation. Henry II also had an acquaintance with Youngren, whom he had met at the Indianapolis automobile races, and whose work he had discussed with several Borg-Warner engineers. When Breech suggested

317

his name, Ford replied: "I have had Youngren in mind, too, so let us see if we can get him." Manufacture at the Rouge did not limp as badly as engineering, but it needed more talent, and to supply this Breech suggested a third man, Delmar S. Harder. Henry II wrote June 14, 1946, that they should try to hire him along with Youngren to deal with these two unsatisfactory parts of the business. "I believe these men could strengthen them considerably."

Youngren was available, for he was dissatisfied at Borg-Warner, where he felt he was too much an executive and too little an engineer. Lunching with Breech and Ford, he promptly agreed to join the company on August 1. He represented a valuable acquisition. "There was no man of Youngren's caliber, not even a third of his caliber, around here at that time," said a perceptive Ford engineer.

As early as April, Ford had asked Breech's advice about a prospect for a third area, purchasing, which Carroll was not managing to his satisfaction. He had fixed an eye on Albert J. Browning, director of the War Department's buying activities during World War II, and now in the Department of Commerce with Henry Wallace. Previously Browning had held the post of merchandising manager for Montgomery Ward. Breech told Ford, "If you can get that man, do it!" Ford acted quickly, and on April 23 announced Browning's appointment to head Purchasing. Two days later he was made vice-president.[2]

Harder was to prove far more difficult to capture. It might well be asked why Ford wanted his services, for the experienced Bricker was in charge of manufacturing, and was ably assisted by Logan Miller, Wiesmyer, and others. But Henry was looking toward the future. He felt that Bricker was "physically slowing up a bit," and "not quite up to the big manufacturing job that Ford Motor Company had ahead." He planned to make Bricker vice-president, fully using his services, but to put overall leadership in Harder's hands. Of Harder's high capacity there could be no question. He had served with Crusoe in Fisher Body for years, had supervised production for General Motors, and was now president of the E. W. Bliss Company. The trouble was that he was completely happy in that position, and in addition had heard tales of the Ford company that made him firmly averse to joining it. He was also doubtful about his possible relationship with Bricker. When Breech approached him, he refused.

But Ford, arranging three separate meetings with Harder, would not accept a rejection. He and Breech assured Harder that his fears were unjustified, that a new company was in the making, and that "if he was interested in a big manufacturing job and really . . . doing something big, there was a lot available here." When Harder asked for a five-year contract, Ford agreed, and finally Crusoe allayed his remaining doubts. In October 1946 he agreed to come, and began work as Vice-President of Operations in December.[3]

During the span between Breech's acceptance and his arrival at Dearborn, the Ford Motor Company was fighting the battle of peace-time conversion. Because of steel and coal strikes, and others against its suppliers, it was obliged to shut down for five weeks in February and March, and again from May 8 to July 2, so that normal production seemed an abnormality. Meanwhile government regulations, including price-fixing for cars, still slowed production and forbade hope of profits; with the volume it could obtain and the prices it could charge, Ford could make no money. Yet between January 1 and May 25, 1946, it produced 187,068 vehicles.

While the company was thus nearing perhaps the greatest change in its history, its founder was apparently unaware of the changes his grandson was making. On March 16 his secretary, Frank Campsall, died, and on April 4 W. J. Cameron, for years his "mouthpiece," left the company. On May 31 the failing, almost eighty-three-year-old Ford appeared with Henry II and Benson Ford at the National Automobile Golden Jubilee in Detroit, where he received a trophy for his past accomplishments.

Even aside from its acquisition of key officials, the new regime had been active that year in preparation for the future. It had started four new assembly plants at St. Louis, Los Angeles, Atlanta, and Metuchen, N.J. In April it had created a Light Car Division, which was to produce a small, cheap car by October 1947—a unit serviceable at least for the French Ford company. The idea of a small car dated back to the late nineteen-thirties, and after twice being abandoned, now seemed certain of realization. Creation of a division to produce it marked the second step in the process of decentralization.[4]

On May 20 Thornton appeared before the Policy Committee and outlined what he and his associates could do to systematize and co-ordinate the activities of the various departments of the company. He noted that no agency in the firm was authorized to set down policy for the company as a whole, "with the result that different departments do overall planning in order to define their own work," a situation resulting in duplicated effort and confusion. Thornton was instructed to undertake overall planning, working directly under Henry II, and discussing his plans with Breech. As a result, he drew up a letter for Ford to sign which gave him very broad authority, and which Henry asked him to show to the future executive vice-president. When Thornton did so, Breech sent word to Ford: "If you sign this letter, there is no use for me to join the company." He suggested that the Thornton group maintain its present status until he himself arrived in Dearborn on July 1.[5]

The day quickly came when Breech assumed authority. He did not minimize the importance of what he was to do. "My job," he said later, "was to develop personnel, organization, and policy methods of the Ford Motor Company." When asked, "To what end, Mr. Breech?" he replied: "To the end of becoming the leading automobile manufacturer in the United States."[6]

This was essentially what Henry Ford II had said nine months earlier. During that period a promise had been established. With the arrival of Breech and Crusoe and the appointment of Youngren the company was acquiring the talent needed to convert promise to performance.

### 2.

Lewis D. Crusoe had never set foot on Ford property, and had never met a Ford. On the day before he reported for duty, he reviewed the rumors he had heard about the company and its officials, and wondered what adjustment he would have to make. Later he laughingly said that he half expected "to have a number tattooed on my chest." He drove around the immense Rouge plant with Mrs. Crusoe. "There it is," he told her. "Tomorrow I have to go in there and find out how it ticks." But he was pleasantly surprised the next day when he was ushered into Henry II's office, and was told, "Call me Henry." He was on the team.

Breech had of course already established full rapport with his new employer, a rapport essential as he faced the need for decisive action in several areas. A quick examination of the company had satisfied him that it was strong in three fields: Sales (J. R. Davis), Industrial

Relations (Bugas), and Purchasing (Browning). While the weakest areas were engineering and finance, the entire company needed reorganization, for in many respects it floundered in inefficiency. There was also, Breech decided, a problem of morale.

He established Crusoe as his executive assistant, and gave him charge of Thornton's group. He already felt that to keep the men together was a mistake, and Ford had raised this question with the Policy Committee on June 6, when "it was decided that Mr. Thornton and his group would be offered an opportunity of joining individually such departments here as might have use for their services. It seemed to everyone that the services of the men could be used to much better advantage in that way than as a group." Actually, the process of distribution was to be slow. The ten had already started working on reorganization, an activity which Crusoe was superbly fitted to supervise, and which would include finance, another area in which he excelled. So for a considerable time he kept the young men together.[7]

Breech was early made aware of the morale problem. A superintendent was ushering him and Bricker through the Rouge when a young man accidentally obstructed their progress. The superintendent "threw him across the room." Another employe had no work at hand and was reading a newspaper. The superintendent kicked it out of his hands and told him to get out: "Don't ever let me see you in the plant again." Breech was outraged. He had understood that Henry II had condemned and altered the old "driver" attitude. Bricker explained that there was still a problem. "You can't make these men over," he advised. "Five years ago they would have been discharged for *not* acting harshly." However, Breech believed that the atmosphere of the plant could be changed.

It seemed desirable to know what Ford employes thought about authority and their personal status. Elmo Roper prepared a questionnaire, and sent it to 124,700 Ford employes. Responses came from 22,461, of whom 84.4 per cent made unfavorable comments on supervision, 81.3 per cent objected in various ways to the company's attitude toward employes, and 71 per cent had little or no idea of the company's personnel policies. Breech laid these results before superintendents and division heads, and reiterated official taboo on harsh discipline. "We cannot have an 'officer caste' in our industry," he announced on November 15, 1946; "we can't have 'brass-hat-ism.'" Ford backed him fully. He declared that for the last twenty years the Ford Motor Company had been built on fear, and that this method would not work. "I don't think that any company can operate in a competitive system, when all their relationships are predicated on fear. . . . [nor can they] build their products as cheaply as they could build them if they had good human relations."

After discharging three officials who could not or would not conform to the new policy, Breech convinced the others that he meant business. The last vestiges of the old driver spirit disappeared in 1947.[8]

But the most urgent problem Breech faced lay in the losses that had marked the company's postwar operations from the beginning. Obviously, to eliminate them would require higher prices on Ford cars. An application for a price increase had just been prepared for OPA, but when Breech studied it, he felt that its very bulk doomed it to defeat. He was convinced also that the increase asked, $136.00 a car, while required at the time to produce a profit, was higher than it would be good policy for the company to accept. He himself estimated that a raise of $60 would soon permit the company to break even.

The Policy Committee meeting of August 6, 1946, saw the question threshed out. The conclusion was that "we should depend upon our own increased efficiency in the future to earn a profit, rather than to ask for prices which would earn the company a profit at its present rate of operations and efficiency." Some increase was imperative; otherwise the firm, which in the first seven months of the year had lost $50,000,000, might plunge into a further loss of $35,000,000. The vote was unanimous to "compromise with OPA" at $80.00 a car.

Breech and Browning went down to Washington and talked there with the head of the automotive section of the OPA, who had formerly worked for General Motors. "You and I are alumni of the same firm," Breech told him. He then astounded the official by proposing an $80 price increase, the Government having expected Ford to ask as much as $150 a car. But Breech was firm. "We don't want any more," he declared. When an application for that amount was submitted, to apply after September 15, a rise of $62.50 was awarded, which exceeded by $2.50 Breech's own private figure. Even in September the company made a profit of $5,000,000, its first since the war. With additional gains during the remainder of the year, it registered a profit of $2000 for the full twelve months.[9]

Improvements in the scheduling of men and materials during this period had helped reduce expenses. Breech checked the schedules of the different departments in relation to available materials, cut them to fit reality, and laid off 8500 workers whose services were not required. At the same time, production proceeded much more smoothly than earlier in the year, and the larger volume meant lower unit costs.

The company was also following through on Henry's new policy of selling off numerous non-productive properties. The Brazilian rubber plantation, sold late in 1945 to the government of Brazil for $250,000, had represented a constant drain, losing more than $20,000,-000 from 1927 to 1945. The soy-bean processing factories had been discontinued during the war, and in November 1946 the principal one at Saline, Michigan, was sold to a commercial company. Much of the elder Ford's farm land had been put up for sale in the spring of 1946, and on July 26 the Policy Committee listed sixteen small plants (village industries) for disposal. These properties, originally costing $3,387,094, now had a book value of $2,450,469. Large tracts of Ford-owned mineral lands were offered to buyers early in 1947 (550,000 acres) and by July had for the most part been sold. Early in 1947 the Ford Fleet was reduced from seven vessels to two—the *Henry Ford II* and the *Benson Ford,* both large ore carriers.[10]

During the fall of 1946 the question of a Ford legal department arose. The company had once maintained a legal staff, but in later years had relied mainly on outside counsel in Detroit. A small department had been set up in 1945, and the firm of Shearman & Sterling & Wright in New York was on call for special service. However, Henry II felt that "we needed strengthening in our legal staff." Breech suggested William T. Gossett, who had been general counsel at Bendix, although not an employe, and after a conference, Gossett joined the company as a vice-president and general counsel in February 1947. He began to build up a legal staff within the company.[11]

Quite as important to the new regime as a satisfactory price on its cars were the designs for new Fords, Mercurys, and Lincolns. Engineering would largely shape the company's tomorrow, and while it was Youngren's special responsibility, Breech's future also hung on it. His first experience with Ford design had been at the test track in April, where he had driven one of the projected 1948 models, and concluded that it was too large. "How much does this car weigh?"

he had asked Ford, who thought it little heavier than the pre-war models. Breech disagreed: "That's a big car." He and Ford talked with the engineers, but got "veiled answers." Now Youngren would come to study what had been done.

Even before his official arrival on August 1, he had surveyed the situation. On a visit to Dearborn he had met the engineering staff, and he had talked several times with Breech. On July 17 Breech reported to the Policy Committee on these conferences. Youngren, he said, was worried about the weights of the new cars. General Motors was making every effort to keep weight down, and Ford should take note. Youngren also suggested that the company should not "place all our hopes on Mr. Gregorie." Breech proposed that the Committee employ an outside styling consultant, and was authorized to approach George W. Walker, an industrial designer who had worked for the Nash Motor Company.

Such was the status of engineering at the time of Youngren's arrival. He was soon to make changes that would brighten the Ford future.[12]

### 3.

If there was one task which all the new officials regarded as urgent, it was reorganization. Ford himself had begun it in September 1945 and though his concern with production, labor, and plant construction had interfered, he had continued his activity. Wiesmyer received a telephone call in Detroit one Friday night early in 1946.

"This is Henry Ford," a recognizable voice told him. "How long would it take you to get out to Los Angeles?"

"I could be there inside of twenty-four hours."

Ford asked him to be on hand the following Monday morning. "We have been talking about setting up the plant managers and separating them from the Sales Department. I'd like to have you and Herman Moekle meet me out there." Thus, starting with Long Branch, California, Ford personally supervised the execution of the recommendations made by J. R. Davis the preceding fall.[13]

The definite allotment of responsibility was a characteristic General Motors practice which Ford had clearly in mind. Equally characteristic of GM was the process of decentralization, of which he had heard but perhaps did not understand fully. The original General Motors of William Crapo Durant was not the smooth-running, powerful organization which led automobile production in the 1930s. Indeed, as noted in *Ford: Expansion and Challenge,* it was a large but vulnerable firm which was rescued from complete shipwreck in the 1920–1921 depression by the Du Ponts, who bought Durant's stock and prepared to remake the sprawling giant in the interests of efficiency.

Pierre S. du Pont became president of the firm in 1921, assisted by Alfred P. Sloan, Jr., a vice-president under Durant who was to take over the supreme leadership after Du Pont relinquished it in 1923. To General Motors with Du Pont in 1921 had come the treasurer of E. I. du Pont de Nemours & Co., Donaldson Brown. He assumed the same office in GM. Brown, who had married into the Du Pont family, but had risen in their domain because of his talent for finance and organization, brought the automotive world the idea of decentralization, then relatively new in American industry.

Sloan quickly assisted in applying it to General Motors. "We . . . set up each of our various operations as an integral unit, complete in itself," he explained later. "We would place in charge of each unit an executive responsible, and solely responsible, for his complete activity." Each division, as a separate unit was termed, not only had its own head, but its own purchasing staff, controller, engineering department, sales force, and so forth. Essentially it was a separate business. Its performance could thus be easily appraised. All six GM cars were produced by self-contained divisions, as were refrigerators, bodies, and other products. The divisions bought from and sold to each other, but also dealt with outsiders. They did not have to deal with General Motors units unless doing so was advantageous. The central staff of the company laid down general policy, allotted funds, and distributed information through a system of committees, but otherwise the divisions were independent. "Of the many policy decisions we have made down through the years," remarked Sloan in 1941, "sometimes the answers have been right and sometimes wrong, but that answer [decentralization] was right. We have never deviated from it. I hope we never shall."

The alternative policy of centralization meant that for the entire company, however varied its products, single executives would direct all purchasing, engineering, sales, manufacturing. This was the Ford practice under Henry I in 1945. But while General Motors knew which of its divisions, if any, was losing money, and which were profitable, and could quickly concentrate on a weak spot, Ford if seeking responsibility for loss could see only the total result of a melange of activities. Purchasing was not only for the Ford car, but also for the Lincoln, Mercury, the Ford tractor, the steel mills, the glass plant, village industries, and other activities, and the share of each in an overall loss was impossible to determine. Centralization was a logical step in American industry when companies were small and each produced a single product; it was illogical in an era of size and proliferation. By 1945 most large companies, like General Electric, International Harvester, Standard Oil, and A.T. & T., had turned to decentralization.

The General Motors system had been improved since 1921. Meanwhile the Harvard Business School, which reached a period of expansion in 1926, had approved it as a tool for bigger business, and in the late 1920s and 1930s Harvard professors like Ross G. Walker and Thomas H. Sanders had thrown light on the related activity of accounting, and Edmund P. Learned on merchandising. As a former colleague of these men, Robert S. McNamara was fully cognizant of their ideas and of Brown's, as in a less special way were all the others in the Thornton group.[14]

In April 1946 appeared a book which vividly interpreted the General Motors accomplishment, Peter F. Drucker's *Concept of the Corporation*. As an outside consultant, Drucker had spent eighteen months studying the gigantic corporation at its own request. His volume not only explained all its chief practices, but also evaluated the modern corporation, with GM as example, as one of the major elements in American life. Drucker pronounced decentralization to be harmonious with national ideals, but pointed out ways in which corporate practice must change. In general, these looked to a fuller participation of employes in leadership training, and their fuller identification with the objectives of the business.

Breech, who knew Drucker, read the book, was delighted, and when he arrived at Ford, brought copies with him. Ford also read it, and agreed heartily that "no institution can exist under one-man rule," and that "under one-man rule there would be nobody in the corporation who has had the opportunity to be trained and tested in independent leadership." Drucker compared the decentralized corporation with the Roman Catholic Church and the Prussian military organization, from which he drew the term "staff and line." To Thornton and his associates, Drucker brought confirmation of ideas they already held.[15]

When Crusoe took the ten former Air Forces men under his direction, they knew more about the Ford Motor Company than he did. He perceived their intelligence, but decided that "they knew nothing about business and the automotive industry. Their knowledge was from books." Crusoe soon began to teach them, usually with full success. "I could not have had better experience than I got under Mr. Crusoe's direction," remarked one of the ten. For the first several months Crusoe bade Thornton continue with the reorganization plans, and both Breech and Crusoe examined and to some extent revised the charts that the group produced. By July 19 Thornton proposed to the Policy Committee that an office be established to develop a comprehensive organizational structure, that an organization committee take charge of this particular work, and that plans be made for a manual to present and explain the eventual structure. The committee would in addition "develop an ultimate plan for organization of the Company, adhering to the principle of decentralized management." He was given authority to proceed with this program.

The planning force consisted of Thornton, Wright, Andreson, Moore, and Bosworth. They worked in the "bull pen" of the Rotunda, in a large open space like a city room, with two girls to assist them. Thornton occupied a wedge at one end of this area. Mills worked on a classification of automotive and business terms, and later on company programming; Reith dealt with budgets; Miller, Lundy, and McNamara were busy with Crusoe on Ford finance.

As Breech's executive assistant, Crusoe had authority from the first to investigate any company activity, and of course knew that finance would require his attention. He took the three former teachers of the Thornton group as his assistants, and spent the first months acquiring information and suggesting minor changes. On September 19 he became head of the newly-created Division of Planning and Control, with Thornton under him directing Planning. His authority was augmented on November 13, 1946, when he became company Controller, and on April 1, 1947, when he became Vice-President in Charge of Finance.

Crusoe and his aides were appalled by the conditions they found. The company had no property records, no certified balance sheet, and "a fantastic cost system." The old merchandising type of accounting was used: "You took the purchases, took the sales, and the difference between the two was profit." Arjay Miller found a large fund in a bank drawing no interest whatever. "The bankers must have loved us," he remarked. Crusoe declared: "The whole system was incredible. I thought I'd never tell anyone but the Lord himself, because nobody would believe it." In milder phraseology, former and present finance officials like G. J. Crimmins and Herman Moekle respectively agreed that a complete renovation was essential. "I wouldn't attempt to defend our old system," said Crimmins later. "It was really ridiculously crude." The job in this area was a modern version of the labors of Hercules.[16]

Crusoe brought in M. E. Sheppard, formerly of Fisher Body, to assist in developing plans which called not only for the rebuilding of the Ford finance department, but for the application of proper financial principles to the process of decentralization. Here his final moves were undoubtedly made in consultation with Breech, who had a firm grasp of financial matters. They and their young assistants invented a term which passed into common usage. Each division became a "profit center," signifying that Ford meant to make, not lose money. Crusoe early began to press for projected balances—i.e. predictions of company finances three or twelve months from the date of estimate. He also established the practice of "project control;" that is, if a project were to be launched, he demanded its cost through an extended period.

Here he encountered an attitude inherited from the original Henry Ford. If a job were to be done, Ford had not wanted to know the cost or have his subordinates estimate it; he would assume all responsibility. One official inured to this practice had proposed a particular measure to Crusoe. "How much is that going to cost?" the latter demanded. "Mr. Crusoe," replied the official, "we don't talk about costs around here." "I have news for you," Crusoe informed him. "From now on you'll begin talking about them."

To bring order into the financial chaos of 1946 proved a prodigious task even for Crusoe and his assistants. Miller finally produced a projected balance, but distrusted it, and Sheppard, trying to ascertain basic figures, seemed to end in worse confusion than when he started. Finally Lybrand, Ross Bros. & Montgomery, an accounting firm, was called in to straighten out the situation.[17] At first, Crusoe had hoped to retain a considerable portion of the existing staff, but this proved impossible. Retraining old employes would have taken precious time, with uncertain results. "We worked under tremendous urgency," recalled Miller. Smart young graduates of colleges or business schools, in contrast, could fit in easily, and so could some men from other companies. Most of the displaced men were shifted to less exacting positions.[18]

Meanwhile the planning activity headed by Thornton and Wright went forward vigorously. A 56-page typescript, "Organizational Problems of the Ford Motor Company," which seems to have been the essence of presentations to the Policy Committee on August 23 and September 13, 1946, shows that the planners proposed three steps. The first was to make "the present structure of the company" clear; the second was the issuance of an Organization Manual to which all company officials could refer, and the development by these units of charts for their own activities; and the third was the development of an "ultimate plan of organization," which should follow "to the maximum extent possible the principle of decentralized operation and centralized control." Provision would be made for a "continuing review and control of organizational development and activities."

The report presented a chart for "present structure" which contained many features that were to mark company organization for years to come. Under the stockholders the President and Executive Vice-President, Ford and Breech, exercised supreme executive power, and from them stemmed the Policy Committee and its sub-committees, the General Counsel, the Director of Public Relations, and various committees which would clarify and help coordinate the work of the company.

Under the chief officers came six vice-presidents in charge of Industrial Relations, Automotive Engineering, Purchasing, Manufacturing, Sales, and Finance (staff officials), and under them the operating divisions, which were listed as Light Car, Ford, Rouge (manufacturing departments and plants), Lincoln-Mercury, and Export. Each of these except Light Car and Rouge had its own engineering, purchasing, production, and sales staffs. Detailed charts for the product divisions, the Rouge, Industrial Engineering, and Sales were included, and the duties of company officers were specified.

Notable in the report was the inclusion of a Ford Division along with the Light Car and Lincoln-Mercury units. For while the company was already manufacturing three types of passenger cars, and with the light car contemplated a fourth, the average American, and most Ford employes, thought of the Ford car as its chief product, and to make a Ford Division in Ford seemed a contradiction in terms. This division would of course have its own purchasing, engineering, and sales, and its own controller. "What are you going to leave *me?*" demanded J. R. Davis when he heard of the plan to set up the division with its own sales manager. Partly because of the difficulty of finding an executive head, however, nearly three years were to elapse before it was actually created and operating.

The report laid out a coherent plan for company structure. On September 13, 1946, Crusoe presented the Policy Committee "a proposed program of operational planning and financial control," which on Breech's motion was approved, with January 1, 1947 as the date when it should be fully operative. On the 27th Arjay Miller presented a fuller program, and the following week Thornton and Wright offered the text of an organizational manual, which was approved that same day.[19] It was one thing to plan a new company and quite another to make the plan live and breathe. Personalities and habitual ways of operating had to be considered, and harmonized with revolutionary changes. There was even a language to be created, so that all could understand what was being discussed. It comprised fundamental terms in company structure like division, department, section, unit, new phrases like project control and profit center, and the designation of parts of the automobile. Here the manual took over the GM classification system, which Breech, Crusoe, Youngren, Harder all knew, and which was consistent and usable.

But the great task was to reorganize activities along the lines of the approved plan. Of immense help in this was the Industrial Relations Division. Bugas assigned one of his able young men, Gordon Walker, to cooperate with the planning unit, and Wright recalled that "Industrial Relations was organized in a jiffy." A relatively easy division to deal with, it provided a model which could be exhibited to others. Aside from Finance, Manufacturing was the most difficult area, but there Bricker gave great assistance. He had been in charge of practically everything from coal mines and forests to assembly plants, on which he did both staff and line work. Once the Policy Committee had adopted the overall company plan, Bricker "pitched in and made it work" in his own area. Eventually this meant the creation of new divisions. Such cooperation was of course indispensable. It was promoted by the management meetings which Henry II and Breech initiated early in 1947. With Ford presiding and Breech speaking freely, these gatherings brought Ford officials together, gave them the benefit of company thinking, invited questions and comments, and promoted a unified attack upon problems that all faced. They became a permanent feature of Ford policy, and continue today.

Breech believed that "a company is never to be considered good until it knows its own weaknesses." These had been discovered, and were now made clear. At the second meeting Ford emphasized that "the first big job was to organize Ford Motor Company along modern organizational lines." Breech took this as a text. "Mr. Ford mentioned the fact that the organization was important. It is THE important thing. Unless it is set up right we know that we will have the pulling and hauling and cancelling of instructions that are common to a poorly organized business. We know we have to have the proper organization to do the job right." Breech became a hard-hitting professor of planning. He displayed large charts to show processes, the progress at Ford, and the unescapable overlapping of staff and line activities. He urged common participation in the task. "By so doing we can look back with pride and say, 'I helped to build that great company.' " [20]

Not only Breech, but all members of the Planning and Control Division, took a hand in teaching. Crusoe and the Thornton group went to officials in various departments saying: "We're going to tell you about costs. This is a tool you should have. It is not your fault that at present you do not have it, for it was not given to you." Crusoe felt that the rank and file of officials welcomed these ministrations. "They were like shipwrecked sailors who haven't eaten for days and see a biscuit." Bosworth, working in other areas, did not recall meeting much enthusiasm, but found no resistance either.

By May 1947 notable progress had been made. Every division had now agreed upon its organizational structure, and was separating staff and operating activities. Three new divisions had been formed on April 1. General Products, under Bricker, included Highland Park manufacturing, with new tractor work, the Rouge automotive, steel, and Northern Michigan activities; Parts and Equipment, under Roscoe Smith, embraced eight surviving village industry plants and the Green Island, N.Y., and Hamilton, Ohio factories; and finally, the Ford Assembly Division under Wiesmyer included all such plants outside the Detroit area. Crusoe, as head of Planning and Control, mildly chided the upper echelons of the company for supervising some of the new divisions too closely; they should be helped, but like young birds taught to depend on themselves. The projected Ford Division, as we have noted, was delayed.[21]

### 4.

Scarcely less urgent than reorganization was the development of the new cars that Ford expected to sell in 1948. Only with superior products could the company hope to recapture its lost leadership in the industry. Arriving on August 1, 1947, Youngren began his work. One result was a motion by Crusoe in the Policy Committee on August 23 that the new Ford designed by Gregorie should become the new Mercury, and that the design of the Mercury should be used for the Lincoln. The Committee formally approved of this program on September 3.

But before doing so it grimly surveyed the probable consequences of such action. There could be no completely new 1948 or even 1949 Ford unless the company decided to alter the existing model (the improved 1942 car), as any wholly renovated automobile would supposedly take three years to develop. Yet such a course seemed a capitulation to disaster, for the Ford was the company's chief product, and there should be no question of its novelty or distinction. After much discussion, the Committee agreed to adjourn until the following morning, leaving Breech deeply disturbed. Driving home that evening, he prayed: "Show us the right way to go." Next day on the way to work an inspiration came to him: "Start afresh!" To the meeting he announced: "I have a vision. We start from scratch. We spend no time or money phoneying up the old Ford, because this organization will be judged by the market on the next car it produces, and it had better be a new one. So we'll have a crash program, as if in war time. Any questions?" He remarked years later, "We've had a series of crash programs ever since."[22]

Youngren set the dimensions for the car. According to Tallberg, he

16. The "electric brain" which directs the automated lines where engine blocks, cylinder heads, and other parts are made at the new Ford Cleveland Engine Plant

17. The Central Office Building at Dearborn, Michigan, center of Ford administrative activity

18. Edsel and Henry Ford II in 1934

19. Henry Ford, his wife Clara, and Henry Ford II

20. Ford officials: TOP LEFT, W. R. Campbell of the Canadian Ford company; TOP RIGHT, John S. Bugas; LOWER LEFT, J. R. Davis; and LOWER RIGHT, John S. Dykstra, President of the Ford Motor Company 1961-1963

21. Ford officials: LEFT, Ernest R. Breech; RIGHT, Lewis D. Crusoe; LOWER LEFT, Robert S. McNamara

22. UPPER RIGHT. "The Team," August, 1950. LEFT TO RIGHT: Delmar S. Harder, Lewis D. Crusoe, Henry Ford II, Ernest R. Breech, Theodore N. Yntemna, John S. Bugas, and Harold T. Youngren

23. LOWER RIGHT. The three Ford brothers, with portraits of their father and grandfather. LEFT TO RIGHT: Benson Ford, Henry Ford II, and William Clay Ford

24. Ford cars. FROM TOP TO BOTTOM: Mercury Monterey, Fairlane 500, Ford Galaxie, Falcon

25. 1963 Comet

26. A portion of the Ford testing track

27. The Ford plant at Cologne, Germany

28. The Ford plant at Windsor, Ontario

was definitely the creator of the new Ford (which actually was not ready until 1949), "because he developed the package, and the package is what . . . these stylists had to work with." That is, he set the length, width, height, and weight of the car, and also developed its transmission. The remainder of the staff worked on various details, and Eugene Gregorie and George Walker took charge of giving the model its final form.

Youngren soon organized his staff, which with two exceptions had comprised Ford talent, by putting Tallberg in charge of Administration, James of Research, Gregorie of Styling, H. H. Gilbert of Lincoln-Mercury and H. S. Currier of Ford passenger cars, Dale Roeder of Commercial Vehicles, and A. W. Frehse of Test Facilities. He also instituted a system of cost control. Later he was to supplement his staff with outsiders. Tactfully, before Youngren arrived, Henry II (July 17) had appointed R. H. McCarroll Director of Chemical and Metallurgical Engineering and Research.[23]

On August 15 the light car still loomed like a beckoning star on the Ford horizon, and on that day in Policy Committee "it was unanimously agreed that . . . Styling and Engineering would make an all-out effort" to produce it. Youngren naturally accepted this mandate, although he must have seen that it would complicate a crowded schedule. Fortunately for him, General Motors, which had also been working on a light model, gave the project up because of too many other problems. Meanwhile Roper, at Breech's suggestion, had conducted surveys which indicated that most Americans wanted larger cars, and were prepared to pay for them. J. R. Davis later summed this up for a sales conference. The public, he pointed out, gave lip service to the cheap car, but nothing more. "We get answers which indicate that people don't want to sacrifice the car features they have been accustomed to. . . . They tell us they don't want a car so light that it will not have the 'roadability' required by the average driver. When we begin to ask about accessories, comments from all areas show conclusively that radios, heaters, lighters, clocks, sun-visors and ash trays are now widely regarded as necessities." By September 13, the company decided to abandon the light car, announcing that Alan B. Pease, *"formerly in charge of the light car division which has been discontinued"* (italics ours) would become Sales Manager for the Ford Central Region.

So temporarily the light car bowed out again, the third time since the late nineteen-thirties. It was nevertheless designed, and appeared in 1948 as the French Ford company's Vedette. It would not come to America for twelve years, in a day of even bigger vehicles and slenderer purses.[24]

Meanwhile work was going forward on the new Ford, with Gregorie, head of the Styling Department, and Walker, as styling consultant, each making mockup designs. By November 22 both had clay models ready, and on December 11 Henry Ford II, Benson Ford, Breech, Bricker, Browning, Youngren and others made a choice at a Products Committee meeting. No one knew who had designed either model, but the choice fell on Walker's. Gregorie resented this decision, for styling had hitherto been his exclusive preserve. As in addition he found working with Youngren difficult, on December 15, 1946, he offered his resignation and left soon afterwards. Walker now took over completely the styling of the new Ford. It was to become the 1949 car, for all the automotive companies found materials so scarce and labor difficulties so harassing that they were unable to produce new cars in 1947 for the 1948 season. Actually, when the Ford was shown in June of the latter year, it was the first popular-priced postwar model to be exhibited.[25]

Early in 1947 the aged Henry Ford and his wife Clara visited Youngren's laboratory and saw the mockup of the 1949 Ford car. Both liked it. Ford now looked benignly on all the activities of his grandson. Clara Ford broke the door handle of the clay model when she tried to turn it. "It looked so real," she explained.[26]

She and her husband spent February and March of 1947 at their winter home in Richmond Hills, Georgia, returning to Dearborn with the beginning of April. Henry seemed to be in good physical condition. On Monday, April 7, he visited the Rouge and Greenfield Village, and watched the return of the ore carrier *Henry Ford II* from its first voyage. That night he and Clara retired early. The Rouge was in flood, and while the rising waters did not touch Fair Lane, thirty feet above the normal level of the stream, they partly covered the power plant a short distance downstream, and deprived the residence of electricity, heat, and telephone.

At 11:15 that night Clara heard her husband call. He complained of a headache and a "dry throat." She dispatched the chauffeur for aid, and he was able to reach Dr. John Mateer of the Ford Hospital. Meanwhile in a house partly heated by wood fire, and without a working telephone, the man who had developed the moving assembly line and the magic of the Rouge was spending his last moments by the light of an oil lamp and flickering candles, with no more mechanical aid at his command than he had known as a boy. At 11:40 he died, and the doctor, arriving a few minutes later, could only certify that the cause had been a cerebral hemorrhage.[27]

The nation paid due homage to Ford. President Truman sent a message of sympathy, and dozens of other eminent men testified to his accomplishments, among them business rivals like Alfred P. Sloan, Jr., and such varied leaders of American life as Orville Wright, Senator Arthur H. Vandenberg, and Governor Thomas E. Dewey of New York. Perhaps a more impressive tribute was paid by the throng, estimated at more than 100,000, that passed through the Recreation Hall in Greenfield Village where Ford's body lay on April 9.

Much praise was showered upon him for accomplishments already described in Chapter X. Some was unqualified. Ford's life-long friend Edgar A. Guest asserted, "His was a sensitive heart and . . . an understanding mind. . . . He had sympathy and pity for the woes of others." Many who had known Ford's arbitrary harshness or stubborn ignorance (as in his anti-Semitic activities) must have smiled wryly at this tribute. But death drew the sting of bitterness and made the world tolerant of his errors and aware of his positive traits. Thousands stood in the rain about St. Paul's Cathedral in Detroit during the funeral rites. Here his entire family gathered, with Clara Ford leaning on the arm of Henry Ford II, who would now carry on alone the work that the older Henry had started forty-four years earlier.[28]

5.

While new Ford plants were rising in half a dozen states, while the design of the 1949 car was growing toward reality, and while the last shadow of Ford the founder flickered and was gone, the new regime was ironing out the last of its major employe problems.

This related to the status of the foremen in Ford plants. During the depression, when every employe needed help and sustenance, the Foremen's Association of America, founded in 1941,* had made rapid prog-

* The Association was founded at the Ford plant, partly as the result of the Ford-UAW agreement of 1941, which reduced the foremen's powers. See Note 29.

ress in enrolling the lowest supervisory officials of the automotive industry. Traditionally, the foreman had identified himself with management rather than with labor, and management tended to assume that he always would. The Ford Motor Company, however, had recognized the FAA as a bargaining agent in 1942, and had dealt with its foremen through the Association ever since.

William T. Gossett, legal head of Ford, later testified that the relationship was unsatisfactory. The union interfered between foremen and company, by insisting on advancement by strict seniority regardless of ability, attaching members to itself rather than to the employer, and tending to make them favor labor unions at company expense. "As the result of hard experience," he said, "we reject the thesis that foremen can be 'employees' for the purpose of mass bargaining with a company over wages and working conditions and yet be part of management when supervising rank-and-file employees." Henry Ford II fully shared this feeling.

In 1946 the company had moved to control its foremen more closely, shifting them from the status of hourly employes to a salaried basis. When on April 8, 1947, the company notified the Association that it intended to terminate the agreement between them, the union reacted belligerently. It made new demands; for example, it asked to be recognized as agent for all foremen, whether members or not, and insisted on a checkoff and stricter seniority provisions. If this program were not accepted, it threatened to strike.

The company did not want a strike, was uncertain whether or not under the Wagner Act it might have to deal with the Association, and had committed itself "to an active program for the constant betterment of personnel relations throughout the organization." It therefore proposed to extend the existing agreement if the FAA would accept in general the company's attitude toward foremen, and put no bar to their climbing the management ladder. The Association refused, and on May 21, 1947, launched its strike. A minority of foremen remained loyal to the company, and it continued production. Then on June 23 the Senate passed over President Truman's veto the Taft-Hartley Act, which specifically freed employers from compulsion to bargain with supervisory unions. When Richard Leonard of UAW offered his services as a mediator, foremen were returning to their jobs, and the company was not interested. On July 3 it made its non-recognition of the union final, and three days later the Association voted to end the strike. None of its demands had been won. However, Ford had lost 123,406 man-days of work.[29]

Henry Ford II later remarked: "I find it difficult to criticize our men [foremen] for joining the union, because frankly I doubt whether in the past very many of them were actually considered or treated as part of management." The company now determined to improve their status. Roper conducted surveys to discover the sources of their dissatisfactions. He found that they complained of unjust discharges, favoritism for promotions, and a feeling that they were mere numbers on the payroll instead of human beings. As a result of these findings, Ford once more admonished his higher officials: "If you have not enough in you to treat those who work for you as human beings, we don't want you in the Ford Motor Company."

But acts spoke louder than words. A record was set up of salaried employes deserving promotions. Time clocks and time cards for foremen were abolished; they were given special parking spaces, individual desks and lockers, special eating facilities, and distinctive overalls. Instead of wearing badges, they carried cards. New vacation plans were made for them. A 10 per cent increase effective June 1, 1947, to all salaried employes earning less than $1000 a month had its effect. Foremen began to consider themselves members of management. Ford could say toward the end of 1947 that "many of the men tell me they have allowed their union membership to lapse." At the same time an order "not to be published" permitted smoking in plants and offices after November 15, 1947—for the first time in Ford history. However, women were requested not to smoke during regular hours.[30]

"We want to do everything in our power," said Ford late in 1947, "to make collective bargaining a far more effective process than it has been in the past." In the middle of that year, the company began four months of negotiations with the UAW. Although the Taft-Hartley Act had in Gossett's view "restored to management-labor relations much of the balance which had been destroyed . . . under the Wagner Act," the union pressed its demands, and finally won a choice of contracts—one providing a 7 per cent wage increase and a pension plan, and the other a straight 15 per cent increase, with no pension. (The cost, the company figured, was identical.) Union negotiators took the two to the workers, who overwhelmingly chose the second. However, Reuther still wanted a pension plan.

The year 1948 was peaceful, with no major strikes. Then in May 1949 came a 24-day stoppage, the union asserting that the company had perpetrated a "speedup" at the Rouge and Lincoln plants. Some 1,716,586 man-days were lost before the two parties accepted arbitration. The result, according to the Ford Annual Report, confirmed the company's right "to establish and enforce reasonable production standards," but outlined general principles for setting them up and applying them.

As the date of the expiration of the Ford-UAW contract, July 15, 1949, approached, threats arose of another strike, but the contract was continued on a day-to-day basis until on September 28 a new one was signed. It provided for a pension plan costing $20,000,000 a year, which guaranteed all workers who had served the company thirty years or more a retirement stipend of $100 a month. (The company paid the difference between what the worker got in social security and this sum.) Employes made no contribution. Retirement was permissible at sixty-five, and mandatory at sixty-eight. Employes who had worked less than thirty years received proportionate benefits. Bugas hailed the contract, which covered a two and a half year period, as "promising a long period of sustained labor peace and productivity," while Reuther called it "a historical step forward in labor's drive to destroy the double economic and moral standards in American industry." The company dropped the security clause of the preceding contract.

Ford was the first automobile company to adopt a pension plan for hourly employes. Under Bugas, it had achieved a steady betterment of relations with all its workers, and increased productivity. The savage tensions of the Bennett era were gone forever.[31]

## 6.

By the spring of 1947 Breech, Browning, Crusoe, Youngren, Gossett, and Harder had all made more than a start in their respective areas. The last major acquisition in personnel was John Dykstra, whose employment by Harder the Policy Committee approved on March 12, 1947. An old Hudson Motor Company and Oldsmobile man, he was a dynamic production manager. While nominally he came as an assistant to Harder, he had been promised an independent post, and soon obtained it. "The first string is now complete," Ford was now quoted as saying.* [32]

The tasks of the Engineering Division for 1947 were numerous and exacting. They included the making of an inproved test track; the continuation of the $50,000,000 engineering center near Greenfield Village; the design of four new cars (Ford, Mercury, Lincoln, Lincoln Cosmopolitan), a number of truck and commercial vehicles, new tractors for both domestic and foreign use, and six new engines; and the improvement of three existing engines.

As previously noted, the test track on part of the Ford Airport had been approved by Henry Ford senior in the 1930s, built, and to some extent used. It was now enlarged to comprise about 360 acres, offering ten miles of test roads and tracks, high speed test loops, mud and waterbath sections, gravel stretches, and a hill with 17 and 30 degree grades. These facilities were being pushed to completion during 1947 and 1948. Further test areas were laid out near Phoenix, Arizona, and in the mountains of Pennsylvania. Cherry Hill Farm near Ypsilanti was acquired to provide tractor testing. It comprised 877 acres, and Youngren remarked that "we shall be able to farm our land at the same time as we get the benefit for testing our tractors and implements." [33]

The $50,000,000 Engineering Center was an eight year project which would furnish few new facilities for some years. Altogether, by the end of 1947 some 667 acres of company property in Dearborn had been allotted to the Engineering Division. By that time the structures in use included the main building near the Henry Ford Museum, and two remodeled structures: the former Airframe Building and the adjacent Hangar, both survivals near the airport from the days when Ford had produced trimotors and other commercial aircraft (1926–1933). These buildings were all on the same side of Oakwood Boulevard as Greenfield Village, while the test track was just opposite the Dearborn Inn on the other or southern side. The new construction went up on the

---

* It was Breech rather than Harder who enlisted Dykstra. The latter had retired to California, where he was managing a small company that did not take his full time. Breech, who knew him well, saw him at a cocktail party there. "What are you doing out on the coast?" he demanded, and when Dykstra explained, he retorted: "You belong in the automobile business; I want you to talk with Henry," and took him over to Ford, who was at the party. The three then met at a breakfast conference. Henry outlined his ideas for the company, and told Dykstra he would consult Harder. He telephoned a few days later: "Well, here's the proposition," and Dykstra accepted it at once. He had always liked the Ford name and spirit. Some of his friends said, "Why are you going with that dying outfit?," but he had confidence in Breech and Henry II. (Interview of January 5, 1960.)

same side as the Inn, some to the east and some to the west of it, and plans in 1947 contemplated a Dynamometer Building, a Styling Center, Body and Exhibit buildings, an Electrical and Chemical Laboratory, and a Laboratory for Human Engineering. The architects were Voorhees, Walker, Foley, and Smith of New York. Part of the Dynamometer Building was completed in 1948 and opened in 1949. During 1947 the engineering staff grew rapidly. From a total of 800 employed in 1939, it mounted to 2600. Among the newcomers were two outstanding men—Earle MacPherson, who soon became Chief Engineer in Charge of Engineering and Research, and John Oswald, soon Executive Engineer in Charge of Styling and Body Engineering. Still, as Youngren said early in 1948, both personnel and facilities were "entirely inadequate," and a great deal of effort went into improving existent facilities while the new buildings were slowly taking form.[34]

The new expansion represented the beginning of a larger manufacturing policy which Harder initiated. "Harder's great contribution," said Dykstra later, "was in expanding Ford facilities." When he arrived, the company depended too much upon suppliers. General Motors was much more highly integrated, manufacturing its own bodies, stampings, axles, drive shafts, wheels, and transmissions. To become competitive, Ford must attain greater self-sufficiency. The new plants at Mound Road and Canton marked strides toward this goal. They produced axles and forgings, respectively. Dykstra was qualified to plan and direct such projects, and soon established a plant in Cincinnati for transmissions. Mound Road and Canton, at first separate divisions, were merged in February, 1948, in the Machining and Forging Division, with Dykstra at its head. He thus won the independent post he had been promised when he joined the company.

In 1949 expenditures for plant and equipment rose further, with Ford acquiring the Kelsey-Hayes wheel plant at Monroe, Michigan, and starting construction on a pressed steel manufactory in Buffalo. A new engine plant and foundry were scheduled for erection in Cleveland, Ohio, which would eventually produce 4000 motors a day. The company now followed a policy of decentralization in a double sense; not only were new divisions created to make new products, but the concentration of Ford facilities at the Rouge was discontinued. Already tractor manufacturing and other activities had been removed from the Rouge and located in Highland Park. Yet the Rouge was to be retained and used fully; further facilities would simply be built elsewhere rather than crowded into an already congested area.[35]

On January 30, 1948, another Ford took a prominent position in the company when Benson, the second brother, became Vice-President in charge of the Lincoln-Mercury Division. He had been working in that and other company units for several years. About the same time the youngest brother, William Clay Ford, became a director and began a period of varied work designed to prepare him for responsibility. His first assignment was to the Sales Division.

The 1949 Ford grew toward completion. On March 12, 1947, Mills and McNamara of the Planning Division had presented a production program to the Policy Committee, and Harder had taken the occasion to say that barring unexpected delays the first postwar Ford should be ready between February 1 and February 15, 1948. But since Breech's decision for a completely new car had supervened, it was of course then far from ready. The first new company products to appear were the Lincoln and Lincoln Cosmopolitan, which were shown by dealers on April 22. Crowding upon them came the new Mercury, which Benson Ford praised for its style and comfort. Meanwhile the new line Ford trucks developed under Roeder's skilful care, had blossomed in 1948 with a choice of 139 different models, the highest number Ford had ever offered. The extra-heavy-duty trucks were the largest in company history, while all models showed completely new cabs, brakes, axles, frames, and steering gear.

The 1949 Ford at length appeared at the Waldorf Astoria Hotel in New York on June 8, 1949, with lavish and colorful publicity. Before the opening, the company entertained the press (including radio and TV representatives), serving champagne at six bars to orchestral music. Each guest received a miniature Ford. Then for six days the public viewed the new car.[36] What they saw was an automobile fundamentally different from its Ford predecessors. At an estimated cost of $118,000,000, the company had produced for the fourth time in its history a notably different car. To the Model T, Model A, and V-8 was now added Model B-A, as unique as any of its three forerunners.

It was a car of attractive lines, almost severely simple in design, with a minimum of chrome trim. Lower and lighter than the 1948 Ford, it had greater seating room front and rear, and improved visibility. The running board had been absorbed into the shapely body. Except for the

V-8 engine, which had been improved, every basic part of the model was new. It carried an improved steering apparatus, an improved ignition system, a new transmission. Redesigned hydraulic brakes, individual front and rear springs (out went the transverse spring, last fetish of the original Henry), direct-action shock absorbers, a Hotchkiss drive, and a re-designed cooling system with new water pumps and a better cooling arrangement in the engine itself, were among its features. It delivered 90 horsepower with a 6-cylinder engine, and 100 with a V-8. As an optional feature, overdrive was offered for the first time.[37]

Hundreds of thousands of potential customers thronged the gold-and-white ballroom where the model was displayed, and orders mounted rapidly. Not all could be filled, for production still lagged behind demand. However, sales of the Ford car only, which had reached 532,646 in 1947 and 486,888 in 1948 (both years reflecting shortages of materials and work stoppages), were to rise to 806,766 in 1949. With 186,629 Mercurys and 37,691 Lincolns sold, the company would pass the million mark for passenger cars (1,031,086). A multitude of men wanted to be automobile salesmen: Davis could have increased his dealer force immensely. He found an "avalanche of applications for franchises to retail the car and truck," fully twenty-five for every available opening.

Despite its success in 1949, the company still stood in third place, less than 5000 cars behind Chrysler. But the important fact was that the Ford Motor Company was now a profitable establishment, and had been since 1947. In that year, after tax deductions, it showed a profit of $66,367,000; this rose in 1948 to $94,346,000 and in 1949 to $177,265,000. It had emerged from the years of meagre gains and disheartening losses.[38]

### 7.

With the appearance of the 1949 Ford, the time approached for the creation of the Ford Division. This had been difficult because it was the greatest change contemplated in organization, and would come more easily after new personnel had been absorbed and the process of reorganization was understood and put into practice. Furthermore, certain high executives were not ready for it. Not only Davis, but Bricker and Youngren objected. Breech followed the policy he had learned from Alfred P. Sloan, Jr. at General Motors: "Wait until the opportune time." Early in 1949 this seemed to have come. Bricker was about to retire to a director-consultant status. Davis had suffered a heart attack, and while he retained his vice-presidency, was replaced as Sales Manager by Walker A. Williams.

Breech and Ford planned the new division, and Ford asked J. O. Wright, who had headed the organizational work in 1946, to organize it. Two years earlier, Crusoe had stated that the new division waited for a dynamic head. It was well that in the intervening period he had presided over the completion of the organizational work, for when the division was created on February 11, 1949, the choice fell on him! He possessed the most varied experience of any Ford executive except Breech, being expert not only in finance, but in purchasing, labor, sales, and business administration. His skill in projecting costs and sales was to be especially valuable, but above all he had the imagination to deal with the problems his new position presented.

One circumstance perhaps helped to hasten the setting up of the new division. The 1949 Ford, despite its promise, showed many minor defects; one of Breech's friends late in 1948 telephoned him that "these cars are a piece of junk," and particularized his assertion. A meeting of the Ford officials concerned took up the complaints. It was difficult to pin down responsibility for them: engineering blamed manufacturing, and vice versa. Breech may well have recognized that with a Ford Division the responsibility would have been easier to fix, and the faults easier to repair.[39]* The new division necessitated drastic changes in company organization. Wiesmyer's Assembly Division became a part of it; so did the Sales and Advertising Division under Walker Williams; and so did part of the Controller's office, a large chunk of Purchasing, and Earl Ward's Service Parts and Accessories.

In the Ford Division the separation of staff and operating activities was a primary principle. Crusoe, of course, gave up his control of company finance. Theodore O. Yntema, a professor of Business and Economic Policy at the University of Chicago, had been acting as a part-time consultant to the company; Kanzler had introduced him to Henry II. In view of Crusoe's impending departure, Breech discussed with Yntema the choice of a successor. Yntema was at a stage where he was prepared to leave academic work. "Ernie, I could do the job my-

---

* Despite its good appearance and a warm reception by Ford dealers, the 1949 Ford did not rate highly with company officials. Its gravest defect was the poor fit of the body shell to the chassis. This allowed dust to sift into the interior, and was not fully remedied until 1952.

self," he said, and Breech, somewhat startled, replied after a pause: "I guess you could, at that." Soon Yntema was installed as Vice-President in Charge of Finance.[40]

Crusoe faced a complicated task. He must weld many divergent elements into an effective team, and he must cope with the complete lack of a physical center. Components of the division were scattered all over Detroit and Dearborn. Ward, for example, worked at Highland Park, Walker Williams at the Administration Building, and Wiesmyer at the Rouge. The greater the difficulties, however, the greater the exhilaration of conquering them.

8.

That Henry II, Breech, and their chief associates had rebuilt the company had by 1949 become generally recognized. Ford had hailed it as an accomplished fact a year sooner. "We were fully satisfied," he said in his report of June 1948, "that if we could bring together the right men and give them the opportunity to be enterprising and successful, we would gain our objectives. The very great progress we have made and are making has been due to the development of a sound, informed, experienced, aggressive organization." The new leadership had revolutionized Ford by clearly allocating responsibility and making possible a quick and accurate appraisal of any company activity on a gain or loss basis.

Engineering had immensely improved since 1945. Manufacturing was bringing the company new plants and greater self-sufficiency, and would soon have the facilities for a dynamic future. Finance had passed from chaos to efficiency. Above all, company officials now had an understanding of the new regime's methods and purposes, and the morale of the wage-earning workers had changed for the better. There was no friction at the top. Ford and Breech worked together so harmoniously that to their associates they seemed almost interchangeable. Discussion of proposed policies could be invoked by any of the "team." "We can get a decision at lunch-time," asserted one vice-president.[41]

The rebuilt company was no proved triumph; it faced tests aplenty. These would show how well or ill it had been constructed. But by mid-1949 there was a quiet confidence throughout the organization that it had the resources for dealing with the unfolding postwar era. Competition would be severe; General Motors had not been standing still while

Ford pressed on. Chrysler, now less of a threat, commanded large resources. The company's slogan had been and was, "Beat Chevrolet!" Amusingly, a sign would soon appear in the General Motors Styling Department, "Beat Ford!" Respect was a two-way street, and the preparations for the clash were intensified by both antagonists.[42]

# XIV

## LIONS IN THE PATH

"IT'LL be a grand fight." These were the words with which Harry Ferguson, who as a Scotch-Irishman risen from the status of machinery salesman to corporation head knew something about fighting, surprised the Ford executives in 1948 by launching a suit against them. The month was January, just as the new management was in the full tide of its regeneration of the company; the sum which Ferguson demanded was a mere $251,000,000. Behind the suit lay not only Ferguson's delight in a shindy but a complicated misunderstanding.

When Henry II returned from naval service, he had found the losses in the manufacture of the Ford tractor, on the basis arranged by the elder Henry and Ferguson, so staggering (they had then reached about $20,000,000) that he gave the subject his earnest attention. Bricker had already taken steps to investigate the situation, and Henry and he continued by transferring the operation from the Rouge to Highland Park, where it could be isolated, studied, and improved. For a time they labored with Harry Ferguson himself and with Roger M. Kyes, the Harvard-educated president of the Ferguson-Sherman Manufacturing Corporation, later Harry Ferguson, Inc., to reduce costs on the tractor.[1]

While doing this, Henry tried to reach some agreement with Ferguson for a better definition of the hazy Ford-Ferguson relationship. Like many another man, he found the inventor "a difficult person to get along with in a business way," and was relieved when the Ulsterite returned to England, leaving negotiations in the hands of Kyes. However, no understanding could be reached. Henry II accepted the testimony of his engineers that the designs for the two principal tractor models were the product of Ford men; Kyes insisted that "Mr. Ferguson did all the designing and development . . . . other than the conventional work of adapting them to the manufacturing practices of your particular plant." This was an honest difference of view which de-manded a compromise.

But the word compromise was not in the Ferguson vocabulary. Though Ernest Kanzler used his best energies as mediator in 1946, and though Breech, when he joined Ford, was hopeful of an agreement be-cause of his long acquaintance with and admiration for Kyes, the im-passe was unbreakable. In vain did Kanzler suggest various solutions: that Ford might acquire an interest in the Ferguson company, or that a new company be created, or that one side sell out to the other. In Ferguson's name, Kyes said no to all proposals. In vain, later, did Breech and Ford propose that they should take part ownership in a dis-tributing company to handle the tractors they made, or a controlling interest in a new company for both manufacture and distribution. On Ferguson's behalf, Kyes repelled both plans.[2]

The upshot, late in 1946, was a severance of relations between the Ford company and the Ferguson interests. Before finally deciding on it, Henry II took care to consult his grandfather, who had made the original arrangement. When he had explained the situation, the elder Ford replied: "Well, use your judgment. Ferguson is a hog anyway, and just keep on building the tractor." Henry II replied, "All right, we will." Talking with Kyes again, he made still another effort to arrange some compromise—once more in vain.[3]

In a last meeting on November 11, 1946, "it was mutually decided," as Henry II puts it, "that we should discontinue our arrangement." Thus the original gentlemen's agreement, "terminable at will," was ended. The event delighted Kyes. "I have never been so relaxed, so happy, so relieved in my life," he wrote Ferguson, who replied from England: "My sincere and warmest congratulations on this truly cheery and splendid news!! 'Glory be—we're free' is just about how I feel over this." It is difficult to escape the conclusion that Ferguson and Kyes had deliberately courted severance. Of course, Ford and Breech were equally delighted.

They immediately completed their plans for a tractor-distributing company, incorporating Dearborn Motors on November 26, 1946. Frank R. Pierce came from General Motors to manage it. Ford had agreed to supply Ferguson with tractors until June 30, 1947, when he expected to have a new model, and when Ferguson would presumably be ready to manufacture for himself. The Ford company, however, raised the price $20 a machine, and Dearborn Motors added another $25, increasing Ferguson's cost by $45. "We felt very strongly," said Henry II, "that since we had broken with Henry Ferguson, Inc., they had no right to make the profit on the tractor that we had been making."[4]

On the establishment of Dearborn Motors, the chief Ford executives were permitted to buy stock in the enterprise, Breech up to 20 per cent of the total. This was the first opportunity they had had to acquire an interest in any Ford undertaking. Henry II had always felt a "moral obligation" to let them do so; the control of Ford Motor Company stock by the Ford Foundation and the family did not permit it, but Dearborn Motors provided an opportunity. Ford himself, however, on Newsom's advice, took no stock whatsoever in the new firm. It began operations in January 1947 and soon enlisted distributors, including a number who had previously served the Ferguson company. It prospered from the start, making profits in the first three months larger than its capital. Then in July 1947, having ceased to manufacture for Ferguson, the Ford company as expected produced its own tractor, the 8N. This machine did not differ greatly from the Ford 2N which Ferguson marketed, for all the latter's basic patents on his hydraulic system had expired, and under the watchful eyes of patent attorney E. C. McRae other features covered by what appeared to be Ferguson patents were simply redesigned.

Meanwhile, Ferguson was not having smooth sailing. As the public financing of his manufacturing program was postponed, Kyes became alarmed, and in November 1947 abandoned a ten-year contract and resigned. Ferguson himself took up the work of tractor production, which he successfully established by October 1948, realizing a profit of $540,968 in the last three months of that year.[5]

Meanwhile, full of fight, he began his quarter-billion-dollar suit against the Ford Motor Company, Dearborn Motors, and the chief officers of both companies. He alleged combination and conspiracy to "restrain and monopolize . . . trade and commerce in farm tractors and implements," to "destroy the Ferguson Company's sources of supply of implements," to "carry the Ferguson system tractor and line of implements (and) infringe the Ferguson patents," to "take over in its entirety the distribution-dealer organization built up by the Ferguson Company," to exclude that company "from access to the market," and to "frustrate the efforts of the Ferguson Company to arrange for the manufacture of its tractor." Claims were advanced for relief against the alleged destruction of the Ferguson business, against patent infringements, and against alleged acts of unfair competition. Ferguson made no effort to conceal his hopes that the suit would furnish abundant publicity for his American enterprise. It assuredly had the distinction of being one of the largest to be brought into an American court.

The Ford Motor Company in a sharp rejoinder at once termed the charges of conspiracy and unfair competition "ridiculous." Said Henry II: "The blunt truth about this relationship is that it made Mr. Ferguson a multi-millionaire and cost the Ford Motor Company $25,000,000 in the process. . . . Our arrangement with the Ferguson people was terminable at will by either party. By 1946 this arrangement had become intolerable. . . . The complaint is full of untruths. Many important facts are omitted, and others have been distorted and twisted out of their true meaning. We will be very happy to meet all of the allegations in the complaint at the proper time and place." On July 25, 1949, the Ford Motor Company and Dearborn Motors filed a full answer which pointed out that Ferguson's business was now flourishing, argued that his patents were invalid, and alleged that as the Ferguson group were "guilty of unclean hands" no relief should be granted them on any count.

A number of sharp issues required answers. Who had designed the tractor, Ford engineers, or Ferguson? Were Ferguson's patents valid? Was the loose agreement between Henry Ford and Ferguson "terminable at will"? Had Dearborn Motors and the Ford Company engaged in unfair practices? Was Ferguson's former business "destroyed," and was the prospering enterprise he now headed a wholly different activity?

Just as the Ford Motor Company was feeling the positive results of three years of reorganization, the Ferguson suit loomed in its path like a boulder dropped by an avalanche. Despite the conviction of company officials that their case was sound, the monumental action cast a shadow over all the constructive activities of the firm.[6]

2.

While Gossett and his aides were framing the answer to the Ferguson complaint, Henry's executive communication of February 11, 1949, established the Ford Division, and partially defined it. "In general terms," he wrote, "the Ford Division will be responsible for determining with the concurrence of appropriate staff officers and subcommittees of the Policy Committee, the design, features, and prices of its products. It will also be responsible for manufacturing and marketing its products." While this seemed to invest the new agency with sweeping powers, practice might trim or enlarge them. How much would the division, which was the heart of the company, defer to the many brilliant leaders who might wish to mold it?

Crusoe did not long leave his colleagues in doubt on these points. The company's Product Planning Committee was considering anew the question of an economy (light) car. A report on February 17 held that there were 4,000,000 potential customers for such a car and that the first company to produce one "would enjoy the distinct advantage of exclusive penetration" of the market, and that public interest warranted at least "continuing and intensifying engineering development work" in the field. However, Earle S. MacPherson of Engineering opposed such activity. "It has to be a kind of religion if the job is to be done successfully," he asserted, and felt that such an absorbing venture would interfere with the discharge of other engineering work.

In the general discussion which followed, some committee members suggested a reduction in the size and weight of the regular Ford car. Crusoe at once protested. The Ford Division, he asserted, "should be allowed to determine what it believed to be the desirable Ford passenger car and make its recommendations to the Committee." No action should be taken until it had made its recommendations. The final decision was that nothing should be done about the light car except by Engineering, which would develop some plans "without interference with the work on other projects already approved."

Crusoe reiterated his right to lead in planning for the Ford car on April 12, 1949. He stated then that while he would welcome advice from all sources, he wanted to "guard the independent thinking of the division" as though it were "an entirely separate company." This, he added, should be true for all divisions. When Breech asked, "Who is going to ride herd on the divisions and their planning?" Crusoe replied: "I think we will be self-starters on it. I don't think it's going to take much needling." [7]

He could speak with confidence. He had a talented crew at his call: Wright, Mills, Tom Lilley, Earl Ward, Walker Williams (all eventually to be Ford vice-presidents), Wiesmyer, and M. W. Welty (industrial relations); he would soon acquire E. B. Richard as controller and A. E. Conn to head purchasing. Jack Clarke would come in before the end of the year to handle public relations. Here was experience and brilliant capacity, which Crusoe used shrewdly. All his crew were soon devising ways to make the Ford car cheaper, stronger, and better.*

The 1949 model helped them, in that it revealed thousands of minor defects (J. R. Davis put them at 8000) which required correction and served as a warning against producing cars in eighteen months. The division reported to the Product Planning Committee on May 26, outlining its ideas for the future. "In the main," it could say, "competitive disadvantages reported by dealers in the present Ford car will be eliminated before or by the introduction of the 1950 model." Crusoe promised that this would be a much improved car, and that a wholly new one would be ready by 1952. One defect, the body shell, could not be fully corrected before that time, for to stop its rains and dust leaks, a wholly new design would be necessary. "We are going to have to live in sin on this shell until we get the 1952 job out," he told regional sales managers. Yet despite its faults, the 1949 car had been a success. Its emergence months ahead of its competitors and its superior styling had pleased everyone. "That car really rang the bell with the dealers," Walker Williams recalled eleven years later.[8]

The dealers had just complaints as to the price of the car, which was higher than those of competing models, and as to the inadequacy of their discounts. When Crusoe said that the price could not be competitive, Davis remarked: "I can't help but remember that Chevrolet took leadership from us when their car was a hundred dollars higher, but they had a gross margin that was good." The Policy Committee soon met one complaint by raising the dealers' discount from 24 to 25 per cent. Crusoe and his young men were meanwhile working to reduce costs. He disassembled Fords and Chevrolets and compared the number and sizes of the parts. He knew from experience what many

---

* The Thornton group had now been broken up. Thornton himself had left in 1948, and in that year was already holding an important post with the Hughes Aircraft Company. While Wright and Mills served in the Ford Division, McNamara on the Finance Staff was Director of the Financial Analysis Department. Miller was Assistant Treasurer. Thornton apparently had felt that his advancement at Dearborn was too slow. However, before leaving he conferred with the other members of the group, assured them that his departure was a personal matter which did not affect them, and that each should follow his chosen course. Thornton found rapid advancement outside Ford, and today is Chairman of the Board for Litton Industries.

of them cost and could often get a figure from a supplier. Checking financial data, he could discover the profit per car. The prices of machine tools were known, for most of them were sold to several manufacturers. Thus Crusoe ascertained cost down to the cent. "This is a nickel and dime business," he said later. "A dime on a million units is $100,000. We'll practically cut your throat around here for a quarter." He knew that Chevrolet was cheaper to make than the Ford. By 1951 he set the difference at $84, but he was working to reduce the figure.

Ford Division even in its first year took part in a notable gain. In 1950 the company soared into second place with 1,518,653 cars, 1,116,267 of them Fords, and 24 per cent of the market, leaving Chrysler with 1,113,794 for all its cars in third place with 17.6 per cent. General Motors with 2,071,078 held 45.5 per cent of all sales. The Ford company never again surrendered second place, and while it had not caught Chevrolet, it was gaining ground.[9]

### 3.

The increase in manufacturing facilities had already been a vital factor in Ford reorganization; but what were "adequate" facilities? They included factories to produce many kinds of fundamental parts hitherto made by suppliers. Hence the plants at Canton (forgings), Mound Road (axles and other products), Monroe (the former Kelsey-Hayes manufactory for wheels), the new pressed steel unit at Buffalo (stampings), the engine and foundry complex at Cleveland, and the transmission factory at Cincinnati. The company continued to expand such facilities, a fact which enabled Crusoe to bring the costs of producing a Ford nearer to those of making a Chevrolet. But quantity and variety were only half the answer. Ford also needed *factories that were better than General Motors factories,* and Harder was keenly aware of this.

The new assembly plants had been carefully located. "Davis could tell us what the market area was," recalls Wiesmyer, "and where they wanted the automobiles by sales district." Most of the new installations were on one level, or partly on two, with ample acreage. There had been two earlier groups of assembly plants; the first built in the Model T period before World War I, when most automotive buildings were multiple-storied and built on small tracts of land, and the second built in the 1923–1925 periods on designs by Albert Kahn as one-or-two-storied structures with ample room for assembly lines, and the parking and yard storage space. Such plants could be modified to the uses of the late 1940s; survivals from the pre-World War I era could not be. The old St. Louis plant, built in 1914, had been a five-storied affair, 144 by 300 feet, occupying 3.74 acres; the new one begun in 1946 was one-storied, measured 520 by 1480 feet, and occupied 99 acres! Incidentally, the Albert Kahn organization drew the plans for all assembly plants erected in 1946.[10]*

At the Rouge the revival of the glass plant, and the expansion of steel facilities have already been noted. In the early postwar period steel had been in great demand, and Ford had a point of superiority over its competitors in being able to supply part of its own metal. In 1946 the company decided to compound this advantage, and a new blast furnace, the enlargement of existing open hearth furnaces, and other additions and improvements by 1949 lifted the steel making capacity from 600,000 to 1,200,000 tons a year. Some steel still had to be procured from outside, but the expansion of capacity was useful. The company also bought five buildings erected at the Rouge for government production during the war, and for $7,000,000 acquired machinery, office furniture, and fixtures. The Armor Plate and Ordnance buildings were utilized in steel-making; the Aircraft Engine Building temporarily served as a warehouse, and later would be remodeled for important manufacturing.

The Ford Motor Company declined an opportunity to acquire the Willow Run property, for the huge aircraft factory was not adaptable to efficient automobile construction. Kaiser-Frazer, its first postwar occupant, did not prosper, although the plant was not the chief reason for its failure to do so.[11]

Even after the removal of various operations, the Rouge was far from the factory it should have been. Charles Patterson, returning in 1945 from Willow Run, had been appalled at the confusion, and said to himself, "Ford is a gone goose!" Patterson himself took a hand in greatly bettering the situation. About the time of the removal of tractor, truck, and bus manufacture, he was put in charge of the motor plant, which according to *Fortune* was "the only spot in the Ford plant that really resembles Charlie Chaplin's *Modern Times* satire." There machines were "bumper to bumper and men worked like demons." Patterson

---

* The Kahn organization did not design all the pre-World War I buildings although among those he did design was the Highland Park plant. Albert Kahn, bearing a great name in industrial engineering, died on Dec. 8, 1942.

overhauled his domain and immensely improved it, establishing a better sequence of operations, a smoother flow of materials, and a sharp reduction of manual operations. "There is more working space," reported *Mill and Factory,* "less handling, less fatigue for workers, less waste motion, better quality products, and increased capacity."

Harder was prepared to renovate the Rouge throughout in a comparable manner. He sent his staff into the various departments to make studies of conveyor as compared to bulk handling, of new machine units, and in general the reduction of lifting, turning, feeding, and stacking. They met resistance. Old patterns of operation had become entrenched, and some managers fought for them. These were usually the "drivers" and were soon replaced by younger and more open-minded men, ready to accept every improvement.[12]

In the midst of innovations at the Rouge the Ford company became involved in a movement that soon promised to revolutionize all American industry. At a staff meeting in 1947 Harder suggested a new department to study the efficient handling of materials. It should be somewhat independent of regular plant activity, but should improve it by developing mechanical methods for handling processes of production which were now manual. Harder groped for a name; "the Automated Handling Department," he suggested, then, "better still, the Automation Department." This seems to have been the first significant appearance of the word. Later, Harder dated its use back to 1936, when he was at Grand Rapids with General Motors. By the diligent efforts of Ford publicity men, and his own impressive accomplishments, Harder came to be known as "the father of automation." John Diebold of the Harvard Business School also claims to have invented the word "automation," but seems to have done so, according to the Ford version, a few days later than Harder's use in 1947.

The definitions of automation vary. Peter Drucker has the simplest: "the use of machines to run machines." Robert Bendiner is more precise: "Automation at its fullest is . . . the controlled operation of an entire factory or process in which the machines as linked units automatically perform their manipulations in specified sequences, with electronic judgment substituted for the perception of the machinist or foreman." Where previously, in the course of producing a unit, manual work supplemented each mechanical performance, the entire process becomes mechanized. Electronic controls built into the machines also inspect the work at various stages and approve it or correct it. Thousands of executives in industry believe that the process represents in Drucker's words, "a major economic and technological change, a change as great as Henry Ford ushered in with the first mass production plant fifty years ago." Obviously, while some processes can be automated in factories built before automation, far greater success is possible when both factories and tools are designed for automation, for its adoption involves a wholly new philosophy of production.

In the Ford plants it was impracticable to automate the entire building of a car (although this is mostly a question of cost versus return), but processes and even whole departments could be and were changed. Ford practice therefore has stood in contrast to varieties of automation which produce complete products under electronic control, such as refined oil, 155 mm. shells, cigarettes, and napalm. This type of automation came into being largely because of the work done in World War II in developing radar, controlled firing mechanisms, and guided missiles. Here the electronic control was dominant. In the postwar period the scarcity of labor, the rise in real wages, and high consumer demand encouraged experiments with manufacturing processes which employed conveyors, compressed air, hydraulic power, and electrical devices to automate certain operations. This was the Ford practice and became known as "Detroit automation." It clearly fits Drucker's definition better than Bendiner's.[13]

Apostles of automation point out that the principle of the new method is very old. Oliver Evans in 1784 constructed a water-driven mill that took grain through the full cycle of grading and cutting operations to finished flour without the aid of a human hand. Men like Dykstra, Ray Sullivan, and D. J. Davis have regarded automation as evolutionary rather than revolutionary, every step that converts a manual act to a machine act leading toward it. Davis told a Congressional Committee how, as a machine designer for Cadillac, he was asked in the 1930s to simplify the milling of connecting rods, where six workers were employed. "I took the overarm on the milling machine and put spring clamps on it. As the worker laid the pieces on, they automatically clamped themselves as they went through the cycle, eliminating manual guidance. This is just as true automation as we are doing today."

The Automation Department at Ford began its work on valves and valve-guide bushings, then automated the manufacture of pistons, then coils and wheels, and then frames and rear axles. Each step was studied before being taken. Would it speed up the pace of manufacture? Usually it would, but the percentage of increase was determined. Would the quality of the product be as good? Usually it would be better. Would the cost of automation as opposed to the cost of ordinary tooling be low enough for the faster rate of production to tip the balance to the new method? Harder when in doubt favored automation, while D. J. Davis tended to feel that the older practice should continue unless proved more expensive.

The Automation Department at first had to work in plants not built for automation. It was forced to redesign tools and alter layouts. In its first year and a half the department approved designs for more than 500 devices, costing in aggregate $3,000,000. It found that on the average production increased 20 per cent, that greater safety was attained, and that 1000 men would have to be transferred. Nobody was discharged. The department itself, starting with five persons in 1947, by the fall of 1948 was using fifty.[14]

Ford engineers began work in 1949 on the first factories built for extensive use of automation, the Buffalo Stamping Plant, which made hoods, doors, floor, and other sheet metal parts, and the Cleveland Engine Plant and Foundry. As Ray Sullivan pointed out in 1955, the manufacture of the larger products represented by these two establishments could not be automated profitably "until we had built new plants from the ground up." The Cleveland plant especially became a focus for the discussion of automation. Already the question was being asked, "What about Labor?" Beyond doubt, men were "losing jobs" in the sense that they ceased to be needed for certain work, and must either be shifted or trained as automation crews.

Walter Reuther, watching the process with ominous intentness, pointed out later how the magic of the modern factory had reduced the time required to make a cylinder block from 24 to 9 hours, and then, with the advent of automation, to 14.6 minutes! "That is just the beginning, because they have drawings on the engineering drawing boards that will now do it in less time." Describing the Ford engine plant at Cleveland, he seemed to find a grim threat in its silent efficiency. But his forebodings never came to the point of an actual attack on automation. The new process produced more goods and required better paid workers; Ford, in a period of expansion, discharged no one for technological reasons. Sullivan could boast in 1954 that since the company had created its Automation Department it had added 50,000 workers to its payrolls.[15]

However, automation remained and still remains today an important factor in Ford thinking, as in that of many industrial corporations. The automotive industry has not seen the last of it: European practice in this field is in some instances going further than American, and represents a challenge. Suppliers are affected. Great problems remain in automation in the further disappearance of jobs, the retraining of men, and cooperation with the labor unions, which see innovations that bring gains to the employers as promising only losses to the workers.

4.

During this period (1947–1950) Ford became the Mecca for an immense number of young men (and some not young) who wanted to rise in the industry. When Breech had brought Crusoe, Youngren, Gossett, and Harder to the company, each had fetched assistants with him. Others pressed after them. The company's youthful president, the talk of overtaking Chevrolet, the expansion and rising sales, the interest of the press in a better day at Ford, all lent an air of opportunity to the organization. As it expanded it would need new captains. At General Motors, where the policy was to hold what the company already had, promotion was relatively slow.

As early as 1948 Henry II and Breech went to see C. E. Wilson about buying hydramatic transmissions from General Motors for the Lincoln, and Wilson agreed to sell. (Youngren was meanwhile perfecting the Ford-o-matic transmission.) But the GM president also complained about the employes whom Ford was taking. Breech pointed out that most of his acquisitions were retired men, or from other firms. "I don't mean your top men," explained Wilson, "but second and third level people." He had counted 150 of these. Dykstra met the same resentment and unquestionably did much to provoke it. In 1947–1949, when starting the Canton and Mound Road plants and planning the Cincinnati transmission center, he had to staff all three. Each needed a controller, purchasing agent, general production chief, experts for chemical and metallurgical work, besides foremen and skilled workers. One day an irate General Motors official reproved him for employing their best switchboard operator. "We miss her terribly!" Said Dykstra, "We'd miss her terribly if we sent her back." But in general he had a convincing reply to all complainers: "It's an ancient American right to change your job." Crusoe had brought some good General Motors men with him, such as Karl Scott and Ken Cassidy in the cost field. Others wanted to come. He made no promises. "If you want to swim away from the shore, okay. I don't know where I'm going." But despite such warnings they came.[16]

The first six months of 1950 represented the best period the company had known since 1929. Ford cars were selling rapidly, and daily production rose to nearly 9000, although on paper the limit was definitely 6300. New plans for expansion were hatching, and those already out of the egg were being pushed with vigor. "We were feeling pretty proud of ourselves," said Breech later. Then came the outbreak of war in Korea.

### 5.

This event, which saw 60,000 well-armed and thoroughly trained North Koreans pour across the border of South Korea, did not give sudden pause to the Ford Motor Company or to the American people. Korea was relatively small and quite remote. The occupation of its northern half by the Russians in the final days of World War II and the formation of a Communist republic there had mildly startled Americans, but they assumed that eventually the North would unite under United Nations auspices with the more populous South. Though they were outraged by the sudden attack on June 24, 1950, President Truman's prompt order to General MacArthur to assist the South Koreans, and his quick appeal to the United Nations, reassured them. The UN condemned the aggressor and arranged for the participation of many nations in an armed intervention. Optimists regarded this as a "police action" which would soon be terminated.

Henry Ford II telegraphed the President on July 19: "I want you to know that all of us at Ford Motor Company stand ready to carry out any assignment the government may give us in view of the present situation." He received an appreciative answer. Meanwhile the company felt no evidence that there was a war. On July 25 the Board of Directors continued its expansion plans, approving expenditures on new assembly plants in Wayne, Michigan, and in Kansas City, voting funds for the modernization of the Rouge and the enlargement of steel operations, and acting on construction at Monroe, Mound Road, Cincinnati, Buffalo, and Cleveland.[17]

But in a week this situation was sharply changed by the continuing successes of the North Koreans. On August 2 the company created a Defense Production Division, shortly renamed the Office of Defense Products. General Motors also organized a Defense Plans Committee. Events then moved rapidly. By early September the Detroit press was headlining ominous news. Truman talked of an army of three million men, and on September 8 signed the Defense Production Act, which gave him power to control credit, stabilize wages and prices, encourage the enlargement of productive capacity, and set priorities and allocations for critical materials. Preparations for equipping American military forces had to be pushed on a new scale. Since 1948 the Air Forces had encouraged Pratt & Whitney to find an automobile company to assist it in manufacturing its 28-cylinder engines for B-36 bombers, and Korea moved the aircraft engine company to do so. In September the Ford Motor Company received an Air Forces letter-contract to build these engines and on the 20th accepted it. Thus for a second time Ford was to produce a Pratt & Whitney engine, although the R-4360 was a far more complicated mechanism than the R-2800 of World War II.

The site chosen was not the Rouge, where the old aircraft engine building was too small and otherwise employed, but the government-owned plant near Chicago where Chrysler's Dodge Division had built Curtiss-Wright engines half a dozen years earlier. Although less publicized than Willow Run, it was the largest factory in the world under a single roof. Dykstra had been deputed by Breech to find a manager. After a fruitless search he heard Ford say to him, "*You* are going to head the Chicago plant." "My God—no!" exclaimed Dykstra, but in an hour he was at the Willow Run airport on his way to Chicago. Here he was paged for a telephone call and found Henry Ford II on the line. "What are you doing out there?" Ford demanded. "Well, you put me in charge of this plant," retorted Dykstra. "I'm going up there to look it over." Ford made no comment on this reply. "I want to be the first," he said, "to congratulate you on becoming a vice-president of the Ford Motor Company." [18]

In Chicago the new vice-president threw a flashlight beam about "a rusted-out plant—no heat, no air, dirty, filthy." Nothing in it could be used. As emblems of the postwar failure of the Tucker Automobile Company, several old Tucker cars stood disintegrating. Dykstra had to make a new layout, tool the great empty shell, gather a staff, and obtain materials. To build up an expert force he brought in 150 Detroit toolmakers and 200 Canadian technicians, took men from Mound Road and Canton, and brought back some Dodge officials who had worked there in World War II. Common labor was available in Chicago, so with a force of 20,000 men he soon drove ahead.

Meanwhile the situation in Korea, which had brightened with a surprise landing at Inchon by the United States marines, the rout of enemy forces, and the penetration of United Nations detachments to the northern border, grew worse in late November when hordes of Chinese "volunteers" struck suddenly. Thinly scattered Allied troops were captured, slaughtered, or pushed southward down the peninsula. In the United States the result was an immediate swing to a war economy. The National Production Authority created by the Defense Act placed more severe restrictions on materials, and the Office of Price Stabilization set price controls. The Ford company reconsidered its resources "in the event of an all-out war," and Harder told a management group early in February: "We have more than 35,000,000 square feet of manufacturing space and more than 140,000 people at the disposal of the government."

The company's building program quickly became integrated with the war program. The projected Lincoln-Mercury assembly plant at Wayne, Michigan, was allocated to a J-40 Westinghouse jet engine Naval contract. The Ford Division assembly plant begun at Kansas City took on the building of Boeing-designed bomber wings. The projected Ford tractor plant at Livonia became a tank factory. The Cincinnati automatic transmission plant was tooled to make aircraft engine parts, and the newly-planned Dearborn Engine Building was also partly devoted to such manufacture. Only a few of the new buildings still held to automotive production—notably the Buffalo Stamping and the Cleveland Engine Plants. Part of the new building program, including the Engineering and Research Center, the staff office building, and the modernization of various assembly plants, was suspended. The Rouge, Highland Park, and other Ford centers continued with automotive production, but on a quota basis.[19]

The Chicago plant made its first deliveries of R-4360 aircraft engines in March 1952. The association with Pratt & Whitney was so happy that the Air Forces, recalls Dykstra, "used to point to our relationship as a good example to other companies that didn't get along harmoniously." On July 11, 1952, less than two years after Ford moved into the Chicago plant, the first B-36 bomber with all-Ford engines was flown at the Carswell Air Force base near Fort Worth, Texas. Even earlier Pratt & Whitney had planned to have Ford build a new engine, the J-57, a turbo jet, and in the middle of 1957 Ford had received a letter-contract authorizing the design of production tools for this motor. Chrysler wanted the contract, but largely because of Pratt & Whitney's loyalty to its Dearborn associate, Ford got it. A pilot model was completed in November 1953, but production did not come until after the war, in the summer of 1954. The R-4360 program ended that season with a total of 3071 engines manufactured by Ford.[20] Meanwhile the company had prepared to manufacture the J-40 Westinghouse jet engine, but changes of plan by the Navy involving a shift to a new plant, and the termination of the contract in the spring of 1953 killed the project.

At Kansas City the veteran assembly plant manager William Rose took charge of Ford Division's bomber wing plant, assisted by young Ben Mills in the negotiation of contracts, purchasing, production programming, and finances. By July 1952 the plant was delivering wings to Boeing, Lockheed, and Douglas. At its new plant in Livonia, Michigan, the company was building T-48 medium tanks, beginning production in June 1952. At the same time it repeated its World War II record by manufacturing tank engines at the Magnesium Smelter Building in the Rouge. At Highland Park the company produced the 3.5 inch bazooka rocket, and at Dearborn Ford engineers worked on plans for a new automatic gun that shot faster than any ever used previously by American forces. This was the M-39, "an electrically-fired, gas-operated, revolver type automatic gun" which the Ford Company designed, and which late in 1952, built elsewhere, became part of the armament of F-86 fighter-planes.

Aircraft engines, bomber wings, tanks, tank engines, a rocket, the M-39, and two types of machine guns comprised the Ford contribution to war in Korea. Bugas told a management group in 1951 that the company had accepted nearly a billion dollars worth of war contracts, and was "committed . . . to an important part in the job of keeping

America strong to meet the threat of Communist aggression." [21] But it felt that while it was making great efforts to furnish weapons to the government, it did not receive proper treatment in the supply of vital materials or in price controls. Indeed, it believed that the government in these two fields had penalized not only its own effort but that of the industry.

The restrictions on materials early covered aluminum, copper, nickel, zinc, and rubber, and were later extended to steel. As Ford was expanding, it paid a severe penalty. For example, its automatic transmission plant, completed after the war began, could get no allocations of aluminum or copper, since the basis for such allocations was production during the six months prior to hostilities. Finally, I. A. Duffy, Browning's successor as vice-president in charge of purchasing, won a concession: the plant would be granted sufficient raw material to permit operation at half capacity!

However, the allotment of materials was soon related to production totals, and the era used as a gauge was 1947–1949. This put Ford at a disadvantage, since its building program and the ensuing rise in productivity did not become a force until 1949–1950. Vice-president William T. Gossett asked the National Production Authority to reconsider the period set, and to base quotas and allotments of materials on the six months or the year prior to the war (the first half of 1950, or that and the last half of 1949). The Authority, however, rejected the Ford petition, and the company appealed. Gossett told the Appeals Board on May 6, 1952, "We feel that an injustice has been done to Ford, and to the public as well." The Ford plea met with vehement opposition from Chrysler and the smaller automotive manufacturers, General Motors remaining silent. Chrysler claimed that a 100-day strike in the early months of 1950 cut down its production and made that period unsuitable. Willys-Overland, Nash, Hudson, Kaiser-Frazer, and Packard all filed briefs giving arguments against the change, for all had produced more in the earlier period.

The dispute became incredibly bitter. Ford submitted that it should be second to General Motors in passenger allocations. Chrysler countered with the charge that Ford was invoking government aid to gain a place "which in a free economy it had been unable to attain in the past seventeen years." * Gossett icily replied, "If the controls were

---

* This was untrue. Ford had surpassed Chrysler in 1945 and 1950, and if the period taken were 1933–1950, also in 1934 and 1935. See *Ward's Reports*.

lifted, we would very quickly demonstrate who is entitled to the second place." He was of course right; Chrysler never again attained it. Courtney Johnson of NPA characterized the Ford plan "discriminating, arbitrary, whimsical, capricious and illusionary." Dr. Sumner Slichter of Harvard termed the 1949–1950 span more representative of normal competitive conditions than 1947–1949. The board of three, under great pressure from the NPA, the smaller companies, and Chrysler, finally rejected the Ford appeal. The *Wall Street Journal* probably expressed the company's feeling when it commented: "Young Mr. Ford can build the best car on the market and sell it at the cheapest price, he can have customers lined up for blocks at his dealers—but for all that he can make and sell no more than 21.1 per cent of the nation's automobiles. Three men have said him nay." [22]

Both the Ford and the Chrysler quotas were raised slightly, to 21.43 and 21.76 per cent. However, when the year 1952 came to an end, Ford, General Motors, Chrysler, and Nash had all oversold their quotas, and even with its lower allotment Ford had managed to outsell Chrysler!

The first freeze of prices had been imposed on December 16, 1950, to apply from December 1. No control had been established on suppliers' prices, and Breech asserted that the passenger car industry "was compelled to hold the dike against inflation alone." When new regulations of April 1951 permitted manufacturers to raise prices in proportion to increases in their labor and materials costs, the situation was not improved for the automobile companies, for passenger cars were specifically exempted!

Courtney Johnson suggested to the Office of Price Stabilization that passenger car prices should not be changed until it could be established that profits in the industry amounted to less than 85 per cent of those from 1946 to 1949. Breech exploded: "If we have reached the day when government mandate is to establish the profits of a particular industry and determine prices of other competing industries by relation to what such agency feels proper profits are, then we face a most serious change in our economic way of life. . . . By no stretch of the imagination is government profit control part of the American way of life." Happily, the Capehart amendment to the Defense Production Act in July 1951 improved the situation, for it forbade using price control as "profit control." On September 14, the Office of Price Stabilization authorized Ford to increase its prices.[23]

6.

Government edicts limiting the production of automobiles for civil-ian use quickly affected the production figures for the industry. Ford sales dropped from 1,518,653 vehicles in 1950 to 1,121,464 in 1951, and to 947,474 in 1952. However, the fundamental methods from which Ford drew success were nurtured and even improved. Some ground won by Harder and his associates from 1947 to 1950 was lost because of the war program. Plans to manufacture an increasing variety of parts, or to modernize assembly operations, were subordinated to military production in Cincinnati, Livonia, Kansas City, and to some extent the Rouge. But the original goals were maintained in other centers, particularly Buffalo and Cleveland. The manufacturing ac-tivities of the company, meanwhile, were improved by further de-centralization.

In January 1951 all manufacturing was divided into three basic groups, each containing a number of divisions. The Basic Products Group (headed by Logan Miller until his retirement in 1952, then by Stanley Ostrander) comprised the Steel, Dearborn General Manu-facturing, and Manufacturing Services Divisions. The Engine and Pressed Steel Group, under Ray Sullivan, included the Metal Stamp-ing, Engine and Foundry, and Parts and Equipment Manufacturing Divisions. The third group, under John Dykstra, the Aircraft Engine, Tractor, and Machined Products Group, was composed of six divisions —Aircraft Engine, Tractor, Highland Park, Canton, Automatic Trans-mission, Mound Road, and Industrial Engine.[24] This organization was to prove essentially sound. Great advances were also made in the quality of manufacturing, particularly through the development of automation. This, as already noted, was first fully employed in the new plants at Buffalo and Cleveland.

The Buffalo plant, the first to be completed, began production in the fall of 1950. The stamped parts, often large, passed for considerable distances from machine to machine, being loaded, unloaded, and transferred mechanically. Workers were chiefly inspectors. The ben-efits of extensive automation became clear when Buffalo production was compared with that of the Dearborn Stamping Plant, which had not been automated. Buffalo production was much higher. The Dear-born unit was shortly automated with the hope of achieving a comparable output, but Buffalo remained superior because it had been planned and constructed with automation in mind. The Cleveland Engine Plant, which began production in September 1951, demonstrated at once the applicability of the new technique to the making of engines. John Diebold called it "spectacular." Harder has described certain of its aspects:

> In our original plant layouts, roller conveyors were considered throughout. . . . Nearly all machine operators had to handle a part in some way. Our Automation Section studied the plant layout and their analyses indicated the need for automation equipment. The plant layout which developed was more compact. . . . The labor required for handling parts approached the vanishing point. The entire department became a synchronized system and functioned as one large transfer machine. . . . it is not necessary for any operator to push, pull, turn over, or position a part.

Said D. J. Davis to a Congressional Committee: "Where once we had 2, 4, or 6 separate manually operated machine tools, we now employ a single multi-purpose machine tool. Where in the past we used chain hoists and conveyors, requiring considerable manual handling of heavy, rough pieces, such parts are now moved automatically from machine to machine and are mechanically loaded, positioned, and unloaded from the machine." In the machining process, 41 in-line-transfer-type machines comprising two basic lines were linked in a continuous process 1200 feet long. Manual handling of the engine block was necessary only once, at the loading point. With the old method, 150 separate machines would have been required, each with a worker.[25]

Everywhere the extension of automation brought lower costs, higher quality, and greater safety, and its success gave the Ford Company an advantage over its competitors. But machine tool manufacturers were ready to sell anybody the essential machines, and other companies quickly began to automate. The effect was marked. "There is no question," said Harder in 1953, "that the future will see new plants with a greater percentage of automatic operations." He was proud to recall in 1959 that practically no opposition had appeared at any of the Ford plants to the spread of automation.[26]

Nor were labor's forebodings of disastrous technological unemployment realized. To be sure, job losses did occur. In 1950, before the new engine plants went into operation, a monthly average of 8253 men worked on the production of engines; in 1954, although the number of engines produced had risen by one per cent, the work force had shrunk to 6399. But the company found jobs elsewhere in its plants for the entire 1954 men displaced. Of course many of the original employes were now serving as supervisors on the automated lines. There were more supervisory jobs, though fewer production jobs, and the moderate rate at which automation was introduced, and the natural limitations upon its use (D. J. Davis pointed out in 1955 that an automated assembly was not practicable) made its extension relatively free of controversy. What its future growth would bring in the way of manufacturing and labor difficulties was a matter for speculation.[27]

### 7.

During the Korean War the Ferguson Suit had continued to disturb the company, for while its heads felt general confidence in their case, the mounting expense of preparation and the time wasted by important officials were exasperating. In the course of the action 555,574 documents were produced, requiring the Ford Motor Company to make an extended search through the files of innumerable offices. Four staff attorneys worked full time on the case, and outside counsel were employed. Between 1948 and 1951 thousands of pages of testimony were taken. They offer a valuable set of statements from Henry Ford II, Breech, J. R. Davis, Newsom and others, covering company history from the 1930s to the time of the suit, but the cost was egregiously high. The strain and expense promised to dwarf those of any previous entanglement of the company, including the Selden Patent Case (1903–1911), the Chicago *Tribune* Case (1915–1917), and the Dodge Suit (1916–1917). The Selden Case had lasted much longer, but had made much slighter demands upon company records and personnel.[28]

The eventual result was a settlement out of court. Some company officials regretted it, feeling that the case could have been fully won, the Ford name and rights vindicated, and the costs laid upon Ferguson, who had invoked the nightmare. Yet to assure such an outcome further outlays of time and money would have been essential, and the attention of high-ranking executives, needed for war production and company development, could ill be spared for an all but interminable procedure.

A consent judgment signed by Judge Gregory F. Noonan on April 9, 1952, upheld most of the Ford contentions. It dismissed all charges of conspiracy to injure or destroy the business of the Ferguson Company, and all allegations of unfair competition. It also completely exonerated the chief Ford and Dearborn Motors executives who had been defendants. But the settlement did give Ferguson $9,250,000 "in full satisfaction of all claims for patent royalties." Four patents were upheld: one on converging links, one on the inlet valve, one on the pump for the hydraulically operated draft control system and the power takeoff shaft, and a fourth on a coupling pin. Dearborn Motors, as chief beneficiary from the use of the patents, paid the award.

Actually, by 1952 the patent on converging links had expired, and Ford had ceased to use a coupling pin on its tractors. However, the company agreed to redesign portions of its machine to avoid infringement of the other patents. The judgment further directed that no costs "shall be allowed to any party." This meant that the Ford Motor Company and Dearborn Motors had to shoulder another large burden, as of course did Ferguson. However, it was possible to write off a portion of both the patent penalty and the legal expenses in taxes. Several minor suits against the company were dismissed with the signing of the consent decree.[29]

The Ferguson decision confirmed Ford's position as a tractor manufacturer, and later, with the acquisition of Dearborn Motors, the Company also took over the marketing of the machines. The suit had demonstrated the wisdom of establishing the Legal Department, and experience during the several years prior to 1952 showed that it was an essential agency for the routine conduct of business. As a large corporation, the Ford Motor Company inevitably found itself facing a succession of suits, some brought for personal injuries, some for defective car parts, some by or about dealers, some involving labor unions. In April 1949 the company was a defendant in 94 such cases in 20 states. In addition, the legal staff watched company relations with vendors, dealers, and foreign branches and companies, for a time handled tax problems, and dealt with leases, patents, and trademarks.[30]

As 1952 advanced, the possibility of relief from the pressures of war gradually brightened. The Truman administration had begun truce negotiations with the North Koreans and "Chinese volunteers" in July 1951, but no definite agreement had been reached by the presidential campaign of 1952. Eisenhower promised a settlement, and seven months after taking office saw an armistice agreement signed on July 27, 1953. The general atmosphere created by the new Republican administration was a cause for rejoicing in Dearborn. "A great many of us," said Breech early in March 1953, "have a greater pride in America than we have had for some time. We feel a renewed confidence in our form of government and our way of life." On March 5, the Office of Price Stabilization ended its curbs on automobile prices, and before July the National Production Authority had lifted all controls on raw materials and automobile production.[31]

### 8.

From the beginning of 1953 Ford could see that the path ahead would soon be cleared, and the drive for a better status begun in 1946 and largely suspended in 1950 could be resumed.

Despite the Ferguson Suit and the emergency of war, the company record for the several years had been encouraging. Its net earnings for 1951 and 1952 had shown a decided drop, attributable chiefly to materials and price controls, and to the quotas laid upon civilian production. After taxes, where 1950 had revealed profits of $238,500,000, 1951 produced only $126,100,000 and 1952 only $116,900,000.* These results were quite explainable and reflected no deterioration in organization, morale, or resources.[32] The main car divisions had made progress, though at a modest rate.

In the Lincoln-Mercury unit, Benson Ford had inherited a difficult situation. He had to sell in the medium-priced and high-priced field two models that had never become outright successes, although the Mercury had shown high promise. Benson was assisted by Stanley Ostrander, but the division lacked an official who could push a point of policy against men like J. R. Davis, Harder, Yntema, Breech, or Henry II. Nevertheless, the Lincoln-Mercury Division held possibilities through the improvement of existing models or the creation of a new one. At this time, the Mercury seemed to offer the chief promise. As Benson put it in 1950, "From the viewpoint of the total Ford Motor

---

* Profits before taxes were in millions, $538.8 (1950), $368.9 (1951), and $281.2 (1952).

Company, what should Ford owners graduate to? The next logical step would be a Mercury." Other possibilities lay in the Lincoln-Continental, a superior and expensive model which had been offered from 1939 to 1948, then discontinued.

The war years saw the division gain some ground, but not much. The Mercury, after an impressive showing in 1950 (318,217 units), sank to 233,339 in 1951 as limitations became effective, and to 185,883 in 1952. This was 4.5 per cent of the total market. Lincoln rose from .5 per cent to .7 per cent. Neither car promised spectacular progress.[33]

Ford Division matured plans for its 1952 car in May 1951, and rejected the idea, still persisting in some quarters, of a new light car. "To the average American," the Division said, "our present car and its size represents an outward symbol of prestige and well-being. It seems reasonable to ask—if we need a smaller car, do we need a smaller refrigerator or a smaller washing machine?" It won its point with the Product Planning Committee, although the war, a poor time for introducing new types of automobiles, was also a factor. The Committee deferred small car development for another year, though Breech indicated that the project might be pursued on a research basis. The Division again opposed the small car in 1952, asserting that the Willys, Henry J., and Nash, had made no showing to alter its previous opinion.

The 1952 Ford was presented in the late spring of 1951, despite the continuing war. It had been styled by George Walker and designed to minimize rattles and squeaks and prevent the sifting in of rain and dust that had marked the 1949–1951 models. Vision had been improved by a large, curved windshield. Customers had a choice in engines between the new 6-cylinder overhead valve model, and the V-8. The car was well received. Ford also introduced a four-door all-steel station wagon to meet the challenge of the Plymouth Suburban, a metal car that had taken leadership in the field, and this new Ford model regained first place with 30.9 per cent of the sales in its special field.

Ford cars even in a time of limited production were able to show gains with respect to their competitors. They captured 17.6 per cent of the passenger car market as against 17 per cent in 1950, while Chevrolet declined from 21.1 per cent to 20.5 per cent, and Plymouth from 10.7 per cent to 10.4 per cent. Ford was now unquestionably the second ranking firm in the industry.[34]

But the future rather than the immediate past was the important thing in the minds of Henry II, Breech, and their associates. Free of the Ferguson Suit, free after June 1953 of government limitations, the company was ready to resume its struggle for supremacy. It was recovering most of the plant facilities it had diverted to the war effort. Morale was high and the market favorable. The entire automotive world would soon be able to appraise the new organization that Henry II and Breech had built in the last six years.

# XV

# FORD BECOMES A CHALLENGE

WHEN on February 13, 1953, the government removed limitations on the production of cars and trucks, it restored competition with growth in industry. Wrote Theodore O. Yntema to the Ford management: "Industrial production is now limited only by material availability and sales demand." [1] But although freedom to manufacture was of the highest moment to company officials, an even more important element was involved. The form the Ford Motor Company would take and the power it might achieve were again wholly in the hands of its leaders. Reorganization with facilities for higher production had been promoted by Henry Ford II and Breech since 1946. Now the time had come to say what should be done with the plant and talent available. Specifically, in what ways should the organization expand? Should it remain essentially a producer selling one good car and several others not very successful, or should Ford activities become broader and better balanced?

## 2.

Interest in the future form of the company, however, seemed temporarily eclipsed by the celebration of its fiftieth year as a producer of motor cars. Planning had begun two years earlier under the expert direction of John R. Davis. Two and a half million calendars by Norman Rockwell, each portraying one of Henry Ford's accomplishments, were issued to commemorate the year. Along with this appeared advertisements carrying Rockwell's paintings, a large flat book illustrated in color, *Ford at Fifty,* which dealt chiefly with the company in 1953, a medallion of Henry Ford I, Edsel Ford, and Henry Ford II designed by the sculptor de Francisi, and a "50th Anniversary Press Packet," outlining the activities of the year. [2]

371

Early in 1951 the company had established the Ford Archives as a research center into which all the correspondence and diaries of Henry and Clara Ford and the complete records of the company were to go, with much additional material on automotive matters. Newsom's firm had been responsible for the idea, which was taken up by the Fiftieth Anniversary Plans Committee. From the International Monetary Fund at Washington, D.C., Henry E. Edmunds, who had once filled a post in the National Archives, was brought to serve as archivist. Later, as the department grew, it came under the general supervision of A. F. Mills of Henry Ford II's office. The archival material comprised books, letters, telegrams, memoranda, diaries, and photographs of Ford cars and events over a span of almost fifty years. Today the department conserves many millions of documents and pictures. One unusual branch of the establishment, embodying an idea taken from Columbia University, was the Oral History Section, where eventually were filed the tape-recorded reminiscences of more than 450 persons closely associated with the Ford story.*

The founding of the Archives was an event in business history. Never before had a great corporation made available to those engaged in research its full records dating from its foundation. Scholars and writers used the collection so promptly that even in its first five years the Archives made possible several published volumes, and was giving assistance to others in progress. At the same time, it began actively to serve numerous branches of the company, providing material for publicity, pictures, and verification of dates and events.

From the beginning, the Archives had been regarded as a repository of materials for a definitive history of the company. The close and dramatic relationship between the Ford story and important changes in modern society—industrial, technological, social—made such a project attractive to Columbia University, which placed the responsibility for seeing the work accomplished upon the authors of this book. The first volume, a fully documented and well-illustrated work of nearly 700 pages, carried the record down to the First World War, and two ensuing volumes were planned to continue the story.**

---

* Assembled under the direction of Owen Bombard, the oral history memoirs include the recollections of friends and relatives of the Fords, and of numerous persons employed by the company or in close contact with it. Of the employes, many were no longer with the company when the reminiscences were taken. All conceivable activities from engineering to sales were covered in the collection, which represents a record of fact and opinion that has unique value.

** The first volume, Ford: the Times, the Man, the Company, appeared in the spring of 1954, written by Allan Nevins in collaboration with Frank Ernest Hill. Dealing with the men, ma-

At first housed in the old Engineering Building at Dearborn, the Archives eventually found a home in Fair Lane, the former residence of Henry and Clara Ford which the company purchased in 1951. Standing on the banks of the wooded River Rouge, almost a mile from the entrance to the estate on Michigan Avenue, it preserved the baronial isolation Ford had created when it was built in 1915–1916. About it lay gardens carefully fostered by Clara Ford, among them the wide expanse of the beautiful rose garden she developed in the 1920s. The Archives were dedicated at Fair Lane on May 7, 1953, when Mrs. Edsel Ford unveiled a plaque as her three sons and her daughter Josephine stood by.[3]

From that moment the anniversary celebration rapidly gathered momentum. In mid-May 400 Ford managers came to Dearborn (officials of assembly plants, manufacturing units, and the like) who were guided through the company's new projects, shown "The American Road," a film telling the Ford story, and invited to the company's birthday party. At this gathering Dwight D. Eisenhower, President of the United States, dedicated the new Research and Engineering Center, paying "tribute to the accomplishments for which the Ford family has been responsible," and looking forward to another fifty years of achievements. An exciting feature of the Center was the new Styling Building with its twelve studios where full-size clay models of cars could be built.

Ed Sullivan's television show on June 14 saluted the company's birthday (it was incorporated on June 16, 1903), and on the 15th an hour-long television program went out over both CBS and NBC channels to between 55,000,000 and 60,000,000 listeners. The theme was America of the past fifty years; the original script had been planned by Frederick Lewis Allen, and Oscar Hammerstein III, Edward R. Murrow, Mary Martin, Ethel Merman, Lowell Thomas, and Marian Anderson appeared in the production, which won the critical approval of journals ranging from *Variety* to the *New York Times*. On June 16 the Rotunda, closed to the public during the war, was reopened, masquerading as a giant birthday cake illuminated for the occasion. In the next four months more than 600,000 visitors viewed its exhibit on research and development in industry.

---

chines, and economic forces that produced the automobile, it described Ford's contribution through the period in which the Model T and mass production were evolved. *Ford: Expansion and Challenge, 1915–1933*, by Allan Nevins and Frank Ernest Hill, continued the account, which the present volume completes.

One of those active in managing the commemoration had been the new director of Public Relations, Charles F. Moore, Jr., a former partner of Earl Newsom who joined the company in April 1952. Throughout 1953 he had worked closely with John R. Davis.[4]

### 3.

As the commemorative year advanced, it also witnessed the growth of its young president in the field of national and world affairs. Henry Ford II, who had already spoken in memorable fashion against governmental bureaucracy and in favor of a harmonious relationship between capital and labor, had won general respect and a position of leadership in the industry. In 1952 he and Breech had been active in promoting the nomination of Eisenhower, and later had worked diligently to elect him president. Early in 1953 Ford appeared in a new public role: that of an advocate of "free trade" in his industry. He proposed to abandon the high protective tariff— "In order for others to buy from us, they must be able to sell to us—" and suggested that a good beginning would be to expunge the 10 per cent tariff on foreign car imports.

His speech was quoted on the front pages of the *Wall Street Journal,* the *New York Times,* and other influential organs. He had not defined a new position, for the Detroit Board of Trade and the National Association of Manufacturers had advanced similar opinions, although less boldly. Furthermore, his own grandfather had consistently opposed tariffs. But Henry Ford II's remarks had been so clear, arresting, and forthright that they had caught the imagination of the journalists. The New York *Herald-Tribune* suggested that "the most notable aspect of Mr. Ford's argument was his readiness . . . . to eliminate tariffs on foreign cars." The New York *Daily News* was "inclined to go along with the general Ford thesis." Americans for Democratic Action congratulated him on proposing "a lasting contribution to the unity of the free world." Others concurred, some demurred, but he won wide attention.

He was soon to speak in larger terms. On the June 15th television program reviewing the last half century of American life he talked about his country. "We're the strongest nation in the world—but we haven't found the best way to use all our strength. We're the richest nation in the world—but we still haven't enough good homes, good

schools, and good hospitals. We have the greatest technical knowhow
—but we've been slow to teach other nations how to use it." He proposed that America act on the facts, and "accept the responsibility the
world expects of us." It was logical for President Eisenhower, late in
July, to ask him to take the post of alternate delegate to the United
Nations. Accepting it, Ford delivered his maiden speech in the Committee on Technical Assistance, approving aid to less advanced countries as "a sound investment in world stability for the future." His
sharp rebuttal at a Thanksgiving Day session to the remarks of a
Soviet delegate showed him an effective impromptu speaker.

Ford's experience with the United Nations convinced him of the
usefulness of that body. In 1945, he recalled, "I could have counted
myself among the skeptics." Now he foresaw a creative role for the
new organization.[5]

4.

The Ford Motor Company celebrated its fiftieth anniversary with
works as well as with words, for it promptly resumed construction on
a number of projects which the Korean war had suspended.

Three additional parts depots, the styling building, and an ore
carrier (the *William Clay Ford*) were completed. A $55,000,000 ex-
pansion of steel operations (begun in 1950), the rehabilitation of the
Rotunda, and additions to the Canton Forge Plant, the Buffalo Stamping Plant, and the Cincinnati Automatic Transmission Plant were
ordered. The Bomber Wing Plant at Kansas City was also converted
to passenger car production, and the Lincoln-Mercury Division's
Metuchen, New Jersey, factory was enlarged. At the same time, a
number of undertakings were begun which dwarfed those already in
process. For example, ground was broken for three new assembly
plants which would serve the expanding Ford Division, one at Louisville, Kentucky, another at San Jose, California, and a third at Mah-
wah, New Jersey.* The last would be the company's largest assembly
center, producing 800 cars and 280 trucks daily.

The same year saw ground broken for two additional manufacturing
plants, both in Cleveland. One, devoted to engines, would use the same
foundry as the Cleveland Engine Plant No. 1; the other was a metal

* These replaced existing but outmoded plants at Louisville, Richmond, California, and Edgewater, N.J.

stamping unit which would house 16 major press lines and employ 2900 people. With these three establishments Cleveland would become second only to Dearborn as a center of Ford production. In addition, four other Ohio projects were planned—a hardware plant at Sandusky, an engine plant at Lima, a new plant for automatic transmissions in Cincinnati, and a Ford Division Assembly Plant at Lorain.[6]

This was prodigal growth, but growth toward what? What would be the form of the Ford Motor Company when it finally emerged as a mature organization?

Henry Ford II and his associates were disappointed with what they had inherited from the old regime—one popular car, the Ford, then struggling to maintain a second place position; a promising but uncertain car in the lower middle range, the Mercury; and a prestige car in the upper price ranges, the Lincoln, that sold rather badly. They had hoped for improvement, and could see it coming in the Ford; however, in the middle-and upper-price fields the Mercury and the Lincoln were not doing well enough. Ford and his "team" had long calculated the risks and advantages of introducing one and perhaps two vehicles in the higher priced markets.

The conception of a broader company with more models had antedated Henry Ford II. Edsel was working toward it when he introduced the Lincoln Zephyr in 1936, and even before the Zephyr had begun to fade, he and John R. Davis had created the Mercury (1939), which despite many ups and downs was well established by the early 1950s. Now, in 1952–1953, Ford officials were thinking of a company with at least four basic cars. This would enable them to become more fully competitive with General Motors and its five models (Chevrolet, Pontiac, Oldsmobile, Buick, and Cadillac), and Chrysler with its four (Plymouth, Dodge, De Soto, Chrysler). They believed a car in the middle-and-upper-middle price field was particularly needed.

Henry Ford II first grappled seriously with the problem when on January 29, 1952, he appointed the "Davis Committee," comprising much of the company's senior talent: J. R. Davis (as chairman), Crusoe, Harder, Walker Williams, Yntema, and Youngren. It got to work at once, and on April 30, 1952, presented a plan to the executive committee. Although Henry II had suggested that a suitable program "may require the introduction of another car name, a new dealer organization, and an additional car division," the report recommended only one of these drastic changes, and that on a rather modest scale. It proposed that a new body be introduced with the 1956 models and used for the Lincoln Cosmopolitan and Capri to compete with the higher-priced Buick and the Oldsmobile, to be known as a Mercury; and that a lower-priced Mercury should be taken from the Ford shell to compete with the Pontiac.

The higher-priced Mercury would be a new car, but the committee explained that if it were launched with a separate name the outlay involved and the risks to be taken would be great, and that the wiser policy would be not to undertake them. It pointed out that General Motors had a record of three new-name car failures: the Marquette (1929, dropped 1930), the Viking (1929, dropped 1931), and the La Salle (1927, dropped 1940). Moreover, if a new name car were established a special dealer organization might be needed, and this would prove difficult and risky to establish. However, the committee called for the separation of the Lincoln and Mercury divisions. It also recommended that the Continental, discontinued in 1948, be revived.

In the ensuing discussion it was proposed that the Mercury made with the Lincoln shell be called the Mercury-Monterey, and that later, if successful, it might drop the first half of its name. Further study was recommended.[7] But it was not long until one feature of the program was accepted. The Executive Committee voted to reintroduce the Continental. First appearing in 1939, this car had never achieved much production (only 5322 units all told) but had won devoted admirers. "The finest car I ever owned!" wrote a North Carolinian, and his praise was echoed by many other owners. *Fortune* announced in 1950 that there was general agreement among dealers that "the Lincoln-Continental was one of the most striking United States automobile designs in the past twenty years." The Museum of Modern Art had given publicity to an exhibit featuring the vehicle. The used car value of the Continental showed half the depreciation of the average car, and compared favorably with that of the Cadillac. Its return to production seemed imperative.[8]

William Clay Ford stated that he would like to handle the Continental, and on July 1, 1952, the Executive Committee established a separate division of which he was head. The youngest of Edsel's sons thus found an opportunity for which his talents seemed to fit him, for he had inherited his father's love of styling. With a B.A. from Yale and three years of experience in the company, he was now assuming his first important responsibility. He assembled a staff, occupying the former Henry Ford Trade School, and on May 12, 1953, was elected a vice-president of the company. By June of that year he was able to show the Executive Committee a model of the new car. He recommended that the company build a plant for its manufacture, and saw the ground broken for the factory on Oakwood Boulevard in Ecorse township on May 20, 1954.[9]

However, the other recommendations of the Davis Committee, while at first favorably discussed, were suspended by the Executive Committee "indefinitely" in January 1953. Among the reasons was the high expense "coming as it does, concurrently with substantial expansion in our facilities programs." The company had however no intention of abandoning the idea of more products.

Company sales in the first "free" year were to be good. For the month of November the Ford car slightly outsold the Chevrolet, with 24.1 per cent of the market as against 23.7 per cent, and though final figures showed the Chevrolet leading for the year with 1,420,399 sales to Ford's 1,166,118, the possibility of a stronger challenge had been indicated. Although Lincoln took a bare .7 per cent of the market, Mercury bounded from its Korean War slump to obtain more than 5 per cent. Buick, Pontiac, Oldsmobile, and Dodge all outsold it, but not by wide margins.[10] It was an encouraging record, with Chrysler definitely in third place, and the executives studied the possibilities of progress on all price levels.

### 5.

By the end of 1953 the automobile industry had recovered from the suppressions of the Korean War period and was in full stride toward its former prosperity. Registrations in 1950 had mounted to 6,326,436, the high figure for 22 years; they were back now to 5,738,989, and leaders hoped that they would continue to rise. The automotive field reflected the general prosperity of the nation. Hostilities had ended, jobs were plentiful, and a Republican president gave most business executives a sense of security. All types of industry were turning to peace-time production, and the public was preparing to buy their products. As for cars, the sales figures showed that the national appetite was still unsatisfied.

That the movement away from the small cars, evident in the 1940s, should continue was taken for granted. The Ford Division, brandishing the results of expert studies,* told the Executive Committee that "as the general standard of living has increased, the consumer has tended to purchase a better car." It looked down its nose at the small car, that annoying incubus that every few years lifted a contentious head into the automotive scene. In 1952, as in earlier years, the Division had firmly opposed the intruder. "To the average American our present car and its size represent an outward symbol of prestige and well-being." It again pointed to small cars struggling in the wake of Ford and Chevrolet sales: the Henry J, the Hudson Jet, the Nash, and the Willys. All but one would soon sink beneath the churning waters marking the progress of their betters.[11]

In pushing toward a more elegant type of low-priced car, the Ford Division was only keeping abreast of its rivals. Chevrolet and Plymouth had been enlarging and improving their models. By 1953 all three had automatic transmissions, and the Fordomatic compared favorably with the others. At this point Chevrolet complicated the situation by attacking Ford's special field of strength. Ever since the V-8 appeared in 1932, Ford had always been able to boast of having the highest engine power of any low-priced car. Chevrolet in 1953 suddenly brought out an engine rating higher than Ford's, a Six, not an Eight, and also announced a V-8 for 1955. At once a race began. Chevrolet eventually offered customers a choice between 162 and 180 h.p., and Ford countered with 162 and 182. Plymouth followed its more successful rivals.

Again, all the cars offered their buyers "power options." Thus power steering, power window lifts, power seat adjustment, and power brakes were available to the customer. He could even have air conditioning if he wanted it. All these features had once belonged exclusively to high-priced cars, but as the Ford Division put it in 1954, "the differences between the highest priced cars and the lowest priced cars are far less today than they were twenty years ago." Along with these special features went greater length, breadth, and color variety, while

* The Ford Division had its own Consumer Research Department under R. J. Eggert.

any buyer could command special trim. In 1954 Ford introduced a new V-8 engine with overhead valves, and offered for the first time independent ball-joint suspension, which reduced steering effort, improved handling, and increased the ease of servicing.

In this year the Ford Division reported "a definite 'swing toward the Ford,'" and was in a neck and neck race with Chevrolet. From one prestige contest it emerged definitely a victor. Chevrolet in 1953 had introduced a sports car, the Corvette, and expected in the ensuing season to dispose of 10,000 units. Ford countered quickly with the Thunderbird, which Crusoe explained was not merely a sports car but "is more truly a personal or boulevard car for the customer who insists on comfort and yet would like to own a prestige vehicle that incorporates the flair and performance characteristics of a sports car." The Thunderbird proved a winner from the start, surpassing even Ford hopes, for in three years 53,166 cars were sold.[12]

All these improvements steadily edged the Ford toward the middle-class market, but apparently the company's leaders saw nothing doubtful in the trend. Certainly they did not seriously consider finding a new small car rather than placing a middle-priced car between the Mercury and the Lincoln. Perhaps in 1954 to do so would not have been a sound move. Buyers of the Ford approved of its being "upgraded," and plenty of customers could be found in the middle-and-upper-price fields which General Motors and Chrysler were holding altogether too successfully. In early 1954 the Lincoln-Mercury Division was still studying how to invade this area, and on May 18 laid some findings before the Executive Committee.

They tallied closely with those of the Davis Committee. The new car should use a Lincoln shell and the Mercury chassis, and should compete in the price class above the Mercury. The only difference, in fact, between this report and that of the Davis Committee was that the Lincoln-Mercury executives did *not* reject a new name for the car. They referred to it as "the Edsel," using the term for "identification purposes." From that time forward it was to be known as "the E car." At this meeting Robert S. McNamara, who had become Assistant General Manager of the Ford Division in 1953, spoke against "putting a lid" on specifications for the Ford car. He also asked: "What is the new car intended to offer the car-buying public?" This shrewd question was not intended to challenge the E car, for he believed in it; however, a full discussion of the point might have been useful.[13]

For a momentus decision had been taken: there was to be a new car with a new name. This might mean that the question of a new dealer organization would have to be faced, together with the expense of advertising the newcomer and the psychological difficulty of establishing it—a feat which both General Motors and Chrysler had failed to perform with the four cars they had introduced and abandoned since 1927. Some Ford officials later believed that the new car could have been launched successfully if the plan just outlined had been followed, but before it made its appearance that plan was to be drastically changed.

Meanwhile the year came to an end in an encouraging fashion, for the 1954 Ford seemed for a time to have bested the Chevrolet. When the dust cleared this was seen to be a delusion, but the two cars finished close, Ford selling 1,400,000 units, Chevrolet 1,417,453. A swing of 9000 cars to Ford would have given victory to the company.[14]

In November 1954 the 1955 line of Ford cars was introduced, ranging from the Mainline series (the basic car) to the Fairlane, a new glamorous creation that had, as Crusoe put it, "all the desirable features we know how to put into a car." In colorful shades, offering optional trim combinations, and providing multiple choices in power services and air conditioning, the Fairline made a bird-of-paradise contrast to the dingy low-priced cars of yesteryear. It was slightly larger than the 1954 model, and with the rest of the line had wrap-around windshields, a new and lower silhouette, a flatter hood, and a longer rear deck. Naturally the Chevrolet and Plymouth also offered their special features, and sought to capture the leadership.

The competition was thus severe, but the market was still the seller's. *Automobile Facts* summed up the trend and the situation as "nothing but the best for the new car buyers." It added: "Auto makers are still ready to provide stylish, dependable transportation in an economy package, but today's average buyer clearly wants and is willing to pay for that 'something extra' that will set his car apart." Crusoe in July confirmed this statement when he told a group of college teachers at the Ford Educational Forum that while the higher-priced Fords flourished, the Mainline, the basic Ford offering, was doing badly. "It is practically non-saleable. People do not want it." This implied a popular rejection of both the smaller car and the really low-priced car. "The kind of automobile that is sold epitomizes our standard of living. People want . . . better cars, better houses, better clothes." [15]

Early in 1955 the Ford administration underwent notable changes. On January 25 Ernest R. Breech was raised from Executive Vice President to a newly-created position as Chairman of the Board of Directors for the company. He continued as in the past to share with Henry Ford II the key management responsibilities. However, his change in status affected others in the organization. Lewis Crusoe was moved from his post as head of the Ford Division to become Executive Vice President, Car and Truck Division, in which capacity he controlled the assembly and distribution of all the company's products, and D. S. Harder at the same time was made Executive Vice President, Basic Manufacturing Divisions. Between them the two covered the entire range of Ford activity. At the same time McNamara, tacitly acknowledged the leader among the seven men of Thornton's former group remaining at Ford, was elected Vice President and General Manager of the Ford Division. D. J. Davis succeeded Harder as the head of Manufacturing. Crusoe also became chairman of the Product Planning Committe, presiding over his first meeting on February 1, 1955; and this body was soon joined by 38-year-old F. C. Reith, recently returned from France, where he had done brilliant work for the company.[16]

To get a full picture of the increasingly powerful Ford organization, we must take account of what was happening in the field of commercial vehicles and tractors.

For years there had been a competition between Ford and Chevrolet in the commercial field paralleling that between their passenger cars. the prize for ascendancy was of course smaller, but had been steadily increasing in value, for the use of trucks and delivery wagons had almost doubled since the 1920s. As previously noted Ford had once outsold its rival, but after 1937 Chevrolet had taken first place. When the Ford Division was formed, the company had 235 truck models, and Crusoe and his assistants, since trucks fell entirely under their control, had begun an uphill battle to regain supremacy.

The field was expanding, favored by the building of better highways, the growth of suburban areas not readily accessible to other forms of freight transportation, and the increasing mechanization of American farming areas. One weakness of Ford had been its failure to produce heavy trucks. In 1947 the F-7 and F-8 models had been introduced to enter this field, and the battle had continued, Ford gaining somewhat but still remaining well behind Chevrolet. (It had always outsold International, Dodge, and other rivals.)

In 1953, as the result of engineering and customer studies, a wholly new series of Ford commercial vehicles was introduced, with better lines, roomier interiors, better driver visibility, better springs and steering. This had its effect. In 1954 Ford sold 267,799 units as opposed to Chevrolet's 293,079, and it was to improve this position slightly, pressing for the leadership but remaining second.[17]

With tractors, as we have seen, from 1938 to 1947 Ford was the manufacturer only, while Ferguson headed the selling organization. However, after 1947 Dearborn Motors acted as the selling agency for Ford until 1953. In 1946 Ford had manufactured and Ferguson had sold 59,742 units, or 23.4 per cent of the American tractor output. After their separations, Ferguson had produced tractors for a while, but eventually ceased to be an important factor in American production.* Meanwhile, the Ford-Dearborn Motors alliance prospered, so that in 1949 the combination made and sold 104,267 units. Sales then fell off slightly, and after a rally in 1951, continued to drop until 1955. Sales patterns were of course affected by the economic situation of the farmer, which was favorable up to 1950, and then deteriorated.

Ford in 1950 stood second in the United States among manufacturers of the wheel-type tractor. The leader was International with 137,500 units, and Ford followed with 97,956. By 1946, when hydraulic lift and linkage patents had expired, and these devices were available to anyone, competition in the tractor field became more severe. Ford determined to make notable improvements in its tractor, and a new line was approved by the Product Planning Committee on February 3, 1949. Among other models it offered one that could handle combines, corn pickers, and feed grinders, and manage other heavy farm jobs. In 1954 Ford was still holding second place, with 21 per cent of

---

* Ferguson had difficulty in getting a factory financed, but finally arranged to manufacture in the United States, and drove the first tractor off the assembly line in October 1948. In 1953 his world-wide enterprises were merged with the Massey-Harris Co. of Toronto, which still produces tractors near Detroit. (N.Y. Times, Oct. 25, 1960; Standard & Poor's, XXII, July 18, 1961, 9121).

all wheel-type tractors. The Company was soon to offer the Fordson Major, a large machine manufactured by the Ford Motor Company, Ltd. of England.[18]

## 7.

Crusoe had added Reith to his staff soon after he had taken over the post of director of the Car and Truck Divisions. "I feel fortunate in securing his assistance in helping to formulate some of our important forward planning," the higher official remarked. Reith at once began to study the Mercury and the E Car. On February 7, 1955, he showed the Product Planning Committee the clay model of the 1957 Mercury already approved, but he also exhibited a second model which embodied certain changes in design. The Committee discarded the first and approved this entirely new model, "Reith's Mercury." It accepted Crusoe's recommendation that the design be more fully developed for a final showing. Later the committee prophesied that the Mercury in its final version "would take a major step forward toward styling leadership."

By this time the 1955 season was well under way, and a spirit of elation infused the automotive centers of the country. "The appetite of the American people for new cars is turning out to be bigger than even the most optimistic leaders of the automobile industry had expected," declared the *U.S. News and World Report*. "At the moment, Detroit is in the middle of a boom, the public has bought two million cars in the off peak season from January to April, and now is established by *Automotive News* to be buying at a 600,000 a month clip. That's a rate of more than 7,000,000 a year." It was an era that encouraged confidence. The present was a road of intoxicating promise, leading into a future that seemed safe and sure. If anything, Ford officials were more sanguine than their rivals, for during its nine years of activity the new regime had marched from triumph to triumph.[19]

In this atmosphere of glowing confidence Reith studied the problem of the E Car, and on April 15, 1955, presented to the Board of Directors an overall plan for the company's future product offerings. He first reminded his listeners of certain basic facts which they already knew. He showed, for example, that in the field of popular low-priced cars the Ford made 43.1 per cent of all sales, but in the middle and upper-priced range, its Mercury and Lincoln obtained a 13.6 per cent. In the portion of this upper field not covered by Lincoln (at the top) or Mercury (at the bottom), the $2400 to $3100 price range, General Motors was selling three cars, and Chrysler two. Ford of course had none. Partly because of this gap the company had far fewer dealers than its rivals, and was especially weak in the middle-priced field. The time, Reith pointed out, was as auspicious as could be imagined. Population was growing, consumer income was rising, and more families than ever before owned cars.

The remedy naturally lay in a better-balanced production. "Too large a percentage of our business [is] in *one* car and *one* price bracket." Ford must introduce cars in the medium-priced area to fill its vacuum there. This would require a stronger dealer organization. He went back to the shells from which Ford cars came, of which there were only two: a Ford shell and a Lincoln shell, the Mercury being taken from the former. As a matter of fact, the Ford shell was used for 97.7 per cent of the company's output, and the Lincoln shell for only 2.3 per cent.

Reith proposed to use three shells—a Ford, a Mercury, and a Lincoln. The Ford shell, however, would appear in two slightly different forms. One would be for the standard Ford cars, the other for the Fairlane and a low-priced E Car. (The 1957 Fairlane and the shell from which it would be taken had been approved before Reith began to study the situation.) We may think of the shells he had in mind as #1 and #1A, just referred to; the #2, which would be used for the Mercury and also for an E Car higher in price than the Mercury; and #3, the shell for a new super-Mercury and for the Lincoln. As arranged below, the lowest-priced car would start the list and reading downward one would go from lower to higher prices.

#1    Ford Mainline and other standard Ford cars
#1A   Ford Fairlane
         #1A lower-priced E Car
#2    Mercury
         #2 high-priced E Car
#3    New super-Mercury
         #3 Lincoln

As expounded by Reith, this range of cars seemed logical and comprehensive. The Ford (including the Fairlane) would compete with Chevrolet and Plymouth. The lower-priced E Car, on a slightly higher level, would challenge the Pontiac and the Dodge. The regular Mercury would vie with the lowest-priced Buick, the high-priced E Car with the De Soto, Oldsmobile and middle-priced Buick, and the super-Mercury with the high-priced Buick and the Chrysler. The Lincoln would compete in the top price ranges against the Cadillac. Reith also proposed three dealer networks, one handling Ford cars, a second the E Car and the Lincoln, and the third the Mercurys.

His entire report was given with crispness and assurance, and he concluded by saying that "the new forward product program is the result of careful and exhaustive study of all the factors which have a bearing on our passenger car lines and the markets in which they must be sold." Its aim was "to broaden and diversify the Company's passenger car lines, with particular emphasis on the medium and higher-priced field, and in doing so to maintain the Company's current earnings as well as to improve its forward earning capacity. . . . As a result, the Company's almost total dependence on the Ford car will be importantly modified by additional strong car lines." [20]

The directors listened closely. Crusoe favored the plan of his protégé, and Reith's reputation and manner put it in the best possible light. There were doubts, particularly about moving the Mercury up in price and about pricing the E Car both below and above it, and such reservations might well have been probed in full discussion. But the plan seemed so convincing that no one was prepared to offer what might appear petty objections. Moreover, the time seemed auspicious, for customer demand appeared insatiable. *Automobile Facts* professed that "the production and use of motor vehicles is headed for new heights," and quoted an industry spokesman: "The nation is growing. We're growing with it." At the end of the year, Henry Ford II and Breech could write that the market "exceeded the most optimistic estimates." The new car seemed essential to a mature Ford Company.[21]

The Board of Directors, on April 15, 1955, after hearing Reith's presentation and after electing a number of new vice presidents, approved of plans that would put Reith's ideas to work.

The Lincoln-Mercury Division became two divisions. Ben Mills became Vice-President of the company and was named General Manager of a new Lincoln unit, while Reith was raised to the same rank and put in charge of the production and sale of Mercurys. A Special Products Division under R. E. Krafve, formerly Assistant General Manager of

Lincoln-Mercury, took charge of the E Car. William Clay Ford continued as Vice President and General Manager of the Continental Division, and also became group director for that unit and the Lincoln. Benson Ford, formerly Vice President and General Manager of Lincoln-Mercury, now became Group Director of the Mercury and Special former three: that is, Ford, Special Products, Mercury, Lincoln, and Continental, took over the work of Ford, Lincoln-Mercury, and Special Products (Continental). Plans went forward for staffing the new divisions and providing the new dealer organizations that would be required.

While results of the year's effort in planning would be tested by the future, the result in sales could be checked immediately. Ford enjoyed its biggest postwar production with 1,573,276 units disposed of, and while this was again short of Chevrolet's 1,640,000, it was again close. In addition, Mercury had climbed by more than 100,000 from its 1954 performance, and took 5.19 per cent of the market. An aura of optimism glows in the *Annual Report for 1955:* "The year 1955 was the most successful in this Company's history. As a result of unprecedented public demand for passenger cars and trucks, the Company's sales, production and profits reached all-time highs."

The progress of the company could be put in other terms. From a net worth of $714,000,000 on December 31, 1946, it had risen to one of $1,848,000,000, and its assets were now $2,585,000,000 as compared with with $868,000,000 nine years earlier. As against a payroll of $328,000,000 in 1946, the company now spent more than a billion dollars to meet its obligations to its employees. Thus financially it represented a citadel of strength from which a strong, bold, and well-calculated venture could be essayed.[22]

The company had also developed methods of financial control that promised well for the future. Early postwar emphasis had been on cost-control—that is, the reduction through more efficient designing, management, operation and so forth of the cost of a unit, which would thereby represent a greater profit for the company. This type of financial control had come from General Motors, where Donaldson Brown understood it well and saw that it was everywhere at work. At Ford two new types of financial control were developed—asset and revenue. The first was simply the most careful and creative use of the company's assets, so that the greatest possible return could be expected from them.

Careful studies were made with this end in view, carrying the practice far beyond the use of mere good judgment. "Revenue control" was a conception introduced at the Ford Motor Company by Robert S. McNamara. It was based on the assumption that the company could make money by studying closely and controlling carefully what it sold, and that perhaps more money could be made by this control of revenue than even by the control of costs.

In principle the practice was old; the novelty lay in the thoroughness with which it was applied. The sale of accessories well illustrates the character of the activity. For example, the company discovered that no particular effort had been made to sell radios as equipment for new cars. But experiment proved that far more buyers wished to have radios than was anticipated, and that others could be easily convinced that this particular accessory was desirable. As it happened the profit on radios was a good one; with greater quantities used it would become greater. But radios represented only one accessory; there were many others. McNamara advocated "a favorable mix of products and accessories, a care in supplying buyers with exactly what they wanted," and prices that would at once attract buyers and satisfy the company. Full profits represented cost control, plus revenue control, plus asset control. The company had earlier lost revenue on radios because "we didn't realize the depth of the market."

By 1956 the Ford Motor Company was becoming a mature organization. The benefits of decentralization were being realized, along with the increase in manufacturing capacity and greater experience in planning. The company was sound financially, and ready to face the uncertainties that always characterize the automotive industry. In the next year it would alter its character profoundly, and find a new relationship to the American people.

# XVI

# FOREIGN SCENE: THE POSTWAR WORLD

By 1948, as progress at home became more assured, the time had come for a fresh start abroad, with new men, new ideas, and firmer principles. The world was settling into a grim division between Communist East and Free West. It was now certain that the United States would join Western Europe in a common defense effort, protecting also the Mediterranean basin, Turkey, and most of the Near East. Moreover, it would do its utmost—with private enterprise to assist the government—to restore these areas to economic health and vigor.

Secretary Marshall had proposed his broad plan of mutual help the previous year, and in April 1948 Congress voted its first massive appropriation for the work. The Economic Cooperation Administration under Paul Hoffman promptly appeared on the European scene with heartening results. Later in the year Russia manifested her hostility in the blockade of Berlin, and the Allies instituted an effective airlift to thwart it. Before the year ended Britain, France, Belgium, the Netherlands, and Luxembourg signed a defensive alliance which laid the foundation for NATO, duly created with twelve member-nations before 1949 was far advanced.

While Congress debated ECA and Harry S. Truman prepared for his battle to keep the Presidency, Henry Ford II and his adviser Graeme K. Howard left for Europe to spend February and March in assessing the wartime damage, the remaining assets, and the prospects for new growth. They had received a preliminary briefing from Lord Perry and Sir Rowland Smith, who had come over in the autumn. The name Ford had always meant world-wide manufacture, assembly, and distribution of cars, but global competition in the postwar period promised to be formidable. As everybody knew, all Europe was hungry for cars, and the production in efficient plants would be limited only by the still-acute shortages of materials, manpower, and credit. Just before war became imminent (1938), the United Kingdom had possessed 2,593,809 automotive vehicles, France 2,250,000, Germany 1,520,000, and Italy 372,767—totals small beside the nearly 30,000,000 vehicles in the United States, but proof of an expanding market. Great Britain then had the largest manufacturing facilities, with Germany in second place and France in third. All manufacturers were eager to start anew.[1]

Although the conflict had practically stopped the making of passenger cars everywhere, war orders had kept plants busy producing carriers of goods and weapons, tanks, and (in Britain particularly) tractors. Throughout Europe government controls of varying strictness still inhibited the work of readjustment to meet peace-time orders. In Ford's three manufacturing centers, Dagenham, Poissy, and occupied Cologne, and at various assembly plants, Henry II and Howard inspected facilities and conferred with managers; while in the capitals they learned the views of political, industrial, and financial leaders.

They saw a continent feebly struggling to its feet, with the prospect sombre in the east and brighter to the west. The sufferings and despondency of the German people, laboring under both material and moral defeat, were pitiable. The land seemed in a state, the two men reported to Dearborn, of "utter hopelessness and despair." Still, the Germans were tidying up their ruins and making a real if slow start; very slow in the motor industry. France was racked by the mutual hatreds of Vichyite collaborationists and the resistance forces, and retarded by governmental instability. In both countries the Ford interests lacked assured leadership. In Germany Dr. Heinrich Albert, now in his mid-seventies, had suffered terribly from the jail sentence the Nazis had given him; he had lost all his property; his son had been killed by the Russians on the last day of the war. The kindly, gentle old man, quite shattered, left the Ford operation after the war. The Dane Vitger, who was in charge of the Cologne plant, had also suffered much. During the war Schmidt had pushed him into a secondary place; then after it the British occupying forces gave him orders. Though the French manager Dollfus was still capable, and his experience as a banker continued useful, his health was increasingly precarious, and he would soon be retired.

Both the Cologne and Poissy factories had suffered less damage, as we have noted, than Dearborn had anticipated, and could be set running efficiently. But they met severe difficulties in getting steel and other materials, in obtaining employes, and in satisfying rigid state controls.

It was in Britain that Henry II and Howard found the situation brightest. The government was anxious to increase the export of British cars of all makes to earn dollars and other foreign currency, and was ready to provide materials for that purpose. The great Dagenham factory was the best in Europe; it had its own blast furnaces to make steel, it enjoyed a connection with the Kelsey-Hayes and Briggs body works on the Dagenham premises which gave it wheels and bodies, and it could readily call upon American technical experience. Henry Ford II during his visit drove the 250,000th car built by Ford Ltd. since the war, a Prefect, off the assembly line. Among the so-called Big Six in Britain (the others were Austin, Morris, Vauxhall, Hillman, and Standard) the company held first place.* Young Henry tactfully gave a warm endorsement to the British export drive, promising that Dearborn would take special pains to sell the English models in America, and approving the plans of the British directors for adding new models to the familiar Consul, Anglia, and Prefect lines.[2]

### 2.

Henry II and Graeme Howard intended to base fundamental policy changes upon their tour, and particularly to tighten both ownership and administration. One immediate decision was that Dearborn should acquire a direct majority control of stock in all the continental companies, thus displacing Dagenham, which through its holding company had maintained control in all countries but France and Germany. In short, with Lord Perry's retirement the Perry plan for English suzerainty would come to an end. Henry II had little trouble in gaining the assent of the English directors. The new intention was to give the American parent firm ownership of controlling stock interests in Ford companies from Copenhagen to Barcelona, facilitating its efforts to coordinate management, sales policy, and capital expansion. It would also bring the continental dividends directly to Dearborn, avoiding double taxation. Ford of England agreed to divest itself of the "associated companies" and to sell the stock in the treasury of its holding

* No registration figures are published in England; this statement is based on the London *Times* supplement on the Motor Industry, October 1949.

company—the Guernsey concern—to the American corporation. At the same time a decision was made to revise the 1928 agreements governing the relationships between the various European Ford companies and the Dearborn Ford company.[3]

While Perry's plan of 1928 had served Ford interests fairly well from its inception to the outbreak of war in 1939, its usefulness had ended. The war had intensified the sense of national identity in each foreign company, loosening the British hold upon the continent, and Nazi arrogance had made the idea of external controls hateful. Now Dearborn alone occupied a position in which it could offer guidance—and help—in welcome forms. The Dagenham executives acquiesced the more readily because they saw that they would have their hands full at home, for a mighty expansion lay just ahead.

The new British leadership exhibited qualities which pleased Henry II and Howard. The two Americans reported that Lord Airedale had "the attributes and character of those men who make English history"; that Sir Rowland Smith had exhibited ability of the highest order in wartime; and that Sir Stanford Cooper was especially well equipped to deal with financial, commercial, and legal problems. But to "build the future of Dagenham," the Americans looked particularly to Sir Patrick Hennessy, a self-made man whose energy and resourcefulness matched even Lord Perry's.

The Dearborn executives decided to leave the French and German enterprises almost untouched for the time being. Dollfus's many problems were dismaying, and he faced the fiercest competition, especially from the Renault cars. The Americans thought he might gain firmer ground by merging Ford SAF with an established French firm, such as Peugeot, but this was a mere hope, not a plan. In Cologne, they decided to give Vitger an opportunity to show what he could accomplish. Henry Ford II and Howard explored the idea of acquiring a 51 per cent interest in the Volkswagen enterprise and of hiring its manager, Heinz Nordhoff, but again this was a hope, a dream, and not a plan.[4]

Ford and Howard reviewed the situation in other parts of Europe, visiting the plants in Holland, Belgium, and Scandinavia. They decided that Spain was hopeless as a site of a foreign-owned automobile company. Franco insisted that cars and trucks be manufactured, not merely assembled, in his country, and this was impracticable. Italy, where the government gave Fiat a thousand advantages, was no more tempting than in Mussolini's day. Sales subsidiaries would suffice there and in Portugal. Holland, Belgium, Denmark, Sweden, and Finland were for the nonce adequately served by assembly plants,* which drew their parts in the main from Britain rather than from the United States, for by placing orders in Europe they reduced transportation costs, eased the dollar pinch, and provided their market with the small cars that were demanded.

The question of the general administration of Ford activities abroad remained. Before leaving on his trip Henry II had become dissatisfied with R. I. Roberge as head of the new International Division at Dearborn, and what he saw abroad increased his irritation. He and Howard reported to their associates that the overseas activities of the five Ford manufacturing centers—in Dearborn, Windsor, Dagenham, Poissy, and Cologne—were totally uncoordinated; each center went its own way, the International Division being "incompetent to give over-all direction." Actually the fault did not rest wholly with Roberge, but was partly traceable to methods and ideas inherited from the oldtime Dearborn system, which had required him to deal with a network of detail while Sorensen and the two Fords had made the significant policy decisions.[5] Coordination was impossible during the war and difficult in the confused postwar scene. When Henry II created the International Division the opportunity came to open a new chapter, but Roberge had failed to seize it.

As Ford and Howard ended their report with an admonition to the company to face its foreign problems realistically, and "act with vision, faith, and courage," everyone understood that Howard would take charge. He became vice-president and director of the International Division April 15, 1948, and Roberge soon resigned.

Howard had a long training for his responsible place. A graduate of Stanford who had attended the Harvard School of Business Administration, he had spent more than a quarter century—he was now in his early fifties—in the overseas activities of General Motors. He had held different managerial posts in India, Denmark, Singapore, and London, finally becoming vice-president in charge of all General Motors' European affairs. Shortly before Pearl Harbor he had written a journalistic volume on America and the world situation.[6] Henry II thought himself

* A new assembly plant was being planned for Sweden, while a new truck assembly had been constructed in Finland in 1946.

fortunate in snatching him for the new group of Ford executives. Lincolnesque in stature, flamboyant in manner, and aggressively self-assertive in presenting his ideas and opinions, he made a dynamic addition to the Dearborn family—perhaps a bit too dynamic. He had brains, energy, and fearlessness, with plenty of brashness thrown in. His wealth of information on the motor industry abroad made him probably the best guide the company could then have found.

The first fruits of his administration of the International Division soon appeared. Toward the end of June 1948, he held a meeting of the overseas managers in Dearborn. More than thirty men streamed in from all parts of the world to exchange experiences and lay plans, for Ford had companies, branches, or dealer organizations in seventy-eight countries. The multilingual * executives who sat down together represented one of the greatest industrial empires placed on a global basis since Standard Oil. The sales abroad this year came to roughly $655,-000,000, a figure which took on meaning when compared with the $625,000,000 of total American sales of the Woolworth stores, or the similar value of the combined domestic and foreign sales of Firestone Tire and Rubber Company. The Canadian and British companies in particular were impressive by any standard of measurement, and Dagenham soon took first place among British corporations earning foreign exchange. The managers had much to discuss in such matters as tariffs, quotas of materials, and currency regulations. Some 350 kinds of foreign exchange transactions figured in the 1948 business.[7]

Soon after this convention Howard paid a quick visit to the Latin-American properties, which were operated by wholly-owned subsidiaries, or by branches of such subsidiaries or of Dearborn. The most important were in Mexico City, Sao Paulo, and Buenos Aires, with smaller establishments in Havana, Cristobal (Panama), Santiago (Chile), and Montevideo (Uruguay). Howard's tour brought out some interesting facts. The assembly plant in Mexico, the first ever opened in the republic, was able to put together about 12,000 Ford cars and trucks annually, while the older assembly in Brazil had a capacity of perhaps 18,000 vehicles. Sao Paulo not only assembled cars, but made its own wooden parts for trucks and station wagons. The well-equipped Buenos Aires plant took equal rank, but the branch in Montevideo was primarily a sales operation.

* The proceedings were in English, which all present understood.

Howard meanwhile was carrying through the plan for the consolidation of Dearborn's control over the continental European companies. Negotiations for the purchase of the stock held by Ford Ltd. of England were concluded in August 1949, and the transaction was consummated late the following January. For £4,256,860 Dearborn obtained all or a majority of the shares of the Danish, Dutch, Belgian, Italian, Spanish, and Egyptian companies, and substantial stock interests in the German and French organizations. The subsidiaries in Portugal, Sweden, and Finland followed their parent concerns into the Dearborn fold.

At the time of purchase by Dearborn of these stock interests, the American company also entered into new agreements with the various European Ford companies and with Ford of Canada which provided for reciprocal patent rights and technical exchanges of information, the supply of products by Dearborn, and an undertaking by Dearborn to furnish administrative and technical advice and services on request.

To cap his work, Howard in 1949 established new offices on Park Avenue, New York, with a staff which swiftly rose to 215. At the same time he established an Overseas Distributors Branch at Harborside in Jersey City to handle shipments of built-up Ford units to markets not served by the foreign assembly plants. These steps seemed logical in view of his ambitious plans for expansion overseas—plans encouraged by the avid postwar demand for cars all over the globe.

Here, however, Graeme Howard's career with Ford abruptly stopped. This dashing individualist left the company in 1950, partly because of the impetuosity and variety of his plans and his incessant fountain of ideas and projects, some brilliant, some less than brilliant, and partly because his personal relationship with Henry II and Ernest Breech became uncomfortable. Company heads, while keeping the Park Avenue offices for the Ford International Division, cut the staff substantially. But the Distributors Branch was retained. Howard had endeavored to move too rapidly on a variety of fronts, but in departing, he left a substantial legacy. He had created order where confusion had reigned, had effectively centralized the foreign business under the American aegis, and had given some high Ford executives a new appreciation of the importance of overseas work.[8]

His place was taken at first by an Ohioan who had also obtained foreign experience with General Motors, A. J. Wieland. Later, after his death in 1957, Tom Lilley and then John Bugas took charge of Ford overseas activities. Under these men the expansion which Howard had anticipated went briskly forward.

The Amsterdam and Antwerp assembly operations began erecting new buildings in 1950, while in Cairo the Egyptian company built the largest and most modern assembly plant in the Middle East. Even the uncertain Poissy factory made additions. Ford-Werke in Cologne, using land acquired two years earlier, commenced a factory for the new Taunus, which was designed partly in Dearborn, partly in Germany. The first new postwar Taunus cars came from the assembly lines in 1952, and met such a demand in their medium-price range that in the summer of 1953 the plant completed its 50,000th car. Ford Ltd. in England made capital expenditures 1950–1953 on buildings and machinery exceeding £15 millions. At the London motor show in the autumn of 1950 Dagenham had exhibited the Consul and Zephyr for the first time, and before long added new models of the Anglia and Prefect, with a Zephyr-Zodiac. The Ford Popular, tiny, cheap and reliable, sold steadily. This was a boom period in automotive manufacture the world over, but also a period of stiffening competition, marked by numerous horizontal mergers and the failure of concerns inefficient in production or design.[9]

3.

Outside North America, Britain led in the boom during the ten years 1946 through 1955. British manufacture of vehicles in the first year of this decade was something over half the 1937 figure; * in 1950 it was almost twice the latter; and in 1955 it reached the record total of 1,400,000 units, or almost three times that of eighteen years earlier. The high consumer and business demand for vehicles was the chief propulsive force. Not until the end of 1955 did a normal balance between demand and supply return. The government lent encouragement by helping in the supply of materials, by tax reductions—the sales tax was always cruelly high in Britain—and by pushing the export drive. British ingenuity in design was also useful. The Austin, Morris, Hillman, and Standard as well as the Ford and Vauxhall became known all over the world; the Rolls-Royce kept its unique place even after its makers

* For cars, trucks, and tractors, 511,456 (1937); 393,605 (1946).

turned mainly to airplane engines; and "specialist" cars like the Jaguar, MG, Austin-Healey, and Triumph found many buyers.[10]

Ford Ltd. held either first or second place before the Big Six were converted into the Big Five in 1952 by the merger of Austin and Morris to form the British Motor Corporation,* and later held second. In 1954, for example, British Motors took 38 per cent of the market with some 290,000 units; Ford took 27 per cent with 204,000 units; and the other three fell far behind, Vauxhall taking only 9 per cent with 72,600 units. In the record written by Ford Ltd., what counted most was the distinguished quality of the leadership. This was supported by the modernity and completeness of the manufacturing facilities, which were steadily enlarged, and the soundness of the engineering and design; still, nothing was so important as the generalship of Sir Patrick Hennessy, Sir Rowland Smith, and Sir Stanford Cooper.

Particularly striking were the foresight and courage of Hennessy. He had pushed his way up the ladder rung by rung. A poor lad in County Cork, he had run away from home to join the British army, in which he became one of the youngest officers. Then he had gone to work in the Ford factory in Cork, had advanced steadily by energy and address, had attracted Sorensen's notice in the early 1930's, and had become manager of purchasing for Dagenham. In that position he was one of the principal agents in getting the cost of the basic car of 1935 down to £100. Visiting America, he became acquainted with Henry and Edsel Ford, who liked him. When the Second World War began he joined Lord Beaverbrook in the Ministry of Aircraft Production, on which the very life of Britain depended, and proved a forceful aide to the driving Canadian, whom he admired. Meanwhile, by wide reading, travel, and friendships, he made himself a cultivated, urbane gentleman.

The Dagenham heads had to meet some grueling perplexities. Attlee's Labour Government temporarily maintained as strict a rationing of raw materials for industry as of food for the people. Steel scarcity in particular compelled car manufacturers to operate below capacity; some increase of supply took place by 1950, but soon rearmament and growing international tensions forced a new cutback. The Government

* The Morris Motors Works at Cowley were built by Sir William Morris, later Lord Nuffield. Statistics are not available for the 1946–1952 period, either for percentages of production by companies, or for numbers of units manufactured.

also exerted pressure to keep the export of cars somewhere near half the total output, a level reached in 1954. Allocation of materials depended partly on the prewar rank of a company, and partly on its efficiency as an exporter; Ford in 1937 had ranked behind Nuffield, the biggest car manufacturer, and Austin. But Hennessy knew that controls would come off, and worked for that day. He cultivated good relations with the British Treasury, won its confidence, and at critical moments had its full support. "I made a point," he states, "of trying to do more for the government than others in the industry." [11]

One of his accomplishments was the introduction in 1950 of the Consul and Zephyr, brand new types well suited to the export trade. A remarkable story of successful design and engineering lay behind both models. Meanwhile, the unique position of the Ford Popular, of prewar design, selling at a price nearly one fifth less than any competitor, was never challenged. The Anglia that appeared in 1953 found its own special niche. It sold at first for £360, the same price as the Austin 30, and less than the Standard (£379) or the Morris (£401). In the competition for the mass market in the decade 1946–1955, Ford Ltd. easily made the greatest advance. Two university economists have tried to analyze the reasons:

The Ford gains cannot be ascribed to a multiplicity of models or to frequent model change. The new post-war range was confined to two basic models, and these continued unaltered until 1956, when the larger model was changed. Nor can it be held that it was the result of aggressive price competition, for, as far as the new models were concerned, the Ford Company accepted the 'going price' and abandoned its pre-war policy of having the cheapest car in each major price class. The explanation may lie on the side of production rather than sales. . . . The production gains could not have been sustained had not Ford cars met with a large measure of public approval. Quality and price always affect the competitive position of a company, and it can be argued that although Ford prices were not the lowest, the value for money offered by Ford was as great as that offered by any other company, and greater than that offered by many.[12]

Another of Hennessy's accomplishments was his introduction of the diesel tractor. In any country where fuel costs are high the diesel engine, which burns cheap heavy oil, offers special advantages; and British taxation made ordinary gasoline very high. Against stubborn opposition, Hennessy insisted on designing a 4-cylinder diesel motor for the tractor, and manufacturing it; he took a tremendous risk, but its success was dazzling. From the original engine, introduced in 1951, he went on to a 6-cylinder diesel. Ford Ltd. and Standard took the lead in British tractor production, sharing four-fifths of the whole output in 1954—an output that came to 133,000 machines. By 1956 Ford of England was producing more tractors than Ford of Detroit (40,991 compared with 39,056). Ford Ltd.'s factory sales of tractors reached an all-time high of 71,455 units in 1960.

In vertical integration Hennessy and his associates showed a timely enterprise. In 1947 as we have seen they bought the Kelsey-Hayes plant at Dagenham. With even more boldness Hennessy in 1953 merged Briggs Motor Bodies, another tenant at Dagenham, into Ford Ltd. He took his courage in his hands; got an option by telephone on American-held shares in the British Briggs company, and also the shares of the Briggs family; and telephoned the news to Henry Ford II on a Saturday —"I told him the terms and he was delighted."

The Briggs purchase was made in the nick of time, for Chrysler soon bought the Briggs properties in the United States, as Hennessy had foreseen—it was a logical step; and if this had happened before Dagenham acquired Briggs of England, Ford Ltd. would have suffered a grave setback. The Briggs holdings included plants at Southampton, Doncaster, Croyden, and Romford as well as Dagenham, bringing the company a combination of "aids and troubles," as Hennessy put it. Moreover, the British Motor Corporation, Ford's greatest rival, shortly amalgamated with Fisher & Ludlow, Ltd., one of the only two remaining suppliers of mass-produced bodies. In April 1958 Briggs celebrated the production of its three millionth body for Ford Ltd., an Anglia painted a "Rochester red." [13]

The growth of Ford Ltd. was given impetus in 1954 by the adoption of a program of modernization and expansion which was estimated in advance to cost £65,000,000, or about $180,000,000. This work was to be financed from its own resources, and was to include a new assembly plant, a new foundry, and large new stamping and machining facilities. In reality, by the time the assembly building was completed in 1959, the costs had risen to $216,000,000, and by 1959 the total of postwar expenditures for growth came to $315,000,000. As new plants were opened, with fresh bodies of workers, Ford Ltd. needed more super-visory personnel. "It was quite obvious that we had to train manage-ment," Hennessy said later. He found it difficult to draw in capable men from the outside. "Dearborn went out and bought management, but we couldn't do this—so we made the officers." Some talent was ob-tained from other carefully-sifted firms, but most of it was home-produced, a fact which would have pleased Henry Ford.

More than other British motor companies, Ford Ltd. tended to plow its profits back into productive assets. Its return on capital for the dec-ade 1947–1956 varied from 15 per cent in the last year to 36 per cent in 1954, and ran for the most part between 22 and 30 per cent. This was net profit in relation to net tangible assets. But its dividend rate was moderate, and it raised absolutely no external capital—in which it dif-fered sharply from Vauxhall, for example. In the period 1947–1956 Ford Ltd. retained in the business 79 per cent of its net earnings, as compared with 68 per cent kept by BMC, 52 per cent by Standard, and 74 per cent by Vauxhall. The natural result was a remarkable in-crease in the net assets of Ford Ltd. By the end of 1956, in fact, they were larger than those of any other British automobile manufacturer, reaching £65,349,000, or several millions more than British Motor Cor-poration, and half again as much as Vauxhall. Nobody could deny that the policy of Hennessy, Cooper, and Smith in financial matters had been both prudent and creative.[14]

Strength was needed, for Britain, like America, had her international troubles, and international competition in marketing cars grew ever keener. The new machine shops at Basildon and Woolwich, the huge new Thames foundry, the improvements in the Leamington foundry, and the new spare parts depot at Aveley, all proved valuable. Thanks partly to them Dagenham in 1957 shipped 23,000 cars to the United States, one-fourth of the whole British exports to America. But other small cars, the Renault, Fiat, and Volkswagen, increasingly invaded the British position. In 1956 German exports of automobiles for the first time surpassed British, and the Suez crisis late that year affected all British business adversely—hitting automobiles particularly by gaso-line rationing. Using an additional factory leased at Slough just west of London, Ford Ltd. made the most of its Thames commercial line of vans and trucks; its tractors, bringing out the light Fordson Dexta in 1957; and its six different passenger cars. Still, the struggle became harder. English executives sometimes remarked that Dearborn did not bestir itself greatly to help sell the Consul and Anglia. To this Ernest Breech replied that while he would give any assistance within reason, Dearborn "has its hands full with a little outfit here called Chevrolet," which demanded first attention.[15]

## 4.

France remained a stubborn depression spot even as the rest of Europe forged ahead. Dollfus retired in 1949, taking considerable magic with him; his successor was François Lehideux. Because the company was mired down in debts, for it had never paid off the Belgian loan taken just before the war, new capital could not be found for a much-needed enlargement of facilities. Moreover, the French factory, unlike those in Britain and Germany, never evolved a car which really penetrated the world market. Its Vedette was a sound product, but too large at a time when small cars were sweeping into international popularity, and priced at a higher level than its rivals; its trucks were sound, but not so saleable as the Thames line of commercial vehicles. Late in 1952 the Dearborn executives were distressed to learn that unless they guaranteed fresh loans to Ford SAF, the corporation would go into a receivership. Wieland made a fervent plea for staving off this disaster, declaring that the company could be placed on a profitable basis for at least long enough to merge it with another concern—or to liquidate it on favorable terms.[16]

His advice was taken. Dearborn did guarantee loans which aggregated $750,000, and in the fall of 1952 sent one of its ablest young executives, F. C. Reith, to Poissy to try to save the sinking ship. Reith labored so skilfully that the French government gave him the ribbon of the Legion of Honor. A bustle of fresh energy pervaded the factory as four new Vedette models were brought out in October 1954. This improvement was so encouraging that some observers believed the company might be rescued. The effort, however, would have taken more money and labor than the Dearborn heads thought it wise to risk, and they decided upon abandonment. Accordingly, the Simca interests acquired Ford SAF for a block of about 15 per cent of their stock, taking over the Poissy factory and the Vedette line. A new French company, Ford (France) SA, was organized to handle the sales of Ford products in

France. Finally, in 1958, Dearborn sold its Simca stock to the Chrysler corporation.*

Ford-Werke, meanwhile, did so well under Vitger with its line of Taunus cars and its Ford-Köln trucks that when Henry II visited Cologne in 1954 he found business satisfactory, trade expanding, and the officers confident of the future. The West German automotive industry, after a slow initial recovery, moved ahead fast during the later 1950s, outstripping the British. Capital stock of Ford-Werke was increased in 1954 from $7,600,000 to $12,000,000, and the new funds were used, along with other resources, in an integration and expansion program which by mid-1958 brought the total of postwar expenditures up to $135 millions. The company which in prewar years had been substantially smaller than Opel or Daimler-Benz, had to meet brisk competition now not only from these cars but from the highly popular Volkswagen. In consequence, its rate of growth, while good, was below the national achievement. While the total German automotive sales in 1959 reached about 1,800,000 units, a gain of one-fourth in a year, Ford-Werke sold only 157,522 units. It lagged far behind its Dagenham counterpart.[17]

The spectacular performance of Germany as a whole was primarily the work of the great Volkswagen establishment at Wolfsburg near Hanover, "the only motor factory in the world that nobody owns," as men long said. This massive plant had been laid out by Dr. Ferdinand Porsche to make 300,000 of his proposed People's Cars a year, and had been built by the DAF, the Nazi labor front. Only a few prototypes had been manufactured when the war diverted the plant to military work. When peace came the DAF was outlawed, and the German trade unions took over its claim. This was at once contested by the West German Government, which asserted ownership, and by some 300,000 Germans who in Nazi days had bought 900 marks worth of savings stamps apiece as payment for a car. The British occupation forces, after getting the works into operation and producing about 20,000 Volkswagen for

* Henry Ford II announced the sale of the entire Ford interest to Simca, the Ford Motor Company receiving in return 15.2 per cent of the Simca stock, on July 31, 1958. (The name Simca stood for Société Industrielle de Méchanique et Carrosserie.) See the Ford news release of that date, Acc. 516. This was the only great retreat of the period, the dropping off of the Spanish unit being a minor matter: in 1954 Ford Iberica had ceased to be a member of the Ford family, and became an entirely independent operating company. The American company surrendered its stock in Motor Iberica (the new firm) in exchange for the latter's shares in Ford Portugal. New contracts were made with the independent company, under which it distributed American, British and German Ford products and was licensed to manufacture certain products of Dagenham and Dearborn. See file on agreements in Ford International Division.

their own personnel, turned the facilities over to the German engineers with the issue of ownership still undecided.

As early as 1953 the Volkswagen cast a long shadow across the world. "The challenge of small cars produced at a volume that no British model can now match is a real one," observed the London *Economist* on February 21, that year. "The huge, over-decorated factory at Wolfsburg has not turned out to be what its begetters dreamed; but it remains one of the largest and most competitive motor production units in Europe." Henry Ford would have admired its product. The air-cooled rear engine, though noisy, gave efficient power, was easily serviced, and furnished the sales department a telling slogan, "Air can't boil and doesn't freeze." As the 1950s advanced the Volkswagen, ideally adapted to meet the universal demand for a cheap small car, first equalled the Anglia, the Renault, the Morris Minor, and the Fiat, and then surpassed them. The Taunus, which cost a good deal more, was left far in the rear.[18]

Ford of Canada, Ltd., which in prewar years had long been the largest automotive manufacturer in the Dominion, holding from two-fifths to nearly one-half the whole production, was in most respects a reduced mirror-image of the American Ford. Only the Detroit River separated them. They made basically the same products, for the Canadians relied almost entirely on Dearborn for designing, styling, and engineering their vehicles. Moreover, Ford of Canada looked to Dearborn for certain vital components that could not yet be manufactured economically north of the border. The principal postwar cars sold from Windsor were the Mercurys, Fords, Monarchs (a Mercury with Canadian styling), and the Meteors (a Ford Canadian-styled). After the war General Motors furnished such active competition that by 1950 Ford lost first place in Canada, and the Windsor group realized that they must accelerate their pace. They did well, net profits in 1949 reaching $17,257,000, and sales and production rising to new peaks in 1951 and 1953; but they did not do well enough.[19]

President R. M. Sale in 1951 therefore announced plans for changing the whole face of the undertaking. They would make Oakville near Toronto their new headquarters, with a large new assembly plant and administrative buildings, and would convert the Windsor facilities into the best-equipped engine factory in the Dominion, with an enlarged foundry and machine shop, and installations to make new overhead-valve engines. At Windsor alone they would spend $30 millions. "Our choice of a site in the Toronto area," they explained, "was simply a matter of moving closer to the bulk market for motor vehicles in Canada." [20] Work progressed so steadily that the Oakville assembly plant began operations on May 11, 1953. The transfer of activities from Windsor was effected in progressive stages over fifteen months in order to minimize unemployment at the old site, but by the end of 1954 all passenger cars and trucks were being put together at Oakville. A new parts and accessories depot was acquired in Montreal, and was made the Ford center for the province of Quebec.

The wholly-owned subsidiaries of Canada in other Commonwealth areas shared in the general growth. Ford of Australia did more and more manufacturing at its Geelong plant, in accordance with the desire of the Australian government for complete automobile production there, while it had assembly operations in four other cities. By mid-1952, in fact, the proportion of Australian-manufactured parts in Ford vehicles completed in that country was about 60 per cent. In 1960 Ford began to manufacture in Australia the compact Falcon car. New Zealand had an assembly plant at Lower Hutt, and South Africa one at Port Elizabeth. The Indian government also indicated its strong desire for complete automobile manufacture, announcing in 1949 that it would prohibit the importation of finished automobile bodies after July 1 of the ensuing year.

Ford of Canada at first consolidated its Indian operations in Bombay, assembling British and Canadian vehicles there, and closing its Calcutta and Madras branches. Then in 1954, as government restrictions grew, it formally placed Ford of India in voluntary liquidation. Ford Malaya in Singapore imported components from both Canada and Britain for its assembly work. Everywhere in the sterling area, of course, the shortage of dollars long favored British products against those of Canada and the United States.

5.

In sheer size, the foreign activities carried on under the Ford name had become tremendously impressive by 1959. Few Americans realized that large Ford assembly plants existed in Antwerp and Alexandria, in Copenhagen and Cork, in Brisbane and Sao Paulo. The company in the late fifties had embarked on manufacturing ventures in Latin America that augured well for the future. These would supplement the assembly plants that had existed on that continent for decades.

The foreign sales of the Ford Motor Company, its subsidiaries, and its branches exceeded one and one half billion dollars in 1959; they had leaped in a single year from $1,389,000 to $1,583,000. Ford of Canada sold more than 125,000 North American type cars and trucks in the Dominion alone; Ford of Germany sold 157,522 cars and trucks; and Ford of England with a sale of 405,100 such units brought the total for these three corporations alone to almost 700,000. The profits were no small element in Ford's vigor and stability. Through its foreign companies, Ford was able to supply vehicles to countries that were short of dollars and whose tariffs, taxes, and low per capita income made the price of an American car prohibitive. As for a generation past, Ford continued to be one of the great names in international manufacture and commerce.

The extent of direct Ford ownership in the foreign companies had markedly increased since the war; while other empires were dissolving, Ford's had extended its stock ownership. The company had purchased a majority interest in Ford of Sweden, owned down to 1955 by Ford of Denmark, and also acquired control of Ford of Finland, formerly a subsidiary of the Swedish company. Ford of Brazil was in 1959 a wholly owned subsidiary, as were Ford of Argentina and the newly-formed Ford of Venezuela. By the end of that year Dearborn owned 99 per cent of the stock of Ford-Werke A.G. It had recently purchased 784,486 shares of the Canadian company, bringing its interest in that corporation to about 75 per cent. It had a common stock equity of 54.6 per cent in the English company, which by a dramatic stroke in 1960 it converted into complete ownership. The theory was that administration was simplified by these enlargements of ownership, and that the purchases were good investments.

Yet, even more than in the old days, the Ford Motor Company kept in mind the paramount interests of the foreign public. It was acutely aware in 1960 that its employes abroad approached 100,000 in number, and its shareholders 10,000. Of its $33,500,000 share in the net income of the foreign subsidiaries and branches in 1958, it had taken only about $13,000,000 in dividends and other income remittances, and put back more than $20,000,000 into various foreign establishments. Proud of its international position, the company recognized that good will, and in the long run profits, depended on an enlightened policy.

# XVII

# THE GREAT TRANSFORMATION

HENRY FORD was probably the supreme individualist of his time. He was an individualist in his ways of making money, his frequent disdain of money, and his use of money; in his unscrupulous exercise and enjoyment of his own power and the denunciation of power held by anyone else; in his love of publicity and hostility to strut; in his confidence that inattention to pattern might result in the best pattern. His was not the individualism of the frontier, for he sprang from a more recent and complex background. Nor could it be said that he resembled other great American individualists: Andrew Jackson, Cyrus McCormick, Walt Whitman, his own friend Thomas A. Edison, or Grover Cleveland, for his personality was unique.

One aspect of Ford's individualism was his complete rejection of organized giving. "I have no patience with professional charity or with any sort of commercialized humanitarianism," he wrote in the early 1920s. "The moment human helpfulness is systematized, organized, commercialized, and professionalized, the heart of it is extinguished, and it becomes a cold and clammy thing." [1] He liked philanthropic projects that were broad enough to have general significance, yet limited enough for his own handling; he preferred to deal with individuals rather than with masses.

Ford's ideas about the use of money in the field of giving conformed to his use of capital and labor in an industrial economy. "Philanthropy, like everything else, ought to be productive," he observed, and therefore "charity is no substitute for reform." He wished to "help others help themselves" rather than to extend aid in ways that made self-help unnecessary. Hence it was that he opposed New Deal proposals for sharing or redistributing wealth on the ground that they poulticed a social malady without curing it. Believing that real wealth lay not in

406

money but in goods and labor, he held that the best way to share it was to establish more well-paid jobs and produce more useful goods. "Industry organized for service removes the need for philanthropy," he asserted.[2]

Similarly, he was contemptuous of labor leaders who declared that the worker laying 200 bricks a day when he might lay 300 made jobs for his mates. On the contrary, argued Ford, "It is the industrious man who is the partner of the industrious manager—who creates more and more business and therefore more and more jobs." This Samuel Smiles doctrine of self-help guided him in his policy of hiring cripples, former convicts, and Negroes, groups who found all too few opportunities for self-support. He once picked up a tramp on the road into Detroit and offered him a job at the Rouge. He asked Sorensen to keep track of the man and assist him, and periodically would himself look in on him, shake hands, and promise a raise. It would be heartening to report a happy result for this experiment, but after six weeks the man yielded to wanderlust and quit his job with the frank remark to Ford, "I want to get out of this jail." Such cases did not shake the industrialist's belief in his general philosophy. He knew that he could turn a sweeper into a metallurgist, and did. He was convinced that his profits were neither his own property, nor that of his labor force; they belonged to those who would benefit, after reinvestment of the money, from more jobs and more goods.

Sometimes Ford's interest seems to have been scarcely philosophical at all, and mainly personal. He had never had a daughter. Meeting a naive and joyous schoolgirl named Ann Hood, he developed a strong interest in her and her father. In 1934 he helped them both make a tour of Britain and the continent, providing cars and drivers, and reading her letters appreciatively. For a decade afterwards he followed her progress through school and college.[3]

As long as Ford actively led the company he gave his money and time in ways that harmonized with his individual tastes and ideas. He was deeply interested in young people. He used to point to children and say, "There is the world that is to be." He believed that good schooling should be practical, teaching the value of hard work and giving full scope for "learning by doing." This conviction he put to work in the "McGuffey type" schools he established in Greenfield Village, in Ways, Georgia, and elsewhere. He insisted that reading, writing, and arithmetic should be emphasized, and that practice go along with study. In the Henry Ford Trade School at Dearborn he trained youth in industrial skills, and won a wide reputation because of the proficiency of its graduates.

At the same time, as noted in Chapter III, Henry Ford wished to preserve the rural values he had loved in his boyhood, and one of his highest ambitions was to weld an effective link between the simple freshness of bucolic life and the efficient energy of large industrial centers. His love for the Arcadian age in America—the old architecture, implements, merrymakings, literary tastes, music and dances, folklore—gave him his oddly individual interest in history. He would have rejected any scientific approach to the past, or any study of such intangibles as political ideas or economic forces. What delighted him was the restoration of historic buildings, the preservation of historic sites, the collection of antique furniture, china, and tools, and the revival of olden tunes. Though his benefactions and his efforts to enrich coming generations were limited by his severely antiquarian and technological interests, within these boundaries he not only gave money but himself.

His individualistic views were not infrequently very modern. He had made a grandiose pledge to give Detroit "the best hospital in the world if you'll all get out and let me build it and run it." His adoption of the system just instituted in the Johns Hopkins Hospital, under which staff members were employed full-time on salaries, and forbidden to engage in private practice, was then a radical and highly controversial act. Ford believed that it would eliminate fee-splitting and keep medical care on a high level whether the patient was poor or rich. His special ideas were also manifest in the use he made of the gifted Johns Hopkins graduate, Dr. Frank J. Sladen, in helping him build up an expert medical group, and of a second Johns Hopkins man, Dr. Roy D. McClure, who had worked with Alexis Carrel at the Rockefeller Institute, as leader of the surgical staff. For another of Ford's beliefs was that the hospital should enlist cooperative specialists in psychiatry, respiratory ailments, cardiaovascular diseases, pediatrics, gynecology, obstetrics, gastro-enterology, and other important fields: he envisioned the medical group-practice that was later to become common.[4]

Despite his convictions, Ford gave some recognition to conventional philanthropy. His son Edsel was more prodigal in this field, donating freely to local charities, the Detroit orchestra, the Detroit Community Chest, and the Red Cross. Henry and Clara gave generously to Martha

Berry's schools in the South. Greenfield Village was of course a philanthropy, and the exhibits in the museum and on the grounds represented
a large expenditure of funds, while they required constant outlay to
preserve them and exhibit them to the public.* Still, formal gifts were
the exception, or were to an extent manifestations of Ford's individualistic attitude.[5]

Ford's philanthropies extended geographically from his Institute of
Agricultural Engineering at Boreham, England, to his George Washington Carver consolidated school for Negroes in Georgia. Though his
"village industries" were not an economic success he cherished them
with loving care, and they reflected both his belief in industrial decentralization and his hopes for the regeneration of small rural communities. He established no university as Rockefeller did; he endowed no
art gallery as Frick and Mellon did; he built no library buildings like
Andrew Carnegie. But recalling the drudgery-ridden life of rural
Michigan in his childhood, he suggested ways of shaping the life of
his mature days in a larger, freer mold. In all his instincts Ford was a
philanthropic man.

But when he had made his contributions to his schools, to Greenfield
Village, to the Ford Hospital, and through large donations to work-and-
study colleges, his great fortune remained. It stood as a downright denial of what Ford had proposed to do with wealth. His contributions
to aid people to help themselves were mere scrapings off this huge acquisition. The fortune could not be handled in an individualistic way;
any disposal of it required the acceptance of a social attitude. There
came a time when Ford was to take a terrific step—the adoption of a
method for dealing with his hundreds of millions. The step was the
creation of the Ford Foundation on January 15, 1936. At that time
Ford did not recognize its importance; possibly he never did. But the
foundation in the end was to receive the bulk of the Ford wealth, and
to use it in ways that would have startled and probably outraged the
man who had amassed it.

3.

In 1916, the year the Dodge Brothers decided to bring their successful suit to compel Ford to distribute profits through dividends, the
Federal Government enacted the first inheritance tax as a permanent

* For Ford's philanthropies, see Nevins & Hill, *Expansion and Challenge*, 277 ff., 340–344,
and 500 ff.

part of its revenue system. All bequests in excess of $50,000 had to pay levies rising at the million mark to 10 per cent. Perceptive men, who realized that levies would soon go much higher, regarded the act as a signal-gun announcing the end of an era. The income tax law of 1913 had shown that it would thereafter be more difficult, though not impossible, to accumulate huge fortunes; the inheritance tax showed that it would be impossible to maintain them intact, or perhaps maintain them at all. By 1924 any fortune exceeding $10,000,000 paid a 40 per cent tax, and though under Coolidge the rate was reduced, in 1932 it went up again to 45 per cent. Twilight was descending upon the grand acquisitors.[6]

The predicament of the Ford family, which since the purchase of the stock holdings of James Couzens, John F. and Horace E. Dodge, Horace H. Rackham and others held complete ownership of the Ford Motor Company, was peculiar. The Standard Oil companies were owned by a long list of men, some of whom gave away money in tens and hundreds of millions; the railroad empires, while dominated by James J. Hill, E. H. Harriman, and the Goulds, had thousands of other stockholders; the large banking houses were based on multiple rather than individual ownership. Meyer Guggenheim had seven sons, and they controlled but by no means completely owned, the so-called copper trust. Carnegie, Rockefeller, and others had endowed great foundations long before the Federal inheritance law was passed. Scanning the economic landscape, observers could see that Henry and Edsel Ford occupied a unique and dangerous eminence. Their sudden death would throw control of their powerful company into other hands, for the heirs would have to issue and sell great blocks of stock to pay the Federal tax levies.

The fact that Henry and Edsel Ford were slow to meet their predicament by the only feasible method, the creation of a foundation, can be explained partly by Henry's ingrained dislike of lawyers and legal expedients; partly by a certain fatalism in the man, and his refusal in years of abounding health to face the fact of death; and partly by the lack of strong social pressures toward such a step. Much of the public was extremely hostile to the fortunes of Carnegie, Rockefeller, and Mellon, which were largely diverted into endowments and foundations; comparatively few were hostile to Ford's, which people felt was usefully employed for social purposes just where it stood. But an interview which Ford had with Judson C. Welliver in 1925 showed that he was interested in the general subject, and was reflecting upon methods of reconciling continued family control of the Ford Motor Company— a very different matter from family ownership—with the national laws on inheritance.

If he continued to think about the problem, his reflections were unquestionably stimulated by the Wealth Tax of 1935. In that year of the Social Security Act and other laws requiring large national expenditures, Huey Long's share-the-wealth agitation gained wide popular support. Responding to President Roosevelt's recommendation that Federal taxes be used as a weapon against "unjust concentration of wealth and power," Congress passed a law, signed August 30, fixing both high income taxes and high estate taxes. Levies on decedents' estates rose to 50 per cent of the initial margin over $4,000,000, and to 70 per cent of all excess over $50,000,000. Taxes on gifts were correspondingly elevated to three-quarters of those on estates. What this meant to a colossal fortune like Henry Ford's was plain. It is clear that he and Edsel began critical consultations with the family lawyers in the autumn of 1935, for the papers they needed were ready by midwinter.

Before the end of 1936 Henry plunged across the line between personal ownership and institutional ownership of the bulk of his fortune. This required several steps. The first had been taken some time earlier, when the existing block of 172,645 shares in the company owned exclusively by the Fords was converted into 3,452,500 shares, of which at first 95 per cent was Class A non-voting common stock, and 5 per cent was Class B voting stock. The second was the establishment on January 15, 1936, of the Ford Foundation, "to receive and administer funds for scientific, educational, and charitable purposes, all for the public welfare and for no other purpose." The third was the drawing up of wills to deal with the two classes of stock and endow the foundation. Henry signed on February 3, 1936, a testament by which he bequeathed all his Class A stock to the Ford Foundation, and all the Class B stock in five equal parts to his son and grandchildren. Edsel executed a similar will, leaving his Class A stock to the Foundation, and his Class B stock to his wife and children.*

The effect of these steps would be to enrich the Foundation with a 95 per cent equity in the Ford Motor Company, but to leave the manage-

* All shares were common stock; the Ford Motor Company never issued any preferred shares.

ment of the corporation entirely in the Ford family. Henry had made sure his heirs would keep authority, and that the government would reap only a minor tax harvest. He had also made sure that the Americans would soon witness the birth of the richest philanthropic organization on the globe.[7]

Initially, the Ford Foundation was so weak that it drew little attention. Its first asset was a gift of $25,000 from Edsel, and its holdings at the end of the first year were only $1,773,850. Though beginning in 1938 Henry and Edsel gave it such considerable amounts that its reports to the Michigan authorities in 1942 listed assets exceeding $30,000,000, it was still small compared with the Rockefeller Foundation and Carnegie Corporation. Edsel served as president, and with a board which included Frank Campsall, B. J. Craig, Clifford Longley, and later Henry Ford II, appropriated an average of perhaps a million a year to such worthy causes as the Detroit Symphony and Edison Institute. Just one important liability rested upon its assets: the wills of Henry and Edsel provided that taxes on the voting stock that went to the heirs were to be paid from the non-voting stock that went to the foundation, a provision further protecting the family control.[8]

The tragic death of Edsel in the spring of 1943 demonstrated the wisdom of these preparations for the inevitable. At that time 3,452,900 shares of Ford Motor Company stock had been issued, the three senior members of the Ford family holding the two classes in the proportion of 95 per cent Class A and 5 per cent Class B. Henry had 55 per cent of the shares, Edsel 41.5 per cent, and Clara Ford 3.5 per cent. Nobody knew the market value of these holdings, for not a share had ever been sold on an exchange. Before Edsel's will was filed, journalists outstripped Munchausen in estimating how much his heirs would have to pay in taxes. While *Newsweek* guessed $178,000,000, the *Commercial and Financial Chronicle* a round $200,000,000, and *Time* $225,000,000, stock brokers in Wall Street were reported rubbing their hands in anticipation of fat commission fees.

If so, they were disappointed. Edsel's will revealed that he had divided his voting stock equally among his wife, daughter, and three sons, and had left his real and other incidental property to his widow, but that the non-voting shares were to go, after expenses and taxes, to the Ford Foundation. A great light dawned upon the world as men saw precisely what the classification of stock effected.

"A legal device of just three pages," wrote one commentator, "was enough to ensure that Ford Motors should remain in control of the family after its creator died." It was also enough to ensure that scientific philanthropy would have the disposal of unprecedented sums. Before long, relates the attorney I. A. Capizzi, a special threat led the Ford family, but especially Henry Ford, to make large additional gifts of non-voting stock to the foundation. Capizzi learned that Attorney-General Tom Clark had written a memorandum to President Roosevelt recommending the enactment of a law limiting tax-free gifts to private foundations to $10,000,000. If such a law passed, large amounts of Ford stock might ultimately have to be sold to pay the inheritance taxes on Henry Ford's estate. Much alarmed, Capizzi consulted members of his staff and high officials of the company, who agreed to try to convince the family of the expediency of an inter-vivos gift of stock to the Foundation. The gift was duly made, a prudent step, although the threatened legislation never passed.[9]

When Henry died in 1947 he bequeathed his estate in the same general way as Edsel. The Ford Foundation now had legacies from the two men which amounted to roughly 90 per cent of the Ford Motor Company assets. Meanwhile, a long wrangle had begun between the government and Edsel's widow over the valuation of the stocks. The government began by placing a figure of $190 on each share, while Mrs. Ford's attorneys asserted that $58 was enough. Finally they reached an agreement on $135 a share. Had the foundation not taken most of the estate, it was estimated that Henry's and Edsel's heirs would have paid federal inheritance taxes of $321,000,000.[10]

Men could now perceive that if the foundation had not been established, and with it the mechanism which made it as residuary legatee responsible for paying the estate taxes, the Ford Motor Company would have confronted a grave financial problem just when its internal organization and efficiency were still near their nadir as a result of Henry Bennett's activities. Had it been necessary to resort to public financing to meet heavy cash demands by the government, the company's unfavorable position would have made it difficult to attract a multitude of stock purchasers. A Wall Street investment house might have intervened, as one did in Studebaker affairs years earlier, and put the inevitable "banker's man" into the treasurer's office. Such an admission of outside interests to ownership and policy decisions could have been disastrous. As it was, the Ford Foundation, with the protracted work of settling the Ford estate, gave Henry II and his associates the breathing space they needed for revamping and revitalizing the company. With family control unimpaired, they had a free hand in accomplishing their skilful reorganization. The foundation helped save the company and itself—for the earning capacity of the rescued company gave the foundation its tremendous resources.

As early as 1930 Evans Clark of the Twentieth Century Fund found that 108 important foundations then active in the United States controlled more than a billion dollars in funds, and spent about sixty millions a year. Even against such a background the Ford Foundation loomed up like a lusty young oak among ferns. Clara Ford's non-voting stock came to it in 1950. The Class A stock was now the property of the foundation. Accepting the low government valuation of $135 a share, it held Ford stock worth nearly $500,000,000, but most experts thought that its total assets were more realistically computed at a figure several times higher. So huge a holding inevitably aroused widespread public curiosity and a good deal of suspicion. One leader, Senator Charles W. Tobey of New Hampshire, began investigating the tax-avoidance aspects of foundations.

It is not astonishing that its trustees, as money poured in from the new corporate regime of Henry II, suddenly became concerned about the colossal problem of spending all their income. Their tax exemption rested upon the understanding that they would engage in philanthropic work, and specialists believed that the government would expect foundations to give away at least three-quarters of their revenues. As Julius Rosenwald had remarked, "It is nearly always easier to make a million dollars honestly than to dispose of it wisely;" and the Ford Foundation expected soon to deal with average annual receipts approaching a hundred millions. Then, too, the officers were anxious to begin. "We all felt that the world had to be saved by next Tuesday," one later remarked.[11]

While a detailed account of foundation policies and activities has no place in these pages, they did sufficiently involve the personnel and reputation of the Ford Motor Company to require brief attention. Henry Ford II, taking preliminary charge, wisely decided in the fall of 1948 to establish a study committee "on policy and program," to ascertain the best principles in planning the promotion of human welfare. The eight men chosen, who included experts in education, medicine, the natural sciences, government, social studies, and the humanities, were headed by a brisk, shrewd San Francisco attorney, H. Rowan Gaither, who had served in the Farm Credit Administration and possessed considerable experience in coordinating the work of scientists, businessmen, and government officials. Gaither himself, with a small staff, traveled a quarter million miles, talked with more than a thousand specialists, and wrote numerous preliminary memoranda.

The final committee report on policy and program filled 139 pages. Its authors, possibly influenced by an article which Edwin R. Embree had published in *Harper's Magazine* called "Timid Millions," castigating the older foundations for excessive attention to medicine and education, and for failing to pour "brains and money into frontal attacks on fresh problems," sought to strike a bold note.

They concluded that the fields where problems were greatest, where the least progress was being made, and where the gravest threats to democracy and welfare lay, were those which "arise in man's relations to man rather than in his relation to nature;" a safe assertion in the aftermath of the Second World War. The five program areas which they recommended therefore emphasized the social studies at the expense of the physical: (1) The Establishment of Peace; (2) The Strengthening of Democracy; (3) The Strengthening of the Economy; (4) Education in a Democratic Society; and (5) Individual Behavior and Human Relations. Henry II and his fellow trustees announced their unanimous acceptance of the committee recommendations. Obviously, no genuflections had been made to the pragmatic spirit of the first Henry, though he would have applauded the precedence given to peace, and would have assented with reservations to other parts of the program.[12]*

If the foundation was to advance with continuous boldness, it must have imaginative and courageous leaders. The trustees made a sound if unconventional choice in naming as first president the resourceful and energetic Paul G. Hoffman, former head of the Studebaker Corporation and administrator of the Marshall Plan or ECA. He obtained explicit assurances that young Henry would sustain the foundation even if some of its activities generated unfavorable pub-

---

* He would have specially liked such later ventures as the community or village development projects in India, with farm demonstration work, initiated in 1951.

licity for the Ford name. Referring to Henry Ford's grandly motivated but much-ridiculed failure to stop the First World War, Hoffman warned: "We might sail twenty Peace Ships, and not a one of them reach shore!" As associate directors, he selected four able men: the brilliant Robert M. Hutchins, known for his daring innovations as chancellor of the University of Chicago; Chester C. Davis, head of the Agricultural Adjustment Administration in New Deal days; Milton Katz, professor of law at Harvard; and Gaither. They had a cheerful readiness to risk bad mistakes and soon put a many-sided and colorful body of activities in motion, ranging from support of the battle against social and racial discrimination to advanced study of behavioral subjects in a center at Stanford.

One after another, independent funds were endowed and staffed. The names of The Fund for the Advancement of Education and The Fund for Adult Education define themselves; The East European Fund labored to integrate refugees from the Soviet regimes into American life. These all emerged in 1951. Next year the foundation established The Fund for the Republic, planned by the imaginative Robert M. Hutchins, which tried to abate restrictions on freedom of thought, speech and inquiry; Intercultural Publications, Inc., to encourage cultural exchanges; and Resources for the Future, Inc., to improve the use and protection of natural wealth. In due course the Council on Library Resources, Inc., emerged to coordinate and improve the nation's libraries. An especially valuable principle was embodied in the National Merit Scholarship Corporation, created in collaboration with the Carnegie Corporation, and the Woodrow Wilson Fellowship Corporation, founded to administer a rapidly broadening program of grants for graduate study; for the Foundation had always been interested in helping talented high school students to enter college, and promising college graduates to pursue advanced research.

Inevitably, some carping ridicule mingled with the general public commendation. When Hoffman established his own office in Pasadena, wags there told of the ladies who telephoned the Ford Foundation for a fitting. One critic compared the agency to a monster with its brain in Pasadena, its vital organs in Dearborn, and its legs in New York, all so maladjusted that the vital organs did the thinking, the brains the traveling, and the legs the digesting. Some academic folk, resentful of Hoffman's wise rejection of small individual pleas and other "retail business" in favor of large undertakings, complained that he rode hobbies, was too anxious to make an international splash. A news magazine sneered at the "projectitis" of the foundation, and its "big and expensive staff of busy people who think up and sort out innumerable projects, to be bestowed with plenty of money upon specially created agencies or upon professors hard pressed to live on their academic salaries." Senator Joseph McCarthy's equation of liberal men and ideas with Communism was then deluding multitudes of people, and his sympathizers tossed such adjectives as "leftist," "pinko," "Socialistic," and "subversive" at the foundation personnel; regarding Hutchins in particular with baleful eye.[13] Hutchins himself in a jovial moment tossed off a bit of verse beginning:

> How firm a Foundation we saints of the Lord
> Have built on the faith of our excellent Ford.

To an overwhelming degree, however, responsible comment on the foundation's activities was favorable. The assistance it gave in ideas and plans as well as dollars to education, to economic research, to labors for world peace, and to the improvement of radio and television was invaluable. And on what a scale it operated! By the end of 1955 it had granted or appropriated some $875,000,000. That year its dramatically sudden allocation of $260,000,000 to much-needed salary-increases in 630 private universities and colleges throughout the United States, of $200,000,000 to extending the services of non-profit hospitals, of $90,000,000 to medical education, and of $20,000,000 to college scholarships for talented high school students—$570,000,000 in all—startled newspaper readers. In a real sense, Henry Ford's factory, his fortune, his life-work, had been socialized.*

Internal friction, differences of opinion on policy, and changes in personnel were measurably evidences of vitality and growth. But foundation trustees were meanwhile greatly disturbed by irresponsible Congressional inquiries into the conduct of such agencies. The most important set of hearings were those conducted in May–July 1954 by

---

* An article by Olga Hoyt, "Ford's $260,000,000 College Grants: What Happened," in the *Saturday Review,* Oct. 25, 1958, states that the gift in itself did not enable the institutions to make substantial salary increases; but coupled with additional funds found or given, it raised salaries in a majority of the schools from 10 per cent to 30 per cent, and in some it doubled the salaries. We may add that it unquestionably stimulated a continuing interest in proper faculty salaries, which had become shockingly low in relation to the cost of living, and led to other gifts and appropriations.

a House Committee under B. Carroll Reece, a Republican Congressman from Tennessee. Like Tobey, he was suspicious of the tax-exemption that these huge reservoirs of wealth enjoyed, and he was also fearful of their possibly malign influence on schools, colleges, and public opinion. The spirit in which he conducted his work was highly discreditable to him, but he gained the support of Hearst newspapers, some 100 per cent Americans antagonistic to all liberal ideas, and a great body of blatherskites. In Los Angeles the Hearst *Herald* led a campaign which brought the rejection of a grant of $335,000 offered by the Fund for the Advancement of Education to the school system.

The foundations conducted themselves creditably under the trying ordeal, and some of their heads, notably Dean Rusk of the Rockefeller Foundation, made courageous affirmations of intellectual freedom. Fortunately, this cloud rapidly blew over. When the Reece report appeared in December 1954 a bare majority of the Congressional committee subscribed to its warnings, and the press was mainly scornful of its critical strictures, while the government took no hostile action. Still, the effect was temporarily depressing. The best that could be said for the investigation was that it had given notice that if expenditures did not tread close on the heels of income, trouble could be expected; and the grants totalling $570,000,000 made in 1955 registered comprehension of the fact.[14]

Henry Ford II had spent some weeks during 1952 at "Itching Palms," Hutchins' gay name for the Pasadena offices, and had not in all respects been favorably impressed. It appears that he and other trustees thought that the foundation needed clearer lines of decision and responsibility, a better coordination of the various sections, and more careful advance planning of enterprises which required large expenditures. Some trustees felt that Hoffman and Hutchins, both ardent reformers anxious to remake the world, were too impetuous and even dictatorial. These two brilliant leaders meanwhile had their own grounds for discontent.

Renovation came in a sudden gust in February 1953. Hoffman resigned under pressure, for a variety of reasons. It was officially said that he wished to remain in Pasadena while the trustees concentrated the foundation offices in New York, but he himself spoke of "a very mild incompatability," with the trustees, and of their dislike of his "militant" activities. He added: "I felt I'd done a first-rate job, and if after two years the trustees didn't agree, I didn't want to keep selling them. I'd rather leave." The government soon gave him a larger sphere of activity. Two of the associate directors, Chester C. Davis and Milton Katz, soon followed. The following year Hutchins became director of The Fund for the Republic, which with $15,000,000 all its own became a detached agency, aggressively useful. The remaining associate director, Gaither, who had always possessed Henry II's warm confidence, rose to the presidency of the foundation. In his first annual report he took pains to assert that it would continue to pride itself upon thrust and experiment, declaring that "timidity characterizes too much of our corporate and individual giving." He also defied its foes in Congress and outside: "Criticism which is based on a wilful misconception of the purposes of a foundation, or which is motivated by partisan or selfish considerations, does a distinct disservice to the public welfare."

For two years Gaither remained head—not altogether happy years, for though he was an able administrator, he let leadership within the foundation begin to slip, adhering too closely to a formal program design that was becoming outdated, and failing to indicate a clear sense of direction. To many he seemed too cool, too deliberate. Then in 1956 he moved to the chairmanship of the trustees, and Henry T. Heald, with a long and varied history of service in engineering, government, and education administration, succeeded him.[15] Heald's record was shrewdly dynamic. As the 1960's opened, the foundation was advancing steadily toward the two billion mark in the total of its grants, was growing more efficient in its numerous undertakings, and had earned prestige and confidence on an international scale. Family influence, as Henry Ford II found his energies fully absorbed elsewhere, meanwhile diminished. Almost every great philanthropy except those of John D. Rockefeller, who took his hands completely off his major gifts, has faced a problem in divesting itself of donor control of policy, but after the first years, the Ford Foundation did not find such control noticeable.

### 5.

One source of misunderstanding remained, and was accurately defined by various friendly writers on the foundation. Should such an endowment—such a powerful implement for good—hold a position where it could not call its own financial shots? demanded one publicist. He answered: "A foundation should have complete freedom in the use and disposition of its resources and its income; and this is manifestly impossible so long as it is tied to a commercial enterprise." At the opening of 1955, the Ford Foundation had a relatively small part of its assets in cash, United States securities, and real estate, the total coming to some $163 millions. The remainder consisted of 3,089,908 shares of non-voting Class A stock of the Ford Motor Company, carried at the estate-tax valuation of $135 a share, but worth far more. This block of stock constituted approximately 88.4 per cent of the total equity of the company.

The situation was manifestly unsatisfactory. Income of the Ford Foundation rose as the company prospered, sank as it met losses. Yet because only the Class B stock, still held entirely by the Ford family, had voting rights, the foundation exercised no direct control over company affairs, although two of its trustees were directors of the Ford firm during this period. They could take part in policy discussions, but not direct policy. The foundation could not control dividend decisions, upon which it relied for more than four-fifths of its income. Theoretically, the Ford family could vote to reinvest all the profit in plant expansion, and the foundation could only wring its hands. Though its wealth was beyond the dreams of avarice, it was really "a pensioner, not a partner." Common prudence required a diversification of assets by the sale of Ford stock and reinvestment of the proceeds in other securities. At the same time, the social and economic reasons which had led Edsel Ford and Ernest Kanzler years before to suggest conversion of a tight family holding into a publicly-owned company had gained force with the years. Great family companies wore an antediluvian look.

The Ford Foundation heads, in consultation with members of the Ford family and company executives, used a host of financial and legal consultants to study the question. Rumors meanwhile filled the press. At last, early in November 1955 the foundation announced that after an important and complicated stock-reclassification, and a drastic splitting of old shares, it expected to sell nearly 7,000,000 new shares of common stock in the Ford Motor Company. The purpose was diversification of the foundation's investments. Obviously, however, other advantages might follow for all parties to the transaction. After the sale it could no longer seriously be suggested that a private business was in a position to dominate one of the world's greatest philanthropic institutions; the company should no longer share, as immediately and directly, any public criticism that might be aroused by foundation enterprises; and the market for Ford products might improve by the appearance of a great body of Ford stockholders.

Countless investors felt a thrill of excitement over the possibility of buying Ford stock in the "first" sale of that commodity, and thus sharing in the "fabulous" company profits. Actually, stock had been sold in 1903—many were the men who now wished they had taken the risk of buying—and recent profits were moderate. These putative investors were also thrilled to learn that the stock bought would be voting shares. The decision to give them that character was taken by company and foundation heads for three reasons, two of them cogent and one imperative; it would improve the market, it would better the company's public relations by affording shareholders a sense of participation in control, and it would meet the rule of the New York Stock Exchange that all stock offered there must carry voting privileges.

Precautions to retain a degree of company control by the Ford family were still perfectly feasible, and they were in fact taken in arranging the complicated reclassification of stock. The gist of the arrangement was that two-fifths of the voting power would be held by the family, and three-fifths would be scattered among the general public and, to a more limited extent, among a number of key employes. Of course as a practical matter these scattered shares could not be mobilized to prevail in any controversy against the family block.[16]*

Actually the equity of the family in the Ford Motor Company, under

* After the split there were three classes of stock, Class A, Class B, and Common. The family's old Class B stock with voting rights was to be split 21-for-1, its shares of new B stock representing ⅖ of the voting rights. The old Class A non-voting stock, the bulk of which was held by the foundation, was to be split 15-for-1 and then divided into two classes. The 10,200,000 shares of common stock offered to the public, for that was the final figure, would become voting stock representing three-fifths of the voting rights. The 36,132,239 shares kept by the foundation would remain non-voting stock. The key employes who held relatively small amounts of the old non-voting shares could now exchange them for voting shares, but this would not make a significant total. The increase in the family equity under the split came to less than 1.75 per cent per share. It may be added that the three-fifths of the voting rights assigned to the publicly owned shares would remain a fixed proportion no matter how many shares sold by the foundation were converted into voting stock. The family holdings would continue to have two-fifths of the voting rights as long as the family possessed at least 2,700,000 Class B shares. All this added up to an ingenious plan for combining family control with a scheme of broad public and foundation ownership. (Prospectus, Ford Motor Company, Jan. 17, 1956; Joseph A. Livingston, Philadelphia investment analyst, in Philadelphia *Evening Bulletin*, December 20, 22, 1955; and Washington *Post*, December 30, 1955.)

the rearrangement, was slightly increased. The largest single block of stock after the reclassification, splits, and sale would be that retained by the foundation, and it would possess no voting rights. Even so, all the public shareholders combined would represent a majority interest in the company, and in theory but probably not in fact might assume control of management. Keith Funston, president of the New York Stock Exchange, correctly termed this break with Ford tradition "a landmark in the history of public ownership."

The eighty days between the first official announcement on November 7, 1955, of the impending stock sale, and the date of distribution on January 26, 1956, witnessed a curious demonstration of the magic of the Ford name among the plain people. Initial enthusiasm for the newly-issued stock seemed overwhelming. Men and women who had never bought stock before, urban and rural, wanted some of this. The enlistment of 722 underwriters across the country to handle the sale made it easy to enter orders. From Los Angeles came word: "Demand for the Ford stock is simply astounding . . ." The mountain area made the same response: "Denver brokers say there never has been anything like the public clamor for the Ford Motor Company stock. Nobody asks the price; everybody just wants some of the stock." In the Middle West the old loyalty to Ford ran high. "It is as though Americans with no previous knowledge of or interest in high finance suddenly discovered one of the key secrets of their own fabulous economy," remarked the Marion (Ohio) *Star*. In the East one Wall Street reporter wrote: "Telephone switchboards at brokerage offices have been lit up here like Christmas trees from dawn to dusk."

Perhaps these statements were exaggerated. But one note was struck again and again. The Wall Street man found that everybody wanted a little stock "for my grandchildren," and the financial editor of the Philadelphia *Bulletin* agreed: "Nobody . . . wants Ford stock for himself or his wife . . . It's always for longterm holding for offspring, nieces, nephews, and an occasional aunt."

In the midst of the excitement some cautionary voices were raised. The prospectus issued by the Ford Motor Company late in December did not impress all readers equally. It recited that the company's assets of $2,483,000,000 ranked it fifth among American corporations, and third among manufacturing concerns, while its sales of $4,042,000,000 in the year which had ended with September placed it behind only

General Motors, Standard Oil, and American Telephone & Telegraph. Since 1945 the company had accumulated $1,536,800,000 in earnings, put in excess of $1,300,000,000 back into the business, and paid more than $439,000,000 in dividends. But various financial critics pointed out that while the automotive industry was at the crest of a decade of post-war prosperity, nobody could be certain that demand and prices would remain high. Some stockholders confidentially advised their clients that at $64.50 the stock seemed overpriced. The London *Economist,* while acknowledging that the Ford Company could not have chosen a better moment for showing its books, warned its readers that "whether this pace can be maintained remains to be seen . . . 1956 may bring retrenchment."

A different type of response came from the respected Senator Joseph C. O'Mahoney of Wyoming, chairman of the subcommittee on monopoly, who after reading in the prospectus that while the Ford family owned only 12.1 per cent equity in the company, it controlled 40 per cent of the votes, spoke in the last days of 1955 of abolishing all forms of non-voting stock. "The small stockholders of America," he declared, "are surrendering their economic freedom to big business management because they are losing control over the vast properties of which they are the real owners." Perhaps the most effective comment on this came from the New York columnist Max Lerner; "I have news for Sen. O'Mahoney. Most Americans don't worry about the giant corporations. What they want is to be cut in—on even a small slice of them." Certainly no general demand arose for abolition of non-voting stock. The desire for a "small slice" was manifest abroad as well, and a part of the offered shares was reserved for sale in Canada, Britain, and other countries. To give everybody at home a chance, the company had an understanding with the underwriters that the buying of huge individual blocks should be discouraged.

Henry Ford II was anxious that investors, whose shares would inevitably fluctuate like all other stocks, should not feel that they had been misled or oversold. At a meeting of underwriters on January 9, 1956, he shook off the gloom. "We at Ford Motor Company are businessmen and not miracle men," he reminded buyers, adding: "I think some people are indulging in wishful thinking about their chances for fast and fabulous financial gains." Certain that 1955 had been the best year the automobile industry and the Ford Motor Company ever had, he felt almost equally sure of another fact: "1956 will not be as good a year as 1955." Though many brokers thought he was foolish to urge caution at that particular moment, his statement was honest and courageous, and events proved him correct. Nevertheless, enthusiasm for the stock was running so high that all the prophets of gloom, led by Jeremiah and Hosea, could not have checked it.

When the foundation agreed to sell the underwriters 10,200,000 shares at $63 a share, the brokers in turn agreed to price the stock at $64.50. This was believed to be the largest corporate offering in history. Trading at a premium began on the Toronto and Montreal exchanges the morning of January 17, shares closing at $69.50; late that afternoon trading began in New York, where the assent of the Securities and Exchange Commission had cost some extra hours, the stock opening at $68.50 and closing at $70.50. This latter price proved just about the peak, however, and in the ensuing weeks and months the quotations fluctuated between a general low mark of $51 and a high mark of $70. The foundation, pocketing something more than its anticipated $631,600,000, could watch these changes impassively.*

The most significant results of the sale were two. With this huge sum in hand for reinvestment, the Ford Foundation was now in great degree independent of the corporation; and the company had acquired approximately 350,000 new holders of common stock, each entitled to one vote a share. The public was naturally most interested in the latter fact. One of the most radical revolutions in the history of industrial ownership had taken place with remarkable quietness and ease. In 1943 the Ford Motor Company had been owned by three persons, Henry, Clara, and Edsel Ford; as late as January 1956 complete voting control was held by Edsel's five heirs; and then in less than a week a third of a million owners shared the old privileges and responsibilities of the family group.[17] For though family control endured, the revolution was real.

Henceforth the directors would feel responsible to all the stockholders, who would demand policies and management able to maintain satisfactory profits and dividends. Henceforth assets, earnings, salaries of officers or directors, and other facts long secret or clouded

* The precise amount realized by the foundation was $640,725,445, which included proceeds from the sale of some 16,000 shares to the company for its stock purchase plan for salaried employes. About 22 per cent of the company's total stock was sold in 1956, but the foundation then still held approximately 67.6 per cent of the whole equity of the company.

would be known to all; automotive competitors would possess data on blunders and successes; labor leaders could measure worker-returns against owner-returns; and accountants and lawyers in Federal departments and commissions could detect any disregard of the public interest. Privacy in management was gone. The Ford leaders had to think in the same terms in which executives of the great railroads, oil companies, electrical companies, and packing-houses had long thought.

Meanwhile, public ownership of shares had been extended in another direction. During 1952, the three Ford brothers, then owners with other members of the family of all the voting stock of the company, decided that it would be wise to grant options for the purchase of shares to Ford executives holding important positions, and thus enhance their interest in the progress of the corporation. In 1953 a number of "incentive" options were distributed. "This," as Henry Ford II said later, "was a difficult bridge to cross because it involved breaking a family tradition"—for the decision was made before the Foundation gave active consideration to its own public sale of stock. The incentive plan worked so effectively that from time to time in later years additional options were granted; the shares thus made available for distribution as the options were exercised aggregating by the end of 1960 approximately 3,600,000, or 6.7 per cent of the total outstanding stock.

Both the Ford business and the Ford philanthropies had been taken from personal power to impersonal control and broad social utility. Both were firmly placed, too, under a new progressive and scientific management that was in consonance with the spirit of the new era. Henry Ford had flourished long after Rockefeller's declaration that "Individualism has gone, never to return;" but times had proved Rockefeller right after all. The company and the foundation continued to broaden their bases. A great new stride in this process was taken in 1959 when a sale of two million shares of common stock was made to the public on March 31 at $56.50 a share, and another of equal size on December 9 at $82; each holder of the common stock being entitled to one vote per share. These two sales permitted a further diversification of the foundation's assets; for although more than 80 per cent of its holdings had once been in Ford stock, by the close of 1959, despite the fact that the value of that stock on foundation books had actually increased, less than 60 per cent of its assets were in the

Ford Motor Company. In May 1961 officers announced that the Ford Foundation was preparing to place a new block of 2,750,000 shares before the public.*

The America which elected John F. Kennedy its chief executive in 1960 was a very different land from the America of President Herbert Hoover thirty years earlier. Wealth was better distributed; collective controls had replaced individual power; the social conscience was more sensitive, and government, business, and philanthropy all felt a larger responsibility for social welfare. In this transformation, the Ford business and Ford fortune offered perhaps the most striking single illustration of change.

* On December 31, 1961, Ford had 55,017,799 shares outstanding, divided into three classes. The Ford Foundation held 27,932,035 Class A shares, the Ford family interests held 6,291,865 Class B shares, and the public held 20,793,899 common shares. All three classes shared equally in dividends. In January 1962 the directors recommended a 2-for-1 stock split, and increased the dividend for the first quarter from 75 cents a share to 90 cents a share. *The Wall Street Journal*, January 11, 1962.

# XVIII

## PRESENT AND FUTURE

LET us turn back, in imagination, to a late spring day in 1896, as Grover Cleveland's second administration drew toward its end, and to the scene in Detroit with which we began our story.

We see the interior of a small brick shed, its grimy walls without paint or plaster, the wooden beams of the roof uncovered, its dusty little windows admitting only a murky light. Every detail spells utility: the rough wooden cupboards full of tools, the wheels and belt of a power lathe overhead, the vise, plane, and wrenches on a shelf in the corner, the potbellied iron stove with its pipe bent in a long L under the ceiling, the electric lights under tin reflectors, and the spatters of oil on the floor. It might be a workshop anywhere in the country, but it happens to be Henry Ford's. In the center is a little rubber-tired vehicle standing on square blocks, with a curious machine under the seat, and beside it are two earnest figures. One, a spare man of thirty-odd, standing erect by his contrivance, and grimly serious as he tinkers with a metal fitting, is Ford himself. The other, a pretty, neatly-dressed young woman seated on a high stool, demurely intent on some embroidery, but casting anxious glances at the husband who as she thinks works excessively long hours, is Clara Bryant Ford. The workshop stands today in Greenfield Village. Of the hundreds of thousands who yearly inspect the shop, many are so familiar with a painting by Norman Rockwell depicting the scene just described that they instantly visualize it: the young couple, the vehicle, the machinery —all irradiated by a dream.[1]

That the dream came true we see as we whirl the hands of the clock forward to a moment sixty years later, in 1956, and a far wider scene. The place is the grounds of the Ford Research and Engineering Center, which looks much like the campus of a university. Trees and lawns stretch into the far background; framing the immediate field are three huge steel, glass, and brick buildings of modern design. A photographer has assembled the members of this particular division, an army of white-shirted men standing as if to attention. This body of fully ten thousand highly-trained employes are all engaged in development and research. They constitute the central core of growth in a plant that, with its equipment, is valued at more than two and a half billion dollars, and that has counted in the previous year an average of 180,000 workers. On these ten thousand rests the responsibility for developing new lines of cars, trucks, and tractors, improving old models, and bettering the materials, methods, and devices used in manufacture.[2] Between the lone tinkerer in the shed and the ten thousand technological experts stretches a direct line.

Obviously the two scenes here described furnish a somewhat conventional type of contrast. The difference between the industrial acorn and oak, between the rudimentary invention of a Watt or Edison and the vast proliferation of men and machines to which it leads, is familiar to all. Written in terms of mere growth, the Ford story would not be basically different from a dozen others. But significant changes accompanied the growth between the beginning and the middle of the century—changes which embraced factors more vital than size.

A much broader meaning, to take one example, attaches to the contrast between the first tiny meetings of Ford Motor Company stockholders, and those which began to take place after the public distribution of shares. Nothing could be more striking than the difference between the meeting held on June 18, 1903, and that held on May 19, 1960, both in Detroit. The original meeting found the company with just twelve owners, and with control tightly lodged in three men, Henry Ford, Alexander Malcomson, and John S. Gray, who held 615 of the 1000 shares. In due course, Henry Ford bought out his associates until *he* was the company (that is, he, his wife, and his son). He had no patience with the idea that the Dodge brothers should compel him to pay out money in dividends which he wished to reinvest in the business, or with the notion that James Couzens should help shape his policies in public relations. He had no desire to see "outsiders" grow wealthy on the earnings of *his* factory. He took such absolute control that for many years no stockholders' meeting was held for the same reason that the Czars held no parliaments; he was dictator, and with his immediate family exercised complete sway.[3]

The meeting of 1960, however, registered a revolution as sweeping as that which had recently overtaken some European dictators. More than 2500 stockholders crowded into the Masonic Temple, where they faced the fifteen directors of the corporation, including Henry Ford II as president. The whole number of owners of the company at the beginning of the year had risen to about 238,000, scattered over the fifty states and fifty-nine foreign countries. Participants in the business of the meeting, in person or by proxy, represented more than 27,750,000 shares, or nine-tenths of all those in existence. The company that was recently a family possession, and that in the not distant past had been as much a one-man domain as Turkey in the time of Suleiman the Magnificent, had been democratized, with property-title and votes open to anyone commanding a few hundred dollars. At the 1960 meeting, in fact, holders of very modest blocks of shares questioned the management in peremptory tones.

It should be pointed out that since September 1945 the former autocratic control of the company had been replaced by a group of expert executives, all of whom had a voice in company affairs. Tried Ford leaders like Bugas, Bricker, and Davis immediately exerted an influence; they were of course soon joined by able recruits from outside the company: Breech, Crusoe, Harder, Dykstra, and also McNamara, Ben Mills, Wright, Arjay Miller, Duffy, and Yntema. Benson Ford soon took an important place and later also William Clay Ford. The shift to public participation was startling, but group administration had been the pattern for eleven years.

An even more striking contrast could be drawn in the field of labor relations. On the one hand we can recall the loose, helpless agglomeration of Ford workers who on January 5, 1914, learned, not from any leaders of their own, and not through any channels of negotiation, but from the newspapers, that the company would thereafter pay a minimum of $5 a day, more than double the old rate of $2.40.[4] On the other hand we can picture the firmly organized UAW-CIO union, a disciplined army, which forty-one years later negotiated with the Ford managers, as equal speaking to equal, one of the memorable agreements in the history of American labor. In the interim the terms of employment had been as drastically revolutionized as the terms of ownership.

Nor was the practically complete unionization of workers, under federal guarantees, the only major change affecting labor, for by the later 1950s the substantive issues under negotiation had become very different from those of earlier times. In 1914 wages had been so much the central question that Ford's five-dollar-day, which instantly became famous, quite eclipsed his simultaneous reduction of hours from nine to eight. By the late 1950s, however, high wages were taken for granted, and emphasis had fallen upon hours, guarantees of tenure, seniority rights, annual vacations, unemployment pay in slack seasons or depressions, and other fringe benefits.[5] Workers who had once been buffeted by harsh bosses, job-competition, and economic vicissitudes, were now protected by powerful union chiefs, friendly laws, and the company's assumption that they were now neither opponents nor dependents.

When Henry Ford and his associates built the Ford Motor Company to its early strength, he and it were helping lead the economic and social advance out of a grimly ruthless situation. Aggressive men and corporations of monopolistic temper towered over the business landscape. J. Pierpont Morgan had just created United States Steel; James J. Hill, E. H. Harriman, and George Jay Gould ruled railroad empires; John D. Rockefeller was still nominally head of Standard Oil. Effective Federal regulation of railroads still lay ahead, and it was far from certain that the anti-trust legislation so often defied since 1890 could be enforced. The predominant public attitude toward labor unions was suspicious or hostile. Slums, poverty, sweatshops, child labor, occupational hazards, and other social malignancies, under the ruling political philosophy, seemed beyond reach of the law; philanthropy might ameliorate such evils, but government could not abolish them.

A half-century later one of the great socio-economic revolutions of history had taken place in the United States. New sources of power, new machines, and new methods had enormously increased the industrial productivity of the nation, inaugurating the age of affluence. In this development the Ford Motor Company had played no small role. Mass-production techniques were a prime element in the change, and mass-production had been born in Ford's Highland Park factory in 1913–1914. The mechanization of agriculture was another prime element, and the Ford tractor had played its part in that revolution.

As political forces in America, using the shock of the depression and the example of Britain and Scandinavia, brought the welfare state into existence, enlightened businessmen responded by creating a welfare capitalism. Here, too, the Ford Motor Company made its contribution with the five-dollar-day, the pioneer welfare work of Sociological Department administered by Dean Marquis, the employment of Negroes and cripples, and the cheap durable car—the Model T that in 1922 reached a low price of $369—which did more than all other vehicles combined to "put America on wheels." If some of Henry Ford's attitudes impeded the revolution, other attitudes favored it, and he never lost his optimistic vision of brighter days ahead. As he said in 1935: "Our times are primitive. True progress is yet to come. The industrial age has scarcely dawned as yet; we see only its first crude beginnings."

Henry Ford and the earlier company, down to the Second World War, were largely creatures of the old laissez-faire era, ahead of it in the main, but sometimes, after the founder lost his early idealism, embodiments of its static or reactionary traits. The end of the war brought the tremendous change in company affairs just traced. The renovated corporation under Henry Ford II and his associates belonged in every respect to the advanced new era of decent union-management relations, government protection of the poor and handicapped, respect for minority rights, greater responsibility in international affairs, and of a better standard of living. If the old company in its last years had lacked realism, courage, and generosity, the new company possessed all three.

Also, it had achieved efficiency. As noted in earlier chapters, Henry Ford II in ten years had transformed a centralized organization about whose separate divisions there was no conclusive information into a decentralized one in which all important activities were separated from each other, their costs and profits known, and the man conducting each one was responsible for the results. Authority went from a supervisory group above to persons in charge of the Ford, Lincoln-Mercury, and manufacturing divisions, and to the vice-presidents of engineering, manufacturing, marketing, and industrial relations. Each of these executives presided over his area, but his decisions, actions, and profits could be checked. Ford was an agglomeration of businesses rather than one business.

Committees at the top coordinated the company's work as a whole, personalities like Breech and Henry II giving it force and direction. The latter's contribution was a willingness to consult with the ablest associates he could assemble and to take from them or supply himself a long and creative view of the future. He delegated authority carefully but fully, encouraging initiative in others. At the same time he never flinched from assuming ultimate responsibility and making decisions himself when to do so seemed to be necessary.

2.

No recent illustration of the transformation in the company's temper and methods is more striking than the labor settlement of 1955.

During the years 1951–1954 Walter Reuther and other UAW leaders had been moving toward a new goal. They were of course interested in improved wages, for which the inflation accompanying the Korean War furnished ample grounds. But they were equally interested in giving the worker some protection against interruptions of employment, for every slump, every change in models, every dispute in suppliers' plants, threw men out of jobs. Reuther began talking about a "guaranteed annual wage," a misleading phrase, for what the workers really wanted was something quite different, a system of unemployment compensation supplementing government insurance; that is, assurance that they would not have to endure long weeks of idleness during layoffs without a pay check. An industry so badly exposed to economic vicissitudes as the automotive business could not pay annual salaries, but it could furnish its workers some lesser protection.

The UAW had determined to launch a drive when its contracts with the automobile companies expired in 1955, and to make Ford the initial target, for a strike there would cost the union far less than one in General Motors and would be as useful in setting an example. Bugas, a believer in what he called "the developing science of industrial relations," made a counter-offer to Reuther's demands. The company, he told labor, wished to alleviate the hardship caused by unemployment; it would gladly sell its workers stock on liberal terms, and then advance them interest-free loans on the stock during layoffs to keep the wolf from the door. The UAW chiefs rejected this proposal. But they began to scale down their demands, and when Ford made an entirely new offer, they accepted it—subject to changes in detail—as a general basis of settlement.

Under the plan adopted June 8, 1955, the company agreed to create two trust funds, one for defense-contract workers, and one for general employes, aggregating $55,000,000. It would establish this reserve by contributing five cents a person for each hour of paid employment. Out of these funds, any hands laid off would be granted benefits which, added to the ordinary state unemployment compensation payments, would amount to 65 per cent of his take-home wages the first four weeks, and 60 per cent thereafter. Duration of the payments, up to a maximum of 26 weeks, would depend on the seniority of the worker, his record of regularity on the job, and the sums in the reserve; precautions being taken against exhaustion of the funds by the first employes laid off, with little or nothing left for those who lost their places later. This "supplemental unemployment benefit plan" was embodied in a three-year contract with the UAW-AFL-CIO.[6]

Since this was the first such contract in the history of the industry, it touched off an explosion of comment, most of it favorable, but in part sharply adverse. Labor reporters hastened to translate the agreement into practical terms. Consider the case of a Ford worker in the Rouge plant earning $100 a week, wrote one—the average weekly wage in 1955 being actually $106.68. His take-home pay after taxes, if he had a wife and four other dependents, was $87.02. "If laid off, he'd get $42 from Michigan. For four weeks, the Ford kitty would contribute a special benefit of $14.56 to bring his weekly pay to $56.56. Then for twenty-two weeks he'd get a regular supplement of $10.21, giving him a total of $52.21."[7] This, said most experts, was mere justice to the workingman, who usually lived with but little margin. The economist Sumner Slichter declared that such supplementary unemployment compensation should be welcomed: "There is no doubt that the unemployment benefits provided by present state laws are too low." Both President Eisenhower and Secretary of Labor James P. Mitchell had in fact been urging that the States increase their compensation. Various men pointed out that although the cost to Ford could not go beyond $55,000,000, the ceiling placed on the trust funds, the plan would nevertheless give the company a strong incentive to keep its plants in nearly constant production. Ideally, it would mean a levelling of output and employment, with pay checks covering 52 weeks of the year.[8]

Other observers, however, made various objections. Some critics asserted that while the rich automotive industry could provide such a largess, most enterprises would find the plan difficult, and depressed industries like coal and textiles utterly impossible. Thus the agreement would seem to presage the growth of a privileged worker class in those large industries possessing healthy reserves. Any attempt to give it a wide application, predicted other businessmen, would cause a shrinkage of employment. "Who would hire a marginal worker if he had to take care of the man the rest of his life?" Others prophesied that it would lead to a wave of mergers as small companies united to escape extinction, for "the big boys will set the pattern and crucify the rest of us." These alarmist views did not carry conviction, for it was clear that the plan could not and would not be widely imitated. Nor did many people accept wild assertions that the new "pattern" would cause an inflationary price rise, or the gloomy prediction of the New York *Herald-Tribune* that, by making employers less willing to hire new men and workers less willing to shift jobs, it would inaugurate a general "hardening and stratification" of the national economy.[9]

It was true that the agreement did something to blur the social and economic lines separating factory hands from white-collar workers and lower-rung executives, but this could be counted a gain. It also did something to cut down absenteeism and turnover, and greater stability of employment, with lessened anxiety over possible layoffs, meant enhanced efficiency. The plan proved a clear success, and since other automotive companies had to follow the Ford example, the management took pride in what with justice it called its "pioneering."

The company during this period had undertaken a wide variety of other enterprises, such as were becoming fairly standard in the most advanced corporations, for its employes. It instituted non-contributory retirement plans for both hourly workers and salaried people in 1950, and improved them in subsequent years. By the end of the decade the normal benefit for a man who retired at 65 after 30 years of work was $67.50 per month—at no cost to himself. Moreover, the company had established a stock investment program for salaried personnel, under which an employe might buy Ford stock and government bonds up to a maximum of 10 per cent of his salary each year, receiving half as much again in stock from the corporation. Group insurance plans were open to all. In addition to paid vacations, Ford employes had seven paid holidays a year. They received premium pay for night-shift work, earned well over three millions within a decade for practical improvements suggested to the management, received length-of-service awards, and could share an educational program in which more than 120 instructors were active during the later nineteen-fifties.

Meanwhile, as the manner in which the company celebrated its fiftieth anniversary had emphasized the leaders' interest in the broad social utility of the corporation, every subsequent year saw that interest extended. While the company grew the Ford Foundation grew, but this was by no means all.

It was fitting that the Fair Lane residence of Henry Ford, with the adjacent grounds, should be offered the University of Michigan in 1956 as a gift from the company, with 210 acres of land surrounding it. The Ford Motor Company Fund simultaneously gave the institution $6,500,000 to establish a Dearborn center, in which students might combine classroom study with experience in an appropriate branch of the company, or some other industrial concern of the area. This gift, the largest single donation ever made to the University, was a use of Fair Lane which Henry would have approved.[10] It was fitting also that Henry II and his principal executives should steadily champion liberal social causes at home, and a liberal internationalism in foreign policy. The company by 1959 had an active Office of Civic and Governmental Affairs, conducted seminars for employes to encourage their participation in politics, and made it a fixed policy to grant leaves of absence to workers who took full-time public office. This pledge to serve the country was put to the test when John F. Kennedy in 1961 chose Robert S. McNamara, the newly-elected president of the company, to serve as his Secretary of Defense. (John Dykstra succeeded him, and in 1963 was followed by Arjay R. Miller.)

### 3.

The automotive business, like others, has its ups and downs. It attained an unprecedented peak of production in 1955, when the Automobile Manufacturers Association reported that 7,950,377 passenger cars were made, and that the output of all motor vehicles came to

9,204,000 units. Another peak, of somewhat lower altitude, was reached in 1960, with a production of 6,750,000 passenger cars, and 7,950,000 vehicle units of all types. The economic importance of the automotive industry remains as tremendous as ever. In 1960 it directly employed about 10,000,000 people, and indirectly gave work to many millions more; for it purchased more than 60 per cent of all the synthetic rubber made in the country, 46 per cent of the lead, and 20 per cent of the steel. Three out of four families in the land that year, or 39,500,000 families, had at least one car; and about 7,000,000 families had two or more. The country now had one automobile for every three Americans, as against one for every five in 1945. The Ford Motor Company, which in 1957 had held 30.4 per cent of the market and hoped to better the figure, was one of the pillars of the nation's economy.

Viewed as a business entity, the renovated Ford Motor Company has had three great oustanding characteristics, one of which stands in a somewhat contradictory relationship to the others. It is imposing for its size, one of the half-dozen largest corporations of the land. It has been remarkable for the velocity and range of its growth; for the pace of its progress and the variety of its products. Finally, it has retained to a striking degree, in spite of size and expansion, a special individuality, so that the name Ford means to the average American something unique.

The sheer magnitude of the Ford assets and undertakings would be less impressive if the company were not highly dynamic, for if it did not grow steadily and competitively its size would soon dwindle. In the automotive industry a company must run as fast as it can, like Alice in Wonderland, just to keep up. It is impressive to say that the total company assets on June 30, 1961, fell barely short of $4,500,000,000, and that the value of the property, plant, and equipment alone, after depreciation, was computed at more than two billions. It is impressive to say that sales in the first nine months of 1961 reached $4,800,000,000, and net income $316,200,000. These figures were spread before the public when in January 1962 the Ford directors recommended a two-for-one stock split, the first since the company's shares were sold to the public; at the same time increasing the first-quarter dividend from 75 cents to 90 cents. More striking still, however, were the evidences of diversification in the expansion.[11]

"We are a growth business in a great and growing American economy," said Henry Ford II to the stockholders at the 1960 meeting. "We are reaching out to tomorrow with all our confidence, all our talents, and all our resources." He had ample reason to say this, for from the end of the Second World War through 1958, the company had spent more than two and a half billions on expansion and modernization.

It had built in this period 22 new manufacturing plants, 21 parts depots, and 17 buildings for engineering research, and office use. They were scattered all over the American landscape: Buffalo (pressed steel works), Nashville (glassmaking), Chicago (a stamping plant), Sandusky, O. (hardware), Cleveland, Cincinnati, Canton, O., Sheffield, Ala., and other cities. Few States had failed to share in the expansion. Some of the buildings had attracted attention for their architectural attractiveness; the Nashville plant, for example, and the gigantic glass, steel, and aluminum office building that glittered on Michigan Avenue in Dearborn near the old Fair Lane homestead, a luminous tall honeycomb rivalling any on Madison Avenue. The expansion was so continuous and ambitious that some observers questioned whether it was not excessive. Time justified it, however. And sound reasons could be given for providing full capacity in anticipation of heavy demand. Overtime is costly, and full capacity would make possible the easy fulfillment of market demands, and a quick seizure of sales that would be lost by delays.

Every year since 1958 had seen further illustrations of the statement of Henry Ford II that he headed a "growth business." Early in 1961 he spoke at ceremonies held on the lighting of a new sheet-glass furnace at the Nashville Plant. "We see a growing market," he said, "not only for replacement glass for . . . automobiles, but also for a wide variety of consumer and industrial uses." The year 1961 witnessed three noteworthy acquisitions. At the beginning of the year the company completed the purchase of the publicly-held shares of its subsidiary in Dagenham, England, for $368,100,000—this step being a measure of its faith in the expanding foreign business. (Some Ford experts thought that the overseas market might even outstrip domestic sales by 1970.) A little later, in April, the company spent $28,200,000 to acquire the spark plug business and a battery plant of Electric Autolite; and as the year neared its end, it acquired Philco Corporation, in the appliance and electronic field, by an exchange of stock.[12] It was especially significant to find the company thus enlarging its facilities in view of the fact that the automotive industry had markedly changed its character in recent years.

It had become far more a replacement industry than ever before. No longer could it expect to enjoy such a spectacular general expansion as the growth between 1925 and 1960, between a society in which one American in seven had a passenger car and a society in which one citizen in three was a car-owner. That kind of growth was gone forever. The industry would have to keep pace with the increase of population, but the ratio of per capita ownership would not change greatly; the best-informed men now anticipated an annual increase of 3 per cent at most. Moreover, the industry was no longer one in which the automobile would necessarily be the most important index of affluence, or conspicuous consumption, or a higher plane of living. Public attitudes had begun to alter. As Lewis D. Crusoe was quoted by Richard Austin Smith in *Fortune:* "People no longer think it's just wonderful to go some place sitting down." [13] They might value a trip to Europe, a postgraduate university education for the brilliant son, a boat or swimming pool, or a library of books and records, more than a new car. The automobile, in short, no longer occupied so easily a place in the center of the stage.

One result of these changes was an increased emphasis upon variety of product. When the National Automobile Show was held in Detroit in October 1960, some 300 models were displayed; giving the purchaser an unexampled range of sizes, prices, and styles. The growing popularity of the compact cars played a large part in this, for American companies had been compelled to bring out numerous effective models of their own to check the invasion of small foreign cars. The Ford Motor Company responded to the general trends of the industry. "Everyone," the general manager of the Ford Division, Lee A. Iacocca, had said in 1960, "is playing it by ear." [14]

However, with the Ford Motor Company the compact car has played a part in a revolutionary development affecting the products of the company as a whole. In 1908 the Model T was the sole car manufactured by the firm, and for twenty-five years one such vehicle seemed to be sufficient. Then with the middle nineteen-thirties came an era in which a single car did not seem enough, and rivals with four or five cars gathered more prestige and prosperity.

Since 1922 the Lincoln had been a quality car advertised by the company, but it sold in all but negligible quantities. In 1938 the Mercury was created to seek a place in the middle-price field, and was modestly successful. Still, the Ford car dominated the two higher-priced ones. This top-heavy situation was the one that Henry Ford II encountered in 1945, and for some time it continued. The Fairlane, a glamorized Ford which appeared in 1953, was a promising creation, and in 1955 came the Thunderbird, a prestige car for the lover of style and smartness. It was a product of the Ford Division, but had a character of its own. The Falcon (1959) and Comet (1960) were Ford entries in a field that by the first quarter of 1960 was responsible for nearly one-third of the industry's sales as against one twenty-fifth four years earlier. Cheaper to run, easier to maneuver and park than the usual American automobile, these models have made a definite place for themselves. In the upper- and middle-price fields the company has offered the new Continental and Galaxie.

The present Ford cars cover a wide if not the complete range of car possibilities. Instead of being a company of one dominant car, Ford today presents eight. The Lincoln Continental, Thunderbird, Mercury Monterey, Galaxie, Mercury Meteor, Ford Fairlane, Comet, and Falcon —the list is long and carefully planned. The company has found a pattern of production that answers every type of public demand.

This comprehensive array was not attained without difficulties and even disasters. Against the success of the Thunderbird, the Galaxie, the Falcon, and the Comet could be set the relatively poor reception of the entirely new Mercury introduced in late 1956, and the failure of the Edsel, presented in September 1957.* Careful preparations had been made for this new line of medium-price cars. The Edsel had not only distinctive styling but several innovations in engineering: an automatic transmission with pushbutton controls in the steering wheel, safety-rim wheels, and self-adjusting brakes. The market had been tested. But for a number of reasons the Edsel proved to be a disaster. By far the most important of these was the recession of 1958, which cut the potential market from under the car. However, there were other causes. For example, the Edsel appeared in several types, some lower in price than the Mercury, others higher. This created a confusion in the minds of

---

* The super-Mercury off the Lincoln shell, as described in Reith's presentation of April 1955 (see Ch. 15) was never introduced. This was the only part of Reith's program that was not implemented.

potential customers which infected the dealer organization selling the car. Again, the field which the car was trying to enter—that of middle-priced automobiles—was already a crowded one, difficult to break into in a time of prosperity, and most forbidding in one of depression. Also catastrophic were a larger number of small defects (every new car has some of these, but the Edsel had far too many) which neither the engineers nor the production staff had managed to detect and remedy. A dislike by some possible customers of the shield (dubbed horse-collar) in front was also a factor. Finally, the publicity and advertising campaign, which had loomed up big and bold at first, faded as the car was unfavorably received. It should have been pressed home with renewed vigor. Perhaps the creation of a special Edsel division with a head relatively young and of a new dealer organization were also unfortunate. The new unit had to struggle for recognition and support sometimes against more powerful and experienced executives than those who could champion its needs.

At any rate, the debut was a failure, and when the Edsel was repositioned in the market, although really a bargain, it still sold badly. Even complete restyling resulted in no substantial improvement, and the company discontinued production in November 1959. It was necessary to find other candidates for the middle-price range.

Financially, the Edsel adventure was a costly one. John Brooks in *The Fate of the Edsel and Other Business Adventures* sets the full amount lost at $350,000,000, and if this is high, it seems to represent a careful assessment of expenditures less recoverable items. That the Ford Motor Company took the adventure in stride is proof of its sound financial condition.[15]

Most Americans knew the names of the principal Ford cars; many could distinguish at sight the Park Lane models in the Mercury line from the Montclair series, and some could identify at a glance the Taunus from the Ford works in Germany, the Consul from Dagenham, and the Meteor Montcalm from the Canadian subsidiary. Not so many knew that Ford trucks were available in a similar variety of forms, and that their factory sales in 1959 amounted to 30.6 per cent of all sales of such commercial vehicles in America. Nor did they know that the tractor and implement division that year was marketing thirty-two models of tractors for farm and industry, and with them a variety of seeding, cultivating, and harvesting machines. The Aeronutronic

Division was busy with research in weapon and space systems, missile range system, instrumentation, and other areas where it might at any moment be asked to undertake extensive projects. At one time, in 1955, the value of defense products, with emphasis on turbo-jet engines and B-47 airplane wings, had reached $259,000,000. Altogether, the company was the third largest manufacturing enterprise in the country, and its Rouge complex remained the largest single integrated manufacturing plant in the world, while its automated factories at Cleveland, Buffalo, and Chicago have introduced or improved new techniques of production. Its engineering buildings at Dearborn, now complete, represent a coordinated effort in research facilities that has been immensely useful in the recent creative period of automotive engineering.

4.

The best definition of a company, one Ford leader said, was people working together: "The cleverest engineering, the most up-to-date plants, the finest tools will not bring success in industry unless teamwork is added." Teamwork the Ford Motor Company had systematically cultivated since the end of the Second World War. A good many public or semi-public agencies might have envied it its thirty-one newspapers scattered over the country, its newsletters and teletyped bulletins, and its regular supervisory and management meetings, which cultivated a sense of unity. Colorful organization gave its eight thousand dealers cohesion, and sound public relations gave them pride in the company.

But no matter how much the company conformed to the general demands of the American economy, no matter how closely its strategy resembled that of the other automotive corporations, it retained an individuality all its own. Since the Second World War it had made enormous gains in flexibility, resourcefulness, and scientific expertness; company executives could safely "play it by ear" because they could shift rapidly to meet changing tastes, altering the emphasis on one market segment or engineering feature. This adaptability owed much to to the new regime, but something also to the spirit of an older day. It was part of Ford tradition to make daring moves, introduce epochal innovations, and meet a sudden challenge with dashing expedients. It was also part of the tradition to divine what the plain people wanted. Ford was a magical name when the first Henry was in his prime, marketing the Model T, smashing the Selden Patent, sailing the Peace Ship, and mobilizing his aides in a burst of creative energy to devise the Model A and the V-8. Ford was made a magical name again by Henry II and his helpers, reorganizing the company, bringing forth an unprecedented variety of useful products, making the Foundation rich and powerful, and fixing new social frontiers in its relations with labor.

With corporations, as with individuals, success depends upon tough and stubborn thinking, hard work, integrity, capacity for stern self-criticism, and the optimism that stimulates enterprise. Companies, like nations, must from time to time be reborn in the sense in which Lincoln at Gettysburg demanded a rebirth. The story of the Ford Motor Company, like other stories of business, politics, war, or any other human endeavor, has unhappy passages. But from its ordeals it took enhanced strength; and when viewed as a whole this is perhaps the pre-eminent American story of a great industrial vision transmuted into hard fact.

As we call in review the principal personages of the tale—Henry Ford, Edsel Ford, James Couzens, Harry Wills, Walter Flanders, Dean Marquis, P. E. Martin, William S. Knudsen, Percival Perry, Charles Sorensen, Henry Ford II, Ernest Breech, and others—we realize how earnestly they wrought, and how valiantly they prevailed: they builded better than they knew. The history of the company included the birth of mass production; it included in Model T the most famous vehicle in human annals, an ever-cheaper car made in ever-greater numbers by workers paid ever-higher wages; it included valiant service in two great wars, with the roar and clangor of Highland Park, Willow Run, and the Rouge helping meet the desperate demands of the nation; it included shining chapters of social progressiveness before the First World War, and after the Second; and it included the rearing of one of the world's greatest pillars of philanthropy and public service. It is simple truth to say that the Ford Motor Company changed the face of American civilization and affected patterns of life throughout half the globe. From the dark threats of its most critical years it emerged in a signal demonstration of its capacity to recreate itself, finding enhanced strength and brightened aims.

# CHAPTER I
## Crisis of 1933

1. *The Public Papers & Addresses of Franklin D. Roosevelt*, N.Y., 1938, II, 11–15 (inaugural address); Arthur M. Schlesinger, Jr., *The Coming of the New Deal*, Boston, 1959, 1–2 (inauguration); Acc. 6, Boxes 150–156 (Edsel's economies); *Ford News*, XIII, Feb. 1933, 26 (Ford's opinions).

2. President's Research Committee on Social Trends, *Recent Social Trends in the United States:* 1 Vol. ed., N.Y., 1933, 141, hereafter cited as *Recent Social Trends; N.Y. Times*, Jan. 8, 1933 (dealers, garages, and filling stations); Allan Nevins and Frank Ernest Hill, *Ford: Expansion and Challenge, 1915–1933*, N.Y. 1957, *passim* (hereafter cited as *Ford: Expansion and Challenge*).

3. Henry Ford in collaboration with Samuel Crowther, *Moving Forward*, Garden City, N.Y., 1931, 11 (overproduction); *N.Y. Times*, Aug. 10, 1930 (on depression); *Ford: Expansion and Challenge*, 529, 574 ($7-day, plant expansion); *Ward's 1939 Automotive Yearbook*, Detroit, 1939 (sales and percentages). The $7-day was abandoned in 1931 for a $6 minimum, which quickly sank to $4.

4. Federal Trade Commission, *Report on the Motor Vehicle Industry*, 75th Cong., 3rd Sess. Wash., D.C., 1939, 515, hereafter cited as *FTC Report* (effects of depression on industry and comparative figures motor industry and all others); Arthur M. Schlesinger, Jr., *The Crisis of the Old Order, 1919–1923*, Boston, 1957, 248 (national income).

5. *FTC Report*, 27 (indep. co. sales), 491 (GM loss), 597 (Chrysler), 649 (Ford); *Ford: Expansion and Challenge*, 572, 585 (cars dropped); E. D. Kennedy, *The Automobile Industry*, N.Y., 1941, 199–249. For emergence of cos. from receiverships see *ibid.* 267, 282, and for Reo's demise (1938), 306–307.

6. *FTC Report*, 498–499, 432–435, 440, 491; Arthur Pound, *The Turning Wheel: the Story of General Motors Through Twenty-five Years, 1908–1933*, Garden City, N.Y., 1934, Chs. 17, 18 (Canada & overseas).

7. *FTC Report*, G.M. Section; Norman Beasley, *Knudsen*, N.Y., 1947; Alfred P. Sloan, Jr. (in collab. with Boyden Sparkes) *Adventures of a White Collar Man*, N.Y., 1941.

8. *FTC Report*, 549 ff. (assets) and 591 (Plymouth sales); *Ford: Expansion and Challenge*, 471–475 and 576–577. See also Chrysler's autobiography (in collab. with Boyden Sparkes), *Life of an American Workman*, N.Y., 1950. The Plymouth appeared in 1930 when it sold 63,287, and rose steadily to 242,315 in 1933.

9. *Ford: Expansion and Challenge*, 596; *FTC Report*, 645. The two totals given are a few million dollars different—$125,000,000 as against $117,923,666 (FTC). Various ways of reporting this total might account for the difference.

10. *Ford: Expansion and Challenge*, Chs. 11, 22; Anne O'Hare McCormick, "Ford Seeks a New Deal for Industry," *N.Y. Times*, May 29, 1932; *FTC Report*, 657.

11. *FTC Report*, 600 (integration), 660 (foreign investments); *Ford: Expansion and Challenge*, Ch. 7 and *passim* (Lincoln Plant); *ibid.*, Ch. 9 (village industries, Ford Fleet, mines, etc.); Report of Controller's Office on Highland Park Plant, 1949. *Ford: Expansion and Challenge* traces the shift of the chief volume of work from Highland Park to the Rouge, and Ch. 21 deals with the Ford overseas empire. In 1932 the Briggs Manufacturing Co. occupied 1,700,-

000 sq. ft. of space and Highland Park, and other outside cos. rented more, using 40% in all. It should be noted that Ford investments by no means represented the full capitalization of overseas companies.

12. Characterizations of Ford executives are based on reminiscences by Ford employes, on Ford correspondence, and on newspaper and magazine accounts. The price ranges for cars are cited from the current press. See also Kennedy, *The Automobile Industry*, Chs. 10, 11, and 12.

13. "Ford vs. Blue Eagle," *Newsweek*, Sept. 9, 1933 and Chicago *Times*, Oct. 19, 1936 (Ford on politics).

14. *New International Yearbook*, 1933, N.Y., 1934, 798 and Dwight Lowell Dumond, *America in Our Times, 1896–1946*, N.Y., 1947, 464 (unemployment); U.S. Dept. of Commerce, Bur. of the Census, *Historical Statistics of the United States, 1789–1945*, Wash., D.C., 1949, 273 (bank failures), 274 (losses to depositors). Dumond states that "at the peak" unemployment was estimated by various experts at from 12,000,000 to 15,000,000; in Mar. 1933 the National Industrial Conference Board set it at 13,203,000 and the Amer. Federation of Labor at 13,689,000.

15. "Highlights of Michigan Banking: History Since the Turn of the Century," *Michigan Investor*, LI, July 26, 1952, 106; Detroit daily press, Feb.–Mar. 1933, *passim;* U.S. Congressional Committee on Banking and Currency, *Stock Exchange Practices*, Hearings 73rd Cong., 2nd Sess., Parts 9–13, testimony of Edsel Ford, 4657–4696, hereafter cited as *Senate Hearings on Banking*.

16. *Ibid.*, testimony E. C. Kanzler, 4570; Committee Exhibit No. 29, 4756 (RFC Loans to Guardian Group to Dec. 19, 1933); testimony National Bank Examiner Alfred P. Leyburn and Edsel Ford, 4627, 4691–4692.

17. Harry Barnard, *Independent Man: the Life of Senator James Couzens*, N.Y., 1958, 225, 227; E. G. Liebold, *Reminiscences; Ford: Expansion and Challenge*, Chs. 1, 4 (Ford-Couzens earlier relationship).

18. *Senate Hearings on Banking*, testimony Edsel Ford, John J. McKee, and Wilson W. Mills, 4692, 4733–4734, 5487, 5511; *Detroit Free Press*, Feb. 15, 1933; Mins. RFC Bd. Dirs. Feb. 13, 1933; "Senator Couzens and His Banking Holiday," *Detroit Saturday Night*, XXVII, Feb. 18, 1933, 1; Liebold, *Reminiscences; N.Y. Times*, Feb. 24, 1933 (Ford on banks).

19. Acc. 285, Box 1520, and *Detroit Free Press*, Feb. 27, 1933 (Ford offer); *Senate Hearings on Banking*, copy letter, Wilson W. Mills to J. K. McKee of RFC, 4753; letters rejecting Ford offer, and data on Manufacturers Natl. Bank, Acc. 285, Boxes 1520, 1521, 1721; "Detroit Gets a Bank," *Business Week*, LXIII, Apr. 5, 1933, 5 (Natl. Bank of Detroit); *First Annual Report of Natl. Bank* of Detroit, Jan. 9, 1935, 3; *Detroit Free Press*, Apr. 2, 1933.

20. Detroit *Times*, Apr. 16, 1933; Detroit *Free Press*, May 9, 1933.

21. *Public Papers*, etc., *op. cit.*, I, 742–755; Basil Rauch, *History of the New Deal, 1933–1938*, N.Y., 1944, *passim*, and Broadus Mitchell, *Depression Decade*, N.Y., 1947, 228–267 (Black-Connery Bill & NIRA); Leverett S. Lyon *et al.*, *The National Recovery Administration: an Analysis and Appraisal*, Wash., D.C., 1935, 3 (FDR attitude); *World Tomorrow*, Mar. 8, 1933 (Ford opinion). While Ford does not name the bill, clearly he has it in mind.

22. Lyon, *op. cit.*, 4; *The Secret Diary of Harold L. Ickes: The First Thousand Days, 1933–1936*, N.Y., 1953, 52–53; Russell Owen, "Gen. Johnson Wages a Peace-Time War," *N.Y. Times* (magazine), July 30, 1933; *ibid.*, July 10, 1933.

23. Detroit *News*, Je. 16, 1933 (Ford on NRA); Kennedy, *Automobile Industry*, 247–249, 253; Detroit *Free Press*, Je. 23, 1933 (sub-com. meetings); H. L. Moekle to J. Crawford, Aug. 11, 1933, Acc. 203, Box 3; Moekle, *Reminiscences*.

24. Transcript telephone conversation, and letter Johnson to HF, Je. 27, 1933, Acc. 52, Box 8; Charles E. Sorensen (with Samuel T. Williamson), *My Forty Years with Ford*, N.Y., 1956, 258–259, hereafter cited as *My Forty Years with Ford;* Hugh S. Johnson, *The Blue Eagle from Egg to Earth*, Garden City, N.Y. 1935, 236, 238; *Detroit News*, July 27, 28, 1933; *Detroit Times*, July 29, 1933. Actually, the Ford work-week at this time was 48 hours, but for long periods earlier had been 40.

25. Moekle, *Reminiscences;* Brisbane to Campsall, Sept. 7, 1933, Acc. 285, Box 1533; *N.Y.*

*Times,* Sept. 10, 1933 (HF and NACC); *Fortune,* VII, Dec. 1933, 132; Ford Notebooks, Ford Motor Co., Dearborn, Brisbane, while advising Ford to sign, supported him when he did not (see column clipped to letter of Sept. 20, 1933, Acc. 285, Box 1533).

26. Peter F. Drucker, "Henry Ford: Success and Failure," *Harpers Magazine,* CXCV, July 1947, 1; *Ford: Expansion and Challenge,* 313, 323, 617–619; *Time,* Aug. 7, 1933 (Chrysler, Chevrolet, Johnson); *Detroit News,* Aug. 15, 1933 (invitation); notes by Liebold on telephone conversation, Acc. 572, Box 19; *N.Y. Times,* Aug. 30, 1933 (Johnson threat).

27. Cleveland *Plain Dealer,* Aug. 31, 1933; *Pittsfield Eagle,* Sept. 5, 1933; *New Republic,* LXXVI, Sept. 13, 1933, 115–117; *N.Y. Daily News,* Aug. 31, 1933.

28. HF to Charles Edison, Oct. 6, 1933, Acc. 1, Box 117; transcript telephone conversation, Cameron-Edison, and letters Edison to HF, Oct. 8, 9, 1933, Acc. 285, Box 9.

29. *N.Y. Sun,* Oct. 27, 1933 and *N.Y. Times,* Nov. 4, 1933 (FDR ruling); Wash. *Times,* Oct. 27, 1933 (Johnson); E. C. Simons, Govt. Sales Mgr. Fleet Sales Dept., Ford Div., on sales in NRA period, Acc. 203, Box 1; *N.Y. Sun,* Oct. 26 (War Dept.); Brooklyn *Eagle,* Oct. 29, 1933 (Sabine bid); Wash. *Herald,* Oct. 28, 1933 (FMC statements).

30. *N.Y. Times,* Oct. 27, Nov. 12, 1933 (McCarl rulings) and Dec. 2, 3, 1933 (award of contract); *N.Y. Sun,* Apr. 7, 1934 and *Newsweek,* Dec. 1, 1934 (later rulings).

31. Corresp. in Acc. 6, Boxes 149–152, Acc. 19, Box 1933, and Acc. 572, Box 19.

32. Acc. 285, Box 1533 (Brisbane's broadcast); Gladys H. Kelsey, "Detroit Sees Ford as Industry's Hero," *N.Y. Times,* Nov. 4, 1933; *ibid.,* Will Rogers's daily message.

33. *Ford News,* XIII, Je. 1933, 105, July, 123, 127, and Nov., 203–204; Acc. 19, Box 1933 (advertisements); corresp., Acc. 6, Boxes 149 ff.; Acc. 285 and 572, *passim.* The letter quoted is from Acc. 6, Box 170, and was sent to Edsel on July 10, 1935 by the Sec'y. of the Detroit Bd. of Commerce.

34. *Ford News,* XIV, Jan. 1934, 10–11; Detroit *Free Press,* Dec. 8, 1933 (HF on FDR); *N.Y. Times,* Jan. 11, 1934 (Ford on NRA).

35. FDR to HF, July 28, 1933, Acc. 587, Box 67 (for HF's birthday); FDR to HF, Nov. 8, 1934 and HF to FDR, Nov. 16, and Marvin McIntyre to HF, Nov. 21 (on Edsel), all in Acc. 285, Box 1676.

36. *Ford News,* XIV, Nov. 1934, 207 (1935 plans); *ibid.,* XV, Apr. 1935, 63, 65 (Rouge expansion); D. D. Hovey, Factory count, Jan. 23, 1935, and comparable figures for other years, Acc. 38, Box 77; Acc. 285, Box 1720 and 1732 (stickers).

# CHAPTER II
## The Troubled March of Labor

1. Interv. Richard T. Frankensteen, July 28, 1958.

2. Leo Wolman, "Labor," in Committee on Recent Economic Changes (Herbert Hoover, chairman), *Recent Economic Changes in the United States,* 2 vols., N.Y., 1929, II, 479 ff.; Preston W. Slosson, *The Great Crusade and After, 1914–1928,* N.Y., 1931, 170–175; Selig Perlman, *A History of Trade Unionism in the United States,* N.Y., 1922, *passim.*

3. Edward Levinson, *Labor on the March,* N.Y., 1938, 42–46.

4. Benjamin Gitlow, *The Whole of Their Lives: Communism in America,* with a foreword by Max Eastman, N.Y., 1948, by a top Communist leader who recanted, treats Communist activities in this era, 145–295.

5. Gitlow, 218–226, covers the Communist campaign against Ford; cf. Sorensen, *My Forty Years with Ford,* 254–256.

6. On Feb. 23, 1932, a Communist meeting was held at the Rouge plant gates, District Organizer R. Baker spoke, and just four workers joined the Communist Party: *Daily Worker,* Feb. 24, 1932. On another occasion, a man threw a brick through a Ford Employment Office window but was released after arrest: Detroit *Free Press,* Mar. 9, 1932.

7. *Detroit News,* Mar. 11, 14, 1932.

8. Gitlow, *The Whole of Their Lives*, 223–226.

9. For press accounts of the affair see Detroit *Free Press*, Mar., 1932; Detroit *Labor News*, Mar. 11, 1932; for comment, *New Republic*, XXXV, Mar. 30, 1932.

10. Harry Bennett, *We Never Called Him Henry*, N.Y., 1951, 92–94. See also Detroit *Mirror*, Mar. 12, 1932.

11. Detroit *Mirror*, Mar. 12; Detroit *Labor News*, Mar. 11, 1932; Irving Bacon, *Reminiscences*, give varying accounts.

12. *Detroit Times*, Mar. 13, *The Nation*, Mar. 30, 1932.

13. *New Republic*, XXXV, Mar. 30, 1932.

14. See Ch. 7 of *The Whole of Their Lives*, "Organized Confusion," 204–240.

15. For the Briggs strike see *Automobile Topics*, Jan. 28, Feb. 4, 1933; *Motor*, Mar. 1933; *Business Week*, Feb. 8, 15, 23, 1933; *N.Y. Times*, Jan. 27 et seq.; Keith Sward, *The Legend of Henry Ford*, N.Y., 1948, 220–222; A. J. Muste, *The Automobile Industry and Organized Labor*, N.Y., 1936, 29.

16. Feb. 8, 1933, 8.

17. *Business Week*, Feb. 15, 1933, 67.

18. Benjamin Stolberg, *The Story of the CIO*, N.Y., 1938, 156–158; Levinson, *Labor on the March*, 41–42, 56–59.

19. *American Year Book, 1933*, 1–49, 343–444.

20. J. M. Clark and others, "National Recovery Administration: Report of the President's Committee of Analysis," 75th Cong., 1st Sess., House Doc. 158, is illuminating.

21. Sidney Fine, "The Ford Motor Company and the NRA," *Business History Review*, XXXII, Winter 1958, 354–385; Levinson, *Labor on the March*, 60; Richard S. Childs, "The New Partnership Comes to Detroit," *Common Sense*, Nov. 1933, 13–16.

22. Henry Ford's ideas on labor were really not so much ideas as a melange of prejudices. In 1923 he had told a *Collier's* reporter that unions were organized by Jewish financiers to interrupt work. Later he suggested to a *N.Y. Times* reporter that union movements to serve the workingmen were really schemes to benefit "The financial interests and divided school of business." High finance, he remarked, wanted control both of management and labor, but labor was too shrewd to be fooled. "I belong to 'labor,' " he said. "It is all I have done all my life." William Richards, *The Last Billionaire*, Bantam ed. N.Y., 1956, 273; Sorenson, *My Forty Years*, 258 ff.; Bennett, *op. cit.*, 96.

23. *Automobile Topics*, July 1, 1933, 323; Sidney Fine, "President Roosevelt and the Automobile Code," *Mississippi Valley Historical Review*, XLV, Jan. 1959.

24. Childs, "The New Partnership Comes to Detroit," *Common Sense*, Nov. 1933, 14.

25. *N.Y. Times*, Aug. 18, 1933.

26. Levinson, *Labor on the March*, 55, 56. For the text, see NRA, *Codes of Fair Competition*, II, 255, 256.

27. Sidney Fine, "President Roosevelt and the Automobile Code," *ut supra*, 26–29.

28. *N.Y. Times*, Aug. 30, 1933.

29. *N.Y. Times*, Sept. 7, 1933; Childs, "The New Partnership," *ut supra*.

30. *Automotive Industries*, Sept. 2, 1933, 267.

31. Fine, "Pres. Roosevelt & the Automobile Code," *ut supra*, 26; Fine, "The Ford Motor Co. & the NRA," *ut supra*, 363; *N.Y. Times*, Aug. 6, 1933; Notes, "Pay Roll Dept.," Ford Archives.

32. Levinson, *Labor on the March*, 76, 77, 98, 191 ff.; Joel Seidman, *Union Rights and Union Duties*, N.Y., 1943, 95–97; Samuel Romer, "That Automobile Strike," *The Nation*, CXL, Feb. 6, 1935, 162.

33. Fine, "The Ford Motor Co. & the NRA," *ut supra*, covers Chester Strike in detail.

34. Fine, *ibid.*, 371–378.

35. Fine, *ibid.*, 378–385; *N.Y. Times*, Jan. 9, 1934.

36. In the Rouge plant the average weekly wage of employes had dropped in the years 1929–1935 from $36.97 to $23.58; and the minimum daily wage paid by the Ford Company had dropped from $7 to $4. *FTC Report*, 668.

37. *N.Y. Times,* Mar.–Apr. 1934; Levinson, *Labor on the March,* 60, 61.

38. Levinson, *op. cit.,* 61.

39. A full record of the "peace plan" terms, and of Roosevelt's remarks on it, may be found in the *N.Y. Times* of Mar. 26, 1934. The President said he looked forward to the development of "a kind of works council in industry in which all groups of employes, whatever may be their choice of organization or form of representation, may participate in joint conference with their employers." Nicholas Kelley was counsel for Chrysler.

40. *N.Y. Times,* Detroit *Times,* Mar. 27, 1934; Fine, "The Origins of the United Automobile Workers, 1933–1935," *Journal of Economic History,* Sept. 1958, 249–282.

41. Interv. Frankensteen, July 28, 1958. Walter Chrysler expressed his views on company unions in *Automobile Topics,* Oct. 14, 1933, 408.

42. Interv. Ed Hall, July 23, 1958.

43. William Collins' attack on the Wolman policy is in the *N.Y. Times,* Apr. 10, 1934.

44. Pickering's letter of Oct. 4, 1934, and Martin's letter of Jan. 19, 1935, are in the Martin Papers.

45. Levinson, *Labor on the March,* 66.

46. Leo Huberman, *The Labor Spy Racket,* N.Y., 1937, 6, 13 ff.; Subcommittee on Education and Labor, Hearings Pursuant to Senate Res. 266, 75th Cong., 1st Sess., 4, *passim.*

47. Interv. John Fitzpatrick, Aug. 28, 1958.

48. *Ibid., passim.*

49. National Labor Relations Board v. Ford Motor Company, No. 7919, Petition of Respondent, 21.

50. Walter Galenson, *The CIO Challenge to the AFL: A History of the American Labor Movement, 1935–1951,* Cambridge, Mass., 1960; A. M. Schlesinger, Jr., *The Coming of the New Deal,* Boston, 1958, 414, 415.

51. This entire subject is covered in Levinson, *Labor on the March,* Chs. 6 and 7; Stolberg, *Story of the CIO,* Ch. 6; and Sidney Fine, "The Origins of the United Automobile Workers, 1933–1935," 273 ff.

# CHAPTER III
## Challenge of the Future

1. *N.Y. Times,* July 28, 1936; *Automotive Industries,* LXXV, Aug. 1, 1936, 134; *Ward's 1939 Automotive Yearbook,* 36–37; *FTC Report,* 531.

2. *Moving Forward,* 148; interv. J. R. Davis, July 25–26, 1960; *Ford: Expansion and Challenge,* 249–253 (FMC engineering 1924–1933); Hartley Barclay, *Ford Production Methods,* N.Y., 1936, 61; Laurence Sheldrick, Dale Roeder, *Reminiscences.*

3. Sheldrick, *Reminiscences;* Reginald M. Cleveland and S. T. Williamson, *The Road Is Yours,* 235 (quoting Sloan).

4. Sorensen, *My Forty Years with Ford,* 225; Roeder, *Reminiscences.*

5. Sheldrick, Roeder, J. L. McCloud, D. J. Hutchins, in their reminiscences. Dozens of reminiscences by Ford engineers support the conclusions set forth here. There is no evidence of any obvious deterioration in Henry Ford prior to the late nineteen-thirties, as indicated in Chap. I. The authors have talked with many persons such as Charles A. Lindbergh and J. R. Davis about Ford's appearance and vigor in the nineteen-thirties, who support this conclusion. Later we have abundant evidence of failure.

6. Barclay, *Ford Production Methods,* 32–33 (expansion program); *N.Y. Times,* May 29, 1938 and E. F. Wait, *Reminiscences; American Machinist,* LXXXIII, Feb. 22, 1939, 69–72 (on second expansion program).

7. Barclay, *op. cit.,* 33; *Iron Age,* CXLII, July 21, 1938, 46–47 and *Metal & Alloys,* VI, Oct. 1935, 259–263 (cast steel); *N.Y. Times,* July 9, 1933 (new enamel) and Dec. 29, 1936 (rear-engine car); *Automobile Topics,* June 1, 1935, 186 (rust-proof).

8. *Ford: Expansion and Challenge*, Ch. 22; Cowling, *Reminiscences;* interv. Walker Williams, Jan. 13, 1960; interv. J. R. Davis; *FTC Report, passim;* Arthur Pound, *The Turning Wheel*, 427–428 (customer research). See also Acc. 78, *passim,* for FMC attitude toward dealers.

9. *FTC Report*, 280 ff. (finance cos.); Acc. 390, Boxes 41–44 (UCC), and *Annual Report of UCC* in Box 43; interv. E. C. Kanzler, Jan. 14, 1960; *FTC Report*, 660–661 (review of UCC); *Automobile Topics*, May 20, 1933, 87 (Ford's statement); Letter, W. C. Cowling to Branch Managers and Dealers, May 17, 1933, Acc. 78, Box 2.

10. Farkas, Roeder, Sheldrick, in their reminiscences. Correspondence in Acc. 38 supports this description of the early days of V-8.

11. Interv. Davis (obstacles to sales); *Ward's Report 1939*, 36; Acc. 78, Box 22 (Elgin Race); *Printer's Ink*, CLXIV, Aug. 24, 1933, 37 (N.H. contest); *Motor*, Aug. 1933, 100, and Acc. 78, Box 2 (re-service plan)

12. *Advertisnig & Selling*, XII, Dec. 21, 1933, 50 (Ford quote); *Ford News*, XIV, Jan., 1934, 6 ff. (Waring, trucks, Lincoln); and Feb. 2 (Jan. Production); *N.Y. Times*, Dec. 10, 1933 (exhibit); *Printer's Ink*, CLXV, Dec. 14, 1933, 17–18 and CLXVI, Jan. 18, 1934, 28 (advertising details). The *Ford News* for Nov. 1933, XIII, 203–204, describes the exhibit.

13. *Ford News*, XIV, Mar. 1934, 46–47 (Gilmore) and 43 (Fair plans); *ibid.*, Apr. 1934, 63 ($5 a day) and 75 (no price increases); *ibid.*, Je. 1934, 104 ff. (Ford at Fair); *Motor*, Aug. 1934, 92 (quote); *Automobile Topics*, Apr. 7, 1934, 381, 386 (prices); *Sales Management*, XXXV, Sept. 1, 1934, 188 (advertising). In the first half of 1933, *Sales Management* pointed out, Ford used 1,493,565 lines of newspaper advertising, and in the same period for 1934, a total of 4,799,618.

14. *Ibid.* (quote); *Magazine of Wall Street*, Je. 23, 1934, 243–244 and *Motor*, Aug. 1934, 92 (strikes); *Ward's Report, 1939*, 36 (sales figs.); *Ford News*, XIV, Oct. 1934, 184 (World Series) and Nov. 1934, 203 (Sun Eve. Hr.); *Motor*, Jan. 1935, 134 (Dalton); Acc. 78, Boxes 24, 25; *Ward's, op. cit.*, (1935 figs.); *Magazine of Wall Street*, LVI, May 25, 1935, 154–155 (Chevrolet troubles).

15. *Ford News*, XV, Nov. 1935, 208 ff. (Lincoln Zephyr and Lincoln) and 203 (Ford cars); *N.Y. Times*, Oct. 27, Nov. 3, 1935 (Plymouth and Chevrolet cars).

16. Interv. Williams; R. Gnau to CES, Apr. 28, 1936, Acc. 38, Box 79; interv. Davis. Davis felt that neither HF nor CES was willing to understand the difficulties of the dealers.

17. Acc. 78, Boxes 26 and 27; *FTC Report*, 653, and FMC Release, Mar. 14, 1958 (sales). *Ward's, op. cit.*

18. Cowling, Sheldrick, Roeder, in their reminiscences; *Ford News*, XIV, Dec. 1934, 226 and 229; *Ward's, op. cit.* (truck sales).

19. Sheldrick, Esper. Roeder, in their reminiscences; R. Gnau to CES, May 13, 1936, Acc. 38, Box 79 (wind tunnel); *Heating, Piping, and Air Conditioning*, Aug. 1938, 530 (temperature control devices) and *Motor*, Aug. 1938, 68 (final form of tunnel).

20. Sheldrick, *Reminiscences; Ford: Expansion and Challenge*, 500–505.

21. *Ford: Expansion and Challenge*, 490–491; *Automotive Industries*, LXXIII, Oct. 26, 1935 (Rouge soy bean plant); Ford Property Management Records, Ford Motor Company, Dearborn.

22. *Ford: Expansion and Challenge*, 226–230; Ford Property Management Records; *Ford News*, V, May 15, 1925, 3 (early plants), XVI, Mar. 1936, 43 (workers), and XIX, Mar. 1939, 53 (on America); W. J. Cameron, *The Ford Sunday Evening Hour Talks, 1934–1942*, 8 vols., Dearborn, 1935–1943, *passim;* W. J. Cameron, "Decentralization of Industry," *Mechanical Engineering*, LIX, July 1937, 487; *Fortune*, VIII, Dec. 1933, 65; Liebold, *Reminiscences*.

23. Detroit press, Nov. 6, 7, 1936; *Ford News*, XVI, Dec. 1936, 223 ff.; interv. Williams.

24. *Ford News*, XVI, Dec. 1936, 229 ff.; *Automotive Industries*, LXXV, Nov. 14, 1936; Cowling to dealers, Nov. 16, 1936 and telegram Feb. 22, 1937, Acc. 78, Box 28; *Ward's Report 1939; FTC Report*, 649 (Ford profit).

25. EBF to Branch Managers, Dec. 22, 1937, Acc. 78, Box 30 and *Detroit News*, Dec. 24, 1937 (Davis's appointment).

# CHAPTER IV
## Overseas Domain

The background of this story of European operations is treated in Nevins and Hill, *Ford: Expansion and Challenge,* Chapters 14 and 21. All lives of Henry Ford neglect his manufacturing activities in foreign lands, and no real attempt has yet been made to treat the history of the automotive industry in Europe.

Considering the turmoil of the nineteen-thirties, documentary sources are fairly ample. In the Ford Archives in Dearborn, Edsel Ford's office file, Accession 6, reflects his close attention to the foreign companies throughout the decade. Sorensen was equally interested, and his office file, Accession 38, contains valuable letters and reports. Accession 58, Boxes 1, 2, etc., offers a mass of correspondence on the German company. Henry Ford's office file is Accession 285, and provides diminishing returns as the years pass, but is not to be neglected. The minutes of Matford are in Accession 334. The audit reports in Accession 415 are valuable on many matters, including finances; see especially "Report on Financial Condition Ford SAF, Historical Section."

Sir Percival Perry sent to Dearborn annual reports of the English company, FMC Ltd., and minutes of meetings of all companies 1932–1939, which are in International Division, Central File; additional material appears in Accessions 320 (Roumania); 606 (France), and 608 (Spain). The useful "Memorandum on European Organizations" by R. I. Roberge, June 20, 1935, is in Accession 507, Box 95. Summaries of the annual reports of British and chief continental businesses were published in the London *Times,* and with useful comment in the London *Economist.* Material on Ford history in Europe, Asia, and Australasia is also available in files of the British magazine *Motor.*

The Reminiscences of R. I. Roberge and H. L. Moekle throw light on personalities, ideas, and policies in the foreign operations.

1. For methods of supervision see Roberge, *Reminiscences,* and letters in Acc. 6 and Acc. 38; Dearborn had no unified foreign division.

2. Dr. Heinrich Albert to CES, Aug. 17, 1936, Acc. 38, Box 33; M. Wiesmyer to Russell Gnau, London, Jan. 5, 1936, Acc. 38, Box 31.

3. Speech of Graeme K. Howard in *Report of Management Meeting No. 15,* Jan. 1949; *Ford: Expansion and Challenge,* 547.

4. FMC Ltd., *Annual Reports 1933–1937;* Craig to Perry, Mar. 3, 1937. Acc. 38, Box 36.

5. *Motor,* Feb. 23, Apr. 13, 30, 1937 (Ford models); London *Economist* May 1, 7, 1937 (profits); Thornhill Cooper; Report production of FMC Ltd., Acc. 38, Box 36.

6. Roberge, *Reminiscences;* corr. in Acc. 6; accounts of Société d'Investissement Ford, Acc. 313, Box 1; mins. FMC Ltd., sharehldrs. mtg., 1932–1934.

7. Roberge, "Memorandum on European Organization," Je. 20, 1935, Acc. 507, Box 95; Albert-Sorensen corr., Acc. 38, Box 40; Thornhill Cooper-Edsel Ford corr. on southeastern Europe, Acc. 390, Box 84; "Greece-Athens Historical Data," International Div. mins. Bd. Dirs., Spanish, Dutch companies, *ibid.*

8. Dollfus-CES corr., Acc. 38, Box 32; Mathis-EBF corr., Acc. 507, Box 63; annual reports Ford SAF Bd. Dirs., 1935, 1936, in *ibid.*

9. Mathis to HF, Aug. 25, 1936, Acc. 6, Box 346.

10. Dollfus-CES corr., Acc. 38, Box 32; Dollfus to EBF, Feb. 27, 1936, Acc. 6, Box 335; Moekle to CES, Feb. 18, 1937, Acc. 38, Box 37. For background see D. W. Brogan, *The French Nation,* N.Y., 1957, 286.

11. Mathis had threatened a suit against Matford and Ford SAF, asking 142 million francs for alleged injuries. Arbitrators ruled Nov. 29, 1939, that his general claims were groundless, that as greater Matford publicity had been given the Ford name than the Mathis name, he was entitled to indemnity. As the Ford attorney warned executives that an appeal would be long

and costly, Mathis finally got the 5.5 million francs. See cables in Acc. 507, Box 66, and mins. Ford SAF Bd. Dirs., Feb. 18, 1942, Acc. 606, Box 2.

12. Dollfus-EBF corr., Acc. 507, Box 67; Riecks and Dollfus corr. with CES, Acc. 38, Box 40; La Chambre to Dollfus, Jan. 31, 1939, Acc. 6, Box 354; mins. Ford SAF Bd. Dirs., 1938, Acc. 38, Box 40.

13. Prince Louis Ferdinand, *The Rebel Prince,* Chicago, 1952, 261.

14. Albert-CES corr., Acc. 38, Box 23; reports by A. L. Byrns and H. L. Moekle, Apr. 15, May 24, 1935, Acc. 415, Box 1.

15. Roberge, *Reminiscences;* Diestel and Albert corr. with Reich government, 1936, Acc. 38, Box 33; Albert, "Memorandum," Mar. 9, 1936, Acc. 6, Box 335; mins. FMC-AG Bd. Dirs.. 1936, Acc. 38, Box 33.

16. Albert's "Strictly Confidential Memorandum" on Diestel, Aug. 17, 1936, is in Acc. 6, Box 335. See the large Perry-CES-Albert corr. in Acc. 38, Boxes 33, 38.

17. On German affairs see Roberge, V. Y. Tallberg, *Reminiscences;* Roberge, "Memorandum," Jan. 4, 1937, Acc. 38, Box 38; manager's reports for 1936, 1937, 1938, in FMC-AG Business Reports and Balance Sheets, Select File; R. H. Schmidt, "Memorandum on Production Program for Cologne, 1939–40," Acc. 6, Box 346.

18. For Spanish affairs see Ubach, "Memo" and letters, Aug. 6, 8, 1936, Acc. 6, Box 335; Perry-CES cables July–Aug. 1936, Acc. 38, Box 34; Perry-Jenkins corr. and Jenkins' reports, *ibid.;* mins. Ford Iberica Bd. Dirs. 1936–1939, Acc. 608, Box 2.

19. Nevins and Hill, *Ford: Expansion and Challenge,* 557–559; Perry-CES corr. 1935, Acc. 38, Box 29; Reports FMC of Egypt, Je. 30, Sept. 30, 1935, Acc. 38, Box 29; FMC Ltd., sales statistics, *ibid.; N.Y. Times,* Oct. 18, Dec. 16, 1935; Perry to Craig, Je. 8, 1936, Acc. 38, Box 34.

20. Perry to CES, Dec. 20, 1937, Acc. 38, Box 85.. Istanbul data in Central Files, International Division; mins. Ford Romana Bd. Dirs., Acc. 320, Box 1; mins. FMC (Belg.) Bd. Dirs., Feb. 3, May 2, 1938, International Div.; corr. Acc. 38, Box 39; corr. on both, Acc. 38, Box 34.

21. Mins. FMC Ltd. Bd. Dirs., Dec. 24, 1936, Acc. 38, Box 31; Perry-CES corr., Apr.–May, 1937, Acc. 38, Box 36; FMC Ltd. *Annual Reports 1938, 1939, 1940,* Acc. 285, Box 22. The London *Economist,* CXLV, Aug. 15, 1942, 214, has a three-year summary on FMC Ltd.

22. Tallberg, *Reminiscences;* Roberge, *Reminiscences;* FMC Ltd. *Annual Reports 1937, 1938, 1939;* "Address to the Shareholders of FMC of Canada, Ltd." by W. R. Campbell, Apr. 28, 1941, Apr. 27, 1942; FMC, *Annual Report 1946,* 41 (in this report investments in the Canadian and British companies are not separated.)

# CHAPTER V

## A Company in the Doldrums

1. Cowling, *Reminiscences* (Davis's role); interv. W. Williams, Jan. 13, 1960; H. C. Doss, *Reminiscences.* Edsel, according to Cowling, sent him an appreciative letter, and undoubtedly recognized his good qualities. Doss, who later succeeded Davis, fully agreed with Williams, who is the official quoted. "Mr. Davis," he said, "had the respect and good will of the managers . . . and I think the thought of Davis going in was very stabilizing."

2. Letters and telegrams, Dec. 19, 1937, Jan. 14, Mar. 31, Je. 17, 1938, Acc. 78, Box 30; interv. Davis, July 25–26, 1960; *Ford News,* XVIII, Apr. 1938, 75 ff. and *FTC Report* (see Ch. 3, Note 1), 99 ff. (used car week); *Motor,* July 1938, 44, & Aug., 45.

3. Klann, Bricker, Black, in their reminiscences, interv. Davis, and *Ford: Expansion and Challenge,* 211, 294, 296, 524–526 (Bennett); Sorensen, *My Forty Years with Ford,* 256–257.

4. Sorensen, *op. cit.;* interv. Davis; Klann, *Reminiscences.*

5. Bennett, *We Never Called Him Henry,* 48, 146–147, 170–173; Sorenson, *op. cit.,* 250 ff.; Sheldrick, *Reminiscences;* Bricker, *Reminiscences;* interv. HF II, June 16, 1959.

6. Doss, Sheldrick, Black, in their reminiscences; interv. Davis; Bennett, *op. cit., passim.*

7. Bennett's own book lists a number of his activities, and a dozen interviews and reminiscences: Davis's, Wibel's, Harff's, Sheldrick's etc., cover the same ground.

8. *Detroit News,* Sept. 28, 1945; *Business Week,* Oct. 6, 1945; Hariff, Crimmins, Wiesmyer, Doss, Black, Norman J. Ahrens, and numerous other reminiscences. Ford correspondence in Accs. 38 and 587 show that Bennett, Gnau, and Campsall were closely related.

9. Interv. Davis (HB's table); Bennett, *passim* (on Edsel); Black, *Reminiscences,* and Sorensen, *My Forty Years with Ford,* Chs. 18–20 (HF's attitude to EBF); Harff, Hicks, Wagner, Bricker and other reminiscences.

10. *Iron Age,* CXLII, Nov. 17, 1938, 62–63 and *N.Y. Times,* Oct. 21, 1941 (consent decrees); Letters and telegrams, Je. 22, 1938 (July program), Je. 24 (on demonstrations), Acc. 78, Box 31; Sheldrick, *Reminiscences;* Farkas, *Reminiscences;* Wibel to Gnau (undated), Acc. 38, Box 86, and Gnau to CES, Apr. 11, 1938, Acc. 38, Box 85.

11. Letters and telegrams, Aug. 5, Oct. 5 (Lincoln Zephyr sales), Sept. 29, Oct. 6, 26, 1938, Acc. 78, Box 31; *N.Y. Times,* Oct. 7, 1938 (Mercury); *Ford News,* XVIII, Nov. 1938, 243 ff. and Dec. 1938, 258 ff. (description, advertising 1939 cars); interv. W. Williams (dealers' attitude).

12. Note on radio interv., Nov. 7, 1938, Acc. 78, Box 31; *FTC Report,* 180 (Ford & Chev.); FMC Information Release, Mar. 14, 1958 (Mercury figs.)

13. Letters and telegrams, Jan. 17, Feb. 3 (models at Fair), Apr. 6 (Mar. figs.), May 26 (meeting), Aug. 19, 1939, Acc. 78, Box 34.

14. *Ford News,* XIX, Apr. 1939, 75–85 (Ford at Fair); *N.Y. Times,* Apr. 23, 1939 (EBF's Manhassett house); *Detroit News,* Aug. 19, 1939 (visitors).

15. Letters and telegrams, Acc. 78, Boxes 34, 36.

16. Interv. Davis; Bennett, *We Never Called Him Henry,* 61–62; C. J. Crimmins, *Reminiscences;* Letters of Oct. 16 (signed GSD) and Dec. 22, 1939 (signed by EBF), Acc. 78, Box 37. Bennett makes no mention whatever of Mack, and says that Davis got into "some domestic difficulties," and Ford insisted on his discharge. "I transferred him to the West Coast, without telling Mr. Ford." Davis's account is followed here, and the sales correspondence tallies with it.

17. Doss, Wibel, Harff, and others in their reminiscences; interv. Williams.

18. Eber Sherman to H. G. Ferguson, Nov. 16, 1937, in "Memorandum Concerning Henry Ford and Ford Motor Co. Tractor;" *Ford: Expansion and Challenge,* Chs. 2, 3 and p. 565.

19. *Detroit News,* Dec. 31, 1937, Jan. 7, 1938; Howard Simpson, Diary, Sept. 21, 1938, Ford Archives, and *Reminiscences.* Schultz's tractor, which Simpson thought was about ready, broke in two in the course of a test, and Ford rejected it.

20. Harry Ferguson, & Harry Ferguson, Inc., v. Ford Motor Co. et al., Dist. Court of U.S., Southern Dist. of N.Y., Dec. 1949 (hereafter cited as "Ferg. v. Ford"), Trial Brief on Behalf of Defendants, 23; deposition Ferguson, Ferg. v. Ford, 2479 (Sorensen in 1917), 744, 760, 2305; deposition Sands, *ibid., passim;* Trial Brief, 7 (Brown).

21. *Ford: Expansion and Challenge,* Ch. 7; Sorensen, *My Forty Years with Ford,* 241 ff; R. B. Darragh, interv. with Sorensen, 35, 37; Sheldrick's Engineering Log., Jan. 23, 1939, Acc. 376, Box 1; Sheldrick, Roeder, Simpson, McCarroll, Wibel, Thomas, in their reminiscences; Counter Claim, Ferg. v. Ford, 11–12, 40, 41; "Invitation to the Dance," *Ford News,* XIX, Aug. 1939, 171–172, 189; *Detroit News,* Je. 29, 1939; Deposition HF II, Ferg. v. Ford, 135, 139; EBF to Ferguson, May 6, 1942, Ferg. v. Ford, 1658.

22. FMC production statistics on tractor, 1940, 1941.

23. FMC, Release, *op. cit.;* FMC, Sales Reports & Analysis (Passenger cars).

24. Sheldrick, *Reminiscences* (6-cyl. engine); Doss, *Reminiscences;* FMC, Sales Reports and Analysis; Federal Works Agency, *Highway Statistics, Registrations, Public Road Administration,* Wash., D.C. 1947, 18 (number vehicles), 58, 79 (roads); *N.Y. Times,* Autumn months of 1939 and 1940 on new cars, particularly Aug. 25, 27, 1939 (signals, tourist information) and Oct. 20, 1940 (Reeves); Roeder, *Reminiscences.*

# CHAPTER VI
## A New Deal for Labor

The basic sources for labor history in the New Deal period are government documents. The *Hearings* of the National Labor Relations Board fill forty volumes (Wash., 1940). The Senate Judiciary Committee published its *Hearings* in the "Investigation of the National Labor Relations Board," 75th Cong., 3rd Sess., in 1938 (Wash., 1 vol.); and the House Committee to investigate the National Labor Relations Board in the same Congress, 1st., 2d., and 3rd. Sessions, issued 30 volumes of *Hearings* (1940). The Senate Labor Committee dealt with "Violations of Free Speech and Rights of Labor," 74th, 75th, and 76th Congs., in *Hearings* published in 75 parts (Wash., 1936–1941). J. M. Landis and Marcus Manoff edited *Cases on Labor Law* (1942), and Charles Aikin edited *National Labor Relations Board Cases* (London, 1939). Among the more famous prosecutions connected with the NLRB, the Jones & Laughlin Case may be found in 301 U.S. 1, the Apex Hosiery Company Case in 310 U.S. 469, and the Hutcheson Case in 312 U.S. 219. C. O. Gregory and H. A. Katz published a valuable analysis in *Labor Law* (N.Y., 1948).

The most useful secondary treatments include Selig Perlman, *Labor in the New Deal Decade* (N.Y., 1945); Herbert Harris, *American Labor* (New Haven, 1939); Robert R. R. Brooks, *When Labor Organizes* (New Haven, 1937) and *Unions of Their Own Choosing* (New Haven, 1939); Edward Levinson, *Labor on the March* (N.Y., 1938); Clinton Golden and H. J. Ruttenberg, *Dynamics of Industrial Democracy* (1942); and Charles O. Gregory, *Labor and the Law* (rev. ed., N.Y., 1946). Benjamin Gitlow has written a useful exposé of Communism in the labor field entitled *The Whole of Their Lives* (N.Y., 1948), and Harold Seidman a volume called *Labor Czars, A History of Labor Racketeering* (N.Y., 1938). Benjamin Stolberg's *The Story of the CIO* (N.Y., 1938) devotes a special chapter to the automobile industry.

Walter Chrysler's and Alfred P. Sloan's biographies, and Charles Sorensen's *My Forty Years with Ford,* all previously cited, have value for the industrial background.

1. General accounts in Stolberg, *The Story of the CIO,* 166–174; Levinson, *Labor on the March,* 175–182, 197, 198; *Fortune,* Nov. 1937, 160–166.

2. Dixon Wecter, *The Age of the Great Depression, 1929–1941,* N.Y., 1948, 113, 114; U.S. Court of Appeals, Sixth Circuit, Oct. Term 1939, No. 8399, 19. *Fortune, ut sup.,* 162, and Stolberg, *ut. sup.,* 167, 168, cover the Flint violence.

3. On the Chrysler strike see Walsh, *CIO, Industrial Unionism in Action,* 126–129; Walter Chrysler, *Life of an American Workingman,* Ch. 6. Henry Ford said just after the Chrysler settlement, that sit-down strikers "are in the same category as housebreakers," and added: "History shows that all improvements in labor have come out of industry, and never out of coercion or politics;" Detroit *News,* Apr. 8, 1937.

4. Levinson, *Labor on the March,* 182–209; Robert R. R. Brooks, *Unions of Their Own Choosing,* 112, 113, 192.

5. Wecter, *The Great Depression,* 114, 115; Stolberg, *The Story of the CIO,* 66–91; *American Year Book, 1937,* 584.

6. Harold L. Ickes, *Secret Diary,* II, 128, 129; *N.Y. Times,* Mar. 21, Apr. 20, May 2, 1937; A. M. Smith of the *Detroit News,* reprint pamphlet, Apr. 29, 1937. See also Sorenson, *Forty Years,* 259, 260.

7. Sorenson, *Forty Years,* 260 ff.; Wecter, *The Great Depression,* 114, 115; Foster Rhea Dulles, *Labor in America,* N.Y. 1949, 308. In NLRB v. Fansteel Metallurgical Corporation, 306 U.S. 240, the Supreme Court declared that to justify a sit-down strike "would be to put a premium on resort to force instead of legal remedies and to subvert the principles of law and order which lie at the foundations of society."

8. Sorensen, *Forty Years,* 260.

9. Sheldrick, *Reminiscences,* emphasizes Edsel's interest in "going along with the times."

A letter of Martin to Bennett, July 17, 1940, shows that Martin became very friendly with Bennett and accepted favors for which he expressed gratitude (Acc. 1, Box 142).

10. Sorensen, *Forty Years*, 256, 257. Bennett's *We Never Called Him Henry*, Ch. 15, is eloquent of the bad manners that Sorensen mentions.

11. Sorensen, *op. cit.*, 261, 262.

12. Ford Motor Company v. United Automobile Workers of America, 4 NLRB, 621 ff. For comments see oral argument of Ford counsel before the U.S. Court of Appeals, Cincinnati, Je. 5, 1940, Acc. 51, Box 6.

13. For the loyalty of many Ford workers see the New York newspaper *PM*, Jan. 5, 1941, a comprehensive article; Sheldrick and J. F. Bossardet, *Reminiscences;* U.S. Court of Appeals, Sixth Circuit, No. 7919, NLRB v. Ford Motor Company, 8, 22–28.

14. On Union plans to organize the Rouge see Detroit *News*, Feb. 20, Mar. 21, Apr. 10, 13, 1937; on union optimism about the effort see *Detroit Free Press*, Apr. 17, 1937; on the opening of union headquarters, *ibid.*, May 25, 1937; of workers for unoin activities prior to the events of May 26 see 14 NLRB, 382–388, 390, 393, 395–398.

15. The Detroit *News* and *Free Press* dealt with the affray May 27, 28. Good general accounts may be found in Levinson, *Labor on the March*, 214–216, and Keith Sward, *Legend of Henry Ford*, N.Y. 1948, 391–394. George Heliker's interview with John Gillespie, July 23, 1958, in the Ford Archives, is illuminating. A responsible Detroit physician asserted that Merriweather's injuries would cause him incapacitating pains for many years, that Dunham might suffer permanent brain injury, and that Tony Marinovich, another union man badly beaten, would probably never be able to work again; 14 NLRB, *passim;* Levinson, 215, 216.

16. NLRB, *Second Annual Report;* Ford Motor Company and UAW, 4 NLRB; the quotation by Ford is cited by Sward from the *N.Y. Times*, Jan. 1, 1938.

17. 26 NLRB, Cases C-1554 to C-1558 inclusive, with Decision and Order, pp. 330–347; *Detroit News*, July 1, 1937 (Dallas affairs).

18. 26 NLRB, 348, 351, 353–365 (Dallas beatings). An article in the *Nation*, Jan. 22, 1938, puts the number at eighteen. See also the Amended Complaint against the Ford Motor Company, Feb. 6, 1940, Acc. 51, Box 5. The head of the "outside squad" or gang, "Fats" Perry, turned against his employers and contributed effectively to the million or more words of testimony on which the NLRB examiner based his report, and the Board its order.

19. M. L. Wiesmyer memorandum to CES and P. E. Martin, Feb. 1, 1937, Acc. 572, Box 31 (Kansas City situation); sample spy reports and memoranda in same box from H. C. Doss to Wiesmyer, Feb. 27, Mar. 8, 1937.

20. Ford Motor Company and UAW, Case No. C-1463, decided May 21, 1941, in 31 NLRB 1001 ff.; Board order, 1006–1018; Doss, *Reminiscences*.

21. *Detroit Free Press*, Oct. 16–18, 1937 (Bennett-McElroy exchanges); *Detroit News*, Oct. 30, Nov. 15, 1937; *Business Week*, Oct. 30, 1937; and Board order, 31 NLRB 1061 ff.

22. *Detroit Free Press*, Dec. 11, 17, 21, 22, 23; Board order, *ut sup.*

23. Board order, 1036, 1039, 1042–1053, 1056, 1060, 1061.

24. R. R. R. Brooks, *Unions of Their Own Choosing*, 21; the governor is quoted in 77th Cong., 3rd Sess. Hearings on S. Res. 207, p. 77.

25. Brooks, *op. cit.*, 1–16 (informal procedures of Board); 16–21, 79, 80, 174–176 (formal procedures). See also first and second *Annual Reports* of the NLRB; Charles O. Gregory, *Labor and the Law*, 289, 333 (NLRB before the courts).

26. Gregory, *op. cit.*, 324 ff.; Brooks, *op. cit.*, 55; NLRB v. Ford Motor Company, U.S. Circuit Court of Appeals, Sixth Circuit, No. 8399, Brief for Respondent, 30 ff.

27. Stolberg, *Story of the CIO*, Ch. 5 (factionalism); (slump in employment), *American Year Book, 1938*, 485, 486; Detroit *News*, Jan. 10, 28, 1938; UAW estimates in Brown Coll., Wayne State Univ. Libr.

28. Levinson, *Labor on the March*, 266–271 (intra-union battles); *Detroit News*, Jan. 1, 1938 (Frankensteen's plans); May 24, 1938 (his removal); Stolberg, *Story of the CIO*, 183–186 (Martin's role). The 1939 Cleveland convention of the CIO published its *Daily Proceedings*, which for the third day give Frankensteen's speeches, pp. 18, 19, 22, 23, 24.

29. *Story of the CIO*, 116.

30. *American Year Book, 1938,* 586.

31. Waggoner, *Reminiscences;* "Direct Quotes from Ford Workers, Dearborn," Brown Coll., Wayne State Univ. Libr.

32. Logan Miller, *Reminiscences;* Herbert Harris, *American Labor,* 271 (wives).

33. Mimeographed copy of Ruskin's speech to 1936 South Bend Convention in Brown Coll.; Acc. 572, Boxes 31, 32 (age levels).

34. Reid's comment on Report of William Haber, Michigan State Emergency Relief Administrator, Oct. 1936, Brown Coll.; Acc. 572, Box 32 (Ford statistics).

35. Reminiscences of John Fitzpatrick, H. S. Ablewhite, Logan Miller, J. M. Waggoner, Charles Patterson, and T. R. Mallon.

36. *ETC Report,* 668 ff. (Ford wages 1929–1937); Henderson, Report on Labor Conditions in the Automobile Industry, NRA Research and Planning Division, Jan. 23, 1935, Appendix B (wages in the industry); intervs. with former Ford workers, James Murdoch, Percy Llewellyn, William Johnson, on labor and wages. Murdoch, vice-president of the MESA, charged in 1937 that the company had laid off 4000 employes, and replaced them with unemployed persons who were paid $4 the first thirty days, $5 the next ninety days, and only after the fourth month the minimum $6 wage. It is impossible to disprove or to verify this statement.

37. All this is set forth in the Ford argument in the appeal against the NLRB before the U.S. Circuit Court, Sixth Circuit, Oct. Term 1939, No. 8399. See accounts of the Rouge in *Ford: Expansion and Challenge, passim.*

38. *Detroit Times,* Sept. 18, 19, 27, 1933; *N.Y. Times,* Je. 29, 1937; James H. Peyton to CES, Je. 15, 1937, Acc. 522, Box 30; Mallon, *Reminiscences.*

39. This "union" was organized in June 1937 by a Detroit attorney named William S. McDowell; Stolberg, *Story of the CIO,* 118.

40. Intervs. Martin, July 15, Aug. 14, 1958.

41. Mielke, *Reminiscences;* Martin to Bennett, July 17, 1940, Acc. 1, Box 142, suggests their relations had grown close.

42. The full story of this agreement, its motivation on both sides, the heated approval and dissent it aroused, and its rapid rejection, would require a small book. Basic documents are 1) the complaint of the majority of the UAW Executive Board against Martin, the Board Minority, the Ford Motor Company, and Harry Bennett filed with the NLRB Jan. 30, 1939; and 2) Martin's bill of complaint filed in the Circuit Court in Detroit in connection with a suit of his faction against the Thomas faction for control of the UAW assets; and 3) collateral material, all in the Brown Coll. Percy Llewellyn published an account in the *United Automobile Worker,* Feb. 11, 1939, and Paul Ste. Marie one in the *Detroit Times,* Jan. 25, 1939. Intervs. Martin and Llewellyn are invaluable.

43. The appointment of Widman was announced in the *N.Y. Times,* Sept. 20, 1940, with comment. The switch of AFL leaders in Ford was noted in the *Detroit News,* Sept. 13, 1940, and is covered in detail in interv. Harry Ross, July 16, 1958. Henry Ford had accepted the Grand Cross of the German Eagle in 1938, and as Harry Bennett elegantly puts it, the company "began getting a bad press on the Nazi stuff," *We Never Called Him Henry,* 120, 127; see also Detroit *News,* May 27, 1940.

44. Al Smith, *Reminiscences;* interv. John Fitzpatrick, July 26, 1958, who said, "During the drive to organize Ford we had our courage bolstered . . . by the knowledge that the UAW boys were doing a very good job in the rest of the industry." Logan Miller, *Reminiscences,* mentions the tearing off of union badges.

45. *United Automobile Worker,* Feb. 1, 1941, on volunteer organizers; editorials in *Michigan Labor Leader,* Jan. 17, Feb. 14, Mar. 28, 1941.

46. NLRB *Annual Report, 1941;* interv. Llewellyn, Feb. 24, 1954; *Detroit Free Press,* Mar. 9, 1941 (Ford statement); interv. Harry Ross, July 16, 1958.

47. Norman Smith had shouted through Gate 4: "The strike is on! Every worker should come out!" interv. Fitzpatrick. The *Detroit News* describes scenes the first day at union headquarters and plant exits, April 2, 1941; Harry Ross deals with Widman's role, and Fitzpatrick gives some vigorous impressions of early events; see intervs.

48. Sorensen, *Forty Years,* 267; Bennett, *We Never Called Him Henry,* 135, 136.

49. The Teamsters Union cooperated with the strikers by refusing to allow any truck to enter the plant; Detroit *Daily Worker*, Apr. 3, 1941. The role of the Negroes is discussed in the Detroit *News*, Apr. 7, and Detroit *Times*, Apr. 3–7, 1941. James Wechsler had asserted in New York *PM* Jan. 5, 1941, that Bennett had hired about 10,000 Negroes. For the fear which they inspired see the *Reminiscences* of Joseph Lawry (foundry boss), E. F. Wait, Arthur Renner, and Charles Patterson.

50. Detroit *Free Press*, Apr. 2, 5, 1941 (Capizzi's Washington trip); Detroit *News*, Apr. 2, 1941 (use of State Police).

51. Gitlow, *The Whole of Their Lives*, 310–323, deals with Communist participation in the strike. While his account is exaggerated, it is a fact that such prominent men in the UAW as Maurice Sugar and Wyndham Mortimer were Communists, that the important Ford organizer William McKie was honored at a Party dinner for his "fanatical devotion" to Communism, and that Reuther in time had to purge numerous Communists from the CIO.

52. Bennett, *We Never Called Him Henry*, 136; Sorensen, *Forty Years*, 263–267. The Ford Motor Company rather desperately applied to the courts for an injunction against the barricades about the plant; Detroit *Times*, Apr. 8, *Free Press*, Apr. 9, 1941. The negotiations and settlement are covered in the *Free Press*, *Times*, and *News*, Apr. 8–12, 1941.

53. Detroit *News*, May 22, 1941 (full totals and percentages of the vote); *ibid.*, Nov. 29, 1941 (results of the elections in the outlying factories, two of which, Saline and Manchester, gave a unanimous vote for the UAW).

54. Sorensen, *Forty Years*, 267; Bennett, *We Never Called Him Henry*, 135, 137; Richards, *The Last Billionaire*, 282, 283; newspapers, June 1–24, 1941; *N.Y. Times*, May 23 (Bennett quote) and May 24, 1941 (Capizzi).

55. Sorensen, *Forty Years*, 268–271.

# CHAPTER VII
## Shadow of War

1. *N.Y. Times*, Aug. 29, 1939; Liebold, *Reminiscences;* Acc. 1, Box 127 (Prince Louis, Bigelow); Detroit *Free Press*, July 31, 1938 (presentation of cross).

2. Liebold, *Reminiscences; N.Y. Times*, Oct. 25, 1938 (Munich) and Dec. 1, 1938 (Ford's defense); *Saturday Evening Post*, CCVIII, Feb. 1, 1936 (war, dictators).

3. Folder: "Religious, Moral Rearmament, 1921–1937," Acc. 1, Box 52 (clippings, correspondence), James Draper Newton and Eva (Mrs. Willard Seely) Worcester were American group members in frequent contact with the Fords.

4. Interv. Charles A. Lindbergh, Oct. 27, 1959, and letters, Lindbergh to authors, Nov. 13 and Dec. 6, 1959; *N.Y. Times*, Aug. 18, Sept. 5, Oct. 12, 13, 20, Nov. 7, 28, Dec. 19, 1938, Jan. 16, Aug. 28, 1940, and Jan. 17, 1960.

5. *Ibid.*, Apr. 15, 20, May 7, Je. 13, 1939; Lindbergh to authors, Dec. 6, 1959. Lindbergh thought he worked for two weeks on the "normal pay of a reserve officer," and for the remainder of his study, without remuneration.

6. *N.Y. Times*, Sept. 16, 17, 1939. In the news story of the 17th, on how the broadcast came to be made, Fulton Lewis, Jr., of MBS, described the events leading up to it.

7. *N.Y. Times*, Sept. 21, 26, 1939 (Ford on Neutrality Act). Ford appeared before the Legion convention, but simply spoke ten words of greeting to the delegates.

8. William F. Langer and S. Everett Gleason, *The Challenge to Isolation*, N.Y. 1952, 193, 194 (general, FDR statements); Acc. 1, Box 147 (Dagmar Renie—later Baroness Ramsey).

9. Langer and Gleason, 474.

10. *Ibid.*, 676; Charles A. Lindbergh, "What Substitute for War?" *Atlantic*, CLXV, Mar. 1940, 304–308; *N.Y. Times*, May 20, 1940 (radio address).

11. *N.Y. Times*, May 29, Je. 4, 11, 12, 1940; Wash. *Evening Post*, Je. 11, 1940; Acc. 285, Box 2412 (Johnson telegram); Lindbergh to authors, Nov. 13, 1959. "Edsel Ford came at my

request to discuss the mass production of engines," the *Times* article of June 1 quoted Secretary Johnson; it indicated that Edsel arrived in Washington on May 29. The aircraft engine was thus the government's first interest, although it acted on the pursuit plane.

12. *N.Y. Times,* Je. 11, 17, 19, 25, 26 and Wash. *Post,* Je. 11, 1940; Acc. 6, Boxes 215, 217, 352 (EBF-Knudsen); Sorensen, *My Forty Years with Ford,* 273–276. The Defense Advisory Commission, June 25, stated that Edsel was told that a separate contract must be made with the British, checked with his father, and accepted the arrangement. He may have understood that a separate contract must be made, but Sorensen and Henry Ford may not have understood it. Again, Edsel himself may not have had this understanding.

13. Folder, "Airplane Motors for England," Acc. 6, Box 359.

14. *Commercial & Financial Chronicle,* Je. 29, 1940, 4057 (Ford on defense contracts); *N.Y. Times,* Je. 29, Aug. 4, 1940 (Lindbergh visit, engine); Acc. 1, Box 141 (Lindbergh-HF corr.).

15. Col. E. J. Hall to EBF, July 9, 1940, and CES to Hall, July 16, 1940, Acc. 38, Box 127 (Douglas); *Business Week,* Aug. 10, 1940, 16, and *N.Y. Times,* Aug. 4, 1940 (Ford engine); Gnau to EBF, Aug. 15, 1940, Acc. 38, Box 137 (P&W); *N.Y. Times,* Aug. 17, 1940 (P&W order); Detroit *News,* May 27, 1940 (Ford's Nazi sympathies); *Automotive Industries,* LXXXIII, Dec. 1, 1940, 602, 605–606 (Thomas); *Detroit News,* Dec. 14, 28, 1940 (Hillman, Knudsen); E. J. Wedge, *Reminiscences*; *N.Y. Times,* Sept. 12, 1940 (plans for plant); *Business Week,* Sept. 28, 1940, 25 (ground broken); Sorensen, *op. cit.,* 276–277; E. O. La Croix, *Record of War Effort,* Acc. 435, Boxes 1–5.

16. La Croix, *Record of War Effort,* Acc. 435, Box 1 (Ford improvements); corr., CES with P&W officials, fall of 1941, Acc. 38, Box 93; Lovett to CES, Je. 6, 1941, Acc. 38, Box 92; FMC, News Release, Dec. 16, 1941, Acc. 38, Box 93 (advantages cast barrels).

17. *Automotive & Aviation Industries,* LXXXVII, Dec. 1, 1942, 18–24, 102, 104; Memo, A. M. Wibel to Ford Execs., Oct. 22, 1940, Acc. 38, Box 89, and CES to Knudsen, Dec. 12, 1941, Acc. 38, Box 92 (all tools and priorities); La Croix, *Record,* Acc. 435, Box 3 (school); H. J. Robinson, *Reminiscences,* and Report of L. S. Hobbs to CES, Oct. 7, 1941, Acc. 38, Box 93 (work force). As to priority, Wibel's memo quoted General Arnold: "Priority A-1 has been given your contract . . . for the manufacture of airplane engines." But other manufacturers also had such priorities.

18. Roeder, Sheldrick, *Reminiscences,* and La Croix, *Record,* Acc. 435, Box 1 (jeep); *Motor,* Jan. 1941, and *N.Y. Times,* Mar. 1, 1941 (midget truck).

19. Lindbergh to HF, Sept. 22, 1940, Acc. 1, Box 147; Anne Morrow Lindbergh, *The Wave of the Future,* N.Y., 1940, *passim*; *N.Y. Times,* Nov. 21, 1940, Jan. 16, Feb. 16, 1941 (HF of war and defense).

20. *N.Y. Times,* Aug. 5, 1940 (Soldiers Field); Lindbergh, "We Are Not Prepared for War," *Vital Speeches,* VII, Feb. 15, 1941, 266–267 (before Sen. Com. Feb. 6); Charles A. Lindbergh, *Of Flight and Life,* N.Y., 1948, v–vii, 25.

21. Clippings, correspondence, statements on *PM* charges, Acc. 285, Box 2375, and Liebold, *Reminiscences; N.Y. Times,* Dec. 22, 1939 (Lindbergh resigns NACA), May 29, 1940 (Lafayette Escadrille), Je. 17, Oct. 17, 25, Nov. 21, 1940 (comment). Lindbergh had his many staunch supporters. While he may have differed with the flyer on national policy, Gen. H. H. Arnold had the highest opinion of his abilities, and urged Sorensen to use him in aircraft production work.

22. Sorensen, *My Forty Years with Ford,* 278–279; letters Russell Gnau (CES's secty.) to CES, Dec. 27, 30, 1940, Jan. 3, 1941, Acc. 38, Box 93. In this correspondence we see plans for the trip maturing.

23. Acc. 6, Boxes 211, 213, 214, 230, 360.

24. *Ibid.*

25. Sheldrick, *Reminiscences;* EBF to HF II, Je. 6, 1940, Acc. 6, Box 360; *ibid.* and *Life,* IX, July 19, 1940, 26–27 (HF II's wedding, the McDonnells); *N.Y. Times,* July 10, 1941 (Benson's wedding).

26. Sorensen, *op. cit.,* 279–286; *N.Y. Times,* Jan. 9, 1941 (Consolidated) and Jan. 12, 1941 (Douglas); *Business Week,* Jan. 18, 1941; CES to Robert E. Gross (Lockheed), R. H. Fleet (Consolidated), and Donald Douglas, all Jan. 20, 1941, Acc. 38, Box 93. Sorensen in his letter

to Fleet notes that Ford engineers and technicians were still working at San Diego. All these letters were acknowledgments of courtesies extended the Ford group in Southern California.

27. CES to Campsall, Feb. 6, 1941 and to General George H. Brett, Air Corps, Jan. 31, 1941, Acc. 38, Box 93 (Ford plan); Detroit *Times*, Feb. 4, 1941; CES to Mead, Feb. 10, 1941, Acc. 587, Box 70; and *ibid.*, Release by McCann-Erickson, Inc. (for FMC) "Ford Speeds Plans to Build Army Bombers," Mar. 4, 1941; Letter from Consolidated to Chief, Materiel Division, Wash., D.C. Feb. 25, 1941, Acc. 38, Box 93 (Consolidated's position); CES to Knudsen, Mar. 11, 1943, Acc. 38, Box 99 (first schedule, May 20, 1941); Detroit *News*, Feb. 7, 1941 (Hillman). In this letter to Knudsen, CES reviews the successive contracts imposed by the Army on the FMC.

28. Sorensen, *Forty Years with Ford*, 283 (mile-long plant); Marion F. Wilson, *The Story of Willow Run*, Ann Arbor, 1956, 19–21; Hanson, *Reminiscences;* CES to Campsall, Feb. 6, 1941, Acc. 587, Box 70. According to the Property Management Office of the FMC, Ford through a subsidiary, the Quirk farms, at the end of 1940 owned 3060 acres of land in the vicinity of Willow Run. Sorensen eventually bought about 1280 acres more, rounding out a block of land 7½ miles square.

29. "Battle of Detroit," *Time*, XXXIX, Mar. 23, 1943, 10–11; Roy Schumann, Frank C. Riecks, Hanson in their reminiscences; FMC, Press Release, "Willow Run," Nov. 18, 1942, Acc. 454, Box 9; La Croix, *Record*, Acc. 435, Box 3 (dimensions of plant, field).

30. Hanson, *Reminiscences;* Sorensen, *op. cit.*, 286–287.

31. Roscoe Smith to CES, Apr. 22, 1941, Acc. 38, Box 93; La Croix, *Record*, Acc. 435, Boxes 15, 19 (methods of companies, breakdown of plane, Consolidated's indoor assembly line); McCloud, *Reminiscences* (pivot of landing gear); Sorensen, *op. cit.*, 286–289 (methods contrasted); Acc. 38, Box 93 (Ford's suggestions for changes); FMC Release, Nov. 18, 1942, Acc. 454, Box 9 (number of parts in plane); Lindbergh to authors, Nov. 13, 1959 (character of B-24 relative to other planes). Other aviation authorities of course define the character of the B-17, B-24, and B-29, but Col. Lindbergh was familiar with the existing planes and the attitude of most pilots toward them.

32. Roscoe Smith, Logan Miller, *Reminiscences*; Press Release, Nov. 18, 1942, *op. cit.*, and La Croix, *Record*, Acc. 435, Box 15 (for events of 1941); also "Chronological Data," Acc. 6, Box 381.

33. *Automotive War Production*, I, Aug. 1942, 4 and II, Feb. 1943, 7 (M-4 and M-3); La Croix, *Record*, Acc. 435, Box 13 (same, and Ford engine); Sheldrick, Robinson, *Reminiscences* (develop. Ford engine).

34. Sheldrick, Robinson, *Reminiscences;* La Croix, *Record*, Acc. 435, Box 13; *Iron Age*, CLXIX, Jan. 1, 1942, 218–220.

35. Robinson, *Reminiscences;* La Croix, *Record*, Acc. 435, Box 8.

36. *N.Y. Times*, Mar. 5, Apr. 9, 22, May 27, Je. 15, 1941 (HF II and Benson); *Ibid.*, Dec. 4, 1941 (HF on war).

# CHAPTER VIII
## Arsenal of Democracy

1. Harold L. Hutchins, ed., *American Goes to War*, Chicago, 1941, 20, 54.

2. *Automotive War Production*, I, Mar. 1942, 1, and July 1; Deptl. Com., L. S. Sheldrick to FMC executives, Oct. 10, 1941, and William K. Frank, Production Divn., OPM, to CES, Dec. 16, 1941, with copy of report on Ford activities (FMC activities in late 1941), EBF to Jones, Dec. 9, 1941, all in Acc. 38, Box 92; *N.Y. Times*, Dec. 13, 1941. Unfortunately *Automotive War Production* never notes the activities of any particular company. Frank's report, made to OPM, after a 3-day survey, praises the defense program of the FMC, the spirit of officials and workers, and discusses its training program, machine tools, sub-contracts, etc.

3. La Croix, *Record of the War Effort*, Acc. 435, Box 3, (original order P&Ws); Brig. Gen. George C. Kenny to CES, Dec. 11, 1941, Acc. 38, Box 93 (proposed new schedule); Maj. Gen.

E. M. Wesson, Chief of Ordnance to EBF, Feb. 16, 1942, noted in LaCroix, *Record*, Acc. 435, Box 8 (directors); *ibid.*, Box 13 (tanks).

4. Sheldrick, *Reminiscences* and La Croix, *Record*, Acc. 435, Box 1, and Jewett, Bush, to EBF, Feb. 24, 1942, Acc. 6, Box 381 (amphibian); LaCroix, *Record*, Acc. 435, Box 12 (supercharger); *ibid.*, Boxes 6, 11 (magnesium, aluminum); Deptl. Com., C. M. Nelles of Purchasing to Ford execs., Dec. 9, 1941, Acc. 38, Box 92 and *The Army Air Forces in World War II*, Office of Air Force History (eds., W. F. Craven and J. L. Cate), 6 vols., Chicago, 1948–1958, VI, 326 (curtailment, termination of civilian auto production); *N.Y. Times*, Feb. 11, 1942 (Ford ends it).

5. *Ford: Expansion and Challenge*, chs. 8, 9, 10, 19 (development of plants, resources, employes); "The Overall Picture," La Croix, *Record*, Acc. 435, Box 23; data on plants in Acc. 672, Box 1; War Production Board, *War Manufacturing Facilities*, Wash., 1945, 134–136, 229–231; 250–257. The WPB publication, listing by company the plants used for war work, shows that Ford like General Motors maintained factories in numerous states (11 compared with GM's 12). Chrysler's manufacturing was more concentrated, all its establishments being in Ohio, Indiana, Michigan, and Illinois.

6. Riecks, *Reminiscences*, also Sheldrick's, Wagner's, Bricker's, and Robinson's reminiscences, and Sorensen's *My Forty Years with Ford*. Ford's own ideas and practices and his attitude toward his subordinates are discussed in *Ford: Expansion and Challenge, passim*.

7. CES to Lt. Col. A. B. Johnson, Dec. 16, 1940, Acc. 38, Box 89; Frank, OPM Report, as cited in Note 2; CES to Knudsen, Dec. 12, 1941, Acc. 38, Box 92; Kenny to CES, Dec. 4, 1941, Acc. 38, Box 93.

8. La Croix, *Record*, Acc. 435, Boxes 1, 3; Chronology Sheet, Acc. 596, Box 1; *Detroit News*, Nov. 20, 1941 (Murray); CES to Brant, Dec. 18, 1940 and Brant to CES, Dec. 21, 1940, Acc. 38, Box 92 (deferment); Memo Prepared on Losses for EBF, Nov., Acc. 6, Box 381; J. A. Reid, Memo, Nov. 9, 1942, Acc. 596, Box 1 (other cos.); A. M. Wibel, to Commdg. Genl. AAF, Dec. 28, 1942, Acc. 38, Box 98; E. A. Dunton, "Deptl. Com.," Jan. 8, 1943, Acc. 38, Box 98 (details of schedule). Subsequent schedules set the 3400 level for Aug., 1944 and then for Sept. 1944, see Acc. 38, Box 98, also see Sorensen to AAF Materiel Command, May 11, 1943, Acc. 596, Box 1.

9. Collis Stocking to W. B. Murphy, WPB, Dec. 18, 1942, Acc. 38, Box 98; CES to AAF Materiel Command, May 11, 1943, Acc. 596, Box 1; *Detroit Times, Detroit News*, Apr. 17, 1943.

10. H. J. Robinson, *Reminiscences;* Malcolm Denise, "Labor Relations and Implementation of Policy in 1943, 1944, and 1945, with Appraisal" (shortened title), 35 page typewritten report dated Dec. 2, 1946. (Denise, now Vice-President in Charge of Labor Relations, was credited by union leaders with being the "brains" behind company labor policy from 1942–1945.)

11. La Croix, *Record*, Acc. 435, Boxes 1, 5; Table in Acc. 596, Box 1; *Army Air Forces*, VI, 353, 356 (totals of engine production). The latter source shows that Pratt & Whitney produced 130,117 engines of all types, five being for units of from 450 to 1350 h.p. Its production of R-2800's is not given, but could hardly have exceeded Ford's. As to aircraft engines in general, an OPM sheet for Aug. 15, 1941 lists Pratt & Whitney, Wright (5 types), Allison (a GM subsidiary); Continental, Jacobs, Kiser, Lycoming, Packard, and Ranger. The Wright R-3350 was the highest powered, eventually delivered 2500 h.p. The P&W R-2800 was next, with an eventual maximum delivery of 2100.

12. Robinson, *Reminiscences;* La Croix, *Record*, Acc. 435, Box 8; Brig. Gen. G. E. Wells to Robinson, Aug. 11, 1943, Acc. 285, Box 2770.

13. La Croix, *Record*, Acc. 435, Boxes 8, 23; Robinson, *Reminiscences*.

14. La Croix, *Record*, Boxes 13, 23; Sheldrick, *Reminiscences;* Testimony R. I. Roberge before Mead Investigating Com. in Detroit, Mar. 1945, Acc. 599, Box 1.

15. La Croix, *Record*, Boxes 13, 23; Robinson, *Reminiscences*, R. Elberton Smith, *The Army and Economical Mobilization* (in series, U.S. Army in World War II—War Dept.) Wash., D.C., 1959, 256 (producers of jeeps).

16. Sheldrick, *Reminiscences;* Transcript of Joint Meeting of Labor and Industrial Subcommittees on General Automotive Problems, Jan. 6, 1942, 76, Acc. 6, Box 362, (C. E. Wilson

on Government and GM: "They want to give us the tough ones"); *Wartime Production Activities*, Report of Chairman, WPB, Oct. 9, 1945, Wash., D.C., 1945, 109 (numbers of tanks, armored cars, scout cars, etc., tank chassis, trucks). In the figure of 2,665,196 vehicles the 2,455,956 tractors manufactured is not listed. This would make the total 5,111,146 vehicles.

17. Keith Ayling, *They Fly to Fight*, New York, 1944, 21–22, 101; Walter G. Nelson, *Reminiscences;* La Croix, *Record,* Acc. 435, Box 13.

18. *Ibid.;* Nelson, *Reminiscences.*

19. La Croix, *Record,* Acc. 435, Box 13. La Croix describes in detail the Ford glider and its first demonstration.

20. Nelson, *Reminiscences;* La Croix, *Record,* Acc. 435, Boxes 13 and 23; Ayling, *They Fly to Fight,* 24 (Arnold quote); Hanson W. Baldwin, *N.Y. Times,* Aug. 6, 1943; Maj. Gen. James M. Gavin, *Airborne Warfare,* Wash., 1947, Chaps. 1 & 2 (Sicily and Italy), and 145–147 (Normandy, general).

21. *Army Air Forces,* VI, 299, 319; *Mill & Factory,* XXX, Feb. 1942, 61.

22. *Fortune,* XXV, Apr. 1942, 79, 120 (Ford's attitude); Sorensen, *My Forty Years,* Chap. 19 (Sorensen's); La Croix, *Record,* Acc. 435, Box 15 (progress) and Chronology, Acc. 6, Box 381 (same); Wibel, Wagner, *Reminiscences.*

23. La Croix, *Record,* Acc. 435, Boxes 15, 19; Logan Miller, Smith, Wagner, Charles H. Patterson, in their reminiscences; various plats of plant in Accs. 435 and 6.

24. Smith, *Reminiscences;* Bennett, *We Never Called Him Henry,* 159; Bricker, *Reminiscences;* Wagner, *Reminiscences;* Bennett says that he hit Smith because the latter had agreed with him about making Willow Run all-Negro, and then in conference spoke against the proposal. Smith and Bennett both agreed that only one blow was struck.

25. CES to Robert A. Lovett, May 18, 1942, Acc. 38, Box 95 (rail vs. trailer, and decision to use trailers); Chronology, Acc. 6, Box 383 (shipment of sub-assemblies and first knockdown); A. E. Raymond, VP Engineering, Douglas, Notes on Conference of Ford, Consolidated, Douglas, Mar. 17, 1941, Acc. 38, Box 93 (plants, problems); C. B. Ostrander to CES, July 23, 1943 (Douglas plant at Tulsa), Acc. 435, Box 16 (first KD shipment). Ostrander writes CES that the Douglas plant is 4020 by 390 feet, and can assemble about 3 planes a day.

26. Harff, *Reminiscences* (Bricker); Chronology for 1942, Acc. 38, Box 99; La Croix, *Record,* Acc. 435, Box 15 ("May 19, M. L. Bricker assigned to Willow Run full time"); EBF to CES, Mar. 12, 1943, Acc. 6, Box 381 (Bricker appointed General manager); Press Release, Acc. 454, Box 9 ("educational plane"). The completion of the regular No. 1 Ford plane is noted in the Acc. 435 Chronology for 1942 (see above) as completed Sept. 10.

27. George R. Clark, "The Strange Story of the Reuther Plan," *Harper's,* CLXXXIV, May 1942, 645–654; Denise Memorandum, as cited in Note 10 above; intervs. Brenan Sexton, Sept. 4, 1958, and Percy Llewellyn, Sept. 24, 1954 (general conditions at WR); "The 'Bomber Local' at Willow Run," *Monthly Labor Review,* LXI, Dec. 1945, 1076.

28. Hanson, *Reminiscences;* Acc. 6, Box 38 (hookup of July 26); *N.Y. Times,* Sept. 12, 1942 (Patterson); Gnau to Campsall, Feb. 26, 1942, Acc. 587, Box 71 (new expressway to Detroit). Gnau had just driven over this, which was completed but not opened. "You certainly make excellent time on this new road," he wrote.

29. *N.Y. Times,* Apr. 19, May 24, 1942 (estimate of workers, housing scarcity, state and government plans, opposition); CES to T. P. Wright, Aircraft Resources Control Officer, Wash., D.C., June 9, 1943, Acc. 38, Box 99 (Sorensen's estimate of workers needed); M. L. Bricker to EBF, Jan. 26, 1943, Acc. 6, Box 381 (report on housing); La Croix, *Record,* Acc. 435, Box 15 (opening of housing units).

30. Acc. 6, Box 381 (school); Acc. 138, Box 95 (Ford reports on production); *Aero Digest,* July 1, 1945 (Figures by year for WR). The article in *Aero Digest,* F. M. Beck's "Willow Run's Achievement," gives an excellent summary of the plant's accomplishment. Sorensen's *Forty Years,* 290, gives figures which do not tally with Beck's or with company records.

31. La Croix, *Record,* Acc. 435, Boxes 20, 41 (buildings); "Dodge Plant to Top Ford's," *Chicago Times,* Dec. 15, 1941; Wibel, *Reminiscences,* and *Fortune,* XXVII, Feb. 1943, 113 (HF at Willow Run); *N.Y. Times,* Apr. 3, 5, 18, 1942 (Lindbergh); *ibid.,* Je. 6, July 1, 25, 31, Aug. 15, Oct. 2, 1942 and Acc. 454, Box 9 (visitors). Sorensen, *Forty Years,* 292–295,

describes the Roosevelts' visit, and Logan Miller, *Reminiscences*, gives an amusing account of it. Details of Lindbergh's activity appear in La Croix, *Record*, Acc. 435, Box 15, and in the interviews and letters from Lindbergh to the authors, cited above. He relates the episode of Ford's and Sorensen's aeronautical ideas.

32. *N.Y. Times*, Nov. 15, 1942 (general comment) and Feb. 16, 1943 (Wallgren); *Fortune*, XXVII, Feb. 1943, 113; 1943 Chronology, La Croix, *Record*, Acc. 435, Box 15 (monthly production); Frank Nolan, Memo of telephone conversation with Justice Frank Murphy, Feb. 17, 1943 and I. A. Capizzi to Harry Bennett, Feb. 19, 1943, Acc. 587, Box 71 (Roosevelt).

33. 1943 Chronology, La Croix, *Record*, Acc. 435, Box 15 (work force); CES to Nelson, March 11, 1943, Acc. 38, Box 99 (draftees); *N.Y. Times*, Dec. 5, 1942 (hiring, quitting); *Automotive & Aviation Industries*, XC, Apr. 15, 1944, 85–88 (losses to armed forces); CES to C. E. Wilson, WPB, Aug. 4, 1943, Acc. 38, Box 99 (hiring and quitting).

34. La Croix, *Record*, Acc. 435, Box 15 (shifting production); *Automotive & Aviation Industries*, XC, Apr. 15, 1944, 85–88; M. L. Bricker, *Reminiscences*. The *Automotive & Aviation Industries* article gives a very full account of sub-contracting, and while doubtless based on Ford data, presents an objective point of view.

35. La Croix, as cited above; corr., Acc. 38, Box 99 (showing Army and Douglas pressure); Fulton to CES, July 9, 1943, telegraphed text of Committee's report, and CES to Fulton, July 1943 all in Acc. 38, Box 99; *Army Air Forces in World War II*, VI, 335–337 (modification and modification centers); Logan Miller, *Reminiscences*. Early Ford planes, as Miller states and a vast amount of Ford correspondence and reports show, seem to have met all specifications; La Croix gives a list of 87 Ford officials in San Diego which shows that all types were represented. Planes were modified by adding armor, guns, communications equipment, or target-finding equipment, or for work against submarines or in the Arctic or the desert. There was thus ample evidence to show that many Committee statements were quite untrue. The two union officials who denounced the WR record were Glenn R. Brayton and Walter Quillico, and they were quoted in the *N.Y. Times* of Sept. 26, 1943. The *Times* carried the company's reply on Sept. 29.

36. La Croix, statement to the authors, Sept. 1960 (on morale); Memorandum of Meeting, WR, Aug. 11, 1943, Branshaw to CES, Sept. 25, 1943, and CES to Branshaw, Sept. 25, 1943, and Ford production in latter months of 1943 all in Acc. 38, Box 99.

37. Bricker, *Reminiscences* (block system); Kroll, *Reminiscences* (inspection); La Croix, *Record*, Acc. 435, Box 41 (visitors, workers).

38. Branshaw to CES and CES to Branshaw, telegrams of Sept. 25, 1943, Arnold to CES (in answer to telegram not included), Oct. 29, 1943, Acc. 38, Box 99; Sorensen, *Forty Years*, 290; La Croix, *Record*, Acc. 435, Box 15 (production); C. E. Wilson to FMC, Mar. 3, 1944, Acc. 38, Box 99; Press Release, FMC, April 10, 1945, Acc. 454, Box 9 (Army-Navy "E").

39. Consolidated to Chief, Materiel Division, Wash., D.C., Feb. 25, 1941, defining position (quote from this), Acc. 38, Box 93; Farkas, Bricker, in their reminiscences (Consolidated's position); proposed bulletin apparently submitted by Consolidated in Apr. 1943 and CES's memorandum on it to AAF, Apr. 29, 1943, Acc. 38, Box 99 (from which his quotation is taken).

40. La Croix, *Record*, Acc. 435, Box 23 (data and totals); Brandt to HF, Dec. 14, 1942, Acc. 38, Box 95; *Washington Manpower Report*, Report No. 19, prepared by Automotive Council for War production, Oct. 27, 1943 (production per employe.)

41. Logan Miller, *Reminiscences* (rubber dies); Lindbergh to authors, Nov. 13, 1959; Wibel, Wagner, Bricker in their reminiscences (lack of training in Ford workers, facilities for making hard-metal dies, necessity of accuracy for unskilled employees—that is, mechanical rather than manual accuracy); *Army Air Force in World War II*, VI, 329. An Article in *Take-off*, III, Mar. 19, 1943, 1, 7, tells the story of North American's first bomber. Although the company had extensive plant facilities and a trained aircraft work force, and received the cooperation of both Consolidated and Ford, the production of the first bomber took 319 days. Many of the parts for it were furnished by the other two companies.

42. War Production Board, *War Manufacturing Facilities*, Wash., Jan. 1945, Introductory statement, 134–136, 229–231, 250–257; FMC News Release, Jan. 16, 1951; La Croix, *Record*,

*passim.* The summary of Ford war production offered by the release is presented in round figures; La Croix in dealing with the various projects gives the exact numbers produced, which except in a few cases he does not touch upon, are used here.

# CHAPTER IX
## Power is the Prize

Much documentary material on the relationships of Henry Ford, Edsel Ford, Harry Bennett, and Charles Sorensen with each other is scattered through the Ford Archives. Edsel Ford's file, Accession 6, Henry Ford's file, Accession 285, and the general executive file, Accession 46, are all valuable. In the Sorensen office file, Accession 38, Boxes 77 to 124 inclusive contain pertinent material. In Accession 587, Folder 26 is labelled "Harry Bennett," and offers letters from operators who did detective work for Bennett, correspondence bearing on his role as confidential agent for Henry Ford, and materials on his activity in securing appointments as manufacturers' agents for his friends. Accession 375, Box 2, holds Henry Ford II's deposition in the Ferguson Case, January 1950, in which pp. 4401–4409 deals with the relations of Henry Ford II and Bennett. Invaluable light on the subject of this chapter is afforded by the Reminiscences of Logan Miller, Laurence Sheldrick, A. M. Wibel, G. J. Crimmins, and Fred L. Black, among others.

Several books are useful, notably Charles Sorensen's *My Forty Years with Ford,* Harry Bennett's *We Never Called Him Henry,* Prince Louis Ferdinand's *The Rebel Prince* (see pp. 157–161), and William C. Richards's *The Last Billionaire* (see pp. 229–232); but Sorensen and Bennett must be used with great reserve. Among the most illuminating magazine articles are "The Rebirth of Ford," *Fortune,* XXX, May 1947, 82 ff.; Robert Coughlan, "Co-Captains in Ford's Battle for Supremacy," *Life,* Feb. 28, 1944, 84 ff.; George Koether, "How Henry Ford II Saved the Empire," *Look,* XVII, Je. 30, 1953, 48–52; John McCarten, "The Little Man in Henry Ford's Basement," *American Mercury,* May 1940, 7–15 and Je. 1940, 200–208; and Joe McCarthy, "The Ford Family," *Holiday,* XXI, Je. 1957, 69 ff.; XXII, July 1957, 60 ff.; Aug. 1957, 64 ff.; and Sept. 1957, 72 ff. The *N.Y. Times, Detroit Times,* and *Free Press,* and *Time* contain scattered reports of value. The authors have had the benefit of talks with Ernest Kanzler, and illuminating letters by I. A. Capizzi.

1. *Time,* Mar. 13, 1944.

2. Sorensen, *Forty Years,* 4–7, 49 ff.

3. The *Reminiscences* of Wibel, Sheldrick, and Black bring out this point.

4. See William B. Harris, "Ford's Fight for First," *Fortune,* L (Sept. 1954), 125; *Iron Age,* Sept. 30, 1943, 66; Andre Fontaine, "Revolution on the Rouge," *Collier's,* Nov. 15, 1947, 58; Bennett, *We Never Called Him Henry,* 162. Sorensen asserts that Henry Ford gave up the presidency in 1919 "ostensibly to bring out another car in competition with Model T, but actually to frighten the few last lingering stockholders to sell out, which they did"; *Forty Years,* 306.

5. Bennett, *We Never Called Him Henry,* 152. According to Bennett, Ford jumped at the conclusion that the Du Ponts were behind a survey made by the Federal Public Housing Administration; but later he "cooled off."

6. Anthony Harff, Sheldrick, *Reminiscences;* see also J. L. McCloud, *Reminiscences,* for plant attitudes toward Bennett.

7. Bennett's *We Never Called Him Henry,* Chs. 3, 4. Asserting that Henry Ford's attitude in many critical situations was "Harry, let's you and him have a fight," Bennett declares that Henry on different occasions assured him that both Sorensen and Edsel were "no friends of yours."

8. *We Never Called Him Henry,* 15, 28, 39, 64, 172, 173; FMC Personnel Off. Records; Irving Bacon, *Reminiscences,* offers many sidelights on Bennett; Acc. 587, Folder "Harry Bennett," contains items upon the special errands he performed.

9. James Sweinhart, "Life Story" of Harry Bennett, *Detroit News*, Sept. 30, 1945; Kenneth F. McCormick, "Meet the Real Harry Bennett," *Detroit Free Press*, Feb. 8, 1942.

10. Black, Voorhees, *Reminiscences;* Bennett's statement that he was closer to Ford than Edsel is in *We Never Called Him Henry*, 5; see also pp. 36–38; Coughlan, "Co-Captains," *op. cit.*, 85, and *Detroit Times*, Je. 13, 1935, are illuminating.

11. *We Never Called Him Henry*, 42.

12. Frank C. Riecks, *Reminiscences*, for Ford's dislike of personal meddling; *Detroit News*, Oct. 1, 1945, on Ford's fear of kidnappers and Bennett's vacation visits to gangsters; John H. O'Brien, "Henry Ford's Commander in Chief," *Forum*, XCIX, Feb. 1938, 70. Bennett's target practice is covered by John McCarten, "The Little Man," *op. cit.*, and Bennett's own book, 42.

13. McCarten, "The Little Man," 10. Other Bennett quotations are from *Detroit Times*, Je. 30, 1937, and *We Never Called Him Henry*, 65; see also Sorensen, *Forty Years*, 257, relating how in 1942 Bennett wished to surround Edsel's house to prevent a kidnapping of his sons. Bennett received some fame for helping break the Jackie Thompson kidnapping; see Acc. 589, Box 68.

14. Bennett gives a blood-curdling account in his book (Ch. 10) of his adventures with "Legs" Laman and his fellow-kidnappers. After trying to murder Bennett, and being paroled to him at the Rouge, Laman at first indicated regret that he had failed.

15. *We Never Called Him Henry*, 69, 70.

16. McCarten, "The Little Man," 10.

17. Wibel, *Reminiscences;* Bennett, *We Never Called Him Henry*, 37, 38.

18. Riecks, *Reminiscences;* Bennett, *We Never Called Him Henry*, 25, 30; and on Edsel's response to the situation, Sorensen, *Forty Years*, 321.

19. Without giving dates except to indicate the general period when the Model A emerged, Sorensen writes: "Relations between Henry and Edsel Ford once reached such a serious state that Mr. Ford told me to tell his son to clear out, go to California, and stay there until ordered to come back." Sorensen delayed, and after two days good feeling returned. *Forty Years*, 222.

20. Wibel, Crimmins, and Frank Riecks, *Reminiscences*, with McCarthy, *op. cit.*, 98, Sorensen, *Forty Years*, 27, 256–262, 302, and *Fortune*, XXIX, Je. 1944, 142 ff., cover Henry Ford's adoption of Bennett as a substitute son. Sweinhart, *Detroit News*, Sept. 28, 1945, and Apr. 21, 1947, describes Ford's morning routine and his pointing at Bennett. See also Anthony Harff, *Reminiscences*.

21. Reminiscences of Wait, Logan Miller, and H. L. Moekle; Sorensen, *Forty Years*, 272.

22. Martindale, *Reminiscences*.

23. Black, Wibel, *Reminiscences*, supplemented by McCarthy, "The Ford Family," *op. cit.*, *passim;* Sorensen, *Forty Years*, 311, 312. The authors have profited by talks with Ernest Kanzler, Henry Ford II, E. G. Liebold, Sorensen, and others involved in the situation.

24. Sorensen, *Forty Years*, Ch. 20, "Henry Ford's Greatest Failure," covers this story graphically, and his *Reminiscences* offer additional detail. Bennett, *We Never Called Him Henry*, 146, states that "everything seemed to conspire to create differences between Edsel and me," and explains how he "got Mr. Ford to think" of certain matters; p. 154.

25. Wibel, *Reminiscences; N.Y. Times*, Apr. 29, 1943.

26. This list is printed as given in Sorensen, *Forty Years*, 320. Clearly two of lines should be turned into one: "Seeing labor leaders [is] Bennett's job, no one else."

27. The *Detroit Free Press, N.Y. Times*, and other newspapers May 26–May 29, 1943 (accounts of Edsel's death and funeral). Details of manoeuvring inside the company as given by Sorensen, 324, 325, Bennett, 166 ff., and others, are widely discrepant. The account given in the text follows the most probable statements.

28. The authors are indebted to Mr. Capizzi for full statements, while the subject is also covered by memoranda of conferences which R. B. Darragh and Edmund J. Gallagher, of the Ford Motor Company legal staff, held with Mr. Capizzi on Feb. 15, 1952, and Oct. 24, 1961. Bennett adverts to the subject in *We Never Called Him Henry*, 87, 132, 174.

29. Minutes, Stockholders' Meeting, Je. 1, 1943 and Board of Directors' Meeting, Je. 1, 1943, both in Secty's Off.

30. *Time*, Je. 14, 1943, 84 ff.

# CHAPTER X
## End of a Legend

This tenebrous chapter in company affairs is given partial illumination by the books of the two principal figures, Charles E. Sorensen's *My Forty Years with Ford,* and Harry Bennett's *We Never Called Him Henry.* Sorensen's book is based on his oral history memoir in the Ford Archives and his diary; Bennett's on his memory only. Both are self-justificatory in dealing with these years, but Bennett reveals more than he probably intended. Sorensen's treatment of the events leading up to his departure shows grasp, and is magnanimous in its attitude toward Henry Ford. Valuable material may be found in Joe McCarthy's article on "The Ford Family" in *Holiday,* XXII, July, Aug. 1957, especially Part III (Aug.). The authors have talked with Henry Ford II, Ernest Kanzler, John S. Bugas, and Sorensen, and Mr. I. A. Capizzi has enlarged on certain points in correspondence with the authors. The oral history reminiscences for the occurrences narrated here are particularly good; those by Sheldrick, Wibel, Crimmins, McCloud, Logan Miller, and Doss may in fact be termed invaluable.

1. Sorensen, *Forty Years,* 328 ff.; interv. Henry Ford II, June 16, 1959 (talk with father); Apr. 22, 30, May 5, 1941, Gnau corr., Ford Archives.

2. Je. 5, 1941, Gnau corr., Ford Archives.

3. Bennett, *We Never Called Him Henry,* 167 (board meetings), 323, 324 (quoting Dr. McClure).

4. Interv. Henry Ford II, Je. 16, 1959.

5. Sorensen, *Forty Years,* 328.

6. *Fortune,* XXIX, Je. 1944, 245.

7. *Look,* XVII, Je. 30, 1953, 48, 49.

8. Quoted by Joe McCarthy, "The Ford Family," *Holiday,* XXII, July, 1957, 98.

9. Acc. 464, Box 2 (speech dated July 21, 1944).

10. Sheldrick, *Reminiscences;* Sorensen, *op. cit.,* 329 (dismisses Sheldrick's ouster in a sentence).

11. Sorensen, *Forty Years,* 329; Liebold, *Reminiscences.*

12. Wait, *Reminiscences.*

13. *N.Y. Times,* Je. 19, 1943.

14. *Detroit News,* Mar. 5, 1944; *Newsweek,* XXIII, Mar. 13, 1944, 72; *N.Y. Times,* Mar. 5, 1944 (with portrait).

15. Interv. Ernest Kanzler, Jan. 14, 1960.

16. Sorensen shortly became president of Willys-Overland at a high salary, with the grant of an option on company stock; *N.Y. Times,* July 13, 1944; for the Canadian posts, *N.Y. Times,* July 4, 1944.

17. *Iron Age,* CLIII, Mar. 9, 1944, 74; *Time,* Mar. 13, 1944; *Fortune,* XXIX, Je. 1944, 139–144, 245–259.

18. James Sweinhart, *Detroit News,* Sept. 30, 1945; Fred L. Black, *Reminiscences.*

19. "The Rebirth of Ford," *Fortune,* May 1947, 82 ff.; McCarthy, *op. cit.*

20. Doss, *Reminiscences.*

21. McCloud, *Reminiscences.*

22. *Look,* XVIX, Je. 30, 1953, 48, 49.

23. Interv. confidential source, Jan. 1960.

24. Doss, *Reminiscences; N.Y. Times,* Apr. 11, 1944.

25. The authors have had the benefit of talks and correspondence with Mr. Bugas. See also Logan Miller, *Reminiscences,* and Bennett, *op. cit.,* 148, 149.

26. Interv. HF II, Je. 16, 1959.

27. This is covered by Joe McCarthy, "The Ford Family," Part III, *Holiday,* XXII, Aug.

1957, an article corrected for the authors by Mr. Bugas. Light is also thrown on the events by information from I. A. Capizzi, Feb. 15, 1952, and Oct. 25, 1961.

28. Acc. 454, Box 2 (HF II's 2 trips); *Atlanta Journal,* Nov. 2, 1944 (Atlanta parts depot).

29. McCarthy, *ut supra;* Andre Fontaine, "Revolution on the Rouge," *Collier's,* CXX, Nov. 15, 1947, 58–60.

30. Logan Miller, *Reminiscences.*

31. Interv. Kanzler, Jan. 14, 1960; McCarthy, *op. cit.*

32. McCarthy, *ut supra;* Min. Bd. Dirs., Sept. 21, 1945, Secty off.; *N.Y. Times* followed its news despatch of June 2 with a hopeful editorial, Je. 6, 1944. Actually, Bennett remained less than a month, later retiring to California.

33. William Richards, *The Last Billionaire; Henry Ford* (Bantam Ed.), N.Y., 1956, 299.

# CHAPTER XI
## Outer Empire: War and Peace

Mr. Hill and Dr. Mira Wilkins, in collecting materials for a separate volume on the foreign undertakings of the Ford Motor Company, have talked with numerous men in London, Paris, Cologne, and other cities. Some of their findings are embodied in a report by Dr. Wilkins, "The European Ford Companies in World War II," (May 1959), and other papers in their files. Hilary St. George Saunders wrote an excellent volume on *Ford at War* (London, no date), covering the British story 1939–1946. For this record and for continental activities the annual reports of the Ford Motor Company, Ltd. are also valuable. The *Ford Times,* English edition, through all the years here covered, throws much light on wartime and post-war activities. The German story is partly covered by a booklet, *Ford in Deutschland* (Munich, 1955). Valuable material on Ford history in Europe, Asia, and Australasia is available in files of the British magazine *Motor.* Accurate summaries of the annual reports of the British and chief Continental companies (when available) were published in the London *Times,* and with useful comment in the London *Economist.*

Considering the turmoil of the war years, documentary sources are surprisingly ample. The minutes of meetings of the European boards of directors are preserved in the Ford Archives in Dearborn, together with minutes of stockholders' meetings; consult Accession 606 (France), Accession 608 (Spain), Accession 20 (Roumania), and for other companies the Secretary's office. Fairly full records of the Dagenham plant are in the Regent Street office of Ford Motor Company, Ltd., and the plant itself. Minutes of the Ford Investment Company (Guernsey) are kept in the Central Files, International Division, Dearborn. Material on the history of the Poissy plant, on the wartime vicissitudes of the Cologne plant, on the de-control of Cologne, and other aspects of the French and German operations, are in Storage B-38 of the International Division, Boxes 97b, 115b, etc. The International Division, Central Files, also contained annual reports, correspondence, and other data on the Ford Motor Company of Canada, Ltd.

The authors gleaned much invaluable material from the folders in "Central Files," Ford International Division. Since the research was done, "Central Files" has been abolished; Miss Charlene Ferrill, formerly head of this department, now has charge of the materials once in that repository. All references in the foot-notes to International Division relate to these documents.

In the Ford Archives at Dearborn, Edsel Ford's office file is Accession 6, and is replete with material on the foreign companies arranged by year. It covers the French and other continental companies through 1942. Sorensen's office file, Accession 38, has much correspondence to the eve of war. Accession 46 contains general executive correspondence, not very useful. Henry Ford's office files make up Accession 285, but offer little light. Data on Machinery Suppliers, Inc. is in Accession 333, and the complete minutes of Matford are in Accession 334. The audit reports in Accession 415, Box 1, cover the French company in enlightening fashion; see especially "Report on Financial Condition Ford SAF, Historical Section." Accession 507, Boxes 61–74, are invaluable for British and French operations.

1. Acc. 6, Box 361.

2. *Ibid.* Operations of Fordair ended with the German conquest of France; see Mins. Ford SAF Bd. Dirs., Aug. 9, 18, 1940, Acc. 606, Box 2.

3. H. C. Møller, Memo, Dec. 11, 1944, Mins. FMC-Denmark Bd. Dirs. International Div., Office of Lord Perry; Report on German Company, International Div.; booklet, *"Ford in Deutschland,"* 5; "Germany Cologne, Ford-Werke, A/G Reports, Audits, 1946–47, International Division; reports in "Germany Cologne Ford-Werke, A/G, De-control, 1945–47." Storage B-38, Box 97B, International Division; Tallberg, *Reminiscences.*

4. Albert to EBF, July 11, 1940, report from Dollfus, July 18, 1940, and numerous subsequent communications from Dr. Albert to EBF, all in Acc. 6, Box 361.

5. Tallberg, *Reminiscences.*

6. Dollfus struck this note repeatedly in letters to EBF, JJuly 18, Aug. 2, Aug. 31, Sept. 18, 1940, Acc. 6, Box 361.

7. Dollfus to EBF, Nov. 27, 1940, Acc. 6, Box 361.

8. Dollfus to CES, May 30, 1941, Acc. 6, Box 369; Dollfus to Edsel Ford, Jan. 29, 1941, Acc. 6, Box 376; Dollfus to EBF, Aug. 21, 1941, Nov. 25, 1941, Acc. 6, Box 369 (expressing great content). Dollfus was delighted with the new Poissy plant.

9. For the Hungarian company see the manager's reports to directors, Select File; for the Roumanian company, mins. Ford Romana Bd. Dirs. Acc. 320, Box 1, and H. S. Cooper, "Memo on Management and Directorate Problems at Bucharest," with Perry's letter to Edsel Ford, Jan. 2, 1941, Acc. 320, Box 1.

10. *Detroit News,* Je. 19, 1940 (Ford announcement); *N.Y. Times,* Je. 19, 20, 1940. Baltimore *Sun,* Je. 19, 1940, was one of the few American papers to note that Ford Ltd. at Dagenham already had a contract to build the same Rolls-Royce engines.

11. Hilary St. George Saunders, *Ford at War; Ford Times* (English edition), X–XII, *passim,* and XIII, Nov.–Dec. 1945, 557–565; Patrick Hennessy to Wibel, July 13, 1942, Acc. 390, Box 84.

12. *N.Y. Times,* July 31, 1941; *Ford Times* (Eng. ed.) IX, Sept.–Oct. 1942; Saunders, *op. cit.,* 48; EBF to Perry, Mar. 12, 1941, in "FMC Ltd., Shares-Dividends, 1938–1946," International Div.

13. Mins. Ford SAF, Bd. Dirs., Apr. 21, Sept. 30, 1942, Feb. 18, 1943, Oct. 19, 1944, Acc. 606, Box 276; Dollfus to EBF, Jan. 28, 1942, Acc. 6, Box 376.

14. Wiskott to Beckers, Oct. 12, Dec. 1, 1943, in "Ford SAF France Poissy Hist. Data, 1940–1948." Storage B-38, Box 115B, International Division. See also Mins. Ford SAF, Bd. Dirs., 1942–1944, Acc. 606, Box 2; Dollfus to EBF, Aug. 15, 1942, Acc. 6, Box 376.

15. Mins. Ford SAF, Bd. Dirs., 1942–1944, Acc. 606, Box 2 (bombings of Poissy); Breckinridge Long to EBF, Sept. 29, 1942, Acc. 6, Box 376; Wibel to Hennessy, Je. 2, 1942, Acc. 390, Box 84; Dollfus to EBF, Aug. 15, 1942, Acc. 6, Box 376. Ford-Werke, *Annual Reports 1938–1951,* International Division (bombings of Cologne); Ford-Werke AG De-control, 1945–47 in Storage B-38, Box 97B, International Division, article by David M. Nichol, Wash. *Evening Star,* Je. 5, 1947.

16. Monthly letters of Cologne managers 1938–1948 in Storage B-38, Box 2A, International Division; and Office of Lord Perry, "Report on German Company," pp. 9b, 9d, International Division; *Ford in Deutschland, passim;* Tallberg, *Reminiscences.*

17. "Ford-Werke AG De-control, 1945–47," in Storage B-38, Box 97B, International Division (German situation); and Office of Lord Perry, "Report on German Company," *ut supra;* Legrand, "Financial Analysis," Oct. 14, 1947 (typescript), in "France Poissy Hist. Data, 1940–48," Storage B-38, Box 115B, International Div. (French situation).

18. FMC Ltd., *Annual Reports 1941–1950;* Roberge, General Executive Corr., Storage B-38, Box 51, International Division; "FMC Hist. Data (A)" International Division, including booklet *Ford Motor Company, Ltd.* London, 1951.

19. Acc. 11, Box 1 and "Report on European Trip," Acc. 536, Box 46 (trip of Ford and Howard); FMC, *Annual Reports 1947–48–49* (the setting); Report of Management Meeting No. 14, Dec. 1948, Acc. 422, Box 1 (Breech's European trip).

## CHAPTER XII
### Reaching for Answers

1. Joe McCarthy, "The Ford Family," Part 4, *Holiday*, XXI, Sept. 1957, 73; interv. Charles E. Bosworth, Dec. 9, 1959; FMC release, Address HF II, Commonwealth Club, S.F., Feb. 8, 1946.

2. Wiesmyer, Moekle, Tallberg, in their reminiscences; N.Y. *World-Telegram*, Je. 6, 1945 (tractor); Report by George S. Armstrong & Co., Inc. (undated, but presumably 1946). The Armstrong Report, to be cited as such hereafter, reveals that for the period 1930–1939 inclusive, the company showed a loss of $62,764,000 on manufacturing operations. With "other income" added, it showed a profit after taxes of approximately $20,000,000. The war years had been modestly profitable.

3. *Steel*, CXVII, Oct. 8, 1945, 92; *Newsweek*, XLV, Je. 20, 1955, 74–76; N.Y. *Times*, Sept. 22, 1945 (goal); *ibid.*, Je. 30, 1945 (surplus); Robert Coughlan, "Co-Captains in Ford's Battle for Supremacy," *Life*, XXXVIII, Feb. 28, 1955, 90; "Henry Ford II Speaks Out—A Conversation with Tom Lilley," *Atlantic Monthly*, CLXXX, Dec. 1947, 26.

4. Memo, HF II to all Dept. Heads, Bldg. Supts., etc., Acc. 516, Box 1 (appointments); Mins., Gen. Planning Com., Oct. 3, 1945, Secty's off.; interv. HF II, Je. 16, 1959; HF II, Office records.

5. Coughlan, *op. cit.*, 90; Wiesmyer, *Reminiscences;* Detroit *News*, Oct. 12, 1945, and *Business Week*, Oct. 6, 1945, 18; Logan Miller, *Reminiscences.* Among other Bennett men who departed were Stanley Fay, assistant personnel director, John Thompson, public relations director, and Clifford Prevost (in Washington, D.C.).

6. Mins. Policy Com., Oct. 3, 1945, Secty's off.; also for Oct. 18, 1945, Jan. 14, 28, 1946; interv. Ernest C. Kanzler, Jan. 14, 1960.

7. N.Y. *Times*, May 25, 1945; Kansas City *Times*, Je. 5, 1945; *Detroit Free Press*, Je. 3, 1945; *Wall Street Journal*, Je. 21, 1945 (Ford quota); N.Y. *Times*, Je. 3, 1945 (new car).

8. N.Y. *Herald-Tribune*, Aug. 16, 1945 (effects of V-J day, Ford statement); Detroit *News*, Aug. 29, 1945 (K-Hayes strike); *ibid.*, Sept. 6, 15; Portland (Mich.), *Press-Herald*, Sept. 15, 1945.

9. Detroit *News*, Oct. 8, 1945 (K-Hayes strike); *ibid.*, Oct. 11 (new strikes); FMC Release 191, Nov. 2, 1945; N.Y. *Times*, Nov. 21, 27, 1945.

10. N.Y. *Times*, Nov. 19, 1945 (prices on new models, comparison with pre-war, etc.); Mins. Policy Com., Oct. 29, 1945; J. R. Davis to Dealers, FMC Release 194 (undated, but apparently early Nov.).

11. Telegram, HF II to John W. Snyder, Jan. 29, 1946, Acc. 454, Box 12; Snyder to HF II, N.Y. *Times*, Feb. 2, 1946; Speech by HF II, "One Solution to Our Problems," Commonwealth Club, S.F., Feb. 8, 1946, Acc. 247, Box 1.

12. *Ibid.*

13. OPA Press Release, Feb. 15, 1946, copy in Acc. 454, Box 10; *Congressl Rec.*, XCII, pt. 1, 79th Cong., 2nd Sess. (Jan. 14–Feb. 18, 1946), 1429; N.Y. *Times*, Feb. 20, 1946.

14. Telephone conversation, Martindale, Crimmins, Newsom, Feb. 19, 1946, Acc. 454, Box 10; HF II to Brent Spence, Feb. 20, 1946, and HF II to Bowles, Feb. 20, 1946, Acc. 454, Box 11; N.Y. *Times*, Feb. 22, 1946 (HF II to Bowles); OPA Orders #14 to MPR 594, Mar. 11, 1946, Acc. 157, Box 61, and Prices and Specifications, genl. ltr. no. 1, May 22, 1946, in unnumbered Box on Ford Prices; FMC, Annual Report, 1946, 28 (strikes and shortages).

15. Keith Sward, *Legend of Henry Ford*, 471; N.Y. *Times*, Nov. 16, 1945.

16. Sward, *op. cit.*, 470–472; N.Y. *Times*, Nov. 21, 22, 24, & 29, 1945; Genl. Planning Mins., Nov. 9, 1945, Secty's off.; Detroit *Times*, Nov. 20, 1945 (start of negotiations).

17. N.Y. *Times*, Nov. 29, Dec. 10, 11, 1945.

18. *Ibid.*, Dec. 13, 18, 21, 25, 1945.

19. Henry Ford II, "The Challenge of Human Engineering," *Vital Speeches*, XII, Feb. 15, 1946, 273–274.

20. *Current Biography, 1946,* 194–195; *Time,* XLVII, Jan. 21, 1946, 19; *N.Y. Times,* Jan. 27, Feb. 27, 1946. For comments on the settlement see also *Steel,* CXVIII, Mar. 11, 1946, 75–76, which has a somewhat skeptical attitude toward the union's promises.

21. *N.Y. Times,* Feb. 27, 28, 1946 (GM, Chrysler), Mar. 13, 1946 (GM settlement); *Time,* XLVII, Jan. 21, 1946, 19. The benefits that UAW received in the GM settlement included the removal of inequities in wage rates (which they estimated in itself to be worth another cent in wages), improved vacation pay, higher overtime pay, and equal rates for women.

22. Interv. HF II, June 16, 1959.

23. Intervs. members of Thornton group. Except in particular instances, it seems undesirable to refer to these interviews separately. Hereafter they will be cited by last names only, and usually several together. Tht dates of the interviews are as follows: Ben D. Mills, Nov. 17, 1959; J. O. Wright, Nov. 18, 1959; Arjay Miller, Jan. 11, 1960; R. S. McNamara, Jan. 8, 1960; C. E. Bosworth, Dec. 9, 1959; J. E. Lundy, July 21, 1960.

24. All intervs. cited in Note 23; FMC, News Bureau Releases, Acc. 157, Box 61; biographies in *Who's Who in America.*

25. Intervs. Wright, Miller, McNamara, Bosworth; interv. Kanzler, *op. cit.*

26. Intervs. Wright, Miller, Bosworth.

27. All intervs. as cited in Note 23 above; H. J. Robinson, *Reminiscences.*

28. *Ibid.*

29. *Ibid.*

30. Intervs. HF II and Kanzler, *op. cit.*

31. Ford Publicity Release, May 17, 1946, Acc. 454, Box 12; deposition E. R. Breech, Ferguson v. Ford, 24–33; *Newsweek,* XXIX, Apr. 21, 1947, 75. *Newsweek* predicted that Breech would succeed C. E. Wilson as President of GM.

32. Intervs. Ford, Kanzler; interv. E. R. Breech, Jan. 6, 1960; deposition Breech, Ferg. v. Ford, 60, 61.

33. Interv. Breech; deposition Breech, Ferg. v. Ford, 270, 289, 294; interv. Kanzler. Actually, there were various complications surrounding a possible sale of stock. The family did not want to sell for a variety of reasons, and while the foundation could, there was a great difficulty as to setting a price. Kanzler felt that a stock option plan was not included because it would have been far too complicated to fix its terms at that time.

34. Deposition Breech, Ferg. v. Ford, 301; deposition HF II, 230, 4789–4795; intervs. Breech, Kanzler.

35. Interv. Kanzler; deposition Breech, Ferg. v. Ford, 648, 649.

# CHAPTER XIII
## To Rebuild a Company

1. Interv. Breech, Jan. 6, 1960; interv. Crusoe, Jan. 12, 1960, FMC, Press Release, Oct. 15, 1953, Acc. 536, Box 24; deposition HF II, Ferg. v. Ford, 120–121, 2984–2985.

2. Deposition Breech, Ferg. v. Ford, 615–616; HF II to Breech, Je. 14, 1946, in deposition Breech, 672–674; *N.Y. Times,* Apr. 23, 1946; FMC, Press Release, Apr. 25, 1946, Acc. 454, Box 12; Tallberg, *Reminiscences;* interv. Breech, *op. cit.*

3. Deposition HF II, Ferg. v. Ford, 4462–4468; interv. Crusoe, *op. cit.* "I was the man who persuaded him to come to Ford," said Crusoe of Harder. His was undoubtedly the final push needed, but both Breech and Ford had already done much.

4. *N.Y. Times,* Mar. 12 (first stoppage); Apr. 5 (Cameron); Je. 2 (HF I's appearance); July 2, 1946 (second stoppage); Je. 5, 1946; Mins. Policy Com., Apr. 15, May 3, 10, 1946 (light car).

5. Mins. Policy Com., May 20, Je. 6, 1946; interv. Breech, *op. cit.*

6. Deposition Breech, Ferg. v. Ford, 4789–4794.

7. Interv. Crusoe, *op. cit.;* interv. Breech; Mins. Policy Com., Je. 6, 1946.

8. Interv. Breech; *N.Y Times,* Nov. 15, 1960; HF II, Speech, Dec. 2, 1946, Acc. 422, Box 1; FMC, *Annual Report 1946; Statistical Abstract, 1958,* 237–239.

9. Interv. Breech; Mins. Policy Com., Aug. 6, 1946; FMC, *Annual Report 1946.* At the time the claim for $2000 was made. Later, the official company figure for the year was a loss of $8,100,000. (This is given in the 1955 report which covers the previous ten years of company activities.) The discrepancy is symptomatic of the financial confusion still existing in 1946.

10. Nevins and Hill, *Ford: Expansion and Challenge,* 232–238; FMC Sales Data, Acc. 384.

11. Deposition HF II, Ferg. v. Ford, 4476–4479. For Ford's earlier legal arrangements, see *Ford: the Times, the Man, the Company* and *Ford: Expansion and Challenge,* which cover the Selden Patent Suit, the Chicago *Tribune* Suit, the Dodge Suit, the Leland Suit, the Sapiro Case, and other actions. Gossett was born in Texas in 1904, studied law at Columbia Univ., and had appeared in notable suits in the 1930s (e.g. U.S. Govt. v. Aluminum Co. of America, 1937–1941). He had been General Counsel for Bendix 1943–1947.

12. Interv. Breech; Mins. Policy Com., July 17, 1946; Tallberg, *Reminiscences.*

13. Wiesmyer, *Reminiscences.*

14. Nevins and Hill, *Ford: Expansion and Challenge,* 155, 402 ff.; Donaldson Brown, "Decentralized Operations and Responsibilities with Coordinated Control" (pamphlet), 1927 (no publisher). In a 1942 reprint the words "in General Motors" were added to the title; interv. McNamara, Jan. 8, 1960; Alfred J. Sloan in collab. w. Boyden Sparkes, *Adventures of a White-Collar Man,* Garden City, N.Y., 1941, 134–135; Breech to Management Meeting No. 2, May 13, 1947, 7, Acc. 422, Box 1; Samuel Eliot Morison, *The Development of Harvard University, 1869–1929,* Cambridge, Mass., 1930, 535.

15. Peter F. Drucker, *Concept of the Corporation,* N.Y., 1946, 26, 27, and *passim;* intervs. HF II, Breech, Wright.

16. Intervs. Crusoe, Wright, Miller; deposition Breech, Ferg. v. Ford, 336–337, 351, 357; HF II, Departmental Communication, Sept. 19, 26, 1946 (Planning and Control Div.), Acc. 536, Box 44; Breech, Deptl. Comm., Nov. 13, 1946, Acc. 536, Box 12; *N.Y. Times,* Apr. 1, 1947; Mins. Com. Pol., July 19, 1946; G. J. Crimmins, *Reminiscences.* Crimmins had been Controller in the old FMC. Moekle and Craig, also in finance, expressed themselves similarly.

17. Intervs. Crusoe, Miller.

18. Interv. Miller.

19. Report, "Organizational Problems of the Ford Motor Company," lent authors by J. O. Wright, 1960; intervs. Crusoe, Breech, Bosworth, Mills, Wright; Mins. Policy Com., Aug. 23, 27, and Oct. 4, 1946.

20. Intervs. Mills, Wright, Breech; FMC Annual Report, 1946 (management meetings); Report of Mgt. Meetg. No. 2, May 13, 1947, Acc. 422, Box 1. Management meetings began in March 1947 and have continued to be held up to the present time. They have attempted to keep FMC officials in touch with the purposes of the company, and to promote a more unified effort. The record of the first meetings show, that there was need for interpretation of company purposes, and reassurance about them, as well as for clear explanations of what was being done.

21. Intervs. Mills, Bosworth, Crusoe, Wright, Miller; "Report on Progress in Organizational Development and Recommendations for Further Action," report signed by Crusoe and pencil-dated, "May 1, 1947," copy with J. O. Wright.

22. Tallberg, *Reminiscences;* Mins. Policy Com., Aug. 23, Sept. 3, 1946; interv. Breech; W. B. Harris, "Ford's Fight for First," *Fortune,* L, Sept. 1954, 122–127 ff.

23. Tallberg, *Reminiscences; Iron Age,* LVIII, Oct. 24, 1946, 126, 128 (assignments); Deptl. Com., HF II to FMC Execs., July 17, 1946, Acc. 536, Box 44 (McCarroll). Of the engineers, James had previously been a Studebaker man, and Currier had served in the Oldsmobile Divn. of GM.

24. Mins. Policy Com., Aug. 15, Sept. 13, 1946; Tallberg, *Reminiscences; Business Week,* May 1, 1943, 65, and *Iron Age,* CLXI, Apr. 22, 1948, 102 (Vedette); J. R. Davis, Speech to N. Eng. Sales Ngt. Cong., Jan. 10, 1947.

25. Tallberg, *Reminiscences;* interv. Breech; Mins. Prod. Com., Nov. 22, Dec. 11, 1946, Acc. 480, Box 3; FMC Personnel Records (Gregorie's departure). There is some question as to when the choice of the Ford car was made, but "approval" is not recorded until the Dec. 11 meeting.

26. Article by Ralph R. Watts, *Ford News*, Je. 18, 1948.

27. *Detroit Free Press*, Apr. 9, 10, 1947; A. H. Allen, "Mirrors of Motordom," in *Steel*, Apr. 14, 1947.

28. *Detroit Free Press*, Apr. 9, 10, 1947; *Time*, Apr. 21, 1947; Drucker, *Concept*, 220 (quote on "maximum profit"); script of Guest broadcast, Ford Archives; magazine and newspaper comment, Apr. 9–30, 1947, particularly *Mich. Mfr. & Fincl. Record*, Apr. 12, 1947, 8, and *Amer. Machinist*, Apr. 24, 1947.

29. Robert D. Leitner, *The Foreman in Industrial Relations*, N.Y., 1948, 88 ff.; Statement of W. T. Gossett before Senate Com. on Labor, Feb. 16, 1949, copy in Off. Editl. Services, FMC; FMC Industrial Rels. Divn., gen. info. on FAA; *N.Y. Times*, May 9–July 18, for factual material; *Newsweek*, XXX, July 14, 1947, 64, 67 (aftermath); FMC, *Annual Report 1947*, 22. The *Times* on July 18 reported the discharge of 32 foremen on the 17th for "violence and terrorism." The Association threatened both a strike and an appeal to the Labor Board. Apparently neither threat was carried out. The Company insisted, "We will not have such men working for us."

30. HF II in Lilley Interv., 30 (see Note 3, Ch. 12); HF II to Mgt. Mtg. No. 6, Dec. 2, 1947, Acc. 422, Box 1; HF II, Exec. Coms., May 28 (salaries), Oct. 29 (smoking), 1947, Acc. 536, Box 44.

31. HF II in Lilley Interv., 30; Addresses: Gossett to Inter-Amer. Bar Assn., May 24, 1949 and Bugas, "Labor Relations and Productivity," Oct. 2, 1947, in Off. Editl. Services, FMC; FMC, *Annual Report 1948; Detroit Times*, Sept. 29, 1949.

32. Interv. Dykstra, Jan. 5, 1960; Mins. Policy Com., Mar. 12, 1947; *Newsweek*, XXIX, Apr. 21, 1947, 72 ff. (Henry's team).

33. H. L. Youngren, Reports to Mgt. Mtg. No. 8, Feb. 16, 1948, and No. 23, Dec. 12, 1949, Acc. 422, Box 1.

34. FMC *Annual Reports 1948–58;* FMC News Release, Je. 4, 1946. Acc. 454, Box 12; *Steel*, CXVIII, Je. 10, 1946, 73–74. HF II in Lilley interv., 27; FMC News Release, Apr. 9, 1952, Acc. 536, Box 115; Report of Youngren to Mgt. Mtg. No. 8, Feb. 16, 1948; FMC *Annual Reports 1948–1950*.

35. FMC, *Annual Reports 1947–1949* (facilities); interv. Dykstra; Records of Organization Planning Office, 1946–48 (Dykstra's Divn.); HF II in Lilley interv. (Mfg. facils.)

36. FMC, *Annual Report 1948* (Benson, trucks); interv. W. C. Ford, Apr. 12, 1960; Mins. Policy Com., Mar. 12, 1947; Lincoln-Mercury News Bur. Releases, Apr. 15, 20, 1948, Acc. 182, Boxes 4, 11; *Detroit News*, Je. 9, 1948; *Business Week*, Je. 19, 1948.

37. *Ibid.*

38. FMC booklet, "Introducing the '49 Ford;" R. L. Polk, Registration Figures; deposition Davis, Ferg. v. Ford, 937; *N.Y. Times*, Apr. 4, 1949 (price of Ford cars); *Detroit News*, Je. 29, 1949 ($1000 car); FMC, *Annual Reports 1947–1949* (position, profits).

39. Intervs. Breech, Yntema, Wright; FMC News Release, Apr. 3, 1949 and May 4, 1950, and HF II, Exec. Com., Apr. 5, 1949, Acc. 536, Box 44; *ibid.*, Feb. 11, 1949 (Ford Divn.).

40. Intervs. Wright, Breech, Yntema; HF II, Exec. Comm., Mar. 15, 1949, Acc. 536, Box 44 (Yntema Appt.).

41. FMC, *Annual Report 1947;* intervs. Wright, Mills, Dykstra.

42. Interv. Crusoe.

# CHAPTER XIV
## Lions in the Path

1. FMC *et al., Counterclaim*, Ferg. v. Ford, 42 (losses); HF II to Roger Kyes, Feb. 15, 1945, in deposition HF II, Ferg. v. Ford, 1675; Robinson, *Reminiscences*. Losses on tractor production were $27,000,000 for the period of 1939–1946.

2. Deposition HF II, Ferg. v. Ford, 2741; Letter Kyes to HF II, Je. 24, 1944, in deposition HF II, 1129–1292; E. C. McRae (patent atty.) to R. I. Roberge, Apr. 26, 1945, in *ibid.*,

5319, and Harry Ferguson to OPA, Mar. 15, 1946, in *ibid.*, 1575; deposition HF II, 2726, 3339; Roger Kyes to Ferguson, Je. 24, 1946, in deposition HF II, 2918; deposition Breech, Ferg. v. Ford, 48–174, 340, 341.

3. Deposition HF II, Ferg. v. Ford, 230, 3032, 3040–3041, 4763–4764, 4770 (covering HF II's part throughout); deposition Breech, 1729–1733; Letter Clinton Davidson to ERB, July 19, 1946, in deposition HF II, 4797.

4. Deposition HF II, Ferg. v. Ford, 268, 370, 3411, 3658; *N.Y. Times,* Nov. 28, 1946; *Motor,* Dec. 1946, 172, and letter F. R. Pierce to C. E. Wilson, Nov. 21, 1946, Doc. 137621, Ferg. Docs. (all Pierce); Ford Trial Brief, Ferg. v. Ford, 17, 96; Mins. Policy Com., Nov. 12, 1946; deposition Breech, Ferg. v. Ford, 2225; FMC Press Release, Nov. 21, 1946, Doc. 137622, Ferg. Docs.

5. Deposition HF II, Ferg. v. Ford, 112 ff. (incorporation, stock); deposition Newsom, 254 (Ford participation); Pierce to Davis, Feb. 3, 1947, Doc. 137582, Ferg. Docs. (dealers); *Time,* L, July 21, 1947, 88 (Dearborn Motors tractor); deposition HF II, 3512 (construction 8N); F. R. Pierce, memo, Apr. 17, 1947, Docs. 137534–536, Ferg. Docs. (on Kyes); trial brief of Defendants, 155–170, and deposition Ferguson, 7684; "Ferguson Shows Profit," *Steel,* CXXIV, Feb. 21, 1949, 80. Newsom counseled Ford not to take DM stock because he might be accused of divided loyalty between the two companies and might be criticised as taking profits from both. The men entitled to buy DM stock were Pierce, Browning, Bugas, Crusoe, Davis, Harder, Moekle, Bricker, and Youngren. Kanzler was also eligible and agreed to buy stock and hold it for new executives to whom HF II might later want to offer it.

6. The complaint, Ferg. v. Ford, Jan. 8, 1948, 19–21, and *passim; Time,* LIX, Apr. 21, 1952, 97–98 (Ferg. quote); FMC Press Release, Jan. 1948, Acc. 536, Box 40; Amended Answer and Counterclaim, Ferg. v. Ford, July 25, 1949, *passim.*

7. HF II, Exec. Com., Feb. 11, 1949, copy in office J. O. Wright; Mins. Planng. Com., Feb. 17, 1949, Prod. Planning Committee Files; *ibid.,* Apr. 12, 1949. It should be noted that from this time forward the Policy Committee, which had taken a leading role in company affairs, begins to be less important, while the Executive Committee and the Product Planning Committee take relatively more important positions.

8. FMC Press Releases, Jan. 6, 1950 and Feb. 20, 1950, Acc. 227, Box 4; Mins. Prod. Plannng. Com., May 26, 1949; J. R. Davis, Transcript of Speech at Regional Managers Meeting, Oct. 20, 1949; Acc. 577, Box 3; *ibid.,* Crusoe quote; interv. W. Williams.

9. Mins. Policy Com., Oct. 25, 1949 (discounts); Transcript Regional Managers Meeting, Oct. 20, 1949, Acc. 577, Box 3 (price, discounts); interv. Crusoe; Robt. Coughlan, "Co-Captains in Ford's Battle for Supremacy," *Life,* XXXVIII, Feb. 28, 1955, 84 ff.; Ford Divn. Presentn., "Competitive Cost-price Position of the Ford Car," Mar. 28, 1951, Acc. 472, Box 1; Mins. Ford Divn. Operating Com., July 19, 1951, Acc. 577, Box 1.

10. Wiesmyer, *Reminiscences;* Nevins and Hill, *Ford: Expansion and Challenge,* 255–257; interv. Dykstra; Acc. 106, Box 16 (new St. Louis Assembly Plant).

11. FMC, *Annual Reports 1946–1949;* Report of Mgt. Mtg., Je. 29, 1949, 6, Acc. 422, Box 1 (Sutherland on importance of steel and additions to plant); Acc. 106, Box 5 (uniqueness of Ford steel plant); FMC Publicity Release, Sept. 19, 1945, Acc. 454, Box 12 (Willow Run); interv. Crusoe (on WR).

12. *Fortune,* XXXV, May 1947, 207–208; interv. Patterson; *Mill & Factory,* XL, Mar. 1947, 100; interv. J. McDougall, Oct. 7, 1959; *Business Week,* Oct. 23, 1948, 70.

13. Interv. McDougall; interv. Harder, Nov. 12, 1959; John Diebold, *Automation: Its Impact on Business and Labor,* N.Y., 1959; Robert Bendiner, "The Age of the Thinking Robot and What It Will Mean to Us," *The Reporter,* XII, Apr. 7, 1955, 12; Peter Drucker, "The Promise of Automation," *Harpers Magazine,* CCX, Apr. 1955, 41 ff.; Paul Einzig, *The Economic Consequences of Automation,* N.Y., 1956; *The Push-Button World,* ed. by E. M. Hugh-Jones, Norman, Okla., 1956; Walter Buckingham, *Automation: Its Impact on Business and People,* N.Y., 1961.

14. Einzig, *op. cit.;* Untitled Pamphlet on Automation, FMC Res. & Info. Dept.; interv. Dykstra; FMC News Release, Ray Sullivan on Automation, Mar. 10, 1955; D. J. Davis, in Hearings Before the Senate Sub-Committee on Economic Stabilization of the Joint Committee on the Economic Report, "Automation and Technical Change," 84th Cong., 1st Sess., Oct.

1955, Wash., 1955, hereafter cited as "Senate Sub-Com. on Automation"; interv. McDougall; Drucker as cited in Note 13 above; *American Machinist*, XCII, Oct. 21, 1948, 107–112.

15. Sullivan as cited in Note 4; Reuther testimony, Senate Sub-Com. on Automation; interv. McDougall. Automation undoubtedly meant the "loss" of many jobs to workers, but its introduction was relatively slow, and the Ford Motor Company was in a period of increasing production and did not discharge employes. Eventually, argued Ford executives (and those of many other companies), the effect of automation would be to increase jobs. This was based on the assumption that the higher production automation brought, with higher pay for those employed, and indirect increases in the work of tool-makers, etc. would actually increase rather than diminish employment. In 1959 Ford still had only about 6 per cent of its employees on automated production.

16. Intervs. Breech, Dykstra, Crusoe.

17. Telegram, HF II to Truman, July 19, 1950, and letter Truman to HF II, July 20, 1950, Acc. 16, Box 1; Mins. Bd. Dirs., July 25, 1950.

18. Organization Planning Off. Data (Defense Prods. Div.); Det. daily papers, Aug. 1950–Feb. 1951; Harder to Managt. Meetg., Feb. 7, 1951, Acc. 422, Box 3; FMC Press Release, Sept. 18, 1950; Mins. Bd. Dirs., Sept. 20, 1950; R. Elberton Smith, *The Army and Economic Mobilization*, Wash., D.C., 1959, 492, and FMC, *Annual Report 1952*, 9; interv. Dykstra; Mins. Exec. Com., Sept. 22, 1955 (Dykstra's election).

19. Interv. Dykstra; E. Robson, "Summary Relationship of Ford Motor Company and Pratt & Whitney," Jan. 1959 (typescript) in Editl. Serv. Off.; Harder to Managt. Meetg., *op. cit.;* R. J. Hampson, Rept. to Bd. Dirs., Sept. 12, 1951.

20. Robson, *op. cit.;* FMC *Annual Report 1952*, 9; Mins. Exec. Com., Je. 20, 1951, and Mins. Bd. Dirs., Nov. 14, 1951.

21. Mins. Exec. Com., Apr. 11, Dec. 12, 23, 1951, Secty.'s Off. (J-40); interv. Ben Mills; FMC, *Annual Report 1952;* FMC Press Release, Apr. 28, 1952; FMC Progress Report 1951, Acc. 422, Box 3; Bugas to Managt. Meetg., Mar. 28, 1951, Acc. 422, Box 3.

22. Breech, Speech in Cincinnati, May 23, 1951; Gossett Statement to NPA Appeals Board, May 6, 1952; *Detroit News*, May 9, 1952; *Detroit Free Press*, May 15, 1952; *Detroit Times*, May 7, 15, 1952; *Wall Street Journal*, July 17, 1952.

23. *Ward's Report, 1953,* 45, 47, 147; *N.Y. Times*, Dec. 17, 20, 1950; Breech, Speech at Cincinnati, *op. cit.; Facts on File*, Aug. 3, Sept. 14, 1951, 262, 303; Mins. Exec. Com., Sept. 14, 1951; Breech, Speech at Dallas, Je. 4, 1952; "Henry Ford II Charges Economic Controls Throttle Industry," *N.Y. Times*, Dec. 1, 1951, also interv. with him, *U.S. News & World Report*, Jan. 25, 1952, 35.

24. *Ward's Report, 1950–1952;* Details of Organization, Organization Planning Off.

25. John McDougall, Presentation to Annual Schenectady Planners and Rate Setters Assn., Oct. 18, 1954 (Buffalo & Cleve. plants); interv. Harder, Nov. 12, 1959 (productivity of Buffalo & Dearborn); *Automotive Industries*, CVII, Aug. 15, 1952, 24–38 (improvements, Dearborn plant); Steel, CXXX, Apr. 7, 1952, 99, and *Iron Age*, CLXX, Nov. 27, 1952, 117–119 (Cleve. plant); Diebold, *Automation*, 9; Harder to Society of Automotive Engineers, Mar. 26, 1953; D. J. Davis at Hearings before Senate Sub-Com. on Automation, 57; FMC, *Annual Report 1952*, 11 (comparisons).

26. Interv. Harder; interv. Patterson, Nov. 12, 1959; Breech to Committee of One Hundred at Miami, Mar. 3, 1953.

27. D. J. Davis at Hearings, *op. cit.,* 51, 57; Paul Einzig, *Economic Consequences of Automation, passim.* See also Davis's testimony in general, Diebold, *op. cit.,* FMC Training Statement, "Advantages and Disadvantages of Automation," May 8, 1957, and John McDougall, "Applied Automation," in *Proceedings of 7th Annual Industrial Engineering Institute* (Univ. of Calif., Berkeley & L.A., Jan.–Feb. 1955), 45 ff.

28. D. Duncan, "Costs Incurred by Ford Motor Company in connection with the IBM indexing projects," typescript, Jan. 1952; Gossett Report to Managt. Meetg. No. 17, Apr. 20, 1949, 14, Acc. 422, Box 1; Nevins and Hill, *Ford: the Times, the Man, the Company*, Chs. 13, 17; *Ford: Expansion and Challenge*, Ch. 4.

29. *Consent Judgment: Order of Dismissal, and Related Settlement Papers*, printed May 15, 1952. These went into effect Apr. 9, 1952. Copy with FMC, General Counsel's Office.

30. Gossett to Managt. Meetg. No. 17, Apr. 20, 1949, Acc. 422, Box 1.

31. Breech to Committee of One Hundred, *op. cit.; Facts on File, 1953*, FMC, *Annual Report 1953*.

32. FMC, *Annual Reports 1950, 1951, 1952*.

33. Mins. Bd. Dirs., Jan. 30, 1948 (Benson); FMC Press Release, Oct. 15, 1948 (Ostrander); Benson to Managt. Meetg., Apr. 19, 1950, Acc. 422, Box 2; Mins. Ex. Com.; July 1, 1952; R. L. Polk figures on new car registrations. The records of the Product Planning Committee show how frequently Crusoe supported a point successfully, and how seldom the Lincoln Mercury Division did. As to Mercury percentages, the 1950 orders represented 5.03 per cent of automotive production, and 1951 4.6 per cent.

34. Mins. Ex. Com., Sept. 22, 1949 and *Annual Report 1949* (Warehouse, 1950); interv. Crusoe (Warehouse, Mar. 1951); FMC Press Release, Nov. 26, 1950, Acc. 277, Box 4 (new office bldg.); Mins. Prod. Planning Com., Jan. 25, 1951 (Ford Divn. on Light Car, and Com.'s decision); Mins. Ex. Com., Jan. 9, 1952 (light car); Crusoe to Members of Merchandizg. Com., May 15, 1951, Acc. 577, Box 1 (1952 car); Mins. Ford Divn. Operating Com., Mar. 18, 1953, Acc. 577, Box 1 (reception of car); *Ward's Report, 1953*, 105 (Ford station wagon); *Ward's Report 1953*, 150–151 (percentages).

# CHAPTER XV
## Ford Becomes a Challenge

1. Yntema to Ex. Com., Feb. 18, 1953, Acc. 577, Box 4.

2. W. J. Mitchel, Jr., "Ford's Fiftieth Anniversary," Oct. 15, 1953. Mitchel was Executive Secretary of the Fiftieth Anniversary Committee. Other sources are current press clippings; *Ford at Fifty*, N.Y., 1953 (prepared by Joseph J. Thorndike), and Fairlane-Ford Motor Company Archives, Bull. No. 1, Dearborn, 1953.

3. *Ibid.* In 1957 the Archives became a part of the Research and Information Dept., with selected accessions in the Department offices at Ford Central Office Building, and the bulk of the materials in the Rotunda. The authors began working in the Archives while it was situated in the Engineering Building, and while its materials were relatively few. Each group of new documents has been called an accession, numbered accordingly, and placed in boxes (4 x 10 x 14 inches), some accessions having thousands of boxes, others two or three. It is amusing to note that in 1952 several people had read practically everything in the Archives. But soon the records began to pour in at a rate of from 50 to 100 boxes a day, or more, and today the most superficial examination of the materials in the repository—say ten or fifteen minutes per box— would be a labor of many years.

4. Same sources as Notes 2 and 3 above.

5. Speech of HF II to Inland Press Association, Feb. 17, 1953, Ed. Ser. Files; *Wall Street Journal*, Feb. 19, 1953; *N.Y. Times*, Feb. 22, 1953; *N.Y. Herald-Tribune*, Feb. 19, 1953; *N.Y. Daily News*, Feb. 19, 1953; Letter Robert R. Nathan, Chmn. Ex. Com. of Amers. for Dem. Action to HF II, Feb. 19, 1953, in Ed. Ser. Files; HF II's Television Address, June 15, 1953, Ed. Ser. Files; *Facts of File, 1953*, 265F (nominated and confirmed as delegate); MS. Speeches of HF II, Acc. 536, Box 51, and (rebuttal speech) Nov. 28, 1953, Ed. Ser. Files; HF II, Progress Report for 1953, 16, Acc. 536, Box 85.

6. FMC, *Annual Report 1953;* Acc. 106, Box 4 (Ohio plants).

7. HF II, to Ex. Com., Jan. 29, 1952, copy in Prod. Planning Off.; Report of Davis Committee Sub-Com. in Prod. Planning Com. Files, Apr. 30, 1952; Mins. Ex. Com., Apr. 30, 1952.

8. Sub-Com. of Future Car Program, Rpt. to Davis Com., Je. 19, 1952, Prod. Planning Off. Files.

9. Ford Press Releases, 1949–1952, Acc. 536, Box 53 (W. C. Ford); Mins. Ex. Com., May 12, Je. 24, July 7, 1953; History of the MEL Div. of the FMC, Res. and Info. Dept. Chronology, 1958 (?).

10. Mins. Ex. Com., Jan. 16, 1953; R. L. Polk Figs. on New Car Registrations.

11. Ward's figs. on new registrations, 1928–1953; Ford Div. to the Prod. Planning Com., Jan. 25, 1951, and to the Ex. Com., Jan. 9, 1952, Apr. 9, 1953, and Je. 2, 1954.

12. Mins. Prod. Planning Com., Jan. 16, 1953 (Chevrolet's 1953 engine power, and its V-8); Ford Div. to the Ex. Com., Je. 2, 1954; *Automotive News*, Nov. 6, 1939 (air conditioning introduced in Packard); AMA Specifications (engine power rivalry and results); Ford Div. to Prod. Planning Com., Apr. 25, 1952 (overhead engine and ball-joint suspensn.); Crusoe and Walker Williams to Yntema, Sept. 22, 1954.

13. L-M Div. to Ex. Com., May 18, 1954, and minutes of ensuing discussion; interv. Breech (he termed this the "Davis car" or "Davis Edsel"); Mins. Ex. Com., May 18, 1954.

14. R. L. Polk new car registration figures.

15. Crusoe at Ford Educatl Forum, July 1955, Proceedings (copy in Room 985, Central Office Bldg.), 322, 324–325; Current press reports on Ford cars, Nov. 1954; *Automobile Facts*, XIII, Dec. 1954, 1.

16. FMC, *Annual Report 1955;* Mins. Prod. Planning Com., Feb. 1, 1955. See Ch. XVI for Reith's activities in France.

17. R. L. Polk, registration figs.; Ford Div. to Prod. Planning Com., June 2, 1954.

18. Report to Planning Off. in Finance, May 7, 1947, Doc. No. 137220, Ferg. Docs. (Ferg. sales); Production Statistics, FMC Files (Ford Sales); Mins. Prod. Planning Com., Dec. 7, 1951 (Ford & rivals); I. A. Duffy, "Ford in Agriculture," Ford Eductl. Forum, Procedings; statistics on tractor exports, FMC Ltd., 1953–1960. John Deere was closest to Ford in the battle for second place. Wheel-type tractors represented 72 per cent of the total tractor output. General Motors was not a rival in the tractor field.

19. FMC Press Release, Jan. 28, 1955 (Crusoe on Reith); Mins. Prod. Planning Com., Feb. 7, 1955; *Automobile Industry*, XXXDVIII, May 13, 1955, 26–28.

20. 2 Vol. Presentation to FMC Bd. Dirs., Apr. 15, 1955, copy in Prod. Planning Off.

21. *Automobile Facts*, XIV, Jan. 1955, 1–2.

22. Mins. Bd. Dirs., Apr. 15, 1955; FMC, *Annual Report 1955* (new divisions, sales, financial data).

23. For General Motors cost policy, see Ch. 13; intervs. McNamara, Miller.

# CHAPTER XVI
## Foreign Scene: The Postwar World

Secondary sources are as yet few. For the British situation the careful volume by George Maxcy and Aubrey Silberston, *The Motor Industry* (London, 1959), one of a Cambridge University series of industrial studies, is highly illuminating. P. Lesley Cook and Ruth Cohen, *The Effects of Mergers* (London, 1958), and John H. Dunning, *American Investment in British Manufacturing Industry* (London, 1958) are useful. PEP (Political and Economic Planning) issued an analytical report on *Motor Vehicles* (London, 1950). P. W. S. Andrews and E. Brunner, *The Life of Lord Nuffield* (London, 1955) contains valuable sidelights. For Germany the booklet *Ford in Deutschland* (Munich, 1955) offers a few bits of value. The annual reports of the Ford Motor Company in these years contain short but accurate summaries of foreign operations, with graphs and maps, and occasional photographs of cars and pictures of executives. Files of the *Ford Times*, English edition, the *London Economist*, which published a "Motoring Supplement" October 23, 1954, with frequent financial reports and critical appraisals, and such British magazines as *Motor* and the *Automobile Engineer*, furnish much not to be found elsewhere.

The documentary records of the International Division in Dearborn are of course indispensable. See comments in Notes on Ch. 11, relating to "Central Files," International Division. The most valuable report of Graeme Howard and Henry Ford II on their European tour of 1948 is in Accession 536, Box 46 of the Ford Archives. Board of Directors Minutes, as cited in Notes on Ch. 11, are useful for the post-war period as well. Dr. Mira Wilkins visited Great Britain, Germany, and other countries in 1960 and Canada in 1961, bringing back notes from the archives of the foreign corporations, and records of conversations with their executives, including an especially valuable statement of Sir Patrick Hennessy. Mr. Frank E. Hill made a similar tour in 1961 with equally fruitful results. Their findings will be published in a volume which will cover in much more detail the story of Ford's overseas activities.

1. Society of Motor Manufacturers and Traders, *The Motor Industry of Great Britain,* London, 1960, 103, 123 ff.

2. Report by HF II and Graeme Howard, Acc. 536, Box 46. Dr. Wilkins talked with Dr. Albert, then near death, in 1960. Ernest Breech's Report on his own European trip of 1948 is in Acc. 422, Box 1. Bristol *Evening Post,* Feb. 11, 1948 reports HF II driving Prefect.

3. HF II and Howard Report, *op. cit.*

4. *Ibid.*

5. *Ibid.,* and Roberge, *Reminiscences;* also see Roberge corr. in Storage B-38, Box 51, International Div.

6. Howard, *America and the New World Order,* N.Y., 1940.

7. Report of Management Meeting No. 15, Acc. 422, Box 1; FMC, *Annual Report 1948.* Ford News Release, Je. 27, 1948 (mgrs. meetg.).

8. Historical Data files, International Div. (Latin American plants); FMC, *Annual Report 1949* (consolidation Dearborn control); folder "Ford International Agreements Relationship, 1948–1956," International Div.; Howard talk to Univ. Club, Feb. 24, 1950, International Div., Storage B-38, Box 49A (215 employes); Report of Managt. Meeting No. 15, Acc. 422, Box 1 (general program); Org. Planning office (Howard's departure); intervs. International Div. executives (reasons for departure).

9. FMC, *Annual Reports* (Bugas, Lilley, facility expansion etc.); Ford-Werke, *Annual Reports* (German activities); Ford Ltd., *Annual Reports* (developments England).

10. SMMT, *The Motor Industry,* 11; Maxcy and Silberston, *Motor Industry, passim* (gen. conditions Brit. industry).

11. Intervs. Sir Patrick Hennessy, by Dr. Wilkins, Aug. 1960.

12. Maxcy and Silberston, 113, 117, 118.

3. Interv. Hennessy, *op. cit.;* Ford Ltd., *Annual Report 1953;* Statistics from Ford Ltd. and from FMC, *Annual Report 1961.*

14. FMC, *Annual Report 1959;* interv. Hennessy, *op. cit.;* Maxcy and Silberston, 176–178.

15. FMC, *Annual Reports 1956–1959;* the *Ford Bulletin,* Jan. 10, Apr. 4, 1958, contains a valuable review of the English business in 1957. The year was notable for what Sir Patrick Hennessy called a "dramatic" rise in exports to America; sales of English Fords in the United States rose to the figure of 23,000 given in the text, and Hennessy rejoiced. Breech to A. R. Smith, Dec. 29, 1949 in "Howard to Breech, Feb. 2, 1950" folder, International Div.

16. Acc. 516 contains material on the French effort; see also Sales Files, International Division.

17. See Ford-Werke, *Business Reports.*

18. The London *Economist,* Feb. 21, 1953, and subsequent dates treats the meteoric rise of the Volkswagen.

19. Ford of Canada issued exceptionally careful, full, and candid annual reports. It also published a series called "Handy Facts About Ford of Canada," of which International Div. has a run.

20. Ford-Canada, *Annual Report 1951,* 16.

# CHAPTER XVII
## The Great Transformation

The authors have benefited from a scholarly typescript monograph by Professor William Greenleaf, "The Ford Philanthropies, 1911–1936," completed in 1956 and in the archives of the Ford Foundation. It offers a documented account of all the family benefactions, including chapters on the Henry Ford Hospital, experiments in self-help, Henry Ford's ventures in education, and "Edsel Ford, Philanthropist." The study closes with the incorporation of the Ford Foundation in January 1936. A supplementary monograph by Professor Greenleaf on the early history of the foundation was not available to the authors. But material is contained in the Annual Reports of the foundation; in the four-part series by Dwight Macdonald entitled "Foundation" in *The New Yorker*, XXXI, Nov. 26, Dec. 3, 10, and 17, 1955, devoted entirely to the Ford Foundation; and in Joe McCarthy's four-part series entitled "The Ford Family," *Holiday*, XXI, Je. 1957, and XXII, July, Aug., and Sept. 1957, clearly based in part on conversations with members of the family. The reminiscences of W. J. Cameron, Ernest G. Liebold, Fred L. Black, Harold M. Cordell, E. J. Cutler, Charles Voorhees, J. L. McCloud, and Mrs. Stanley Ruddiman are useful. Of the published books, Henry Ford's collaborative works with Samuel Crowther, *My Life and Work* and *Today and Tomorrow* (Garden City, N.Y., 1923, 1926), and William L. Stidger's *Henry Ford: The Man and His Motives* (New York, 1923), contain the most relevant items. Something may be found also in Samuel S. Marquis, *Henry Ford; An Interpretation* (Boston, 1923), Charles E. Sorensen, *My Forty Years with Ford* (N.Y. 1956) and William C. Richards, *The Last Billionnaire, Henry Ford* (N.Y., 1948). The public sale of Ford Motor Company stock in 1956 is described in a 43-page "Prospectus" issued by the underwriters on January 17th of that year. The company statement filed with the Securities and Exchange Commission was published in the *New York Times* of December 22, 1955. Much information may also be gleaned from the voluminous Composite Registration Statement for the subsequent stock sale in 1959 filed with the S.E.C. in March 1959.

1. Ford and Crowther, *My Life and Work*, 206, 207; Sorensen, *Forty Years*, 21–23.

2. Henry Ford, *My Philosophy of Industry*, An authorized interv. by Fay Leone Favrote, N.Y. 1929, 104 and *passim*.

3. Acc. 1, Box 138 (Ann Hood).

4. Liebold, *Reminiscences* (Henry Ford Hospital); Nevins and Hill, *Ford: Expansion and Challenge*, 494–496; Sward, *Legend of Henry Ford*, 136–140, 480.

5. Nevins and Hill, *Ford: Expansion and Challenge*, 506–507.

6. E. R. A. Seligman, *The Income Tax*, N.Y., 1914, and W. J. Shultz, *The Taxation of Inheritance*, Boston, 1926 are standard treatises. Technically, the national government imposes an estate tax, not an inheritance tax.

7. See description of common stock in Registration Statement of the Ford Motor Company to the S.E.C., Mar. 1959, 19 ff. Much evidence exists suggesting that Edsel and his attorney Longley were leaders in creating Ford Foundation and writing the wills which endowed it with a heavily preponderant equity in the company.

8. The early financial resources of the Ford Foundation are described in *Detroit News*, Je. 3, 1943; *Motor*, July 1943, 102; and Greenleaf, "The Ford Philanthropies."

9. Dwight Macdonald, *The New Yorker*, Dec. 10, 17, 1955; *Time*, XLI, Je. 17, 1943, 81, 82; *Fortune*, XXIX, Je. 1944, 254 ff.; *Commercial and Financial Chronicle*, Je. 10, 1943, 2189; Memorandum by R. B. Darragh of a conference with Mr. Capizzi, Oct. 24, 1961.

10. The *N.Y. Times*, Apr. 13, 1950 (Federal taxes on Edsel's estate, $24,635,093; those on Henry Ford's estate were presumably larger).

11. Robert L. Heilbroner, "The Fabulous Ford Foundation," *Harper's Magazine*, CCIII, Dec. 1951, 31 ff.; Dwight Macdonald, *The New Yorker*, Dec. 17, 1955. Income and expenditures for the Ford Foundation for the years 1936–1959 are charted in its *Annual Report 1959*, 92.

12. Edwin Rogers Embree, "Timid Billions," *Harper's Magazine*, CXCVIII, Mar. 1949, 28–37.

13. Heilbroner, *op. cit.*, 29, 30; Raymond Moley, "The Ford Foundation," *Newsweek*, XLVII, Jan. 9, 1956, 76.

14. MacDonald, *New Yorker*, Nov. 26, 1955, summarizes Reece's investigation. See *N.Y. Times*, Feb. 13, Apr. 7, May 1, 1954, with his majority report for the committee Dec. 20, 1954. An earlier investigation under Representative Edward E. Cox is reported in *N.Y. Times*, Nov. 16, 19, 1952.

15. MacDonald, *New Yorker*, Dec. 17, 1955, gives the most complete account of the dropping of Hoffman.

16. "Prospectus," Jan. 17, 1956; *N.Y. Times*, Dec. 22, 1955; and numerous magazines and newspapers, Jan.–Feb. 1956 (sale of Ford stock), *N.Y. Times, Herald-Tribune, Detroit Free Press*, Jan. 18, 1956, cover the first day's trading. Prices are given in Ford Foundation, *Annual Report 1956*, 147, 148.

17. FMC, *Annual Report 1955*, 6, gives the figure of 350,000 stockholders; the *Annual Report 1956*, 17, showed a drop to about 300,000.

# CHAPTER XVIII
## Present and Future

A general picutre of the Ford Motor Company since 1955 can be obtained from the *Annual Reports* of the company, which are full and lucidly written; and from the published accounts of the annual meetings of stockholders, which are not complete transcripts of the proceedings, but fair and intelligent summaries. Minutes of the Executive Committee, the Product Planning Committee, and various divisional operating committees are carefully kept. The authors have had the benefit of talks with all principal executives. Little of the copious magazine material is profitable; an exception is "On the Frontier: Complex Plant Machinery," *Fortune*, LI, May, 1955, 88 ff. The speeches by Henry Ford II, Ernest Breech, John S. Bugas, and others are useful.

1. The workshop is pictured in the dust cover of Allan Nevins and Frank E. Hill, *Ford: The Times, The Man, The Company;* and pictures of Henry Ford in his first automobile appear between pp. 208 and 209 of that volume. Norman Rockwell's painting has been frequently reproduced.

2. This photograph is in the Ford Motor Company *Annual Report 1959*, 22.

3. For the emergence of Henry Ford's autocracy, see Nevins and Hill, *op. cit.*, Ch. 21.

4. Nevins and Hill, *op. cit.*, Chs. 20, 21.

5. Statement of Vice-President William T. Gossett to Senate Labor Committee, Feb. 16, 1949.

6. John S. Bugas published as a company brochure, dated Je. 1955, a full analysis of "The Ford Motor Company's Supplemental Unemployment Plan."

7. *Boston Globe*, Je. 11, 1955.

8. Comments summarized in *Business Week*, Je. 11, 1955.

9. *Washington Star*, Je. 10; New York *Herald Tribune*, Je. 11, 1955.

10. *Annual Report, 1956.*

11. Ford Motor Company, Sales Reports and Statistics; *Annual Reports 1957, 1959, 1960.*

12. *Annual Reports 1960, 1961.*

13. Richard Austin Smith, "Detroit Is Flying By The Seat Of Its Pants," *Fortune*, LXIII, Jan. 1961, 80–85, 189–200.

14. Quoted by Smith, *ut supra*, 81.

15. John Brooks, *The Fate of the Edsel and Other Business Adventures*, New York, 1963, 67–68.

# APPENDICES

# INDEX

## APPENDIX I: FORD MOTOR COMPANY PRODUCTION REPORT, 1903 THRU 1955

### UNITED STATES, INCLUDING BU AND KD

| Year | 1) Ford Passenger | 2) Ford Truck | 3) Metro-Coach | 4) Mercury | 5) Lincoln | 6) Tractor | 7) Total U.S. |
|---|---|---|---|---|---|---|---|
| 1903†† | 1,708 | | | | | | 1,7 |
| 1904 | 1,695 | | | | | | 1,6 |
| 1905 | 1,599 | | | | | | 1,5 |
| 1906 | 8,729 | | | | | | 8,7 |
| 1907 | 14,887 | | | | | | 14,8 |
| 1908 | 10,202 | | | | | | 10,2 |
| 1909 | 17,771 | | | | | | 17,7 |
| 1910 | 32,053 | | | | | | 32,0 |
| 1911 | 69,762 | | | | | | 69,7 |
| 1912 | 170,211 | | | | | | 170,2 |
| 1913 | 202,667 | | | | | | 202,6 |
| 1914 | 308,162 | | | | | | 308,1 |
| 1915 | 501,462 | | | | | | 501,4 |
| 1916 | 734,811 | 209 | | | | | 735,0 |
| 1917 | 622,351 | 41,725 | | | | 254 | 664.3 |
| 1918 | 435,898 | 62,444 | | | | 34,167 | 532,5 |
| 1919 | 820,445 | 120,597 | | | | 56,987 | 998,0 |
| 1920† | 419,517 | 43,934 | | | | 67,329 | 530,7 |
| 1921 | 903,814 | 67,796 | | | | 35,338 | 1,006,9 |
| 1922 | 1,173,745 | 127,322 | | | 5,512 | 66,752 | 1,373,3 |
| 1923 | 1,817,891 | 193,234 | | | 7,875 | 101,898 | 2,120,8 |
| 1924 | 1,749,827 | 172,221 | | | 7,053 | 83,010 | 2,012,1 |
| 1925 | 1,643,295 | 268,411 | | | 8,380 | 104,168 | 2,024,2 |
| 1926 | 1,368,383 | 186,082 | | | 8,858 | 88,101 | 1,651,4 |
| 1927 | 356,188 | 61,100 | | | 7,141 | 93,972 | 518,4 |
| 1928 | 633,594 | 110,342 | | | 6,362 | 8,001 | 758,2 |
| 1929 | 1,507,132 | 355,453 | | | 7,672 | 0 | 1,870,2 |
| 1930 | 1,155,162 | 272,897 | | | 3,515 | 0 | 1,431,5 |
| 1931 | 541,615 | 186,394 | | | 3,592 | 0 | 731,6 |
| 1932 | 287,285 | 105,283 | | | 3,388 | 0 | 395,9 |
| 1933 | 334,969 | 92,662 | | | 2,007 | 0 | 429,6 |
| 1934 | 563,921 | 191,861 | | | 2,149 | 0 | 757,9 |
| 1935 | 942,439 | 250,282 | | | 3,915 | 0 | 1,196,6 |
| 1936 | 791,812 | 223,779 | | | 22,001 | 0 | 1,037,5 |
| 1937 | 848,608 | 268,621 | | | 29,293 | 0 | 1,146,5 |
| 1938 | 410,048 | 150,858 | 221 | 17,282 | 19,751 | 0 | 598,1 |
| 1939 | 532,152 | 184,572 | 608 | 76,198 | 22,578* | 10,233 | 826,3 |
| 1940 | 599,175 | 202,545 | 552 | 82,770 | 24,021* | 35,742 | 944,8 |
| 1941 | 600,814 | 249,789 | 803 | 80,085 | 17,756* | 42,910 | 992,1 |
| 1942 | 43,407 | 177,959 | 1,344 | 4,430 | 1,276* | 16,487 | 244,9 |
| 1943 | 0 | 141,488 | 869 | 0 | 0 | 21,163 | 163,5 |
| 1944 | 0 | 152,733 | 2,028 | 0 | 0 | 43,444 | 198,2 |
| 1945 | 34,439 | 122,473 | 1,827 | 2,848 | 569 | 28,749 | 190,9 |
| 1946 | 372,917 | 198,767 | 2,513 | 70,955 | 13,496* | 59,773 | 718,4 |
| 1947 | 601,665 | 247,832 | 2,256 | 124,612 | 29,275* | 85,589 | 1,091,2 |
| 1948 | 549,077 | 301,791 | 363 | 154,702 | 43,688* | 103,462 | 1,153,0 |
| 1949 | 841,170 | 244,613 | 170 | 203,339 | 33,132 | 104,267 | 1,426,6 |
| 1950 | 1,187,122 | 345,801 | 50 | 334,081 | 35,485 | 97,956 | 2,000,4 |
| 1951 | 900,770 | 317,252 | 0 | 238,854 | 25,386 | 98,442 | 1,580,7 |
| 1952 | 777,531 | 236,753 | 0 | 195,261 | 31,992 | 82,041 | 1,323,5 |
| 1953 | 1,184,187 | 317,151 | 0 | 320,369 | 41,962 | 72,548 | 1,936,2 |
| 1954 | 1,394,762 | 302,796 | 0 | 256,729 | 35,733 | 51,490 | 2,041,5 |
| 1955 | 1,764,524 | 373,897 | 0 | 434,911 | 41,226 | 66,656 | 2,681,2 |
| Total | 32,787,370 | 7,671,719 | 13,604 | 2,597,426 | 546,039 | 1,760,929 | 45,377,0 |

† Aug. 1 to Dec. 31, 1919
†† Fiscal year Figures; Aug. 1 to July 31, inclusive

\* — Includes Continental, Mark I — 5,322 units
▲ — Includes Continental, Mark II — 1,231 units

(Note that production figures will not tally exactly with sales figures.)

| CANADA, INCLUDING BU AND KD | | | FOREIGN | | | | TOTAL: U.S., CANADA, AND FOREIGN | |
|---|---|---|---|---|---|---|---|---|
| Passenger | 9) Truck | 10) Total Canada | 11) Passenger | 12) Truck | 13) Tractor | 14) Total Foreign | 15) Year | 16) Accumulated |
| | | | | | | | 1,708 | 1,708 |
| | | | | | | | 1,695 | 3,403 |
| 117 | | 117 | | | | | 1,716 | 5,119 |
| 99 | | 99 | | | | | 8,828 | 13,947 |
| 327 | | 327 | | | | | 15,214 | 29,161 |
| 324 | | 324 | | | | | 10,526 | 39,687 |
| 486 | | 486 | | | | | 18,257 | 57,944 |
| 1,280 | | 1,280 | | | | | 33,333 | 91,277 |
| 2,805 | | 2,805 | | | | | 72,567 | 163,844 |
| 7,543 | 80 | 7,623 | | | | | 177,834 | 341,678 |
| 12,215 | 304 | 12,519 | | | | | 215,186 | 556,864 |
| 14,033 | 350 | 14,383 | | | | | 322,545 | 879,409 |
| 27,626 | 1,241 | 28,867 | | | | | 530,329 | 1,409,738 |
| 32,072 | 1,599 | 33,671 | | | | | 768,691 | 2,178,429 |
| 54,772 | 3,120 | 57,892 | | | | | 722,222 | 2,900,651 |
| 29,744 | 9,901 | 39,645 | | | | | 572,154 | 3,472,805 |
| 31,877 | 17,649 | 49,526 | | | 303 | 303 | 1,047,858 | 4,520,663 |
| 36,119 | 12,122 | 48,241 | | | 3,626 | 3,626 | 582,647 | 5,103,310 |
| 34,473 | 7,875 | 42,348 | | | 1,445 | 1,445 | 1,050,741 | 6,154,051 |
| 35,012 | 15,254 | 50,266 | | | 2,233 | 2,233 | 1,425,830 | 7,579,881 |
| 48,416 | 31,874 | 80,290 | | | 0 | 0 | 2,201,188 | 9,781,069 |
| 44,475 | 26,895 | 71,370 | | | 0 | 0 | 2,083,481 | 11,864,550 |
| 50,741 | 28,546 | 79,287 | | | 0 | 0 | 2,103,541 | 13,968,091 |
| 66,779 | 33,872 | 100,651 | | | 0 | 0 | 1,752,075 | 15,720,166 |
| 26,109 | 11,286 | 37,395 | | | 0 | 0 | 555,796 | 16,275,962 |
| 49,356 | 25,859 | 75,215 | | | 0 | 0 | 833,514 | 17,109,476 |
| 56,980 | 30,818 | 87,798 | | | 9,686 | 9,686 | 1,967,741 | 19,077,217 |
| 49,594 | 20,659 | 70,253 | | | 15,196 | 15,196 | 1,517,023 | 20,594,240 |
| 21,966 | 8,886 | 30,852 | 5 | 5,485 | 3,501 | 8,991 | 771,444 | 21,365,684 |
| 19,975 | 5,273 | 25,248 | 12,986 | 14,313 | 3,088 | 30,387 | 451,591 | 21,817,275 |
| 19,049 | 7,477 | 26,526 | 39,219 | 17,298 | 2,807 | 59,324 | 515,488 | 22,332,763 |
| 35,376 | 12,332 | 47,708 | 42,124 | 21,497 | 3,589 | 67,210 | 872,849 | 23,205,612 |
| 58,500 | 21,664 | 80,164 | 57,722 | 24,361 | 9,256 | 91,339 | 1,368,139 | 24,573,751 |
| 42,861 | 17,618 | 60,479 | 94,905 | 28,129 | 12,838 | 135,872 | 1,233,943 | 25,807,694 |
| 48,618 | 24,196 | 72,814 | 111,527 | 28,140 | 19,198 | 158,865 | 1,378,201 | 27,185,895 |
| 48,429 | 19,488 | 67,917 | 89,002 | 31,840 | 10,647 | 131,489 | 797,566 | 27,983,461 |
| 41,072 | 19,943 | 61,015 | 69,707 | 36,823 | 15,712 | 122,242 | 1,009,598 | 28,993,059 |
| 32,486 | 63,963 | 96,449 | 10,919 | 27,089 | 20,276 | 58,284 | 1,099,538 | 30,092,597 |
| 26,880 | 84,507 | 111,387 | 1,869 | 29,498 | 22,210 | 53,577 | 1,157,121 | 31,249,718 |
| 4,442 | 100,298 | 104,740 | 853 | 38,310 | 27,650 | 66,813 | 416,456 | 31,666,174 |
| 0 | 75,653 | 75,653 | 40 | 41,942 | 26,300 | 68,282 | 307,455 | 31,973,629 |
| 0 | 62,418 | 62,418 | 0 | 37,505 | 23,845 | 61,350 | 321,973 | 32,295,602 |
| 0 | 46,344 | 46,344 | 2,324 | 26,577 | 17,770 | 46,671 | 283,920 | 32,579,522 |
| 40,780 | 39,493 | 80,273 | 32,726 | 41,492 | 25,290 | 99,508 | 898,202 | 33,477,724 |
| 63,408 | 37,776 | 101,184 | 47,148 | 45,879 | 34,215 | 127,242 | 1,319,655 | 34,797,379 |
| 54,554 | 42,461 | 97,015 | 69,524 | 53,705 | 50,561 | 173,790 | 1,423,888 | 36,221,267 |
| 72,868 | 39,262 | 112,130 | 104,126 | 49,881 | 33,375 | 187,382 | 1,726,203 | 37,947,470 |
| 94,161 | 34,865 | 129,026 | 141,588 | 51,124 | 42,275 | 234,987 | 2,364,508 | 40,311,978 |
| 79,371 | 39,485 | 118,856 | 141,655 | 51,496 | 35,868 | 229,019 | 1,928,579 | 42,240,557 |
| 84,189 | 48,001 | 132,190 | 138,864 | 53,881 | 30,444 | 223,189 | 1,678,957 | 43,919,514 |
| 126,201 | 29,425 | 155,626 | 214,960 | 55,123 | 29,575 | 299,658 | 2,391,501 | 46,311,015 |
| 104,259 | 18,322 | 122,581 | 262,221 | 64,451 | 45,689 | 372,361 | 2,536,452 | 48,847,467 |
| 139,902 | 25,808 | 165,710 | 293,166 | 94,110 | 48,872 | 436,148 | 3,283,072 | 52,130,539 |
| ,972,721 | 1,204,262 | 3,176,983 | 1,979,180 | 969,949 | 627,340 | 3,576,469 | 52,130,539 | |

## APPENDIX II:
### FORD MOTOR COMPANY AND AFFILIATES: VEHICLE PRODUCTION
### 1956 THROUGH 1962

| | Accum. 1903 thru 1955 | 1956 | 195 |
|---|---|---|---|
| **UNITED STATES** | | | |
| Passenger | 35,930,835 | 1,669,166 | 1,889 |
| Truck | * 7,685,323 | 297,308 | 337, |
| Tractor | 1,760,929 | 39,097 | 39 |
| Totals | 45,377,087 | 2,005,571 | 2,266 |
| **CANADA** | | | |
| Passenger | 1,972,721 | 121,768 | 112, |
| Truck | 1,204,262 | 27,098 | 21 |
| Totals | 3,176,983 | 148,866 | 134, |
| **FOREIGN** | | | |
| Passenger | 1,979,180 | 284,395 | 300, |
| Truck | 969,949 | 86,051 | 83 |
| Tractor | 627,340 | 40,991 | 46 |
| Totals | 3,576,469 | 411,437 | 429, |
| **TOTAL** | | | |
| Passenger | 39,882,736 | 2,075,329 | 2,302, |
| Truck | .9,859,534 | 410,457 | 442, |
| Tractor | 2,388,269 | 80,088 | 85, |
| Totals | 52,130,539 | 2,565,874 | 2,830, |

* Includes 13,604 Metropolitan Coaches.

| 1958 | 1959 | 1960 | 1961 | 1962 | Accum. 1903 thru 1962 |
|---|---|---|---|---|---|
| ,219,422 | 1,745,409 | 1,892,003 | 1,689,940 | 1,935,203 | 47,971,683 |
| 242,890 | 331,348 | 337,468 | 338,985 | 375,410 | * 9,945,855 |
| 46,315 | 47,633 | 25,482 | 23,718 | 26,705 | 2,009,564 |
| ,508,627 | 2,124,390 | 2,254,953 | 2,052,643 | 2,337,318 | 59,927,102 |
| 90,151 | 100,259 | 94,557 | 98,307 | 118,310 | 2,708,630 |
| 15,348 | 17,791 | 18,776 | 16,567 | 25,442 | 1,346,874 |
| 105,499 | 118,050 | 113,333 | 114,874 | 143,752 | 4,055,504 |
| 398,800 | 451,085 | 610,144 | 588,668 | 688,731 | 5,301,113 |
| 88,298 | 120,283 | 141,787 | 132,935 | 148,188 | 1,771,178 |
| 58,518 | 67,238 | 71,578 | 72,391 | 74,954 | 1,059,124 |
| 545,616 | 638,606 | 823,509 | 793,994 | 911,873 | 8,131,415 |
| 1,708,373 | 2,296,753 | 2,596,704 | 2,376,915 | 2,742,244 | 55,981,426 |
| 346,536 | 469,422 | 498,031 | 488,487 | 549,040 | 13,063,907 |
| 104,833 | 114,871 | 97,060 | 96,109 | 101,659 | 3,068,688 |
| 2,159,742 | 2,881,046 | 3,191,795 | 2,861,511 | 3,392,943 | 72,114,021 |

## APPENDIX III:

## FINANCIAL RECORD OF THE FORD MOTOR COMPANY AND CONSOLIDATED SUBSIDIARIES (1946-1960)

### 10 YEAR FINANCIAL SUMMARY

| | 1960 | 1959 | 1958 | 1957 | 1956 | 1955 | 1954 | 1953 | 1952 | 1951 |
|---|---|---|---|---|---|---|---|---|---|---|
| **RESULTS FOR YEAR** (Dollar amounts in millions) | | | | | | | | | | |
| Sales | $5,237.9 | 5,356.9 | 4,130.3 | 5,771.3 | 4,647.0 | 5,594.0 | 4,062.3 | 4,211.3 | 2,640.2 | 2,741.8 |
| Income before income taxes | $ 774.7 | 842.5 | 182.5 | 580.6 | 490.4 | 985.6 | 510.7 | 520.4 | 289.2 | 379.3 |
| Provision for income taxes | $ 346.8 | 391.4 | 66.3 | 286.6 | 242.2 | 531.4 | 268.1 | 341.3 | 164.4 | 242.9 |
| Net income | $ 427.9 | 451.4 | 116.2 | 294.0 | 248.2 | 454.2 | 242.6 | 179.1 | 124.8 | 136.4 |
| As a percent of sales | 8.2% | 8.4% | 2.8% | 5.1% | 5.3% | 8.1% | 6.0% | 4.3% | 4.7% | 5.0% |
| Dividends paid | $ 164.6 | 153.5 | 109.4 | 130.7 | 129.6 | 174.7 | 89.8 | 51.8 | 34.5 | 34.5 |
| Retained income | $ 263.3 | 297.9 | 6.8 | 163.3 | 118.6 | 279.5 | 152.8 | 127.3 | 90.3 | 101.9 |
| Capital expenditures for expansion, modernization and replacement of facilities (excluding special tools) | $ 128.2 | 75.0 | 89.0 | 328.7 | 486.9 | 214.0 | 279.9 | 151.5 | 176.8 | 217.6 |
| Retirements of property, plant and equipment (excluding special tools) | $ 40.4 | 66.2 | 45.4 | 50.2 | 49.8 | 30.2 | 58.2 | 30.5 | 32.6* | 43.1 |
| Depreciation | $ 164.0 | 172.9 | 187.3 | 177.1 | 133.5 | 116.0 | 90.2 | 74.0 | 54.9 | 45.8 |
| Expenditures for special tools | $ 160.5 | 154.8 | 148.0 | 218.9 | 273.5 | 93.0 | 137.1 | 55.6 | 38.1 | 109.0 |
| Amortization of special tools | $ 143.6 | 188.3 | 215.9 | 208.8 | 128.2 | 122.9 | 71.0 | 57.7 | 65.9 | 19.1 |
| **EMPLOYE DATA** | | | | | | | | | | |
| Payroll | $1,193.9 | 1,151.6 | 954.5 | 1,204.6 | 1,086.7 | 1,117.6 | 964.3 | 988.4 | 722.6 | 625.4 |
| Average total hourly labor costs, (in dollars) per hour worked, including fringe benefits | $ 3.59 | 3.44 | 3.33 | 3.09 | 2.96 | 2.77 | 2.66 | 2.56 | 2.48 | 2.33 |
| Average number of employes working | 160,181 | 159,541 | 142,076 | 191,759 | 178,061 | 181,616 | 171,019 | 178,032 | 139,782 | 136,993 |
| **YEAR END POSITION** | | | | | | | | | | |
| Cash and marketable securities | $ 454.1 | 666.3 | 451.6 | 265.1 | 215.1 | 568.3 | 327.6 | 299.5 | 347.0 | 386.9 |
| Current assets | $1,198.3 | 1,357.7 | 1,102.6 | 1,091.3 | 967.2 | 1,269.0 | 869.2 | 926.5 | 863.8 | 779.6 |
| Current liabilities | $ 560.6 | 528.5 | 532.1 | 656.2 | 683.1 | 643.6 | 445.9 | 386.3 | 367.5 | 268.0 |
| Net working capital | $ 637.7 | 829.2 | 570.5 | 435.1 | 284.1 | 625.4 | 423.3 | 540.2 | 496.3 | 511.6 |
| Current ratio | 2.1 to 1 | 2.6 to 1 | 2.1 to 1 | 1.7 to 1 | 1.4 to 1 | 2.0 to 1 | 1.9 to 1 | 2.4 to 1 | 2.4 to 1 | 2.9 to 1 |
| Property, plant and equipment | $2,678.4 | 2,574.0 | 2,598.7 | 2,623.3 | 2,335.4 | 1,754.0 | 1,601.0 | 1,314.1 | 1,196.2 | 1,110.9 |
| Accumulated depreciation | $1,162.7 | 1,037.7 | 925.4 | 781.0 | 649.3 | 561.6 | 474.9 | 441.4 | 395.0 | 396.7 |
| Net property, plant and equipment | $1,515.7 | 1,536.3 | 1,673.3 | 1,842.3 | 1,686.1 | 1,192.4 | 1,126.1 | 872.7 | 801.2 | 714.2 |
| Long-term debt | $ 239.4 | 249.5 | 250.0 | 250.0 | 58.6 | — | | | | |
| Total assets | $3,756.8 | 3,462.2 | 3,133.5 | 3,265.3 | 2,932.2 | 2,713.3 | 2,194.2 | 1,985.4 | 1,833.3 | 1,657.1 |
| Stockholders' equity | $2,879.6 | 2,614.8 | 2,312.9 | 2,300.3 | 2,127.0 | 1,996.2 | 1,704.0 | 1,542.2 | 1,414.9 | 1,321.6 |
| **PER SHARE**** (In dollars) | | | | | | | | | | |
| Net income | $ 7.80 | 8.24 | 2.12 | 5.40 | 4.60 | 8.51 | 4.59 | 3.39 | 2.36 | 2.58 |
| Dividends | $ 3.00 | 2.80 | 2.00 | 2.40 | 2.40 | 3.27 | 1.70 | .98 | .65 | .65 |
| Stockholders' equity | $ 52.44 | 47.66 | 42.24 | 42.22 | 39.38 | 37.24 | 33.26 | 29.10 | 26.29 | 25.02 |

RESULTS FOR YEAR
*(Dollar amounts in millions)*

| | 1955 | 1954 | 1953 | 1952 | 1951 | 1950 | 1949 | 1948 | 1947 | 1946 |
|---|---|---|---|---|---|---|---|---|---|---|
| Net sales | $5,594.0 | 4,062.3 | 4,211.3 | 2,640.2 | 2,741.8 | 3,029.5 | 2,249.4 | 1,971.2 | 1,501.7 | 894.5 |
| Income before taxes on income | $968.4 | 495.9 | 507.1 | 281.3 | 369.0 | 540.6 | 294.9 | 170.5 | 108.5 | (7.4) |
| Provision for taxes on income | 531.4 | 268.1 | 341.3 | 164.4 | 242.9 | 280.3 | 117.8 | 74.5 | 45.8 | .7 |
| Net income | $437.0 | 227.8 | 165.8 | 116.9 | 126.1 | 260.3 | 177.1 | 96.0 | 62.7 | (8.1) |
| As a percent of sales | 7.8% | 5.6% | 3.9% | 4.4% | 4.6% | 8.6% | 7.9% | 4.9% | 4.2% | (0.9%) |
| Dividends paid | $174.7 | 89.8 | 51.8 | 34.5 | 34.5 | 96.7 | 27.6 | 19.0 | 6.9 | (8.1) |
| Retained income | $262.3 | 138.0 | 114.0 | 82.4 | 91.6 | 163.6 | 149.5 | 77.0 | 55.8 | — |
| Gross additions to property, plant and equipment* | $214.0 | 279.9 | 151.5 | 176.8 | 217.6 | 109.7 | 34.9 | 79.3 | 94.4 | 56.5 |
| Retirements of property, plant and equipment* | $30.2 | 58.2 | 30.5 | 32.6** | 43.1 | 21.1 | 23.4 | 24.7 | 19.9 | 18.3 |
| Depreciation charges† | $116.0 | 90.2 | 74.0 | 54.9 | 45.8 | 41.3 | 40.7 | 37.9 | 33.0 | 31.3 |
| Payroll | $1,117.6 | 964.3 | 988.4 | 722.6 | 625.4 | 582.1 | 469.4 | 484.6 | 413.4 | 328.4 |

YEAR END POSITION

| | 1955 | 1954 | 1953 | 1952 | 1951 | 1950 | 1949 | 1948 | 1947 | 1946 |
|---|---|---|---|---|---|---|---|---|---|---|
| Current assets | $1,269.0 | 869.2 | 926.5 | 863.8 | 779.6 | 934.8 | 763.4 | 604.9 | 548.7 | 488.3 |
| Current liabilities | $643.6 | 445.9 | 386.3 | 367.5 | 268.0 | 264.2 | 188.2 | 212.5 | 198.6 | 145.1 |
| Net working capital | $625.4 | 423.3 | 540.2 | 496.3 | 511.6 | 670.6 | 575.2 | 392.4 | 350.1 | 343.2 |
| Gross property, plant and equipment | $1,754.0 | 1,601.0 | 1,314.1 | 1,196.2 | 1,110.9 | 847.2 | 760.8 | 777.0 | 714.0 | 626.6 |
| Reserves for depreciation | $561.6 | 474.9 | 441.4 | 395.0 | 396.7 | 386.4 | 364.6 | 343.6 | 325.8 | 309.2 |
| Net property, plant and equipment | $1,192.4 | 1,126.1 | 872.7 | 801.2 | 714.2 | 460.8 | 396.2 | 433.4 | 388.2 | 317.4 |
| Total assets | $2,585.3 | 2,083.5 | 1,889.4 | 1,750.6 | 1,582.3 | 1,477.4 | 1,207.8 | 1,077.4 | 981.9 | 868.1 |
| Stockholders' equity | $1,868.2 | 1,593.3 | 1,446.2 | 1,332.2 | 1,246.8 | 1,155.3 | 984.8 | 835.2 | 758.1 | 714.4 |

PER SHARE††
*(In dollars)*

| | 1955 | 1954 | 1953 | 1952 | 1951 | 1950 | 1949 | 1948 | 1947 | 1946 |
|---|---|---|---|---|---|---|---|---|---|---|
| Net income | $ 8.19 | 4.31 | 3.14 | 2.21 | 2.39 | 4.93 | 3.35 | 1.82 | 1.19 | (.15) |
| Dividends | $ 3.27 | 1.70 | .98 | .65 | .65 | 1.83 | .52 | .36 | .13 | — |

* Excluding special tools
** Exclusive of adjustments to record the results of a physical inventory of property, plant and equipment
† Excluding amortization of special tools
†† After adjustment to give effect to the January, 1956, reclassification of stock

# CORPORATE STRUCTURE OF FORD MOTOR COMPANY

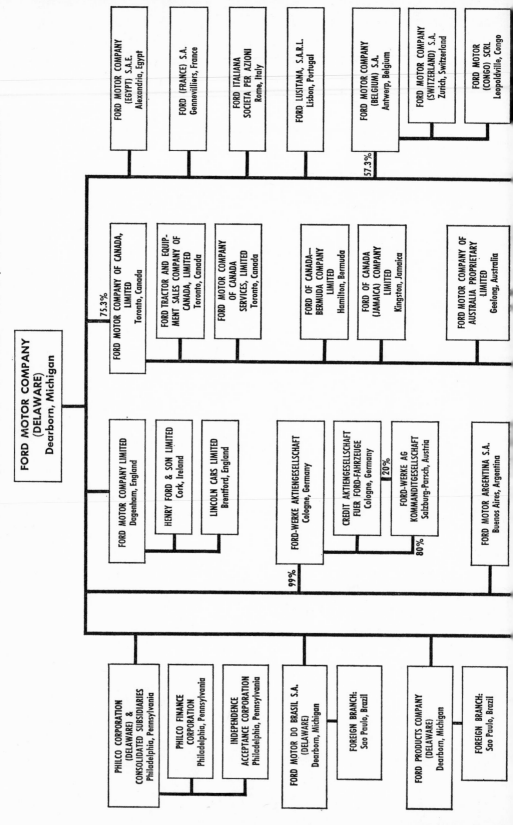

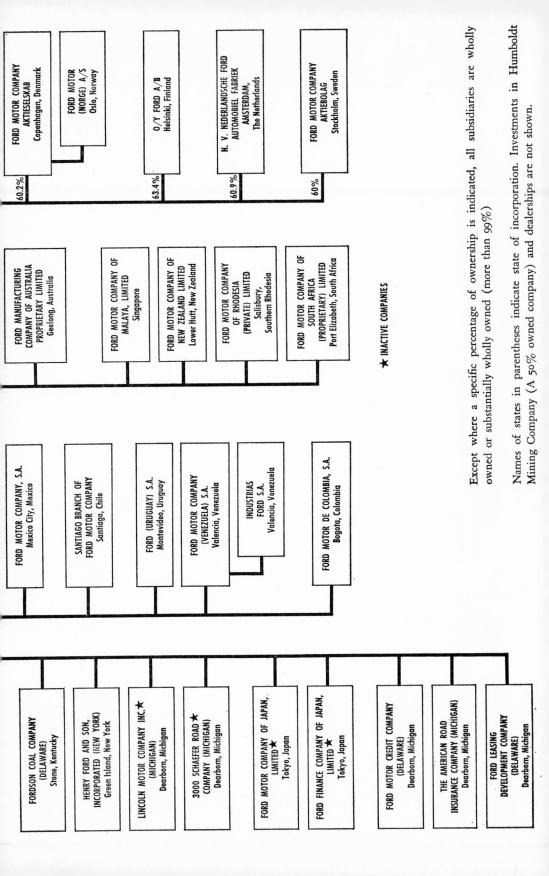

**FORD MOTOR COMPANY AKTIESELSKAB**
Copenhagen, Denmark

**FORD MOTOR (NORGE) A/S**
Oslo, Norway

60.2%

**O/Y FORD A/B**
Helsinki, Finland

63.4%

**N. V. NEDERLANDSCHE FORD AUTOMOBIEL FABRIEK**
AMSTERDAM, The Netherlands

60.9%

**FORD MOTOR COMPANY AKTIEBOLAG**
Stockholm, Sweden

60%

**FORD MANUFACTURING COMPANY OF AUSTRALIA PROPRIETARY LIMITED**
Geelong, Australia

**FORD MOTOR COMPANY OF MALAYA, LIMITED**
Singapore

**FORD MOTOR COMPANY OF NEW ZEALAND LIMITED**
Lower Hutt, New Zealand

**FORD MOTOR COMPANY OF RHODESIA (PRIVATE) LIMITED**
Salisbury, Southern Rhodesia

**FORD MOTOR COMPANY OF SOUTH AFRICA (PROPRIETARY) LIMITED**
Port Elizabeth, South Africa

★ **INACTIVE COMPANIES**

**FORD MOTOR COMPANY, S.A.**
Mexico City, Mexico

**SANTIAGO BRANCH OF FORD MOTOR COMPANY**
Santiago, Chile

**FORD (URUGUAY) S.A.**
Montevideo, Uruguay

**FORD MOTOR COMPANY (VENEZUELA) S.A.**
Valencia, Venezuela

**INDUSTRIAS FORD S.A.**
Valencia, Venezuela

**FORD MOTOR DE COLOMBIA, S.A.**
Bogota, Colombia

**FORDSON COAL COMPANY (DELAWARE)**
Stone, Kentucky

**HENRY FORD AND SON, INCORPORATED (NEW YORK)**
Green Island, New York

**LINCOLN MOTOR COMPANY INC.★ (MICHIGAN)**
Dearborn, Michigan

**3000 SCHAEFER ROAD COMPANY ★ (MICHIGAN)**
Dearborn, Michigan

**FORD MOTOR COMPANY OF JAPAN, LIMITED ★**
Tokyo, Japan

**FORD FINANCE COMPANY OF JAPAN, LIMITED ★**
Tokyo, Japan

**FORD MOTOR CREDIT COMPANY (DELAWARE)**
Dearborn, Michigan

**THE AMERICAN ROAD INSURANCE COMPANY (MICHIGAN)**
Dearborn, Michigan

**FORD LEASING DEVELOPMENT COMPANY (DELAWARE)**
Dearborn, Michigan

Except where a specific percentage of ownership is indicated, all subsidiaries are wholly owned or substantially wholly owned (more than 99%)

Names of states in parentheses indicate state of incorporation. Investments in Humboldt Mining Company (A 50% owned company) and dealerships are not shown.

# INDEX